CHRIST
THE IDEAL OF THE MONK

CHRIST
THE IDEAL OF THE MONK

SPIRITUAL CONFERENCES
ON THE MONASTIC AND RELIGIOUS LIFE

by
Blessed Columba Marmion, O.S.B.

Preface by
Abbot Xavier Perrin, O.S.B.

Guided by the Gospel let us walk in the path of Christ.
— St. Benedict, *Rule.*

Christ the Ideal of the Monk was first published in French in 1922. First published in English in 1926 (translated from the French by a Nun of Tyburn Convent), this Cenacle Press edition is based on the 8th edition of that translation (published by the B. Herder Book Co.), which bore the *Nihil Obstat* of Alb. Boone, S.J. (Brugis, 11a Februarii 1926), and the *Imprimatur* of H. Van Den Berghe, *Vic. Gen.* (Brugis, 11a Februarii 1926).

This revised edition, published in 2022 by The Cenacle Press at Silverstream Priory, provides translation of Latin texts left untranslated in the original English edition. It also incorporates some corrections to the footnotes and references, and a few minor changes to the main text.

The translations introduced to this new edition are taken from the following sources: Aquinas translations are sourced from the *Opera Omnia* published by The Aquinas Institute. Patristic quotations appearing in the *Summa* have been taken from the same source. Used with permission. Except for translations of the *Rule* of St Bendict, which are taken from or based upon Abbot McCann's version, and translations of St Gregory's *Moralia*, which were made with reference to John Henry Parker and J. Rivington's translation of 1844, all other translations are original and Copyright © 2022 by Silverstream Priory.

The Cenacle Press at Silverstream Priory
Silverstream Priory
Stamullen, County Meath, K32 T189, Ireland
www.cenaclepress.com

ppr ISBN 978-1-915544-16-2
cloth ISBN 978-1-915544-17-9

Interior layout by Kenneth Lieblich.
Cover design by Silverstream Priory.
Detail of St Augustine of Canterbury from an
opus sectile altarpiece in Westminster Cathedral, London
(Photograph: Lawrence Lew, OP).

CONTENTS

THE LIFE OF UNION WITH CHRIST (*...et secuti sumus te*)

PREFACE TO THIS EDITION

by Abbot Xavier Perrin, O.S.B.

I HAVE never forgotten the two sisters encountered on a visit to a poor Passionist convent in France in the 1980s. These two venerable nuns, well into their eighties, were in charge of the cooking, at least on certain days of the week. They had on the kitchen table a worn copy of the present book. "We take turns," they explained with a great smile, "while one is cooking, the other reads out from the book. When we have finished, we begin again from the beginning. We are never bored. It is so beautiful!"

Like these two sisters, generations of monks and nuns have fed on the rich teaching of Blessed Columba Marmion. Because it leads directly to Christ, it is inexhaustible. It goes to the heart of the *Rule* of St Benedict. Indeed, it touches the heart of hearts of any monastic soul. Contemplative and doctrinal by the constant grounding of every aspect of the monk's life in the person of Christ, it is also very practical. For the Abbot of Maredsous builds on a great experience of monastic communities. He knows the challenges monks face, the spiritual illnesses they sometimes suffer from, the fruits of holiness which faithful and generous observance quietly bears. He has read the best of monastic literature and is able to present it in a way which is both accessible and profound.

One hundred years after its publication, one turns with joy the pages of this little *chef-d'œuvre* in which many a piece of advice has not aged. Full of wisdom and simplicity, it provides an almost complete commentary on the *Rule*. One feels in it the power of the Gospel and the real grandeur of monasticism. It is able to give to monks and nuns, oblates and friends of monasteries, as well as to many Christians, a renewed trust in Christ and in St Benedict's sure guidance. Moreover, the text, albeit written by a secretary, puts us in contact with the soul of a man of great charm, unabated faith and exquisite charity, who is also a Blessed to whom one can pray. May he inspire the new start—from the *Rule* and from Christ—and the constant conversion monastic houses always need if they want to remain convincing and appealing "schools of the service of the Lord."

Quarr Abbey, Holy Week 2022
✠ *Fr Xavier Perrin, Abbot*

AUTHOR'S PREFACE

CHRIST Jesus is the sublime Ideal of all holiness, the Divine Model presented by God Himself to the imitation of His elect. Christian holiness consists in the complete and sincere acceptation of Christ by faith, and in the expansion of this faith by hope and charity; it implies the stable and total hold exercised by Christ upon our activity through the supernatural influence of His Spirit. Christ Jesus, the Alpha and Omega of all our works, becomes by the communication of His own life, the very life of our Souls: *Mihi vivere Christus est.*[1] This is what we have tried to show, in the light of the Gospels and the writings of St. Paul and St. John, in a first series of conferences entitled *Christ the Life of the Soul.* As a logical consequence, these dogmatic truths required the concrete showing forth of the very existence of the Incarnate Word. This existence is manifested to us by the states and mysteries, the actions and words of the Sacred Humanity of Jesus. Christ's works, during His terrestrial life are at once models to be imitated and sources of holiness: from them ever goes out a powerful and efficacious virtue to heal, enlighten and sanctify those who by faith come in contact with the mysteries of Jesus with the sincere desire of walking in His footsteps. We have studied, under this aspect, the Incarnate Word, in a second volume: *Christ in His Mysteries.*

But besides the precepts laid down by Christ to His disciples as condition of salvation and essential holiness, there are to be found in the Gospels some counsels that Christ proposes to those who wish to make the ascension of the Sublime heights of perfection: *Si vis perfectus esse, vade, vende omnia quae habes, et veni, sequere me.*[2]

---

1 "For to me, to live is Christ," Philip. i, 21.

2 "If thou wilt be perfect, go sell what thou hast... and come follow Me," Matth. xix, 21.

These are only counsels, undoubtedly: "If thou wilt," *Si vis,* said the Master. But the magnificent promises made by Him to those who follow them show the value that He Himself attaches to their observance: this observance has for its aim a more complete and more perfect imitation of the Saviour. Here again, He is the Way and the Model: religious perfection is but the full acquisition and the entire taking possession of the soul by the teaching and example of the Word Incarnate: *Veni, sequere me... Perfectus omnis discipulus erit si sit sicut Magister ejus.*[1]

These are the thoughts that we have endeavoured to comment upon in the present volume. We have constantly placed the Divine Figure of Christ before the eyes of privileged souls called to walk in the path of the counsels: nothing is so efficacious as this contemplation to touch and draw souls, and to obtain from them the necessary efforts in view of remaining faithful to so high a vocation and one so rich in eternal promises.

Many of these pages explain the religious life such as St. Benedict understands it; but, as we shall fully see in the sequel, in the eyes of the Patriarch of monks, the religious state, taken in what is essential, does not constitute a particular form of existence on the borders or at the side of Christianity: it is this same Christianity lived in its fulness in the pure light of the Gospel: *Per ducatum Evangelii pergamus itinera Christi.*[2] The extraordinary supernatural fecundity of which the Rule has given proof throughout so many centuries, is only to be explained by this essentially *Christian* character imprinted by St. Benedict on all his teaching.

A glance cast on the *Index of the Conferences,* at the beginning of the volume, will show the simplicity of the plan adopted. The first part gives, in broad outline, a general view of the monastic idea and institution, such as they appear to those who wish to cross the threshold of the cloister. The second part develops the programme to be filled by those desirous of adapting themselves to this idea and of embracing this institution in such a way as to assimilate all its spirit. This work presents a two-fold aspect: The necessary detachment from created things in order to cleave to Christ; the way of detachment, thus embraced, leading to the life of

---

1 "Come follow Me... every one shall be perfect, if he be as his Master," cf. Luc. vi, 40.

2 "Following the guidance of the Gospel, let us walk in the paths of Christ," Prologue of the Rule.

union: "Behold we have left all things—to follow Thee," *Ecce nos reliquimus omnia,—et secuti sumus te.* That is the whole substance of the practice of the counsels, the secret of perfection.

It will be seen that this plan closely follows the one adopted in *Christ the Life of the Soul.* This is not to be wondered at, since religious perfection is so essentially akin to Christian holiness.

May these pages serve to make a great number of souls better understand the nature of this perfection to which God so widely invites Christians; to increase in some of these the esteem of the religious vocation sometimes misunderstood by our age; to help some chosen ones to realise in themselves the call of grace or to triumph over the obstacles that natural affections or the spirit of the world oppose to its call... May they above all quicken the first fervour of such consecrated souls whose perseverance perhaps is wearied by the length of the way, obtain for those who are faithful to their vows the resolution of applying themselves without relaxing to attain the summit of the virtues; finally, stimulate among them the best of ambitions, ever unsatisfied, that of holiness!

Confident that the Heavenly Father will recognise in our humble labour the traditional teachings of His Saints,[1] and will vouchsafe to bless our efforts to prepare His field—*Apollo rigavit*[2]—we earnestly beseech Him to throw therein the divine seed by handfuls and to bring it to maturity—*Deus autem incrementum dedit.*[3]

For this let us render Him even now our humble and filial thanksgiving!

D.C.M.
Maredsous Abbey, *Solemnity of St. Benedict.* July, 11th, 1922.

---

1 Among Benedictine authors, we have chiefly quoted those who, by their teaching or life, have more particularly laid stress on the central idea expressed by the title of this book; this explains why we have by preference utilised the writings of St. Gregory, St. Bernard, St. Gertude, St. Mechtilde and Blosius.

2 "Apollo watered," I Cor. iii, 6.

3 "But God gave the increase," Ibid.

GENERAL VIEW OF THE MONASTIC INSTITUTION

TO SEEK GOD

SUMMARY.—Importance of the end in the human life.—I. "To seek God," the end of the Monastic Life.—II. To seek God in all things.—III. To seek Him only.—IV. Precious fruits of this search.—V. How Christ Jesus is the perfect Model of this seeking after God.

WHEN we examine the Rule of St. Benedict, we see very clearly that he presents it only as an abridgement of Christianity, and a means of practising the Christian Life in its fulness and perfection.

We find the great Patriarch declaring from the first lines of the Prologue of his Rule, that he only addresses those who wish to return to God under Christ's leadership. And in ending the monastic code he declares that he proposes the accomplishment of this rule to whomsoever, through the help of Christ, hasteneth to the heavenly country: *Quisquis ergo ad patriam caelestem festinas, hanc... regulam descriptam, adjuvante Christo, perfice.*[1]

To his mind, the Rule is but a simple and very safe guide for leading to God. In writing it, St. Benedict does not wish to institute anything beyond or beside the Christian life: he does not assign to his monks any special work as a particular end to be pursued; the end is, as he says, "to seek God": *Si revera quaerit Deum.*[2] This is what he requires, before all, of those who come to knock at the door of the monastery to be there received as monks; in this disposition he resumes all the others; it gives, as it were, the key to all his teaching, and determines the mode of life he wishes to see led by his sons. This is the end that he proposes, and this

1 Rule, ch. lxxiii. 2 Ibid. ch. lviii.

is why we ought always to have this end before our eyes, to examine it frequently, and above all only to act in view of it.

You know that every man, as a free and reasonable creature, acts from some deliberate motive. Let us imagine ourselves in a great city like London. At certain hours of the day the streets are thronged with people; it is like a moving army. It is the ebb and flow of a human sea. Men are coming and going, elbowing their way, passing to and fro, and all this rapidly—for "time is money"—almost without exchanging any signs among themselves. Each one of these innumerable beings is independent of the others, and has his own particular end in view. *Quid quaerunt?* What are they seeking, these thousands and thousands of men who are hurrying in the City? Why are they in such haste? Some are in search of pleasure, others pursue honours; these are urged by the fever of ambition, those by the thirst for gold; the greater number are in quest of daily bread. From time to time, a lady goes to visit the poor; a Sister of Charity seeks Jesus Christ in the person of the sick; unnoticed, a priest passes by, the pyx hidden upon his breast, as he carries the Viaticum to the dying... But out of this immense crowd pursuing created things, only a very small number are working for God alone.

And yet the influence of the motive is predominant in the value of our actions. See these two men who are embarking together for a far-off destination. Both leave country, friends, family; landing on a foreign shore, they penetrate into the interior of the country; exposed to the same dangers, they cross the same rivers and the same mountains; the sacrifices they impose upon themselves are the same. But the one is a merchant urged on by the greed of gold, the other is an apostle seeking souls. And this is why, although the human eye can scarcely discern the difference, an abyss which God alone can measure separates the lives of these two men; this abyss has been created by the motive. Give a cup of water to a beggar, a coin to a poor man; if you do so in the name of Jesus Christ, that is to say from a supernatural motive of grace, and because in this poor man you see Christ Who said: "As long as you did it to one of these my least brethren, you did it to Me,"[1] your action is pleasing to God; and this cup of water, which is nothing, this small coin, will not remain without a reward. But pour out handfuls of gold into the hand

1 Matth. xxv, 40.

of this poor man in order to pervert him: on this account alone, your action becomes abominable.

Thus then, the motive from which we act, the end that we pursue, and that is as it were to direct our whole life, is for us of capital importance.

Never forget this truth: a man is worth that which he seeks, that to which he is attached. Are you seeking God? Are you tending towards Him with all the fervour of your soul? However little removed you may be from nothingness by your condition of creature, you raise yourself, because you unite yourself to the infinitely perfect Being. Are you seeking the creature? gold, pleasures, honours, satisfaction of pride, that is to say yourself under all these forms? Then, however great you may be in the sight of men, you are just worth as much as this creature, you lower yourself to its level, and the baser it is, the more you debase yourself. A poor Sister of Charity, a simple Lay Brother, who, seeking God spend their lives in humble and obscure labours in order to accomplish the Divine will, are incomparably greater in the sight of God—Whose judgment alone matters, for He is eternal—than a man who has heaped up riches, or is surrounded with honours, or lives only for pleasures.

Yes, a man is worth what he seeks. This is why St. Benedict, who shows us the adepts of the cenobitical life as "the most strong race," *coenobitarum fortissimum genus*,[1] requires so supernatural and perfect a motive from one who wishes to embrace this career: the motive and ambition of possessing God, *si revera Deum quaerit*.[2]

But, you may say, what is it to "seek God?" And by what means are we to find Him? For it is needful to seek in such a way that we may find. To seek God constitutes the whole programme; to find God and remain habitually united to Him by the bonds of faith and love, in this lies all perfection.

Let us see what it is *to seek God*;—let us consider the conditions of this seeking; we shall next see the fruits that it brings to whomsoever applies himself to it. We shall have pointed out at the same time, with the end that we pursue, the path that will lead us to perfection and beatitude. For if we truly seek God, nothing will prevent us from finding Him, and, in Him, we shall possess all good.

---

1 Rule, ch. i. 2 Ibid. ch. lviii.

I

We must seek God.

But is God in some place where He must be sought? Is He not everywhere? Assuredly, as we know, God is in every being by His Presence, by His Power, and by His Essence. In God the operation is not separated from the active virtue whence it is derived, and the power is identical with the essence. In every being, God operates by sustaining it in existence.[1]

In this manner God is in every creature, for all exist and continue to exist only by an effect of the Divine action that supposes God's intimate presence. But reasonable beings can, moreover, know and love God, and thus possess Him in themselves.

However, this kind of immanence was not sufficient for God as regards us. There is a more intimate and elevated degree of union. God does not content Himself with being the object of a natural knowledge and love on man's part, but He calls us to share His very life and His own beatitude.

By a movement of infinite love towards us, God wishes to be for our souls not only the Sovereign Master of all things, but a Friend, a Father. It is His will that we should know Him as He knows Himself, the source of all truth and of all beauty. It is His Will that we should possess Him, the Infinite Good, here below in the dimness of faith, and above in the light of glory.

To this end, as you know, He raises our nature above itself by adorning it with sanctifying grace, infused virtues and the gifts of the Spirit. God wills, by the communication of His infinite and eternal life, to be Himself our perfect beatitude. He does not wish us to find our happiness apart from Himself, the plenitude of all good; He leaves to no creature the power of satisfying our heart: *EGO merces tua magna nimis*[2] "It is I myself who am thy reward exceeding great." And Our Lord confirmed His promise when about to pay the price thereof by the sacrifice of His Precious Blood. "Father, I will that where I am, they also whom Thou hast given Me may be with Me; that they may see My glory... that the

1 St. Thomas, II *Sentent. Dist.* xxxvii, q. I, a. 2.

2 Gen. xv, 1.

love wherewith Thou hast loved me, may be in them."[1]

Such is the unique and supreme end to which we must tend; we have to seek God; not only the God of nature, but the God of Revelation. For us Christians, then, "to seek God" is to tend towards Him, not only as simple creatures who move towards the first principle and last end of their being, but supernaturally, that is to say as children who wish to remain united to their Father with all their strength of will urged by love, and through that mysterious participation in the very nature of God, of which St. Peter speaks;[2] it is to have and to cultivate with the Divine Persons an intimacy so real and so profound, that St. John calls it, the "fellowship with the Father, and with His Son Jesus Christ," in their common Spirit.[3]

It is to this the Psalmist alludes when he exhorts us to "seek the face of God" *Quaerite FACIEM ejus semper*:[4] that is to say, to seek the friendship of God, to seek His love, as when the bride looking upon the bridegroom seeks to behold in his eyes the depth of his soul telling her of his tenderness. God is to us a Father full of goodness. He wills that even here below we should find our happiness in Him, in His ineffable perfections.

St. Benedict has no other views for his disciples. From the first lines of the Prologue, he warns us not to grieve by our evil deeds the God Who has vouchsafed to count us among His children.

"To attain to God," this is the end that St. Benedict wishes us to have ever before our eyes. This principle, like a life-giving sap, circulates through all the articles of the monastic code.

We have not come to the monastery then, in order to devote ourselves to science, nor the arts, nor the work of education. It is true that the great Patriarch wishes us at all times to serve God with the good things He has given us: *ei (Deo) omni tempore de bonis suis in nobis parendum est*:[5] He wishes the house of God to be wisely governed by prudent men;[6] doubtless this recommendation primarily foresees the material organisation, but it can be equally applied to the moral and intellectual life of the monastery. St. Benedict does not wish the talents given by God to remain hidden, he permits the cultivation of the arts; a constant tradi-

1 Cf. Joan. xvii, 24, 26.
2 II Petr. i, 4.
3 I Joan. i, 3.
4 Ps. civ, 4.
5 Prologue of the Rule.
6 Rule, ch. liii.

tion, which we ought humbly to respect, has in the same way sufficiently established for monks the legitimacy of studies and apostolic labours, and the Abbot, the head of the monastery, will certainly have it at heart to preserve the diverse manifestations of monastic activity; he will endeavour to develop for the common good, for the service of the Church, for the salvation of souls, and for God's glory, the various aptitude that he finds in each of his monks.

But once again, the end does not lie in this. All these works are only means in view of an end; the end is higher: it is in God, it is God sought for Himself, as the Supreme Beatitude.

Thus as we shall see later, the Divine worship itself neither constitutes nor can constitute the direct end that the monastic institution established by the Rule wills to attain. St. Benedict will have us seek God,—seek Him for His own glory, because we love Him above all things. He would have us seek to unite ourselves to Him by charity. There is not, for us, any other end, or any other perfection. The worship of God proceeds from the virtue of religion, doubtless the highest of the moral virtues, and it is united to the virtue of justice, but it is not a theological virtue. The infused theological virtues: faith, hope, and charity are the specific virtues of our state as children of God. Properly speaking, the supernatural life is based here below on these three virtues. They regard God directly inasmuch as He is the author of the supernatural order. Faith is like the root, hope the stalk, and charity at once the flower and the fruit of the supernatural life.

Now, it is this charity, whereby we are and remain truly united to God, that constitutes the end assigned by St. Benedict and the very essence of perfection: *Si revera Deum quaerit.*

This end establishes the true greatness of the monastic life; it also establishes the true reason of its existence. In the opinion of Pseudo-Denys the Areopagite, we are given the name of "monks" μονος "alone, one" on account of this life of indivisible unity, whereby, withdrawing our mind from the distraction of manifold things, we hasten towards divine unity and towards the perfection of holy love.[1]

1 Cf. "*Of the Ecclesiastical Hierarchy.*"

II

The ambition of possessing God:—such is the primal disposition that St. Benedict requires of the postulant who presents himself at the door of the monastery; he sees in this a proof of a sure vocation; but this disposition must extend to the monk's whole life.

For the abbot himself, the great Patriarch wishes that first and foremost he should seek "the Kingdom of God"[1] in charity, as Christ commanded; that he should have care, above all to establish this kingdom in the souls entrusted to Him.[2] All material activity exerted in the monastery ought to have but this one end in view: *Ut in omnibus glorificetur Deus*: "that in all things God may be glorified,"[3] for in all things love refers everything to His glory.

Let us carefully notice these words: "in all things," *in omnibus*. This is one of the conditions of our seeking God. In order for it to be "true," as St. Benedict requires, our seeking after God must be constant; we must "seek His face *evermore*": *Quaerite faciem ejus* SEMPER. You may say: but do we not possess God from the time of our baptism, and as long as we are in possession of sanctifying grace? Undoubtedly. Then why seek God, if we possess Him already?

"To seek God," is to remain united to Him by faith, it is to attach ourselves to Him as the object of our love. Now we know that this union of faith and love admits of a vast number of degrees. "God is everywhere present," says St. Ambrose, "but He is nearest to those who love Him, He dwells far from those who neglect His service." *Dominus ubique semper est: sed est praesentior diligentibus, negligentibus abest.*[4] When we have found God, we can still seek Him, that is to say we can always draw nearer to God, by an ever intenser faith, an ever more fervent love, an ever more faithful accomplishment of His will, and this is why we can and ought *always* to seek God, until the day when He will give Himself to us in an inamissible manner in the glorious splendour of His indefectible light.

If we do not attain this end, we shall remain useless and unprofitable. The Psalmist says,—and St. Benedict quotes these words in the Prologue in commenting upon them,—that "the Lord hath looked down from

1 Rule, ch. ii (Cf. Matth. vi, 33).
2 Ibid.
3 Ibid. chap. lvii.
4 St. Ambrose.

heaven upon the children of men, to see if there be any that understand and seek God. They are all gone aside, they are become unprofitable together." *Dominus de caelo prospexit super filios hominum ut videat si est intelligens aut requirens Deum; omnes declinaverunt, simul inutiles facti sunt.*[1] How many men indeed do not understand that God is the source of all good and the supreme end of every creature? These men have turned aside from the road that leads to the end, they have become unprofitable. Why is this? What is a useless being? It is one that does not correspond to the end for which it was created. For instance, in order to fulfil the end for which it is purchased, a watch must show the time. It may well be of gold, studded with diamonds, encrusted with precious stones, but unless it keeps time it is useless.

We too become useless beings if we do not tend unceasingly to the end for which we came to the monastery. Now, this end is to seek God, to refer all to Him as to our Supreme End, to place in Him our sole beatitude; all the rest is "vanity of vanities."[2] If we do not act thus, we are useless, it is in vain that we spend ourselves; even though this spending of ourselves should appear remarkable in the eyes of the world, in God's sight, it would be that of profitless beings, who do not fulfil the conditions required by their existence, and have lost sight of the end to which their vocation predestined them. How terrible is the uselessness of a human life! And how much there is that is useless sometimes in our life, even our religious life, because God is absent from our actions!...

Do not let us, then, be of those foolish people of which Scripture speaks, who are stayed by vain and passing trifles.[3] Let us be attentive to seek God in all things: in the Superiors, in our brethren, in all creatures, in the events of life, in the midst of contradiction as in hours of joy.

Let us seek Him always, so as to be able unceasingly to put our lips to this source of beatitude; we can always drink from it, without fear of seeing the waters exhausted, for, says St. Augustine, their abundance surpasses our need: *Fons vincit sitientem.* It is of them that Christ Jesus said that they become in the soul "a fountain of water, springing up into life everlasting."[4]

1 Ps. xiii, 2–3. 2 Eccle. i, 2. 3 Sap. iv, 12. 4 Joan. iv, 14.

III

Another condition of the sincerity of our seeking is that it be *exclusive*. Let us seek God solely; I look upon this condition as capital.

To seek God solely, that is without doubt the same as saying to seek God Himself. Notice the term "God," not the gifts of God, although they help us to remain faithful; nor His consolations, although God wills that we taste the sweetness of His service;[1] but we ought not to stop at these gifts nor be attached to these consolations. It is for God Himself that we have come to the monastery; our seeking will then only be "true," as St. Benedict wishes it to be, it will only be pleasing to God, if we are attached to nothing apart from God.

When we seek the creature, when we are attached to it, it is as if we said to God: "My God, I do not find all in Thee." There are many souls who have need of something *with* God, of something *more* than God; God is not *all* for them; they cannot, like the Saint of Assisi, look at God and say to Him, with all the truth of their being: "My God and my All": *Deus meus et omnia*. They cannot repeat after St. Paul: *OMNIA detrimentum feci et arbitror ut stercora ut Christum lucrifaciam*: "I count *all things* to be but loss for the excellent knowledge of Jesus Christ my Lord; for Whom I have suffered the loss of all things, and count them as dung that I may gain Christ."[2]

Never forget this extremely important truth: as long as we experience the need of a creature, and are attached to it, we cannot say that we seek God *solely*, and God will not give Himself entirely to us. If it is our will that our search be sincere,—*si REVERA quaerit*,—if we want to find God fully, we must detach ourselves from all that is not God, and that would shackle in us the operation of His grace.

This is the doctrine of the saints. Listen to what St. Catherine of Siena said on her death bed. Feeling her end approaching, she gathered her spiritual family around her, and gave them her last instructions which have been collected by her confessor, the Blessed Raymund of Capua: "Her first and fundamental teaching was that he who enters into the service of God, ought necessarily, if he truly wishes to possess God, to root out from his heart all sensible affection, not only for persons but

---

1 Cf. Ps. xxxiii, 9. 2 Philip. iii, 8.

moreover for any creature whatever, and tend towards His Divine Creator in the simplicity of an undivided love. For the heart cannot be given entirely to God if it is not free from all other love, and if it does not open itself with a frankness exclusive of all reserve."[1]

St. Teresa, speaking from the same experience says, "We are so miserly, so slow in giving ourselves to God that we never finish putting ourselves into the necessary dispositions. And yet Our Lord will not allow us to enter into the enjoyment of so precious a treasure (the perfect possession of God) without paying a high price for it. I see clearly that there is nothing upon earth wherewith it can be purchased." However, the Saint adds, "if we did all that depended upon ourselves not to cling to anything earthly, if our conversation and all our thoughts were in heaven, such a treasure I am convinced would be granted to us." The Saint next shows by some examples how it often happens that we give ourselves to God, entirely, but afterwards take back little by little what we have given; and she concludes: "A nice way forsooth to seek the love of God! We must have it at once and "in handfuls" as the saying is, but on condition of retaining our affections. To take possession of it, we do not make any effort to fulfil our good desires, we allow them to drag miserably upon the earth. And with all this, we must moreover have many spiritual consolations! Truly, they will not be granted to us. In my opinion, these two things are quite incompatible. Therefore *it is because our gift is not entire* that we do not receive without delay the treasure of divine love."[2]

It is to find God, "to please Him alone," that, after the example of the great Patriarch, we have left all: *Soli Deo placere desiderans*, says St. Gregory.[3] We must always remain in this fundamental disposition. It is only at this price that we shall find God. If, on the contrary, forgetting little by little our initial gift, we allow ourselves to turn aside from this supreme aim, if we cling to some person, some employment, some charge, some work or occupation, some object, then, let us be convinced of this, we shall never possess God fully.

Oh! if we could say, and say in all truth, what the Apostle Philip said to Jesus: "Lord, shew us the Father, and it is enough for us!" But in or-

1 *Life* by Raymund of Capua.
2 *Life by herself*, ch. xi.
3 *Dialogues*. Lib. ii.

der to be able to say this in truth, we must also be able to say with the Apostles: "Lord, we have left all things and have followed Thee..." Happy are they who carry out this desire to its end, to extreme, actual and perfect renunciation! But let them not say: this trifle to which I cling is nothing. Do you not know the nature of the human heart? However little we leave to it, it will not be content till it has obtained all its desire. Tear all away, break all asunder, hold to nothing. Happy indeed are they to whom it is given to carry out this desire to the end, to pursue it even to attainment.[1]

IV

If we seek God in spite of every trial, if each day, each hour, we give Him this homage, so extremely pleasing to Him, which consists of placing in Him, and in Him alone, our beatitude; if we never seek anything but His will; if we act, in such a way that His good pleasure is the true motive power of all our activity, God will never fail us. "God is faithful";[2] He cannot forsake those who seek Him: *Non dereliquisti quaerentes te, Domine.*[3] The nearer we approach Him by faith, confidence and love, the nearer we approach our perfection. As God is the principal author of our holiness, since it is supernatural, to draw near to Him, to remain united to Him by charity constitutes the very condition of our perfection. The more we set ourselves free from all sin, from all imperfection, from all creatures, from all human springs of action, in order to think only of Him, to seek only His good pleasure, the more, too, life will abound in us and God will fill us with Himself: *Quaerite Deum, et vivet anima vestra.*[4]

There are souls who so sincerely seek God that they are wholly possessed by Him, and no longer know how to live without Him. "I declare to you," a holy Benedictine nun, the Blessed Bonomo, wrote to her father, "that it is not I that live, but another in me Who has entire possession of me; He is my absolute Master. O God! I know not how to drive Him from me!..."[5]

1 Bossuet, *Meditations upon the Gospel,* The Last Supper, 2nd part, 83rd day.

2 Thess. v, 25. 3 Ps. ix, 11.

4 "Seek ye God, and your soul shall live," Ps. lxviii, 33.

5 D. du Bourg, *La Bse J. M. Bonomo, moniale bénédictine,* Paris 1910, p. 56.

When the soul is thus wholly given to God, God also gives Himself to the soul; He takes a particular care of her; one might at times say that for such a soul God forgets the rest of the universe. Look at St. Gertrude. You know what a special love Our Lord manifested towards her; He declared that He had not then upon the earth "any creature towards whom He stooped with more delight";[1] to the point that He added He would always be found in the heart of Gertrude, whose least desires He loved to fulfil. One who knew of this great intimacy dared to ask Our Lord what were the attractions whereby St. Gertrude had merited a like preference. "I love her in this way" replied Our Lord, "on account of her liberty of heart wherein nothing enters that can dispute the sovereignty with Me." Thus because, entirely detached from every creature, she sought God only in all things, this Saint merited to be the object of divine delight truly ineffable and extraordinary.

Let us, then, seek God always and in all, after the example of this great soul, herself a worthy daughter of the great Patriarch; let us seek Him sincerely, from the depth of our hearts. Let us often say to Him like the Psalmist: "Thy face, O Lord, will I seek." *Faciem tuam, Domine, requiram.*[2] "For what have I in heaven, and besides Thee what do I desire upon earth?... Thou art the God of my heart, and the God that is my portion for ever" *Quid enim mihi est in caelo, et a te quid volui super terram? Deus cordis mei et pars mea Deus in aeternum.*[3] My God, Thou art so great, so beautiful, so good, that, as Thou knowest, Thou dost fully suffice me. Let others cling to human love, not only dost Thou permit it but Thy Providence has established that it should be so, and this mission of preparing the elect for Thy Kingdom is a great and high mission: Thy Apostle says: *Sacramentum hoc magnum est*;[4] Thou givest abundant blessings to those who observe Thy law in this state.[5] As for me, I want Thee alone so that my heart may be undivided and solicitous only for the interests of Thy glory and may cleave to Thee without impediment.[6]

1 *The Herald of Divine Love,* Bk. i, ch. 3.
2 Ps. xxvi, 8.
3 Ps. lxxii, 25–26.
4 "This is a great sacrament," Eph. v, 32.
5 Ps. cxxvii.
6 I Cor. vii, 32, 35.

And when created things present themselves to us, let us say inwardly: *Discede a me, pabulum mortis*: "Depart from me, for thou art the prey of death."[1]

If we act in this way, we shall find God, and with Him all good things. "Seek Me," He says Himself to the soul, "with that simplicity of heart which is born of sincerity, for I am found by them that tempt me not, and shew Myself to them that have faith in Me."[2]

In finding God, we shall likewise possess joy.

We were made to be happy; the human heart has a capacity for the infinite; only God can fully satisfy us. "Thou didst make us for Thyself, O Lord, and our heart is restless until it finds its rest in Thee": *Fecisti nos ad te, et inquietum est cor nostrum, donec requiescat in te.*[3] This is why when we seek anything apart from God or from His will, we do not find stable and perfect happiness.

It may be said that in any rather numerous religious community, different categories of souls are to be met with. You will see some living in continual gladness. Their inward joy radiates outwardly. I am not now speaking of that sensible joy which often depends upon the temperament, the state of health, or of circumstances independent of the will, but of joy abiding in the depth of the soul which is like a foretaste of heavenly bliss. Have these souls then never any trials? Have they no conflicts to sustain, nor contradictions to undergo? Certainly they have, for each disciple of Jesus Christ has to carry his cross;[4] but the fervour of grace and divine unction make them endure these sufferings joyfully. Other souls do not feel this gladness; inwardly, and often even outwardly, they are troubled, distressed, unhappy. Whence comes this difference?

Because the first seek God in all things, and seeking Him alone they find Him everywhere, and, with Him, supreme good and unchanging bliss: *Bonus est Dominus animae quaerenti illum.*[5] The others are either attached to created things or seek themselves, by egotism, self-love,

1 Office of St. Agnes, 1st Ant. I Noct.

2 Sap. i, 1–2.

3 St. Augustine, *Confessions. Lib.* i, ch. 1.

4 Cf. Luc. ix, 23.

5 "The Lord is good to them that hope in him, to the soul that seeketh him," Thren. iii, 25.

levity; and it is themselves too that they find—themselves, that is to say nothingness, and this cannot content them, for the soul, created for God thirsts after perfect good. "What fills your mind? Where your thoughts naturally turn, there is your treasure, there is your heart. If it is God, you are happy; if it is anything mortal, unceasingly consumed by rust, corruption, mortality, your treasure will escape you, and your heart will remain poor and arid."[1]

When a man of the world tires of his own hearth, he forgets his boredom by seeking distractions outside; he goes to his Club, or he travels. But the religious has not these resources; he has to stay in his monastery, where the regular life, with its successive exercises for which the bell inexorably rings, is uninterrupted by those natural distractions which people in the world may lawfully seek; with souls for whom God is not all, weariness easily slips into that monotony inherent to all regular life; and when the monk does not find God, because he does not seek God, he is very near estimating that the burden he has to carry is too heavy.

He could, doubtless, become absorbed in an occupation, forget himself in his work, but, says Blosius, this is an insufficient and illusory diversion: *Quidquid praeter Deum quaeritur mentem occupat, non satiat.*[2] And why is this? Because, especially in the monastery, there are always hours when a man has to come face to face with himself, that is to say with his own nothingness; the soul in its depths does not taste that transporting joy, it does not experience that deep and peaceful fervour which is given by the intimate nearness of God; it does not go straight to God; it hovers unceasingly around Him without ever finding Him perfectly.

But when the soul seeks God, and seeks Him alone, when it tends towards Him with all its energies, when it clings to no created thing, God fills it with joy, with that overflowing joy of which St. Benedict speaks when he says that in the measure wherein faith, and with it hope and love

1 Bossuet, *Meditations on the Gospel*, Sermon on the Mount. 29th day.

2 Whatsoever is sought apart from God occupies the mind, but does not satisfy it. *Canon vitae spiritualis*, ch. 15. The great Abbot was moreover in this but the echo of an old monk: *Ad imaginem Dei facta est anima rationalis; caeteris omnibus occupari potest, repleri non potest; capacem Dei quidquid Deo minus est non implebit* (The rational animal is made unto the image of God; he is able to be occupied by all other things, but he cannot be filled by them; whatever is less than God will not fill the one capable of God). *P. L. t.* 184, col. 455.

increase in the soul of the monk, he runs, "with heart enlarged and unspeakable sweetness of love, in the way of God's commandments": *Dilatato corde, inenarrabili dilectionis dulcedine curritur via mandatorum Dei.*[1]

Let us then often repeat like that great monk St. Bernard: *Ad quid venisti?* "Wherefore have I come?" Why have I left the world? Why have I separated myself from all who were dear to me? Why have I renounced my liberty? Why have I made so many and such great sacrifices? Did I come to give myself up to intellectual labours? To gain knowledge? To occupy myself with the arts, or with teaching?

No, we came, never let us forget this, for one thing, and one thing only: "to seek God." *Si revera Deum quaerit.* It was to win this one precious pearl of the possession of God that we renounced everything: *Inventa una pretiosa margarita vendidit omnia quae habuit et emit eam.*[2]

We should examine ourselves to see to what degree we seek God, to what point we are detached from the creature. If we are loyal, God will show us what there is in us that hinders us from going to Him with all our heart. Our end and our glory is to seek God; it is a very high vocation, that of belonging to the race of those who seek God: *Haec est generatio quaerentium eum;*[3] in choosing the one thing necessary, we have chosen the better part: *Hereditas mea praeclara est mihi.*[4]

Let us remain faithful to this sublime vocation. We shall not arrive at the realisation of our ideal in a day nor yet in a year; we shall not arrive at it without difficulty or without sufferings, for that purity of affection, that absolute detachment, full and constant, which God requires of us before giving Himself entirely to us, is only gained by much generosity; but if we have decided to give ourselves completely to God, without reservation, and never to bargain with Him for the least corner of our heart, to admit no attachment, however slight it may be to any creature, let us be assured that God will reward our efforts by the perfect possession of Himself, wherein we shall find all our beatitude. "With what mercy God treats a soul," says St. Teresa, "when He bestows upon her

---

1 Prologue to the Rule.

2 "Who when he had found one pearl of great price, went his way, and sold all that he had, and bought it," Matth. xiii, 46.

3 Ps. xxiii, 6.

4 "For my inheritance is goodly to me," Ps. xv, 6.

grace and courage to devote herself generously and with all her might to the pursuit of such a good! Let her but persevere, God refuses Himself to none: little by little He will increase her courage, and finally she will gain the victory."[1]

"When we are thoroughly resolved," wrote a soul who had understood how God is everything, and knew faithfully how to seek God alone, "it is only the first steps that count; for from the moment that our well beloved Saviour sees our good will, He does all the rest. I will refuse nothing to Jesus Whose love urges me. You know how eloquent is the voice of Jesus. Besides, no one is foolish enough to give up the whole for a part. The love of Jesus, that is the whole; the rest, whatever one may think, is but a negligable quantity, despicable even, in contrast with our unique treasure. I am resolved to surrender myself to the love of Christ. I am indifferent to all else; I wish to love Him even to folly; men may break and crush my will and understanding, all that you will, but I do not intend to let go of the sole good, our Divine Jesus, or rather I feel that it is He Who will not let me go. It is needful that our souls should please Jesus, but no other person."[2]

V

In this seeking after God, the principle of our holiness, we cannot find a better model than Christ Jesus Himself.

But, you will at once say, how is this, can Christ be our Model? how could He "seek God," since He was God Himself?

It is true that Jesus is God, the true God come forth from God, the Light arising from the Uncreated Light,[3] the Son of the Living God, equal to the Father. But He is likewise man; He is authentically one of us, through His human nature. And although this human nature is united in an indissoluble way to the Divine Person of the Word, although the holy soul of Jesus has ceaselessly enjoyed the delights of the Beatific Vision, although it has been drawn into the divine current which necessarily bears the Son towards the Father, it remains true to say that

---

1 L. c. p. 145.

2 Une âme bénédictine, D. Pie de Hemptinne. 5° édit., p. 264.

3 Credo of the Mass.

Christ's human activity, which was derived from His human faculties as from its immediate sources, was sovereignly free.

It is in the exercise of this free activity that we can find in Jesus that which we call the "seeking after God." What are the innermost aspirations of His soul, those to which He Himself refers all His mission, and in which He sums up all His life?

St. Paul tells us; he raises for us a corner of the veil to enable us to penetrate into the Holy of Holies. He tells us that the first throb of the soul of Jesus on entering into this world was one of infinite intensity towards His Father: *Ingrediens mundum, dicit:... Ecce venio, in capite libri scriptum est de me: ut faciam, Deus, voluntatem tuam.*[1]

And we see Christ Jesus, like a giant, rejoice to run the way, in the pursuit of the glory of His Father. This is His primal disposition. Let us hear how, in the Gospel, He clearly tells us so. "I seek not My own will, but the will of Him that sent Me."[2] To the Jews, He proves that He comes from God, that His doctrine is divine, because He seeks the glory of Him that sent Him.[3] He seeks it to such a degree that He has no solicitude for His own.[4] He has ever these words upon His lips: "My Father"; His whole life is but the magnificent echo of this cry: *Abba, (Pater)*. All for Him is summed up in seeking the will and the glory of His Father.

And what constancy in this search! He Himself declares to us that He never deviated from it: "I do always the things that please [my Father]": *Quae placita sunt ei facio semper*;[5] at the supreme hour of His last farewell, at the moment when about to deliver Himself up to death, He tells us that all the mission He had received from His Father was accomplished.[6]

Nothing, moreover, stayed Him in this search. It was to pursue it that at the age of twelve years He left His Mother, the Blessed Virgin, at Jerusalem. Never did child love his Mother as Jesus loved the Blessed Virgin. Put together all the love that can animate the heart of a son; it is only a flickering spark beside this furnace of the love of Jesus for His Mother. And yet, as soon as it concerns His Father's will, or His glory, one would say that this love no longer counts for anything. Jesus knew

1 "Wherefore when He cometh into the world, He saith:... Behold I come: in the head of the book it is written of Me: that I should do Thy will, O God," Hebr. x, 5–7.

2 Joan. v, 30.
3 Ibid. vii, 18.
4 Ibid. viii, 50.
5 Ibid. viii, 29.
6 Ibid. xvii, 4.

into what an abyss of anguish He plunged His Mother's heart during three days, but the interests of His Father required it, and hence He did not hesitate: "Did you not know that I must be about My Father's business?"[1] These words fallen from the lips of Jesus, are the first that have been gathered up by the Gospel. Christ therein sums up all His Person, condenses all His Mission.

The sorrows and the ignominies of the Passion, even death itself, does not diminish this burning fervour of the Heart of Jesus for His Father's glory; quite the contrary. It is because in all things He seeks the will of the Father, as manifested by the Scriptures, that He delivers Himself, out of love, to the torments of the Cross: *Ut impleantur scripturae.*[2] The waters of a river do not rush towards the ocean with more majestic impetuosity than the soul of Jesus tended inwardly towards the abyss of sufferings wherein the Passion was to plunge Him. "That the world may know that I love the Father; and as the Father hath given Me commandment, so do I": *Et sicut mandatum dedit mihi Pater, sic facio.*[3]

If, as God, Jesus is the term of our seeking, as Man, He is the unique Exemplar wherefrom we ought never to turn our gaze. Let us take to ourselves these words and say: *Ingrediens monasterium, dixi: Ecce venio.* On the day of my entering the monastery I said: Behold I come. In the head of the Rule, which is for me the book of Thy good pleasure, it is written that I should seek Thee in doing Thy will, for it is to Thee, O My heavenly Father, that I will to attain.

And in the same way as Christ Jesus rejoices "to run the way" *ad currendam viam*,[4] let us run in His train, since He is Himself the Way. "Run," says St. Benedict, "while ye have the light of life"; carried along by the holy desire of reaching the Kingdom where our heavenly Father awaits us, let us press forward unceasingly in the practise of good deeds; that is the indispensable condition for attaining the goal. *Nisi illuc bonis actibus currendo minime pervenitur.*[5]

And again in the same way as Christ Jesus, coming down from heaven, only finished His glorious course when He gained the height of heaven;

1 Luc. ii, 49.
2 "But that the scriptures may be fulfilled," Marc. xiv, 49.
3 Joan. xiv, 31.
4 Ps. xviii, 6.
5 "Except we run thither with good deeds we shall not arrive," Prologue to the Rule.

Et occursus ejus usque ad summum ejus,[1] so let us not grow weary, as we follow after Him, in seeking God, in seeking Him solely, until we arrive at that which the great Patriarch so well calls, at the close of his Rule, the *culmina virtutum*, the *celsitudo perfectionis*,[2] the "lofty summits of virtue," "the heights of perfection." The soul thus "arrived" lives habitually united to God Whom she seeks, she has already a foretaste of the delights of the ineffable union which is attained in the beatitude of the Father's Bosom: *apud Patrem*.

"O Lord, my God, my one hope, hear me so that I may never weary of seeking Thee, but that with unfailing ardour my soul may ever seek Thy Countenance. Grant the strength to seek Thee, O Thou Who givest the grace to find Thee after having more and more given the hope of attaining Thee."[3]

NOTE: "SEEKING AFTER GOD," ACCORDING TO ST. BERNARD.

"It is a great good, this will to seek God. In my opinion it deserves to be esteemed second to none of all the goods of the soul. It is the first grace which the soul receives, and it is also the last advance she makes in her progress towards perfection. It follows after no virtue, neither does it yield place to any. What virtue can it be supposed to follow, since it is preceded by none? Or to what virtue can it give place, since it is itself the crown and consummation of all? For how can any virtue be ascribed to the man who has not the will to seek God? And as to him who does seek God, what term shall be appointed for his seeking? "Seek His Face evermore," says the Psalmist, by which he implies, as it seems to me, that even after God has been found He shall not cease to be sought. For it is not by bodily locomotion that we have to seek God, but by fervent desire. Now this desire, so far from being extinguished by the happy at-

1 Ps. xviii, 7. 2 Rule, ch. lxxiii.

3 *Domine Deus meus, una spes mea, exaudi me, ne fatigatus nolim te quaerere, sed quaeram faciem tuam semper ardenter. Tu da quaerendi vires qui invenire te fecisti, et magis magisque inveniendi te spem dedisti!* St. Augustine. *De Trinitate*, I, xv, ch. 28.

tainment of its Object, is on the contrary greatly intensified. How is it possible that the consummation of joy should be the exclusion of desire? It would be more true to say that the former is to the latter as oil to flame, because desire is in truth a flame. So it is, my brethren. The joy is made perfect, yet there is no end to the desire, and by consequence no end to the seeking. But conceive (if you can) of this eager seeking as implying no absence of what is sought, and of this ardent desire as being accompanied by no solicitude. For absence is incompatible with possession and solicitude with security of tenure." *In Cantica*, Serm. LXXXIV, 1, translated by a priest of Mount Melleray.

THE FOLLOWING OF CHRIST

SUMMARY.—In consequence of sin, the "seeking after God" takes the character of a "returning to God"; this is carried into effect by following Christ.—I. Christ is the Way by His teaching and example.—II. He is the supreme High Priest Who binds us to God.—III. The Fountainhead of grace wherefrom we may draw the necessary help.—IV. These truths apply to religious perfection: Christ is "the Religious" supereminently.—V. How the Rule of St. Benedict is permeated with these truths; its character is "Christocentric."

THE object of our life is "to seek God"; that is our destiny, our vocation. This vocation is incomparably high, because every creature, even the angelic creature, is of its nature infinitely far removed from God. God is the fulness of Being and of all perfection; and every creature, however perfect it may be, is only a being drawn out of nothing and possesses only a borrowed perfection.

Moreover, as we have said, the end of a free creature is, in itself, proportioned to the nature of this creature; as every created being is "finite," the beatitude to which it has a right by nature is necessarily limited. But God, in immense condescension, has willed to admit us to share His intimate life in the bosom of His Adorable Trinity, to enjoy His own Divine Beatitude. This Beatitude, placed infinitely beyond our nature, constitutes our last end and the foundation of the supernatural order.

You know that from the time when He first formed man, God has called us universally to this beatitude: Adam, the head of the human race, was created in supernatural "justice"; his soul, filled with grace, illuminated with divine light was entirely set towards God. He possessed the gift of integrity by which his lower faculties were fully subjected to reason while reason was fully subjected to the Divine Will: all, in the head of our race, was perfectly in harmony.

Adam sinned, he separated himself from God, and drew all his descendants after him into his revolt and misery. All—the Blessed Virgin Mary excepted—are conceived with the imprint of his apostacy; in each one of us God beholds the trace of our first father's rebellion: that is why we are born "children of wrath," *filii irae*,[1] sons of disobedience, far removed from God, turned away from God.

The consequence of this state of things is that "the seeking after God" takes for us the character of a "returning to God" Whom we have lost. Drawn into the original solidarity, we have all forsaken God by sin in order to turn to the creature; the parable of the Prodigal Son is but the picture of all the human race that has left the Heavenly Father and must return to Him. It is this character of a "return" deeply imprinted on the Christian life that St. Benedict teaches, as a master, from the first lines of the Prologue to whomsoever comes to him: "Hearken, O my son... incline the ear of thy heart... that thou mayest return to Him from Whom thou hast departed": *Ausculta, O fili... et inclina aurem cordis tui ut AD EUM... REDEAS a quo... recesseras*. This is the well-determined and precise end.

Now, by what path are we "to return to God?" It is extremely important that we should know it. In fact if we do not take this path, we shall not come to God; we shall miss our end. For we must never forget that our holiness is a supernatural holiness, we cannot acquire it by our own efforts. If God had not raised us to the supernatural order, if He had not placed our beatitude in His intimate glory, we might have been able to seek Him by the light of reason, and attain, by natural means, a natural perfection and beatitude. God did not will this: He has raised man to a supernatural state, because He destined him for a beatitude which surpasses all the exigences and powers of our nature. Outside this destiny there is nothing but error and damnation.

And what is true of the way of salvation, in general, is equally so of perfection and of holiness which are but a higher way of salvation: they likewise belong to the supernatural order; a man's most finished perfection in the merely natural domain has of itself no value for eternal life.

1 Eph. ii, 3.

There are not two states of perfection for us nor two beatitudes, the one purely natural, the other supernatural, between which we may make our choice. Now, as God is the sole Author of the supernatural order, He alone "according to His good pleasure," *secundum beneplacitum ejus*,[1] can show us the road whereby to arrive at it; hence we must seek God as God wishes us to seek Him, otherwise we shall not find Him.

This is one of the reasons why so many souls make such little progress in the spiritual life. They imagine a holiness for themselves, they want to be the architects of their own perfection, built up according to their personal conceptions; they do not understand God's plan as it concerns them, or else they do not adapt themselves to it. These souls make some progress, certainly, because the goodness of God is infinite and His grace ever fruitful; but they do not fly in the way that leads to God; they go haltingly all their life. The more I come in contact with souls, the more assured I am that it is already a most precious grace to know this Divine Plan; to have recourse to it is a source of continual communication of divine grace; to adapt oneself to it is the very substance of sanctity.

But has God made known to us His Will? Yes, as St. Paul says, He has revealed to us the secret "hidden from eternity": *Sacramentum absconditum a saeculis*.[2] And what is this secret? What are these Divine thoughts? St. Paul has disclosed to us the Divine Plan in four words: *Instaurare omnia in Christo*.[3] God has willed "to re-establish all things in Christ" or better, according to the Greek term "to recapitulate all things in Christ."

The Christ, the Divine Word, Son of God, become Son of Adam by being born of the Blessed Virgin Mary, is constituted the Head of the race of the elect in order to bring all those who believe in Him to God His Father. As Man-God, Christ will repair the sin committed by Adam, will restore to us the Divine adoption, re-open the gates of Heaven and bring us thither by His grace. This is in a few words the Divine Plan.

Let us contemplate for a few moments this plan of God for us and try to comprehend its height and depth, *comprehendere... quae sit... sublimitas et profundum... ut impleamini in omnem plenitudinem Dei*,[4] that

1 Eph. i, 9. 2 Cf. Ibid. iii, 9; Col. i, 26. 3 Eph. i, 10.

4 "You may be able to comprehend... what is the... height and depth... that you may be filled unto all the fulness of God," Ibid. iii, 18–19.

we "may be filled unto all the fulness of God." God wishes to give us all things, to give Himself entirely to us, but He only gives Himself by Christ, in Christ and with Christ: *Per Ipsum, cum Ipso, in Ipso.*[1] This is God's secret for us. Let us contemplate it with faith and reverence, for it infinitely surpasses all our conceptions. Let us also contemplate it with love, for it is itself the fruit of love: *Sic Deus dilexit mundum.*[2] It is because God loved us that He has given us His Son, and through Him and in Him, every good.

What then is Christ Jesus for us?

He is the Way; He is the High Priest; He is the Fountainhead of grace. He is the Way by His doctrine and example; He is the supreme High Priest, Who was merited for us, by His sacrifice, the power to follow in the way which He has established; He is the Fountain of grace wherefrom we draw strength to persevere in the path that leads to "the holy mountain": *Usque ad montem Dei.*[3]

We will first of all listen to the very words of the Holy Spirit; next we will take up in respectful parallelism the corresponding teaching repeated by the one who was, according to St. Gregory, his first biographer, "filled with the spirit of all the just."[4]

I

Christ is the *Way.*

God wills that we should seek Him as He is in Himself, in a way conformable to our supernatural end. But, says St. Paul, God "inhabiteth light inaccessible,"[5] He dwells in very holiness: *Tu autem in sancto habitas.*[6] How then are we to attain to Him? Through Christ. Christ Jesus is the Word Incarnate, the Man-God. He it is Who becomes "our Way": *Ego sum via.*[7] This way is sure, infallible, it leads to eternal light: *Qui sequitur Me non ambulat in tenebris, sed habebit lumen vitae,*[8] but above all, never let us forget, this way is unique, there is no other. As Jesus says: "No man cometh to the Father but by Me": *Nemo venit ad*

1 Canon of the Mass. 2 Joan. iii, 16. 3 III Reg. xix, 8.
4 St. Gregory, *Dialogues*. Lib. ii, ch. 8. 5 I Tim. vi, 16.
6 Ps. xxi, 4. 7 Joan. xiv, 16.
8 "He that followeth Me, walketh not in darkness, but shall have the light of life," Ibid. viii, 12.

Patrem nisi per Me.[1] *Ad Patrem*, that is to say to life everlasting, to God loved and possessed in Himself in the intimate secret of His beatifying Trinity. So then in order to find God, to attain the end of our search, we have only to follow Christ Jesus.

And how is Christ the Way that leads us to God? By His teaching and His example: *Coepit facere et docere.*[2]

As I have said, God wills that we should seek Him as He is. We must therefore first know Him. Now Jesus Christ Who is "in the Bosom of the Father," *in sinu Patris*,[3] reveals God to us: *Unigenitus... ipse enarravit*;[4] God is made known to us by the word of His Son: *Deus... illuxit in cordibus nostris ad illuminationem scientiae claritatis Dei in facie Christi Jesu*,[5] Jesus tells us: It is I Who reveal My Father, your God; I know Him, for I am His Son; "My doctrine is not Mine, but His that sent Me";[6]... "I speak that which I have seen with My Father": *Ego quod vidi apud Patrem meum loquor*;[7] I do not deceive you, for I "have spoken the truth to you": *Veritatem vobis locutus sum*;[8] "I am the Truth": *Ego sum veritas*;[9] those who seek God must do so "in spirit and in truth": *In spiritu et veritate oportet adorare*;[10] "the words that I have spoken to you are spirit and life;[11] if you continue in My word... you shall know the truth" *Si vos manseritis in sermone meo... cognoscetis veritatem.*[12]

"I have not spoken of Myself: but the Father Who sent Me, He gave Me commandment what I should say and what I should speak. And I know that His commandment is life everlasting": *Quia ego ex meipso non sum locutus, sed qui misit Me Pater, ipse mihi mandatum dedit quid dicam et quid loquor; et scio quia mandatum ejus vita aeterna est.*[13]

The Father moreover confirms this testimony of the Son: "Hear ye Him"; for He is My own Son in Whom I have placed all My delights: *Ipsum audite.*[14]

Let us then hear this word, this doctrine of Jesus: it is first of all through this doctrine that He is our Way; let us say to Him with ardent faith, like St. Peter: "Lord, to Whom shall we go? Thou hast the

---

1 Ibid. xiv, 6. 2 Act. i, 1. 3 Joan. i, 18. 4 Ibid.

5 "For God... hath shined in our hearts, to give the light of the knowledge of the glory of God, in the face of Christ Jesus," II Cor. iv, 6.

6 Joan. vii, 16. 7 Joan viii, 38. 8 Ibid. 40. 9 Ibid. xiv, 6.

10 Ibid. iv, 24. 11 Ibid. vi, 64. 12 Ibid. viii, 31-32.

13 Ibid. xii, 49-50. 14 Matth. xvii, 5.

words of eternal life": *Verba vitae aeternae habes.*[1] We truly believe that Thou art the Divine Word, come down on our earth in order to teach us; Thou art truly God, speaking to our souls; for God "in these days, hath spoken to us by His Son": *Novissime locutus est nobis in Filio.*[2] We believe in Thee, O Christ, we accept all that Thou dost tell us of the Divine secrets, and because we accept Thy words, we give ourselves to Thee in order to live by Thy Gospel. Thou didst say that if we would be perfect, we must leave all to follow Thee;[3] we believe this and we have come, having left all things[4] to be Thy disciples. Lead us, Thou, Indefectible Light, for in Thee we have the most invincible hope. Thou wilt not reject us; we come to Thee that we may be brought to the Father. Thou hast declared: "Him that cometh to Me, I will not cast out": *Et eum qui venit ad me non ejiciam foras.*[5]

Again Jesus is the Way by *His example.*

He is perfect God, the sole-begotten Son of God: *Deum de Deo*;[6] but He is also perfect Man; He belongs authentically to our race. You know that from His two-fold nature flows a two-fold activity; a divine activity, and a human activity, but these two activities are not confounded, any more than the two natures are confounded, although ineffably united in one and the same Person.

Christ is the revelation of God adapted to our weakness; He is the manifestation of God under a human form. "He that seeth Me," Christ has said, "seeth the Father also": *Qui videt me, videt et Patrem.*[7] He is God living amongst us and showing us by this tangible human life how we ought to live in order to please our Father in Heaven.

All that Jesus accomplished was perfect, not only because of the love wherewith He accomplished it, but also in the manner He brought it to fruition; and all that Jesus did, even His least actions, were the actions of a God and infinitely pleasing to His Father: they are consequently for us examples to be followed, models of perfection: *Exemplum dedi vobis ut quemadmodum ego feci ita et vos faciatis.*[8] In imitating Christ

1 Joan. vi, 69. 2 Hebr. i, 2. 3 Matth. xix, 21. 4 Ibid. 27.
5 Joan. vi, 37. 6 Credo of the Mass. 7 Joan. xiv, 9.
8 "For I have given you an example, that as I have done to you, so you do also," Ibid. xiii, 15.

Jesus, we are sure of being like Him, although under a different title, pleasing to His Father. "The life of Christ," said a holy monk who spoke from experience, "is an excellent book for the learned and the ignorant, the perfect and the imperfect, who desire to please God. He who reads it carefully and frequently, attains high wisdom, and easily obtains... spiritual light, peace and quietness of conscience, and a firm confidence in God in sincere love."[1]

Let us then contemplate in the Gospel the example of Jesus: it is the norm of all human sanctity. If we remain united to Jesus by faith in His doctrine, by the imitation of His virtues, especially His religious virtues, we shall surely attain to God. It is true that there is an infinite distance between God and us; God is the Creator, and we are creatures, the last rung on the ladder of intellectual creation; God is spirit, we are spirit and matter; God is unchanging, we are ever subject to change; but with Christ we can bridge this distance and establish ourselves in the immutable, because, in Jesus, God and the creature meet in an ineffable and indissoluble union. In Christ we find God. "Unless you apply yourselves," says again the venerable Abbot of Liessies, "to imprint upon your soul the loveable image of Christ's Humanity, it is in vain that you aspire to the eminent knowledge and enjoyment of His Divinity."[2] "The soul cannot see the Lord in the light of love, be fixed in God and clad, as it were, with the form of the Divinity unless it has become the perfect image of Christ, according to the spirit, according to the soul, and even in the flesh."[3]

For it is to the Father that Jesus leads us. Listen to what He says on leaving His disciples: "I ascend to My Father and to your Father, to My God and to your God";[4] the Word has come down from Heaven to take upon Himself our flesh and to redeem us; His work accomplished, He ascends to Heaven, but He does not ascend alone; He virtually takes with Him all who believe in Him. And why? In order that—in Him again—the union of all with the Father should 'be accomplished: *Ego in eis et tu in Me.*[5] Is not this Jesus' supreme prayer to His Father? "That

---

1 Blosius, *The Mirror of the Soul,* ch. x, 7.
2 *Sanctuary of the Faithful Soul.*
3 *A Book of Spiritual Instruction,* ch. xii, 2.
4 Joan. xx, 17.
5 "I in them, and Thou in Me," Ibid. xvii, 23.

I may be in them, O Father,—by My grace—as Thou in Me, that they may contemplate, in the Divinity, the glory which Thou hast given Me."[1]

Never let us wander from this way, for that would be to run the risk of losing ourselves; to follow it, is to journey infallibly to the light of eternal life. When we take as our Guide the One Who is the true Light of the World, *Lux vera quae illuminat omnem hominem*,[2] we walk with sure and certain steps, and cannot fail to reach the sublime goal of our vocation: Father grant they may be with Me, even to the sharing of My glory: *Ut ubi sum ego et illi sint mecum!*[3]

II

It is not enough to know the way, we must also be able to follow it. It is likewise to Christ Jesus that we owe this power.

St. Paul[4] declares that the riches brought to us through the mediation of Christ, our Redeemer, are inexhaustible; under the Apostle's pen, terms abound which express the manifold aspects of this mediation, and give us a glimpse of its inestimable treasures. The Apostle above all reminds us that Christ redeems us, reconciles us with the Father, and creates anew within us the power of bearing fruits of justice.

We were the slaves of the devil—Christ delivers us from this bondage; we were the enemies of God—Jesus reconciles us with the Father; we had lost our inheritance—the Only-begotten Son restores to us this inheritance. Let us for a few moments contemplate these aspects of Jesus' work of mediation. These truths are doubtless known to us, but is it not always a joy for our souls to return to them?

When "the fulness of time" fixed by the eternal decrees had come, says St. Paul, "God sent His Son, made of a woman, that He might redeem them who were under the law."[5] It was then that "the grace of God our Saviour hath appeared to all men... that He might redeem us from all iniquity."[6]

Such is the essential mission of the Word Incarnate, signified by His very name: "Thou shalt call His name Jesus," says the Holy Gospel—

1 Cf. Ibid. 24. 2 Ibid. i, 9. 3 Joan. xvii, 24. 4 Eph. iii, 8.
5 Gal. iv, 4–5. 6 Tit. ii, 11 and 14.

Jesus, that is to say Saviour—"for He shall save His people from their sins."[1] Therefore, adds St. Peter, "There is no other name under heaven given to men, whereby we must be saved";[2] this name is unique as the Redemption wrought by it is universal.

And from what does Christ deliver us? From the yoke of sin. What did Jesus say at the time of His Passion when about to consummate His Sacrifice? *Nunc princeps hujus mundi ejicietur foras.* "Now shall the prince of this world be cast out. And I, if I be lifted up from the earth, will draw all things to Myself."[3]

It was indeed by His immolation upon Mount Calvary that our King destroyed Satan's reign. St. Paul tells us that Christ, snatching from the devil's hands the sentence of our eternal bondage, destroyed it "fastening it to the cross": *Delens quod adversum nos erat chirographum decreti... affigens illud cruci.*[4] His death is the ransom of our deliverance. What is the song that resounds in the holy splendor of heaven from the innumerable choir of the redeemed? To Thee, O Lord, be all honour, praise and glory for it is by Thy immaculate Blood, O Divine Lamb, that we have become Thy Kingdom![5]

Christ delivers us from eternal damnation in order to bring us to the Father and reconcile us with Him. He is "the one Mediator between God and men": *Unus mediator Dei et hominum homo Christus Jesus.*[6]

Son of God, God Himself, enjoying all the prerogatives of the Godhead, Christ, the Word Incarnate, can treat as an equal with the Father. When about to shed His Blood as the price of our redemption, He asks His Father that we may be united to Him. *Volo, Pater*;[7] "I will, O Father." The absolute character of this prayer shows the oneness of the Divine Nature in which Jesus, as the Word, lives with the Father and their common Spirit.

He is also Man: the human nature bestows on Jesus the power of offering to the Father all the satisfaction that love and justice demand: *Holocautomata... non tibi placuerunt, corpus autem aptasti mihi, ecce*

---

1 Matth. i, 21. 2 Act. iv, 12. 3 Joan. xii, 31-32.

4 "Blotting out the handwriting of the decree that was against us... fastening it to the cross," Col. ii, 14.

5 Cf. Apoc. iv, 11; v, 9. 6 I Tim. ii, 5. 7 Joan. xvii, 24.

venio ut faciam, Deus, voluntatem tuam.[1] The sacrifice of this Divine Victim appeases God, and makes Him propitious to us: *Pacificans per sanguinem crucis ejus.*[2] As Mediator, Christ Jesus is Pontiff; as Man-God, He forms the bridge over the gulf made by sin between heaven and earth. He binds us to God through His Manhood wherein "dwelleth all the fulness of the Godhead corporeally."[3]

St. Paul also tells us that "God indeed was in Christ, reconciling the world to Himself": *Deus erat in Christo mundum reconcilians sibi,*[4] so that we "who some time were afar off, are made nigh by the blood of Christ": *Vos qui aliquando eratis longe, facti estis prope in sanguine Christi.*[5] At the foot of the Cross, justice appeased and peace restored give each other the kiss of reconciliation: *Justitia et pax osculatae sunt.*[6]

Rightly does the Apostle conclude by saying: *In quo [Christo] habemus fiduciam et accessum in confidentia per fidem ejus.*[7] Through faith in Christ we may indeed have the boldness to draw near to God with confidence. How can we lack confidence when Christ, the Son of the Father, having become our Surety and the Propitiation for our iniqui-

1 "Holocausts... did not please Thee, a body Thou hast fitted to Me, behold I come that I should do Thy will, O God," cf. Hebr. x, 5–7.

2 Col. i, 20.

3 Ibid. ii, 9. Let us quote this beautiful text of the great Pope St. Gregory, the biographer of St. Benedict, where we find something more than a simple reminiscence of the Prologue of the Rule: *Redire ad Deum. "Dei Filius adjuvit hominem factus homo ut quia puro homini via redeundi non patebat ad Deum, via redeundi fieret per Hominem-Deum. Longe quippe distabamus a justo et immortali, nos mortales et injusti. Sed inter immortalem et justum, et nos mortales et injustos, apparuit mediator Dei et hominum, mortalis et justus, qui et mortem haberet cum hominibus, et justitiam cum Deo, ut quia per ima nostra longe distabamus a summis, in seipso uno jungeret ima cum summis, atque ex eo nobis via redeundi fieret ad Deum, quo summis suis ima nostra copularet."* (The Son of God, having been made man, helped man, that because the way of returning to God was not open to mere man, there should be made a Way of returning through the God-Man. Of course, we were far removed from the Righteous and Immortal One, since we were mortal and unrighteous. But between the Immortal and Righteous One and ourselves the mortal and unrighteous, appeared the mediator of God and man, Mortal and Righteous, Who might both hold death with mortals and righteousness with God; that because by our things below we were far removed from the things above, He might join as one in Himself things below with things on high, and that herein there might be a Way made for us of returning to God, in the degree that He joined ours beneath with His own on high.) St. Gregory, *Moralia in Job*, Lib. xxii, in ch. 27. P. L. 76, col. 327-328.

4 II Cor. v, 19.

5 Eph. ii, 13.

6 Ps. lxxxiv, 11.

7 Eph. iii, 12.

ties, has expiated and paid off all? Why should we not draw near to this High Priest, Who, like unto us in all things, sin excepted, chose to experience all our infirmities, to drink of the chalice of all our sufferings, to find, in the experience of sorrow, the power of compassionating our miseries more deeply?

So powerful indeed is this High Priest, so effectual is His mediation that the reconciliation is perfect. From the moment when Jesus paid the price of our salvation with His Blood we entered into the rights of the heavenly inheritance. When about to accomplish His essential work of mediation, our Lord reveals the inmost sentiments of His Sacred Heart in the prayer He addresses to His Father. He prays that we may be with Him: *Ut illi sint mecum.* And where does He desire this union should be realised? In the glory full of delights which, from all eternity, is His own: "That they may see My glory which Thou hast given me... before the creation of the world": *Ut videant claritatem quam dedisti mihi... ante constitutionem mundi.*[1]

Tertullian says[2] somewhere in his writings: *Tam Pater nemo* [*quam Deus*]: "No one is a father like God is." We might say too: *Nemo tam frater quam Christus*: "No one is a brother like Christ is." St. Paul calls Christ "the Firstborn amongst many brethren": *Primogenitus in multis fratribus*;[3] but, he adds, Christ is not ashamed to call us brethren: *Non confunditur fratres eos vocare.*[4] Indeed what does Jesus Himself say to Magdalen when already in the glory of His Resurrection? "Go to My brethren": *Vade ad fratres meos.*[5] And how great is His "fraternity!" God as He is, this Only-begotten Son takes upon Himself our infirmities, He makes Himself responsible for our sins, in order to be like unto us. Because, says St. Paul, we are formed of flesh and blood, Christ has willed to take upon Himself our nature, sinful in us, that by His death, "He might destroy him who had the empire of death, that is to say, the

---

1 Joan. xvii, 24.

2 *Quis ille nobis intelligendus Pater? Deus scilicet: tam pater nemo, tam pius nemo* (Who is that Father to be understood by us? Certainly God: for no one is a father, no one so loving as He). *De Poenitentia*, ch. 8.

3 Rom. viii, 29. 4 Hebr. ii, 11. 5 Joan. xx, 17.

devil,"[1] and restore to us the possession of the eternal Kingdom of Life with the Father.

And he concludes by bidding us who are called to be "partakers of the heavenly vocation" to "consider the Apostle and High Priest of our confession, Jesus," Who faithfully fulfilled the command of Him by Whom He was established Head of His Kingdom. This Kingdom, this house of God, continues St. Paul, "are we, if we hold fast the confidence and glory of hope unto the end."[2]

Truly what a glory for us is this hope we have in Jesus, now that He is our Elder Brother, our High Priest filled with compassion for us, and our all-powerful Mediator. St. Paul is very expressive on this point. On the day of the Ascension, the Humanity of Jesus takes possession of this glorious inheritance in a wonderful manner. But the Man-God only enters into Heaven as our Forerunner: *Praecursor pro nobis introivit.*[3] And there, for the soul of each one of us, He offers to the Father the infinite price of His Passion in a perpetually living mediation: *Semper vivens ad interpellandum pro nobis.*[4]

So our confidence ought to be boundless. All the graces that adorn the soul and make it blossom forth in virtues from the time of its call to the Christian faith until its vocation to the religious life, all the streams of living water that gladden the city of God which is the religious soul, have their inexhaustible source on Calvary: for this river of life gushed forth from the Heart and Wounds of Jesus.

Can we contemplate the magnificent work of our powerful High Priest without exulting in continual thanksgiving: *Dilexit me et tradidit semetipsum pro me*:[5] "Who loved me," says St. Paul, "and delivered Himself for me." The Apostle does not say, although it be the very truth: *dilexit nos*: "He loved us"; but "He loved me," that is to say His love is distributed to all, while being appropriated to each one of us. The life, the humiliations, the sufferings, the Passion of Jesus—all concern *me*. And how has He loved me? To love's last extremity: *in finem dilexit.*[6] O most gentle High Priest, Who by Thy Blood hast re-opened to me the doors of the Holy of Holies, Who ceaselessly dost intercede for me, to Thee be all praise and glory for evermore!

1 Hebr. ii, 14-15.
2 Ibid. iii, 1–2 and 6.
3 Ibid. vi, 20.
4 Ibid. vii, 25.
5 Gal. ii, 20.
6 Joan. xiii, 1.

Secondly, Christ's merits are so much our own that we may justly appropriate them to ourselves; the satisfactions of Jesus compose an infinitely precious treasure whence we can continually draw in order to expiate our faults, repair our negligences, provide for our needs, perfect our deeds, supply for our shortcomings. "The servant of God," says the Venerable Blosius, "should form the holy custom of offering all his works by a pure intention for the honour of God. He should be careful to join and unite all he does and all he suffers to the actions and sufferings of Christ, through prayer and desire. In this way, the works and trials that are in themselves, and when looked at as belonging to the servant of God himself, vile, worthless and imperfect, will become noble, of the highest value, and most pleasing to God. They receive an unspeakable dignity from the merits of Christ, to which they are united, as a drop of water poured into a vessel full of wine is entirely absorbed by the wine, and receives the full flavour and colour of the wine. The good works of those who piously practise this union with Christ's actions incomparably excel the good works of those who neglect it."[1]

Therefore this great monk, so versed in spiritual ways, does not hesitate to exhort his disciples to unite all their actions to those of Jesus: it is the surest way of attaining perfection. "Confide your good works and exercises to the most holy and sweetest Heart of Jesus that He may correct and perfect them: this is the most ardent wish of His loving Heart ever ready to complete our defective works in the most excellent manner. Rejoice and exult with gladness in that, poor as you are in yourself, you possess such riches in your Redeemer Whose will it is to make you a partaker in His merits... In Him is laid up for you an immense treasure provided you have true humility and goodwill."[2]

This is what our Lord Himself said to a Benedictine nun, Mother Deleloë, whose wonderful inner life has but recently been revealed: "What more can you desire than to have within you the true source of all good, My Divine Heart?... All these great things are yours, all these treasures

1 *A Book of Spiritual Instruction,* translated from the Latin by the late Bertrand A. Wilberforce of the Order of Preachers. Ch. 9. All this chapter should be read.

2 *The Mirror of the Soul,* ch. vii, 4.

and riches are for the heart that I have chosen... Draw as much as you desire of these infinite delights and riches."[1]

III

It did not suffice for our Heavenly Father to give us His Son as Mediator; He has appointed Him the universal distributor of every gift; "the Father loveth the Son: and He hath given all things into His hand": *Pater diligit Filium et omnia dedit in manu ejus.*[2] Christ communicates to us the grace that He has merited for us.

Many know that our Lord is the only way that leads to the Father: "No man cometh to the Father, but by me": *Nemo venit ad Patrem nisi per me;*[3] that He has redeemed us by His Blood; but they forget—at least to all practical purposes—another truth of capital importance: it is that Christ is the Cause of every grace and that He acts in us by His Spirit.

Christ Jesus possesses in Himself the plenitude of every grace. Hear what He Himself says: "As the Father hath life in Himself, so He hath given to the Son also to have life in Himself": *Sicut Pater habet vitam in semetipso, sic dedit et Filio habere vitam in semetipso.*[4] And what is this life? It is an eternal life, an ocean of divine life containing all the perfections and beatitude of the Godhead. Now Christ Jesus has this Divine Life "in Himself" *in semetipso*, that is to say by nature, being fully entitled to it, for Christ is the Incarnate Son of God. When the Father beholds His Christ, He is ravished, for this Infinite God beholds His equal in Christ His Son, and He declares: "This is my beloved Son": *Hic est Filius meus dilectus.*[5] He sees nothing in His Son except what comes from Himself: "Thou art My Son, this day have I begotten Thee": *Filius meus es tu, ego hodie genui te.*[6] Christ is truly "the brightness of His glory and the figure of His substance;[7] and it gives the Father infinite joy to behold Him: *In quo mihi bene complacui.*[8] Thus Christ, because He is the Son of God, is "Life" supereminently: "I am the Life," *Ego sum vita.*[9]

---

1 *La Mère Jeanne Deleloë,* Collection "Pax." See also further on, p. 41–42 the same doctrine set forth by St. Mechtilde.

2 Joan. iii, 35. 3 Ibid. xiv, 6. 4 Ibid. v, 26.
5 Matth. iii, 17; xvii, 5. 6 Ps. ii, 7. 7 Hebr. i, 3.
8 Matth. xvii, 5; cf. Ibid. iii, 17. 9 Joan. xiv, 6.

This Divine Life that Jesus possesses personally and in its plenitude, He wills to communicate and lavish upon us: "I am come that they may have life, and may have it more abundantly": *Ego veni ut vitam habeant et abundantius habeant*;[1] He wills that the life which is His through the hypostatic union, should be ours by grace, and it is "of His fulness we all have received": *Vidimus [eum] plenum gratiae et de plenitudine ejus nos omnes accepimus*.[2] Through the Sacraments, through the action of His Spirit in us, He infuses grace into us as the principle of our life.

Bear this truth well in mind: there is no grace of which a soul can have need that is not found in Jesus, the Fount of every grace. For if "without [Him] we can do nothing"[3] that brings us nearer to Heaven and to the Father, in Him are laid up "all the treasures of wisdom and knowledge": *In quo sunt omnes thesauri sapientiae et scientiae absconditi*.[4] And they are there laid up that they may be transmitted to us. If we can sing that only Jesus Christ is holy: *Tu solus sanctus*,[5] it is because no one is holy except by Him and in Him.

There is perhaps no truth upon which St. Paul, the herald of the mystery of Christ, more insists when commenting upon the Divine Plan. Christ is the second Adam and, like Adam, is the head of a race, but this is the race of the elect. "By one man sin entered into this world, and by sin death; and so death passed upon all men... if by one man's offence death reigned through one; much more they who receive abundance of grace, and of the gift and of justice shall reign in life through one, Jesus Christ"[6]... With this difference, however, that "where sin abounded grace did more abound."[7]

Christ has been established by His Father the Head of the race of the redeemed, of the faithful, with whom He forms one body. His infinite grace is to flow into the members of the mystical organism, "according to the measure of the giving of Christ": *Unicuique nostrum data est gratia secundum mensuram donationis Christi*.[8] And, by this grace which flows from Himself, Christ renders each of the elect like unto Himself, and pleasing, as He is, to the Father. For in the eternal decrees the Father does not separate us from Christ Jesus: the act by which He predestined

1 Ibid. x, 10.
2 Ibid i, 14 and 16.
3 Ibid. xv, 5.
4 Col. ii, 3.
5 *Gloria of the Mass.*
6 Rom. v, 12 and 17.
7 Ibid. 20.
8 Eph. iv, 7.

a human nature to be personally united to His word is the same act by which He predestined us to become the brethren of Jesus.

We cannot work out our salvation without Christ, without the help of the grace that He gives to us. He is the one, the true Life that saves from death: *Ego sum vita.*[1]

IV

These essential truths apply to salvation; they are equally to be understood of perfection. You are perhaps surprised that I have spoken at such length of Christ Jesus before speaking to you of religious perfection. It is because Christ is the foundation of monastic perfection that He is "the Religious" pre-eminently, the Example of the perfect religious; more than that, He is the very source of perfection, and the consummation of all holiness, "the author and finisher of faith."[2]

The religious life is not an institution created on the borders of Christianity; plunging its roots into the Gospel of Christ, it aims only at expressing the Gospel in all its integrity. Our religious "holiness" is but the plenitude of our Divine adoption in Jesus; it is the absolute tradition of the whole of ourselves through love, to the will of the Most High. Now His Will is essentially that we should be His worthy children. He has predestined us "to be made conformable to the image of His Son": *Praedestinavit (nos) conformes fieri imaginis Filii sui.*[3] All that God enjoins upon us and asks of us, all that Christ counsels us, has no other end than to give us the opportunity of showing that we are God's children and the brethren of Jesus; and when we attain this ideal in everything, not only in our thoughts and actions, but even in the motives from which we act, then we reach perfection.

Perfection can indeed be resumed in this inward disposition of the soul seeking to please the Heavenly Father by living habitually and totally in the spirit of its supernatural adoption.

Perfection has love for its habitual motive; it embraces the entire life, that is to say it makes one think, will, love, hate, act,—not only according to the views of nature vitiated by original sin, nor yet merely according to nature in so far as it is upright and moral (although this is

1 Joan. xiv, 6. 2 Hebr. xii, 2. 3 Rom. viii, 29.

certainly always requisite), but in the spirit of this divine "superaddition" infused by God: to wit, grace which makes us His children and friends.

He alone is perfect who lives *habitually* and *totally* according to grace; it is a failing, an imperfection, for a man adopted as a child of God to withdraw any one of his acts from the influence of grace and from charity which accompanies grace. Jesus has given us the watchword of Christian perfection: "I must be about My Father's business": *In his quae Patris mei sunt* OPORTET *me esse.*[1]

The result of this disposition is to render all the actions of a soul, thus fully living according to the meaning of its supernatural adoption, pleasing to God, because they are all rooted in charity.

Let us listen to St. Paul: "Walk worthy of God," he writes, "in all things pleasing": *Ut ambuletis digne Deo per omnia placentes.*[2] The Apostle tells us we are to do this by walking worthy of the vocation in which we are called. *Ut digne ambuletis vocatione qua vocati estis.*[3] And this vocation is to the supernatural life and the glorious beatitude that crowns it: *Ut ambularetis digne Deo qui vocavit vos in* SUUM *regnum et gloriam.*[4]

So then, to please our Heavenly Father, in order that He be glorified, that His Kingdom be established within us and His will be done by us totally and steadfastly—that is perfection: "Stand perfect, and full in all the will of God": *Ut stetis perfecti et pleni in omni voluntate Dei.*[5]

This attitude towards God avails to make us "fruitful in every good work": *Per omnia placentes, in omni bono opere fructificantes.*[6] And does not Our Lord Himself declare that this perfection is glorious to God? "In this is My Father glorified: that you bear very much fruit": *In hoc clarificatus est Pater meus ut fructum plurimum afferatis.*[7]

Whence are we to draw the sap which is to make all our actions fruitful in order that we may bring to the Father this abundant harvest of good works whereby we shall glorify Him?

This fruitful sap which is grace comes to us through Jesus only. It is only by remaining united to Him that we can be divinely fruitful: "He that abideth in Me, and I in Him, the same beareth much fruit": *Qui*

---

1 Luc. ii, 49. 2 Col. i, 10. 3 Eph. iv, 1.

4 "That you walk worthy of God, who hath called you unto His kingdom and glory," I Thess. ii, 12.

5 Col. iv, 12. 6 Col. i, 10. 7 Joan. xv, 8.

manet in Me et Ego in eo HIC *fert fructum multum.*[1] If without Him we can do nothing that is worthy of His Father, with Him, in Him, we bear much fruit: He is the Vine, we are the branches.[2]

You will perhaps ask how we are to "abide" in Jesus? By faith, first of all. St. Paul tells us that it is by our faith Christ dwells in our hearts: *Christum per fidem inhabitare in cordibus vestris.*[3] Next by love: "Abide in My love": *Manete in dilectione mea,*[4] the love that, joined to grace, gives us up entirely to Christ's service and the keeping of His commandments: "If you love Me, keep My commandments": *Si diligitis Me, mandata mea servate.*[5]

This doctrine is true of the perfection in which every Christian ought to live according to his state; it is true above all of religious perfection. Perfection can only exist where the orientation of the soul towards God and His will is habitual and steadfast.

We find many obstacles to perfection in ourselves and all around us: the triple concupiscence of the flesh, and of the eyes, and the pride of life solicits and divides the poor human heart, and impairs the integrity necessary to perfection. The religious puts aside, in principle, all the obstacles to his progress by entering into the way of the evangelical counsels: by the vows, he places himself irrevocably in a *state* of perfection which shields him, if he is faithful, from the fluctuations and solicitations which might disturb and divide his heart; in this state, the grace of adoption has more freedom and is able to bear more fruit. "I would," says St. Paul, "have you to be without solicitude. He that is without a wife is solicitous for the things that belong to the Lord: how he may please God. But he that is with a wife is solicitous for the things of the world: how he may please his wife. And he is divided... And this I speak for your profit... which may give you power to attend upon the Lord, without impediment": *Volo vos sine sollicitudine esse... quod facultatem praebeat sine impedimento Dominum obsecrandi.*[6]

This is why Christ Jesus said to the young man enamoured of the ideal: "If thou wilt be perfect, go, sell what thou hast and give to the poor

1 Ibid. xv, 5. 2 Ibid. 3 Eph. iii, 17.
4 Joan. xv, 9. 5 Ibid. xiv, 15. 6 I Cor. vii, 32, 35.

and thou shalt have treasure in heaven. And come follow me": *Si VIS perfectus esse, vende omnia quae habes, et veni, sequere me.*[1]

The religious, the monk, despoils himself, detaches himself from everything: *Reliquimus omnia*;[2] he puts away all the obstacles that could retard his progress and shackle his flight towards God. In him, faith, whereby Christ dwells in souls, is more ardent, love, whereby they dwell in Christ, is more generous and far-reaching. In this blessed state, the soul can more fully cleave to God, because it follows Christ more closely: *Et secuti sumus te.*[3]

Perfection has then grace for principle, love for its mainspring, and the degree of union with Jesus for its measure. Of this perfection Jesus is the initiator by the supernatural vocation; secondly, He is its one model, at once divine and accessible; finally and above all, it is He Who gives it to us as a participation in His own perfection. We must be perfect as our Heavenly Father is perfect;[4] this is what Christ tells us, but it is God alone Who can make us perfect and He does so by giving us His Son.

Therefore all is summed up in constant union with Jesus, in ceaselessly contemplating Him in order to imitate Him, and in doing, at all times, for love, as He did: *quia diligo Patrem*[5]—the things that please the Father:—*Quae PLACITA sunt ei facio semper.*[6] This is the secret of perfection.

It is related in the life of St. Mechtilde, that one Saturday, during the singing of the Mass *Salve sancte parens*, she saluted the Blessed Virgin and besought her to obtain for her true holiness. The glorious Virgin replied: "If thou desirest true holiness, keep close to my Son; He is Holiness itself, sanctifying all things." While St. Mechtilde was asking herself how she could do this, the sweet Virgin said to her again: "Unite thyself to His most holy Childhood, beseeching Him that by His innocence, the faults and negligences of thy childhood may be repaired. Unite thyself to His most fervent Boyhood ever unfolding in a more burning love which alone had the privilege of giving sufficient matter to the love of God. Unite thyself to His Divine virtues, which have power to ennoble and elevate thine. Secondly, keep close to My Son by directing all thy thoughts, words, and actions towards Him in order that He may blot out all that is imperfect therein. Thirdly, keep close to my Son

1 Matth. xix, 21. 2 Ibid. 27. 3 Ibid.
4 Ibid. v, 48. 5 Joan. xiv, 30. 6 Ibid. viii, 29.

as the bride keeps close to the bridegroom who, out of his possessions, furnishes her with food and clothing, while she cherishes and honours, for love of him, the friends and family of her bridegroom. Thus, thy soul will be sustained by the Word of God as with the best sustinence, and clad and adorned with the delights she takes in Him, that is to say with the example that He gives her to imitate... Thus thou wilt be truly holy, according as it is written, with the holy thou shalt be holy, in the same way as a queen becomes queen in sharing the lot of the king."[1]

"Therefore, beloved brethren," concluded the Saint on another occasion when the same doctrine was revealed to her, "receiving with deep gratitude this high favour from the divine Clemency, let us take possession of Christ's most holy life that we may supply for all that is lacking to our merits. Let us also strive, as far as we are able, to be conformed to Him by our virtues for this will be our supreme glory in eternal beatitude. What glory indeed could be greater than, by a certain resemblance, to approach Him Who is the splendour of everlasting light?"[2]

V

St. Benedict lived on these fruitful truths; from these springs of living water he slaked the thirst of his great soul; in this beneficent light he wishes to see the lives of his disciples transfigured. Let us go back to the beginning of his Prologue: he supposes that a postulant presents himself in order to be received as a monk and asks what he must do. St. Benedict replies that he must return to God by following Christ. "To thee, therefore, my words are now addressed who... desirest to fight for the Lord Christ, our true King": *Ad te ergo nunc meus sermo dirigitur quisquis... Domino Christo vero Regi militaturus*. It is not a mere formula with St. Benedict; this idea impregnates the entire Rule and gives it that eminently *Christian* character, so much admired by Bossuet.[3] The holy Legislator points out by these opening words of his Rule that he intends to take Christ fundamentally as Example and to consider Him as the

1 *The Book of Special Grace,* 1st Part, ch. 37, *How to obtain true holiness.*

2 *The Book of Special Grace,* 3rd Part, ch. 14, *How a man can attribute to himself all the Life of Jesus Christ.* Cf. also 2nd Part, ch. 34; 3rd Part, ch. 15 and 16; 4th Part, ch. 22, *How Jesus Christ supplies for what is lacking to us.*

3 *Panegyric of St. Benedict.*

source of perfection. His Rule is "Christocentric." So he tells us again and again "to prefer nothing to the love of Christ,"[1] "to hold nothing dearer than Christ";[2] and, in ending his Rule, he condenses all the ascetic programme of the monk in a sentence of absolute devotion to Christ: "Let nothing whatever be preferred to Christ, Who deigns to bring us all alike to everlasting life": *Christo OMNINO NIHIL praeponant qui nos pariter ad vitam aeternam perducat.*[3]

These are the great Patriarch's last words, as it were the supreme farewell that he bids his sons upon leaving them; these words echo those that open the Rule. Christ is the Alpha and Omega of all perfection.

In the chapter that serves as the epilogue and crown of the monastic code, St. Benedict repeats this truth that we shall find the way to our eternal country in Christ, and that it is by His grace alone we can fulfil the Rule traced out, and thus attain the end proposed at the head of the first page: "to seek God": *Quisquis ergo ad patriam caelestem festinas, hanc Regulam descriptam adjuvante Christo perfice.*[4]

So throughout our life, whatever be the state of our soul and the circumstances that may arise, we ought never to turn our gaze away from Christ. St. Benedict constantly places the Divine Model before our eyes. If he tells us we ought to deny ourselves, it is that we may follow Christ: *Abnegare semetipsum sibi ut sequatur Christum.*[5] All our obedience—and what is the whole of our life but a continual obedience?—is to be inspired by the love of Christ: *Haec convenit his qui nihil sibi a Christo carius aliquid existimant.*[6] Are we a butt to temptation? We must have recourse to Christ, it is against Him as against a rock that we must dash our evil thoughts the instant they come into the heart: *Cogitationes malas cordi suo advenientes mox ad Christum allidere.*[7] Our tribulations, our adversities, must be united to Christ's sufferings: *Passionibus Christi per patientiam participemur.*[8] The whole existence of a monk is to consist in walking in the path traced out by the Divine Master in the Gospel: *Per ducatum Evangelii pergamus itinera ejus.*[9] Finally, if we come to a state of perfect charity, which is the bond of perfection, it is the love of

1 Rule, ch. iv. 2 Ibid. ch. v. 3 Ibid. ch. lxxii.

4 "Whoever, therefore, thou art that hastenest to thy heavenly country, fulfil first of all by the help of Christ this Rule," Ibid. ch. lxxiii.

5 Ibid. ch. iv; cf. Matth. xvi, 24. 6 Rule, ch. v. 7 Ibid. ch. iv.

8 Prologue to the Rule. 9 Prologue to the Rule.

Christ that has brought us thither and because He is the mainspring of all our actions: *Ad caritatem Dei perveniet illam quae perfecta... universa custodit... amore Christi.*[1]

You see how for St. Benedict Christ must be everything to the monk. In all things he would have the monk think of Christ, lean upon Him; the monk is to see Christ in everyone, in the Abbot,[2] in his brethren,[3] in the sick[4], in the guests[5], in strangers,[6] in the poor,[7] and, if need be, he is to pray for his enemies *in Christi amore.*[8] The love of Christ brought the postulant to the monastery; it is the love of Christ that keeps him there and transforms him into the likeness of his Elder Brother.

We understand why it was that St. Benedict told a hermit who had bound himself by chains in his cave: "If thou art the servant of God, do not bind thyself by an iron chain but by the chain of Christ": *Non teneat te catena ferri, sed catena Christi,*[9] that is to say by the love that binds thee to Christ.

May it be the same for us; may the love of Christ hold us united to Him: *Teneat te catena Christi!* There is no other way so traditional for us. Read the most authentic and most magnificent monuments of Benedictine asceticism, and you will see they are overflowing with this teaching.

---

1 "The monk will presently come to that perfect love of God... he observes all those precepts... for love of Christ," Rule, ch. vii. At the end of the chapter on *Humility*, St. Benedict borrows a quotation from Cassian; it is textual, saving the addition of the words: *amore Christi* to indicate the first motive power of all our deeds. It is a remarkable fact that these two words have sufficed to change essentially the "physiognomy" and the bearing of the quotation, and to open out a special perspective, unknown to Cassian but revealing the thought of the great Patriarch. In reference to Cassian, it has moreover been remarked with justice that "in the same extent that St. Benedict is indebted to Cassian in what concerns the observance and organisation of the claustral life, he differs from him in his teaching on grace. St. Benedict's originality does not then consist only in the manner wherein he adapts the asceticism of the East to Western conditions, but also in the clearness with which he repudiates rationalistic tendencies and entirely subjects the natural to the supernatural: hence results, in his conception of asceticism, the indubitable subordination of the letter to the spirit, and of the matter of the act to the intention." D. M. Festugière in the *Revue Bénédictine,* 1912, p. 491.

2 Rule, ch. ii and lxiii.

3 Ibid. ch. ii.

4 Ibid. ch. xxxvi.

5 Ibid. ch. liii.

6 Ibid.

7 Ibid.

8 Ibid. ch. iv.

9 St. Gregory, *Dialogues.* Lib. iii, ch. 16.

It explains the ardent aspirations of St. Anselm towards the Word Incarnate, the tenderness of St. Bernard's love for Christ, the astonishing familiarities of St. Gertrude and St. Mechtilde with the Divine Saviour, the burning outpourings of Ven. Blosius to the Sacred Humanity of Jesus.[1] These great souls so pure and high in holiness, had fully made proof of this line of conduct proposed by the great Patriarch whose faithful disciples they were: *Nihil amori Christi praeponere*: "To put the love of Christ before all things."[2]

This way of making everything converge to Christ Jesus, which is so characteristic of St. Benedict, is extremely advantageous for the soul. It makes the life of the soul powerful, for it concentrates it in unity; and in the spiritual life, as in everything, sterility is the daughter of dispersion. It renders it attractive, for nothing can more delight the mind and more easily obtain the necessary efforts from the heart than to view the Adorable Person of Christ Jesus. "It requires very little experience of life to know how necessary it is for every one to have ever ready some sort of idea or word or thought—which by practice comes instinctively to our aid in times of difficulty or mental stress and gives us courage and strength to walk in the right path. This—a veritable talisman to the soul if we will only let it be so—is to be found in the sacred Name of our Blessed Lord. His should be an ever abiding presence to us, not a theoretical and abstract personality but a living actuality ever with us, 'Christ in the mind, Christ in the heart, Christ in the hands'—the abiding thought of Christ, the abiding love of Christ, the constant and conscious following of Christ—this secures the union of our souls with God and makes our service real and a work of love... Of all the means which St. Benedict proposed to his disciples as aids to the spiritual life, this constant keeping of our Lord before the mind and following His example is perhaps insisted on most frequently and clearly."[3]

1 And so many others like St. Odilo, St. Hildegarde, St. Elisabeth of Schönau, St. Frances of Rome, Mother Deleloë, favoured, long before St. Margaret Mary, with the revelations of the Sacred Heart, Blessed Bonomo, etc. For the period previous to the 13th century, see D. Besse: *Les Mystiques Bénédictins* (Paris, 1922); for the Abbot of Liessies, see the excellent article *La place du Christ dans la doctrine spirituelle de Louis de Blois,* by Dom P. de Puniet, in *La Vie Spirituelle,* August 1920, p. 386 seq.

2 Rule, ch. iv, v and lxxii.

3 Card. Gasquet, *Religio Religiosi: The Object and Scope of the Religious Life.*

THE ABBOT, CHRIST'S REPRESENTATIVE

SUMMARY.—The monk is to seek God by walking in Christ's footsteps; he belongs to the cenobitical society, the authority of which is concentrated in the hands of the Abbot.—I. The Abbot, the representative of Christ, is to imitate Him as Pastor.—II. As Pontiff.—III. He is to be conspicuous for his discretion.—IV. For his kindness.—V. Attitude of the monk towards the Abbot: humble and sincere love.—VI. Docility of spirit.—VII. Obedience of action.

To seek God by walking in Christ's footsteps: such in a few words is the sublime vocation that St. Benedict assigns to his sons. When a secular wishes to be admitted into the Community, this question is put to him: "What do you ask?" and the Church places upon his lips this reply exactly appropriate to the situation: "The mercy of God and your fellowship," *Misericordiam Dei et vestram confraternitatem.*[1]

Every vocation, even the simple Christian vocation, comes from God. Our Lord Himself says "No man can come to Me, except the Father draw him": *Nemo potest venire ad me nisi Pater traxerit eum.*[2]

But it is God's love for us—and as we are born miserable, it is His merciful love—which is the origin of this call: *attraxi te miserans.*[3] This vocation is great, and this first loving glance cast upon us by God is the first link in the chain of graces which He bestows upon us throughout the course of our existence; all the Divine mercies towards us have for

1 *Rituale monasticum.* 2 Joan. vi, 44.
3 Jerem. xxxi, 3. See also St. Paul, Tit. iii, 5, 7.

their first principle this invitation to share, by adoption, in the Sonship of Christ Jesus.

The monastic vocation itself only aims at perfecting this adoption, at making it more extensive, by a deeper participation in Christ's grace, by a more finished imitation of the Divine Model. But it is also an act of mercy, and a signal mercy. Christ Jesus does not oblige all men to follow Him thus closely; the counsel is given, but "all men take not this word": *Non omnes capiunt verbum istud.*[1] You know the call of Jesus to the rich young man: "If thou wilt be perfect… follow Me."[2] You know too the refusal that the Divine Master met with. Jesus had at first only pointed out the common way: "If thou wilt enter into life, keep the commandments": *Si vis ad vitam ingredi, serva mandata.*[3] Then after the rejoinder of the young man: "All these things I have kept from my youth,"[4] Jesus wished to show him a higher way, a way which leads to a more intimate degree of union, a more perfect beatitude. These successive and ascending calls had love only for their source: "Jesus looking on him, loved him": *Intuitus eum, dilexit eum.*[5] It is the love of God which draws us to the cloister, which invites us to serve Him in the cenobitical life, "the fellowship of the brethren": *Et vestram confraternitatem.*

The monastery is the basis of a society. What is a society? It is an assembly of men whose wills conspire towards a determined end, under a recognised authority. In order to form a society it is not enough for men to be materially united, for example like a crowd of curious people grouped together in a public place: that would be simply an accidental conglomeration without consistency; men must have an identical aim to which all tend by common consent: this aim gives to the society its direction and specification. But as men are unstable, as discussions often arise among them, and as individual liberty has to be directed, it is especially necessary for the constituting and functioning of a society that there should be an authority maintaining the union of the members in pursuit of the social ends and keeping them united as to the means.

We at once see the importance of this latter element: without one supreme authority recognised as incontestable by all, any society, however nobly inspired we might otherwise suppose it to be, is fatally con-

1 Matth. xix, 11. 2 Matth. xix, 21; Marc. x, 21; Luc. xviii, 22.
3 Matth. xix, 17. 4 Ibid. 20. 5 Marc. x, 21.

demned to dissensions and ruin: "Every kingdom divided against itself," Christ has said, "shall be brought to desolation": *Regnum in seipsum divisum desolabitur*.[1] St. Benedict remarks this in one of his chapters, and we shall nowhere else see the Lawgiver of monks express himself with such warmth: he declares as "absurd"[2] the existence of an authority that would be, in any degree, independent, and consequently a rival of the supreme authority; he heaps up terms depicting the disastrous consequences that would ensue. Dissensions inevitably follow disunion, and from these dissensions "souls are endangered... and run to destruction": *Necesse est sub hac dissensione animas periclitari... eunt in perditionem*.[3]

I have pointed out the primal object that St. Benedict wishes us to pursue, namely, to seek God,[4] to return to Him: *Ut ad Eum redeas*;[5] I have shown how the great means that he places in our hands is courageously to follow Christ the true King; *Domino Christo vero Regi militaturus*.[6] By its end, as well as by the means employed to attain this end, the monastery forms a supernatural society. But before studying the monastery from the cenobitical point of view, it is necessary first of all carefully to analyse the authority which is its mainstay: this authority is concentrated in the hands of the Abbot.

There is a striking analogy between the Church and the monastery, both envisaged as societies. Christ founded a society to continue among men His mission of redemption and sanctification. Now what means did He, Infinite Wisdom, take in order to constitute His society? It is remarkable that the first time Christ speaks of His Church it is to indicate its foundation. Christ, the wise Architect,[7] first of all lays the foundation; this foundation is Peter. *Tu es Petrus, et super hanc petram aedificabo Ecclesiam meam*.[8] Authority being once established, the rest is regulated without difficulty.

The great Patriarch, whose Roman genius and Christian spirit appear so clearly in the Rule, uses no other logic. After a preliminary chapter where he sets aside the different forms of religious life in order to retain

---

1 Luc. xi, 17; cf. Matth. xii, 25; Marc. iii, 24.
2 Rule, ch. lxv.
3 Rule, ch. lxv.
4 Ibid. ch. lxviii.
5 Prologue of the Rule.
6 Ibid.
7 Prov. ix, 1.
8 "Thou art Peter; and upon this rock I will build my Church," Matth. xvi, 18.

only the cenobitical form, he at once and before all speaks of the Abbot: *Qualis debeat esse abbas.*[1] And this Abbot he defines from the opening of the chapter as the head of the monastery: *Abbas qui* PRAESSE *dignus est* MONASTERIO...[2] St. Benedict, in this, imitates Our Lord. He first and foremost lays the foundation, the corner stone, upon which the edifice is to rest, and he devotes one of the most beautiful, if not the most beautiful chapter of his Rule, to detailing the qualities and mission of the head of the monastery.

Let us then say a few words as to the ideal that the great Patriarch forms of the head of the monastery: in this he has certainly traced—unknown to his humility, be it understood!—his own portrait, for in St. Gregory's words "he did not ordain otherwise than he lived."[3]

The Abbot will appear to us, after the example of Christ Whom he represents, as *Pastor*, and as *Pontiff*; we shall next see how he is to show forth his *discretion* and thus imitate the loving kindness of the supreme Pastor; from these considerations will quite naturally follow *the monk's attitude* towards the Abbot, an attitude which is summed up in love, docility of spirit and obedience of action.

I

If we want to understand the ideal that the lawgiver of monks forms of the head of the monastery, it is not enough to study the two chapters of the Rule treating *ex professo* of the Abbot;[4] we must know the mind and spirit of the great Patriarch, such as they appear in the Rule taken as a whole, and in its thousand details, as well as in St. Benedict's life itself. For our Blessed Father cannot propose to the Abbot any other ideal than that which he himself contemplates in prayer, the principles

1 "What kind of man the abbot should be," Rule, ch. ii.

2 "An abbot who is worthy to rule a monastery," Ibid.

3 *Dialogues*. Lib. ii, ch. 36.

4 St. Benedict devotes two chapters to the Abbot: in ch. ii he describes the qualities that the head of the monastery ought to possess; in ch. lxiv (to be found in that section of the Rule concerning the order to be observed in the different elements of the monastic city) he first shows the mode of procedure to be followed in the election of the Abbot, and completes the advice given in Chapter ii. Let us add that, in the course of the Rule, the great Patriarch constantly mentions the abbatial power.

of which he explains in his monastic code, and accomplishes in his own government.

According to his custom, St. Benedict begins by laying down a supreme principle whence he deducts all his teaching, and that gives unity, cohesion and supernatural fecundity to the whole ordering of the society which he intends to found.

This principle is thus announced: *Abbas... Christi agere vices in monasterio creditur.*[1] "The Abbot is believed to hold the place of Christ in the monastery." In this axiom is condensed the whole synthesis of the chapter of the Rule concerning the Abbot; all the remainder is but development and application. Thus St. Benedict wishes the Abbot to be penetrated with this fundamental thought and to adapt himself to it in order to find the norm of his conduct and the rule of his life. "Let the Abbot, since he is considered to represent the person of Christ, be called Lord and Father... out of reverence and love for Christ. Let him be mindful of this and show himself to be worthy of such an honour": *Abbas quia vices Christi agere videtur, Domnus et Abbas vocetur... honore et amore Christi. Ipse autem cogitet, et sic se exhibeat ut dignus sit tali honore.*[2] In the mind of St. Benedict, the Abbot represents Christ in the midst of his monks; he ought therefore, in the measure possible to human frailty, to reproduce in his life and in his government the person and actions of Christ Jesus.

Now in the Church which is His Kingdom, His "family" (that is the idea of St. Paul),[3] Christ appears as Pastor, and as Pontiff.

The Apostle tells us that Christ, as Man, did not arrogate to Himself the honour of the Priesthood, but that He was called to this dignity by the Father.[4] It is the same as regards Christ's office of Pastor. God proclaims by His prophet Ezechiel that He will set up one Shepherd Who shall lead His flock: *Suscitabo super eas Pastorem unum qui pascat eas... et ipse erit eis in Pastorem.*[5] Jesus Himself declares that He is this Shepherd. In sublime words addressed to His Father at the Last Supper, He confesses that it is from His Father that He has received the guardian-

1 Rule, ch. ii. 2 Ibid. ch. lxiii. 3 Eph. ii, 19.
4 Hebr. v, 5–6. 5 Ezech. xxxiv, 23.

ship of souls: *Tui erant, et mihi eos dedisti,*[1] "Thine they were; and to Me Thou gavest them."

This twofold office has conferred upon Jesus the fulness of all power: *Data est mihi omnis potestas.*[2] He wills to share this power with certain men, whom He chooses, according to the designs of His eternal providence, to co-operate with Him in the charge and sanctification of souls, and to whom He distributes the measure of His gifts; *Secundum mensuram donationis Christi.*[3] St. Paul writes that Christ appointed some as apostles, others as pastors, for the edifying of the Mystical Body.

It is a like mission that the Abbot has to fulfil: it is this twofold ideal he must strive to attain. Called to receive a participation in the dignity, office and grace of the universal Pontiff and supreme Pastor, the Abbot will find his greatness, his perfection and joy in the care wherewith he acquits himself of this supernatural commission.

This is why St. Benedict encompasses the appointment of the Abbot with all that can guarantee the authenticity of the Divine call, in the first place as concerns the election itself. This election is to be made "in the fear of God";[4] it is an election that must be ratified by the supreme power, in the person of the Sovereign Pontiff, in order that he who is elected may be legitimately invested with the authority of the head of the monastery. St. Benedict likewise specifies the conditions as to aptitude for the office which the future Abbot must satisfy, and explains to the electors the qualities that they must look for in their head; then he sets before the Abbot-elect the principles he should follow in his government and the spirit that should inspire him in the guidance of souls.[5]

From St. Benedict's point of view the Abbot then appears first of all as *pastor*. The ideal corresponding to this word is one particularly dear to St. Benedict, familiarised as he is with Holy Writ.[6] It is to be remarked how often the terms "pastor," "flock," "sheep," occur under his pen when he wishes to characterise the relations of the Abbot with the other members of the monastic society.[7] "Let him imitate the loving

1 Joan. xvii, 6. 2 Matth. xxviii, 18. 3 Eph. iv, 7.
4 Rule, ch. lxiv. 5 Rule, ch. lxiv.
6 This image is frequent, especially in the Old Testament, Israel having led the pastoral life. 7 Rule, ch. xxvii and xxviii.

example of the Good Shepherd," *Pastoris boni pium imitetur exemplum.*[1] It is the shepherd's first duty to feed his flock: *Nonne greges a pastoribus pascuntur.*[2] And what is the food that he must give them? God answers us by the mouth of the prophet: "They shall feed you with knowledge and doctrine," *Et pascent vos scientia et doctrina.*[3] Christ Jesus Himself declares: "Not in bread alone doth man live, but in every word that proceedeth from the mouth of God."[4]

This is why St. Benedict so insistently requires of the Abbot the perfection of doctrine and the knowledge of the Divine law: *Ergo cum aliquis suscipit nomen abbatis, duplici* DEBET *doctrina suis praeesse discipulis...* OPORTET *ergo eum esse doctum in lege divina.*[5]

The great Patriarch does not here mean the theoretic knowledge of philosophy and theology. A man may possess all the treasures of human knowledge, even in theological matters, and yet produce no fruit for souls. Hear how St. Paul insists on this subject: "If I speak with the tongues of men and of angels, and have not charity, I am become as sounding brass, or a tinkling cymbal. And if I should have prophecy and should know all mysteries and all knowledge... and have not charity, I am nothing": *Si noverim mysteria omnia, et omnem scientiam... factus sum velut aes sonans aut cymbalum tinniens.*[6] He speaks elsewhere of those who spend their lives in learning without ever arriving at the profitable knowledge of the truth: *Semper discentes, ei nunquam ad scientiam veritatis pervenientes.*[7]

The knowledge of which St. Benedict speaks and that he requires of the Abbot is a knowledge of God and holy things, obtained from the Scriptures, a knowledge enlightened by the rays of the Eternal Word and fructified by the Holy Spirit. This Spirit tells us that the wisdom of the Saints is true prudence: *Scientia sanctorum prudentia.*[8] It is therefore a question here of a knowledge of holiness, gained in prayer, assimilated and lived by the one who is to transmit it to souls. Such is the "wisdom

---

1 Ibid. ch. xxvii. 2 Ezech. xxxiv, 2. 3 Jerem. iii, 15.

4 Matth. iv, 4, Luc. iv, 4.

5 "Therefore, when anyone has received the name of abbot, he ought to rule his disciples with a twofold teaching... it behoves him, therefore, to be learned in the divine law," Rule, ch. ii and lxiv.

6 I Cor. xiii, 1–2. 7 II Tim. iii, 7. 8 Prov. ix, 10.

of doctrine," *sapientia doctrina*,[1] wherein the Abbot ought to excel; such is the treasury of knowledge whence he should unceasingly find the traditional maxims and also new lights for the directing of those who are at "the school of the Lord's service":[2] *Ut sciat unde proferat nova et vetera*.[3] In the ritual for the blessing of the Abbot, the Church implores for him from God the *thesaurum sapientiae ut sciat et habeat unde nova et vetera proferat*.

In this as in all things, Christ, "the Wisdom of God," *Sapientia Dei*, remains the Model. "I am the Truth," Jesus has said. He came into this world to render testimony to the truth.

The Abbot is to remember that he has received a participation in the dignity and mission of the Prince of Pastors; he is to strive ever to contemplate in prayer the Divine law brought by Christ, and to be united with Him by faith. Then only will he be in his turn a beacon-light of truth enlightening the hearts of his monks with the pure rays of heavenly doctrine. For, to use another metaphor, his great duty is to infuse this divine truth into the minds of his disciples like the leaven which is to permeate every action: *Ejus doctrina fermentum divinae justitiae in discipulorum mentibus conspergatur*.[4]

Hence the necessity of perfect orthodoxy in the doctrine taught. Christ, in making Peter the shepherd of the sheep and lambs, gave him the privilege of never erring in the faith; this privilege is not granted to the Abbot, hence the necessity of his taking constant care to assure the perfect orthodoxy and purity of his doctrine, not only that he may feed his flock, but also defend it against enemies who would give poisoned food to the sheep. The Abbot must be ever vigilant lest error or dangerous opinions find their way into the sheepfold. If St. Benedict so emphatically requires that the Abbot "be learned in the law of God," *doctum in lege divina*,[5] it is in order that he may discern errors and pitilessly condemn them. Listen to the grave warning wherewith the holy Patriarch shows how great is the responsibility that lies with the head of the monastery: "The Abbot ought not (God forbid!) to teach, or ordain,

1 Rule, ch. lxiv. 2 Prologue of the Rule.

3 "So that he may have... knowledge whence he may bring forth things new and old," Rule, ch. lxiv; cf. Matth. xiii, 52.

4 Ibid. ch. ii. 5 Ibid. ch. lxiv,

or command anything contrary to the law of the Lord. Let the Abbot be ever mindful that at the dreadful judgment of God, an account will have to be given both of his own teaching and of the obedience of his disciples. And let him know that to the fault of the shepherd shall be imputed any detriment, however small it be, which the Father of the household may find that His sheep have suffered..."[1] For the reading before Compline the Abbot must allow only the canonical Scriptures or the writings of the Fathers who are acknowledged as orthodox and "Catholic."[2] In the divine worship he is to be inspired by the traditions of the Roman Church, *Sicut psallit Ecclesia romana*.[3]

You see the constant solicitude that appears throughout the Rule; as shepherd, the Abbot is to keep in continual contact with Him in Whose place he stands so as to guide the flock, entrusted to his care, into fertile pastures "even to the mountain of God": *Usque ad montem Dei*.[4]

This is a redoubtable responsibility upon which St. Benedict, in several passages, insists with more than ordinary force. Let the Abbot, he says, hold it of indubitable truth that it is not only for his own soul, but for the souls of all his disciples that he will have to give a strict account on the Judgment Day. This wholesome fear of God's inevitable judgments, adds the holy Lawgiver, will make the Abbot attentive, and in the care he must take in directing Christ's sheep, he will find the occasion of keeping himself pure and stainless in God's sight.[5]

It is on this condition alone that St. Benedict guarantees to him that heavenly bliss promised by God to the faithful steward who in due season distributes to his fellow servants the bread of revealed doctrine, the wheat of divine wisdom: *Dum bene ministravit, audiat a Domino quod servus bonus, qui erogavit triticum conservis suis in tempore suo: amen dico vobis, ait, super omnia bona constituet eum*.[6]

II

To the ideal frequently evoked in the Rule by the word *pastor*, the Church, in her ceremonial for the blessing of the Abbot, joins that of *pontiff*.

1 Rule, ch. ii.
2 Cf. ix, and lxxiii.
3 Ibid. ch. xiii.
4 Cf. iii. Reg. xix, 8.
5 Rule, ch. ii.
6 Ibid. ch. lxiv; cf. Matth. xxiv, 47.

By the formulas of her invocations, her rites, the exterior insignia wherewith she invests the one elected, the Bride of Christ signifies in the eyes of all the quality of pontiff which she attaches to the function of the head of the monastery blessed by her.

In this again, the Abbot represents Christ; he is to seek, in the measure of his weakness, to attain this lofty ideal by the holiness of his life. This is what St. Benedict requires of him; at the same time as "the wisdom of doctrine," the abbot is to possess moral merit: *vitae meritum*.[1]

Personal holiness is indeed necessary to a Pontiff. Every high priest, says St. Paul, is an intermediary between God and man;[2] it is through him that the people's petitions are offered to God, and that God's gifts are communicated to souls. He cannot draw near to God and effectually plead the cause of the people unless he is, by reason of his purity, pleasing to God.

Christ, called by the Father to be the unique High Priest, by His own right, is "holy, innocent, undefiled, separated from sinners, and made higher than the heavens"[3] being the very Son of God; He is the object of God's delight. This is why He can efficaciously plead our cause. To the grace of personal holiness is added, in Jesus, the *gratia capitis*, which makes of Him "our Head" an all-powerful Mediator, Whose life and sanctity are communicated to His whole Mystical Body. Each action of Jesus is at once a homage of supreme love for His Father and a source of grace for mankind.

As far as human frailty allows, something analogous ought to be the case with the head of the monastery. As soon as the Abbot is canonically appointed, the Church beseeches God to communicate to him "the spirit of the grace of salvation"; she prays that it may please God to "pour upon him the dew of abundant blessings." The Bishop, extending his hands over the head of the one elected, prays that he who is made Abbot by the laying on of hands may ever be "the Lord's elect, worthy of being sanctified by Him."

From this moment, the Abbot has to endeavour to live and to become holy, no longer for himself alone, but for his brethren. He should be able to say, like the Supreme High Priest, Whose legitimate representative he henceforward is; "For them do I sanctify myself": *Et ego pro eis sanc-*

1 Rule, ch. lxiv. 2 Cf. Hebr. v, 1. 3 Ibid. vii, 26.

tifico meipsum.[1] As well as glorifying God by his personal perfection, he has, after the abbatial blessing of the Church, to procure God's glory by the holiness and fruitfulness of souls confided to him, "that the people who serve the Lord may increase in merit and in number": *Et merito et numero populus tibi serviens augeatur.*[2]

Each degree of the union of his soul with God, each step that he takes in the path of holiness, will render him more powerful with God, more fruitful in his supernatural action on minds and hearts.

This it is that gives such vast importance to the personal holiness that St. Benedict requires of the Abbot.

The Abbot is constantly to remember, says St. Benedict, that he has to bring souls to God.[3] Now in a supernatural society, the head is to be the pattern of his flock: *Forma gregis ex animo.*[4]

It is incontestable that the Abbot leaves his own impression on the monastery, and casts upon it his own reflection. It is exact to say: as the Abbot, so is the monastery. If you read monastic history, you will see how this truth is verified. The first Abbots of Cluny: Odo, Odilo, Majolus, Hugh, are four great admirable Saints whom the Church has placed on her altars. Such glory did their holiness shed on the celebrated Abbey that it was called "the court of Angels": *Deambulatorium angelorum.*[5] And as each one of them had a long reign, the history of the two first centuries of Cluny reads like a fairy tale of holiness. After them came an Abbot who was far from possessing the holiness of his predecessors; Cluny visibly fell away from the path of perfection; to bring it back, the efforts of a new Saint, Peter the Venerable, were needed.

This example among a thousand others proves that the Abbot is truly the living Rule, fashioning to his own image the monastery that he governs.

Again personal holiness is necessary to the Abbot in order that he may be enabled to fulfil his office of mediator. St. Gregory says somewhere in his writings that if an ambassador is not *persona grata* with the sovereign to whom he is sent, far from promoting the cause he is charged to plead, he risks compromising it. He says further that the

1 Joan. xvii, 19.
2 Collect *super populum* for Tuesday in Passion Week.
3 Rule, ch. xi.
4 I Petr. v, 3.
5 *Vita S. Hugon. auct. Hildeberto*, Migne, P. L. t. 159, 885.

pontiff cannot effectually intercede for his flock unless he is, by the sanctity of his life, a familiar friend of God.[1] It is not sufficient, therefore, that a conduct pure and beyond reproach should be required from the Abbot so that he may, by his example, draw his sons after him in the way of holiness; he must be conspicuous for "the merit of his life," *vitae meritum*,[2] in order the more effectually to plead the cause of his flock with God. We here touch on the highest condition of vital radiation that the head can exert on the members of the monastic society. Do we not often see, in the Old Testament, the heads of Israel, such as Moses, obtain Divine favours for the people because they were, by their holiness, the friends of God?

Was not Moses in this an anticipated figure of Christ, the one Mediator, Who was to appease the Father's justice, restore the heritage to us, and bring us all heavenly gifts? But why did our Divine Pontiff say that He was always heard by the Father, if not because being "holy, innocent, undefiled... and made higher than the heavens,"[3] He is, essentially, "the Son of His love?"[4]

If then the Abbot wishes to fulfil worthily his mission of head of the monastic society, he must strive unceasingly to remain united to the Godhead. In Christ Jesus, the Humanity was united hypostatically to the Divine Word, and, through this union, obtained floods of graces which overflowed from the Sacred Humanity upon souls. By analogy, in the measure which his lowly condition as man permits, the Abbot should live united to the Word that he may draw from His "treasures of wisdom and knowledge" the graces he is to shed upon his flock.

He will only attain to this fruitful union by a life of prayer. Like Moses upon the mountain, he must remain on terms of familiarity with God, that he may be able to communicate to his brethren the Lord's

---

1 *Qua mente apud Deum intercessionis locum pro populo arripit qui familiarem se ejus gratiae esse per vitae meritum nescit?* (With what frame of mind does he assail the place of intercession before God for the people, who does not know that he is a friend of His favor through the merit of his life?) *Reg. Past.* i, 10. *Lex levitarum* by Bishop Hedley. Under the pen of the great Pope are to be remarked the terms *vitae meritum* employed by St. Benedict.

2 Rule, ch. lxiv. 3 Hebr. vii, 26. 4 Col. i, 13.

commandments, and the lights received in assiduous intercourse with the Father of Lights from Whom comes down "every perfect gift."[1]

III

We shall have but an imperfect idea of the mission that St. Benedict assigns to the Abbot if we do not bring forward two dominant qualities which the Lawgiver of monks emphatically declares to be necessary to him. These are *discretion* and *kindness.*

Discretion is one of the characteristics of St. Benedict's Rule, as St. Gregory[2] remarks in contrasting it with the other ascetical Rules of Christian antiquity. But this quality shines out especially in the chapter concerning the Abbot. In the guidance of souls, St. Benedict wills the Abbot to exercise discretion "the mother of virtues."[3] What are we to understand by discretion?

It is the supernatural art of discerning and measuring all things in view of the end; of adapting every means, each according to its nature and circumstances, to the obtaining of the end. This end is to bring souls to God: *Ut animae salventur.*[4] And to bring them in such a manner that the monks may fulfil their task willingly. Therefore, says the holy Legislator, the Abbot must "well temper all things": *Omnia temperet;*[5] and explaining his thought more fully, he summarises from this point of view, the work of the Abbot in a very precise and significant formula: He is "to accommodate himself to the diversity of characters": *Multorum servire moribus.*[6]

Such is the golden Rule laid down for the practical conduct of the Abbot towards his brethren; such is the noble device which, if well observed, will make him successful in the delicate and arduous art—St. Gregory calls it "the art of arts"[7]—of ruling souls: *Sciat quam difficilem et arduam rem suscipit regere animas.*[8]

In this domain, St. Benedict requires of the Abbot a combination of contrasting qualities: strength linked with gentleness, authority tem-

1 Jac. i, 17.
2 *Dialogues.* Lib. ii, ch. 36.
3 Rule, ch. lxiv.
4 Ibid. ch. xli.
5 Ibid. ch. lxiv.
6 Ibid. ch. ii.
7 *Regula pastoralis,* I, 1.
8 "Let him realise also how difficult and arduous a task he has undertaken, of ruling souls," Rule, ch. ii.

pered by love. See with what perfect tact he selects the terms designed to characterise the exercise of the aforesaid virtue of discretion. He wishes the Abbot to be zealous without anxiety, prudent without timidity,[1] ever seeking "the Kingdom of God and His justice,"[2] and yet in nowise neglecting the material care of the monastery which he has to administer wisely, with prudence and justice;[3] "loving the brethren but hating sin";[4] using prudence even in correction for fear lest "in seeking too eagerly to scrape off the rust, the vessel be broken";[5] the Abbot is to vary his conduct with great pliability, according to the circumstances and dispositions of each: one is of an open character, another is reserved; in one the intellect predominates, in another sensibility; here he finds docility, there self-will; he must adapt himself to every temperament: *Miscens temporibus tempora terroribus blandimenta*;[6] showing the severity of a master to the disobedient disciple: *Dirum magistri*; to the upright soul seeking God, the tenderness of a father: *Pium patris ostendat affectum.*[7] To the well-endowed souls, eager to find God, it suffices for the Abbot to set before them the heavenly doctrine: *Capacibus discipulis mandata Domini verbis proponat*; to those of simpler minds or of a more difficult temperament, the pastor will point out the way by his own example: *Duris vero corde et simplicioribus factis suis divina praecepta demonstret.*[8] One he must win by kindness, another by reproofs, yet another by persuasion and force of reasoning: *Et alium quidem blandimentis, alium vero increpationibus, alium suasionibus.*[9] It is only at this price that "far from having to suffer any detriment in the flock committed to his care he will be able to rejoice in its increase in goodness."[10]

In summing up this magnificent teaching on discretion, the holy Lawgiver gives us finally this lapidary formula dictated by his great experience of souls and his distinctly Roman genius, so skilful in the management of men: "Let the Abbot so temper all things that strong souls may give rein to their holy ambition, and the weak need not be discouraged": *Sic omnia temperet ut sit et fortes quod cupiant et infirmi non refugiant.*[11]

---

1 Ibid. ch. lxiv.
2 Ibid. ch. ii.
3 Ibid. ch. iii and *passim.*
4 Ibid. ch. lxiv.
5 Ibid. ch. lxiv.
6 Ibid. ch. ii.
7 Ibid. ch. ii.
8 Ibid. ch. ii.
9 Rule, ch. ii.
10 Rule, ch. ii.
11 Ibid. ch. lxiv.

IV

Is discretion the sole dominant virtue that St. Benedict requires of the Abbot? No, he furthermore wishes him to add love thereto; or rather it is to be the love of souls which will make his supernatural tact more delicate. It is because he loves souls well and individually that he will have it at heart to bring them to Christ, according to their talents and aptitudes, their weaknesses, needs and aspirations.

Let us raise our gaze for an instant towards the Adorable Trinity. There we contemplate the Word Who, with the Father, is the principle of the Spirit of Love: *Verbum spirans Amorem*. Christ, the Word Incarnate, has become the Good Shepherd Who gives His life for His sheep[1] and thereby gives testimony to the greatest love of all: *Majorem hac dilectionem nemo habet.*[2] And St. Paul explicitly tells us that Christ took upon Himself in His Human Nature all our infirmities, sin excepted, in order to become a compassionate High Priest Who knows how to be merciful to human weakness: *UT misericors fieret.*[3]

St. Benedict, so full of the spirit of the Gospel, lets this spirit of mercy abound throughout his Rule. See with what goodness he will have the Abbot or the officials who replace him treat children,[4] old men,[5] the brothers in delicate health,[6] pilgrims,[7] the poor;[8] what humanity full of noble delicacy he shows to guests and strangers;[9] what attentive solicitude he requires towards the sick:[10] how the chapters he consecrates to Christ's suffering members reveal the great Patriarch's tenderness!

But it is especially in the chapter on the Abbot that St. Benedict gives a precept of love to the Father of the monastery: *Diligat fratres.*[11] The Abbot is to love the monks, and love them deeply, with equal love for all: *Non unus plus ametur quam alius,*[12] because, adds St. Benedict, "we are all one in Christ; and in Christ there is neither bond nor free"; for all are called to the same grace of adoption, and to be partakers of the same heavenly inheritance.

However, in the same way as God looks with more complacency on those who most bear in themselves the features of His Son Jesus—since

1 Joan. x, 11 and 15.
2 Ibid. xv, 13.
3 Hebr. ii, 17.
4 Rule, ch. xxxvii.
5 Ibid.
6 Ibid. ch. xxxvi.
7 Ibid. ch. liii.
8 Ibid.
9 Ibid.
10 Ibid. ch. xxxvi.
11 Ibid. ch. lxiv.
12 Ibid. ch. ii.

that is the ideal of our predestination—so the Abbot may evince more love towards those who most nearly approach this Divine Model by their good deeds and obedience: *Nisi quem in bonis actibus aut obedientia invenerit meliorem.*[1]

St. Benedict insists much on this love that the Abbot ought to have for his sons. He wishes the Abbot "to study to be loved rather than feared": that is to say his government ought to be free from any tyranny, *Studeat plus amari quam timeri.*[2] And this love of the Abbot for his monks ought to go to the utmost extent. Read the chapter where St. Benedict sets forth in detail the solicitude that the Abbot should show to those who fall into any fault: *Omni sollicitudine curam gerat abbas circa delinquentes fratres.*"[3] And the Legislator of monks recalls the example of the Good Shepherd Who leaves the ninety-nine faithful sheep to go after the one that is lost.

This kindness is in nowise to degenerate into culpable weakness. Look at Jesus Christ. Full as He is of love and pity for souls, He is equally full of hatred for evil. He forgives Magdalen, and the woman taken in adultery; He bears, with how much goodness! the shortcomings of His disciples; but what severity he shows to vice, above all to pharisaical pride!

So the Abbot, holding the place of Christ, ought to strive—however "difficult and arduous the task": *difficilem et arduam rem*—to imitate in this, the Divine Model: "Let him love the brethren but hate vice": *Diligat fratres, oderit vitia.* If a monk has to be corrected in anything, the Abbot should rebuke him with great charity and fatherly love. It is certain that a too severe Superior can do much harm to souls; it is no less true that fervour will suffer in a monastery where an easy-going Abbot does not correct faults, and never refuses anything to anyone. However, in all this matter, it is charity that must be the motive power of his conduct. It may happen that during a long time a monk does not give what is rightly to be expected of him. What is to be done in this case? Is the Abbot to cease to concern himself about this soul? On the contrary, he will with great patience await the hour of grace. He will remember too that all souls are not called to the same degree of perfec-

1 Ibid. ch. ii. 2 Ibid. ch. lxiv. 3 Ibid. ch. xxvii.

tion, and he will show more indulgence towards those whose ascent is slower and more painful.

But what is the Abbot to do when he has to deal with one who has a truly bad spirit? St. Benedict wishes him to use severity, "the sword of separation": *ferrum abscissionis*, "lest" he says, "one diseased sheep should infect the whole flock."[1] However, as long as he does not meet with incorrigible obstinacy, the Abbot is to "abound in mercy," after Jesus Christ's example: *Superexaltet misericordiam judicio*, so that, as Christ has promised in the Beatitudes, he may benefit by a like indulgence, *Ut idem ipse consequatur*,[2] for "he ought ever to remember his own frailty": *suamque fragilitatem semper suspectus sit*.[3]

The beautiful words uttered by the Patriarch in reference to the administration of the cellarer are first to be verified in the government of the Abbot: "Let no one in the monastery, which is 'the house,' 'the family,' of God be troubled or grieved": *Ut nemo perturbetur neque contristetur in domo Dei*.[4] In simple and upright hearts, sincerely seeking God and living by His grace, joy should superabound, and, with joy, "the peace that passeth all understanding."[5]

V

We have seen that at the very beginning of the chapter concerning the Abbot, St. Benedict lays down this fundamental principle: in the monastery the Abbot holds the place of Christ; this we must believe: *Abbas Christi agere vices in monasterio creditur*. This principle may also serve correlatively to characterise the attitude of monks faithful to their vocation.

This is a thought of capital importance to us, because the monastery constitutes a supernatural society where we live by faith: *Justus meus ex fide vivit*.[6] Notice the word *creditur*. It is an eminent act of faith that is to illumine all our conduct and make all our deeds fruitful. Either you believe or you believe not. If you do not believe with a firm faith, then you will, little by little, insensibly but infallibly, end by detaching yourself from the Superior, from his person and his teaching. But at the

1 Rule, ch. xxviii. 2 Ibid. ch. lxiv. 3 Ibid. ch. lxiv.
4 Ibid. ch. xxxi. 5 Philip. iv, 7. 6 Hebr. x, 38.

same time, and to the same extent you will separate yourself from the principle of grace, for we must know, says St. Benedict, that it is by this path of obedience that we come to God: *Scientes se per* HANC *obedientiae viam ituros ad Deum.*[1]

If you believe that the Abbot represents Christ, your attitude towards him will be ruled by this belief. This attitude will be composed of love, docility of mind, obedience of action.

The Abbot, as the name which St. Benedict wishes to retain for him itself denotes, is "Father": *Abba Pater*. And the holy Lawgiver requires that his monks shall have "a sincere and humble affection for *their* Abbot": *Abbatem* SUUM *sincera et humili caritate diligant.*[2]

It is in nowise requisite to have a sensible love or one of enthusiasm; it would be childishness to claim this; but it must be a supernatural love given to God, Who is seen by faith in the person of the head of the monastery.

St. Benedict wishes that this love be "sincere and humble," sincere because humble. The whole list of qualities that he requires in the Abbot is so complete and so remarkable, that it is almost impossible to find it perfectly realised in one man. Few Superiors combine in themselves that harmonious sum of diverse perfections which the great Patriarch has gathered together in one full sheaf. The Abbot has certainly graces of state, but these do not essentially modify his nature; and every man, with the best will in the world remains inferior to his ideal.

What are we then to do in presence of the deficiencies, failings and imperfections which may be discovered in the Abbot, *our* Abbot, says St. Benedict, he who, *for us*, represents Christ? Are we going to bring up these shortcomings, analyse or discuss them with others in order to criticise or censure them? Such a way of acting would destroy the spirit of faith, and be far from that "humble and sincere affection," *sincera et humili caritate*, desired by the holy Legislator. Nothing would do more harm to a soul because nothing is more contrary to the letter and spirit of our religious profession.

---

1 Rule, ch. lxxi. St. Benedict uses these words in reference to the obedience that the brethren are to have one to the other. But this mutual obedience supposes obedience to the Superior, and what is said of the spiritual fruits of the first applies *a fortiori* to the latter.

2 Rule, ch. lxxii.

Let us know how to abstain with the greatest care from these criticisms and recriminations. And if a brother should come to us to complain of the Superior in a critical spirit, the greatest charity we could show him would be to recall to him his Profession and bring him back to the spirit of generous donation and humble submission vowed on that day. Let us throw a cloak of love over the imperfections of the Superior, following the example of two of Noe's sons: far from imitating their brother in his mockeries, they covered their father's nakedness with a mantle. You know how they were blessed for doing so, and what a curse the unhappy Cham brought upon himself.[1] All the murmurings and criticisms, not to speak of railleries, against the Superior do nothing to change the situation that one may think blameworthy or open to disapproval; they often only embitter it, casting trouble into souls, and thereby depriving them of peace and joy and diminishing their intimate union with God: such things draw down upon those who thus Separate themselves from the Superior, the malediction fallen upon Cham.

It is a like chastisement that St. Benedict himself, full as he is of compassionate loving kindness, calls down upon the turbulent and disobedient who, despising or making light of the advice given to them, still rebel against their Pastor's care: death itself, having the last word, shall be their punishment: *Paena sit eis praevalens ipsa mors*.[2]

Do we not find the equivalent of a malediction in the grave words one day addressed by Our Lord Himself to St. Margaret Mary on this subject? We cannot read them without trembling. Listen attentively to these words falling from the lips of Truth itself: "All religious who are not united to their Superiors may look upon themselves as vessels of reprobation—in which good liquors are corrupted; on whose souls the shining of the Divine Sun of Justice has but the same effect as the sun shining on the slime of the earth. These souls are so far removed from My Heart that the more they strive to approach me by means of the Sacraments, prayer and other pious exercises, the further I withdraw Myself in horror from them. They will go from one hell to another, for it is this disunion which has been the loss of so many, and which will be the ruin of so many yet to come, because every Superior, whether he be good or bad holds My place. That is why the inferior, thinking to harm

1 Gen. ix, 21-25. 2 Rule, ch. ii.

the Superior, inflicts so many, and such mortal wounds on his own soul. After all, it is in vain for him to sigh at the gates of mercy—he will not be heard if I do not hear the voice of the Superior."

VI

This humble and sincere love for the Abbot is to be manifested by a great docility of mind to his teaching and a generous obedience to his commands. Here again faith is the true light.

God, Who does all things with wisdom, adapts His action to our nature. He speaks to the intellect in order to touch the will, light becomes the source of action. Therefore, says the Apostle, "It pleased God, by the foolishness of our preaching, to save them that believe": *PLACUIT Deo per stultitiam praedicationis salvos facere credentes.*[1] This good pleasure of God, like all His ways, is adorable. Remark that Christ did not ordain His Apostles to write, but to preach, and by this means, God has renewed the face of the earth. It is the Word Who sanctifies souls, but to reach them He took a human and tangible form. This same Word likewise takes a sensible form by preaching. While the word from the lips of men strikes the bodily ears, the internal Word reaches the mind and is instilled sweetly and mightily into the will: *Fides ex auditu.*[2]

But, continues the Apostle, how are men to believe unless preachers are sent? *Quomodo credent nisi mittantur?*[3] Christ has provided for that: "Behold I send you... Go preach to every creature": *Ecce mitto vos: ite, praedicate Evangelium omni creaturae.*[4] And those sent by Christ do not speak in their own name but in His: "He that heareth you heareth Me; and he that despiseth you, despiseth Me": *Qui vos audit me audit, qui vos spernit me spernit.*[5] God exhorts through these ambassadors of Christ: *Pro Christo legatione fungimur tamquam Deo exhortante per nos.*[6] Hence the word they speak is not "as the word of men, but (as it is

1 I Cor. i, 21.
2 "Faith then cometh by hearing," Rom. x, 17.
3 Ibid.
4 Luc. x, 3; Marc. xvi, 15.
5 Luc. x, 16.
6 II Cor. v, 20.

indeed) the word of God."[1] For do you not know, says St. Paul again, it is "Christ that speaketh in me": *In me loquitur Christus?*[2]

Thus the obligation that all lawful pastors have of distributing the bread of doctrine to their flock cannot suffer dispensation. This obligation reaches the Abbot who, as we have seen, according to the will of St. Benedict, and in virtue of his appointment, is *missus,* that is to say established by the Church over a portion of Christ's flock.

But the word of the Abbot, like that of each one sent by Christ, like that of Christ Himself, does not always produce the same effects. What was said of the Humanity of Jesus, namely, that it was "set for the fall, and for the resurrection of many": *Ecce positus est hic in ruinam et in resurrectionem multorum,*[3] is true of every evangelical word. It is a seed of life, but it only bears fruit, as the Word declares, in well disposed hearts.[4] Christ is the Son of God, Eternal Wisdom; all His teaching, full of the unction of the Holy Ghost, is, as He Himself declares, "spirit and life."[5] And yet during the years of His ministry what did those men say who listened to Him while their hearts were not right with God, those who tried to entrap Him in His speech? "This saying is hard; and who can hear it?" *Durus est hic sermo, et quis potest eum audire?*[6] Were these hearers, these disciples, lacking in intelligence? No, but their hearts resisted. And the result of this inward attitude was that they left Jesus to their own great loss "and walked no more with Him": *Et jam non cum illo ambulabant.*[7] Consider the behaviour of the Apostles under these same circumstances. They hear the same Jesus pronounce the same words, but, for these simple upright hearts, they are the words of salvation: "Will you also go away?" asks the Master. And they answer: "Lord, to whom shall we go? Thou hast the words of eternal life."[8] Whence arises the difference between these two groups of souls? From the dispositions of the heart.

There is an important word at the beginning of the Prologue. The great Patriarch invites us to receive his teaching "with joy," *libenter*, and tells us to incline the ear of our heart towards his word that we may the better put it into practice. *Inclina aurem cordis tui.*[9] If the mind alone

1 *Cum accepissetis a nobis verbum auditus Dei, accepistis illud non ut verbum hominum, sed sicut est vere Verbum Dei, qui operatur in vobis qui credidistis.* I Thess. ii, 13.

2 II Cor. xiii, 3. 3 Luc. ii, 34. 4 Ibid. viii, 15. 5 Joan. vi, 64.

6 Ibid. 61. 7 Ibid. 67. 8 Ibid. vi, 68-69.

9 St. Gregory likewise employs this expression more than once: *Si ipse verba Dei*

hears without the heart's co-operation, God's word does not bring forth all its fruit. If you do not listen to the word of him, who holds the place of Christ towards you, with faith, humility and in a childlike spirit, as St. Benedict desires (*admonitionem patris*),[1] but in a spirit of criticism or simply with a closed heart, this word, even if it came from a saint, would remain barren and might even be hurtful.[2] And on the day of judgment we shall be asked to give an account of all the teachings by which we have not chosen to profit. Therefore the Psalmist exclaims: "Today if you shall hear [the Lord's] voice, harden not your hearts": *Hodie si vocem eius audieritis, nolite obdurare* CORDA *vestra*.[3] And how do we harden our hearts? By pride of spirit.

"Yea rather, Blessed are they who hear the word of God and keep it," even when they are, or think themselves, more learned than the one who speaks: *Beati qui audiunt verbum Dei*.[4] Receiving this word (it is still the same idea) with "a good and perfect *heart*": CORDE *bono et optimo*, they will bring forth at the heavenly harvest that "hundredfold," that "very much fruit" which alone rejoices our Heavenly Father because in this is He glorified: *In hoc clarificatus est Pater meus, ut fructum plurimum afferatis*.[5]

VII

To docility of mind, St. Benedict wishes the monk to join obedience of action and "for the love of God to submit himself to his superior in all obedience": *Pro Dei amore omni obedientia se subdat majori*.[6] But as the great Patriarch devotes a special and important chapter to this virtue, we will treat of it further on. What is to be noted here is a twofold aspect very characteristic of St. Benedict's teaching. On the one hand there is a

---

audit qui ex Deo est, et audire verba ejus non potest quisquis de illo non est, interroget se unusquisque si verba Dei IN AURE CORDIS *percipit; et intelliget unde sit* (If he who is of God hears the words of God, and whoever is not from Him cannot hear His words, let each one ask himself if he perceives the words of God in the *ear of his heart;* and he will understand whence it comes). *Homilia 18 in Evang.*

1 Prologue of the Rule.

2 St. Paul speaks of the enlightening of the eyes of the heart as necessary for knowing the truth. (Eph. i, 18.)

3 Ps. xciv, 8. 4 Luc. xi, 28. 5 Joan. xv, 8. 6 Rule, ch. vii.

rare width of view in the material organisation of the monastic life; on the other hand, an almost boundless fidelity to the least details of the observance, when once established by authority, is required.

Far removed from all *parti-pris*, from all formalism, the Lawgiver of monks leaves the regulation of many details, sometimes even points of consequence, to the Abbot's power of discretion. Thus in the matter of food, he refrains from fixing the quantity or quality with too much precision, for "everyone has his proper gift from God"[1] in what regards corporal necessities; in case of illness or delicate health, he allows the use of meat,[2] and more generally a moderate use of wine;[3] when the labour of the monks is harder than usual, the Abbot has the faculty of increasing the customary portion.[4] St. Benedict leaves a like latitude in what concerns the quality of the clothing: the Abbot is to decide according to the requirements of the climate and other considerations.[5] In the matter of penances and punishments for faults committed, much is left again to the Abbot's judgment: *Culparum modus in abbatis pendet arbitrio*;[6] we find the same discretion—and this seems astonishing—relative to the distribution of psalms in the Divine Office: in proposing an order to be adopted in the psalmody, the holy Legislator adds that he does not wish to impose this order; if any Abbot finds a better arrangement, he is free to adopt it.[7]

The extent of the Abbot's authority is, in some ways, indefinite. All, from the prior and cellarer down to the last of the brethren, must submit to the decision of the Abbot; *In abbatis pendeat arbitrio, ut quod salubrius esse judicaverit, et cuncti obediant*;[8] every action done knowingly without the Abbot's authorisation is imputed to presumption and, however slight a matter it may be, its author will be subjected to a penance: *Vindictae regulari subjaceat qui praesumpserit... quippiam quamvis parvum sine abbatis jussione facere.*[9] This entire submission naturally extends to the use of material objects: "It is not licit to have anything whatsoever that the Abbot has not given, or authorised to receive": *Nec quidquam liceat habere quod Abbas non dederit aut permiserit.*[10] St. Benedict goes still

1 Rule, ch. xl.
2 Ibid. ch. xxxvi and xxxix.
3 Ibid. ch xl.
4 Ibid. ch. xxxix.
5 Ibid. ch. lv.
6 Ibid. ch. xxiv.
7 Ibid. ch. xviii.
8 Ibid. ch. iii.
9 Ibid. ch. lxvii.
10 Ibid. ch. xxxiii.

further; even the supererogatory acts of mortification that the monks wish to undertake are accounted by him presumption and vainglory, and as unworthy of reward, if the Abbot has not been consulted in this respect and if they have not had the blessing of his consent and of his prayers. "Let everything then be done with the approval of the Abbot": *Ergo cum voluntate abbatis omnia agenda sunt.*[1]

How are we to explain these apparently contradictory attitudes? How reconcile these extreme requirements with these broad views? St. Benedict had too enlightened a mind to place monastic perfection in such or such a detail of the common life taken in itself: it would have been a pharisaical tendency repugnant to his great soul. These details undoubtedly have their importance, but they do not constitute the matter of perfection. The form of perfection is something far higher. It is the absolute tradition of the monk to God's Will by a loving and generous obedience. This is why St. Benedict shows himself so exacting once this Will is manifested, "for the obedience which is given to superiors is given to God": *Obedientia quae majoribus praebetur, Deo exhibetur.*[2] Therefore, he adds, "Those who burn with love of eternal life... desire to have an Abbot over them." Our holy Father St. Benedict does not say that they "support" the authority of the head of the monastery, but that they "desire" it: *Abbatem sibi praeesse DESIDERANT.*[3] So true is it that the holy Legislator sees in the obedience given through love the very path that leads us to God: *Scientes se PER HANC VIAM ituros ad Deum.*[4]

Ever faithful to his essentially Christian method, the great Patriarch places before the eyes of his sons the One Example of all perfection: Christ Jesus. By obedience to their Abbot, they will imitate Him Who said: "I came not to do Mine own will, but the will of Him Who sent Me."[5]

Never let us lose sight of this essential principle placed by St. Benedict at the very head of his Rule; it perfectly synthesises our whole life; it lights us all along our path like a luminous and kindly beacon. The Abbot holds the place of Christ. He is the head of the monastic society, the high priest and pastor. The monks should show him a humble and sincere affection, great docility of spirit and perfect obedience.

1 Ibid. ch. xlix. 2 Rule, ch. v. 3 Rule, ch. v.
4 Ibid. ch. lxxi. 5 Ibid. ch. vii; cf. Joan. vi, 38.

A Benedictine community animated by such sentiments becomes veritably the palace of the King, a Paradise where Justice and Peace give one another the kiss of union.[1] From such souls who are "truly seeking God" goes up the inward, silent cry: "Father, Thy will be done on earth as it is in Heaven": *Pater, fiat voluntas tua sicut in coelo et in terra!* By humble prayer, constant dependence on Eternal Wisdom, and close union with the Prince of Pastors, the Abbot will endeavour to know this Divine will and set it before his brethren; it is for them to do it with generous obedience inspired by love.

And when (again to take up St. Benedict's words),[2] the Lord looks down to see if there be any who seek Him, He will find, in such a Community, hearts that are pleasing to Him because they imitate the Son of His love; He will behold the realisation, as it were, of that ideal whereof He Himself speaks by His Spirit in the Scriptures: "This is the generation of them that seek Him, of them that seek the face of the God of Jacob": *Haec est generatio quaerentium Eum, quaerentium faciem Dei Jacob.*[3]

Nothing more vividly translates all this admirable and fruitful supernatural doctrine than the conventual Mass celebrated by the Abbot surrounded by his sons. Vested in the insignia of his dignity, the head of the monastery offers the Sacred Victim to God, or rather, through his ministry, Christ, the Supreme High Priest and universal Mediator, offers Himself to the Father. The Abbot offers up to Heaven the homage, the vows, the very hearts of his monks, whence arises a perfume of sacrifice and of love, which the Father receives, through Christ, in the odour of sweetness: *in odorem suavitatis.*[4]

In this solemn moment of the holy Oblation, when voices are blended in one and the same praise, hearts uplifted in the same spirit of adoration and love towards God, the Abbot worthy of the name can repeat the words uttered in the presence of His Disciples by the Divine Pastor, when He was about to give His life for His sheep: "Father, Thine they were, and to me Thou gavest them... I pray not that Thou shouldst take them out of the world, but that Thou shouldst keep them from evil..." May they be one among themselves and with me, as Thy Son is One with

---

1 Ps. lxxxiv, 11. 2 Prologue of the Rule.
3 Ps. xxiii, 6. 4 Exod. xxix, 41.

Thee... may Thy love abide in them, and to all may it one day be given to contemplate the glory of Thy Christ, and to be partakers of Thy blessed fellowship with Thy beloved Son and the Holy Spirit.

THE CENOBITICAL SOCIETY

SUMMARY.—I. Hierarchical relations of the Abbot with the monks.—II. Forms of activity that are to be manifested in the monastic society: prayer.—II. Work; the spirit that should inspire it.—IV. Stability in the common life.—V. Mutual relations of the members of the Cenobitical society.—VI. Stability likewise attaches monks to their cloister.

THE foundation stone of the cenobitical society having been laid in the person of the Abbot, it remains for us, in order to complete our broad outline of the Benedictine idea, to examine more closely the divers elements whence result the organic life and intimate existence of this society.

We will first treat of the Abbot's relations with the monks from the hierarchical point of view;—we will next see what sort of activity ought to be manifested in the framework of this organisation, an activity which is summed up in prayer and work; then stability in the common life will appear to us as one of the characteristic elements of cenobitical existence;—and we will conclude by indicating what should be the dispositions of those who dwell in the monastery, so that the ideal formed by the great Patriarch may be attained.

I

We have already remarked that there is a striking analogy between the government instituted by St. Benedict and that of the Church, and this should in nowise astonish us in a Rule coming from one in whom the Christian sense is so closely allied to the Roman genius.[1]

---

1 This is evidently only an analogy; if points of similitude exist between the Church

You know that the constitution given by Eternal Wisdom to His Church establishes a monarchical and hierarchical form of government, reflecting upon earth God's supreme monarchy in Heaven and the hierarchy which reigns there.

At the basis of the visible body which is His Church, Christ Jesus has placed a visible foundation, Peter and his successors. From them all power and jurisdiction is derived. In the same way, our Blessed Father makes the entire organisation of the monastery depend upon the Abbot; *Nos vidimus expedire... in abbatis pendere arbitrio ordinationem monasterii sui.*[1] From the supreme abbatial authority flows all the activity of the monastery, and all delegation: the principal officials in the monastery, the prior, cellarer, deans are instituted by the Abbot. St. Benedict says that the Abbot is to appoint the Prior himself and for himself: *Ordinet ipse sibi praepositum.*[2] Not only does the first investiture of these officials depend on the power of the Abbot, but in the exercise of their charges, they must not undertake or carry out anything beyond the orders or wishes of the Abbot.[3]

This centralisation of power within the hands of the Abbot is one of the most distinct ideas in the monastic code.

Absolute as is the Abbot's authority, we know however that it is not arbitrary. The Sovereign Pontiff, in his teaching, must follow Christ's doctrine and the spirit of tradition; in the same way, the Abbot, says

---

and the monastery, there are also differences, and some are considerable. We at once see those that are most important; in certain cases the Sovereign Pontiff is infallible, the head of the monastery never enjoys this privilege; the Pope's authority is universal, that of the Abbot is restricted, etc.

1 "We have judged it expedient... that the abbot should have the appointment to all offices in his monastery," Rule, ch. lxv. 2 Ibid.

3 *Praepositus illa agat cum reverentia quae ab abbate suo ei injuncta fuerint, nihil contra abbatis voluntatem aut ordinationem faciens,* (Let the prior respectfully perform what is enjoined him by his abbot, and do nothing contrary to the abbot's will or regulations) *(c. lxv); cellarius... sine jussione abbatis nihil faciat, quae jubentur custodiat... Omnia quae ei injunxerit abbas ipsa habeat sub cura sua; a quibus eum prohibuerit non praesumat* (The cellarer... let him do nothing without the abbot's order, but keep to his instructions... let him have under his care all those things which the abbot has assigned to him, but presume not to deal with what he has forbidden him) *(xxxi); decani sollicitudinem gerant... in omnibus... secundum praecepta abbatis sui* (Let the deans take charge... in all things... observing the instructions of their abbot) *(xxi).*

St. Benedict, must not teach, ordain, or command anything contrary to the Divine precepts; in all things he must, like his brethren follow the Rule: *Omnes in omnibus sequantur Regulam*; but, as Christ's Vicar is the authorised interpreter of the laws of the Church, so it is for the Abbot to regulate and, if needs be, to decide the meaning of the letter of the monastic code, make modifications and permit the exceptions that he judges expedient for the good of the community.[1]

Moreover the Abbot is not left to his own lights. The Council of Cardinals surround the Pope and guide him in many circumstances; the Abbot likewise finds counsel in the "seniors," *seniores*, who enlighten him in manifold ordinary occasions where the life of the Abbey is interested.

St. Benedict goes further. In affairs where the spiritual or temporal interests of the monastery are seriously concerned he wishes the Abbot to call together the brethren, and himself lay before them the matter in question and ask their advice. And the reason our holy Legislator gives for this consultation is that it is often to the younger of the brethren that the Lord gives the most judicious views.[2] And this shows us once more the supernatural spirit that guided St. Benedict's pen in the drawing up of the Rule. This consultation is however very different from those which are held in parliaments. St. Benedict wishes "the brethren to give their advice in all humility and subjection, without stubbornly upholding their opinion." Then, the advice having been heard, it belongs to the Abbot to examine the matter himself and take the course which he considers to be best: *Et audiens consilium fratrum tractet apud se, et quod utilius judicaverit faciat*.[3] Doubtless, the Abbot must regulate everything with foresight and equity; for he will have to render rigorous account of his administration to One Who is Infinite Justice. Furthermore, the Church in her canon law has fixed the guarantees which surround several determined cases, such as the reception of novices, in which the conclusion of the affair depends on the vote of the Community.

As long as the question is in suspense, one ought to speak with humble frankness, at need with respectful boldness; but once the Abbot has

1 It is however to be noted that the Sovereign Pontiff is more than the interpreter of the Church's laws since he himself is the lawgiver.

2 Rule, ch. iii. 3 Ibid.

taken his decision, all, says St. Benedict, must obey: *Ei cuncti obediant.*[1] To murmur then, to discuss the matter judged, *contendere*, is an attitude that the holy Legislator rigorously condemns, because it is unworthy and disloyal; besides, nothing is more opposed to the spirit of faith and to the loving submission which should characterise the true monk.

That *patria potestas* granted to the Abbot by our Blessed Father St. Benedict gives us an insight into the family character which the cenobitical life ought to bear. The Kingdom of God is a family. We see that the liturgy often uses the expression "God's household"[2] to designate the Church. All Christians, God's children by the grace of adoption, form, in fact, one family of whom the eldest is the Only-begotten Son, the Son of the Heavenly Father's delight. All the other members are to resemble this eldest Son, according to the degree of their union with Him; they are pleasing to God in the measure of perfection wherewith they reproduce the features of this Only-begotten One become the Firstborn of a multitude of brethren. This is indeed their divine "predestination"; *Praedestinavit [nos] conformes fieri imaginis Filii sui, ut sit ipse primogenitus in multis fratribus.*[3]

In this household of God, upon earth, the Sovereign Pontiff is the visible Father. The Abbot holds the same role in the little monastic family; he is truly, according to the great Patriarch's own words, "the Father of the monastery" who has to provide for all the needs of his children: *Omnia a Patre monasterii sperare.*[4] All is ordered in this household which our Blessed Father calls "the house of God"[5] in such a way that the members may reproduce in themselves the features of the Eldest Brother, in Whose footsteps they are to tread.

From this same principle of the *patria potestas* likewise flows the following application, generally confirmed by tradition, although the letter of it is not explicitly found in the Rule: the power of the Abbot, like that of the Sovereign Pontiff, is for life, that is to say, Providence alone is to put an end to the exercise of his authority at the same time as to his days.

1 Ibid. ch. iii.

2 Collect for fifth Sunday after Epiphany; first Sunday in Lent; twenty-first Sunday after Pentecost, etc.

3 Rom. viii, 29. 4 Rule, ch. xxiii. 5 Ibid. ch. xxxi.

In other institutes of more modern times, the Superiors called Priors, Guardians, Rectors, are elected every three years; for these institutes this is a condition of vitality and perfection; in the Monastic Society which forms one family, the Abbot, called "Father," normally keeps in power during his life. This is one of the characteristics of the cenobitical life, and cannot be modified without, at the same time, striking a blow at one of the essential principles of our institution. For the monk, this continuity of the Abbot's power secures to him in a larger measure that "good of obedience" which he came to seek in the cloister. Moreover this form of government is traced upon that which Christ Himself, Eternal Wisdom, has given to His Church.

No one would think of denying that this institution has its disadvantages; experience has shown that there have been bad Abbots, as, in ecclesiastical history, unworthy popes are to be found. But no human system is exempt from disadvantages. Against these, moreover, the Church has provided its guarantees and remedies in the monastic government, by Canonical visitations, General Chapters and other stipulations.

However this may be, the monarchial and absolute character of the authority of the head of the monastery remains: undoubtedly neither the democratic spirit of the age, nor yet human pride, are in accordance with this, but it is still the one most in conformity with the letter and spirit of the Rule of the Lawgiver of monks. Where monks "sincerely seek God," the closest union knits the sons to their father, and peace, the fruit of the Spirit of Love, reigns in minds and hearts.

II

We have now to see what is to be the kind of activity developed in the religious family thus constituted. This activity is summed up in two points: prayer and work, *ora et labora*.

Our Blessed Father, in founding the cenobitical life, had no particular end in view such as the care of the poor, the evangelisation of nations, literary studies, scientific labours. This it is that radically distinguishes the Monastic Order from several later orders and institutes. If we here permit ourselves to establish such or such a comparison with other forms of religious life, it is not to exalt the one and depreciate the other. Certainly nothing is further from our mind. Religious orders are the flowers wherewith the Holy Spirit has adorned the Church, the Garden of the Spouse. Each of them has its particular beauty, its special splendour; each occupies a place in Christ's Heart and glorifies the Heavenly Father by its works. But, according to the thought of St. Thomas, in order to grasp the nature of a thing, it is useful to comprehend not only what it is but also what it is not; in order to define, it is necessary to distinguish.

All religious leave the goods of this world that they may imitate Christ: "Behold we have left all things, and have followed Thee": *Ecce nos reliquimus omnia, et secuti sumus te.*[1] However, the manner of following or imitating Christ differs for religious orders according to the nature of their particular vocation. Some are for the evangelisation of the poor; others for that of the heathen; here, an institute is founded for the education of children; there, another makes preaching its special end. We at once see that this particular end, by subordinating all energies and efforts to its influence gives the society its direction, its specific character and its own modality.

The monk "seeks God" in Himself,[2] for Himself; that is the adequate goal of all monastic life, that which gives it all its value and beauty. The different forms of activity of work, zeal or charity do not constitute the goal of his life, but are at once the consequences and manifestations of this seeking after "the one thing necessary,"[3] according to the perfection of the Saviour's counsels.

The holy Patriarch, in writing his Rule, wished to found a supernatural society, a school of perfection in the practice of evangelical holiness taken in all its amplitude, a centre of the pure Christian spirit. The members of this society who have left all worldly possessions in order to follow Christ, this Christ to Whom nothing must be preferred: *Cui nihil praeponendum*,[4] strive to attain to union with God by the practice, as perfect as possible, of the precepts of the Gospel and the counsels of Christ: *Per ducatum Evangelii pergamus itinera ejus.*[5] To this society St. Benedict gives an organisation modelled upon that which the Word Incarnate has chosen for His Church. Now in the works that the Christian has to perform, all have not the same importance in God's

1 Matth. xix, 27. 2 Rule, ch. lviii. 3 Cf. Luc. x, 42.
4 Rule, ch. iv and lxxii. 5 Prologue of the Rule.

sight; those are more pleasing to Him that spring most directly from the highest virtues or are most closely allied to them, such as the theological virtues and the virtue of religion. This is why certain duties relating to the virtue of religion are so grave that they are commanded to all Christians without distinction, such as assistance at Holy Mass, the reception of certain sacraments, prayer—while as for other works the greatest liberty is left to each one; no occupation is imposed in preference to another, no honest profession is interdicted, as long as it does not hinder the obligations of religion.

In a "school of Christian perfection,"[1] we must naturally expect to see this principle affirmed and accentuated. In the supernatural society founded by St. Benedict, of which the aim is to pursue the perfection of evangelical holiness, a preponderant place will naturally be given to the practice of the virtue of religion. This is one of the reasons why the holy Legislator dedicates so many chapters of his Rule to organising the Divine Office.[2] This constitutes the work of works, that to which "nothing is to be preferred," and that is to become for the monk, with the *lectio divina*, labour, and what is furthermore ordained by the vows, especially that of obedience,[3] the most authentic means of attaining the end that he proposes to himself: union with God. Therefore this work is indispensable in every monastery, and other works depend on the circumstances of place, time, and persons, and can only be undertaken in the measure that they do not interfere with the primal character of the Divine Office. That is and must remain the chief work excelling all others, because it is, according to St. Benedict's beautiful expression, "the Work of God": *Opus Dei*,[4] the one that directly glorifies God, at the same time that it becomes for the monk the most natural, important and fruitful source of his inmost prayer and assiduous intercourse with our Lord.

---

1 Ibid.

2 It is noteworthy that, historically and critically, the considerable developments that St. Benedict gives to the *opus Dei* in the text of his Rule come from the fact that, in the 5th century, the "Breviary" was not yet uniformly constituted. It was necessary to give a *regulation* to his monks.

3 Evidently, obedience accepted for love is the supreme means. *Per accidens,* the monk can sanctify himself without office in choir, it is in nowise the same without obedience.

4 Rule, ch. xliii, xlvii and lii.

III

Important as is the Divine Office, it is not, as we have seen, and it cannot be the end and aim of the monastic life: that aim must necessarily be sought for higher; neither is it the exclusive work nor the chief characteristic of our vocation; we are not Canons and we have not been gathered together *directly* for office in choir. In fact, neither the Rule, which wishes the monk to give himself in a very notable measure to reading and work, nor tradition authorises us to admit that the work of God constitutes a special prerogative of our Order.[1]

To Liturgical and mental prayer, work must necessarily be joined: *Ora ET LABORA*. The whole of monastic tradition shows us that when these two means, prayer and work, have been most held in honour the most abundant fruits of monastic holiness have been brought forth.

It is clear *a priori* that work is necessary to the monk in order to attain the holiness of his vocation. We must not forget indeed that work is an essential part of the homage that the reasonable creature owes to God. Fashioned in the divine image, man ought to imitate his Creator. Now, God is the great Worker: "My Father," said Jesus, "worketh until now; and I work": *Pater meus usque modo operatur et ego operor.*[2] Although God finds all happiness in Himself, He has willed to rejoice in the works of His hands; He saw that creation was "very good": *valde bona*,[3] that it perfectly responded to His eternal thoughts: "The Lord shall rejoice in His works": *Laetabitur Dominus in operibus suis.*[4] God also delights in the harmonious play of the activity of His creatures which glorify Him by acting in conformity to the laws of their nature.

---

1 "In short, Canonical prayer is, without doubt, the noblest of the elements of the Benedictine life, because it refers directly to God; but, after all, it leaves room for many kinds of activity without being the necessary and indispensable end of all the rest. Its chosen place among all the exercises of the monk, corresponds with that which it held in the regard and in the daily life of the Primitive Christians." *The Ideal of the Monastic Life Found in the Apostolic Age,* by D. G. Morin, O.S.B., translated from the French by C. Gunning, p. 105. In this little volume of great originality, the author has established how the religious life is linked to the life led by the faithful of the primitive Church such as the *Acts* have brought them down to us as a lasting example to Christians of all time, and as the model of holiness, fortitude and fruitfulness in the *Ecclesia perennis.*

2 Joan. v, 17. 3 Gen. i, 31. 4 Ps. ciii, 31.

Work is one of the laws of human nature, as we see in the book of Genesis. After the narration of the creation of the world, it is added that God placed man in a garden of delight. What was he to do there? Pass his life in repose and contemplation? No, to cultivate this garden and to keep it: *Ut operaretur et custodiret illum.*[1] Thus even before the fall, God wished Adam to work, because work allows of the exercise of human powers and energies. Only, by innocent man work was done with ease and delight; it was moreover a hymn of praise, a song arising from the whole human being towards God.

After sin entered the world the Lord renewed to man the promulgation of the law of labour; but this law was henceforth to cost Adam the sweat of his brow: *In sudore vultus tui.*[2] Toil became painful, arduous, thankless; it is, with death, the great penance, the supreme mortification inflicted on sinful man. Our Blessed Father does not speak explicitly in his Rule of the hair shirt and discipline,[3] but he devotes several chapters to work; work is a true penance, and it is impossible for one who shirks it to advance in union with God. Why indeed did we come to the monastery? "To seek God." And our law is to find God not only in prayer, but also in labour. We find Him in the measure in which we glorify Him, and we glorify Him by freely putting forth our energies in the service of His sovereign will. To seek our ease and a base well-being in idleness is to go against the Divine Plan, and such behaviour cannot incline God to give us His favours.

Let us contemplate, too, how God acts with His Divine Son when this Son is made man. The Father wills that, in imitation of Himself and for our example, Christ Jesus shall be a "workman"; an artisan; and Christ accepts and carries out this will. Is He not called in the Gospel "the carpenter's son": *Fabri filius?*[4] Although He is conscious of His Godhead, of the greatness of the work that He comes to do upon earth, He passes thirty years of His life in the obscure labour of a poor workshop. His apostolic journeys during His public life, what are they but

---

1 Gen. ii, 15. 2 Ibid. iii, 19.

3 Special practices of afflictive penance are clearly indicated, although not in so many words, in treating of the observance of Lent (ch. xlix); but they are simply suggested, and individual initiative—always however controlled by the Abbot—here plays a large part. Cf. infra the conference *Self Renunciation*.

4 Matth. xiii, 55.

continual and indefatigable toil, offered for His Father's glory and the salvation of souls?

If it is true that the monk ought to carry out to perfection the programme of Christian life which finds in Christ its first and authentic Exemplar, he must necessarily give to work an important part of his life.

The forms and objects of this work are manifold.

According to the letter of the Rule, the time that the monk has to dispose of, outside the time of Divine Office, is devoted to manual work or to reading, taken in the wide sense of the word, which helps towards "the seeking after God." The holy Legislator devotes a whole chapter to manual labour;[1] he allows arts and crafts to be practised in the monastery;[2] but it is only in case of necessity that the monks themselves are to gather in the crops.[3]

Little by little, in consequence of an evolution which had its principle in the Rule itself, and has been accentuated since monks were raised to the priestly dignity, intellectual work has taken the place of manual labour.

We cannot consider here the manifold aspects of the work accomplished by monachism in the course of ages. What it is especially important to establish at this moment, is the inner spirit that is to vivify and sanctify all the work of the monk. And what is this spirit? That of obedience. The great Patriarch did not intend to found an agricultural or industrial concern, nor to institute a university, but *a school of perfection*.[4] And here we do not come to seek the satisfaction of self-love, the pleasure of the mind, the joys of dilettantism. We come here "to seek God";[5] otherwise we might have stayed in the world: we could have done there just as well what we do here.

But we know the most direct path whereby we find God in the monastery is that of obedience: *Scientes se per hanc obedientiae viam ituros ad Deum*."[6] St. Benedict accounts as "presumption and vain glory"[7] the mortifications that the monk undertakes without having submitted

1 Rule, ch. xlviii.
2 Ibid. ch. lvii.
3 Ibid. ch. xlviii.
4 Prologue of the Rule.
5 Rule, ch. lviii.
6 Ibid. ch. lxxi.
7 Cf. Rule, ch. xlix.

them to the approbation of authority. It is the same for work; that too is to be undertaken and performed with the blessing and permission of the Abbot: *cum [Abbatis] fiat oratione et voluntate.*[1] It is obedience that blesses our efforts, and assures success as God sees it, because it is obedience that brings down upon us and our works light from above, the first source of all fruitfulness. "May the brightness of the Lord shine upon us, and direct, O God, the works of our hands": *Et sit splendor Domini super nos, et opera manuum nostrarum dirige.*[2] Such is the prayer which was formerly recited at the Chapter immediately before the distribution of the day's work.

The monk who lives in God's light knows well that every work that obedience does not impose or ordain, approve or uphold, is barren for himself and for the Kingdom of God: it is in vain that we labour to build up the city of souls, unless God, by the way of obedience, helps us by His grace and blessing: *Nisi Dominus aedificaverit domum, in vanum laboraverunt qui aedificant eam.*[3]

IV

One of the characteristics of cenobitical life, as conceived and organised by St. Benedict, is "stability."

The great Patriarch wishes the monastery to possess, as far as can be, all that is necessary to its subsistence, for "it is by no means expedient for their souls that monks should go abroad uselessly": *vagari foras.*[4] The world for which Christ Jesus declared that He prayed not,[5] has its maxims, its morals, its ways of acting which are opposed to the Christian and supernatural spirit; its atmosphere is fatal to the soul that wishes to safeguard the fragrance of the life hidden in God: *Vita vestra est abscondita cum Christo in Deo.*[6] It is the cloister that, properly speaking, constitutes the social and moral *sphere* of the monk where his soul will most *naturally* unfold in God. Therefore the true monk in nowise seeks, even under pretext of zeal, to go out of his cloister; he leaves himself on this point to the prescriptions of obedience.

---

1 Cf. Ibid. ch. xlix.
2 Ps. lxxxix, 17; Office of Prime.
3 Ps. cxxvi, I.
4 Rule, ch. lxvi.
5 Joan. xvii, 9.
6 Col. iii, 3.

Unknown before St. Benedict's time, stability becomes in the Rule the object of a vow: the monk is attached until the end of his life to his abbey and the community of which he makes a part. But this vow will only be well pleasing to God if we observe the spirit of it by our loving observance of the practices of cenobitical life.

To understand clearly the importance of this point, it is needful to recall a principle which you already know, but which is so capital that it is always useful to bring it again to light.

All God's mercies towards us come from our predestination in Jesus Christ. This is one of the most explicit notions of St. Paul, of that Apostle who was chosen and formed by Christ Himself and caught up to the third heaven. From the solitude of his prison, he writes to the Ephesians that the aurora of every grace is the eternal election that God has made of us in His Word, in His Son: "Blessed be the God and Father of our Lord Jesus Christ, Who hath blessed us with spiritual blessings in heavenly places in Christ; as He chose us in Him": *Benedictus Deus et Pater Domini nostri Jesu Christi, qui benedixit nos in omni benedictione Spirituali... sicut elegit nos in ipso.*[1] By a free movement of love, God willed to elect the human race, to choose us to be His children; but, before all things, He began, if we may thus speak, by predestinating the Humanity of His Son Jesus Christ.

In the Divine thought, Christ Jesus is "the Firstborn of every creature": *Primogenitus omnis creaturae.*[2] Therefore God showers upon this Human Nature "all the treasures of wisdom and knowledge";[3] so that it is truly "full of grace and truth,"[4] the object, consequently, of all the Father's delight.

But Christ draws and unites to Himself the whole of humanity that He comes to redeem and save; and God, in Christ and by Christ, extends His graces and good pleasure upon the Mystical Body of Jesus. All which is not in union with Christ does not exist, so to speak, for God; union with Christ is the essential condition of our salvation and holiness, as it was of our election: it was in Him that we were chosen: *Elegit nos in ipso.*

Now how do we abide in Christ, *in ipso?* Through the Church. Since the Ascension, the normal regular way of our union with Christ, and of safeguarding this union, is to make part of the visible organisation

1 Eph. i, 3–4. 2 Col. i, 15. 3 Ibid. ii, 3. 4 Joan. i, 14.

that He founded. In the same way as the body of Jesus united to His soul was "the instrument of the Divinity" and the channel of graces, so grace reaches us only if we belong to the body of the Church. Baptism which incorporates us to this body is, with faith, the first condition of all grace as of all salvation. "All power," Christ has said, "is given to Me in heaven and in earth." "Going therefore, teach ye all nations";[1] "he that believeth and is baptised, shall be saved."[2] Such is the law established by Christ Himself and ratified by the Father Who "hath given all things into His hand."[3] "No man cometh to the Father," is pleasing to the Father, receives the gifts of the Father, but by Jesus: *Nemo venit ad Patrem nisi per me*;[4] no man, (I am speaking of the law and of the normal way; we know that in certain cases, the baptism of desire suffices and that many of our "separated brethren" live in entire good faith), no man, we say, is united to Christ except through the Church, nor receives His doctrine nor partakes of His grace except through the Church. This is in fact, because Christ is the head of His Mystical Body; the Church is "of His flesh, and of His bones,"[5] says St. Paul; now, continues the Apostle, "no man ever hateth his own flesh; but nourisheth and cherisheth it" that it may come to perfection. This is what Jesus does through His vivifying Spirit.

We at once understand that the more we live by the life of the Church, through acceptation of her teaching, obedience to her precepts and the practice of her worship, the more abundant share we have in the blessings that Jesus ceases not to pour out upon His Bride. Truth and the light that shines from it in the soul are more fruitful in so far as we are more closely united to the Church.

We likewise understand what a terrible penalty it is for a soul to be separated from the Church by excommunication; it is to be separated from the very fount of grace; like a branch cut off from the stem, the nourishing sap no longer reaches it; it is no longer good for anything but to be cast into the fire. As the etymology of the word indicates, excommunication cuts the soul off from the communion of Saints, from the solidarity of the "blessed of the Father,"[6] and from all the graces of light and strength that God sheds upon souls in His Son Jesus; it is like the

1 Matth. xxviii, 18-19.
2 Marc. xvi, 16.
3 Cf. Joan. iii, 35; v, 22.
4 Ibid. xiv, 6.
5 Eph. v, 30.
6 Matth. xxv, 34.

anticipated shadow of final excommunication and supreme malediction: "Depart from Me, ye cursed": *Discedite a me, maledicti.*[1]

Such is, in broad outline, the Divine plan established by the Father, Who has predestined us to share, as children, in His infinite beatitude. Every perfect gift which gladdens our souls comes from Him,[2] through His Son Jesus; Christ unites us to Himself only in His Church, the dispenser of her Bridegroom's graces. In order to partake of these graces, we must abide in this visible organisation and live by its life.

The religious Orders and Institutes raised up by the Spirit of God, recognised and approved by the Church, and associated in an official and canonical manner to the Church, possess, on this account, a closer union with the Bride of Christ; their members, having thus become the privileged ones of the Church, acquire a new and special title to Divine blessings.

But these singular graces only reach our souls in the same measure that we live by the organic life of the Society whereof we are members. This is an important truth. In the same way that we enter into contact with Jesus through the Church on the day of our Baptism, so we enter into the current of religious grace on the day of our Profession: henceforward we have an effectual part in it, according to the degree in which we live the common life.

What do we ask on the day of our Clothing? "God's mercy and the companionship of His servants." It is the one that brings us the other. If we put aside the common life, which is the sign of our particular divine election, we shall be like wrecks stranded on the riverbank, doubtless still lapped by the tide, but no longer lifted up and borne along on its impetuous living waters.

You see then of what capital importance it is for the religious to live the common life, in the framework of the established and accepted organisation; for the monk, as for the Christian, excommunication even in the simply monastic sense, such as instituted by St. Benedict, constitutes a terrible penalty.

There are some minds, says the holy Legislator, unable to grasp the greatness of this penalty, or the great harm that can be wrought in the

1 Ibid. 41. 2 Jac. i, 17.

soul by being excluded from the common life by the Superior. The great Patriarch has pronounced excommunication for certain transgressions; but do not let it be supposed that the excommunicated brother is therefore placed beyond the encircling fatherly love that the Abbot is to have for his monks. Human love, after the example of Divine love, does not always exclude severity; it is manifested quite as much by the just application of salutary chastisements as by rewards and caresses. That he may cure the one confided to him, does not the doctor use, when there is occasion, prohibitions, separations, and very bitter remedies?

It is rarely that the Abbot, to whom alone belongs the power of pronouncing excommunication, ought to apply this penalty, which moreover admits of degrees. But, unless we take care, we can practically excommunicate ourselves. And this is equally to be dreaded, perhaps even more so, in that a wholesome reaction is less to be hoped for.

How can this case occur? By wilful and habitual infidelities; by our self-will which gradually withdraws us from the exercises and usages of the common life. Some souls have the tendency of preferring what they do alone to what is done by the Community, as such; they imagine, for example, that it would be more useful for them to spend the time of recreation in the oratory rather than in the midst of their brethren; this kind of piety is not only false in itself, but it is practically sterile, if not worse. How could God give Himself to souls who put themselves outside the current of grace that He has established? It is impossible. God only communicates Himself to the docile and faithful soul; and such we are when, obedient to legitimate authority, we are where this authority wills us to be, and at the hour and employment it wills us to be. If God does not find us where He looks for us, He will not bless us. "Blessed are those servants whom the Lord, when He cometh, shall find watching": *Beati servi illi, quos, cum venerit Dominus, invenerit vigilantes.*[1]

No outward circumstance, besides, can hinder the Divine action and its beneficial effect in the soul. Was it not in the middle of the street, as she was returning home one evening with her young brother Stefano, that St. Catherine of Siena had her first vision, when she saw our Lord, seated upon a magnificent throne, smile lovingly upon her and trace

1 Luc. xii, 37.

upon her the sign of the cross? "And so powerful was this blessing of the Eternal God, that transported out of herself, the child, who by nature was timid, remained standing there, upon the public way, her eyes raised to Heaven, in the midst of the passing to and fro of men and animals."[1]

What happens in the case of the saints, comes to pass, all proportion guarded, in every faithful soul: Christ Jesus sometimes chooses the moments which, humanly speaking, appear the least favorable to calm and recollection, to communicate to us His lights;—lights which He renders so much the more abundant in that the soul is the more attentive not to seek self-satisfaction, but to be conformed by obedience to the good pleasure from on high;—lights sometimes lavished to such a degree that the impression of the Bridegroom's embrace remains ineffaceable, and the soul is for a long time embalmed with the fragrance of the Divine visit...

A monk can excommunicate himself not only by withdrawing himself, by unfaithfulness or by mistaken piety, from the exercises, customs and traditions of the common life, but also by making himself singular. Everything can serve as an opportunity for singularity, even things of piety and devotion. Some find the best pretexts for justifying themselves in their own eyes; they are persuaded that they are showing a wider understanding of what should be done, they think they are performing brilliant actions.

Now, St. Benedict himself, gives us to understand that this is often only foolish pride. In fact does it not seem like saying: "I know better than others what ought to be done": *non sum sicut caeteri*?[2] However ordinary, however indifferent may appear the common ways and customs, it is giving a proof of humility to hold to them and not to do anything to draw attention to oneself: "The eighth degree of humility is when a monk does nothing except what is commanded by the common Rule of the monastery or by the traditions of the seniors."[3]

This point is very important, because grace is hidden in the humble observance of common customs and traditions. God gives His grace to

1 Jörgensen, *St. Catherine of Siena.* 2 Luc. xviii, 41.
3 Rule, ch. vii.

the humble: *Humilibus dat gratiam*,[1] whilst pride, the most frequent principle of singularity, separates us from God, and renders us, even if we do not see it, insupportable to our neighbour. Look at our Divine Saviour. What more perfect model of holiness can we contemplate and imitate? He is God, Eternal Wisdom Incarnate. All that He does is infinitely pleasing to the Father: *Quae placita sunt ei facio semper*;[2] and that not only because He is the Son of God, but because He brings to all His actions a Divine perfection. Now, during thirty years, He remains in such self-effacement—just the contrary to singularity—that when He begins His public life, He is not known otherwise than as "the carpenter's son": *fabri filius*.[3] The sublimity of His teaching, the greatness of His miracles, cause astonishment because until then He had not brought Himself into notice. And in the acts of His public life, what admirable simplicity! He possesses all the treasures of wisdom.[4] What is our personal wisdom, what is all human wisdom in face of His? Nothingness and foolishness.

The true monk, whose gaze is ever fixed upon the Divine Model, follows with simplicity and uprightness the customs common to the Community he has entered and which are a sign of the unity that Christ wishes to see reigning among the members of His Mystical Body. Here exteriorly written for him, as it were, is the practical programme of the perfection he has vowed to seek. If the devil tries to beguile us, to make us think that we shall remain more easily united to God by living apart, and making ourselves singular, do not let us listen to him. If truly, one day, we arrive at the height of sanctity which St. Benedict requires for hermits, and if God so designs, then a cell shall be built for us in a solitary corner, and we shall be surrounded with the veneration and regard due to so sublime a vocation!

In the meanwhile—whether we be simple monks, or whether the confidence of the Abbot has invested us with a share in his authority—let us keep to the loving observance of the common life: it is the path the holy Patriarch invites us to follow, it is the path God wills for us. This observance will be like the sign of our stability in good, as also that of the permanence of God's grace within us. For therein we shall find Christ Jesus; and the Father, seeing us united to His Son in all things,

1 I Petr. v, 5; Jac. iv, 6.
2 Joan. viii, 29.
3 Matth. xiii, 55.
4 Col. ii, 3.

will shower upon us, for His sake and through Him, all heavenly blessings: *Benedixit nos in omni benedictione spirituali.*[1]

V

From the point of view of the cenobitical life, the notion of excommunication can take other shades of meaning and suggest other lessons.

It may happen, and this is no less grave, that a monk may himself "excommunicate" his brethren. This may be done by failing in charity; by excluding someone, if not from his heart, at least from the radiation of his effective love. Again one may "excommunicate" someone from the hearts of others by exciting them to distrust him... This is a sin so utterly contrary to the Christian spirit that we should especially be on our guard against it and act in this matter with the greatest delicacy.

The cenobitical family is *one*, the cement that joins together its different members is charity. If that is diminished, the divine life also tends to be lowered in the social body. What, in fact, is the distinctive sign whereby the members of the Christian family are infallibly recognised, the sign given by Christ Himself? It is mutual love: *In hoc cognoscent omnes quia discipuli mei estis, si dilectionem habueritis ad invicem.*[2] It is the same for the monastic family, and the true mark of the protection of Christ Jesus over a religious Community is the charity that reigns between its members. Woe to those who impair, in whatever manner it may be, this spirit of charity. In rending the robe of the Bride, they tear from their own soul the Christian sign excelling all others.

Christ is one; He tells us that what we do to the least of *our* brethren—of *His* brethren—of good or evil, we do to Himself.[3] St. Benedict reminds the Abbot of this, when he enjoins upon him to love all the brethren without distinction. He wishes too that we should testify towards one another a fervent though chaste love: *Caritatem fraternitatis casto impendant amore.*[4] He wills us to translate this love by forgetting ourselves, preferring what seems good for others rather than what seems good for ourselves;[5] it is this love, he again says, which will fill the hearts of the brethren with the greatest patience so that they may mutually en-

1 Eph. i, 3.
2 Joan. xiii, 35.
3 Matth. xxv, 40 and 45.
4 Rule, ch. lxxii.
5 Ibid. ch. lxxii.

dure their infirmities of body or defects of character: *Infirmitates suas sive corporum sive morum patientissime tolerent.*[1]

This love will be itself manifested by "obedience one towards another," in matters where nothing contrary has been commanded by the will of the Abbot; a ready submission which can be exercised in many circumstances when some slight service is asked of us: *Etiam sibi invicem obediant fratres.*[2] *Obedientiam sibi certatim impendant.*[3]

And because he wishes this love to be chaste, St. Benedict requires it to be accompanied with respect; he recalls St. Paul's recommendation to simple Christians: "In honour preferring one another": *Honore se invicem praeveniant.*[4] What is the underlying reason for this mutual respect? It is that every soul, in a state of grace, is the temple of the Holy Spirit. We ought to have that respect for others which strikes us in presence of something sacred. It is especially on the part of the young towards the seniors that the holy Legislator requires this attitude and sense of respect: "To reverence the seniors": *Seniores venerare,*[5] in the same way as he wishes that love should be shown especially on the part of the seniors towards the young brethren: *Juniores diligere*[6]—but certainly nothing ought to dispense from respect; it preserves from that wrong kind of familiarity which is said to breed contempt.

Respect, obedience, love, such is the three-fold character of the relations which the great Patriarch wishes to see reigning between the members of the cenobitical family. Happy, thrice happy, the community inspired by these dispositions and where the members form but one heart and one soul! Our Lord will assuredly shed upon it His most abundant blessings for it realises the most ardent longing of His Sacred Heart, the supreme wish of His life: "That they may be made perfect in one": *Ut sint consummati in unum.*[7] "The sole means that we have," said Venerable Bede, "of showing others that Christ dwells within us, is the spirit of holy and undivided charity": *Docet eos non posse aliter dare experimentum Christi in se inhabitantis nisi per spiritum sanctae ac individuae caritatis.*[8] In which this great monk was but the faithful echo of

1 Ibid. ch. lxxii.
2 Ibid. ch. lxxi.
3 Ibid. ch. lxxii.
4 Ibid.
5 Rule, ch. iv.
6 Ibid.
7 Joan. xvii, 23.
8 *Vita Bedae,* auctore anonymo pervetusto, P. L. 90, col. 51.

Christ Himself: "By this shall all men know that you are My disciples, if you have love one for another."

VI

In attaching ourselves to the monastic family, our vow of stability binds us likewise to the monastery: therefore the monk ought to extend his love to the very walls of his cloister. The Abbey is for him the *Jerusalem sancta*, the "City of peace" where he loves to dwell under the Eye of God, in obedience to Christ's representative, in prayer and labour. For this Jerusalem, he repeats each day the Psalmist's prayer: "Let peace be in thy strength: and abundance in thy towers!"[1] For his monastery, the true monk, who has a horror of selfishness (that principle of spiritual sterility) knows how to forget himself, how to spend himself in hard unremitting toil and the most obscure tasks. Feeling that the love he bears towards it ennobles the humblest services and fructifies the most thankless labours, he shrinks from nothing that can profit the common good of this portion of the earth, for him blessed amongst all others. His thoughts, his love, his wishes, his prayers, his labours, his life, he gives them all even to his last breath: "Let my tongue cleave to my palate, if I do not remember thee": *Adhaereat lingua mea faucibus meis, si non meminero tui!*[2]

In this Jerusalem, the Church is the centre of the monk's love. The abbatial church is truly for him the building where all is sacred to God, the cherished dwelling echoing with the harmony of his praises and jubilation and proclaiming to all the fervour of his faith in the one thrice holy Lord.[3] There, several times a day, with all the members of the cenobitical family, the monk extends his suppliant arms, like Moses on the mountain, for the intention of his brethren fighting in the plain; he knows that he can obtain, through the ardour and constancy of his prayer, the victory for the armies of Israel over the enemies of God and of His people. Therefore his gaze, enlightened by faith, reaches out to

1 Ps. cxxi, 7. 2 Ps. cxxx, 6.

3 *Omnis illa Deo sacra—et dilecta civitas—plena modulis in laude—et canore jubilo—Trinum Deum unicumque—cum fervore praedicat.* Hymn for the Dedication of a Church at Lauds.

all that touches God's Kingdom; his charity stirs up the flame of his devotion, it would reach all the souls who are struggling in ignorance, error, doubt, misery, temptation, suffering, sin; all who are spending themselves in promoting Christ's reign upon earth; all those too who are filled with the intense desire of being nearer to our Lord. To render his intercession more efficacious, he joins his prayer to the all powerful and ever-answered prayer of the Divine Victim with arms stretched out upon the new Calvary which is the high altar...

With what veneration he surrounds this high altar of the abbatial church, this stone upon which holy oil was poured and sacred incense burnt! This altar has lost nothing of that which was solemnly bestowed upon it on the day of its consecration; quite the contrary! The conventual Mass which, day by day, gathers the cenobitical family around it, consecrates it more and more. Therefore it ought to be dear to the heart of the monk as it is dear to the Heart of God. Is not this altar, with the five crosses engraved on its stone to represent Christ's Wounds, the image of "the Son of His love?" Is it not here that on the blessed day of our vows, we all placed with our own hands the chart of our monastic profession, thus uniting our oblation more closely to the Sacrifice of Christ Jesus that it may rise up to God in the odour of sweetness? *Ecce odor filii mei sicut odor agri pleni, cui benedixit Dominus.*[1]

In this church where the very stones breath forth adoration, immolation, thanksgiving, supplication, the monk will often stay his steps before the image of the great Patriarch to learn from him the unique science of Divine things. Was not our holy Lawgiver, "the Man of God," *vir Dei*, the great Seer who, at every hour of his magnificent life walked before God in perfection: *Ambula coram me, et esto perfectus*?[2] Is he not the new Abraham, to whom God promised, as a sign of supreme blessing, to make his name illustrious by a numerous and powerful posterity? *Faciam te in gentem magnam, et benedicam tibi, et magnificabo nomen tuum, erisque benedictus.*[3]

1 "Behold the smell of my son is as the smell of a plentiful field, which the Lord hath blessed," Gen. xxvii, 27.

2 "And I will make of thee a great nation, and I will bless thee, and magnify thy name, and thou shalt be blessed," Ibid. xvii, 1.

3 Ibid. xii, 2.

St. Benedict appears to us holding in his hand the Rule, which his profound humility makes him declare to be only a sketch or "rough outline."[1] But we know with what spirit of holiness this immortal code overflows; we know what innumerable cohorts of monks it has sanctified in the course of an era of many hundred years; we know with what powerful help it has served Christ's Church and what signal fruits of Christian civilisation its observance has gained for the world. "Who can measure the extraordinary influence that these few pages [of the Rule] have exercised, during fourteen centuries, over the general development of the western world? Yet St. Benedict thought only of God and of souls desirous to go to God; in the tranquil simplicity of his faith he purposed only to establish a school of the Lord's service: *Dominici schola servitii*. But, just because of this singleminded pursuit of the one thing necessary, God has blessed the *Rule of Monks* with singular fruitfulness, and St. Benedict has taken his place in the line of the great patriarchs."[2]

The holy Rule, indeed, teaches us that, for the monk, everything lies in "seeking God" in order to give Him to others; in sure characters, for they are all borrowed from the Gospel of which it is the pure reflection, it marks out the path of most sublime perfection, then it guides us to this end by following Christ in the way of obedience, prayer and work. It is by the Rule that the monk sanctifies himself individually, that socially the Kingdom of Christ is built up, and that the Heavenly Father is glorified. By it, the great Patriarch continues to live in the Church, for it is the Rule that maintains in those who follow it, that spirit of sanctification which eminently made of him the "Blessed of God."

This is why before the image of the holy Lawgiver, we may greatly rejoice and return most humble thanks to God, in that we, although unworthy, belong to the holy race that forms his magnificent posterity. And we should repeat for ourselves, for our brethren, for every soul in the city of God, this prayer that the Bride of Jesus places on our lips: "Raise up, O Lord, in Thy Church the spirit that animated our Blessed Father Benedict, Abbot, that being replenished with this same spirit,

1 Rule, ch. lxxiii. See *Note* at the end of this conference.

2 *Commentary on the Rule of St. Benedict,* by the Abbot of Solesmes, *Introduction*, ii, translated from the French by Dom Justin McCann. We shall more than once quote this remarkable work of Dom Delatte.

we may strive to love what he loved and in our actions to practise what he taught": *Excita, Domine, in Ecclesia tua, spiritum cui Beatus Pater noster Benedictus abbas servivit, ut eodem nos repleti, studeamus amare quod amavit et opere exercere quod docuit.*

NOTE

(The Rule, which his profound humility makes him declare to be only an "outline": *Hanc minimam inchoationis regulam*, p. 82).

We must not take these words of the holy Patriarch too literally: Here we certainly have an expression of humility, but there is something more. The Rule of St. Benedict contains both relatively slight material observances and very lofty ascetical directions. In this place, he is only considering the first; he draws a comparison between what he regulates in the way of common ordinances and what was done by men such as Antony, Macarius, and even Pachomius.

"From the individual point of view, the Rule embraces not only the phases of asceticism denominated the 'purgative way' and 'illuminative way': but furthermore it gives to souls—without expecting too much of human strength,—counsels of heroic virtue, and opens out to them—without seeking to outstrip grace,—the perspectives of the unitive life." (D. Festugière *l. c., p.* 92).

We see the holy Lawgiver writing that he in nowise wishes to discourage weak souls who climb slowly, but for all that, he does not intend to hinder the holy ascensions of the valiant up the heights of perfection: *Ut et sit quod infirmi non refugiant et fortes quod cupiant*. We have but to read the 4th degree of humility to see to what a summit of heroism he invites his disciples to rise.

Moreover the value of the Rule of St. Benedict is sufficiently proved by the rapidity with which it supplanted, in a relatively short time, all the Rules then in use, although these rules were made by personages remarkable for their holiness. Again it is proved by the extraordinary supernatural fruitfulness whereof it has been the principle in the course of ages. It is only necessary to survey the long line of saints who found their perfection in the school of him whom St. Gregory the Great calls "the most excellent master of the perfect life": *Magister optimus arctissimae vitae.*

"Is there, apart from the Gospel"—D. Delatte very truly writes in his *Commentary on the Rule* (p. 495)—"a book which has been able, as it has, to adapt itself to all the needs of Christian society from the sixth century to our own day?... We should recognise for a last time that the Rule has lent itself with wonderful adaptability to works of extremely various kinds, that it has accommodated itself better than any other to times and circumstances, and that it has furnished a solid legislative framework to several founders of Orders or Congregations. To devise a Rule so wide as to embrace all, so strong as to contain all, so divinely simple as to be understood by the unlettered Goth and to charm St. Gregory the Great, so perfect as to deserve for ever the appellation of 'the Rule,' the monastic Rule *par excellence*: is not this a work of surpassing supernatural genius?"

STARTING POINT AND TWO-FOLD CHARACTER OF MONASTIC PERFECTION

OUR FAITH, THE VICTORY OVER THE WORLD

Haec est victoria quae vincit mundum fides nostra.[1]

SUMMARY.—I. How by faith we overcome the world.—II. How precious this victory is and of what life it is the prelude.—III. Faith is also the starting point of our monastic perfection, the "deifying light" wherewith St. Benedict wishes the whole life of a monk to be enlightened.—IV. The stability resulting therefrom for the inner life. —- V. Exercise of the virtue of faith and the joy of which it is the source.

IN the preceding conferences, we have tried to view the Benedictine ideal and institution taken as a whole. "To seek God" only, by following Christ Jesus, such is the supreme end of the monastic life; the monk proposes to himself to attain this end in the cloister, in the midst of his brethren, living with them under the guidance of the abbot who holds the place of Christ, sharing with them a life of obedience divided between prayer and labour.

We are now going to see how one desiring to embrace this ideal realises it in practice. We shall see that it is faith that makes him cross the threshold of the cloister and love that keeps him there by means of the religious profession, in the same way as the neophyte, at the moment of being received into the Church, performs an act of faith and becomes a member of the supernatural society by Baptism, which is the Sacrament of adoption and initiation. Faith and the religious profession are

1 "This is the victory which overcometh the world, our faith," I Joan. v, 4.

indispensable in order to enable him to cleave to Christ in the state of monastic perfection.

Let us call to mind what takes place in the case of the simple Christian.

The example that God proposes to men's imitation is His Son Jesus. Twice—the first time upon the banks of the Jordan, and again on Mount Thabor—God breaks the eternal silence in order to present to us this same Son, the living expression, under human form, of Divine perfection. And however high may be the summits of holiness which souls attain, this perfection is never anything else than the reflection of the holiness of the Word Incarnate.

Now, how do we become one with Christ? How do we participate in his grace and holiness? First and before all, by faith. What, in fact, does St. John say? Those have received Christ who have believed in Him: *Quotquot autem receperunt eum... his qui credunt in nomine ejus.*[1] This is "the work" that God requires first of all from us: That we "believe in Him Whom He hath sent": *Hoc est opus Dei ut credatis in eum quem misit ille.*[2]

Faith is the primary disposition of one who would follow Christ; it must be the first attitude of the soul in presence of the Incarnate Word.[3]

Christianity is nought else than the acceptation, by faith—a practical faith — of the Incarnation with all its consequences; the Christian life is but the constant putting into practice of this act of faith made to Jesus. "Thou art the Christ, the Son of the Living God."[4] Without this act of faith, which involves all our life, there is no means of being a Christian. If you accept the Divinity of Jesus Christ, you must, in consequence, accept His will, His words, His institutions, the Church, the Sacraments, the reality of His Mystical Body.

What is true of the simple Christian is yet more true of the monk. The monk aims at realising in himself the perfection of Christianity; we shall then be monks only if we are first of all Christians; we shall only be perfect monks if we are perfect Christians. Now, as I have just been saying, it is above all faith in Christ that makes us Christians, disciples of Christ, and by His grace, children of God.

---

1 Joan. i, 12. 2 Ibid. vi, 29.

3 We have developed these important ideas in the conference. Faith the foundation of the Christian life, in our volume, *Christ, the Life of the Soul.*

4 Matth. xvi, 16.

Let us consider what this faith is to us. It is the principle of our victory over the world—a victory that comes to us from Christ through the faith that we have in Him and that makes us God's children. Again it is the foundation and the root of monastic perfection as of the Christian life; thence comes what St. Benedict calls "the deifying light": *deificum lumen*.[1] This having been said, it remains for us to explain how we are to live by faith and what fruits this life bears for us.

I

What is faith? It is the homage that our intellect gives without any reservation to the Divine veracity.

God tells us when showing us His Son co-equal to Himself: "Hear ye Him."[2] And Christ tells us in His turn that He is the Only-begotten Son of God and what He sees of the eternal secrets He reveals to us; that His word is infallible, for He is the Truth.[3] And when we accept this testimony of Jesus, when we give the assent of our intellect to His word, to all that He says, we make an act of faith.

But this faith must be complete, its object must extend to all that Christ Jesus says or does. It is not only in Christ's word that we must believe, but in the divinity of His mission, in the infinite value of His merits and of the satisfaction He made: faith embraces the whole Christ.

And when this faith is living, ardent, it casts us at the feet of Jesus that we may accomplish His will in all things; it attaches us to Jesus never more to leave Him: this is perfect faith which blossoms into hope and love.

In order to be a Christian it is necessary to have this faith in Jesus Christ; one cannot be a Christian unless one prefers Christ's words, will and commands to his own ideas and personal interests.

Of course the monk has this faith, but with him it goes further; it even makes him leave the world that he may attach himself to Christ alone. Why have we left the world? Because we have believed in these words of Jesus: "Come, follow Me, and you shall be perfect."[4] And we have said to our Lord: "Thou callest me? Behold here I am. I have such

1 Prologue of the Rule.
2 Matth. xvii, 5.
3 Cf. Ibid. xi, 27; Joan. xiv, 6.
4 Cf. Matth. xix, 21.

faith in Thee and in Thy word; I am so persuaded that Thou art the Way, the Truth and the Life, I am so convinced that in Thee I shall find all, that I wish to cleave to Thee alone. Thou art so powerful, that Thou canst make me attain even to our Father in Heaven; so powerful that Thou canst, by Thy grace and infinite merits, make me like unto Thyself in order that I may be pleasing to Thy Father; so powerful, that Thou canst make me reach the highest perfection and supreme beatitude; and because I believe this, because I have confidence in Thee and Thou art the infinite Good beyond which all is vain and barren, I wish to leave all to follow Thee and serve Thee alone": *Ecce nos reliquimus omnia et secuti sumus te.*[1] This is a pure act of faith in the omnipotence and in the infinite goodness of Jesus Christ.

Now, this act of faith, says St. John, "is the victory which overcometh the world": *Haec est victoria quae vincit mundum, fides nostra.* And he immediately adds that this faith "which overcometh the world" is that which we have in Christ, the Son of the Living God: *Quis est qui vincit mundum, nisi qui credit quoniam Jesus est Filius Dei?*[2] Let us meditate for a few moments on these words for they are of a great importance for our souls.

What is the meaning of *Vincere mundum*: "to overcome the world"? The world does not here mean Christians, faithful disciples of Jesus Christ, whose condition obliges them to live in the world, but those men for whom the natural life alone exists, who confine their desires and enjoyments to the life here below. This world has its principles, its maxims, its prejudices, all borrowed, according to St. John's words, from "the concupiscence of the flesh and the concupiscence of the eyes and the pride of life."[3] It is this world for which our Divine Saviour says that He does not pray.[4] And why does He not pray for it? Because between this world and Christ there is absolute incompatibility. The world rejects the maxims of the Gospel; for it, the Cross is foolishness and a scandal.

This world which surrounds us has offered us its riches, its honours, its pleasures; it flatters the natural man, it tempts us with its attractions. But in following Christ in order to attach ourselves to Him alone, we have rejected the world; we have risen above all the natural satisfactions

1 Ibid. 27. 2 I Joan. v, 4–5. 3 Ibid. ii, 16. 4 Joan. xvii, 9.

that it could offer or promise us, we have been insensible to its charms: this is to "overcome the world."

And what has enabled us to win such a victory? Faith in Jesus Christ. It is because we believe that Jesus is the Son of God, is God, and consequently is very perfection and beatitude, that we have joined ourselves to Him. See the rich young man in the Gospel who comes to Jesus that he may be His disciple. He asks what he must do to obtain everlasting life. Our Divine Saviour Who loves him as soon as He looks upon him, *intuitus eum dilexit eum,*[1] first points out to him the keeping of the commandments. "All these things I have observed from my youth,"[2] replies the young man. Then our Lord shows him the higher way of the counsels. "If thou wilt be perfect, go sell what thou hast and give to the poor and thou shalt have treasure in heaven. And come, follow Me."[3] But, says the Gospel, the young man having heard these words "went away sad,"[4] and did not follow the Saviour. Why was this? Because he had great possessions: the world held him enchained by wealth. And because he did not believe that Christ was the Infinite Good, surpassing every other good, this young man was unable to overcome the world.

Christ Jesus gave us this light of faith on the day of our vocation; and it is owing to this light which showed us the vanity of the world, the emptiness of its pleasures, the barrenness of its works, and revealed to us the state of perfection in the absolute imitation of Christ, that we have "overcome the world": *Haec est victoria quae vincit mundum, fides nostra.*

Blessed victory which set us free from one of the worst states of bondage to give us the full liberty of the children of God, in order that we might join ourselves perfectly to Him Who alone deserves our love!

II

What truly makes our victory so precious is that it is in itself a signal gift of love which Christ makes to us: He has purchased it with His Blood. Listen to what our Lord said to His disciples at the close of His

1 Marc. x, 21. 2 Ibid. 20. 3 Matth. xix, 21. 4 Ibid. 22.

life: "Have confidence. I have overcome the world": *Confidite, ego vici mundum.*[1]

And how did He overcome the world? With gold? With the splendour of exterior actions? No, in the eyes of the world, Christ was only the son of a carpenter of Nazareth: *fabri filius.*[2] He was humble all His life. He was born in a stable, He dwelt in a workshop; during His apostolic journeys, He had not always a shelter, or even anywhere to lay His head.[3] The wisdom of the world would have scouted the idea that it could be overcome by poverty and renunciation. Did He overcome the world by the immediate temporal success of His undertakings or by other human advantages likely to impress or dominate it? Again no. He was derided and crucified. In the eyes of the "wise" of that time His mission ended in lamentable failure upon the Cross. His disciples are scattered, the crowd wag their heads; the Pharisees laugh Him to scorn: "He saved others: Himself He cannot save... Let Him now come down from the Cross, and then—but then only—we will believe in Him."[4]

And yet the failure was only apparent; it was precisely at this moment that in reality Christ won the victory; in the sight of the world, from the natural point of view, He was overcome;—but in the sight of God, He was the Victor over the prince of darkness and over the world. "Have confidence. I have overcome the world": *Confidite, ego vici mundum.* And from that hour Christ Jesus has been appointed by His Father King over the nations.[5] "There is no other name" that is for us a cause of salvation and grace,[6] and His enemies are made His footstool.[7]

Jesus gives to His disciples likewise the power of overcoming the world. But how does He make them share in His victory? By bestowing upon them, through the faith they have in Him, the divine adoption that makes them the children of God. There is here a profound teaching given by St. John which it is important to bring forward.

God is Being, Life. God knows and comprehends Himself perfectly; He says to Himself, by an Infinite utterance, all that He is: this utterance is the Word. The Word expresses the whole of the Divine essence, not only taken in itself, but also inasmuch as it is imitable. In the Word,

1 Joan. xvi, 33.
2 Matth. xiii, 55.
3 Ibid. viii, 20.
4 Matth. xxvii, 42.
5 Cf. Ps. ii, 6.
6 Act. iv, 12; Ps. cix, 1.
7 Hebr. i, 13; x, 13.

God contemplates the exemplar of every creature, even of the creature merely possible; in this Word all being has life. "In the beginning was the Word... and the Word was God... All things were made by Him, and without Him was nothing made that was made: in Him was life": *In principio erat Verbum... et Deus erat Verbum... Sine ipso factum est nihil quod factum est; in ipso vita erat.*[8]

Our natural life, which has its first source in the Word, comes to us from those immediate agents who are our parents.

But, as you know, we are called to a yet higher life, called to share God's own life by becoming "partakers of the Divine nature": *Efficiamini divinae consortes naturae.*[9] This vocation to infinite beatitude is supereminently the work of love which crowns and, in a profound sense, explains all the others. If our natural life comes from God's Hands: *Manus tuae fecerunt me et plasmaverunt me totum in circuitu,*[10] it is from His Heart that the supernatural life springs forth. "Behold," says St. John, "what manner of charity the Father hath bestowed upon us, that we should be called and should be the sons of God": *Videte qualem caritatem dedit nobis Pater, ut filii Dei nominemur et simus.*[11] This divine life does not destroy the natural life in what it has that is positive and good, but, surpassing its possibilities, its exigences and rights, it raises and transfigures it.

Now, it is still in the Word that the source of this divine life and its outpourings is to be found: God beholds us in His Word, not only as simple creatures but also in our being of grace. Each of the predestined represents an eternal thought of God. "Of His own will hath He begotten us by the word of truth": *Voluntarie enim genuit nos verbo veritatis;*[12] Christ, the Incarnate Word, is truly the image in conformity with which we must be and remain the children of God: *Praedestinavit [nos] conformes fieri imaginis Filii sui;*[13] He is, as I have said, the Son of God by nature, we by grace; but it is the same Divine life that inundates Christ's Humanity and our souls with its fulness. This Only-begotten Son, born of God in the holy splendours of an eternal and ineffable generation, is the Son of the Living God, for He possesses Life in Himself; He is very

8 Joan. i, 1–4.
9 II Petr. i, 4.
10 Job. x, 5; cf. Ps. cxviii, 73.
11 I Joan. iii, 1.
12 Jac. i, 18.
13 Rom. viii, 29.

Life, *Ego sum vita,*[1] and He has become incarnate in order to make us partakers of this life: *Ego veni ut vitam habeant.*[2]

And how do we participate in this life? By receiving Christ through faith. "As many as received Him, He gave them power to be made the sons of God, to them that believe in His name, who are born... of God": *Quotquot autem receberunt eum, dedit eis potestatem filios Dei fieri his qui credunt in nomine ejus... qui ex Deo nati sunt.*[3] Our access to this new life is a veritable birth; and this birth is brought about by faith and Baptism, the Sacrament of adoption: *Renatus ex aqua et Spiritu Sancto.*[4] Thus St. John writes that "Whosoever believeth that Jesus is the Christ is born of God": *Qui credit quoniam Jesus est Christus, ex Deo natus est.*[5]

As you see in order to be "born of God," to be "children of God," we must believe in Jesus Christ and receive Him. Faith is the foundation of this supernatural life which makes us share, in an ineffable manner, in the Divine Life; faith introduces us into that supernatural sphere which is hidden from the eyes of the world. "Your life is hid with Christ in God": *Vita vestra est abscondita cum Christo in Deo.*[6] The only true life, because it does not end, like the natural life, in death, but has its fruition in the unalloyed happiness of eternity.

The world sees only, or rather wishes to see and know only, the natural life both for the individual and for society at large; it only esteems and admires that which appears, which shines and obtains temporal success; it judges by outward appearances, according to the eyes of flesh; it relies only upon human effort, upon the natural virtues: that is its way of judging and acting. It neglects, it systematically ignores the supernatural life, and smiles at the idea of a perfection that goes beyond reason alone. Human reasoning, in fact, can only produce human results; purely natural effort can only be the cause of effects in the purely natural order. "That which is born of the flesh is flesh," says St. John: *Quot natum est ex carne, caro est;*[7] that which is the result of nature, outside the supernatural, "profiteth nothing" in God's sight: *Caro non prodest quidquam.*[8] A man who has not faith, who has not grace, may attain by force of energy, of will and perseverance, to a certain natural perfection; he may be good,

1 Joan. xiv, 6.
2 Ibid. x, 10.
3 Ibid. i, 12–13.
4 Ibid. iii, 3–5.
5 I Joan. v, 1.
6 Col. iii, 3.
7 Joan. iii, 6.
8 Ibid. vi, 64.

upright, loyal, just, but this is but a natural morality which, furthermore, ever remains deficient in some particular. Between it and the supernatural life lies an abyss. It is however with this natural perfection and this natural life that the world contents itself.

At a single flight, faith rises higher and uplifts the soul above all the visible universe, bringing it even to God. This faith which causes us to be "born of God," which makes us children of God, through Christ, makes us also conquerors over the world. Such is the wonderful doctrine of St. John in his Epistle: "Whatsoever is born of God overcometh the world..." "Who is he that overcometh the world, but he that believeth that Jesus is the Son of God?" *Omne quod natum est ex Deo vincit mundum... Quis est qui vincit mundum, nisi qui credit quoniam Jesus est Filius Dei?*[1]

III

To this glorious destiny every Christian is called. Whoever receives Baptism, morally breaks with the world, by disowning its maxims, its principles, and its spirit, in order to live according to Christ's Gospel.

But, for the monk, how much more complete are this severance and this transformation!

The divine life that we received at Baptism with grace is the germ of all our monastic sanctification, as it is of the simple Christian life. Our perfection is not of an essentially different order from that of Christian perfection; both intrinsically belong to the same supernatural order. Religious perfection is but the development, in a given form and state, of our divine adoption. A simple Christian is a child of God; a monk is likewise a child of God, but one who seeks, in the largest possible degree and by especially adapted means, to develop this condition of a child of God. The Christian is allowed, without essential detriment to his state as child of God, the lawful use of certain creatures; the monk chooses to adhere to God alone, and his chief work is to put away from him or destroy all such created things as are opposed to the perfect expansion of the divine life in him. But for the religious as for the simple Christian, faith in Jesus Christ is the door whereby he enters into this

1 Ibid. v, 4–5.

divine life: it is as the Council of Trent says, "the foundation and root of all justification."[1]

Faith is a foundation. Think of an edifice which attracts attention by its grandeur and the harmony of its proportions. What is it that gives it solidity? The foundations. If these are shaken, at once the walls crack and the building is in danger; unless it be consolidated, it is doomed to ruin. This is an image of the spiritual life. It is an edifice which God, together with us, constructs in us, to His glory; it is a temple wherein He would dwell. But if we do not lay a firm foundation, it is impossible to build the edifice. And the higher it is to be raised, the deeper and firmer must be the foundation. When a spiritual man thinks to arrive at the summit of perfection, at the height of contemplation, without his faith, which is the basis of real love, being strong in proportion, all must come to ruin.

The Holy Council again compares faith to a root. Look at a majestic tree, with mighty trunk, vigorous branches, and abundant foliage. Whence comes to it this strength and beauty? From something unseen: the roots. These are plunged in the soil there to take a firm hold and draw the nourishing sap necessary to the life of this giant. Should the roots dry up, the tree will decay.

The root of the Christian life is faith. Without faith all withers away, dries up and perishes. It is the necessary condition of all life and all spiritual progress.

If faith be the basis of all Christian life, it is likewise upon faith that the whole monastic life rests; it is faith that explains and maintains it. The monastic life, like the Christian life, is the practical consequence of an act of faith. Why are we Christians? Because we have said to Jesus Christ: "Thou art the Christ, the Son of the Living God; Thou art He Who alone canst bring us to the Father, to eternal life." Why have we become monks? Because we have said to Jesus Christ: "Thou art the Christ; Thou art the Way that alone leads to the Father; Thou art the Fountainhead of all life, of all good, of all perfection, of all beatitude." And this initial act of faith explains the whole of our conduct.

1 Sess. vi, ch. 8.

Without faith in Jesus Christ, the life that we lead has no meaning; the world indeed takes us for fools: *Vitam illorum aestimabamus insaniam.*[1] But the terrestrial man, "the sensual man" as St. Paul calls him, "perceiveth not those things that are of the Spirit of God"; they are foolishness for him, and he cannot know them, because it is by the Spirit of God, and not by the spirit of the world, that they are discerned.[2]

In the eyes of faith, our life constitutes that "better part," *optimam partem*,[3] that Christ reserves to those upon whom He has cast His look of special love: *Intuitus eum dilexit eum*;[4] already it is for us the assured pledge of a "goodly inheritance": *hereditas praeclara.*[5]

And what is true of our life taken as a whole, remains true of the detail of our days.

Regarded from the natural point of view, from the world's point of view, the thousand details of our life of prayer, of obedience, humility, abnegation and labour, may appear trifling, narrow and insignificant. When a man who allows himself to be led by the spirit of the world sees us chanting the psalms in choir and learns that we spend so many hours in praising God, he shrugs his shoulders: "What a pity to see men waste their time like that!" It is because he does not understand and cannot understand, because he is lacking in faith: his reason is too limited to allow him to go beyond natural horizons; he has not the light of faith that would enable him to enter into God's secrets; he cannot comprehend that our life of prayer is a life most pleasing to the Lord and most profitable for souls.

So it is with all the elements of our monastic life. Faith shows us their value for eternity; faith places us above the judgments of the world, the wisdom of the world which, according to St. Paul, is "foolishness with God."[6] "We have received not the spirit of this world, but *the Spirit that is of God*: that we may know the things that are given us from God." For "the Spirit searcheth all things, yea, the deep things of God."[7]

---

1 Sap. v, 4. 2 I Cor. ii, 14. 3 Luc. x, 42. 4 Marc. x, 21.
5 Ps. xv, 6. 6 I Cor. iii, 19. 7 Ibid. ii, 10-12.

And because we adhere to this Spirit by faith, faith becomes, as our Blessed Father so well calls it, the "deifying light" that illumines and uplifts our whole life: *deificum lumen.*[1]

Faith is, in fact, for us the true divine light. To the natural life, God gives the light of reason: the intellect is the faculty that directs the specifically human activity. To the supernatural life God also gives an appropriate light. What is this light? In Heaven, where the supernatural life attains its perfection, it is the radiant light of glory, the visual power of the Beatific Vision. "In Thy light we shall see light": *In lumine tuo videbimus lumen.*[2] Here below it is the veiled light of faith. The soul that would live the true life must be guided by this light which makes it a partaker of the knowledge that God has of Himself and of all things.

In this Christ Jesus is as ever our perfect Example, and the Ideal we are predestined to reproduce. The motive power of Christ's activity was the light that shone for His Blessed Soul in the Beatific Vision. As you know, from the first instant of Its creation, the Soul of Jesus contemplated God, and from this Vision arose the light wherein It regarded all things and that directed It in all its ways. Jesus says that He reveals to us that which He Sees; He tells us only that which He hears,[3] He does nothing but what He sees the Father doing: *Non potest Filius a se facere quidquam, nisi quod viderit Patrem facientem*;[4] "Nothing of Himself, nothing for Himself; He only does that which the Father reveals to Him, and all that the Father does, He also does, but yet He does it in a like manner, with the same dignity and the same perfection, because He is the Sole-begotten Son, God of God, perfect God of perfect God."[5]

For us upon earth, the light of faith preludes the power of the Beatific Vision. The child of God knows God and beholds all things in this light.[6] God, first of all: for if no one here below has ever seen God Who "inhabiteth light inaccessible,"[7] God has, however, revealed Himself to us through His Son Jesus: *Illuxit in cordibus nostris... in facie Christi Jesu.*[8] The Only-begotten Son Who is ever in "the bosom of the Father," *in sinu Patris*,[9] manifests God to us: "He that seeth Me, seeth

1 Prologue of the Rule.
2 Ps. xxxv, 10.
3 Joan. iii, 11.
4 Ibid. v, 19.
5 Bossuet, *Meditations on the Holy Gospel.*
6 Joan. i, 18.
7 I Tim. vi, 16.
8 II Cor. iv, 6.
9 Joan. i, 18.

the Father also": *Qui videt Me, videt et Patrem.*[1] In accepting the testimony of the Son, the Word, the soul knows the secrets of the Divine life. In this celestial light, the soul likewise judges all things as God sees, considers and estimates them. It regards creation with the same eyes as do those who have not the faith; but the universe reveals to this soul what is not disclosed to others: to wit, that it is the reflection of the perfections of its Author. In the ceremonies of the Church, the believing soul does not see only the exterior side of actions and symbols, that outward aspect which all eyes may behold, but it penetrates to the depths of the rites, therein to recognise God's ideal, the intentions of the Church, the hidden mystery of the worship, the realisation of the Divine thought, the perfections of God made manifest, the glory of God procured; and with the incense of the sanctuary, the hymn of the loving and grateful heart rises up to God. In like manner, under ordinary and commonplace appearances, under the unexpected, painful or enigmatical aspect of daily events, the child of God discerns the work full of love that an infallible and maternal Providence pursues.

When this life of faith is intense, it leads to the highest perfection, just as we have seen that the Sacred Humanity of Jesus derived its principle of perfection and activity from the Beatific Vision. Doubtless, the soul that lives by faith leads outwardly the ordinary existence of the rest of mankind; it exerts its human activity like other souls, but it exerts this activity in the higher light of Divine truth. Christ is the Truth, the Light: he who lives in truth is a child of light, *filius lucis.*[2] He lives in this truth, his life abounds in those fruits of light which are, says St. Paul, "goodness and justice and truth": *Fructus enim lucis est in omni bonitate et justitia et veritate.*[3]

Can we then be surprised that St. Benedict requires of us that we should be guided in all things by the light of faith? It must be understood once for all that the holy Patriarch always places the monk from the outset on supernatural grounds. He wishes us to have "each day," *quotidie*, our gaze fixed on the "deifying light,"[4] that we may constantly receive its rays; he would have his disciples' whole conduct based on faith.

1 Ibid. xiv, 9. 2 Ibid. xii, 36. 3 Eph. v, 9.
4 Prologue of the Rule.

On the strength of these words, we will consider some passages taken from the Holy Rule. Why must the monk obey his abbot? Simply because the abbot "holds the place of Christ": *Abbas Christi agere vices creditur.*[1] Why must the monks remain perfectly united to one another? Because "all are one in Christ."[2] Why must guests, at whatever hour they arrive—and in St. Benedict's time they were very numerous, *nunquam desunt,*[3] and arrived at unlooked for hours—be received with eagerness and joy? Because it is Christ Who is received in them, because it is before Christ that we prostrate when we bow down before them: *CHRISTUS in hospitibus ADORETUR qui et SUSCIPITUR... omnes supervenientes hospites TAMQUAM CHRISTUS suscipiantur.*[4] Again why must the poor and strangers be more especially cared for? Because it is above all in these disinherited members that Christ presents Himself to our faith: *Pauperum et peregrinorum maxime susceptionum cura sollicite exhibeatur: quia in ipsis MAGIS CHRISTUS suscipitur.*[5] And it is to be the same as regards the care given to the sick in the monastery. St. Benedict most urgently recommends that the sick are to lack nothing of the succour that their infirmity requires. This point appears astonishing since the monastic state is one of abnegation. And yet St. Benedict is very precise on this point: "Before all things and above all things, care is to be taken of the sick": *Infirmorum cura ante omnia et super omnia adhibenda est.*[6] Why such insistence? Because here again faith sees Christ in His suffering members: "They are to be served as if they were Christ in person, for He hath said: 'I was sick and ye visited Me'": *Ut sicut revera Christo, ita eis serviatur, quia ipse dixit: Infirmus fui et visitastis me.*[7]

This faith, this supernatural point of view, is extended by the great Patriarch from persons to the actions of the life of the monk: whether the monk be in choir, or serve at table, or set out on a journey, everywhere St. Benedict would have him bathed in this light of faith. If the great Legislator carefully enumerates the natural qualities to be desired in the principal officials, he requires before all things that they should

1 Rule, ch. ii and lxiii.
2 Ibid. ii; cf. Gal. iii, 25.
3 Ibid. ch. liii.
4 Ibid. ch. liii.
5 Ibid. ch. liii.
6 Ibid. ch. xxxvi.
7 Ibid. ch. xxxvi; cf. Matth. xxv, 36.

have hearts "fearing God";[1] he requires of the master of novices that he should especially "be skilled in gaining souls."[2]

He envelops even the material things of the monastery with this light of faith. Because the monastery is "the house of God," *domus Dei*,[3] he would have us "look upon the vessels and goods of the monastery as if they were the consecrated vessels of the altar": *Omnia vasa monasterii cunctamque substantiam, ac si altaris vasa sacrata conspiciat*.[4] The world will find such a recommendation very trifling, very simple and useless, but the holy Legislator judged quite otherwise. And this was because his faith was strong, and he understood that all things are only of any value in God's sight according to the measure of our faith.[5]

IV

Such then is the supernatural atmosphere wherein St. Benedict wishes the monk to live and breathe continually, *quotidie*; he wishes him, as St. Paul wishes the Christian, to "live by faith": *Justus ex fide vivit*.[6] The just man, (that is to say one who in Baptism has put on the new man created in justice) lives, in so far as he is just, by faith, by the light that the Sacrament of illumination brings to him. The more he lives by faith, the more he realises in himself the perfection of his divine adoption. Notice this expression carefully: EX *fide*. The exact meaning of this is that faith ought to be the root of *all* our actions, of *all* our life. There are souls who live "with" the faith: CUM *fide*. They have faith, and one cannot deny that they practise it; but it is only on certain occasions, for example, in exercises of piety, Holy Mass, Holy Communion, the Divine Office, that they remember their faith to any purpose; it is impossible that faith should not come into play in these actions because, of their nature, these actions relate directly to God and, properly speaking, concern the supernatural economy.

---

1 Ibid. ch. xxxi and liii. 2 Ibid. ch, lviii. 3 Rule, ch. xxxi.

4 Ibid.

5 "Faith, or rather what we would call *the spirit of faith*, the supernatural spirit, is manifested in the Rule in a thousand ways that are as touching and edifying for the believer as they are paradoxical and even laughable in the eyes of the world: the *mihi fecistis* of the Gospel is there carried to the supreme degree." D. M. Festugière, *The Catholic Liturgy*. 6 Hebr. x, 38.

But one would say that these souls restrict themselves to this; and that as soon as they leave these exercises, they enter into another sphere, and return to a merely natural life. If obedience then commands them something irksome or inconvenient, they murmur; if a brother-monk is in need of something, they pay no attention to it; are their susceptibilities touched, they are irritated. At these moments the outlook of their souls is not enlightened by faith. They do not live *by* faith; theoretically, doubtless, they know that the Abbot represents Christ, that Christ is in each of their brethren, that we ought to forget ourselves in order to imitate Christ in His obedience. But, practically, these truths do not exist for them; these truths have no influence on their life; their activity does not spring *from* their faith; they make use of faith under certain circumstances, but, these circumstances having passed, they bid farewell, as it were, to their faith. Then it is the natural life that is uppermost, the natural spirit that becomes master. Certainly this is not to live by faith: *ex fide vivere.*

Now, such a life, so devoid of homogeneity, cannot be firm or stable; it is at the mercy of impressions, of every sally of temperament or mood, of the chances of health or temptation; it is a spiritual life that fluctuates and is tossed about by every wind that blows. It changes day by day, at the will of the capricious rudder that serves it as guide.

But when faith is living, strong, ardent, when we live by faith, that is to say when in everything we are actuated by the principles of faith, when faith is the root of all our actions, the inward principle of all our activity, then we become strong and steadfast in spite of difficulties within and without, in spite of obscurities, contradictions and temptations. Why so? Because, by faith, we judge, we estimate all things as God sees and estimates them: we participate in the Divine immutability and stability.

Is not this what our Lord has said? "Everyone therefore that heareth these My words and doth them"—that is to live by faith—"shall be likened to a wise man that built his house upon a rock. And the rain fell and the floods came and the winds blew, and they beat upon this house. And it fell not." "For," Jesus Christ immediately adds, "it was founded on a rock."[1]

1 Matth. vii, 25.

This is truly what we experience when our faith is deep and intense. Faith causes us to live the supernatural life; by it we are of God's family, we belong to that house of God, whereof Christ, as St. Paul says, is "the chief corner stone": *Ipso summo angulari lapide Christo Jesu.*[1] By faith, we adhere to Christ, and the edifice of our spiritual life becomes thereby firm and stable. Christ makes us share in the stability of the divine rock against which even hell's fury cannot prevail: *Portae inferi non praevalebunt.*[2] Thus divinely sustained, we are conquerors over the assaults and temptations of the world and of the devil, the prince of this world: *Haec est victoria quae vincit mundum, fides nostra.*[3] The devil, and the world which the devil uses as an accomplice, offer violence to us or solicit us; by faith in the word of Jesus we come out victorious from these attacks.

You will have remarked that the devil always insinuates the contrary to what God affirms. Look at the sad experience that our first parents made of this. "In what day soever thou shalt eat of [the forbidden fruit], thou shalt die the death";[4] such is the Divine word. The devil impudently declares the contrary: "You shall not die the death": *Nequaquam morte moriemini.*[5] When we lend an ear to the devil, we put our trust in him, we have faith in him, and not in God. Now, the devil is "the father of lies and the prince of darkness,"[6] while God is "the Truth"[7] and "in Him is no darkness."[8] If we always listen to God, we shall always be victorious. When our Lord was tempted, He repulsed temptation by placing the authority of God's Word in opposition to each solicitation of the Evil One. We ought to do the same and repulse hell's attacks by faith in Jesus' word. The devil says to us: "How can Christ be present under the species of bread and wine?" Answer him: The Lord has said: "This is My Body, this is my Blood.[9] He is the Truth, that is enough for me." The devil tells us not to let an injury or an affront pass without retorting. Answer him: "Christ has said that all we do to the least of His brethren, we do to Himself,[10] therefore any feeling of coldness voluntarily shown to our brethren or entertained towards them is shown to Jesus in person."

What is true of the devil is true of the world: it is by faith that we overcome it. When a man has a living faith in Christ, he fears nei-

1 Eph. ii, 20,
2 Matth. xvi, 15.
3 Joan. v, 4.
4 Gen. ii, 17.
5 Ibid. 4.
6 Cf. Eph. vi, 12.
7 Joan. xiv, 6.
8 Ibid. i, 5.
9 Matth. xxvi, 26-28.
10 Ibid. xxv, 40.

ther difficulties nor opposition, nor the world's judgments because he knows that Christ abides in us by faith and because he relies on Him. Our Lord explicitly gave such assurances to St. Catherine when He gave her missions far and wide for the good of His Church, especially the mission of bringing back the Sovereign Pontiff from Avignon to Rome. The Saint, in her weakness and humility, feared a mission in the course of which she foresaw insurmountable difficulties; but Christ said to her: "Because thou art armed with the might of faith, thou wilt triumph happily over all adversaries."[1] Again, later on, in her *Dialogue*, Catherine speaks of faith with holy enthusiasm: "In the light of faith," she says addressing the Eternal Father, "I gain that wisdom which is found in the wisdom of the Word, Thy Son; in the light of faith, I become stronger, more constant, more persevering. In the light of faith, I find the hope that Thou wilt not let me faint upon my way. It is also this light which shows me the path along which I must journey. Without this light, I should walk in darkness, and, therefore, I beseech Thee, Eternal Father, to enlighten me with the light of most holy faith."[2]

V

Let us, too, beseech the Father and Christ Jesus, His Word, to grant us this light of faith. We have received the principle of it in Baptism; but we ought to guard and develop this divine germ. What is the co-operation that God expects of us in this matter?

He first of all expects us to pray. Faith is a gift of God; the spirit of faith comes from the Spirit of God: "Lord, increase our faith": *Adauge nobis fidem.*[3] Let us often say to Christ Jesus, like the father of the dumb boy in the Gospel: "I do believe, Lord, help my unbelief": *Adjuva incredulitatem meam.*[4] It is truly God alone Who can, as the Efficient Cause, increase faith within us; our part is to merit this increase by our prayers and good works.

This is to say that having obtained faith, it is our duty to exercise it. At Baptism, God gives us the *habitus* of faith; it is a "force," a "power"; but this force must not remain inactive, this "habit" must not become

1 *Life by Bl. Raymund.* 2 *Life by Bl. Raymund.* 3 Luc. xvii, 5.
4 Marc. ix, 23.

ankylosed, so to speak, from want of exercise. This *habitus* ought to go on getting ever stronger by corresponding acts. We must not be of those souls in whom faith slumbers. Let us often renew our acts of faith, not only during our exercises of devotion, but furthermore, as the great Patriarch wishes, in the least details of our life. It is "every day," *quotidie*, that we must, in accordance with his counsels, walk in this light.

And you will remark that with St. Benedict, faith is always practical; he never separates it from deeds; he wishes us "to have our loins girded with faith, and the performance of good works": *Succinctis fide vel observantia bonorum actuum lumbis nostris*;[1] he promises us joy and blessedness only on condition that we "go forward in good works and in faith": *Processu vero conversationis et fidei*.[2] Let us regard all things from the point of view of faith, the supernatural point of view, which is the only true one; let all our actions be in accordance with our faith, let us do everything in its light. Under these conditions it can be said that faith is manifested by love: it becomes logically and practically perfect, because it is through love that the soul devotes itself to works of faith.

Thus spiritually armed, we shall avoid routine which is one of the great dangers of the regular life. The intensity of our faith should animate our least actions. If we apply ourselves to this, our life will be full of light and joy. The tiniest details of the day will appear to us as precious pearls which we want to gain, that with them we may compose our heavenly treasure. And in the measure that we advance in faith, in the measure that it becomes firmer, more ardent, more active, joy will more and more superabound in our souls. Light is added to light, hope, beholding its horizons widening, is strengthened day by day; love, feeling itself more ardent, makes everything easy; and we run in the path of the Lord's commandments. The great Patriarch himself assures us of this, and, without any doubt, he speaks from experience. Listen to what he says at the end of the Prologue, after having determined the end and shown the way: "In the measure that we go forward in the observance of the precepts which is the putting into practice of our faith, it is with hearts enlarged that we shall run the way of perfection with unspeakable sweetness of love": *Processu vero conversationis et fidei, dilatato corde, inenarrabili dilectionis dulcedine curritur via mandatorum Dei*. St. Benedict does not say it will

1 Prologue of the Rule. 2 Prologue of the Rule.

sometimes happen that the monk will find joy; he promises to all his sons that their hearts will dilate with joy. In Heaven the source of our joy will be the certain, perfect and inamissible possession of sovereign and immutable good, in the full light of glory; here below, the source of our joy is the possession, already begun, of God, the anticipated union with God: this possession, this union is so much the more intimate the more we are bathed in the light of faith.

The joy that faith gains for us is necessary here upon earth. God Himself fashioned our hearts, and He has fashioned them in such a way that they have need of gladness. Doubtless there are souls who live entirely in the hope and expectation of the joys of eternity, but this is the happy privilege of a small number. As for us, we have left all things to follow Christ! *Ecce nos reliquimus omnia et secuti sumus te.*[1] We cannot go begging happiness from creatures. We must expect everything from Christ What is it then that we expect? *Quid ergo erit nobis*?[2] Christ Himself promises us the hundredfold even here below. Now, joy makes part of this hundredfold, and it is faith above all that maintains joy.

Faith in fact shows us the grandeur and beauty of this supernatural life to which God has called us: "It is I, I Myself, Who will be thy Reward exceeding great": *Ego merces tua magna nimis*;[3] it shows us the height and sublimity of our monastic vocation which causes us to live in Christ's intimacy, since as St. Benedict says, it is our love for Christ, that has made us prefer Him to all things.[4]

Faith is yet again the fount of joy because it is the fount of truth and hope; it is the supreme testimony of promised good, it already puts us in anticipated possession of the good things to come: *Sperandarum substantia rerum.*[5] Supersensible realities, the only realities that eternally remain, are made tangible to us by faith.

Let us then live the life of faith as intensely as we can with Christ's grace: let our whole existence be, as our great Patriarch would have it to be, deeply impregnated, even in the least details, with the spirit of faith, the supernatural spirit. Then temptation will be unable to take any hold

1 Matth. xix, 27.
2 Ibid.
3 Gen. xv, 1.
4 Rule, ch. iv, v and lxxii.
5 Hebr. xi, 1.

on us, for our house will be built upon the rock of God's stability; we shall be victorious over the assaults of the devil and the world.

Thus delivered from our enemies, we shall live in the light of the spirit and in joy of heart. When Our Lord revealed to His disciples, at the Last Supper, the divine secrets that He alone possessed, what were the intimate meaning and end of these ineffable revelations of God's love for His children? They were to fill our hearts with joy, to pour into them His own divine joy: "These things I have spoken to you, that My joy may be in you, and your joy may be filled": *Haec locutus vobis ut gaudium MEUM in vobis sit, et gaudium vestrum IMPLEATUR.*[1]

1 Joan. xv, 11.

MONASTIC PROFESSION

SUMMARY.—The necessity, in order to be a monk, of being incorporated in the monastic society by religious profession.—I. Monastic profession constitutes an immolation of which Christ's oblation is the model.—II. Character of a holocaust attached to religious profession.—III. To unite this act to the oblation which Christ made of Himself.—IV. Blessings bestowed by God upon those who make the vows of religion.—V. Necessity of remaining constantly faithful to our Vows.

IN order to draw the Christian life at its authentic source and to be Christ's disciple, it is necessary to belong not only to the soul but likewise to the body of the Church. It is necessary to become a member of the visible organism of the Church. This incorporation is made by the profession of faith and the reception of Baptism, the Sacrament of Christian initiation; it is maintained by participation in the other Sacraments, the rites of religion and by obedience to the authorities ordained by Christ.

The same analogy holds good as regards the monastic life. To be truly a monk, is it sufficient to live according to the spirit of the great Patriarch? No, it is further necessary to be received and incorporated in the monastic society. When about to receive the holy Habit, the postulant asks to be admitted to the fellowship of God's servants: *Vestram confraternitatem.*[1] His incorporation takes place on the day of his profession. Faith brought him to the threshold of the cloister, love expressed by a solemn engagement will attach him to the monastic life: that will be the work of his Profession.

---

1 Ritual for the Clothing.

The Profession is to the monastic life what Baptism is to the Christian life; certainly it is not a sacrament but its consequences are in some manner comparable with those of baptism. Baptism places the neophyte in God's family and seals him with the character of Christian; the Profession or emission of vows places the novice in the monastic family and consecrates him to God's service that he may become a perfect disciple of Christ Jesus.[1]

Let us then analyse the meaning of the monastic profession; we shall see that it is an immolation of our whole being which, made with love, is extremely pleasing to God—that it becomes, for those who remain faithful to it, the starting-point towards perfection—and an unfailing source of spiritual blessings.

I

It is an acquired truth for us that, in the work of our perfection, we ought to keep our gaze always fixed on Christ Jesus, Who is not only the one Model of our perfection but also the Fount of holiness for us.

When Our Lord calls His disciples to Him, He invites them to leave everything so as to follow and imitate Him, and this they do: "Leaving all things they followed Him": *Relictis omnibus, secuti sunt eum.*[2] Our Lord even tells us that we cannot truly be worthy or perfect disciples, capable of partaking in the glory of "His Kingdom," unless having left all things to follow Him, we have the persevering strength not to look back. *Nemo mittens manum suam ad aratum, et respiciens retro, aptus est regno Dei.*[3]

Now as we are by nature weak and inconstant, St. Benedict wills that he who presents himself at the door of the monastery in order to return to God by following Christ, shall first of all be tried during the space of a

1 The numerous analogies existing between Monastic Profession and Christian Baptism have nowhere been shown so remarkably (although briefly) as in *The Ideal of the Monastic Life Found in the Apostolic Age* (C. VI). These pages full of sure knowledge show how, in the spirit of ecclesiastical tradition, religious Profession is a second Baptism. Setting aside this aspect of the question, we will especially confine ourselves to pointing out in what way religious Profession is an oblation; we shall see how this concept is placed in relief by St. Benedict.

2 Luc. v, 11. 3 Ibid. ix, 62.

year to ascertain if he truly seek God: *Si revera Deum quaerit.*[1] In a general manner, the Orders founded in the course of the Middle Ages adopted the same "probation" of a year. The Council of Trent appropriated this delay, in enacting the Canonical Noviceship. After having persevered in his purpose during this space of time, the novice will confirm it in an irrevocable way by a promise made to God, a promise of his stability, conversion of his manners, and obedience.[2] This is monastic profession, which having once made, the monk is definitely considered as a member of the community: *Et jam ex illa hora in congregatione reputetur.*

The holy Legislator encompasses this promise with much solemnity: he wishes it to be put into writing—to be read aloud "in the oratory"—"before all the members of the monastery"—and made "in the name of the saints whose relics enrich the altar": *Ad nomen sanctorum quorum reliquiae ibi sunt.* His solemn engagement publicly made, the monk is to go and "cast himself at the feet of his brethren that all may help him with their prayers"; *Tunc prosternatur singulorum pedibus, ut orent pro eo.*

The "promise" is at the same time a "prayer," a "petition." The novice asks to be received; he especially asks that God's help may be obtained for him; he asks God Himself to accept him and not let the expectation of his soul be in vain. The terms "engagement," "oath" denote therefore only one side (that of the human will, the secondary cause) of monastic Profession, which is eminently regarded by St. Benedict as an act of *co-operation* wherein God's action works, wherein human liberty co-operates.

One detail is especially to be noted: St. Benedict links this profession to the Sacrifice of the Altar. When the novice has read and signed the document that bears his promise, he goes to place it, with his own hand, on the altar: *Et manu sua eam super altare ponat,* as if to join the tangible and authentic testimony of his engagement to the gifts that are offered to God in sacrifice; the monk then unites his immolation with that of Christ Jesus. This is in fact what our holy Father St. Benedict intends. We see how this intention is expressed in a complementary chapter where he treats of the reception of children; St. Benedict wishes the parents to wrap their child's hand and the act of profession

1 Rule, ch. lviii.

2 This and the following texts cited are taken from the same chapter lviii of the Rule.

in the altar cloth, at the same time as the elements destined to become the matter of the Sacrifice.[1]

Monastic Profession is indeed an immolation, and this immolation derives all its value from its union with Christ's holocaust. Now whence does the Holy Sacrifice of the Mass derive its value? Is it not from the Sacrifice of the Cross which the oblation of the altar renews and reproduces? It is in contemplating this Sacrifice of the Cross, in taking the immolation of Jesus as our example, that we shall learn the qualities that the offering of ourselves in Profession ought to have. Christ's immolation has three special characters: it is a holocaust *worthy of God*, a *full* holocaust, a holocaust offered *out of love*. These characters should be found again in our Profession.

It is first of all a holocaust *worthy of God*.

St. Paul tells us that at the moment when Christ entered into the world through the Incarnation, the first movement of his soul was to cast His gaze upon the by-gone centuries, upon the sacrifices that had been offered to God under the Old Law. The Divine Word, Who knows His Father's infinite perfection, does not find these sacrifices worthy of the Father: "Holocausts for sin did not please Thee": *Holocautomata non tibi placuerunt.*[2] But Christ has seen that His own Body is destined to be the true Victim of the only sacrifice worthy of God, "A body Thou hast fitted Me": *Corpus autem aptasti mihi.*[3] Why is the immolation of this Body to be the only sacrifice pleasing to the Father? First of all, because this Victim is pure and spotless; secondly, because the Priest Who offers this sacrifice is "holy, innocent, separated from sinners":[4] this Victim and this Priest are identified in the Person of the Father's Well-beloved Son, "the Son of His loves."[5] If all that Jesus does is accepted by His Father Whose good pleasure He ever accomplishes: *Quae* *PLACITA SUNT ei, facio semper*,[6] this is above all true of His Sacrifice.

The plenitude of this Sacrifice further augments its value.

It is a holocaust. We ought not to consider Christ's Sacrifice as offered only at the time of the Passion. Christ is a Victim from the moment of

1 Rule, ch. lix. 2 Hebr. x, 6. 3 Ibid. 5.
4 Ibid. vii, 26. 5 Col. i, 13. 6 Joan. viii, 29.

the Incarnation, and it is as Victim that He offers Himself; in entering into the world, He beheld the sum of suffering, humiliation, abjection and ignominy that He was to endure from the Crib to the Cross: He accepted to fulfil all that was decreed: He said to His Father: "Behold I come": *Ecce venio.*[1] The initial act of offering whereby He wholly yielded Himself up, virtually contained all His sacrifice; from that instant His immolation began; and His whole life of suffering was but the continuation of this immolation. Let us clearly understand the meaning, at once present and retrospective, of the words our Lord utters upon the Cross, before breathing forth His last sigh: "All is consummated": *Consummatum est.*[2] This word is like the supreme echo of the *Ecce venio.*

Our Lord's sacrifice is *one*; it is perfect in its duration; it is also perfect in its plenitude. It is Himself, the whole of Himself, that Jesus Christ offers: *Semetipsum obtulit,*[3] and that He offers unto the last drop of His Blood, unto the fulfilment of the last prophecy and of His Father's last desire. There is nothing so perfect as this holocaust; it is so perfect that this oblation which Jesus Christ made, once for all, of His own Body suffices to sanctify us: *In qua voluntate sanctificati sumus per oblationem corporis Jesu Christi SEMEL.*[4] By this "one oblation He hath perfected for ever them that are sanctified": *UNA enim oblatione consummavit in sempiternum sanctificatos.*[5]

What completely renders this holocaust infinitely pleasing to God is the perfection of love wherewith it is offered.

What, in fact, is the inward motive power which urges the soul of Christ Jesus to embrace the Father's will and to confess, by His oblation and immolation, God's infinite perfections and sovereign rights? It is love. "Behold I come. In the head of the book it is written of Me that I should do Thy will: O My God, I have desired it, and Thy law in the midst of my heart": *Ecce venio, in capite libri scriptum est de me; ut faciam voluntatem tuam! Deus meus volui, et legem tuam in medio cordis mei.*[6] It is in the midst of His Heart that Jesus places His Father's will: this is as much as to say it is love that urges Him to offer Himself entirely to God's good pleasure. Our Divine Saviour gives this clearly to be understood

1 Ps. xxxix, 8; Hebr. x, 7.
2 Joan. xix, 30.
3 Hebr. ix, 14.
4 Hebr. x, 10.
5 Ibid.
6 Ps. xxxix, 8–9: cf. Hebr. x, 7.

when the moment comes to complete, to consummate, upon the Cross, the Sacrifice inaugurated by the Incarnation. Doubtless He dies for love of His brethren: "greater love," He says, "than this no man hath, that a man lay down his life for his friends," *Majorem dilectionem nemo habet ut animam suam ponat quis pro amicis suis.*[1] But His fraternal charity is itself totally subordinate to the love He bears towards His Father and to the zeal that devours Him for His Father's glory and interests, and He would have the whole world know the supremacy that this love exerts over all that He does: *Ut cognoscat mundus quia diligo Patrem... sic facio.*[2]

II

We shall find these characters again in the Holy Sacrifice of the Mass.

Our Lord has willed that the immolation of the Altar shall renew the immolation of the Cross, by reproducing it in order to apply its fruit to every soul. It is the same Christ Who offers Himself to His Father "in the odour of sweetness": *cum odore suavitatis*;[3] this unbloody oblation is as acceptable to God as the Sacrifice of Calvary: here Jesus is the Victim, as He was when upon the Cross, and as He was when He came upon earth. Upon the altar, Christ Jesus comes again into this world every day as Victim; every day He repeats his oblation and His immolation for us. Doubtless He wishes us to offer Him to the Father; but neither does He ever weary of urging us to offer ourselves to His Father, in union with Him, that we too may thus be accepted, and, having shared in His Sacrifice here below, may likewise share in His eternal glory.

Our condition as creatures already obliges us to offer ourselves to God, for His dominion over us is sovereign: "The earth is the Lord's and the fulness thereof: the world and all they that dwell therein": *Domini est terra et plenitudo ejus, orbis terrarum et universi qui habitant in eo.*[4] We ought to confess, by our adoration and the sacrifice of our submission to God's will, His supreme perfection and our absolute dependence.

But our condition as members of Jesus Christ also obliges us to imitate our Divine Head. St. Paul addresses these words to Christians: "I beseech you, therefore, brethren, by the mercy of God,"—that is to say

1 Joan. xv, 13.
2 Ibid. xiv, 31.
3 Ordinary of the Mass, offering of the Chalice.
4 Ps. xxiii.

because of God's infinite bounty towards you—"that you present your bodies a living sacrifice, holy, pleasing unto God, your reasonable service": *Obsecro vos, fratres, per misericordiam Dei, ut exhibeatis corpora vestra hostiam viventem, sanctam, Deo placentem, rationabile obsequium vestrum.*[1]

These words ought to be especially true of those who offer themselves to God by religious profession.

Christians in the world offer sacrifices to God. On account of our fallen nature, a certain self-abnegation is necessary for all, a certain self-immolation, in order to obey God's commandments. But with the ordinary Christian this immolation has its limits; he may offer his possessions to God, but he keeps the free disposal of his person; he must love God, but he may also give a legitimate share of his love to creatures.

He who gives himself to God by religious profession, renounces everything; he comes to God with all that he has, all that he is: "Behold I come," *Ecce venio*; and he offers all this to God, keeping nothing back. This is what it means to be a living sacrifice, to offer a holocaust. At our profession, it is as if we said: "My God, my nature gives me the faculty of possessing; but I abdicate earthly goods that I may possess Thee alone. It allows me to love creatures, but I wish to love Thee alone. It authorises me to dispose of myself, but I wish to lay my liberty at Thy feet." We give up not only earthly possessions and the right of making a home of our own, but we renounce what is dearest to our being: our liberty; and because we surrender this citadel of the will, we surrender our entire being, the very root of all our activity, we keep back nothing. From this day we have not even, as our holy Father St. Benedict says, the disposal of our own bodies: *Ex illo die nec proprii corporis potestatem se habiturum sciat.*[2] We make the tradition of everything in the joyful simplicity of our love: *Domine, in simplicitate cordis mei laetus obtuli* UNIVERSA.[3]

That great monk St. Gregory says: "When a soul offers to the Divine Omnipotence all that it has, all that is within it, all that pleases it, that is a holocaust": *Cum quis omne quod habet, omne quod vivit, omne quod*

---

1 Rom. xii, 1. 2 Rule, ch. lviii.

3 "My God... I also in the simplicity of my heart, have joyfully offered all these things," I Par. xxix, 17.

sapit omnipotenti Deo voverit, holocaustum est.[1] St. Thomas expresses the same thought: "A holocaust consists in offering to God all that we have": *Holocaustum est cum aliquis totum quod habet offert Deo.*[2]

By this immolation we acknowledge that God is the First Principle of all things; we lay down at His feet all that we have received from Him, we offer ourselves up entirely, in order that all that we are and all that we have may return to Him.

Moreover, in order to make this holocaust more perfect, more complete, and, as far as possible, perpetual, we offer it by a solemn public promise, accepted by the Church: this is the Profession, the emission of the vows. It is true that from the day we entered the monastery, we effectively left all to follow Christ Jesus; but the great moral threshold was not crossed: it is the part of the vows to consecrate the donation and make it, of itself, irrevocable. The vows of religious require, as you know, a deliberate act of the will, bound by a public promise made to the Church. St. Benedict evidently means it to be so: the novice is to consider well within himself for some length of time, before binding himself for ever by a promise: *Et si habita secum deliberatione, promiserit se omnia custodire.*[3]

O God, Infinite Being, Who art very Beatitude, what an immense and inestimable grace Thou dost give to Thy poor creatures in calling them to be, with the Son of Thy love, acceptable sacrifices, wholly consecrated to the glory of Thy Majesty!

III

For this holocaust to be "pleasing unto God," *Deo placens*, as St. Paul says, it must be united to the sacrifice of Christ Jesus.

This is a truth of capital importance: it is Christ's oblation which gives value to ours, and makes it worthy of the Heavenly Father. It is in order to manifest outwardly this union of our immolation with that of Christ, that St. Benedict wishes the Profession to be made during the Holy Sacrifice, and the novice to place upon the altar, with his own hand, the

1 *Super Ezech.*, 1, 1 homil. 8, n° 16.
2 II-II, q. clxxxvi, a. 7.
3 Rule, ch. lviii.

parchment that contains his written promise. As everything laid upon the altar as an offering is consecrated to God, this act of profession is the symbol of the immolation that the newly professed brother has just made in the sanctuary of his own soul.

How is this union of our sacrifice with that of Jesus carried into effect? Through love. Love it is that unites. It is because we love Christ that we wish to cleave to Him and prefer Him to every creature. "Come, follow Me," says Jesus; *Veni, sequere me*;[1] and like Jesus when entering into this world, we have said to Him: "Behold I come," *Ecce venio*; I wish to cleave to Thee alone. Because I believe that Thou art God, very Perfection and Beatitude; because I trust in the infinite value of Thy merits and of Thy grace; because in Thee I love the Supreme Being, and "for Thy Name's Sake"; *propter nomen tuum*,[2] I have left all things and I even relinquish that which is most near and dear to me—my liberty. *Ecce nos reliquimus omnia, et secuti sumus te*.[3]

Doubtless what we have given to God is, taken in itself, a very small thing. We are poor creatures who have received everything from our Heavenly Father, and God has no need of our goods: *Bonorum meorum non eges*.[4] But what God asks is our heart, our love; and, as St. Gregory says, when love gives all, however little this "all" may be, the gift is very pleasing to God, because the giver keeps nothing back. "In this transaction, it is the love that must be considered rather than the thing itself": *Hac in re affectum debemus potius pensare quam censum; multum reliquit qui sibi nihil retinuit; multum reliquit qui quantumlibet parum, totum deseruit*.[5] The holy Pontiff remarks that the Apostles Peter and Andrew materially left nothing but their fishing nets, but that, having left these things for love's sake to follow Christ, they relinquished all right and power of possessing.

Separation from all that is earthly, all that is created, is the first aspect of holiness; the donation of oneself to God is the second. But it is necessary to be "separated" in order to be "consecrated." The vows give us the power of reaching the highest possible degree of separation from the creature, since we renounce our own will. We can truly say:

---

1 Matth. xix, 21. 2 Cf. Marc. x, 29-30.
3 Matth. xx, 27; cf. Marc. x, 28; Luc. xviii, 28.
4 Ps. xv, 2. 5 Lib. I *Homil. v in Evangel.* n° 2.

"We have left all," *Reliquimus omnia*. But we must not delay to add: "that we may follow Thee," *Et secuti sumus te*. Such is the formula of union with God, the second aspect of holiness: we give ourselves, we consecrate ourselves to God; and we can say to God in our monastic profession: "Uphold me, O Lord, according to Thy word, and I shall live; and let me not be confounded in my expectation": *Suscipe me, Domine, secundum eloquium tuum, et vivam, et non confundas me ab exspectatione mea.*[1]

When a soul thus gives itself fully to God, through love, to seek Him alone, when it is detached, as far as possible, from every creature, from itself, from all human springs of action, in order to cleave only to God, then it is a "holy sacrifice": *Hostiam sanctam*. It is a spotless sacrifice, unstained by earth. If, on the contrary, a soul retains its attachment to created things, it remains glued to the earth, it is not "holy." The Heart of Christ Jesus was attached only to the Father: *Ego vivo propter Patrem.*[2] Therefore St. Paul says that Christ was an unspotted sacrifice offered to God: *Qui semetipsum obtulit immaculatum Deo.*[3] The monk who makes profession casts away from him, in principle, every creature, all that could turn him away from God; he is freed from every fetter that he may be perfectly bound to Christ, and seek solely the will of His Father. This is an act of perfect love extremely pleasing to God. And because Profession is the expression of so complete a love, God outpours immense blessings and unceasing joy upon the soul that gives itself to Him through the vows and remains faithful to them.

IV

The most inestimable of the blessings that religious Profession brings to the soul is, assuredly, that of rendering it very pleasing to God. It is solidly established in ecclesiastical tradition that Profession is like a second baptism which restores to the Christian his entire purity;[4] at the moment of the emission of vows, God forgets all the past and grants a universal forgiveness to the professed: He sees before Him only a crea-

1 Ps. cxviii, 116; Rule, ch. lviii.

2 "I live by the Father," Joan. vi, 58.

3 Hebr. ix, 14.

4 See D. G. Morin: *L'idéal monastique,* p. 60.

ture totally renewed: *Nova creatura.*[1] At this blessed hour, the soul is given to Jesus as the bride to the bridegroom; the mystical tomb wherein the soul is buried may be compared to the baptismal font wherein the neophyte was plunged. The Heavenly Father can say of this soul as of the newly baptised who has just "put on Christ": "This is My beloved child in whom I am well pleased." What bounty is lavished upon this soul while God so lovingly beholds it in His Son!

The second blessing that God gives to the new religious is that all his actions henceforward possess great value. These actions all participate in the virtue of religion.

As you know, every virtue has its own form, its particular beauty and special merit. But the act of a virtue can be the fruit of a superior virtue, for example an act of mortification or humility, may be inspired by the virtue of charity, which is the queen of virtues. Then besides its own splendour and intrinsic value, this act of temperance or of humility assumes the beauty and merit of an act of charity. Now in the life of a monk, all acts of virtue assume, by the fact of his profession, the value of acts of religion. "The acts of the different virtues," says St. Thomas, "become better and more meritorious, when they are performed in virtue of a vow: on this head they appertain to Divine worship, as if they were sacrifices": *Opera aliarum virtutum... sunt meliora et magis meritoria, si fiunt ex voto, quia sic jam pertinent ad divinum cultum, quasi quaedam Dei sacrificia.*[2] Thus Profession communicates to the monk's whole life the character and virtue of a holocaust; it makes of our life a perpetual sacrifice. The act of profession itself only lasts a few moments, but its effects are permanent and its fruits eternal. As Baptism is the starting point of Christian holiness, so is Profession that of our monastic perfection. It should appear to us like the gradual developing of an initial act of immense weight. "The property of the vows," says St. Thomas, "is to immobilise the will in good. And the acts which proceed from a will thus fixed in good, appertain to perfect virtue": *Per votum immobiliter voluntas firmatur in bonum. Facere autem aliquid ex voluntate firmata in bonum, pertinet ad perfectionem virtutis.*[3]

1 Gal. vi, 15. 2 II-II, q. 88, a. 6. 3 II-II, q. 88, a. 6.

But here a precision is necessary: the perfection assigned to us is of a definite type. In the same way as the baptismal vows are the initial point of our *supernatural* holiness, so monastic profession is the first impulsion towards our *Benedictine* perfection. It is not, in fact, either a Dominican perfection, nor a Carthusian perfection which is to arise from our profession: it is a Benedictine perfection; for our vows have in view the practice of the Rule of St. Benedict and of the Constitutions which govern us: *Promitto... obedientiam secundum regulam S. P. Benedicti in congregatione nostra.*[1] The Rule, interpreted by our Constitutions—and not the Rule of another Order, or the constitutions of another Congregation—is what we have vowed to observe. The Rule contains moreover all that is necessary for our perfection and holiness: it is in giving themselves to God by the bonds of this Rule that so many monks are made holy and come to the highest perfection, to the summit of sanctity.

As it is the starting point of our perfection, so our profession is also the origin of our joy. "Lord, in the simplicity of my heart, I have gladly given Thee all": such are the accents of the soul, at the moment of offering itself to God. But God repays this joyful generosity of the soul with a further increase of joy. "God loveth a cheerful giver": *Hilarem datorem diligit Deus*, says St. Benedict,[2] repeating the expression of the Apostle.[3] And as God is the source of all beatitude and we have left all things in order to cleave to Him alone, He says to us: It is I Myself Who will be Thy reward, a reward "exceeding great": *Ego merces tua magna nimis.*[4] *EGO*: Myself! I will not leave the care of crowning thee to any other, God says to the soul; because thou art My victim, because thou art wholly Mine, I will be all thine, thy inheritance, thy possession, and thou shalt find in Me thy beatitude: *Ego merces tua!*

Yes, Lord, it is thus indeed: "For what have I in Heaven and besides Thee what do I desire upon earth?... Thou art the God of my heart, and the God that is my portion for ever": *Quid enim mihi est in caelo, et a te quid volui super terram? Deus cordis mei et pars mea Deus in aeternum.*[5]

---

1 "I promise... obedience to the Rule of our Holy Father Benedict in our congregation," Ceremonial of the Monastic Profession.

2 Rule, ch. v.

3 II Cor. ix, 7.

4 Gen. xv, 1.

5 Ps. lxxii, 25–26.

V

But in order to taste these joys, we must keep ourselves at the height of our profession; we must remain in this state of absolute oblation; we must, during our whole life, be faithful to our vows. In the same way as, by baptism, the Christian engages himself for ever "to die to sin" and to strive ever "to live unto God,"[1] so the monk, by his profession, obliges himself to be ever more and more detached from all that is created, in order to follow Christ more and more closely.

This is an arduous task which requires of us great generosity, because our fallen nature ever tends to take back something of what it has given. We cannot withdraw the offering of ourselves once made; if we do so by wilful infidelities, we incur God's anger. Our holy Father St. Benedict himself warns us of this in dramatic terms: "Let him who acts otherwise than as he has promised, know that he will be condemned by Him Whom he mocketh": *Ut se aliquando aliter fecerit, ab eo se damnandum sciat quem irridet*.[2] Never let us forget indeed that our chart of profession is registered in Heaven in the book of Predestination, and that we shall be judged not only as to our baptismal promises, but also as to the vows which we have pronounced before the holy altar: *Stas in conspectu Dei ante hoc sacrosanctum altare*.[3] The thought of not having faithfully observed the vows by which he freely bound himself would be a cause of terrible anguish for a religious at the hour of death. God judges according to the truth; He even judges our justices: *Ego justitias judicabo*.[4] Let us therefore often examine the object of our threefold offering and see if we are faithful, despite opposition and difficulties, in keeping our vow of stability, in labouring at the conversion of our manners, in living in obedience under the guidance of the one who, for us, represents Christ and holds His place.

Doubtless, this faithfulness is perfectly compatible with our miseries, our infirmities, the faults that escape us and that we deplore and try to repair; but it cannot be reconciled with habitual and unresisted tepidity or with deliberate infidelities. A religious, whether monk or nun, who

---

1 See *Baptism, Sacrament of Initiation and Adoption* in *Christ, the Life of the Soul*.

2 Rule, ch. lviii.

3 "You stand in the sight of God before this most holy altar," Ceremonial of Monastic Profession.

4 Ps. lxxiv, 3.

bargains with Christ, who thinks that too much is asked, who makes reservations in the gift of self, who "looks back,"[1] is not worthy of Him. For such souls, neither perfection nor intimate union with God is possible.

We must then fervently strive to remain generously faithful. Strange aberration of certain souls who imagine that the profession once made, they can "take things easily!" But in reality it is quite the contrary; then it is that the true life of intimate union with Jesus in His sacrifice begins for us.

Union in sacrifice, we say, but also in our inward ascensions; for God has likewise bound Himself on His side, if I may thus speak: He is bound to help us, to make us attain to holiness. And be assured that He will keep His contract. *Fidelis Deus*:[2] "God is faithful"; He will never fail the soul who sincerely seeks Him. Our Lord clearly tells us so: "Everyone that hath left house, or brethren, or sisters, or father, or mother... or lands for My Name's sake, shall receive an hundredfold, and shall possess life everlasting." And Christ Jesus confirms this promise by a kind of oath: "Amen, I say to you."[3] His word is that of Truth itself; it is infallible. If we are faithful to cleave to Jesus alone, we shall receive even here below, and without any possible miscalculation, the promised hundredfold; we shall have our hands filled with great, immense blessings. He is for our souls the most sincere of Friends, the most faithful Bridegroom.

Let us ask our Lord for the grace never to leave Him. *Juravi et statui*: O Lord Jesus, "I have sworn and am determined to keep the judgments of Thy justice," *Custodire judicia justitiae tuae*.[4] Like Thee, for love of Thee, I am determined to keep my Rule even to the least detail; not so much as an iota, not so much as a comma, shall be taken away by me from Thy law: *Iota unum aut unus apex non praeteribit a lege donec omnia fiant*.[5]

Christ offered Himself to His Father on entering into the world. At that moment, He, so to speak, made His profession; from that moment He gave everything, although this donation was to be manifested throughout His whole life until His death upon the Cross. He never retracted aught of this tradition of Himself, He took back nothing from this holocaust. He sought only what pleased His Father, even when the chalice that His Father proffered Him overflowed with bitterness. He

1 Luc. ix, 62.
2 I Cor. i, 9.
3 Matth. xix, 28–29.
4 Ps. cxviii, 106.
5 Matth. v, 18.

could therefore say in all truth before dying: *Consummatum est.*[1] Let us often contemplate Christ Jesus in the supreme and immutable fidelity with which He fulfilled His mission, let us beseech Him to give us the grace to take nothing back of what we have given. Like Him, and for love of Him, we gave all at the moment of our profession: all the good we have done since is but the daily and exterior manifestation of a will and determination rendered irrevocable by our vows.

St. Paul writing to his disciple Timothy exhorts him to "stir up" within himself the grace which he received on the day of his ordination, whereby he became a partaker of Christ's eternal Priesthood.[2] It is for us likewise a salutary practice to revive within us the grace of Profession by renewing the promises we then made. This monastic sacramental is always at our disposal: when we have recourse to it a new influx of divine life flows into our souls.

After Holy Mass, there is no action so pleasing to God as the self-oblation of religious Profession: there is no state so precious in His sight as that of constancy in the dispositions wherein the soul was at that moment. It is a holy practice then to renew our profession daily, for example at the offertory of the Mass. Let us unite our sacrifice with that of Christ Jesus. Let us offer ourselves with Him "in the spirit of humility, and with a contrite heart that our sacrifice may be pleasing in the eyes of the Lord": *In spiritu humilitatis et in animo contrito suscipiamur a te, Domine, et sic fiat sacrificium nostrum in conspectu tuo hodie, ut placeat tibi, Domine Deus.*[3] O Eternal Father, receive not only Thy Divine Son, but ourselves with Him of Whom we say that He is "a pure Host, a holy Host, an immaculate Host": *Hostiam puram, hostiam sanctam, hostiam immaculatam.*[4] Of ourselves, we are only poor creatures, but, miserable as we are, Thou wilt not reject us, for the sake of Thy Son Jesus Who is our Propitiation, and to Whom we would be united, so that through Him, and with Him, and in Him, all honour and glory be to Thee, O Father Almighty, in the unity of the Holy Ghost: *Per ipsum, et cum ipso,*

1 "It is consummated," Joan. xix, 30.
2 II Tim. i, 6.
3 Ordinary of the Mass.
4 Canon of the Mass.

et in ipso est tibi Deo Patri omnipotenti, in unitate Spiritus Sancti, omnis honor et gloria.[1]

When with all our heart we thus associate ourselves with our Lord's Sacrifice, our daily life becomes the practical expression of the oblation made at the hour of our profession: it is like the prolongation of the Mass wherein Christ our Divine Head is immolated, and hence, our whole existence is transfigured into a hymn of praise, a continual *Gloria* rising up to God like the incense of the sacrifice, "in the odour of sweetness"; *cum odore suavitatis*, an act of perfect adoration indefinitely renewed. The vows nail us to the Cross with Christ, and it may be said that these mystical nails were forged by the Church, the Bride of Christ, since it is she who approves our vows. It is the Church's explicit intervention which guarantees that our vows are so pleasing to our Lord and so useful to our souls. Doubtless the religious state is hard for nature, for it obliges us to constant abnegation. When St. Gertrude, on one All Saints Day, contemplated the legions of the elect, she saw that religious figured in the ranks of martyrs: the vision signified that profession makes of our life a perpetual holocaust.[2] "Do not say," an author of the first centuries had already exclaimed, "do not say that in our days the conflicts where martyrs triumph no longer exist. For peace itself has its martyrs. To repress anger, to flee from impurity, to keep justice, despise avarice, to beat down our pride, is not this to accomplish the principal acts of martyrdom?"[3]

But the generous and faithful soul finds in this ever renewed self-oblation an inexhaustible joy, an ever increasing joy, because this joy comes from One Who is infinite and immutable Beatitude. It is this Divine Beatitude that we wished to gain when we left all things, like to the mer-

1 Ibid. 2 *The Herald of Divine Love,* Bk. iv, ch. 55.

3 *Nemo dicat quod temporibus nostris martyrum certamina esse non possint; habet enim pax martyres suos. Nam iracundiam mitigare, libidinem jugere, justitiam custodire, avaritiam contemnere, superbiam humiliare, pars magna martyrii est.* Migne, P. L. p. xxxix, col. 2301. (Sermons attributed to St. Augustine.) The same thought is found again with St. Gregory: *Quamvis occasio persecutionis desit, habet tamen et pax nostra martyrium suum: quia etsi carnis colla fero non subjicimus, spirituali tamen gladio carnalia desideria in mente trucidamus.* (Although the occasion of persecution has ceased, yet our peace has its own martyrdom: for even if we do not expose our head of flesh to the wild beast, yet do we slay fleshly desires in the soul with the sword of the spirit) *Homil. LIII in Evangel.* Of course, the word "martyrdom" here is not to be taken literally, and the *aureola* of martyrdom belongs only to one who has shed his blood for the faith.

chant, "who when he had found one pearl of great price... sold all that he had, and bought it": *Inventa autem una pretiosa margarita... vendidit omnia quae habuit, et emit eum.*[1] This happiness we shall find if we are ever seeking it; we shall possess it one day in all its perfection, or rather we shall lose ourselves in its infinity: so much the more deeply lost in it according to the measure wherein here below we are the more detached from creatures in order to cleave exclusively to Christ: *Ecce nos reliquimus omnia et secuti sumus te.*

1 Matth. xiii, 46.

THE INSTRUMENTS OF GOOD WORKS

SUMMARY.—Religious Profession inaugurates the true monastic life.—I. Why St. Benedict compares the monastic life to a "spiritual workshop."—II. The instruments he puts in our hands that we may excel in it.—III. In what way we are to make use of them; divers stages.—IV. The part that, in our ascetic industry, proceeds from the divine co-operation.—V. Love is the supreme mainspring of this undertaking.—VI. Fruits of a life guided by love.—VII. Persevering strength requisite in order to attain final success.

IT is under the guidance of Christ Jesus that we must return to God. Christ is the Leader Who shows us the way and brings us to the supreme end. Faith yields us up to Christ, by causing Him to reign in us—a reign which is accepted in substance on the day of Baptism, and renewed in its full extent on the blessed day of our monastic Profession: at that hour we overcame the world by an act of practical faith, in order to surrender ourselves entirely to Christ and attach us to Him alone without looking back: "Behold we have left all things, and have followed Thee": *Ecce nos reliquimus omnia et secuti sumus te.*[1]

But religious Profession is only the beginning of our real monastic life, as the donation that Christ made of Himself to His Father's good pleasure on entering into the world, was but the ineffable prelude to all His humano-divine activity. The faith that gave us up to Christ when we pronounced our Vows ought to continue to be a daily principle of action in us; it ought, if it is to be perfect, to blossom into love, and,

1 Matth. xix, 27.

through a motive of love, set all our energies in motion, in order that we may work out our union with Christ Jesus.

It is truly thus that our Holy Father, "filled with the spirit of all the just," according to the saying of St. Gregory,[1] conceives the cenobitical life which we have embraced by our profession. See for yourselves. The first vow that he makes us pronounce is that of stability which binds us to the cenobitical society and fixes us in the monastery until death: *Usque ad mortem in monasterio perseverantes.*[2] But under what aspect does he present this monastery? Under that of a "spiritual workshop." Trades are not learnt there, but the soul is exercised in seeking God. The spiritual workshop is also "a school of the Lord's service": *Dominici schola servitii.*[3] In this workshop, in this school, the holy Legislator places what he calls the "instruments of good works," the "tools of the spiritual craft": *Instrumenta bonorum operum, artis spiritualis.*[4]

Let us try to understand the profound teaching hidden under these expressions. Why does St. Benedict compare the monastic life to a "spiritual craft"? What are the "instruments" that he places in our hands that we may learn to excel? In what manner are we to make use of them? We shall have to recognise the part that, in our ascetical industry, proceeds from the Divine operation; finally we will explain how love must be the supreme mainspring of the whole of this undertaking, and with what firm perseverance we must continue in it so that it may be crowned with success.

I

The essentially practical terms that our Holy Father employs sufficiently emphasise that an urgent work of activity is traced out for us.

For St. Benedict, the necessity of good works is evident. The lofty aim he sets before us, namely, to find God, is not to be obtained without good works. "If we wish," he says in the Prologue, "to dwell in the tab-

1 *Dialogues.* Lib. ii, ch. 8.
2 Prologue of the Rule.
3 Prologue of the Rule.
4 Rule, ch. iv. The metaphor of "instrument," "workshop" is an inheritance that comes to us from the East; we find these terms in the language of the asceticism of the first centuries and of the Fathers of the Desert. Cf. likewise St. Thomas, II-II, q. 184, a. 3, c. fin; q. 188, a. 8, c. fin.

ernacle of His Kingdom, we must run thither"—and he uses this term *run*[1] time after time—"by good works..." We shall only become heirs of the Kingdom of Heaven if we fulfil by our deeds the requisite conditions for obtaining this inheritance. It is for this reason, he adds, that a "delay," a "respite" is granted to us by God in this present life.[2]

What are the works that the holy Legislator exhorts us to accomplish and for which he gives us "instruments of the spiritual art"?

First of all, remark the exactitude of this last expression. *Ars,* says St. Thomas, *est ratio recta aliquorum operum faciendorum.*[3] Art consists in giving a faithful material reproduction of an idea, of an ideal. Consider a work of art. It exists, to begin with, in the thought of the artist: it is this thought that guides his hand; and when the work is executed it is often but an imperfect reflection of the ideal formed and cherished by the master's genius. God, if we may thus speak, is the greatest of artists. The whole creation is but the outward expression of the ideal that God forms to Himself of all things in His Word. As the artist finds his delight in the work that reproduces his thought, so creation, in coming forth from God's hands, was seen by Him to be "very good," because it responded perfectly to the ideal of its Divine Author: *Viditque Deus quae fecerat et erant valde bona.*[4] The Holy Spirit stirs up the Psalmist to contemplate nature thereby to glorify the God of creation. *Domine, Dominus noster, quam admirabile est nomen tuum in universa terra*:[5] "O Lord, our Lord, how admirable is Thy name in the whole earth!" *Omnia in sapientia fecisti*: "Thou hast made all things in wisdom."[6] We do the same as the Psalmist when, at the chanting of the *Benedicite* of Lauds, we lend to all beings the accents of our lips, the life of our understanding and of our heart, in order to praise God for having made them.

But there remains a great difference between us and material things. They are but a vestige, a far-off reflection of the Divine Beauty. Man, on the contrary, was created with an intellect and a heart in the image of God: *Faciamus hominem ad imaginem et similitudinem nostram.*[7] Such is the secret of the dignity of man and the ineffable love that God bears towards him. "My delights are to be with the children of men": *Deli-*

1 Cf. Ps. xviii, 6; cxviii, 32: *Viam mandatorum tuorum cucurri.*
2 Prologue of the Rule.
3 I-II, q. 57, a. 3.
4 Gen. i, 31.
5 Ps. viii, 1.
6 Ps. ciii, 24.
7 Gen. i, 26.

ciae meae esse cum filiis hominum.[1] God loves His image in us. Now, as you know, this image has been degraded, disfigured by original sin and by our personal sins. All spiritual art is hence to consist in repairing the consequences of this degradation, and of restoring to the soul its primitive beauty, in order to give God the joy of seeing His image more perfectly reflected in us.

God is the first to work at this restoration. To this end, He sends His Son, "perfect God and perfect Man": *Perfectus Deus, perfectus homo.*[2] As God, Christ is "the image of the invisible God and the brightness of His glory":[3] He is the adequate and substantial image of the eternal perfections; He is perfect God, pure and spotless Light, begotten by Light. As Man, He is likewise perfect, surely the most beautiful of the children of men; His soul is immaculate, adorned with the plenitude of grace. Christ is the beloved Son in Whom the Father recognises Himself; in the midst of creation, He is the Divine Masterpiece in Whom is all the Father's delight.

And it is Christ Who becomes for us the type, the example which we must reproduce in order to restore the divine beauty to our souls and to be admitted into the heavenly kingdom. How many times have we not meditated on these truths? He Who created us has willed that Christ shall be the very form of our predestination: *Praedestinavit [nos Deus] conformes fieri imaginis Filii sui.*[4]

The "new creature": *nova creatura,*[5] who is the child of adoption in Christ Jesus, reproduces in God's sight the traits of His beloved Son. God's great desire is that we should resemble His Son Jesus as perfectly as possible. Therefore the whole method of the spiritual art consists in keeping the eyes of the soul unceasingly fixed upon Christ our Model, this humano-divine Ideal, in order to reproduce His features in us. It is thus that we shall rehabilitate our nature and raise it to its first splendour; and it is thus we may be assured of the delight and liberality of the Heavenly Father, because then He will recognise in us the many brethren of the First-born: *Ut sit ipse primogenitus in multis fratribus.*[6]

1 Prov. viii, 31.
2 Creed attributed to St. Athanasius.
3 Col. i, 15; Hebr. i, 3.
4 Rom. viii, 29.
5 Gal. vi, 15.
6 Rom. viii, 29.

But you will say: Has not baptism washed away sin and has it not clad us with Christ Himself? *Quicumque in Christo baptizati estis, Christum induistis.*[1] Assuredly. However, we have as yet but the principle of our progressive assimilation; evil tendencies remain in us ever ready to break out in sinful deeds which disfigure the soul. On the one hand it is in removing these stains and overcoming these tendencies, and on the other hand in developing this resemblance to Christ by the practice of virtues, that we tend to perfection.

What in fact is a Christian? "Another Christ," all antiquity replies. And who is Christ? The Man-God. And He comes to destroy sin by His death; He brings life whereof He has the fulness. To renounce sin and participate in this life, such is the programme so clearly traced out by St. Paul to the neophyte on the day when by his baptism he becomes Christ's disciple: "So do you also reckon, that you are dead to sin, but alive unto God, in Christ Jesus": *Ita et vos existimate, vos mortuos esse peccato, viventes autem Deo, in Christo Jesu.*[2] And this twofold formula is the summary of the whole work of the Christian and of all religious asceticism.

Manifestly St. Benedict makes this the starting point of the perfection that he wishes to develop in his monks. Through Christ's grace, the Christian dies to sin and lives to God: St. Benedict wishes us to carry out this plan to its full achievement. Like the simple Christian, the monk is the child of God, called by God to eternal beatitude, having Christ as Head and being sustained by the grace of Christ. But if he starts from the same point as the simple Christian, the monk goes further in order to reach a beatitude which, substantially the same, is yet capable of degrees reaching to ever ascending heights. The simple Christian dies to sin: the monk, by his vows, renounces created things, renounces himself. The simple Christian lives, through grace, for God; the monk must have in view perfect charity where every human motive power disappears. The monk seeks to bring to realisation the fulness of the Christian life; he must possess within himself a deeper degree of "death," but also a more powerful intensity of "life" than is the case with the ordinary faithful. To the precepts the observance of which leads to the Kingdom of Heav-

1 "For as many of you as have been baptised in Christ, have put on Christ," Gal. iii, 27. 2 Rom. vi, 11.

en, he adds the practice of the counsels which give a greater vigour and perfection to the merely Christian life.

Hear how the great Patriarch himself presents these ideas: he first makes the monk listen to the Divine voice: "The Lord," he says, "seeks His workman in the multitude of the people, and cries out: 'Who is the man that will have life, and desireth to see good days.'" The end is here indicated: the divine life, God's beatitude shared here below in faith, up above in the brightness of eternal light. "And if," continues the holy Legislator, "thou respondest to this invitation by the words 'I am he': what will be the Lord's reply? 'Turn from evil, and do good; seek peace, and pursue it.'"[1] Here is characterised the twofold work to which St. Benedict would have us apply ourselves while living in the monastery: Avoid evil and do good; and by the same fact, possess peace. Very general terms in which he summarizes the spiritual craft.

So true is it that our Holy Father sees in monastic holiness only the normal but full expansion of baptismal grace, for his spirituality—I cannot insist too much upon this—proceeds directly from the Gospel; it is all steeped in it, and this it is that gives it that seal of greatness and simplicity, of strength and sweetness, which especially characterises it.

II

In practice, the fulfilment of this maxim "to turn from evil and do good" is apportioned according to specifically divers precepts and manifold acts.[2] St. Benedict thus furnishes his spiritual workshop—the monastery—with various instruments, which the workmen—the monks—have to learn how to handle and continue to use.

But what are these "instruments"? The holy Lawgiver calls by this name sentences taken for the most part from Holy Scripture, others borrowed from the ancient Fathers of the Church and the early monastic writers. These are sentences, aphorisms, maxims which point out some fault to be avoided, some vice to be uprooted, some virtue to be practised. These axioms which, by their concise form, recall the formulas of

1 Prologue of the Rule.

2 We know that this maxim constitutes, according to the philosophers, the first principle of the moral order.

the Decalogue, are easily retained by the memory, and the mind turns them over to derive fruit from them, and puts them into practice when the moment comes: they are to help us to overthrow the obstacles opposed to the Divine action in us and to practise acts of virtue.

As souls are different and have not the same tendencies to evil, or identical aptitudes for good, our Holy Father has multiplied instruments: seventy-three are to be counted. When a man of the world reads over the list,[1] he is nearly always astonished to see St. Benedict giving his sons recommendations which concern only the order of natural morality or the life of the simple Christian. "To love God with all one's heart, all one's soul, all one's strength; to love one's neighbour as oneself; to honour all men; not to do to another what one would not have done to oneself; to tell the truth from heart and mind; not to kill, not to steal, not to bear false witness; to relieve the poor; to visit the sick; to console the afflicted."

Why does our Blessed Father thus blend counsels so general or so specifically Christian with exhortations of purely monastic inspiration? It is undoubtedly because, in his time, Christian civilisation had not penetrated everywhere and the atmosphere that Christians breathed was yet laden with evil effluvia, the persistant remains of Paganism or relapses into barbarism.[2] In his monasteries were to be found noblemen who had known the most decadent periods of Roman society; there were also Goths scarcely freed from their brutal passions. For the use of such kind of disciples, it was necessary to publish anew even the precepts of the natural law and the current truths of the Gospel. We know moreover that these precepts implicitly contain all the perfection of the corresponding virtues.

Another and deeper reason guided the Holy Lawgiver in his choice: in thus blending sentences of the Christian life with those that concern monks only, St. Benedict wished to emphasise the plainly "Christian" character that he meant to give to his spirituality. The monk was to be first of all a man who observes the natural law, and then fully practises

1 Rule, ch. iv.

2 Cf. St. Gregory, *Dialogues*. Lib. ii, ch. 8. St. Benedict is seen overthrowing the idols of Monte Cassino; before this he had endured the infamous proceedings of a bad priest; he had only just escaped being poisoned by the wicked monks in the neighbourhood of Subiaco.

the Christian law. Religious perfection comes from the same root as Christian perfection in general; the holy Legislator combines the precepts and the counsels in close conjunction: never has the Evangelical ideal appeared more indivisible.

This is why the Patriarch does not arrange his instruments according to an altogether systematic order which would result from a methodical plan all traced out in advance. In this again, he resembles the Gospels, he is eminently simple—which does not prevent him from being sure—in his manner of leading souls to God. However, certain groups stand out clearly: here are instruments that concern our duties towards God; there are those that regulate our relations with our neighbour; finally others that more directly concern ourselves.

But whatever be the number and diversity of the said instruments, we must use them with discernment. We cannot attempt to employ them all at the same time, any more than we can practise all the virtues at the same time; souls are different and needs are various.

Some of the sentences recall general dispositions that ought always to animate us: "To love God with all our heart and with all our soul;—to prefer nothing to the love of Christ;—to desire eternal life with all the intensity of our love;—to keep guard at every hour over the actions of our life;—not to forget that God beholds us everywhere."

Other instruments are to be utilised at certain hours, for example at the moment of temptation: "To dash down at the feet of Christ evil thoughts as soon as they arise in the heart."

Others are particularly fitted to root out some vice or repress some evil inclination. It is for each soul to see what are the perverse inclinations that have the ascendency and tend to disfigure the divine image within it. When the soul is attached to the creature, it is fashioned to the image of this creature, and every bad tendency that is not striven against becomes, by the deeds that proceed from it, the origin of many stains that we have to remove in order to be made like Christ Jesus. With one soul it is pride that dominates and becomes the principle of a host of reprehensible deeds. To such a one our Blessed Father gives proper instruments for repressing the divers manifestations born of his pride: "Not to love contestations;—to fly from vainglory;—if one sees any good in oneself, to attribute it to God, and not to oneself;—on the contrary, to impute to oneself the evil that one does and to believe oneself the cause of it;—to hate one's own will;—not to wish to be esteemed as holy before one is so; but first of all to be holy that it may be with more truth that one is so called."

With another, it is levity of mind that hinders divine union; in the morning this soul is recollected; at Communion Our Lord descends into it and embalms it with the perfume of His Divinity; but, having left the oratory, this soul gives way to dissipation, indulges in useless words. If this imperfection is not fought against it will, during the day, make the monk lose a part of the fruits of his union with Christ. What ought he to do? Take the instruments appropriate to his defects: "Watch over his actions at every moment of his life;—keep his tongue from all unruly discourse;—not love much speaking." And so forth.

It is for each one to know himself in the light from on high and to seek what is still wanting to him; there is no one, however advanced, who will not find in this workshop the necessary instrument for perfecting in his soul the ineffable traits of the Divine Model.

III

Not only are souls different, but one and the same soul goes through different stages which our Holy Father has well defined.

The spiritual craft has its beginnings, and like all beginnings; these are painful. The entrance into the way of salvation is always narrow: *Via salutis non est nisi angusto initio incipiendo.*[1] Why is this? Because it is a "conversion" which we have to bring about. A man must divest himself of *his* way of envisaging things, of *his* manner of acting; he must renounce himself, go against his vicious habits, the tendencies of concupiscence, apply himself to uprooting vices, to destroying and rectifying, feature by feature, that caricature of God to which a soul plunged in sin may be likened; and this with so much the more perseverance as habits contrary to the virtues predominate in us. To get a statue out of a block of marble, one must first rough-hew the block. When we arrive at the monastery, we are a little like these rough blocks. In His goodness, God

1 Prologue of the Rule.

subjects us to His interior action, but gives us also into the hands of our Superiors and to our own personal efforts in order that from this work may come forth little by little the realisation of the Divine ideal. If we do not courageously take the necessary instruments and employ them faithfully, we shall remain very nearly in the state of unhewn blocks. Then as we are yet novices in the art to be practised, we are awkward, clumsy in the use of the instruments; hence we must feel our way; there are hesitations, perplexities, doubts, which may further increase what is rough in the work itself. It is a laborious stage to be gone through, but it is a necessary one.

Moreover St. Benedict takes care to encourage the soul at the outset. In this spiritual workshop, in this school where we learn to seek God, he has it at heart, he says, to establish nothing rigorous or too arduous.[1] He uses very great discretion; he is a father. To one who comes to place himself under his direction, he says: "If for the amendment of vices or the preservation of charity, things are a little strictly laid down": *Si quid paululum restrictius... processerit,* "take care, lest, under a cowardly emotion, you fly from the way of salvation of which the entrance is strait": *Non illico favore perterritus refugias viam salutis.*[2]

What argument does he employ? Does he relax anything of the vigour of the precepts? Does he dissemble the obligation of self-renunciation? Far from it, as we have seen. But he shows already the facilities and joys of acquired virtue, and gives a foretaste of the intimate rewards promised to effort. "In the measure one advances in the observance and in faith," he says, "the heart is enlarged and enables one to run with unutterable sweetness of love in the way of God's commandments": *Processu vero conversationis et fidei, inenarrabili dilectionis dulcedine curritur via mandatorum Dei.*[3] When one is generous from the outset, and attentive to the light of faith, love increases, for God gives Himself the more; and, with the presence of God, the joy of being in His service abounds. The heart is enlarged, our Blessed Father affirms. That is as much as to say the heart is the capacity of loving, and this capacity is infinite as regards the object whereto the soul must tend. "Thou hast made us for Thyself, O God, and our heart is restless till it rests in Thee": *Fecisti nos ad Te, et*

1 Ibid. 2 Ibid. 3 Ibid.

inquietum est cor nostrum donec requiescat in Te.[1] The actual capacity of the heart is measured by the object of its present affections: if this object is small, the heart becomes small; if this object is infinite, the heart enlarges its power even to the infinite. To one who sees God, creatures appear small: *Videnti Creatorem angusta est omnis creatura*, say St. Gregory,[2] in speaking of St. Benedict himself.

Now, when one truly seeks God, without going aside after creatures, without any self-seeking, the heart is gradually enlarged; God fills it and, with God, joy floods it.

Furthermore, this very joy augments the capacity of love; and then, says our Holy Father,—this is the second stage—one runs in the way of the commandments: there are no longer those painful beginnings, those oft repeated efforts with which one struggled, but, with the ever increasing *light* of faith, fervour stirs one up in God's service and renders that service full of sweetness. Then, whatever be the vicissitudes of life, the monk "never departs from the teaching of the Divine Master," Who is the Truth, "but perseveres in His doctrine," the light of the soul; and if he shares in Christ's sufferings it is that he may deserve by patience also to enjoy the bliss of His Kingdom.[3]

The last stage marked out by St. Benedict is that of perfect charity. This stage, he says, is attained when the soul is "purified from its vices and sins" *munda a vitiis et peccatis.*[4] Not only does the soul no longer obey its vicious habits, for it has uprooted them all as far as a creature can; but, in its activity, it no longer has any human mainspring of action, for all that it does, it does solely for the love of Christ and the attraction of virtue: *UNIVERSA... incipit CUSTODIRE, non jam timore gehennae, sed AMORE CHRISTI... et delectatione virtutum.*[5] The soul has placed the love

1 St. Augustine, *Confessions.* Lib. i, ch. 1.

2 *Dialogues.* Lib. ii, ch. 35.

3 Prologue of the Rule.

4 Rule, ch. vii.

5 "He begins to keep... all those precepts... no longer for fear of hell, but for love of Christ... and delight in virtue," Rule, ch. viii. St. Augustine, *Tract. V in I Joan.* n° 4, thus characterises these three stages: *Caritas cum fuerit nata nutritur; cum fuerit nutrita roboratur: cum fuerit roborata perficitur* (As soon as charity is born it is nourished; when it is nourished it grows strong; and when it grows strong it is made perfect). St. Thomas (II-II, q. 24, a. 9) classes the three categories of souls after this manner:

of Christ in the centre of itself, and this love makes it find everything light, however painful it be: then with great facility and perfection it acquits itself of labours that formerly with manifold efforts it only accomplished imperfectly. Virtue has become to it almost a second nature: *Absque ullo labore, velut naturaliter.*[1]

The state that we are describing is that of perfect charity, of the perfection of union with God: the soul no longer seeks aught but Him alone; it no longer wills anything except His glory; it no longer acts except by the movement of the Holy Spirit. Are there then no more trials to undergo? no more sufferings to endure? Yes, indeed; but the unction of grace sweetens every trial, and love finds in the cross a new opportunity of manifesting itself and increasing. Love is the principle of those wonderful interior ascensions that the Lord, by the action of His Spirit, operates and manifests in purified souls: *Quae Dominus in operario suo mundo a vitiis et peccatis Spiritu Sancto dignabitur demonstrare*![2]

IV

But whatever be the stage in which the soul is, its work, however, is never anything but a work of co-operation. The soul is not alone: God works in it and with it: for He is ever the first Author of its progress.

Doubtless, at the outset, when the soul is yet encumbered with vices and evil habits, it must needs apply itself with virility and ardour to remove these obstacles which are opposed to divine union. The co-operation that God requires of it at this period is particularly great and active, and is revealed very clearly to the conscience. During this period, God grants sensible graces that uplift and encourage. But the soul experiences inward vicissitudes: it falls, then rises up again; it labours, then rests; it takes breath again, and then goes forward on its way.

As far and in the measure as the soul advances, and obstacles give way, the inner life becomes more homogeneous, more regular, more uniform; the action of God is felt to be more powerful, because it is more free to

---

the *incipientes*, the *proficientes*, the *perfecti* (beginners, those who are progressing, the perfect).

1 Rule, ch. vii.

2 "And this will the Lord deign to show forth by the power of his Spirit in his workman now cleansed from vice and from sin," Ibid.

act and because it. meets with less resistance and more suppleness in the soul: then we rapidly go forward in the path of perfection.

All this economy of our religious life is explained by the fact that all holiness is of its essence supernatural. God alone is the Author of it; and if He does not Himself build the house it is in vain that the masons labour: *Nisi Dominus aedificaverit domum in vanum laboraverunt qui aedificant eam.*[3] Our Lord has so clearly given us this fundamental doctrine. "I am the Vine, you are the branches; abide in Me that you may bear fruit, for without Me you can do nothing": *Sine me nihil potestis facere.*[4] "Let no one," says St. Augustine in commenting upon this passage, "imagine that he can, by himself, bear the least fruit. Whether it is a matter of doing much or doing little, one can only succeed through the help of Him without Whom we can do nothing. If the branch does not remain united to the vine and does not draw the nourishing sap from the stem, it cannot by itself produce the least fruit": *Sive ergo parum, sive multum, sine illo fieri non potest sine quo nihil fieri potest... nisi in vite manserit et vixerit de radice, quantumlibet fructum a semetipso non potest ferre.*[5]

St Benedict well knows these important truths and their different aspects. He does not tell us to abstain from good works; quite the contrary, as we have seen at the beginning of this conference: we must do all that depends upon us. Although our Lord is the Fountainhead of our sanctification, He sees it good to leave to us a share of work to perform; for we are causes, really such, although entirely subordinate to the Divine causality. It is only on the condition that we generously and faithfully contribute the said share that He will continue and consummate in us the work of our sanctification. To imagine then that Christ will take upon Himself all the work would be a dangerous illusion; but to believe that we could do anything whatsoever without Him would be no less perilous. We must be convinced too that our works are only of value by reason of our union with Jesus.

Among the instruments that the Holy Legislator puts into our hands there is one which expressly concerns this necessity of referring everything, in the work of our perfection, to Divine grace: "To attribute any good one sees in oneself to God, and not to oneself: as to the evil always to impute it to oneself and recognise it as one's own": *Bonum*

3 Ps. cxxvi, 1.   4 Joan. xv, 5.   5 *Tract. in Joan.* lxxx, 3.

aliquod in se cum viderit, Deo applicet, non sibi; malum vero semper a se factum sciat et sibi reputet. But in what way does St. Benedict teach us how to make this conviction enter into the very trend of our life?

First, he inculcates the necessity of prayer, *at the very beginning* of every undertaking. In his Prologue, after having shown the end—to seek God—and marked the way—Christ—he immediately tells us not to put our hand to any good work without earnestly beseeching God to bring it to a good end: *In primis, ut quidquid agendum inchoas bonum, ab eo perfici instantissima oratione deposcas.* Weigh well all these terms, for each has its value. *In primis*: "first of all," "before all," the thing that he most wishes to teach us, is to have recourse to the One Who is the first and principal Author of our sanctification, because without His grace we can do nothing.

Quidquid... bonum: "whatever be the work proposed," that is to say a "good" work, morally good, which procures the glory of God, for it evidently cannot be question of an evil work, of a work wherein the creature, or the seeking after self enters as the principal end, or from which God would be absent. *Instantissima oratione*: "with most earnest prayer," for it is necessary to knock that God may open, to seek so that we may find, to ask so that we may receive. And what must we ask? That God will perfect our work: *ab eo perfici.* Manifestly, the holy Patriarch here has in mind the text of the Apostle: "For it is God Who worketh in you, both to will and to accomplish, according to His good will": *Deus est qui operatur in vobis et* VELLE ET PERFICERE *pro bona voluntate.*[1]

And see how our Holy Father himself applies this recommendation in his Rule. When monks go on a journey or return from one;[2] on entering into their functions as weekly servers at table and on ending their week's service;[3] in receiving guests;[4] in all these actions, so simple and ordinary in the course of our life, and in yet others, he wishes that the Community should go to the oratory there to invoke God's help.

The work ended, the good achieved, St. Benedict further wishes that we should refer the glory to Him without Whom we can do nothing. Those who seek God, he writes in his Prologue, are not to be puffed up by their good observance; "knowing that the good which is in them comes

1 Philip. ii, 13. 2 Rule, ch. lxvii. 3 Ibid. ch. xxxv.
4 Ibid. ch. liii.

not from their own power but is wrought by the Lord, they magnify the Lord Who worketh in them": *Operantem in se Dominum magnificant*, "saying with the Prophet, Not unto us, O Lord, not unto us, but unto Thy name give the glory."[1] "Again" he adds, "the Apostle Paul attributed nothing of the success of his preaching to himself, but said: By the grace of God I am what I am,[2] and elsewhere: He that glorieth, let him glory in the Lord."[3]

You will say: Are not our works our own? Certainly they are, since it is we who act; but these works are good *only* if we accomplish them, moved by grace, in the faith and love of Christ. We are the branches, Christ is the root. Is it the root that bears fruit? No, it is the branch, it is we ourselves; but it is the branch, inasmuch as it is united by the trunk to the root and draws its sap from the root; it is we, inasmuch as we are united to Christ Jesus and draw grace from Him. If, at the sight of a branch covered with beautiful fruits, we believe they are produced by the branch, abstraction made of its union with the root, we are in error; the branch only produces fruits by drawing from the root the sap necessary for their formation. So it is with us; never let us forget this; the branch separated from the trunk, from the root, is a dead branch: such is our lot unless we remain united to Christ by grace.

This union comprises moreover an indefinite number of degrees; the intenser and stronger it is, that is to say the fewer obstacles we oppose to grace, and the deeper our faith and love,—the more numerous will be the fruits that we shall bear.

It is, then, very important to direct our mind and heart towards God, with faith and love, before beginning anything whatsoever it may be: our mind, in order to have no other end before us but the glory of our Heavenly Father; our heart in order to have no other will save His: a twofold result which is the realisation of the "very earnest prayer" required by St. Benedict. This prayer which ought to be oft repeated throughout the course of the day, need not be long: being most often reduced to a simple turning towards God, to a spiritual spark rising up to Him, it rather resembles in form what in these latter days we call ejaculatory prayer. What gives it price and value is the rectitude of intention, the purity of our faith and the intensity of love. All this teaching wonder-

1 Prologue of the Rule; Ps. cxiii. 2 I Cor. xv, 10. 3 II Cor. x, 17.

fully harmonises with our Holy Father's assertion that a soul's progress towards perfection goes together with progress in faith. Faith increases love; love as it becomes greater, surrenders the soul more and more to the action of Christ Who works in us by His Spirit, and this action of Christ becomes more and more powerful and more fruitful in the measure that vices are uprooted, that the soul becomes more detached from creatures and that every human mainspring of action vanishes.

The great Patriarch strives in his Rule to open widely the avenues of our souls so that the grace of the Gospel may abundantly penetrate therein and produce all its effects of holiness: *OPERANTEM IN SE Dominum magnificant.*[1] He has no other end in organising the workshop of the spiritual craft and in giving us entry into it, than to ensure all freedom for the Divine action within us. He wishes us to seek God by our good works, but at the same time to rely solely upon His Divine Son Christ Jesus.

Once being thoroughly and practically convinced that all good comes from God, we are forever guaranteed against discouragement. Indeed if, without union with Christ by faith and love, we can do nothing, with this union we can do everything that God expects of us. Our oneness with Christ accords very well, not with sin—above all deliberate or habitual sin, even venial—but with our weaknesses, our miseries, and the short-comings inherent upon our fragility. Our Lord knows that "the spirit indeed is willing, but the flesh weak."[2] Let not our faults then cast us down nor temptations discourage us. The last instrument that our Holy Father marks out is "never to despair of the mercy of God": *Et de Dei misericordia nunquam desperare*. Even though we only know how to handle the other instruments imperfectly, let this one at least never be out of our grasp, *nunquam*. The devil delights, throughout the course of our spiritual life, in urging us to sadness, to discouragement, because he well knows that when the soul is sad it is led to abandon the exercise of good works, and that to its great detriment. When therefore a like sadness arises in our heart, we may be assured that it comes from the devil or from our own pride, and that, if we give way to it, we shall be

1 "They magnify the Lord working in them," Prologue of the Rule.

2 Matth. xxvi, 41.

listening to the devil who is so clever at playing upon our pride. Could a movement of distrust, of despair, come from God? Never, *nunquam*. Were we to fall into great faults, were we to have the unhappiness of living a long time in unfaithfulness, the Holy Spirit would doubtless urge us to penitence, to expiation, to immolation: St. Benedict exhorts us to weep for our past sins and to amend them,[1] but he would also stir us up to hope, to confidence in God "rich in mercy."[2] To distrust? To discouragement? To despair? Never. As long as we are here below we must never lose confidence: because the satisfactions and merits of Christ Jesus are infinite, because the Eternal Father has willed to place in Him all the treasures of grace and holiness that He destines for souls, and these treasures are inexhaustible; because Jesus prays and pleads for us with His Father: *Semper vivens ad interpellandum pro nobis*.[3] Our strength is in Him, not in ourselves: *Omnia possum in eo qui me confortat*.[4]

"O Lord, let the action of Thy mercy direct our hearts, for without Thee we are not able to please Thee": *Dirigat corda nostra quaesumus, Domine, tuae miserationis operatio: quia tibi sine te placere non possumus!*[5]

V

Praiseworthy though it be ardently to seek God by good works and especially by works of the Rule, we must yet be forearmed against a certain erroneous conception of perfection, which is sometimes to be met with in not very enlightened souls. It may happen that these place the *whole* of perfection in the *merely outward and material observance*. Although the word I am going to use is severe, I do not hesitate to pronounce it: the abovesaid prejudicial idea would border upon pharisaism or would risk leading to it and that would be a great danger.

You know what our Divine Saviour, Who is very Truth and Goodness, said to His disciples: "Unless your justice abound more than that of... the Pharisees, you shall not enter into the Kingdom of Heaven."[6] These words are truly those of Christ. He Who would not condemn the woman taken in adultery; Who vouchsafed to speak with the Samaritan

1 Rule, ch. iv. 2 Eph. ii, 4. 3 Hebr. vii, 25.
4 "I can do all these things in him who strengtheneth me," Phil. iv, 13.
5 Collect for the eighteenth Sunday after Pentecost. 6 Matth. v, 20.

woman and reveal heavenly mysteries to her in spite of her guilty life: He Who consented to eat with the Publicans, socially disqualified as sinners; Who allowed Magdalen to wash His feet and wipe them with the hairs of her head; He Who was so "meek and humble of heart,"[1] publicly hurled anathemas at the Pharisees: "Woe to you... hypocrites, because you shut the kingdom of heaven against men, for yourselves do not enter in."[2]

The Pharisees passed in the eyes of the multitude as holy personages. They esteemed themselves saints, and made all perfection consist in the exactitude of outward observances. You know too how their fidelity to the letter and this exactitude were so fastidious that the examples given of their formalism are sometimes ludicrous.[3] Not content with thus scrupulously keeping the Law of Moses, which already constituted a heavy burden, they added thereto a whole catalogue of prescriptions of their own invention—what our Lord called "the tradition of men."[4] All this was so well observed exteriorly that in this respect there was nothing with which to reproach them: impossible to find more correct disciples of Moses. Call to mind the Pharisee whom Christ depicts going up to the Temple to pray. What is his prayer? "My God, I am a man altogether irreproachable; I fast, I give tithes: Thou canst not find me in fault on any point, Thou oughtest to be proud of me."[5] And in the literal sense, what he said was true: he did observe all these things. However, what judgment does Jesus pass upon him? This man went out of the Temple without being justified, his heart empty of God's grace. Why this condemnation? Because the unhappy man glorified himself for his good actions and placed all his perfection in merely outward observance, without troubling himself about the inward dispositions of his heart. Therefore our Lord tells us that unless our justice is greater than that of the Pharisees we shall have no part in the Kingdom of Heaven.

Do we enter into the deep signification of these words? What is the Christian life? A list of observances? In nowise. It is the life of Christ within us, and all that Christ has appointed to maintain this life in us; it is the Divine life overflowing from the bosom of the Father into Christ

---

1 Ibid. xi, 29. 2 Ibid. xxiii, 13.

3 See *Christ in His Mysteries,* ch. 11. *Some Aspects of the Public Life.*

4 Marc. vii, 8. 5 Cf. Luc. xviii, 11–12.

Jesus and, through Him, into our souls. There is the supernatural life in its foundation and at its fountainhead; and without this all the rest is nothing. Are we to understand by this that the exterior prescriptions of Christianity are to be disdained? Far from it. Their observance is at once the normal condition and the obligatory manifestation of the interior life. But the first is the more important, as the soul, in man, is more important than the body: the soul is spiritual, immortal, created to the image of God; the body, a little earthly clay; but the soul is only created at the moment of being united to the body, and the exercise of its faculties depends on the good constitution of the body. In the Church of Christ, there are also the soul and the body. Following the normal law, it is necessary to belong to the body, to the visible Church, and observe her commandments, in order to participate in her intimate life, the life of grace; but the Christian life must not be placed principally in the outward observance of material ordinances.

In the same way, the essence of the monastic life does not consist in the horarium of our daily life. It may happen that a monk succeeds by force of will and energy in keeping all the rules, and yet has no monastic spirit, no true inner life: there is the body, but not the soul. And in fact it is not so rare to find religious whose spiritual progress is very slow, although their outward exactitude lends itself to no reproach. It is because there is often only self-seeking and self-complacency in this exactitude, or because they look down on their brethren who do not appear to be so faithful; or else because they put their perfection in the exterior observance itself. Now, *of themselves* these observances are small matters: one is worth as much as another.[1] As Christ Himself said, John the Baptist drank no wine, and he was blamed; the Son of man ate of what was set before Him, and the Pharisees still disapproved of Him, for they were a race of "hypocrites."[2]

If it is then somewhat indifferent, in itself, what our exterior practices be, it does not the less remain that we have promised to keep them: hence, this observance, when animated by love, is extremely pleasing to God. I say: "animated by love." It is in the heart that perfection lies; for love is the supreme law. Christ Jesus "searches hearts and He sees that one

1 See what we have said above p. 68 on the width of St. Benedict's views on this matter. 2 Cf. Matth. xi, 18–19; Luc. vii, 33–34.

who says and believes he loves, but without proving it by deeds, does not love. But likewise one who exteriorly keeps Christ's words, and does not act from love, does not truly keep these words. *We must join the doing of His word with His love*, because His chief word, and the abridgment of His doctrine is that we must love."[1]

The observing of the Rule does not constitute holiness, but it constitutes a means of arriving at holiness. You may say: Must we not observe all that is prescribed? Certainly we must; for oftentimes an habitual and wilful infidelity upon such or such a point of the Rule—prayer, charity, silence, work—suffices to shackle our progress in the path of perfection. Only, bear this well in mind:—What is important in our observance is the *inner principle* that animates us. The Pharisees observed all things exactly but it was that they might be seen and applauded by the multitude: and this moral deviation utterly spoiled all their works. As to the outward observance, kept mathematically, but for its own sake and without anything to ennoble it, we may at least say that it is in nowise perfection.

The interior life must be the soul of our exterior fidelity. It must be the result, the fruit and manifestation of the faith, confidence and love that govern our heart. The Rule is the expression of God's Will. Now the fulfilling of the Rule out of love constitutes fidelity. Fidelity is the most precious and delicate flower of love here below. Up above, in heaven, love will blossom out into thanksgiving, in delight and enjoyment, in the full and entire possession of the beloved object; here, upon earth, it is manifested by a generous and constant fidelity to God, despite the obscurity of faith, despite trials, difficulties, oppositions.

After the example of our Divine Model, we ought to give ourselves unreservedly, as He gave Himself unreservedly to the Father on entering into the world: *Ecce venio*, "Behold I come... that I should do Thy will": *Ut faciam voluntatem tuam*.[2] Each morning, when, after Holy Communion, we make but one with Him, let us renew our disposition of wishing to belong entirely to Him. O Jesus, I wish to live by Thy life, through faith and love; I wish Thy desires to be my desires, and, like Thee, out of love for Thy Father, I wish to do all that may be pleasing to

1 Bossuet, *Meditations on the Gospel,* The Last Supper, 93rd day.

2 Ps. xxxix, 8–9. Heb. x, 7 and 9.

Thee: I have placed "Thy law in the midst of my heart": *Et legem tuam in medio* CORDIS MEI.[1] It is pleasing to Thee when I faithfully keep the prescriptions of the Christian law which Thou hast established and those of the monastic code which I have accepted; as proof of the delicacy of my love for Thee, I wish to say as Thou hast said Thyself: Neither a jot nor a tittle shall be taken away by me from Thy law: *Iota unum aut unus apex non praeteribit a lege donec omnia fiant*;[2] grant me Thy grace that I may not let the least thing pass that could give Thee pleasure, in order that, according to Thine own word, being faithful in small things, I may likewise become so in great things;[3] grant above all that I may ever act out of love for Thee and for Thy Father: *Ut cognoscat mundus quia diligo Patrem*;[4] my sole desire is to be able to say like Thee "I do always the things that please Him," *Quia placita sunt ei, facio semper*.[5]

This is the programme that our Lord traced out for the Blessed Bonomo, an Italian nun: "Before each of thy actions, offer all to Me, with thy whole being, asking of Me the help and grace to do nothing except for Me: for I am thy End, thy God, and thy Lord Whom thou oughtest to please."[6]

All things done in love—love being the mainspring of all our activity and the guardian of all our fidelity: is not this the very formula of perfection? Love it is that measures, in the last resort, the value of all our actions, even of the most ordinary.

Thus St. Benedict points out as the first "instrument" the love of God: "In the first place, *in primis*, to love the Lord God with all one's heart, all one's soul and all one's strength." This is as much as to say: Place love in your heart before all things; let love rule and guide you in all your actions; it is love that is to put in your hands all the other instruments of good works; it is love that will give a high value to the most insignificant details of your days. Little things, says St. Augustine, are little in themselves, but they become great through the faithful love with which

1 Ps. xxxix, 8–9. 2 Matth. v, 18. 3 Cf. Luc. xvi, 10.
4 Joan. xiv, 31. 5 Joan. viii, 29.
6 *La B^se Bonomo, moniale bénédictine* by D. du Bourg, p. 54. Read above all in *The Book of Special Grace* of St. Mechtilde, chapter xxvii of the 3rd part: *How the heart of man is united to the Heart of God.*

they are done: *Quod minimum est, minimum est; sed in minimis fidelem esse magnum est.*[1]

Outward observance, sought after for its own sake, without the inward love which quickens it, is a formal show—even a Pharisaical show. An interior love pretending to dispense with the exterior faithfulness which is its fruit, would be an illusion, for our Lord tells us that he who loves Him keeps His commandments.[2] And this is true of the monastic life as it is of the Christian life. Christ Jesus says to us: You protest that you love Me? It is for My Name's sake that you have left all things: *Propter nomen meum*?[3] Then keep faithfully the least points of your Rule.

The ideal we ought to have in view is the exactitude of love: not scruple, nor anxiety never to make a mistake, nor the wish of being able to say: "I will never be found in fault": there is pride in this. It is from the heart that the inner life springs; and if you possess it, you will seek to fulfil by love all you have to do with the greatest purity of intention, and the greatest care possible. *Universa custodire... amore Christi*:[4] St. Benedict says, the monk ought to be faithful in all things "for the love of Christ."

Let us take care then not to content ourselves with regulating the outward behaviour; God must have His own spectacle; that is to say, a heart which seeks Him in secret.[5] And this is what our great Patriarch asks of us: that we should seek God in the sincerity of our hearts: *Si revera Deum quaerit.*[6]

VI

In this exactitude which is born of love there is something easy, wide, free, lovable, joyous. On the contrary, if a monk places *all* his perfection in *merely* outward observance, it often happens that, when even without any fault of his own, he is unable to carry out such or such a prescription he is troubled and upset; he imagines that his spiritual edifice is about to crumble into ruins, and that perfection is not for him. If this happens repeatedly he gets discouraged, and this sense of discouragement

---

1 *De doctrina christiana,* Lib. iv, ch. 18. Was it not Pascal who wrote: "Do small things as well as great for the sake of the majesty of Jesus Christ Who does them in us?"

2 Joan. xiv, 21. 3 Matth. xix, 29. 4 Rule, ch. vii.

5 Bossuet, *Meditations upon the Gospel,* The Sermon on the Mount, 20th day.

6 Rule, ch. lviii.

is easily to be understood, since, for him, all is summed up and made to consist in outward observance.

On account of this same false principle, it will sometimes occur that he fails in charity towards his brethren and creates friction. Having to choose between the observance and an accidental occasion of helping someone, he will not hesitate: "The observance before everything!" This is servitude to the "letter," with its aridity and hardness. See how the Pharisees reproached our Divine Saviour for healing the sick on the Sabbath day:[1] under the pretext that the Sabbath was a day of rest,[2] they even reproached the disciples because, being hungry, they rubbed the ears of corn in their hands to eat.

Opposed to this, one who loves Christ Jesus and does all for love, enjoys, at the same time, a great liberty in regard to observances. In fact, not placing his perfection principally in material practices, he does not seek them for themselves; and when, in consequence of some circumstance, he is prevented from accomplishing them, he is not unduly troubled, because he is not attached to them. And if, as may happen, he sees one of his brethren in need, he does not hesitate, first of all, to help his brother, even if such or such a prescription—we are supposing, of course, that it does not oblige under sin—has to be put aside. Some might say as the Pharisees said of Jesus: "This man is not of God, who keepeth not the sabbath";[3] but this is taking scandal in a Pharisaical spirit to which no attention must be paid.

Let us learn by this that we ought not generally to make ourselves the judges of how our brethren observe the Rule. There are some who, outwardly, may appear less correct than others, yet whose inner life is more intense. The ideal would be doubtless that there should be nothing to blame in them, but it is not for us to set ourselves up as censors of our brethren. Let us not then be Pharisees; lest thinking so much of being a monk, it may befall that one is no longer either Christian, or human, and fails in the great natural precept of charity.

See how well these truths were understood by our great Lawgiver. He assuredly esteemed the monastic observances which after a long experience he had himself laid down. But none the less he knew how to make them cede to a higher motive. When for example on a fast day a guest

---

1 Luc. vi, 11. 2 Matth. xii, 2. 3 Joan. ix, 16.

arrives, St. Benedict wishes that, out of humanity and charity for this guest, the prior who receives him shall break his fast: *Jejunium a priore frangatur propter hospitem.*[1] A Pharisee would not have acted thus: he would have fasted and... made his guest fast! But our Holy Father "full of the spirit of all the just,"[2] places perfection before all things in charity, whether it goes directly to God, or is manifested to Christ in the person of the neighbour.

You will not mistake my meaning. I in nowise mean to sanction failings in the observance, nor to excuse negligences, the letting things go; far from that; I only want you to appreciate each thing at its true value. Never forget that the very source of the value of our deeds is in our oneness with Christ Jesus by grace, in the love wherewith we perform our actions. To this end, we must, as our Holy Father says, direct our intention towards God before each good work that we undertake, with great intensity of faith and love: *Quidquid agendum inchoas bonum, ab eo perfici instantissima oratione deposcas.*[3]

VII

What we have undertaken for God and put under His protection, we must never, by our own fault, cease to pursue. It is only at the cost of persevering faithfulness, says St. Benedict, that we shall deserve the reward promised to the good servant.

Perseverance is, in fact, the virtue that consummates and crowns all the others.

We must be careful to distinguish this virtue from the gift of final perseverance by which we "die in the Lord"; this gift is purely gratuitous, and, says the Council of Trent, "none can, with absolute certitude, be assured that it will be granted to him."[4]

However, the Holy Council adds, "we ought to have and to keep the most lively confidence in God's help, for God is all-powerful to finish in us the good that He has begun, unless we ourselves be unfaithful to grace": *Nisi ipsi illius gratiae defuerint.*[5]

---

1 Rule, ch. liii.
2 St. Gregory, *Dialogues.* Lib. ii, ch. 8.
3 Prologue of the Rule.
4 Sess. vi, ch. 13.
5 Ibid.

The means then given to us in order that we may count upon this infinitely precious gift, the gift exceeding all others, is daily fidelity; and we shall carry out well and to its end the great work of our whole life, if we carry out well and to its end each work that we undertake for God: this is the object of the virtue of perseverance.

St. Thomas[1] most justly links this virtue to the virtue of fortitude. What indeed is fortitude? It is a disposition of steadfastness which inclines the soul to support valiantly all evils, even the worst and most continuous, rather than forsake good; pushed to the supreme degree, fortitude goes so far as to endure martyrdom.

This virtue of fortitude is particularly required by cenobites living together in a monastery. It seems truly as if Providence, in instituting cloisters, had, besides its principal design, a secondary one. The principal design is to create the *coenobitarum fortissimum genus*,[2] the secondary design to receive now and then weak souls who rely upon the strong. Thus in a forest of giant trees, beautiful and powerful, shrubs are not completely excluded from the soil where the former flourish. Here and there shrubs live in the shade of their great elders and protectors, but they do not make the forest. St. Benedict does not intend to discourage weak souls, but it is chiefly to the ambition of the strong that he opens the avenues to perfection. It is in conformity with the spirit of the great Patriarch that the abbot does not always repulse a postulant who avows his fears in face of the temptations of the world and declares that one of the reasons that brings him to the cloister is the desire of security, provided that this postulant "truly seeks God," and that there is an underlying seriousness in his character. But the holy Lawgiver addresses himself above all to resolute souls; they alone are able to attain these "summits of virtue": *culmina virtutum*,[3] indicated by St. Benedict.

This in fact is because fortitude is not only the principle of "aggression" *aggredi*, but it is likewise that of "endurance" *sustinere*; and as this requires more steadfastness of soul than the former, it constitutes, says St. Thomas, the principal act of the virtue of fortitude: *Principalior actus fortitudinis est sustinere*.[4] Now, the religious life, *faithfully* led in the cloister, at once demands and teaches this endurance; of its nature, it

1 II-II, q. cxxxvi, a. 2.

2 "The most strong race of cenobites," Rule, ch. i.

3 Rule, ch. lxxii.

4 II-II, q. cxxiii, a. 6.

tends to establish in the soul a steadfastness which can even go so far as to be heroic, and this so much the more real in that it is the more hidden.

This is because, on the one hand, the changeableness of our nature is extreme, and, in the long run, the life tells on the firmest will. On the other hand, the life led in community offers nothing to poor nature that can flatter or distract it. Daily to bear generously and in the obscurity of faith,[1] the monotony inherent to the claustral life, stability in the same place, the accomplishment of the same ever repeated exercises, however minute they may be, the yoke of obedience, above all when it goes against or offers violence to nature; and that, as St. Benedict wishes, "with patience, in silence, without growing weary or giving in." *Tacita conscientia patientiam amplectatur et sustinens non lassescat vel discedat.*[2] Daily to acquit oneself carefully of the task assigned by obedience, however humble, hidden from sight, or thankless it may be, without that strong incentive to human activity which is the struggle against exterior obstacles, without seeking compensation from creatures, without encountering those distractions those diversions, so frequent in the world, which break the uniformity of occupations,—all this requires of the soul singular endurance, self-mastery and firmness.[3]

We understand God's saying in Holy Scripture: "The patient man is better than the valiant: and he that ruleth his spirit, than he that taketh cities"; *Melior est patiens viro forti, et qui dominatur animo suo expugnatore urbium*;[4] we understand why St. Benedict qualifies disobedience as "sloth,"[5] and the weapon of obedience which he gives to his disciples, as "strongly tempered,"[6] and it is enough to read the fourth degree of

1 All things being otherwise equal, it requires more faith for anyone living the hidden life with God (Whom he does not see experimentally) than for one who performs outward works of which he can estimate the progress and measure the result of his efforts.

2 Rule, ch. vii.

3 One day Mabillon was asked to reveal the extraordinary actions, which to his way of thinking would manifest or testify to the perfection of life of one of the most eminent religious of the Congregation of St. Maur, D. Claude Martin. This great monk wrote but two lines, but they contain a most profound truth: "I know nothing of Dom Martin except what everyone has seen, but his constant and uniformly good life holds for me the place of a miracle." *Vie de D. Claude Martin,* Tours 1697, p. 388.

4 Prov. xvi, 32. 5 Prologue of the Rule. 6 Ibid.

humility in order to see to what heights of heroic endurance he invites his sons to climb.[1]

Thus, if faithfully observed, the Rule becomes a principle of fortitude; in disciplining the will, it tempers it as steel is tempered; directing the will, it increases its energies tenfold and saves it from dispersing them.[2] It has become a commonplace to speak of the patience of true monks at work, of their holy pertinacity and faithfulness to their task.[3] They have given the example of conscientious and persevering toil under every form. Thus they became, in the middle ages, the pioneers of Christian civilisation in Europe.[4] Would such results have been possible if the cloisters had only contained feeble souls? Assuredly not.

We are not then astonished that the great monks showed themselves to be strong souls. Where, if not in the cloister, did holy missionaries like Boniface and Adalbert find the secret of crowning with martyrdom a long apostolic life and incessant labours? Where did such as Anselm, Gregory VII and Pius VII obtain that wonderful steadfastness of soul which sustained them in their memorable conflicts for the liberty of the Church? Again it was in the cloister. It was the common life of the cloister that tried and moulded their souls, strengthened their characters and made them so intrepid and magnanimous that no danger affrighted them, no obstacle held them back, who, according to the noble saying of Gregory VII himself to the monks of Cluny, "never bent beneath the domination of the princes of this world and remained the courageous and submissive defenders of St. Peter and of his Church... Monks and abbots have not failed this Holy Church their Mother."

It is this daily endurance in the common life, this toilsome fidelity, that St. Benedict requires of us in this workshop where he distributes

---

1 It is remarkable that in this single paragraph the great Patriarch heaps up terms signifying endurance: once the words *sufferre, non discedere, non lassescere* (suffer, do not withdraw, do not grow weary); twice the word *patientia* (patience) and four times that of *sustinere* (endure).

2 Read on this subject the beautiful pages of Buathier, in *Le Sacrifice,* ch. 16, *Le Sacrifice et la Volonté.*

3 The holy Lawgiver wars against every form and manifestation of instability, versatility, caprice. See for example, ch. xlviii; he will have the monks to read *per ordinem ex integro* (right through consecutively) the books given them by the abbot to be read during Lent.

4 Cf. Berlière, L. c., ch. 2 and 3, *L'apostolat monastique; l'œuvre civilisatrice.*

our tasks and provides us with the instruments of our sanctification. It is "day and night" *die noctuque*, that is to say "unceasingly," *incessabiliter*,[1] that he would have us use these instruments, without being wearied by the length of the task, without being discouraged by our want of success, without letting ourselves be cast down by our failures.

The virtue of fortitude constantly exercised, preserved and sustained until our last day constitutes perseverance. And it is to acquire this that our great Patriarch exhorts us so explicitly when he tells us never to depart from the teaching of the Divine Master, but to persevere in His teaching in the monastery until death: *Ab ipsius nunquam magisterio discedentes, in ejus doctrina usque ad mortem in monasterio perseverantes*.[2]

In order to quicken and sustain us in the practice of endurance, our Holy Father places the Divine Ideal before our eyes; he appeals to the supreme motive: the love of Christ Jesus: "That we may by patience share in the sufferings of Christ": *Passionibus Christi PER PATIENTIAM participemur*.[3]

Indeed it is to Christ Jesus we must cleave. We cannot be His disciples if, having put our hand to the plough, we look back[4] and shirk the weary labour. Only he who perseveres unto death shall be saved: *Qui perseveraverit usque in finem hic salvus erit*.[5] Christ Jesus prepares a place in His Kingdom only for those who have continued with Him in trial: *Vos estis qui permansistis mecum in tentationibus meis, et ego dispono vobis regnum*.[6]

Let us listen to these grave words of teaching from the infallible Truth. Let us ask God daily, for the gift of final perseverance, and repeat the prayer that the Church puts upon our lips each day at Holy Mass: "O Lord, establish our days in Thy peace, deliver us from eternal damnation, and vouchsafe to number us in the flock of Thy elect."[7] "Make us ever adhere to Thy commandments and never suffer us to be separated from Thee."[8]

If we are faithful, despite temptations and difficulties, the day of reward promised by God will come for us; this is the assurance the great Patriarch gives us in ending this chapter on "The Instruments of Good Works": *Illa merces nobis a Domino recompensabitur quam ipse promisit*.

1 Rule, ch. iv.
2 Prologue of the Rule.
3 Ibid.
4 Luc. ix, 62.
5 Matth. x, 22.
6 Luc. xxii, 28–29.
7 Canon of the Mass.
8 Prayer before the Communion.

If we have had that constant application which love brings to the perfect fulfilment of our Heavenly Father's wishes, if we have done "always the things that please Him," *Quae placita sunt ei facio* SEMPER,[1] we shall certainly receive the magnificent reward promised in these words by Him Who is Faithfulness itself: "Well done, good and faithful servant: because thou hast been faithful over a few things, I will Place thee over many things: enter thou into the joy of thy Lord."[2]

Each Saint on entering into Heaven hears these blessed words that form the welcome he receives from Christ Jesus. And what are these things in which Our Lord gives him a share? God Himself, in His Trinity and His perfections; and, with God, all spiritual good. The soul will be like unto God for it will "see Him as He is": *Similes ei erimus, quoniam videbimus eum sicuti est.*

Through this ineffable vision, which succeeds to faith, the soul will be fixed in God, and will find in Him the Divine stability; it will for ever be knit in a perfect embrace, and without the fear of ever losing Him, to the Supreme and Immutable Good: *Participatio incommutabilis boni.*[3]

Whilst waiting till the splendours of eternal light shine before our purified sight, let us often repeat this prayer of the Church which well epitomises the different points of this conference: "O God, Who in Thy love dost restore the beauty of innocence, direct towards Thee the hearts of Thy servants: that the fervour of love which is born of Thy Spirit may make them steadfast in faith, and faithful in practising Thy Law": *Deus innocentiae* RESTITUTOR *et amator,* DIRIGE AD TE *tuorum* CORDA *servorum: ut spiritus tui* FERVORE *concepto, et* IN FIDE *inveniantur* STABILES, *et* IN OPERE EFFICACES.[4]

1 Joan. viii, 29. 2 Matth. xxv, 21.
3 St. Augustine. *Epist. ad Honorat.* cxl, 31.
4 Feria iv post Dominicam II Quadragesimae.

THE WAY OF ABNEGATION

Reliquimus Omnia

COMPUNCTION OF HEART

SUMMARY.—The "return to God" is only possible on condition of first removing the obstacles opposed to it.—I. Compunction, most efficacious means of putting away sin; it is the habitual sense of contrition.—II. What the Saints of the Church think of this disposition.—III. Far from being incompatible with confidence and complacency in God, compunction strengthens them.—IV. It makes us strong against temptation.—V. How we ought to resist temptation.—VI. Means of acquiring compunction; prayer, frequent contemplation of the sufferings of Jesus.

FROM the first lines of the Prologue of the Rule, St. Benedict, addressing himself to the soul, presents the monastic life as "a returning to God": *Ut ad Eum redeas a quo recesseras.* You know the reason of this: it is that sin has, from our birth, turned us away from God: *Eratis longe,*[1] says St. Paul. By sin, the soul turns away from God, the Infinite and Immutable Good, to give itself to the creature, which is but transitory good; this is the definition that St. Thomas gives of sin: *Aversio ab incommutabili bono et conversio ad commutabile bonum.*[2] If then we wish "to seek God sincerely," we must sever all inordinate at-

1 Ephes. ii, 13.

2 "The turning away from the immutable good... and the turning to mutable good," I-II, q. lxxxvii, a. 4 and II-II, q. clxii, a. 6.

tachment to the creature in order to turn entirely to God. This is what St. Benedict calls "conversion": *Veniens quis ad conversionem.*[1]

Our holy Father in speaking of "conversion" does not here attach to the word the very particular and precise meaning that we commonly give to it, but he views as a whole the actions whereby the soul, in turning away from sin and setting itself free from the creature and every human motive, exerts all its powers to remove the obstacles that hinder it from going to God and seeking Him alone.

Between sin and God there is, as you know, absolute incompatibility; there is not, says St. Paul, any possible concord between Christ and Belial, the father of sin.[2] And therefore to imagine that God will allow Himself to be found by us, will give Himself to us without our having to leave sin is to be under an illusion; and this illusion, more frequent than we think, is dangerous. We should ardently desire the Divine Word to be united to us; but this desire should be effectual and urge us to destroy all that is opposed in us to this union. There are some minds that find admirable—as indeed it is—what they call the "positive side" of the spiritual life: love, prayer, contemplation, union with God, but forget that all this is only to be found with certainty in a soul purified from all sin, from all evil habits, and that constantly tends, by a life of generous vigilance, to abate the sources of sin and imperfection. The spiritual edifice is very fragile when it is not based upon the constant flight from sin, for it is built upon sand.

When one sees the terrible examples of those who abandon their priesthood, of those religious who "make the angels weep,"[3] one asks oneself: "How can these things be possible? Whence come these falls? Do these disasters come about all at once?" No; these are not sudden falls; it is often necessary to go a long way back to trace the beginning of them. The foundations of the house were long since undermined by pride, self-love, presumption, sensuality, the lack of the fear of God. At a given moment, a great wind of temptation arose which shook the edifice and overthrew it.

Thus St. Benedict is very careful to point out to us the necessity of working at personal self-conquest, the logical preliminary to all development, to all preservation of the divine life in the soul. And because in

1 Rule, ch. lviii. 2 II Cor. vi, 15. 3 Cf. Isa. xxxiii, 7.

us these roots of sin, which are the triple concupiscence of the eyes, of the flesh and of the pride of life, are never entirely destroyed, this work never completely ceases; although in the measure that it advances, the soul, gaining spiritual liberty, moves more at ease, it still must never renounce vigilance.

The holy Legislator therefore wishes this work to become the object of a promise that obliges us throughout life. This is the meaning of the second of our vows, the vow of "conversion of manners": *Promitto... conversionem morum meorum.*[1] By this vow we are bound to tend to perfection, that is to say to union, through love, with God and His holy will.

There are obstacles that prevent this union: hence the seeking after perfection requires of us that we should first remove these obstacles from our path. St. Benedict is very explicit on this point; he puts within our hands the "instruments" destined to root out vices: "Not to give way to anger; not to harbour a desire of revenge; not to foster guile in one's heart; not to give marks of affection that are not sincere; not to return evil for good; to keep one's mouth from evil and wicked words,"[2] etc. He likewise wishes that we should "daily confess to God in prayer, with tears and sighs, our past sins, and amend them for the time to come": *De ipsis malis de cetero emendare.*[3]

Then, furthermore, he declares that it is only when the soul is purified from vice and sin, that the Holy Spirit will fully act within it, and perfect love reign as the principle of its life.[4]

You see that this work of destroying sin and attachment to sin is necessary, if we wish to go to God and find Him alone. Doubtless, we shall not give ourselves up to this labour for the sake of the labour itself; we shall embrace it as a condition of life, as the means for the development and preservation of divine union within us. Let us then examine, with some detail, how we ought to devote ourselves to it. It will be apparent that one of the best ways of succeeding in it is compunction of heart;—we shall see what the saints and the Church think of this sense of com-

1 Cf. Rule, ch. lviii. We do not take it upon ourselves to affirm anything as to the true reading of the word *conversio* or *conversatio,* but we take the expression *conversio morum* in the traditional sense.

2 Rule, ch. iv. 3 Ibid. 4 Ibid. ch. vii.

punction;—the precious advantages that it brings to the soul;—finally, the sources that foster it.

I

The essential obstacle to divine union is mortal sin, while deliberate venial sin is opposed to all progress.

By mortal sin the soul turns away entirely from God in order to make the creature its end; separation from God is radical, and union is destroyed. This is so true that if death surprises the soul in this state it is forever fixed in this separation from God: "Depart from Me, ye cursed": *Discedite a me maledicti.*[1] The Heavenly Father does not recognise the likeness of His Son in the sinner, who is therefore eternally excluded from the inheritance. As you know, it is by perfect contrition and the Sacrament of Penance that this state is destroyed; in the Sacrament, Christ's infinite merits are applied to the soul to purify it from its sins.

There is no need to have recourse to the Sacrament of Penance for venial sins, although it is an excellent thing to do so.

An act of charity, a fervent Communion, suffices to blot out venial sins provided one has no attachment to them, but, in formulating this last condition, we set forth a truth which, in the spiritual life, has great importance.

Indeed when it is a question of perfection, we must carefully distinguish between venial sin and venial sin. A venial sin, a sin of surprise, which escapes us from weakness, cannot keep us back in our seeking after God; we rise from it with humility, and find in the remembrance of it a new stimulus for loving God the more. But bear this well in mind, it is quite otherwise with venial sin, habitual or fully deliberate. When a soul regularly commits deliberate venial sins, when it coolly consents without remorse, to wilful and habitual infidelities against the Rule, even though the Rule does not oblige under sin, it is impossible for this soul to make true and constant progress in perfection. It is not our weaknesses, our infirmities of body or mind that impede the action of grace; God knows our misery and remembers that we are but dust. But it is a disposition that, so to speak, paralyses God's action within us; it is the attachment

1 Matth. xxv, 4.

to our own judgment and self-love, which is the most fruitful source of our infidelities and deliberate faults. A few days before His blessed Passion our Divine Saviour beholding Jerusalem began to weep over the city: *Flevit super illam.*[1] "How often would I have gathered together thy children... and thou wouldst not": *Et noluisti.*[2] Weigh well this word: *noluisti.* When our Lord meets with resistance, even in small matters, He feels, so to speak, the powerlessness of His work in the soul. Why is this? Because this soul fosters habits which form and maintain obstacles to Divine union. God would communicate Himself, but these barriers prevent the fulness of His action; He finds no response to His Divine advances; the soul, day by day says "no" to the inspirations of the Holy Spirit Who urges it to obedience, humility, charity and self-forgetfulness. It is then impossible for it to make any real progress.

Not only does this soul no longer mount towards God, but it is much to be feared that it will fall into grave sins. The above mentioned venial sins are the first step towards the severance of divine union. There is no longer, in such souls, enough vigour to resist temptation. The Holy Spirit ends by being silent when He is "grieved"—it is St. Paul's word[3]—by wilful resistance; and simply a shock is often enough to cause the soul to fall into a mortal sin; experience abundantly proves this.

This state of tepidity is particularly dangerous when it concerns sins of the mind, pride, disobedience; it places as it were a wall between God and us; and as God is the source of all our perfection, the soul that closes itself to the divine action shuts itself out from all progress.

One of the best means of avoiding this perilous state is to cultivate compunction of heart.

For us, who are bound to seek perfection, this point is of extreme importance. If so many souls make little progress in the love of God; if there are so many who easily accomodate themselves—alas for them!—to venial sin and deliberate infidelities, it is because they are not touched with compunction. What then is compunction?

It is an abiding state of habitual contrition. Here is a good man who has given way to a grievous fault; this unhappily can befall, for in the world of souls there are abysses of weakness as there are heights of ho-

1 Luc. xix, 41. 2 Matth. xxiii, 37. 3 Eph. iv, 30.

liness. The Divine Mercy gives this man the grace of rising again; he confesses his sin with deep and true repentance. It is quite evident that at the moment when he grieves so sincerely at having committed this fault he will not go and commit it anew.

Look at the Prodigal Son on his return to his father's house. Do we picture him taking careless, free and easy airs, as if he had been always faithful? No, indeed. You may say: has not his father forgiven him everything? Certainly he has; he has received his son with open arms without making any reproach. He did not say: "You are a miserable wretch"; no, he pressed him to his heart. And his son's return has even given the father such joy that he prepares a great feast for the penitent. All is forgotten, all is forgiven. The conduct of the prodigal's father is the image of the mercy of our Heavenly Father. But as for the prodigal now he is forgiven, what are his feelings and attitude? We can have no doubt but that they are the same that he had when, full of repentance, he threw himself down at his father's feet: "Father, I have sinned against you, I am not worthy to be called your son; treat me like the last of your servants." We may be certain that during the rejoicings with which his return was celebrated, those were his predominant dispositions. And if later the sense of contrition is less intense, it is never altogether lost, even after the boy has retaken forever his former place in the paternal home. How many times he must have said to his father: "I know you have forgiven me everything, but I can never weary of repeating with gratitude how much I regret having offended you, how much I want to make up, by greater fidelity, for the hours I have lost and for my forgetfulness of you."

Such should be the sentiment of a soul that has offended God, despised His perfections, and brought its share to the sufferings of Christ Jesus.

Let us now suppose in this soul no longer *an isolated act* of repentance, but *the habitual state* of contrition: it is almost impossible for this soul to fall anew into a deliberate sin. It is established in a disposition which, essentially, makes it repulse sin. The spirit of compunction is precisely the sense of contrition reigning in an abiding manner in the soul. It constitutes the soul in the habitual state of hatred against sin; by the interior movements that it provokes, it is of sovereign efficacy in preserving the soul from temptation. Between the spirit of compunction and sin, there is irreducible incompatibility: compunction of heart renders the soul firm in its horror of evil and love of God. Thus St. Bernard more than once uses the term "compunction" instead of "perfection." So much does the sense of compunction, when it is real, keep one from offending God.

II

We cannot help being struck by the fact that the spirituality of past times communicated a singular character of stability to its adepts. Whilst taking inevitable exceptions into account, it is indeed to be remarked that the interior life of the monks of old, who were sometimes recruited from a much rougher class of society than ours, rapidly attained a great degree of stability, while with many souls of our days—even religious souls consecrated to God—the spiritual life is of appalling instability. The fluctuations to which it is subject are countless; and its inward ascensions are unceasingly meeting with opposition to such a point that all progress may be compromised.

The reason of this vacillation is most often to be found in the lack of compunction. There is no surer means of rendering the spiritual life firm and steadfast than to impregnate it with the spirit of compunction.

Yet it seems that, speaking generally, modern authors do not insist as much on this subject[1] as did ancient ascetic writers who are never weary of dilating on the importance of compunction, for spiritual progress; and we see the greatest saints constantly cultivating and recommending this disposition of soul.

"You know," said St. Paul to the Ephesians, "from the first day that I came into Asia, in what manner I have been with you, for all the time, serving the Lord with all humility and with tears."[2] It was because he remembered how he once persecuted the Church of God.[3]

He does not fear to recall to his disciple Timothy how he "was a blasphemer, and a persecutor and contumelious"; he declares himself the chief of sinners. And he adds: "But for this cause have I obtained mercy, that in me first Christ Jesus might shew forth all patience, for

1 See however Father Faber: *Growth in Holiness,* ch. 19, *Abiding sorrow for sin.*

2 Act. xx, 18–19. 3 Philip. iii, 6.

the information of them that shall believe in Him unto life everlasting." And the Apostle, remembering this infinite mercy towards him, cries out in gratitude: "Now to the King of ages, immortal, invisible, the only God, be honour and glory for ever and ever!"[1]

It was another "convert," the object of similar mercy, Augustine, who wrote:[2] "To speak much when praying is to do a necessary thing with superfluous words. To pray much is to knock for a long time with the movements of the heart at the door of Him to Whom we pray; prayer, in fact, consists more in sighs and tears than in grand discourses and many words. God puts our tears in His sight; our sighs are not ignored by Him Who created all things by His word, and has no need of our human words."

Our holy Father echoes the words of the great Doctor. "If anyone desire to pray in private, let him do so quietly ... with tears and fervour of heart."[3] Again he says: "Let us remember that not for our much speaking, but for our purity of heart and tears of compunction shall we be heard": *Non in multiloquor, sed in puritate cordis et compunctione lacrymarum nos exaudiri sciamus.*[4] Certainly our great Patriarch does not affirm this truth without deep conviction and, I dare to say, an experimental conviction. Look too at this portrait of a perfect monk that he draws for us when he comes to the 12th degree of humility: this monk, he says, has reached the point where the perfection of charity and divine union are about to be realised: *Mox ad caritatem Dei perveniet illam, quae perfecta foras mittet timorem.*[5] And what is this monk's attitude? He considers himself unworthy, on account of his sins, to appear before God.

This is truly what all holy souls feel. A lady of high rank, who was converted after having lived in vanity and luxury, wrote to St. Gregory that she would give him no peace until he had assured her in the name of God that her sins were forgiven. The holy Pontiff, full of the spirit of the Rule, answered her that her request was as difficult as it was detrimental: difficult, because he did not esteem himself worthy of having revelations; detrimental also for this soul, as it was in the interest of her salvation that she should not be assured of forgiveness: [with an absolute certainty that excluded all doubt and cast away all fear] until the

1 I Tim. i, 13 seq. 2 *Epist.* cxxx, ch. 10. 3 Rule, ch. lii.
4 Ibid. ch. xx. 5 Rule, ch. vii.

last moment of her life, when she would no longer be in a state to weep for her faults and to deplore them in God's sight; until this last hour came, she ought ever to live in compunction and not to let a day pass without washing away her stains with her tears.[1] See our St. Gertrude, that lily of purity. She said to our Lord with the deepest self-abasement: "The greatest miracle in my eyes, Lord, is that the earth can bear such a worthless sinner as I am."[2] St. Teresa, formed to perfection by our Lord Himself, had placed under her eyes in her oratory, in order to make it as it were the refrain of her prayer, this text of the Psalmist: *Non intres, Domine, in judicium cum servo tuo.*[3] It is neither an exclamation of love, nor an act of sublime praise that we hear from this seraphic soul, who is declared by her historians never to have sinned mortally, but it is a cry of compunction: "Enter not, O Lord, into judgment with Thy servant."[4] St. Catherine of Siena did not cease to implore divine mercy; she always ended her prayers with this invocation: *Peccavi, Domine, miserere mei*: "Have pity upon me, O Lord, for I have sinned."[5]

With all these souls, it was not a question of isolated acts and transitory impulses. The words we have repeated were but the outward manifestation of an inward abiding sense of compunction eager to find outlet.

This habitual sense of compunction is so precious that, according to St. Teresa, souls that are the most forestalled with divine favours are the most filled with it. Speaking of souls that have reached the sixth mansion of the interior castle, she puts them on their guard against forgetfulness of their faults: "Souls to whom God has granted these graces will understand what I say," she writes... "Sorrow for sin increases in proportion to the divine grace received, and I believe will never quit us until we come to the land where nothing can grieve us any more... A soul so advanced

---

1 Cf. *Epistolae,* Lib. vii, ch. 25.
2 *The Herald of Divine Love,* Bk. i, ch. 12.
3 Ps. cxlii, 2.
4 *Life of St. Teresa,* according to the Bollandists. Vol. ii, ch. 11.
5 Drane, *Life of St. Catherine of Siena.* 1st Part. ch. 4. We know that St. Catherine has in her *Dialogue* a whole treatise on tears. Bl. Raymund of Capua relates, that marvelling at the works of Catherine, he desired to have an undeniable proof that they came from God. The inspiration came to him to ask the Saint to obtain for him from the Lord an extraordinary contrition for his sins, for, he added, "no one can have this contrition unless it comes from the Holy Ghost, and a like contrition is a great sign of God's grace." We know how St. Catherine obtained "a bull of pardon" for her disciple. *Life of St. Catherine* by Bl. Raymund of Capua. 1st Part, ch. 9.

as that we speak of does not think of the punishment threatening its offences, but of its great ingratitude towards Him to Whom it owes so much, and Who so justly deserves that it should serve Him, for the sublime mysteries revealed have taught it much about the greatness of God. The soul wonders at its former temerity and weeps over its irreverence; its foolishness in the past seems a madness which it never ceases to lament as it remembers for what vile things it forsook so great a Sovereign. The thoughts dwell on this more than on the favours received, which... are so powerful that they seem to rush through the soul like a strong, swift river. The sins, however, remain like a mire in the river bed, and dwell constantly in the memory, making a heavy cross to bear."[1]

The Church herself gives us, in her Liturgy of the Mass, striking examples of compunction of heart.

Look at what the priest does at the moment when about to offer the Holy Sacrifice, the most sublime homage that the creature can render to God. The priest is necessarily supposed to be in a state of grace and in possession of God's friendship; otherwise, in celebrating, he would commit a sacrilege. Yet the Church, his infallible teacher, begins by making him confess before all the faithful there assembled, his condition not only of a creature, but of a sinner: *Confiteor Deo omnipotenti... et vobis, fratres, quia peccavi nimis.*[2] Then in the course of the holy action, the Church multiplies upon his lips formulas imploring forgiveness that he may steep his heart and mind in them: *Aufer a nobis, quaesumus, Domine, iniquitates nostras*: "Take away from us our iniquities, we beseech Thee, O Lord, that we may enter with pure minds into the Holy of Holies." In the midst of the song of the Angels, the priest blends cries for mercy with these exclamations of love and holy gladness: "Thou Who takest away the sins of the world, have mercy on us." When he offers the Immaculate Host to God, it is for his "innumerable sins, offences, and negligences." Before the consecration, he prays "to be delivered from eternal damnation": *Ab aeterna damnatione nos eripi.* After the consecration in which he is even identified with Christ Himself, the priest

1 *The Interior Castle,* translated by the Benedictines of Stanbrook, p. 202.

2 "I confess to Almighty God... and to you, brethren, that I have greatly sinned," The Roman Mass.

beseeches God to grant him some part and fellowship with the Saints *notwithstanding his sins.* *NOBIS QUOQUE PECCATORIBUS... non aestimator meriti, sed veniae quaesumus largitor admitte.*[1] Then comes the moment when he is about to unite himself sacramentally with the Divine Victim. He strikes his breast, like a sinner: "Lamb of God... regard not my sins... grant that this union of my soul with Thee may not turn to my judgment and condemnation."

We think how many holy priests and pontiffs, held up to our veneration, have said these words: *Pro innumerabilibus peccatis meis.*[2] And the Church obliges them to repeat: "Lord, I am not worthy." Why does the Church do this? Because without this spirit of compunction, one is not at the "right pitch," the "diapason" of Christianity. When the priest beseeches that his sacrifice may be united with that of Christ, he says: "May we be received by Thee, O Lord, in the spirit of humility and with a contrite heart." The oblation of Jesus is always pleasing to the Father; but, inasmuch as it is offered by us, it is only so on condition that our souls are filled with compunction and the spirit of self-abasement that results from it.

Such is the spirit that animates the Church, the Spouse of Christ, in the action that is the most sublime, the holiest she can accomplish here below. Even when the soul is identified with Christ, united to God in communion, the Church wishes us never to forget that we are sinners; she wishes the soul to be steeped in compunction: *In spiritu humilitatis et in animo contrito suscipiamur a te, Domine.*[3]

III

No one doubts that these sentiments of compunction prescribed by the Church for the Mass are perfectly fitting. But perhaps the thought may occur that they should be reserved for the renewing of the Sacrifice of the Cross, for the reception of the Sacraments, in a word for the Liturgy. Elsewhere, in the ordinary course of the interior life, would

---

1 To us sinners also... we implore You to admit us, not weighing our merits, but freely granting us pardon," Roman Canon.

2 "For my innumerable sins," Offertory of the Mass.

3 "In a humble spirit and a contrite heart may we be received by Thee, O Lord," Offertory of the Mass.

they not be pious exaggerations, would not this be going a little too far? Certainly not.

Listen to St. John in his divinely inspired Epistle: "If we say that we have no sin, we deceive ourselves, and the truth is not in us."[1] As regards great and holy souls, this assertion is luminous. The nearer they come to God, the Sun of Justice, and spotless Holiness, the better they perceive the stains that disfigure them; the brilliance of the Divine light in which they move, makes their least faults and failings appear in more striking contrast. Their inner gaze, purified by faith and love, penetrates more deeply into the Divine perfections; they have a clearer view of their own nothingness; they are better able to measure the abyss that separates them from the Infinite. Their more intimate union with Christ causes the sufferings endured by Him for the expiation of sin to touch them to the quick. Having a higher notion of the life of grace, they better grasp all that is horrible in offence committed against the Heavenly Father, in despising the Saviour's Passion, in injurious resistance to the Spirit of Love.

We understand that the fact of having offended God, were it but once in their existence, moves these souls with intensest grief. And there is, in their habitual attitude of repentance and detestation of sin, a constant proof of supernatural delicacy which cannot fail to please God, and draw down His infinite mercy upon them.

Moreover, the state of soul we are studying is in nowise, as might be imagined at first sight, incompatible with confidence and spiritual joy, with outpourings of love and delight in God. Quite the contrary! St. Augustine, St. Benedict, St. Gregory, St. Bernard, St. Gertrude, St. Catherine of Siena, St. Teresa, all these souls filled with the spirit of compunction, were they not also inflamed with divine love and carried away by the overflowing joy of the Holy Spirit? Had they not come to a sublime degree of union with God?

Far from love and joy finding a hindrance in the habitual attitude of repentance which constitutes compunction, they find in it a firm basis and one of the greatest incentives for soaring Godwards. Whence in fact is compunction chiefly derived? From the remembrance of the offence against God considered as Infinite Goodness. By its very nature, it hence concerns perfect contrition, one of the purest forms of love. It

1 I Joan. i, 8.

unceasingly stirs up generosity and love which want to repair the past by a greater fervour; it makes the soul distrustful of self, but wonderfully pliant under the hand of God, extremely attentive to the action of the Holy Spirit. Compunction could not admit such a dangerous hindrance to the supernatural life and one so contrary to our religious state as wilful dissipation of mind and habitual levity. Neither could it tolerate in relation to God any irreverence or wrong kind of familiarity, than which nothing is more perilous for the soul. Compunction avoids this danger. Father Faber says:[1] "It leads to a more fruitful, because a more reverent, humble, and hungry use of the Sacraments, and no grace that comes to us is wasted while this sorrow possesses our souls... Lukewarmness is incompatible with this holy sorrow and cannot co-exist with it." This sense of compunction is at times so deep and intense that it becomes the principle of a new life full of love, entirely consecrated to God's service. St. Gregory says that it then often renders the penitent soul more pleasing to God than would be an innocent life passed in sluggish security: *Et fit plerumque Deo gratior amore ardens vita post culpam, quam securitate torpens innocentia.*[2]

The source of humility as of generosity, compunction again inclines the soul to accept the Divine will in its fulness, whatever be the form under which this will is manifested, and whatever be the trials to which it subjects the soul. The soul then regards these trials as means whereby to avenge upon itself God's perfections and rights ignored or outraged by sin. It so much regrets having offended Love, that, if anything disappointing, hard or painful befalls, the soul generously accepts it and this becomes an immense source of merits. You know that episode in the life of David. At the end of his reign, David is forced to flee from Jerusalem in consequence of Absalom's revolt. In the course of his flight he is met by a man, a kinsman of Saul, named Semei. This man at once begins to throw stones at the old king and to curse him, saying: "Come out, come out... thou man of Belial... behold thy evils press upon thee, because thou art a man of blood." One of David's servants wants to intervene and punish the insult, but the king prevents him: "Let him alone," he says. "Behold my son, who came forth from my loins, seeketh my life: how much more now [shall this stranger]? Let him alone that

1 *L. c.* 2 *Reg. pastor.* III, ch. 28. P. L. t. 77, col. 107.

he may curse as the Lord hath bidden him. Perhaps the Lord may look upon my affliction,[1] and the Lord may render me good for the cursing of this day."[2] Remembering his sins, his heart full of the sense of compunction from which the *Miserere* overflowed, the holy king accepted every outrage in expiation.

This sense of compunction is also the principle of ardent charity towards our neighbour. If you are severe in your judgments, exacting with others, if you easily bring up the faults of your brethren, compunction does not dwell in you. Indeed one who is possessed by this sense, sees only his own faults, his own weaknesses, such as he is before God; this is enough to make the spirit of self-exaltation die within him and to render him full of indulgence and compassion for others.

Once again, do not let us suppose that joy is absent from such a soul. Far from that! By awakening love, quickening generosity, and preserving charity, compunction purifies us the more, and makes us less unworthy of being united to our Lord; it strengthens our confidence in God's forgiveness and confirms our soul in peace. Thus it takes nothing away from spiritual joy and the amiability of virtue. Let us trust St. Francis of Sales who, better than any other, knew how to speak of Divine love and the joy that flows from it. "The sadness of true penitence," he writes, "is not so much to be named sadness as displeasure, or the sense and detestation of evil; a sadness which is never troubled nor vexed, a sadness which does not dull the spirit, but makes it active, ready and diligent; a sadness which does not weigh the heart down, but raises it by prayer and hope, and causes in it the movements of the fervour of devotion; a sadness which in the heaviest of its bitternesses ever produces the sweetness of an incomparable consolation..." And quoting an old monk, a faithful echo of the asceticism of bygone ages, the great Doctor adds: "The sadness, says Cassian, which works solid penitence, and that desirable repentance of which one never repents, is obedient, affable, humble, mild, sweet, patient—*as being a child and scion of charity*: so that spreading over every pain of body and contrition of spirit, and being in a certain way joyous, courageous, and strengthened by the hope of doing better, it retains... all the Fruits of the Holy Spirit."[3]

1 The Massorites read: "My tears." 2 II Reg. xvi.

3 *Treatise on the Love of God,* Bk. xi, ch. 21. 2. Translated by the Rev. H.B. Mackey,

These are the natural fruits of this compunction. Far from discouraging the soul, compunction rather makes it full of gladness in God's service; and is not that the note of true devotion? Thus when the soul, at the remembrance of its faults—a remembrance that ought to dwell on *the fact* of having offended God, and not on the circumstances of the sins committed—humbles itself before God; when it plunges in the flames of contrition in order to be purified of any remaining rust, when it sincerely declares itself to be unworthy of the Divine graces, *Exi a me, quia homo peccator sum, Domine,*[1] God looks down upon it with infinite goodness and mercy: *Cor contritum et humiliatum, Deus, non despicies.*[2] "God is quicker to hear our tears than the movement of our lips," says St. Augustine: *Fletus citius audit quam voces.*[3] And St. Gregory writes, "God does not delay to accept our tears; He dries our tears which are but momentary with joys that abide": *Nec mora erit in fletibus, quia tergent citius transeuntes lacrymas mansura gaudia.*[4]

Penetrated with these same thoughts, our Holy Father wishes that we should *each day* confess to God, in prayer, with tears and sighs, our past sins: *Mala sua praeterita cum lacrymis vel gemitu* COTIDIE *in oratione Deo confiteri.*[5] Remark this *cotidie*; St. Benedict does not say "from time to time" but "daily." Why does he make such a recommendation? Because he is assured—and he wants us to share this assurance—that it is on account of this humble attitude of a contrite soul that we shall be heard: *In compunctione lacrymarum nos exaudiri sciamus.*[6] It is not without deep reason that these words of the holy Legislator have passed into an incontested axiom of monastic asceticism.[7]

O.S.B.

1 "Depart from me, for I am a sinful man, O Lord," Luc. v, 8.

2 "A contrite and humbled heart, O God, Thou wilt not despise," Ps. l, 19.

3 Sermon xlvii of the appendix to the works of St. Augustine. P. L. 39, col. 1838.

4 *Homil. in Evangel.,* Lib. ii, hom xxxi, 8. P. L. 76, col. 1232.

5 Rule, ch. iv. 6 Ibid. ch. xx.

7 St. Benedict wants to keep our souls habitually in the "tonality" of the *Miserere:* the interior state of David, penitent yet full of confidence in the Divine Mercy, David indefinitely alternating in his psalms between contrition and love. D. M. Festugière, *L. c.*

IV

Another of the most precious fruits of the spirit of compunction is that it renders us strong against temptation. By fostering in the soul the hatred of sin, compunction puts it on guard against the snares of the enemy.

Temptation plays such a large part in the spiritual life that it is necessary to treat of it; we shall see how compunction is furthermore one of the most effectual arms for resisting temptation.

We come across people who imagine that the interior life is but a pleasant easy ascent, along a flower-bordered path. You know it is not generally so, although God, the Sovereign Master of His gifts, can lead us by such a path if He pleases. Long ago God said in Holy Writ: "Son, when thou comest to the service of God"—and it is for that we have come to the monastery, which is a school where we learn how to serve the Lord: *Schola dominici servitii,*[1]—"prepare thy soul for temptation": *Fili, accedens ad servitutem Dei, praepara animam tuam ad tentationem.*[2] In fact, it is impossible under the conditions of our present humanity, to find God fully without being beset by temptation. And the devil is most often infuriated against those who seek God sincerely and in whom he sees the most living image of Christ Jesus.

But is not temptation a danger for the soul? Would it not be highly preferable not to be tempted? We are spontaneously inclined to envy those whom we may imagine are never tried by temptation. "Happy the man," we would willingly say, "who has not to undergo its assaults." That is what our human wisdom might suggest, but God, Who is the infallible Truth, the source of our holiness and beatitude, says quite the contrary: "Blessed is the man that endureth temptation": *BEATUS VIR qui suffert tentationem...*[3] Why does the Holy Spirit proclaim this man "blessed" when we should have been inclined to think quite otherwise? Why does the Angel say to Tobias: "*Because thou* wast acceptable to God, it was *necessary* that temptation should prove thee": *QUIA acceptus eras Deo, NECESSE FUIT ut tentatio probaret te.*[4] Is it for the sake of the temptation itself? Evidently not, but because God uses it in order

---

1 Prologue of the Rule. 2 Eccli. ii, 1. 3 Jac. i, 12.
4 Tob. xii, 13.

to obtain a proof of our fidelity, which, upheld by grace, is strengthened and manifested in the conflict and wins at last a crown of life. *Cum probatus fuerit, accipiet coronam vitae.*[1]

Temptation patiently borne is a source of merit for the soul and is glorious for God. By its constancy in trial, the soul is the living testimony of the might of grace: "My grace is sufficient for thee: for power is made perfect in infirmity": *Sufficit tibi gratia mea, nam virtus in infirmitate perficitur.*[2] God awaits this homage and glory from us.

Look at the holy man Job. Scripture lends God a kind of pride in the perfection of this great just man. One day—the sacred writer has dramatised the scene—when Satan stands before Him, God says to him: "Whence comest thou?" And Satan replies: "I have gone round about the earth, and walked through it." The Lord says again: "Hast thou considered My servant Job, that there is none like him in the earth, a man simple and upright, and fearing God, and avoiding evil?" Satan sneers and asks what merit Job has in showing himself perfect when all prospers with him and smiles upon him. "But," he adds, "put forth Thy hand, and touch his bone and his flesh and then Thou shalt see that he will bless (or rather curse) Thee to Thy face."[3] God gives Satan leave to strike His servant in his possessions, in his family, even in his person. And now see Job, despoiled little by little of all his goods, covered with ulcers, seated upon his dunghill, and obliged over and above this to undergo the sarcasms of his wife and friends who would excite him to blaspheme. But he remains unshaken in his fidelity to God. No feeling of revolt rises from his heart, not a murmur passes his lips, only words of wonderful submission: "The Lord gave and the Lord hath taken away... blessed be the name of the Lord!... If we have received good things at the hand of God, why should we not receive evil?"[4] What heroic constancy! And what glory is given to God by this man who, overwhelmed with such woes, blesses the Divine Hand! And we know how God, after having tried him, renders testimony to him, and restores all his possessions while multiplying them. Temptation had served to show the extent of Job's fidelity.

---

1 Jac. i, 12. 2 II Cor. xii, 9. 3 Job. i, 7–11.
4 Ibid. 21; ii, 10.

In many a soul, temptation does another work which nothing else could do. Souls there are, upright but proud, who cannot attain divine union unless they are first humbled down to the ground. They have, as it were, to fathom the abyss of their frailty, and learn by experience how absolutely dependent they are on God, so that they may no longer trust in themselves. It is by temptation alone that they can measure their powerlessness. When these souls are buffeted by temptation, and feel themselves at the edge of the abyss, they realise the necessity of humbling themselves. At that moment a great cry escapes them and rises up to God. And then comes the hour of grace. Temptation keeps them in a state of vigilance over their weaknesses, and in a constant spirit of dependence upon God. For them, temptation is the best school of humility.

Trial profits others by preserving them from lukewarmness. Without temptation, they would fall into spiritual sloth. Temptation is for them a stimulus, for in combating it love is quickened while fidelity finds an opportunity of manifesting itself. Look at the Apostles in the Garden of Olives. In spite of the warning given them by their Divine Master to watch and pray, they sleep; all unconscious of danger, they let themselves be surprised by the enemies of Jesus, they take to flight, forsaking their Master, despite all their previous protestations. How different was their conduct from what it had been when they were struggling against the tempest on the Lake. Then in face of the imminent peril of which they are fully aware, they awake Jesus from His sleep with cries of distress: "Lord, save us, we perish": *Domine, salva nos, perimus!*[1]

Again, temptation gives us the great formation of experience. This is a precious fruit because we become skilled in helping souls when they come to us seeking light and help. How can anyone instruct or effectually help another who is tempted, if he himself does not know what temptation is? St. Paul says of Jesus Christ that He willed to be tempted as we are, though without sin, that He might have compassion on our infirmities: *Tentatum per omnia absque peccato;*[2] *in eo enim in quo passus est ipse et tentatus, potens est et eis qui tentantur, auxiliari.*[3]

Let us then not be afraid of the fact of temptation, nor of its frequency or violence. It is only a trial; God never permits it save in view of our greater good. However much it besets us, it is not a sin, provided that

1 Matth. viii, 25. 2 Hebr. iv, 15. 3 Ibid. ii, 18.

we do not expose ourselves wilfully to its attacks and never *consent* to it. We may *feel* its sting or its seductions; but as long as that fine point of the soul which is the will remains steadfast against it, we ought to be tranquil. Christ Jesus is with us, in us; and who is stronger than He?

V

But from wherever it comes,—from the devil, the world, or our evil tendencies,—and whatever be its nature, we must, for our part, resist temptation with courage and above all with promptitude.

Our Holy Father was a model of this generous resistance. You know that one day tempted by the remembrance of worldly joys, he stripped himself of his garments and rolled among thorns until his body was all torn.[1] The great Patriarch knew then by personal experience what temptation was, and how strongly it must be resisted. Now what is the conduct he prescribes to us in presence of temptation? Speaking in the language of his own asceticism, let us say that he furnishes us with three "instruments": "To keep guard at all times over the actions of our life. To know for certain that God sees us everywhere. To dash down at the feet of Christ our evil thoughts the instant that they come into the heart."[2]

Watchfulness has been sovereignly recommended to us by our Lord Himself: *Vigilate*.[3] Now, how are we to keep this vigilance? By the spirit of compunction which keeps us ever upon our guard. A soul, knowing its weakness by experience, has horror of anything that could expose it to offending God anew. On account of this loving fear, it is careful to avoid all that could turn it away from God Who beholds us night and day.

And as it distrusts itself, it has recourse to Christ: *Et orate*.[4] He is a true disciple of Christ, says our Holy Father, who when tempted by the Evil One casts him and his suggestions far from his heart, and brings him to naught.[5] And how are we to bring the Evil One and his malice to naught? By seizing the first "offspring" of the evil thought and breaking it against the feet of Christ.[6] St. Benedict compares evil thoughts to the offspring of the devil, the father of sin; he tells us to cast them

1 St. Gregory, *Dialogues*. Lib. ii, ch. 11.
2 Rule, ch. iv.
3 Matth. xxvi, 41.
4 Matth. xxvi, 41.
5 Prologue of the Rule.
6 Ibid.

out as soon as they appear: *Mox ad Christum allidere.*[1] Note this little word: "*Mox*," immediately. When we play with temptation, we let it grow and increase in strength while at the same time the energy to resist it diminishes in us. We must give evil suggestions no time to grow, but dash them down while they are yet little and weak like beings just born. In this expression *ad Christum allidere*—our Holy Father has in mind the maledictions of the Psalmist against Babylon, the city of sin: "Blessed be he that shall take and dash thy little ones against the rock."[2] Christ, says St. Paul, is "the chief corner stone" of our spiritual edifice: *Ipso summo angulari lapide Christo Jesu.*[3]

Recourse to Christ Jesus is indeed the most certain means of overcoming temptation; the devil fears Christ and trembles at the Cross. Are we tempted against faith? Let us at once say: "All that Jesus has revealed to us He receives from His Father. Jesus is the Only-begotten Son Who from the bosom of the Father has come to manifest to us the Divine secrets which He alone can know. He is the Truth. Yes, Lord Jesus, I believe in Thee, but increase my faith!" If we are tempted against hope, let us look at Christ upon the Cross: has He not become the Propitiation for the sins of the whole world? Is He not the holy High Priest Who has entered for us into Heaven and ever intercedes with the Father on our behalf: *Semper vivens ad interpellandum PRO NOBIS*.[4] And He has said: "Him that cometh to Me, I will not cast out": *Et eum qui venit ad Me non ejiciam foras.*[5] Does want of confidence in God seek to insinuate itself into our heart? But who has loved us more than God, more than Christ: *Dilexit me et tradidit semetipsum pro me*?[6] When the devil whispers thoughts of pride, let us again look on Christ Jesus; He was God and He humbled Himself even to the ignominious death on Calvary. Can the disciple be above the Master?...[7] When wounded self-love sug-

1 "Dash them at once on the rock of Christ," Rule, ch. iv.

2 Ps. cxxxv. St. Jerome, (Epist. xxii, 6), St. Hilarius. (Tract. in Ps. cxxxvi, 14) and St. Augustine make use of the same language: "*Qui sunt parvuli Babyloniae? Nascentes malae cupiditates... Cum parvula est... ad petram elide. Petra autem erat Christus.*" (Who are the little ones of Babylon? Evil desires being born... When it is little... dash it against the rock; and the Rock was Christ.) Enarr. in Psalm cxxxvi, § XXI.

3 Eph. ii, 20. 4 Hebr. vii, 25. 5 Joan. vi, 37.

6 "Who loved me, and delivered Himself for me," Gal. ii, 20.

7 Cf. Luc. vi, 40.

gests that we should return the injuries done to us, let us yet again look at Jesus, our Model, during His Passion: He did not turn away His Face from them that spat upon and struck Him: *Faciem meam non averti ab increpantibus et conspuentibus in me.*[1] If the world, the devil's accomplice, holds before our eyes the reflection of senseless, transitory joys, let us take refuge with Christ to Whom Satan promised the kingdoms of the world and the glory of them if He would adore him: "Lord Jesus, it was for Thee that I left all things, that I might follow Thee more closely, Thee alone; never suffer me to be separated from Thee!" *A te nunquam separari permittas.*[2] There is no temptation but that can be brought to nothing by the remembrance of Christ: *Mox ad Christum allidere.*

And if it continues, if above all it is accompanied by dryness and spiritual darkness, do not let us allow ourselves to be discouraged: it is because God wishes to delve deep down in our soul to enlarge its capacity in order to fill it with His grace: *Purgabit eum ut fructum plus afferat*;[3] only let us cry out to Jesus, like His disciples: "Save us, O Lord, for without Thee, we shall perish!"[4]

If we thus act immediately the temptation arises, *mox*, while it is yet weak; if above all we keep our soul in that inward attitude of habitual repentance which is compunction, let us be assured that the devil will be powerless against us. Temptation will only have served to exercise our fidelity, to strengthen our love and make us more pleasing to our Father in Heaven.

VI

But where are we to obtain this spirit of compunction which is such a great gain?

To begin with, by asking it of God. This "gift of tears" is so precious, so high a grace, that it is in imploring it "from the Father of lights" from Whom every perfect gift comes down upon us[5] that we shall obtain it. The missal contains a formula *pro petitione lacrymarum.*[6] The old monks often recited this prayer. Let us repeat it after them: "Almighty and

---

1 Isa. l, 6.
2 Ordinary of the Mass, prayer before Communion.
3 "He will purge it, that it may bring forth more fruit," Joan. xv, 2.
4 Cf. Matth. viii, 25.
5 Jac. i, 17.
6 For the petition of tears.

most merciful God, Who, to quench the thirst of thy people, madest a fountain of living water to spring out of the rock, draw from our stony hearts the tears of compunction, that effectually bewailing our sins, we may through Thy mercy deserve to obtain pardon for them."

We may also borrow from Holy Writ certain prayers that the Church has made her own; for instance, David's prayer after his sin. You know how dear the great king was to the Heart of God Who had lavished His benefits upon him. Then David falls into a great sin; he gives to his people the scandal of murder and adultery. The Lord sends a prophet to him to excite him to repentance. And David, at once humbling himself and striking his breast, cries out: "I have sinned." This repentance wins pardon for him: "The Lord also hath taken away thy sin," says the prophet: *Transtulit peccatum tuum*.[1] The king then composed that inspired Psalm, the *Miserere*, at once full of contrition and confidence. "Have mercy on me, O God, according to Thy great mercy; wash me yet more from my iniquity; against Thee only have I sinned, and my sin is ever before me; cast me not away from Thy face, and take not Thy Holy Spirit from me." That is contrition. Here is the hope which is inseparable from it: "Restore unto me the joy of Thy salvation... Thou wilt open my lips, and my mouth shall declare Thy praise... A sacrifice to God is an afflicted spirit, a contrite and humbled heart, O God, Thou wilt not despise."[2]

Such accents indeed cannot but touch God's Heart: "Thou hast set my tears in Thy sight": *Posuisti lacrymas meas in conspectu tuo*.[3] Has not Christ Jesus declared "Blessed are they that weep."[4] "But amongst all those who weep, none are sooner consoled than those who weep for their sins. In every other case, sorrow, far from being a remedy for the evil, is another evil which increases it; sin is the only evil that is cured by weeping ... the forgiveness of sins is the fruit of these tears."[5]

To the prayer imploring the gift of compunction from God, is naturally joined all spiritual means capable of awakening it within us: the most powerful is incontestably the frequent contemplation of our Divine Saviour's Passion.

If you contemplate with faith and devotion the sufferings of Jesus Christ you will have a revelation of God's love and justice; you will know,

1 II Reg. xii, 13. 2 Ps, l. 3 Ps. lv, 9. 4 Matth. v, 5.
5 Bossuet, *Meditations upon the Gospel*, Sermon on the Mount, 4th day.

better than with any amount of reasoning, the malice of sin. This contemplation is like a sacramental causing the soul to share in that Divine sadness which invaded the soul of Jesus in the Garden of Olives—Jesus, the very Son of God, in Whom the Father, Whose exigencies are infinite, was well pleased. And yet His heart was full of sorrow—"sorrowful even unto death": *Tristis est anima mea usque ad mortem.*[1] Great cries arise from His breast, as tears arise from His eyes; *cum clamore valido et lacrymis.*[2] Whence come this sadness, these sighs and tears? They come from the weight of the burden of the world's crimes: *Posuit Dominus in eo iniquitatem omnium nostrum.*[3] Christ is like the scape-goat laden with all our sins. Certainly He could not be a "penitent"; He could not have contrition, compunction, such as we have defined it, for the soul of Jesus is entirely holy and immaculate; the debt to be paid off is not His own, but ours: *Attritus est propter scelera nostra.*[4] However, because of this substitution, Jesus has willed to experience that sadness which the soul must feel in presence of its sin; He has willed to undergo the blows of outraged love and justice, and therefore to be crushed by the greatest of sorrow: *Dominus voluit conterere eum in infirmitate.*[5]

"I have not loved thee in jest," our Lord says one day to the Blessed Angela of Foligno. "This word," writes the Saint, "struck a deadly pain into my soul, because straightway the eyes of my soul were opened and I saw clearly that what He said was most true. For I saw the works and the effect of that love, and I saw all that this Son of God worketh by reason of that love." The Saint specifies the object of her vision. "I saw that what He underwent in life and in death, this God-Man, Who suffered His Passion by reason of His ineffable tender love, and I understood that the aforesaid word is most true, namely, that He loves me not in jest, but that by a most true and most perfect and most tender love, hath He loved me." And what was the result of this contemplation for Angela's soul? A deep sense of compunction. Hear how she judges herself in the divine light. "And I saw that in me it was just the opposite... Then, too, my soul cried out and said: 'O Master... I have never loved Thee save in jest and with falsehood and hypocrisy; and never have I desired to come near to Thee in truth, so as to feel the labours that Thou hast willed to

1 Matth. xxvi, 38. 2 Hebr. v, 7. 3 Isa. liii, 6. 4 Ibid. 5.
5 Ibid. 10.

feel and to suffer for me; and never have I served Thee truly and for Thy sake, but with double-dealing and negligently.'"[1]

You see how holy souls are touched and how they humble themselves when they consider Christ's sufferings. On the night of the Passion, Peter, the Prince of the Apostles to whom Christ had revealed His glory upon Thabor, who had just received Holy Communion from Jesus' own hands, Peter, at the voice of a servant-maid, denies His Master. Soon afterwards, the gaze of Jesus, abandoned to the caprices of His mortal enemies, meets that of Peter. The Apostle understands; he goes out, and bitter tears flow from his eyes: *Flevit amare.*[2]

A like effect is produced in the soul that contemplates the sufferings of Jesus with faith: it, too, has followed Jesus, with Peter, on the night of the Passion; it, too, meets the gaze of the Divine Crucified, and that is for it a true grace. Let us often keep close in the footsteps of the Suffering Christ, by making the "Way of the Cross." Jesus will say to us: "See what I have suffered for thee; I have endured a three hours' agony, endured the desertion of My disciples, and having My Face spat upon, the false witnesses, the cowardice of Pilate, the derision of Herod, the weight of the Cross beneath which I fell, the nakedness of the gibbet, the bitter sarcasms of My most deadly enemies, the thirst which they would have quenched with gall and vinegar, and, above all, the being forsaken by My Father. It was for thee, out of love for thee, to expiate thy sins that I endured all; with My Blood I have paid thy debts; I underwent the terrible exigences of Justice that mercy might be shown to thee!" Could we remain insensible to such a plea? The gaze of Jesus upon the Cross penetrates to the depths of our soul and touches it with repentance, because we are made to understand that sin is the cause of all these sufferings. Our heart then deplores having really contributed to the Divine Passion. When God thus touches a soul with His light, in prayer, He grants it one of the most precious graces that can be.

It is a repentance, moreover, full of love and confidence. For the soul does not sink down in despair beneath the weight of its sins: compunction is accompanied with consolation and comfort; the thought of the Redemption prevents shame and regret from degenerating into

---

1 *The Book of Visions,* ch. 33. Translated from the Latin by "A Secular Priest," Publ. by the Art and Book C°, Leamington. 2 Matth. xxvi. 75.

discouragement. Has not Jesus purchased our pardon superabundantly: *Et copiosa apud eum redemptio*?[1] The sight of His sufferings, at the same time as it gives birth to contrition, quickens within us hope in the infinite value of the sufferings by which Christ satisfied for us, and this brings us ineffable peace, *Ecce in pace amaritudo mea amarissima*.[2]

Perhaps in looking back upon the past, we see many miseries and stains. Perhaps we are tempted to say to Christ: "Lord Jesus, how shall such as I ever be able to please Thee?" Let us then remember that Christ came down to earth to seek sinners,[3] that He Himself has said: the angels rejoice over the conversion of one sinner more than over the perseverance of many just.[4] Each time that a sinner repents and obtains forgiveness, the angels in Heaven glorify God for His mercy: *Quoniam in aeternum misericordia ejus*.[5]

Let us think too of these words: "Thou, Who didst absolve Mary [Magdalen] and hear the Good Thief, hast not left me without hope."[6] They are words full of confidence. Christ Jesus forgave Magdalen; more than that, He loved her with a love of predilection; He made her, who had been the shame of her sex, pure as a virgin.

What Christ wrought in Magdalen, He can do again in the greatest of sinners; Christ can rehabilitate the sinner and bring him to holiness. This is a work reserved to Divine Omnipotence: *Quis potest facere mundum de immundo... nisi tu qui solus es?*[7] He is God: and God alone has this power of renewing innocence in His creature: it is the triumph of the Blood of Jesus.

But this ineffable renewal is only wrought upon one condition: it is that one imitates the sinner of the Gospel in her loving repentance. Magdalen is truly a perfect model of compunction. Look at her, at the feast in Simon's house, prostrate at the Saviour's feet, watering them with her tears, wiping them with the hairs of her head, the adornment wherewith she had seduced souls, humbling herself in presence of all the guests, and pouring out her contrite love at the same time as her perfumes. Later, she will generously follow Christ to the foot of the Cross,

1 Ps. cxxix, 7. 2 Isa. xxxviii, 17. 3 Matth. ix, 13.
4 Luc. xv, 7, 10. 5 "For His mercy endureth forever," Ps. cxxxv.
6 Sequence *Dies irae*.
7 "Who can make him clean that is conceived of unclean seed? Is it not Thou Who only art?" Job. xiv, 4.

upheld by the love which make her share the sorrows and reproaches with which Jesus is overwhelmed. Love again will bring her the first to the tomb, until the Risen Christ, calling her by her name, rewards the ardour of her zeal and makes her the apostle of His Resurrection to the disciples: *Remittuntur ei peccata multa quoniam dilexit multum.*[1]

Let us too often stay with Magdalen, near the Cross. After the application of the merits of Jesus in the Sacrament of Penance, after assistance at the Holy Sacrifice of the Mass which reproduces the immolation on Calvary, there is truly no surer means than the exercise of compunction for destroying sin and arming us against it.

Let us then seek to keep ourselves in this disposition of which the fruits are so precious. Nothing will give more solidity to our spiritual life, more sureness to our perseverance. Speaking of compunction, Father Faber says: "It is as life-long with us as anything can be. It is a prominent part of our first turning to God, and there is no height of holiness in which it will leave us."[2]

1 Luc. vii, 47. 2 *L. c.*

SELF-RENUNCIATION

SUMMARY.—Acts of Christian renunciation ought to correspond with sincere compunction. —I. The expiation of sin concerns, for different reasons, both Christ and the members of His Mystical Body.—II. Practice of renunciation: mortifications imposed by the Church.—III. Mortifications inherent to common life and the observance of the Vows.—IV. The mortifications which every one of good will may practise on his own initiative; essential condition which St. Benedict lays down on this point.—V. Practices of self-renunciation constitute only a means, and their value is derived from their union with the sufferings of Jesus.

ACCORDING to the Divine Plan which the Eternal Father has traced out for us, He wills that we should only go to Him by walking in the footsteps of His Son, Christ Jesus. Our Lord has given us the formula of this fundamental truth: "I am the Way... No man cometh to the Father but by Me": *Nemo venit ad Patrem nisi per Me.*[1]

Compunction of heart, as we have seen, by fostering the habitual detestation of sin, works very efficaciously at dissolving the obstacles which would hinder us from following the Divine Model.

However our inward dispositions must logically become a part of our conduct, ruling and inspiring our deeds. To sincere compunction will necessarily correspond acts of Christian renunciation. Did not our Lord bequeath this maxim to all His disciples: "If any man will come after Me, let him deny himself, and take up his cross, and follow Me": *Si quis vult post Me venire, abneget semetipsum et tollat crucem suam et sequatur Me.*[2]

This precept, in one sense characteristic of Christian asceticism, has naturally passed into our Holy Father's teaching, which is the faithful

1 Joan. xiv, 6. 2 Matth. xvi, 24.

reflection of the Gospel. Before detailing the practice of renunciation among the instruments of good works, the very words of the Word Incarnate are recalled to us by the Holy Patriarch: "To deny oneself, in order to follow Christ": *Abnegare semetipsum sibi ut sequatur Christum.*[1]

Let us then study the way wherein Our Lord has gone before us, that we, in our turn, may walk in it. And if this way appears hard to our nature of flesh and blood, let us ask Jesus Himself to uphold us; He is the Life as well as the Truth and the Way; by the unction of His Almighty grace, He will give us the power to contemplate Him as we should, and to follow Him whithersoever He goes.

I

Since Adam's fall, man can only return to God by expiation. St. Paul tells us in speaking of Christ that He is "a High Priest, holy, innocent, undefiled, separated from sinners": *Pontifex sanctus, innocens, impollutus et segregatus a peccatoribus.*[2] Jesus, our Head, is infinitely far from all that is sin; and yet He has to pass through the sufferings of the Cross before entering into His glory.

You know the episode of Emmaus related by St. Luke. On the day of the Resurrection, two of Jesus' disciples set out to this town, a short distance from Jerusalem. They speak to one another of their disappointment caused by the death of the Divine Master, and the apparent downfall of all their hopes concerning the restoration of the kingdom of Israel. And behold, Jesus, under the guise of a stranger, joins them and asks them the subject of their discourse. The disciples tell Him the cause of their sadness. Then the Saviour, Who has not yet revealed Himself to them says, in a tone of reproach: "O foolish and slow of heart to believe... Ought not Christ to have suffered these things, and so to enter into His glory?": *Nonne haec oportuit pati Christum et ita intrare in gloriam suam?*[3]

Why then "ought" Christ to have suffered? If He had so willed, could not God have universally forgiven sin without requiring expiation? Assuredly He could. His absolute power knows no limits; but His justice has exacted expiation, and, first of all, Christ's expiation.

1 Rule, ch. iv. 2 Hebr. vii, 26, 3 Luc. xxiv, 26.

The Word Incarnate, in taking human nature, substituted Himself for sinful man, powerless to redeem himself; and Christ became the Victim for sin. This is what our Lord gave His disciples to understand in telling them that His sufferings were necessary. Necessary, not only in their generality, but even in their least details: for if a single sigh of Christ would have sufficed, and far more than sufficed, to redeem the world, a free decree of the Divine will, touching all the circumstances of the Passion, has accumulated therein an infinite superabundance of satisfaction.

You know with what love and abandonment to the will of His Father, Jesus accepted all that He had decreed. He suffered from His first entrance into the world, that He might fully accomplish this Divine will of which He knew the full extent: *Ecce venio*.[1] All was to be accomplished to the last detail with most loving faithfulness: *Iota unum aut unus apex non praeteribit a lege, donec omnia fiant*.[2]

We find a singular testimony of this Divine exactness in St. John's Gospel. Fastened to the Cross, suffering with thirst, on the point of expiring, Christ Jesus remembers that a verse of the prophecies is not yet fulfilled; and, in order that it should be so, He says: "I thirst."[3] Then, having said this, our Lord pronounces the supreme words: *Consummatum est*.[4] "It is consummated." O Father, I have fulfilled all: since the moment when I said: "Behold I come to do Thy will," I have omitted nothing; now I have drunk to the dregs the chalice Thou gavest Me to drink: there is nothing left for Me to do but commend My spirit into Thy hands.

But if our Divine Saviour suffered that He might redeem us, it was also to give us the grace to unite our expiation to His own and thus render it meritorious. For, says St. Paul, "they that are Christ's, have crucified their flesh, with the vices and concupiscences": *Qui sunt Christi carnem suam crucifixerunt cum vitiis suis*.[5] The expiation required by Divine Justice touches not only Christ Jesus; it extends to all the members of His Mystical Body. We share in the glory of our Head only after having shared in His sufferings; it is St. Paul again who tells us so: *Si tamen compatimur ut et conglorificemur*.[6]

---

1 Ps. xxxix, 8 and Hebr. x, 7.
2 Matth. v, 18.
3 Joan. xix, 28.
4 Ibid. 30.
5 Gal. v, 24.
6 Rom. viii, 17.

Having solidarity with Christ in suffering, we are however condemned to bear it for a quite different reason. He had but to expiate the sins of others: *Propter scelus populi mei percussi eum.*[1] We, on the contrary, have first to bear the weight of our own iniquities: *Digna factis recipimus, hic vero nihil mali gessit.*[2] By sin, we have contracted a debt towards God's justice; and, when the offence has been remitted, the debt still remains for us to pay. This is the role of satisfaction.

Moreover, the spirit of self-renunciation assures perseverance. Every actual sin turns the soul in the direction of evil. Even after forgiveness, there remains a tendency, an inclination, latent for the moment, but real, which, engrafted upon our native concupiscence, finds the first opportunity of producing fruit. It is for mortification to uproot these vicious tendencies, to counteract these habits, to annihilate this attachment to sin. Mortification pursues sin inasmuch as sin is an obstacle between the soul and God; therefore mortification must continue until these perverse tendencies of our nature are mastered; otherwise, these tendencies will end by dominating by being the source of numerous faults which will compromise, or, in any case, will keep at a very low level, our union with God and the life of charity in us. We have made a fervent Communion in the morning; our soul is entirely united to God. But if, in the course of the day, in the midst of our occupations, the "old man" awakens to incline us to pride, to touchiness, to anger, we must immediately repress these movements. Otherwise we might be surprised into giving consent; and the life of charity, the union of our soul with God would be lessened. If, for example, we are strongly inclined to self-love, accustomed to consider self in everything and direct everything towards self, we shall be touchy, hurt by a nothing, we shall be sullen and show bad temper; a quantity of reprehensible actions will be almost instinctively born of this self-love and will impede the action of Christ in it; this is why we must mortify this self-love, so that in the end the love of Jesus Christ may alone reign within us. Our Lord expects of us to repress the ill-regulated movements that urge us to sin, and imperfection; do

---

1 Isa. liii, 8.

2 "And we indeed justly, for we receive the due reward of our deeds; but this man hath done no evil," Luc. xxiii, 41.

not let us suppose we can pretend to the state of union if we allow bad habits to govern our heart.

As you see, renunciation is necessary, not only as satisfaction for our past sins, but also as a means to preserve us from falling into them again, thanks to the mortification of the natural tendencies that incline us to evil.

It is this twofold motive that our Holy Father, ever filled with the spirit of the Gospel, indicates first of all to those who enter the monastery, when he speaks of the mortifying of vicious habits: "*the amendment of vices*" or "*the preservation of charity.*" *Si quid paululum restrictius, dictante aequitatis ratione, propter EMENDATIONEM VITIORUM vel CONSERVATIONEM CARITATIS processerit.*[1]

To those who are more advanced "in the observance and in faith,"[2] who by Christ's grace have already gained the strength to overcome evil tendencies and "to run in the way of God's commandments,"[3] St. Benedict brings forward another motive—a higher and not less powerful one: the participation in Christ's sufferings: *Passionibus Christi per patientiam participemur.*[4] Indeed, for faithful and holy souls who have made satisfaction for their faults, whose union with God is more assured against the assaults of the enemy, self-renunciation becomes the means and proof of a more perfect imitation of our Lord. These souls willingly embrace the cross to "help" Christ in His Passion: Calvary is the chosen place where they are led and held by Love.

II

The need of mortification once recognised, we must learn in what measure we ought to practise it,—and first of all how we are to appreciate specifically the value of the different acts of renunciation proposed to us. Their hierarchy is as follows: in the first place, the mortifications which the Church, the Bride of Christ, prescribes;—next those, which are prescribed by the Rule, or are inherent to the daily observance of the monastic life;—finally, those we choose for ourselves or that are sent to us by God.

1 Prologue of the Rule.
2 Ibid.
3 Prologue of the Rule; cf. Ps. cxviii, 32.
4 Ibid.

To begin with the mortifications that the Church prescribes for us.

We find in a letter of St. Paul some words that at first sight seem astonishing: "I rejoice in my sufferings for you, and fill up those things that are wanting of the sufferings of Christ, in my flesh, for His body, which is the Church": *Adimpleo ea quae desunt passionum Christi in carne mea, pro corpore ejus, quod est Ecclesia.*[1] What do these words mean? Is something then wanting to the sufferings of Christ? Certainly not. We know that in themselves they were, so to speak, measureless: measureless in their intensity, for they rushed like a mighty torrent upon Christ; measureless above all in their value, a value properly speaking infinite, since they are the sufferings of a God. Moreover, Christ, having died for all, has become by His Passion, the Propitiation for the sins of the whole world.[2] St. Augustine explains the meaning of this text of the Apostle: to understand the mystery of Christ, we must not separate Him from His Mystical Body. Christ is not the "Whole Christ," according to the expression of the great Doctor, unless He is taken as *united* to the Church. He is the Head of the Church which forms His Mystical Body. Hence since Christ has brought His share of expiation, it remains for the Mystical Body to bring its share: *Adimpletae fuerunt passiones in capite, restabant adhuc passiones in corpore.*[3]

In the same way as God had decreed that, to satisfy justice and crown His work of love, Christ was to undergo a sum of sufferings, so has he determined a share of sufferings for the Church to distribute among her members. Thereby each of them is to co-operate in the expiation of Jesus, whether in expiation of one's own faults, or in the expiation endured, after the example of the Divine Master, for the faults of others. A soul that truly loves our Lord desires to give Him this proof of love for His Mystical Body by means of these mortifications. Here is the secret of the "extravagances" of the saints, of that thirst for mortifications which characterises nearly all of them: "To fill up those things that are wanting" to the Passion of their Divine Master.

The Church has naturally to legislate as to the work of expiation which concerns her as a whole. She has fixed for all her children a share of mortification which notably comprises the observances of Lent, of Fridays, of the Ember Days and Vigils. One who is little enlightened

1 Col. i, 24. 2 I Joan. ii, 2. 3 St. Augustine. *Enarrat. in Ps. lxxxvi,* 5.

prefers his own mortifications to these; but it is beyond doubt that the expiations imposed by the Church are more pleasing to God and more salutary for our souls.

The reason for this is clear. All the value of our sufferings and self-denial is derived from their union, through faith and love, with the sufferings and merits of Jesus, without Whom we can do nothing. Now, who is more united to Christ than the Church, His Bride? The mortifications she lays upon us are her own; it is as His Bride that she adopts and officially presents them to God; these mortifications become like the natural prolongation of Christ's expiations; presented by the Church herself they are extremely acceptable to God Who sees in them the closest and deepest participation that souls can have in the sufferings of His Beloved Son.

Moreover, these mortifications are very salutary for us.

The Church herself tells us, at the beginning of Lent, that she has "instituted them as a salutary remedy not only for our souls but also for our bodies": *Animabus corporibusque curandis salubriter institutum est.*[1]

Do not forget either that in the course of the holy forty days, the Church prays daily for those who submit to these expiations; she unceasingly beseeches God that these works may be accepted by Him; that He will make them beneficial to us; that He will give us strength to perform them with the piety befitting disciples of Christ and with a devotion that nothing can trouble: *Ut jejuniorum veneranda solemnia et congrua pietate suscipiant et secura devotione percurrant.*[2] This constant prayer of the Church for us is powerful over the Heart of God, and becomes a fount of heavenly benediction which makes our mortifications fruitful.

If then we wish "to be Christ's," as St. Paul says, let us accept, with great faith and generosity, these mortifications of the Church; in God's sight, they have a value and a power of expiation which other afflictive practices do not possess.

We shall therefore not be astonished that our great Patriarch, the heir in this of the piety of the first ages, consecrates a long chapter of his Rule to the observance of Lent. He desires that during this holy season,

---

1 Collect for the Saturday after Ash Wednesday.

2 "That they may begin the venerable solemnities of fasting with becoming piety, and may persevere to the end with steadfast devotion," Collect for Ash Wednesday.

besides the fast and abstinence, we should keep ourselves "in all purity of life; and repair the negligences of other times": *Omnes negligentias aliorum temporum his diebus sanctis diluere.*[1] "This is what we shall worthily do," he adds, "if we abstain from all vices, and apply ourselves to prayer with tears, to holy reading, compunction of heart and abstinence." You see that to the expiation that afflicts the body, St. Benedict is careful to join inward mortification and especially the exercise of that sense of compunction which is, as it were, the will to do uninterrupted penance.

III

After the penances instituted by the Church rank the mortifications and self-renunciation inherent to the monastic state.

We must first name the common life. However much it be sweetened by fraternal charity, however fervently mutual love reigns, the common life still bears with it a great deal of suffering. We love one another very much mutually, with sincere affection, and yet, without wishing it, we jar upon one another. This is part of the very condition of our poor human nature. Since sin entered the world, we are all, says St. Augustine, men subject to death, infirm, weak, bearing earthen vessels, which rub against each other: *Sumus homines mortales, fragiles, infirmi, lutea vasa portantes, quae faciunt invicem angustias.*[2]

The history of the lives of the saints is full of this want of concord, these misunderstandings and dissensions resulting from temperament, from character, the turn of mind, education and the ideal formed by each one. Were there in monasteries none but holy religious, worthy of canonisation, they would still have to suffer from the common life; and this suffering can be so much more acute in as far as the mind is more refined and the soul more delicate. No community, however fervent it may be, to whatever Order it may belong, escapes this law, any more than the greatest saints have escaped it.

Look at the Apostles. Were they not at the best school of sanctity? During three years, they were able to contemplate Jesus, to listen to His teaching and be under the direct influence of His Divine grace. Now what do we read in the Gospel? Two of them, to the exclusion of the

1 Rule, ch. xlix. 2 *Sermo X de Verbis Domini.* P. L. 38, Sermon lxix.

others, ask for a special place in Christ's Kingdom;[1] before the Last Supper there is again "a strife amongst them, which of them should seem to be the greater," to such a degree that our Lord has to rebuke them anew.[2] Later, St. Peter and St. Paul are at variance; St. Barnabas who, for quite a long time, had accompanied St. Paul in his preaching, has one day to separate from him: they no longer agree. St. Jerome and St. Augustine do not always understand one another, any more than St. Charles Borromeo and St. Philip of Neri.

Thus human nature has at times such weaknesses and deficiencies that even souls who sincerely seek God and are most united together in the charity of Christ, are true subjects of mortification for one another. And this happens in every clime, in every latitude, in every community in the world. Now, to endure this friction daily, with patience, with charity, without ever complaining, constitutes a very real mortification.

Thus our holy Patriarch, who had such great experience of the human heart, who knew that everywhere human nature, even among the best, has its infirmities and miseries, insists upon our duty of patiently enduring one another's infirmities: *Infirmitates suas sive corporum sive morum* PATIENTISSIME *tolerent*.[3] When these little dissensions arise which he so well calls "thorns of scandal," *Scandalorum spinea*,[4] he will not have us let the sun go down upon our resentment lest it be given time to take root: *Cum discordante ante solis occasum in pacem redire*.[5] On this subject he introduces into the holy liturgy itself a practice inspired by the purest spirit of the Gospel. He prescribes that the Abbot shall say the *Pater noster* aloud every day in choir, at Lauds and Vespers, in the name of the monastic family,[6] so that when we ask our Heavenly Father to forgive us our own offences, we may not forget in our turn to forgive our brethren if they offend us.

So true is it that the common life easily becomes a continual source of friction for our weak nature. But for those who seek God, this life is transformed into one of boundless and unremitting charity: *Si angustiantur vasa carnis, dilatentur spatia caritatis*![7]

1 Matth. xx, 26–28; Marc. x, 35–45.
2 Luc. xxii, 24–25.
3 Rule, ch. lxxii.
4 Rule, ch. xiii.
5 Ibid. iv.
6 Ibid. xiii.
7 St. Augustine. *L. c.*

To the mortifications of common life which result from the *social* order of things, are to be added those of the *vows* with their precise object and character of a contract between us and God. Constant fidelity to our engagements constitutes a veritable mortification: we are, by nature, so inclined to independence, so fond of liberty and change! It is true that faithful souls observe their vows with gladness, fervour and love; but this observance remains none the less an immolation for nature. Let us again look at our Divine Saviour in His Passion. We know that He accepted it out of love for His Father, and that this love was immense: "That the world may know, that I love the Father": *Ut cognoscat mundus quia diligo Patrem.*[1] But did He not suffer despite this love? Certainly He did: what suffering has ever equalled His suffering which He accepted on coming into this world? Hear the cry which escapes from His Heart crushed beneath the burden: "My Father, if it be possible, let this chalice pass from Me. Nevertheless not as I will, but as Thou wilt."[2] Love for His Father lifted Him above the shrinking of His sensitive nature. And yet His agony was terrible, His sorrows indescribable. His Heart, says the Psalmist, became like wax, melting beneath the intensity of suffering.[3] But because He remained fastened to the Cross by love, He gave His Father infinite glory, worthy of the Divine perfections.

We, too, fastened ourselves to the cross on the day of our profession; we did so out of love; and if we remain faithful to our post of immolation it is still through love. This does not prevent nature from feeling pain. You may ask: Is not the monastery the ante-chamber of Heaven? Assuredly it is; but to stay a long time in a place of waiting, and there to bear monotony and annoyances, can become singularly burdensome and require a big dose of endurance.[4]

We must however remain firm and be patient till God's good time: *Viriliter age et sustine Dominum.*[5] God is never so near to us as when He places His Son's Cross upon our shoulders; never do we give our Father

1 Joan. xiv, 31. 2 Matth. xxvi, 39. 3 Ps. xxi, 15.

4 See above, what we said about fortitude, p. 163.

5 "Do manfully... and wait thou for the Lord," Ps. xxvi, 41.

in Heaven more of the glory that He receives from our patience than in these moments: *Afferunt fructum in patientia.*[1]

The vows being established to procure the practice of the corresponding virtues, it is not astonishing that as regards renunciation, they lead us very far. It is true one finds souls who, after a time, *submit* to obedience, *endure* stability: this they do from force of habit. With them, the vow may, strictly speaking, remain intact; but the virtue is absent or very enfeebled. Such a disposition is very poor in love of God. Let us, on the contrary, strive to practise from love, in all its extent and perfection, the virtue that serves as a stimulus to the vow. This love will solve all the difficulties that can arise in our life, will brave all the renunciations to which our profession obliges us.

Difficulties, disappointments, contradictions, are ever to be encountered in whatsoever part of the world we may be. It is so much the more impossible to escape them in that they have less to do with circumstances than with our human condition. Our Holy Father, the most discreet of religious law-givers, warns us of this. Although he wishes to establish in his Rule "nothing too harsh or rigorous,"[2] he will however have the Master of Novices show the postulants "the hard and rugged things," *dura et aspera,*[3] that fallen nature will inevitably meet with upon the path that leads to God. But, he says,[4] like St. Paul, love makes us overcome in all things: *Quis nos separabit a caritate Christi?... Propter te mortificamur tota die.*[5] It is for Thy sake, O God, and to show Thee our love, that all the day long we deny ourselves.

If we truly love Christ Jesus, we shall not try to avoid the difficulties and sufferings that occur in the faithful practice of the vows and observances of our monastic life; we shall embrace them as our Divine Lord embraced His Cross when it was offered to Him. Some have a heavier cross than others; however heavy it may be, love gives them the strength to bear it; the unction of divine grace makes them cling to it instead of seeking how to cast it away, and in the end they come to feel affection for it as a means of continually testifying to their love: *Aquae multae*

1 "Bring forth fruit in patience," Luc. viii, 15. 2 Prologue of the Rule.

3 Rule, ch. lviii. 4 Ibid. ch. vii.

5 "Who will separate us from the love of Christ?... For Thy sake we are put to death all the day long," Rom. viii, 36. and Rule, ch. vii.

non potuerunt exstinguere caritatem.[1] If a monk who for love of Christ to Whom he gave himself for ever on the day of his profession, were to remain constantly faithful to what he then promised, if he were to live in a spirit of poverty and never admit into his heart a too human and too natural affection, if his whole life were to be spent in absolute dependence on his Rule and on those who represent Christ towards him, if he were to bear, without ever murmuring, the burden of the day and the uniformity inherent to the regular life of the cloister—this monk would give our Lord continual proofs of love and find God perfectly. He would have brought to naught within himself every obstacle that could have been opposed to perfect divine union. But who will show us this religious, that in him we may celebrate the summit of virtue! *Quis est hic, et laudabimus eum? Fecit enim mirabilia in vita sua...*[2]

IV

If the first place is reserved by right, in our estimation and in our life, to the penances prescribed by the Church and by the Rule, the preference given to them of course does not tend to dissuade from and depreciate the mortifications wherein everyone of goodwill takes the initiative. Indeed in the monastery, personal initiative remains entire. Not only does St. Benedict safeguard it, but he positively encourages it. On this subject it suffices to read the chapter in his Rule on Lent. He wishes that during these forty holy days, we should add something to that which is ordinarily appointed to us as regards God's service, *AUGEAMUS nobis aliquid solito penso servitutis nostrae*;[3] private prayers, a greater abstinence from food and sleep, and a tighter rein on our liberty of speech. These are only a few points proposed by the holy Legislator, for the field in this direction is vast, and private initiative can be given free course: *UNUSQUISQUE super mensuram sibi indictam aliquid PROPRIO VOLUNTATE... offerat.*

This liberty left by St. Benedict to private initiative is not limited to the season of Lent; it extends to the whole life of a monk; the holy Patriarch himself makes this understood at the beginning of the abovesaid

1 "Many waters cannot quench charity," Cant. viii, 7.

2 Eccli. xxxi, 9. 3 Rule, ch. xlix.

chapter. If at no time would he discourage the weak, he always leaves free scope to the holy ambition of the valiant: *Ut sit quod fortes cupiant.*[1] These are the works of supererogation which the valiant alone have the strength to undertake. To those on the contrary who find the integral accomplishment of the common observance beyond their physical powers, the idea will come spontaneously of imposing upon themselves some slight penances, so that if they are obliged to renounce the "letter" of the regular discipline they may at least have some modest pledges to give to its "spirit."

But whatever be the reason that instigates the exercise of free choice in this matter of penitential practices, St. Benedict subjects it to one essential condition: every project of mortification foreign to the rule laid down, is to be first of all submitted to the approbation of those who hold the place of Christ towards us.[2]

The end that is here proposed by the holy Legislator is altogether worthy of a clear-sighted director of souls: "If obedience intervenes, it will not be to reduce initiative or manly resolution, but to guide them and make them fruitful";[3] he especially takes precautions against self-will; he would avoid the danger of vainglory which so easily creeps in with those who undertake mortifications of their own choice: "All that is done without permission of the spiritual Father shall be accounted as presumption and vainglory and deserve no reward": *Quod sine permissione patris spiritualis fit, praesumptioni deputabitur et vanae gloriae, non mercedi.*[4]

Our holy Father furthermore exhorts us to offer to God, with the joy that emanates from the Holy Spirit, something beyond the measure appointed to us: *Offerat Deo cum gaudio sancti Spiritus.*[5] Let us be happy to have the opportunity of offering God some acts of penance: fervour and joy must needs accompany what we give to God; magnanimity and generosity are joyful in the giving: *Hilarem datorem diligit Deus.*[6]

1 Rule, ch. lxiv. 2 Ibid. ch. xlix.

3 Abbot of Solesmes. *Commentary on the Rule of St. Benedict,* translated by Dom Justin McCann, p. 319.

4 Rule, ch. xlix. 5 Rule, ch. xlix. 6 I Cor. ix, 7 and Rule, ch. v.

However, before approaching the question itself of exceptional mortifications, we must well understand the attitude St. Benedict recommends to us in general regarding the created things with which God surrounds us in our exile here below, and the legitimate pleasure we derive from them. The holy Patriarch gives us a valuable counsel in this matter: "Not to embrace delights," *delicias non amplecti*.[1] What harms the soul in this domain, is to *give* oneself up to them in excess. Christ Jesus partook of food, contemplated the beauties of nature, and enjoyed the charms of friendship, but He only *gave* Himself to His Father and to souls. In the same way, self-renunciation forbids us to let ourselves be carried away in the use of permitted created things; and it is in following this line of conduct indicated by St. Benedict that we acquire, little by little, that holy liberty of soul and heart in regard to all creatures—a liberty that was one of the characteristic virtues of our great St. Gertrude and won for her most precious favours from Christ.

To return to outward mortifications or afflictive penances, let us say that in this matter itself, a certain discretion must be kept. The degree of voluntary mortification must be measured according to the past state of the soul, and the obstacles to be avoided; it is for the director to fix this degree.

It would be dangerous temerity to undertake extraordinary mortifications without being called to do so by God. In fact, to be able to give oneself to constant macerations of the body is a gift of God. And this gift often constitutes one of His most precious favours. When God grants it to a soul, it is because He wills to lead her far in spiritual ways; often He prepares her in this manner to receive ineffable communications of His Divine grace; He delves deep down in the soul in order to empty her entirely of self, and possess her undividedly. Only, before entering into this way, it is necessary that we should be called to it by God; there is danger in entering it of our own accord. To be able to sustain these great mortifications, we need a special grace which God will only give us if He calls us to it; without this grace we break down physically and in consequence have to take special care of our health. And this easily

1 Rule, ch. iv.

opens the door to relaxation, not without great detriment to the soul; one then becomes a burden to others and to one's self.[1]

It is therefore with great wisdom that the holy Legislator has prescribed, as we have just seen, that in the matter of exterior renunciation, nothing should be done "without permission of the spiritual Father," for "every one hath his proper gift from God": *Unusquisque proprium habet donum ex Deo, alius sic, alius vero sic.*[2]

The domain where all latitude may be taken is that of interior mortification, which is likewise the most perfect. This mortification represses the vices of the mind, breaks our self-love and attachment to our own judgment; it refrains tendencies to pride, independence, vanity, touchiness, levity, curiosity, and subjects us to the common life, that penance of penances. Let us take the order of our day: To rise at the first sound of the bell, to go to the choir whether inclined to do so or not, there to praise God with attention and fervour; to accept the thousand details of the rule as they are laid down for work, meals, recreation, sleep; to submit oneself continually to these things without ever murmuring or being in any way singular, forms an excellent penance which makes the soul greatly pleasing to God, and altogether docile to the action of the Holy Spirit. Consider silence, for instance. How many times, during the course of the day, occasions occur which tempt us to speak needlessly! But we say to ourselves: "No, out of love for Christ, to keep the perfume of His Divine presence in my soul, I will not speak." A single day may be thus made up of acts of mortification which are so many acts of love. Again another point in which virtue may be frequently practised, is in immediate obedience to the voice of God calling us to the different exercises: *Mox exoccupatis manibus,*[3] says St. Benedict. It needs great virtue to put constantly into action what these few words signify. We are busy at our work; the bell rings. We are often tempted to say "It will only take a few moments to finish this." If we listen to this suggestion what is it that we do? We prefer our own will to God's Will. This is not "forsaking" our own will, nor is it what St. Benedict wants: *Quod*

1 This is the teaching that God gave to St. Catherine. See *Dialogue on the Gift of Discernment*, ch. 7.

2 I Cor. vii, 7 and Rule, ch. xl.

3 "Right then, with hands disengaged," Rule, ch. v.

agebant imperfectum relinquentes.[1] Little things? Yes, in themselves; but great by reason of the virtue they require, great by reason of the love that observes them, and the holiness to which they lead. "He who desires for My sake to mortify his body with many penances," said the Eternal Father to St. Catherine of Siena, "but without renouncing his own will is wrong in thinking that this is pleasing to Me."[2] We only please God when we seek to do His good-pleasure in all things.

Let us also accept willingly the mortifications sent to us by Providence: hunger, cold, heat, small inconveniences of place or time, slight contradictions coming from those around us. You may again say that these things are trifles; yes, but trifles that form part of the Divine plan for us. Is not that enough to make us accept them with love?

Finally, let us accept illness, if sent to us by God, or what is sometimes more painful, a state of habitual ill-health, an infirmity that never leaves us; adversities, spiritual aridity; to accept all these things can become very mortifying for nature. If we do so with loving submission, without ever relaxing in the service we owe to God, although heaven seems to be cold and deaf to us, our soul will open more and more to the Divine action. For, according to the saying of St. Paul, "all things work together unto good" to those whom God calls to share His glory: *OMNIA cooperantur in bonum iis qui secundum propositum vocati sunt sancti.*

V

Whatever be our mortifications, corporal or spiritual, those that afflict the body or those that repress the ill regulated tendencies of the mind, they are however only a means. In some institutes, exercises of penance and expiation play so preponderant a part that they constitute the very reason of their existence. These institutes have their own mission in the Holy Church, a special function in the Mystical Body; for the diversity of functions, of which St. Paul speaks, exists for religious orders as it does for the individual. Those who make profession in these institutes are "victims"; the life of continual immolation gives them a particular character and splendour. Happy the souls whom God calls

1 "Leaving the work they were engaged in unfinished," Ibid.

2 *Dialogue.* ch. 10.

to the bareness of the cross! It becomes for them an inexhaustible fount of precious graces.

The spirit of St. Benedict is rather to form Christians who simply aim at practising every virtue in a high degree without specialising in any of them. Our Patriarch, in this domain, has quite other conceptions than some of those which prevailed with the Fathers of the desert and the anchorets of the East in the matter of afflictive practices. Without neglecting, as we have just seen, exterior mortification, his asceticism is however brought to bear upon the virtues of humility and above all of obedience: it is to them that he chiefly looks for the destruction of the "old man" necessary to the fruition of the soul's union with God.[1]

Finally, one truth upon which it is important to insist here, in relation to exterior mortification, is that, although renunciation is an indispensable means, afflictive practices have no value *in themselves* in the plan of Christianity. Their value comes to them from their union through faith and love with the sufferings and expiation of Christ Jesus. Our Divine Saviour came down upon earth to show us how we must live in order to be pleasing to His Father. He is the perfect Model of all perfection. Now the Gospel tells us He ate what was set before Him, without making any distinction, so much so that the Pharisees took scandal thereat. And our Lord tells them: "Not that which goeth into the mouth defileth a man: but what cometh out of the mouth, this defileth a man."[2] Let us then not place our perfection in exterior mortifications, even extraordinary ones, considered in *themselves*. What is above all important is that we mortify ourselves and bear our sufferings out of love for our Lord as a participation in His Passion.

"True perfection and true holiness," says a great master of the spiritual life, the Venerable Louis Blosius, heir in this of the best Benedictine traditions, "does not lie in frightful macerations nor the excessive use of instruments of penance; they consist in the mortification of self-will and of our vices, as well as in true humility and sincere charity."[3] Great aus-

---

1 Rom. vi, 6. Cf. D. Morin, *The Ideal of the Monastic Life in the Apostolic Age.* ch. 3. *Do Penance.* This perfectly characterises St. Benedict's method on this point.

2 Matth. xv, 16.

3 *The Mirror of the Soul,* ch. vii, 3. St. Catherine in her *Dialogue* sets down the same teaching of the Eternal Father: "Those who are nourished at the table of penance are good and perfect, if their penance is founded in me with befitting discernment... with

terity of life is excellent when added to these fundamental dispositions, but everyone is not capable of this, while everyone can lead a life of true and holy mortification if they are careful to offer continually "to God the Father, the fasts, watchings and tribulations of Christ's most bitter Passion,"[1] and to accomplish the little they do in union with these sufferings of the Saviour and in honour of His continual and total submission to His Father's Will. He who knows how to offer to God the complete submission of his free-will, after the Saviour's example, has a soul that is "truly detached and mortified like unto a ripe, tender and delicious grape"; he who knows not this self-renunciation is, on the contrary, for God, like "unripe fruit, hard and sour to the taste."[2]

This thought is a very useful one to encourage us in our work of self-renunciation. During the day let us think of our morning Mass. We were then united to the immolation of Jesus and placed upon the altar with the Divine Victim; let us therefore accept generously the sufferings, the vexations, the burden of the day and the heat thereof, the difficulties and self-denial inherent to the common life. Thus we shall practically live our Mass. Indeed, is not our heart an altar whence the incense of our sacrifice and our submission to His adorable Will unceasingly rises up to God? What altar could be more pleasing to Him than a heart full of love constantly offered up to Him. For we can always sacrifice upon this altar, and offer ourselves with the Son of His love, for His glory and the welfare of souls.

This is the teaching that our Lord Himself gave to St. Mechtilde. "One day whilst she was thinking that her illness made her useless and that her sufferings were unavailing, the Lord said to her: 'Place all thy pains in My Heart and I will give them the most absolute perfection

great humility, and the constant study to judge according to My will and not according to the will of man. If they are not thus clad with My will through true humility, they will very often put obstacles in the way of their perfection, by making themselves judges of those who do not follow the same path as they do. And knowest thou why they do not attain perfection? Because they have exerted their zeal and desire much more in mortifying their body than in slaying their self-will."

1 *The Mirror of the Soul,* ch. vii, 3.

2 *A Book of Spiritual Instruction.* The whole of this passage is taken from the article of D. P. de Puniet: *La place du Christ dans la doctrine spirituelle de Louis de Blots.* (*La Vie Spirituelle.* Aug. 1920, p. 393, sq.)

that suffering can possess. As My Divinity drew to itself the sufferings of My Humanity and made them its own, so will I transport thy pains into My Divinity, I will unite them to My Passion and make thee share in that glory which God the Father has bestowed on My Sacred Humanity in return for all its sufferings. Confide, therefore, each of thy pains to Love in saying: 'O Love, I give them to thee with the same intention that thou hadst when thou didst bring them to me from the Heart of God, and I beseech thee to offer them to Him again, made perfect by intensest gratitude...'" "My Passion," added Christ Jesus, "bore infinite fruit in Heaven and upon earth; thus thy pains, thy tribulations offered to Me and united to My Passion will be so fruitful that they will procure more glory for the elect, new merit for the just, forgiveness for sinners, and an alleviation of their pains for the souls in Purgatory. What is there indeed that My Heart cannot change for the better, since it is from the goodness of My Heart that all good flows both in Heaven and on earth?"[1]

Such is the Catholic doctrine on this point. God is the first Author of our holiness, the source of our perfection, but we must labour at removing the obstacles that hinder His action in us; we must renounce sin, and the tendencies that give rise to it; we must free ourselves from created things in as far as they prevent us going to God. One who will not submit himself to this law of mortification, who seeks his ease and comfort, who is anxious to escape suffering and does all he can to avoid the cross, who puts no constraint upon himself to keep all the observances of common life, will never arrive at intimate union with Christ Jesus. This union is so precious that it must needs be bought with labour and toil and perpetual self-denial. We can only find God fully after having removed all obstacles from our path, and destroyed all that displeases Him in ourselves. St. Gregory—whose words are evidently a commentary on the first lines of the Prologue of the Rule—says that in cleaving to ourselves and to creatures, we separate ourselves from God. In order to return to Him, *Ut ad Eum redeas*, it is to Christ, and to Christ crucified, that we must cleave; we must carry the cross with Him along the path of compunction, obedience and self-forgetfulness.[2] It is only by passing

1 *The Book of Special Grace*, 2nd Part, ch. 36. See also 3rd Part, ch. 36.

2 *Regio nostra paradisus est, ad quam, Jesu cognito, redire per viam qua venimus prohibemur. A regione enim nostra superbiendo, inobediendo, visibilia sequendo, cibum*

through the sorrows of Calvary and the poverty of the Cross that we shall come to the triumph of the Resurrection and the glory of the Ascension: *Nonne oportuit Christum pati et ita intrare in gloriam suam.*[1]

With this thought we will end our conference after the example of our great Patriarch who thus closes his Prologue: *Passionibus Christi per patientiam participemur, ut in regno ejus mereamur esse consortes.*[2] Mortification and self-denial are but for a time; the life that they safeguard and foster in us is everlasting. It is true that here below, where we live by faith, the splendour of this life is hidden from our eyes: *Vita vestra abscondita est*;[3] but in the light of heaven where there is no more darkness it will shine for ever; there will be no more crying, no more suffering; God Himself will wipe away the tears from the eyes of His servants; He will make His elect sit down at the heavenly feast, and will inebriate them at the ever flowing torrent of unalloyed delights: *Et torrente voluptatis tuae potabis eos.*[4]

We shall then see the fulfilment of those words that the Church, the Bride of Christ, applies to us on the day of our religious profession. At that decisive hour when we responded to the Divine call, the Abbot showed us the Rule. He told us by what path of renunciation we must go to God. And we chose to enter upon this path, to labour at the soil of our soul that heavenly virtues might spring up among the thorns and briars. "They that sow in tears shall reap in joy." Now they plough the furrows in the sweat of their brow, and the seeds they cast therein they water with their tears. The hour will come of overflowing joy when they will bring their full sheaves to the Lord of the Harvest: *Euntes ibant et*

---

vetitum gustando discessimus; sed ad eam necesse est ut flendo, obediendo, visibilia contemnendo atque appetitum carnis refrenando redeamus (Our kingdom is Paradise, to which, though Jesus is known, we are not permitted to return by the way we came. For we departed from our kingdom by being proud, disobeying, chasing after visible things, enjoying forbidden food; but to go back, it is necessary that we return by weeping, obeying, condemning visible things, and refraining from the appetite of the flesh). *Homil. 10 in Evang.* The Church has inserted this passage in the Octave of the Epiphany as the interpretation applied to the "*per aliam viam reversi sunt*" (they went back another way) of the Magi.

1 Luc. xxiv, 26.

2 "We shall share by patience in the sufferings of Christ, that we may deserve to be partakers also of his His kingdom," Prologue of the Rule.

3 Col. iii, 3. 4 Ps. xxxv, 9.

flebant mittentes semina sua: venientes autem venient cum exsultatione portantes manipulos suos.[1]

1 Ibid. cxxv, 5–7.

POVERTY

SUMMARY.—Necessity for one who seeks God of renouncing every creature, material goods to begin with.—I. St. Benedict's requirements concerning individual poverty.—II. How everything necessary is to be hoped for from the Abbot.—III. Exercise of the virtue of poverty inseparable from that of hope.—IV. Christ, the Model of poverty; deep aspect of poverty in the inner life of Christ.—V. Precious blessings that God bestows on those who are detached.

IN our seeking after God, we are hindered by the obstacles we find upon our way or within ourselves. To find God perfectly, we must first of all be freed from every creature in so far as it keeps us back on the path of perfection. The young man of the Gospel who comes to our Lord and asks what he must do to have life everlasting, is given this answer: "Keep the commandments." "All these have I kept from my youth," replies the young man. Then our Divine Saviour adds: "If thou wilt be perfect, go sell what thou hast, and give to the poor, and... come follow Me." At these words the young man goes away sorrowful. "For" says the Gospel, "he had great possessions."[1] Riches held his heart captive and because of them he could not follow in the footsteps of Jesus.

Our Lord has given us the immense grace of letting us hear His Divine voice calling us to perfection: *Venite post Me.*[2] By an act of faith in His word and in His Divinity, we have come to Him and have said like St. Peter: "Behold we have left all things, and have followed Thee": *Ecce nos reliquimus omnia et secuti sumus te.*[3] We have relinquished material goods, in order that being voluntarily poor, no longer having anything

1 Matth. xix, 16–22. 2 "Come after Me," Marc. i, 17. 3 Matth. xix, 27.

to hold us back, we may fully consecrate ourselves to the pursuit of the one true immutable Good.

If we keep ourselves in the fervour with which we totally abandoned all worldly possessions, we shall surely find the Infinite Good even here below. "What therefore shall we have?" Peter asked our Lord: *Quid ergo erit nobis?* And Christ replies: "You shall receive an hundredfold and shall possess life everlasting."[1] God is so magnificent in His dealings with us, that in return for the things we leave for Him, He gives Himself to us even now and here with incommensurable generosity. "Amen, I say to you... there is no man that hath left house, or brethren, or sisters, or father or mother, or children, or lands for My sake... who shall not receive an hundred times as much, now in this time": *Amen dico vobis: Nemo est qui reliquerit domum... propter Me... qui non accipiat centies tantum NUNC IN TEMPORE HOC.*[2] He puts no bounds to His Divine communications, and this is the one source of our true beatitude: "Blessed are the poor in Spirit: for theirs is the kingdom of heaven": *BEATI pauperes spiritu, quoniam ipsorum est regnum caelorum.*[3]

Only it is important that we always remain in that disposition of faith, hope and love, whereby we left all to place our beatitude in God alone; it is important that we should no longer be attached to what we have given up for ever. And this is often very difficult.

Thus as St. Teresa remarks, our nature is so subtile that it seeks to take back, in one way or another, what it has once given. "We resolve to become poor," she writes, "and it is a resolution of great merit; but we very often take care not to be in want, not simply of what is necessary, but of what is superfluous; yea, and to make for ourselves friends who may supply us; and in this way we take more pains, and perhaps expose ourselves to greater danger, in order that we may want nothing, than we did formerly, when we had our own possessions in our own power." And the great Saint adds these words which I have already cited but which are always good to read again: "A pleasant manner this of seeking the love of God! We retain our own affections, and yet will have that love, as they say, by handfuls... This is not well, and we are seeking things that are incompatible one with the other."[4]

1 Ibid. 2 Marc. x, 29–30. 3 Matth. v, 3.
4 *Life by Herself*, ch. 11, translated from the Spanish by David Lewis.

You see that if voluntary poverty is an indispensable condition for finding God fully, for being perfect disciples of Christ Jesus, it is extremely important, in the course of our monastic life, not to take anything back from what we have once given as regards the renunciation of exterior goods. Let us then see in what this renunciation consists, how far it extends, and with what virtue we ought to link it so as to practise it in its perfection. We shall see that our Holy Father shows himself singularly exacting upon this point of individual poverty, and the practice of this renunciation to be a very lofty form of the theological virtue of hope.

I

Although St. Benedict does not make the word "poverty" enter into the formula of the vows, he prescribes, however, that the monk at his profession shall distribute his goods to the poor, or bestow them on the monastery; he is to reserve nothing for himself: *Nihil sibi reservans ex omnibus.*[1] Even when parents offered their sons to the monastery, they had to promise that never, either of themselves, or through anyone else, would they give anything whatsoever to their son once he has become a monk, lest occasion should be given him of violating, to the detriment of his soul, the poverty that he has promised.

Moreover, the practice of poverty enters into this *conversio morum*[2] which we vow at the moment of our profession. For, by this vow, we are bound to seek the perfection of our state. Now the exercise of poverty is necessary for one who wishes to be a perfect disciple of Christ. Thus we see our Holy Father consecrate a very remarkable chapter, in his Rule, to the ascetical matter which he has not especially mentioned in the act of profession. He calls private ownership for the monk, "a vice": *vitium proprietatis*; a "baneful vice": *vitium nequissimum*[3] which must be cut off at all costs.

And yet has not man a natural right to possess? The simple Christian living in the world can fully use his faculty of having possessions without compromising his salvation and perfection; for, in this matter, it is not a precept but a simple counsel that our Lord gives when He speaks of leaving everything in order to be His perfect disciple. The action of Divine

1 Rule, ch. lviii. 2 Ibid. 3 Rule, ch. xxxiii.

grace in the soul of the simple Christian is fettered only by the ill-regulated attachment which makes the soul a captive of exterior possessions.

But for us who for love of Christ, and in order to follow Him more freely, have voluntarily renounced this right, it would be in some measure a sin to attempt to take it back unduly.

Our Holy Legislator wishes to eliminate this vice in every form. As you know there is nothing, absolutely nothing, that the monk can receive or give, without leave of his Abbot, nothing that he can possess as his own: *Ne quis praesumat aliquid dare aut accipere sine jussione abbatis, neque aliquid habere proprium, NULLAM OMNINO REM*;[1] "neither books, nor writing-tablets nor pen, nor anything whatsoever: *Neque codicem, neque tabulas, neque graphium, sed nihil omnino*.[2]

What is still more significant is the *last means* he points out by which a monk may dipossess himself of every object: the monk has not even power over his own body or his own will: *Quippe quibus nec corpora sua nec voluntates licet habere in propria voluntate*.[3] This is the application of the words of the Gospel: *Ecce nos reliquimus omnia*. Our Holy Father goes so far to the root of the matter that he does not tolerate that one should account as *his own*, even in words, anything whatsoever: *Nec quisquam suum esse aliquid dicat*.[4] The monk may not receive anything, "neither letters, nor eulogies,[5] or the least gifts without the order of the Abbot," and as to the gifts which have lawfully found their way into the enclosure it remains in the power of the head of the monastery to give them to whomsoever he pleases: *Quod si jusserit suscipi, in abbatis sit potestate cui illud jubeat dari*.[6] St. Benedict takes care to warn the monk for whom the gift had originally been intended by those outside "not to be grieved, lest occasion be given to the devil."[7]

Why does the great Patriarch, ordinarily so wide in his views, enter here into such minute regulations? It is because a question of principle is at stake, and when it concerns a principle, as we have many times seen, he knows how to show himself uncompromising. The principle here

1 Rule, ch. xxxiii. 2 Ibid. 3 Ibid. 4 Ibid.

5 Ibid. ch. liv. The eulogy is properly speaking the morsel of blessed bread distributed to the faithful during the solemn Mass; it symbolised the union that should exist among Christians. By extension, this term has been applied to fruit, holy pictures, medals, relics.

6 Ibid. 7 Ibid.

involved is that of dependence on authority, and detachment of heart. To give or receive anything without the Abbot's permission, is an act of independence, and nourishes the spirit of ownership. And nothing is so contrary to the absolute detachment that we have vowed.

We must then have nothing of our own. You perhaps say to yourself: 'I am quite at rest on that point.' If it be so, thank God for it, for it is a great grace to be fully detached. However, let us examine things more closely, for there is more than one way of having anything of one's own.

It cannot even be a question here of hoarding. At the last Day we should fear to appear before God, if we had possessed the least hoard. But, without going so far as this, there are different fashions of making any object whatsoever "one's own." It may happen, for example, that a religious makes himself from the very first so difficult that he surrounds some book or other object with a hedge of thorns, so to speak, and in such a way that no one dare ask it from him. In theory, this object is for the common use; in fact, it has become the property of this religious. Little things, in themselves; but the detachment resulting from them can become dangerous for the soul's liberty; the principle of our perfection itself is at stake.

"Let all things be common to all," says our Holy Father. That is one of the characters of monastic poverty such as he intends it to be: *Omnia omnibus sint communia*:[1] by these words he refers to the community of goods that existed between the faithful of the early Church. He ordains that "anyone who treats the things of the monastery in a slovenly or negligent manner shall be punished."[2] Why this severity? Because the monastery being the "house of God," all things in it ought to be considered "as if they were the consecrated vessels of the altar": *Omnia vasa monasterii cunctamque substantiam, ac si altaris vasa sacrata conspiciat*.[3]

Once more in this lofty motive, we see the deeply supernatural and "religious" character with which the holy Legislator wishes to steep the monk's whole existence, even in the least details.

1 Rule, ch. xxxiii. 2 Ibid. ch. xxxii. 3 Ibid. ch. xxxi.

II

The care of these goods, "sacred" in the sight of the great Patriarch, is confided to the Abbot. It is for him to provide for all the necessities of his monks; he is the shepherd of the flock, the father of the family, and it is from him, says St. Benedict, that the monk must hope for everything: *Omnia a patre sperare monasterii.*[1] A profound saying and one which marks the character of our poverty.

The monk is to look for everything from the Abbot. At our profession we despoiled ourselves of everything and put ourselves in the hands of the Abbot; it is through him that God will give us what is necessary.

Our Holy Father follows this chapter on poverty with another chapter entitled: "Whether all ought alike to receive what is necessary."[2] Again citing, in his reply, the Acts of the Apostles, where it is said: "distribution was made to everyone according as he had need," St. Benedict adds that the Abbot "ought not to have respect of persons but consideration for infirmities." Necessities are not mathematically the same; one has need of more, another of less. As the Abbot has not infused knowledge, we ought to tell him our needs with simplicity, and to confide ourselves to him, for he is the father of the monastic family. What does not come from the Abbot does not come from God; never let us then try to obtain anything, however small it may be, by roundabout means; do not let us be diplomatic in order, as St. Teresa says, to make friends who will give us what we want.

A trait in the life of St. Margaret Mary shows how pleasing to God is this manner of expecting everything from our Superior. The Saint had revelations sometimes from the Saviour touching the line of conduct that her director, Père de la Colombière, should follow. One day when the latter was setting out for England, she sent him some words of advice amongst which the following were contained: "that he should take great care not to draw good (*direct*) from its source." She further told him that this short saying contained much which God would give him to understand according to the way he acted on it. Père de la Colombière read and re-read this phrase without at first comprehending its meaning; but, some days later, during prayer, our Lord gave him light on it.

1 Ibid. ch. xxxiii. 2 Ibid. ch. xxxiv.

On account of the difficult situation in which he found himself, being in a land of persecution, he received a small pension from his relations. This was not without his Superior's permission but the pension did not pass through the latter's hand; and Christ gave Père de la Colombière to understand that this was not pleasing to Him. "I understood," wrote P. de la Colombière, "that this saying contains much because it concerns the perfection of poverty... and that this is the fount of a great inward and outward peace."[1]

It is the same for us. Everything is to be looked for from the father of the monastery: *Omnia a patre sperare monasterii*. For all that has to do with the health, clothing, food, exceptions, and all else, let us with confidence tell our wants to the Abbot or to those whom he has delegated to replace him in this domain. See what our holy Legislator writes on this subject; his words show, as ever, with much exactitude and discretion, the supernatural line of conduct that we should follow: "Let him who has need of less give thanks to God, and not be grieved thereby; and let him who requireth more be humbled by his infirmity and not be made proud by the mercy shewn to him."[2] And St. Benedict concludes with this sentence so full of his spirit: *Et ita omnia membra erunt in pace,*[3] "and thus all the members of the family will be at peace." Peace is the fruit of detachment; the soul has no longer any disquietude; it belongs altogether to God.

It certainly requires great faith to conform ourselves perfectly to this programme: but we may be persuaded that if we observe all the points of it, God will not fail us in anything, and our soul will taste deep peace because it will look for everything from Him Who is the Beatitude of all the Saints.

As to the Abbot, he is to provide for all things. To enable him to do this, St. Benedict leaves the monastery the power of possessing. In the practice of poverty the great Patriarch does not understand it as it has been understood and carried out since St. Francis of Assisi's day.[4] St. Paul

1 Cf. *Vie de la Bienheureuse Marguerite-Marie,* by Hamon, ch. 7. *Journal des retraites du R. P. de la Colombière,* Edition Desclée, 1896, p. 164, 169.

2 *Qui minus indiget, agat Deo gratias, et non contristetur; qui vero plus indiget, humilietur pro infirmitate, non extollatur pro misericordia.* 3 Rule, ch. xxxiv.

4 On this subject see the suggestive commentary made by D. G. Morin, in *The Ideal of the Monastic Life.*

says, there is but one Spirit Who governs and directs the Church of Jesus but the inspirations of this Spirit are manifold.[1] It is the same as to the ways that He opens out: these are very varied although they all have in view the perfection of Christ's Mystical Body: *In aedificationem corporis Christi*.[2] To the wonderful *Poverello* of Assisi, the Holy Spirit inspired a radical form of poverty touching not only individuals, but the convent itself; and for the sons of St. Francis this is an inexhaustible fount of precious graces. The same Spirit gave to our holy Legislator another direction, supernatural also and not less fruitful. In the Benedictine Order, individual detachment is to be carried as far as possible, but the monastery may have possessions.

Our Holy Father bids the postulant, about to make profession, to choose either to distribute his goods to the poor or give them to the monastery, and in this latter case, he takes care to wrap this donation in solemn legal forms: *Res si quas habet aut eroget prius pauperibus, aut facta solemniter donatione, conferat monasterio*.[3] In the intention of St. Benedict, the monastery keeps the faculty of possessing, and our whole tradition, in accord with the Church, has confirmed this concept.

We know, moreover, how the splendour of Divine worship has benefited with us from this state of things; again it is thanks to this, that, in the course of centuries, our abbeys have so often been able to relieve Christ in His disinherited members with abundant alms. Certainly this use of earthly goods had been clearly foreseen by our Holy Father.

For all that concerned charity towards the neighbour, he showed himself great and wide-hearted. We see how in a time of famine he ordered that the small quantity of oil remaining in the monastery should be distributed to the poor; you know how he caused the vessel of oil, that the disobedient cellarer had kept in spite of his command, to be thrown out of the window and what miracle God wrought at St. Benedict's prayer in order to reward this charity.[4] We likewise see by the life of our Patriarch that the monastery of Monte Cassino had provisions;[5] St. Benedict, full of the spirit of the Gospel, intends that even material misery shall be succoured; he wishes guests, pilgrims, and the poor

1 Cf. I Cor. xii, 4 seq.
2 "For the edifying of the body of Christ," Eph. iv, 12.
3 Rule, ch. lviii.
4 St. Gregory, *Dialogues*. Lib. ii, ch. 29.
5 Cf. Ibid.

to be welcomed at the monastery.[1] Among the "instruments of good works" he points out that of "relieving the poor": *pauperes recreare,*[2] and he orders the monk, charged with the temporal administration of the monastery, to have especial care of the poor: *Pauperum cum omni sollicitudine curam gerat.*[3] It is evident that these very clear precepts of the holy Legislator could only be carried out if the monastic confraternity had goods at its disposition.

III

Let us return to that individual poverty which the monk ought to embrace so closely and let us try to enter more fully into its spirit. We should understand it wrongly if we limited it to material privation. There are some rich people who are detached from their riches, according to the saying of St. Paul, "who use this world, as if they used it not";[4] in the midst of their wealth, their heart is free; they are of those poor in spirit to whom Christ has promised His Kingdom. There are some poor people, on the contrary, who covet riches, and cling with attachment to the little they possess; their poverty is only material. Have these poor people the virtue of their state? Certainly not! As the Kingdom of God is within the heart,—*Regnum Dei intra vos est*[5]—it is above all in our heart that the virtue of poverty is perfected and developed: one can be poor while wearing the robes of a king. The man who is perfectly poor will be ready to seek God alone: never let us forget that this is the end that St. Benedict points out to us: to seek God in the sincerity of our heart, that is to say, solely: *Si revera Deum quaerit.*[6]

Now the practice of the virtue of poverty is inseparable from that of hope under a lofty form. What in fact is hope? It is a supernatural habit which inclines the soul to regard God as its one Good, and from Him to hope for all necessary graces whereby to attain the possession of this supreme Good. "Thou art, O Lord, the portion of my inheritance": *Dominus, pars hereditatis meae.*[7] When in the soul there is living faith it comprehends that God infinitely surpasses all earthly goods; as St. Gregory says, speaking of St. Benedict, "*all* creatures appear as small" to the

1 Rule, ch. liii. 2 Ibid. ch. iv. 3 Ibid. ch. xxxi.
4 I Cor. vii, 31. 5 Luc. xvii, 21. 6 Rule, ch. lviii. 7 Ps. xv, 5.

soul that contemplates the Creator: *Videnti Creatorem angusta est* OMNIS *creatura*.[8] Faith shows us in the perfect possession of God that precious pearl of which the Gospel speaks;[9] to gain it, we sell all, we leave all; it is a homage rendered to the Divine Goodness and Beauty. Faith blossoms into hope. The soul is so enamoured of God that it no longer wishes for any other good, and the privation of any good, except God, does not trouble it. *Deus meus et omnia*.[10] My God, to such as extent art Thou my All that I need nothing besides Thee; I want nought but Thee; I could not bear to have anything besides Thee for my heart to cling to; Thou alone sufficest me, "For what have I in Heaven? and besides Thee what do I desire upon earth?" *Quid mihi est in caelo, et a te quid volui super terram*? "Thou art the God of my heart, and the God that is my portion for ever": *Deus cordis mei et pars mea Deus in aeternum*.[11] Like St. Paul, the soul counts all things as dung, *ut stercora*, that so it may perfectly gain Christ: *Ut Christum lucrifaciam*.[12] Neither is it attached to the gifts of God, although it may ask for them, not for their own sake, but because they help the soul to advance; neither is it attached to consolations from on high, although God never severs it for ever from the sweetness of His service: it wants God alone.

This is why the soul despoils itself, disengages itself, in order to have more liberty; and if, even when God hides Himself, even when He leaves the soul in dryness and desolation, or gives Himself only in the nudity of His Divinity in order to detach it not only from the earth but from itself; if, I say, the soul remains faithful to seek God only, to place its beatitude in Him alone, it may be assured of finding at last, never more to lose Him and to enjoy Him in all peace, this God Who surpasses all treasures: *Vade, quaecumque habes vende... et habebis* THESAURUM *in caelo*.[13]

Hope has another aspect: it is that of inclining us to look to God for all that is necessary for our sanctification.

Monastic profession, as we have said, is a contract. When, having left all things for Christ Jesus, we remain faithful to our promise, Christ must, if I may thus express myself, bring us to perfection. He has bound Himself to do this. "Wilt thou be perfect?" He says to us, "Go, sell what-

8 *Dialogues*. Lib. ii, ch. 35.
9 Matth. xiii, 6.
10 St. Francis of Assisi.
11 Ps. lxxii, 25 and 26.
12 Philip. iii, 8.
13 Marc. x, 21.

soever thou hast... and come."[1] God is a father, says our Lord Himself; when a child asks his father for bread, will he give him a serpent? And if, adds Jesus, you who are evil, "know how to give good things to your children, how much more will your Father Who is in Heaven" give you what is necessary for you.[2]

And how true this is! St. Paul tells us that the tenderness, as well as the authority, of the fathers of this world has its source in the Heart of God.[3] And if our Heavenly Father loves us, what will He not give us? While we were His enemies He reconciled us to Himself by the death of His Son: He gave Him to us that He might be our salvation,[4] and, says St. Paul, "how hath He not also, with Him, given us all things?" *Quomodo cum illo non omnia nobis donavit.*[5] All that we can desire for the perfection and holiness of our souls, we find in Christ Jesus; in Him are all the treasures of the Godhead: *Omnes thesauri sapientiae et scientiae.*[6] The indubitable will of the Eternal Father is that His beloved Son should be *our* redemption, *our* justice, *our* sanctification;[7] that all His merits, all His satisfactions—and their value is infinite—should be ours. You are made so rich in Christ, exclaims St. Paul, "that nothing is wanting to you in any grace":[8] *Ita ut nihil vobis desit in ulla gratia.*[9]

Oh, if we know the gift of God! *Si scires donum Dei!*[10] If we knew what inexhaustible riches we may possess in Christ Jesus, not only should we not go begging happiness from creatures nor seeking it from perishable goods but we should despoil ourselves of them as much as possible in order to increase our soul's capacity for possessing true treasures. We should be watchful not to attach ourselves to the least thing that could keep us back from God.

It is this that gives assurance to our hope and renders it invincible: when our heart is *truly* loosened from all things, when we place our beatitude in God alone; when for love of Him we detach ourselves from every creature, and look but to Him for all necessary graces, then God shows Himself magnificent towards us: He fills us with Himself: *Ego*

1 Ibid.
2 Matth. vii, 9 and 11.
3 Eph. iii, 15.
4 Cf. Rom. v, 10.
5 Ibid. viii, 32.
6 Cf. Col. ii, 3.
7 Cf. I Cor. i, 30.
8 I Cor. i, 7.
9 Ibid.
10 Joan. iv, 10.

merces tua magna nimis:[1] I, Who am God, will leave to none other the care of assuaging your thirst for beatitude!

IV

To arrive at this supreme degree of adherence to God, it has first been necessary to leave the world and despoil ourselves of all ownership. We must remain in that first fervour which made us forsake all things for love of Christ. Let us then be watchful that the observance of our vow of poverty remains intact. For example, let us often make the inventory of what we have for our use, and if we find that we have a fondness for anything, or that we have such or such an object that has not been given or permitted by the Abbot, let us restore it to the common use, let us cast it from us, *projice abs te*,[2] for it might become a veritable obstacle to the development of the perfection we have vowed. Thus to break off from everything needs an effort, it needs generosity; but if we have a living faith in Christ, if our hope is sincere, if our love for Him is ardent, we shall find in Him, through prayer, this strength and this generosity. We have all made great sacrifices to give ourselves to God on the day of our entering the monastery. How can we allow ourselves, after this, to be held captive by the nothings which keep back the soul from winging its flight to God!

Let us contemplate our Lord Who is our Model in all things, Whom we wish to follow for love's sake. What does His life teach us? He, so to speak, espoused Poverty.

He was God: *Non rapinam arbitratus est esse se aequalem Deo*;[3] legions of angels are His ministers; with a single word, He drew heaven and earth out of nothing; He decked them with riches and beauty which are but a pale reflection of His infinite perfections: *Domine, quam admirabile est nomen tuum in universa terra*![4] His power and magnificence are so extensive that, according to the Psalmist's expression, He has but

1 Gen. xv, 1. 2 Matth. v, 29-30

3 "Thought it not robbery to be equal with God," Philip. ii, 6.

4 "O Lord, how admirable is Thy Name in the whole earth," Ps. viii, 2.

to open His hand to fill "with blessing every living creature": *Aperis tu manum tuam, et imples omne animal benedictione.*[1]

And behold this God becomes incarnate to bring us to Himself. What way does He choose? That of poverty.

When the Word came into this world, He, the King of Heaven and earth, willed, in His Divine Wisdom, to dispose the details of His birth, life and death, in such a manner that what most transpired was poverty, contempt for the things of this world. The poorest are born at least under a roof; He first sees the day, as He lies upon straw, *in praesepio*, for "there was no room" for His Mother in the inn.[2] At Nazareth, He leads the obscure life of a poor artisan: *Nonne hic fabri filius?*[3] Later on, in His public life, He has nowhere to lay His Head although, "the foxes have holes."[4] At the hour of His death, He is stripped of His garments and fastened naked to the Cross. He leaves His executioners to take possession of that tunic woven by His Mother; His friends have forsaken Him; of His Apostles, He sees only St. John near Him. At least, His Mother remains to Him: but no; He gives Her to His disciple: *Ecce mater tua.*[5] Is not this absolute renunciation? Yet He finds a means of going beyond this extreme degree of destitution. There are still the heavenly joys with which His Father inundates His Humanity; He renounces them, for now His Father abandons Him: *Deus meus, ut quid dereliquisti me?*[6] He remains *alone*, hanging between heaven and earth.

This is the example that has filled the world with monasteries, and peopled these monasteries with souls in love with poverty. When we contemplate Jesus poor in the manger, poor at Nazareth, poor upon the Cross, holding out His hands to us and saying: "It is for you," we understand the follies of the lovers of poverty.

Let us then keep our eyes fixed on this Divine Poor One of Bethlehem, of Nazareth and of Golgotha. And if we feel some of the effects of poverty, let us accept this generously; do not let us look upon it as a world-wide calamity! And let us not forget that we ought not to be poor merely out of convention, but because we have promised Christ really to leave everything to follow Him. It is at this price that we shall find in Him all our riches; for if He has taken our miseries upon Him-

1 Ps. cxliv, 16. 2 Luc. ii, 7. 3 Matth. xiii, 55.
4 Luc. ix, 58. 5 Joan. xix, 27. 6 Matth. xxvii, 46.

self it is in order to enrich us with His perfections; the poverty of His Humanity serves Him as the means of coming near to us and bringing even to our souls the riches of His Divinity: *Scitis enim gratiam Domini nostri Jesu Christi quoniam propter vos egenus factus est, cum esset dives, ut illius inopia vos divites essetis.*[1]

Such is the wonderful exchange made between the Divine Word and ourselves. He brings His infinite riches: but, let us remember, He brings them to those who are poor: *Esurientes implevit bonis*;[2] and those who most despoil themselves receive the most.

We can never go too far in this voluntary detachment. There is one aspect of the inner life of Christ Jesus that St. John brings forward and of which the imitation forms a very thorough exercise of the virtue of poverty. To understand this aspect, let us raise our hearts and minds as far as the mystery of the Adorable Trinity; but let us raise them with faith and reverence, for these things are only to be well understood in prayer.

In the Trinity, as you know, God the Father has an attribute proper to Himself which is distinctive from His Person: He is the First Principle, proceeding from none: *Principium sine principio.* This is true only of the Father; the Son is a principle, yes; He Himself has told us so: [*Ego*] *principium qui et loquor vobis*,[3] only this is relatively to us; with the Father and the Holy Spirit, He is the fount of all life for every creature. But when we speak of the Three Divine Persons, the Father alone is the Principle proceeding from no other Person; from Him proceeds the Son; and, from the Father and the Son, proceeds the Holy Spirit. This attribute is personal to the Father.

The Son, even as God, holds everything from the Father: *Omnia quae dedisti mihi abs te sunt.*[4] The Son, in beholding His Father, can say to Him that all that He is, all that He has, all that He knows, is from His Father because He proceeds from Him, without there being between the First and Second Person, either inequality, or inferiority, or succession of time. This is one side of the mystery.

1 "For you know the grace of our Lord Jesus Christ, that being rich He became poor, for your sakes; that through His poverty you might be rich," II Cor. viii, 9.

2 Luc. i, 53. 3 Joan. viii, 25. 4 Ibid. cvii, 7.

This sublime truth is especially revealed to us in the Gospel of St. John[1] where Our Lord constantly protests that He holds everything from His Father. Consider for a moment the mystery of the Incarnation. The Sacred Humanity of Christ Jesus is perfect, integral; nothing is wanting to It which can constitute and adorn human nature; *Perfectus homo.*[2] And yet it has no proper personality: there is no human person in Christ. It is the Word Who, in Him, is the Person, and it is in the Word that the Human Nature subsists. This is an ineffable mystery.

In the words of Jesus we shall find some expressions of this mystery. He tells us,—and it is the Incarnate Word Who speaks—"My doctrine is not Mine, but His that sent Me": *Mea doctrina non est mea, sed ejus qui misit Me.*[3] He says again, "I do nothing of Myself, but as the Father hath taught Me, these things I speak": *A meipso facio nihil, sed sicut docuit me Pater, haec loquor.*[4] He then adds in all truth that He seeks not His own will nor His own glory, but that of Him Who sent Him.[5] This glory is to refer everything to His Father, by Whom He is begotten: the Father gives all to Him and the Son refers all to His Father, as the Principle whence He proceeds: *Pater, mea omnia tua sunt, et tua mea sunt.*[6] True of the Humanity of Jesus, it is likewise so, in a very lofty sense, of His Divinity. The Son has not anything that He has not received from the Father; He proceeds from Him wholly; when the Father beholds His Son, He sees that there is nothing in this Son that does not come from Him; and this is why all is Divine in the Son, all is perfect, and this is also why the Son is the object of His Father's love. *Filius dilectionis suae.*[7]

This aspect, one of the deepest and most essential in the life of Jesus Christ, should enlighten us as to what our poverty ought to be. Let us imitate Christ in being not only materially poor but poor of spirit; let us imitate Him in despoiling of ourselves of all that is our own, of all that comes from self: attachment to our own judgment, our self-love, our self-will, which are so many forms of "the vice of ownership," in order that we may no longer have any but the thoughts, the desires, and the will of God, and no longer act save from motives that come from on high. Then, everything in us will proceed, as it were, from God. God

1 Ch. v, vii, viii, xiv.
2 Creed attributed to St. Athanasius.
3 Joan. vii, 16.
4 Ibid. viii, 28; cf. xiv, 10.
5 Ibid. viii, 50.
6 Ibid. xvii, 10.
7 Cf. Col. i, 13.

will see in us the realisation of the Divine idea that, from all eternity, He has formed for us. When in our thoughts and actions we add something that is not from God, something that comes from our own self, sin or imperfection, we impair God's image within us. God then sees in us some *proprium*; and as this *proprium* does not come from Him, it does not go, it cannot go, to God. The great obstacle to heavenly grace, to the love of God, is this "vice of ownership" which in our case is manifested not only by possessing or disposing of material things, or even by simple attachment to these things, but still more by inordinate attachment to what is personal or proper to ourselves. In the two following conferences we will point out in detail how, by humility and obedience, we can arrive at entirely despoiling ourselves of self-love, self-esteem, and self-will. But it has been expedient for us now to bring together the different aspects of the same vice, this "vice of ownership" which forms a radical obstacle to Divine communications and produces a thousand fruits of sin and death. "Pride," said our Lord to Blessed Angela of Foligno, "can exist in those alone who possess anything or believe that they possess anything. Man and angel fell, and fell by pride, because they believed they had something of their own. But neither angel nor man has aught of himself; all belongs to God."[1]

We hence understand why St. Benedict, so enlightened upon the ways of God, wishes that the spirit of ownership in us should be "cut off by the roots": *Radicitus amputetur*.[2]

V

When this holy destruction has been wrought, God puts no bounds to His graces: the Kingdom of God is promised by Jesus to "the poor in spirit." This Kingdom is first of all within us; it is established in us in the very measure that we strip ourselves of every creature and of self. All our spiritual life consists in the imitation of Christ Jesus. The Word, being the Son of God, proceeds entirely from His Father, He lives by Him, He lives for Him: *Ego vivo propter Patrem*;[3] this sums up the whole life of Jesus, the Incarnate Word. It will be proportionately the same for us; the more that our life and aims flow from God, the more that

1 *Book of Visions*, ch. 55. 2 Rule, ch. xxxiii. 3 Joan. vi, 58.

our activity finds the source of its inspirations in the will of God—the higher and more supernatural will our life too become. We need great abnegation in order to establish this disposition in us and never to seek the principle of our actions save in God; for the natural instinct of man urges him to make himself his own centre and to seek the principle of his life in himself alone, in that which is personal and proper to himself. On the contrary the life of our soul must be entirely subject to the Divine good pleasure and must have no movement that does not come from the Holy Spirit.

This is what we ask of our Lord each morning at Prime, on beginning the day. "O Lord our God, King of heaven and earth, vouchsafe this day to direct and sanctify, to rule and govern our hearts and our bodies, our feelings, our words, and our works, according to Thy Law, and in the doing of Thy commandments... O Saviour of the world, Who livest and reignest world, without end": *Dirigere et sanctificare, regere et gubernare dignare, Domine Deus, Rex caeli et terrae, hodie, corda et corpora nostra, sensus, sermones et actus nostros, in lege tua, et in operibus mandatorum tuorum.* We here ask the Word to direct, to take in hand all that is in us; our thoughts, our feelings, our actions, all that we are, all that we have, all that we do. All that is ours will then come from God through Jesus Christ and His Spirit, and will return to God. We shall bring our personality into subjection to Christ Jesus, in order to destroy what is bad in us, and to make all that is good converge towards the doing of His Divine will: then without ceasing to remain ourselves, we shall do everything under the impulsion, by the action of His grace and of His Spirit. It will be no longer in our self-love, our self-esteem, nor our self-will, that we shall seek the mainspring of our thoughts, words, and deeds, but in the love of Christ's will, in cleaving to His law: *In lege tua et in operibus mandatorum tuorum.* We shall have laid down our personality to put on Christ: *Christum induistis.*[1] Doubtless, in this union of ourselves with the Word, two distinct persons always remain, for this union is only moral, but we can strive to subject our personality in the order of activity so perfectly to the Word, that this personality will disappear as far as possible leaving to the Divine Word all the initiative of our life.

---

1 Gal. iii, 27.

The same prayer contains moreover the principle on which it rests, namely, that the Word is King, King of heaven and of earth. The Word lives and reigns in God: *Vivit et regnat Deus*. Christ only lives where He reigns; He is essentially King; He lives in us in the degree that He governs all in us, that He reigns over our faculties, that He rules our activity. When all within us comes from Him, that is to say when we no longer think save as He thinks, when we no longer will save as He wills, when we act only according to His good pleasure, we place our whole self in subjection at His feet; then He reigns in us; all that is proper to us, all that is personal, disappears to give place to the thoughts and will of the Divine Word. This domination of Christ within us must be complete. We ask this a hundred times a day: *Adveniat regnum tuum!* May that day come, O Lord, when Thou wilt reign entirely in me; when no selfish motive will hinder Thy power in me, when, like Thee, I shall be entirely yielded up to the Father, and nothing within me will be opposed to the Holy Spirit's action!

On that day we shall have done all that within us lies, to bring our own personality to naught before the dominion of Christ. He will truly be for us "All in all": *Omnia in omnibus*;[1] morally speaking, we shall no longer have anything of our own; all will be subject, all will be given to Him; this is to be *pauper spiritu*. Who are those whom Our Lord calls *pauperes spiritu*?[2] Those who own nothing either in mind, heart, or will, who wish to have nothing except from God. Daily they lay down their own judgment, their manner of seeing things, their will, everything, at the feet of Christ; they say to Him: "I do not want to have anything of myself; I want to have only what comes from Thee, to do only that which, from all eternity, Thou, as the Word, hast decided for me: to realise Thy own divine ideal concerning me." They can then make their own the words which literally belong to St. Paul: *Vivo autem, jam non ego; vivit vero in me Christus*.[3] "I live, now not I, but Christ liveth in me"; but this will not be without having heroically taken the same means as he did. The Apostle did not arrive in one day at this consummate union, for his personality was of a rare power. A succession of immolations had made all that was contrary to the Christ-life die within him, and leave the initiative of all his movements to the Spirit.

1 I Cor. xv, 28. 2 Matth. v, 3. 3 Gal. ii, 20.

This is perfection at its height. On the day of our profession we renounced the principal motives which bring all natural human activity into play: money, love, independence; we are in the best conditions for the divine life to be able to take full possession of us. Let us then try to despoil ourselves as completely as possible, not only of created things but even, in the domain of our activity, of our personality; let us try to act in such a way that, through prayer and through our eyes being ever fixed upon our Model, all our motives may be supernatural, so that the Father's Name may be sanctified, His Kingdom come and His Will be done—then our whole life will be truly deified.

Then, too, our whole life, returning to God, will become like an unceasing hymn of praise, extremely pleasing to our Heavenly Father. Enlightened, inspired, united, through His Word and His Spirit, *Spiritu Dei aguntur,*[1] we shall be able to say: "The Lord ruleth me": *Dominus regit me.* And at once we shall add with the Psalmist: "And I shall want nothing": *Et nihil mihi deerit.*[2] For the Father, beholding in us only what comes from Himself, from the grace of His Son and the inspiration of His Spirit, beholding us, according to His desire, united in all things to His Son, embraces us with the same love of complacency that He bears to His own Son and pours out upon us the inexhaustible riches of His Kingdom. Our work has been to lay aside self that we may be led to God by Christ. Christ Jesus then carries us with Him to His Father, *in sinu Patris;*[3] for it is essential to the Son "to belong to His Father"; and, all that belongs to the Son belongs to the Father: *Mea omnia tua sunt.*

But likewise all the benedictions poured out upon the Son become our lot and our inheritance: *Tu es qui restitues hereditatem meam mihi.*[4] God abandons to the nothingness of their pretended riches those who, believing themselves to possess something, confide in themselves; but His infinite mercy fills the needy, who hope only in Him, with gifts from on high: *Esurientes implevit bonis, et divites dimisit inanes.*[5]

1 Rom. viii, 14.
2 Ps. xxii, 1.
3 Joan. i, 18.
4 Roman Pontifical, *Ordo ad clericum faciendum.*
5 Luc. i, 53.

HUMILITY

SUMMARY.—One of the greatest obstacles to the Divine outpourings is formed by pride; humility removes this obstacle.—I. Necessity of humility.—II. St. Benedict's concept of humility and the important place he gives to it in the inner life. Nature of this virtue.—III. What St. Thomas, following the example of St. Benedict, assigns as the root of humility: reverence towards God, to which the holy Patriarch allies the most absolute confidence.—IV. Degrees of humility laid down by St. Benedict; the two first degrees of interior humility equally concern simple Christians.—V. The degrees that are, properly speaking, monastic.—VI. Exterior humility; its necessity, its degree.—VII. How humility accords with truth and is allied to confidence.—VIII. The most precious fruit of this virtue: it most efficaciously prepares the soul to receive the abundance of Divine outpourings, and perfect charity.—IX. Means of attaining this virtue: prayer; contemplation of the Divine perfections; consideration of the humiliations of Christ Jesus.—X. Christ makes the humble soul share in His heavenly exaltation.

ONE of the greatest revelations that Our Lord has given to us through His Incarnation is that of God's immense desire to communicate Himself to our souls in order to be their beatitude. God might have dwelt throughout eternity in the fruitful solitude of His one and triune Divinity; He has no need of the creature, for nothing is wanting to Him Who, alone, is the fulness of Being and the First Cause of all things: *Bonorum meorum non eges.*[1] But having decreed, in the absolute and immutable liberty of His sovereign Will, to give Himself to us, the desire He has of realising this Will is infinite.

1 "For Thou hast no need of my goods," Ps. xv, 2.

We might be tempted at times to believe that God may be "indifferent," that His desire to communicate Himself is vague, inefficacious; but these are human conceptions, images of the weakness of our nature, too often unstable and powerless. In God all is pure act; that which in our miserable language we call "Divine desire," is an act really indistinct from the Divine essence, and consequently infinite.

In this, as in all that touches our supernatural life, we must allow ourselves to be guided not by our imagination, but by the light of Revelation. It is God Himself to whom we must listen when we wish to know the Divine Life; it is towards Christ that we must turn, towards the Beloved Son Who is ever "in the Bosom of the Father," *in sinu Patris,*[1] He Who has Himself revealed the Divine secrets: *Ipse enarravit.* What does He tell us? That God so loved men, that He has *given* them His Only-begotten Son: *Sic Deus dilexit mundum ut Filium suum unigenitum daret.*[2] And why has He given Him? That He may be our justice, our redemption, our holiness. Christ Jesus, in obedience to His Father, *Sicut mandatum dedit mihi Pater,*[3] delivered Himself up to us even to the death of the Cross, even to the state of the Host, even to be our Food: *in finem.* Would God have carried love to these extremes if He did not infinitely desire to communicate Himself to us? For, according to the thought of St. Thomas, God's love is not a passive love, since being the First Cause of all things, He cannot receive anything: it is an efficacious love, necessarily efficient.[4] And because God loves us, He wishes with an unbounded love and an efficacious will, to give Himself to us.

But then, one might ask, why does He not give Himself infallibly? Why are souls to be found to whom God does not communicate Himself? Why so often such parsimony in the outpouring of the Divine gifts? Why are there so many souls who seem as if they ought to abound in graces, and are yet so destitute of gifts from on high? When we study the action of grace in souls, we are astonished, in passing from one to another, to notice the difference in the effects produced. With some, grace blossoms in an abundance of lights and gifts; these souls advance visibly; they are filled with something divine, which is often manifested by the spiritual and beneficial influence which radiates from them. With others, on the contrary, it is quasi-sterility; the Sacraments, Mass, holy

1 Joan. i, 18. 2 Ibid. 3 Ibid. xiv, 31. 4 I-II, q. cx, a. 1.

reading, the observance of the Rule, all these means, which although they are authentic channels of Divine grace produce little effect in them. And yet, when one examines these souls, nothing is to be discovered, at least at first sight, which explains such a difference. Why does their outward regularity leave them without habitual union with God, and without any real progress?

The answer to this question is easily to be found in certain pages of our preceding conference. Among the souls we have been considering, some are "rich in spirit": *Divites spiritu*, the others are "poor in spirit": *Pauperes spiritu.*[1] For the latter there is the Kingdom of God, with the abundance of all good things; *Esurientes implevit bonis*; for the former, the destitution of their utter nothingness: *Divites dimisit inanes.*[2]

We all have obstacles within us that hinder God's action: sin, the roots of sin, perverse tendencies not fought against; for "what fellowship hath light, with darkness?"[3] These obstacles are overcome by souls who renounce everything,—created things, and themselves,—who increase their capacity for what is divine, by detachment from all that is not God. They look only to God for all they need; they are humble in themselves, they rely only upon God; God fills these *pauperes spiritu* with good things. As to the others, they bear within them a tendency particularly qualified to form an obstacle to God; this tendency is pride. Pride is radically opposed to the Divine communications; God cannot give Himself to these self-satisfied *divites spiritu*. This is a fact often to be met with.

In studying this fact more deeply, we shall acknowledge how necessary humility is for the life of the soul; we shall understand how right our holy Father was in wishing this virtue to be placed as the very basis of our monastic life; then we will specify its nature and character. We will examine next the "degrees of humility," such as St. Benedict defined them; we shall be enabled to follow the manifestations of the virtue, and finally to point out the means conducive to its development in our souls.

Let us ask Christ Jesus Whom we want to imitate more closely, after having left all things to follow Him, to teach us this humility. It is the virtue to which He willed especially to draw the attention of our souls. One phrase of the Holy Gospel begins with these words: "Learn of Me..."

1 Matth. v, 3. 2 Luc. i, 53. 3 II Cor. vi, 14.

Discite a Me.[1] What is this thing that we are most specially to learn of Him? Is it that He is God? the sovereign Being, All-powerful, full of wisdom? "What we must learn of Him," says St. Augustine, "is not that He has formed the world, created all things visible and invisible, that in this world which is His handiwork He has wrought miracles, and raised the dead to life": *Discite a me non mundum fabricare, non cuncta visibilia et invisibilia creare, non in ipso mundo miracula facere, et mortuos suscitare.*[2] Does He wish us "to learn" from Him the most heroic virtues, that He was obedient unto death, that He delivered Himself up wholly to His Father's will, that He was devoured with zeal for the interests of the Father's glory and those of our salvation? Without doubt He practised all these virtues with wonderful perfection: but what He wants us especially to learn of Him is that He is "meek and humble of heart," those virtues of self-effacement and silence, virtues unperceived by men, or even disdained by them,[3] but which He justly urges us to make our own: *Discite a Me quia mitis sum et humilis corde.* Let us beseech Him that, through His grace, He will make our hearts like unto His, for perfection lies in this constant imitation, through love, of our Divine Model: *Hoc enim sentite in vobis quod et in Christo Jesu.*[4]

I

Holy Scripture, as you know has strange expressions to signify, in human language, God's attitude towards the proud. It says, "God resisteth the proud": *Deus superbis resistit.*[5] If it is a terrible thing for a man to be forsaken by God, what is it when God begins to resist him?

We cannot think without terror of this divine resistance. God is the sole fount of our holiness, because He is the Author of every grace. Now what grace is to be hoped for from God, if God not only does not give Himself to us, but resists us, rejects us?

What is there then that is so evil, so contrary to God in pride, for God so mightily to thrust it far from Him?

1 Matth. xi, 29.

2 St. Augustine. *Sermo 10 de Verbis Domini.* P. L. *Sermo* 69, n. 2.

3 See the Encyclical *Testem benevolentiae,* (22nd Jan. 1899) of Leo XIII on Americanism.

4 Philip. ii, 5.

5 I Petr. v, 5 and Jac. iv, 6.

The reason of this antagonism is derived from the very nature of Divine Holiness. God is the Beginning and the End, the Alpha and Omega[1] of all things; He is the First Cause of every creature and the Fountainhead of all perfection. All life comes from Him, all good flows from Him; but also every creature has to return to Him, all glory to be referred to Him. God has made everything for His glory: *Universa propter semetipsum operatus est Dominus.*[2] In us, a like conduct would be egotism, supreme disorder; in God, to Whom the term of egotism can in nowise be applied, it is a necessity founded upon His very nature. It is essential to God's sanctity to bring back everything to His own glory; otherwise God would not be God, because He would be subordinate to another end than Himself. Listen to the Prophet Isaias. He shows us the Angels singing the holiness of God, because His glory fills heaven and earth: *Sanctus, Sanctus, Sanctus, Dominus Deus Sabaoth; plena est omnis terra gloria ejus.*[3] In the same way St. John at Patmos declares he saw the elect cast themselves down before the throne of God and heard them repeat this canticle: "Thou art worthy, O Lord our God, to receive glory, and honour, and power; for all things have received being and life at Thy hands."[4] God Himself declares "I will not give my glory to another."[5] This is because in contemplating Himself He beholds that He merits infinite glory on account of the plenitude of His Being and the ocean of His perfections; God cannot, without ceasing to be God, without ceasing to be Holiness, tolerate that His glory be attributed to another than Himself. He gives us many graces; He gives us His beloved Son: *Sic Deus dilexit mundum ut Filium suum unigenitum daret*:[6] He gives Him to us entirely for ever, if we will have it so; He gives us all good things in His Son, through His Son. *Cum illo omnia nobis donavit*;[7] He gives us that supreme good which is eternal and unending bliss, He grants us to enter into the intimate fellowship of His Blessed Trinity; but there is one thing which He neither will nor can communicate to anyone—and this thing is His glory: *Ego Dominus; gloriam meam alteri non dabo.*

Now what is it that the proud man does? He attempts to rob God of this glory which God alone merits and of which He is so jealous, in order to appropriate it to himself. The proud man lifts himself up above

1 Apoc. xxii, 13. 2 Prov. xvi, 4. 3 Isa. vi, 3. 4 Apoc. iv, 11.
5 Isa. xlii, 8. 6 Joan. iii, 16. 7 Rom. viii, 32.

others, he makes himself the centre; he glories in his own person, in his perfection, his deeds; he sees in himself alone the principle of all that he has and all that he is; he considers that he owes nothing to anyone, not even to God, He would deprive God, of that Divine attribute of being the First Principle and Last End. Doubtless, in theory, he may think that all comes from God, but, in practice, he acts and lives as if all came from himself.

Such being the antagonism that pride sets up between man and God,[1] it is needful that God should "resist" the proud; God cannot but repulse him as an unjust aggressor: *Superbis resistit.* "The Lord is high, and looketh on the low: and the high He knoweth afar off": *Excelsus Dominus et humilia respicit, et alta a longe cognoscit.*[2] Commenting on these words, an ancient author writes: "God beholdeth the proud from afar off, in order to oppress them more rigorously": *alta, id est, superba, de longe cognoscit ut deprimat.*[3] Is there a more terrifying perspective for the soul than that?

Our Divine Saviour, so merciful, so compassionate, teaches us these same lessons again under the impressive parable of the Pharisee and the Publican. Look at the Pharisee: he is a man convinced of his own importance full of and sure of himself; the "Ego" of this man seeks to advertise itself by words and attitude. He stands in the careless posture of one conscious of his personal worth and perfection, one who owes nothing to anyone, and, inversely, esteems himself to have need of nothing. He complacently displays before God all that he has done; it is true that he returns thanks to God; but, remarks St. Bernard, this false homage is but a lie added to pride; the Pharisee has "a double heart"[4] as the Psalmist says; the contempt that he has for the Publican shows that he believes himself to be much more perfect than he, and thus it is to himself that in reality he reserves the glory that in appearance he gives to God.[5] He does not ask anything from God, because

1 Cf. St. Thomas, II-II, q. clxii, a. 6, *Utrum superbia sit gravissimum peccatorum* (Whether pride is the most grievous of sins). 2 Ps. cxxxvii, 6.

3 *Sermo 2 de ascens. Domini* 177 de tempore, 3. 2. (Appendice to the works of St. Augustine.) 4 Ps. xi, 3.

5 *Quia gratias agendo probas te tibi nihil tribuere, sed Dei esse dona tua merita, prudenter agnoscere, certe caeteros aspernando, prodis te, quod in corde et corde locutus sis, altero commodans linguam mendacio, altero veritatis usurpans gloriam. Non enim judi-*

he does not consider he has need of anything: he suffices for himself; he rather presents his conduct to God's approbation. Can we not almost hear him saying: "My God, You must be very content with me, for I am truly irreproachable; I am not like other men, not even like this publican." In fact this personage is practically persuaded that all his perfection comes from himself. We read moreover in the evangelical text that our Lord spoke this parable to those Jews, "who trusted in themselves as just."

Now look at the other actor in the scene, the Publican. He stands at a distance, scarcely daring to lift up his eyes, for he feels how miserable he is. Does he think he has any plea that can prevail with God? He has none. He is aware only of his sins. "My God, I am only a guilty wretch, have pity on me." He confides only in the Divine mercy; he looks for nothing, he hopes for nothing except from that; all his confidence, all his hope, is placed in God.

Now, how does God act with these two men? Quite differently. "I say to you," declares Christ Jesus, "this man (the Publican) went down into his house justified rather than the other."[1] Was not the Publican, however, a sinner? Assuredly. The Pharisee, on the other hand, was he not, at least outwardly, a faithful observer of the Law of Moses? No less certainly he was. But he, full of himself, showed by his contempt of the publican that he was puffed up in his own heart by reason of these good works he had done. Therefore God repulses him: *Dispersit superbos mente cordis sui.*[2] To the poor publican who humbles himself, He, on the contrary, gives an abundance of grace: *Humilibus autem dat gratiam.*[3]

And Christ Jesus, in ending the parable, Himself lays down the fundamental law which rules our relations with God; He brings forward the essential lesson we have to learn: "Everyone that exalteth himself shall

---

cares publicanum contemnendum prae te, si non prae illo te honorandum censeres. (But when giving thanks, you show that you attribute nothing as your own, you wisely acknowledge that your merits are really gifts of God. When despising others, however, you reveal yourself, that you are speaking from a double heart, with one lending your tongue to a lie, with the other usurping the glory due to truth. For you would not judge the publican as more condemnable than yourself if you did not consider yourself as more honourable than him.) St. Bernard *Sermo 13 in cantica* P. L. clxxxiii, 1302.

1 Luc. xviii, 14. 2 Ibid. i, 51. 3 Jac. iv, 6; I Petr. v, 5.

be humbled: and he that humbleth himself, shall be exalted": *Omnis qui se exaltat humiliabitur et qui se humiliat exaltabitur.*[1]

You see to what a degree pride is opposed to the soul's union with God; there is not, says St. Thomas, any sin, or tendency, that bears more patently the character of an obstacle to Divine communications: *Per superbiam homines maxime a Deo avertuntur.*[2] And as God is the principle of all grace, pride is the most terrible of all dangers for the soul; while there is no surer way of attaining holiness and of finding God than humility. It is pride that above all prevents God from giving Himself; if there were no longer any pride in souls, God would give Himself to them fully. Humility is indeed so fundamental a virtue that without it, says the Abbot of Clairvaux, all other virtues go to ruin: *Virtutum siquidem bonum quoddam ac stabile fundamentum humilitas. Nempe si nutet illa, virtutum aggregatio nonnisi ruina est.*[3] This is because, by reason of our fallen nature, there are in us obstacles opposed to the expansion of the inner life; if these obstacles are not removed, they end by stifling the virtues. Now, the greatest obstacle is pride, because it is a fundamental obstacle, radically opposed to Divine union itself, and consequently to the grace whereof God alone is the source and without which we can do nothing. Humility, again says St. Bernard, receives the other virtues, guards and perfects them: *Humilitas virtutes alias accipit, servat acceptas... servatas consummat.*[4]

The humble soul is ready to receive all the gifts of God, first because it is empty of self, because it looks to God for all that is necessary to its perfection, and because it feels itself to be poor and miserable. All that God has done for us since the Fall into which we have been drawn, is the effect of His mercy. The Angels who have no miseries hymn the sanctity of God; we hymn His mercy: *Misericordias Domini in aeternum cantabo.*[5] God, beholding fallen man, encompassed with weaknesses, subject to temptation, at the mercy of his inclinations which change with the times and seasons, with health, surroundings, education, is touched by this misery, as if it were His own; this Divine movement which inclines

1 Luc. xviii, 14. 2 II-II, q. clxii, a. 6, concl.
3 *De consideratione,* Lib. v, ch. xiv, 32.
4 *Tractatus de moribus et officio episcopi,* ch. v, 17. 5 Ps. lxxxviii, 2.

the Lord towards our misery in order to relieve it, is mercy: *Quomodo miseretur Pater filiorum, misertus est Dominus timentibus se, quoniam ipse cognovit figmentum nostrum.*[1]

So profound is our misery that it may be compared to an abyss, which calls upon the abyss of the Divine mercy: *Abyssus abyssum invocat;*[2] but it only *calls* upon it in so far as this misery is recognised, confessed; and it is humility that wrings this cry from us: *Domine, miserere mei!* Humility is the practical and continual avowal of our misery, and this avowal attracts the eyes of God. The rags and wounds of the poor plead for them; they do not strive to hide them, on the contrary, they display them so as to touch the hearts of those who behold them. In the same way, we ought not to strive to dazzle God by our perfection, but rather to draw down His mercy by the confession of our weakness. Each one of us has a sum of miseries sufficient to draw down the pity of our God. Are we not all like that poor wayfarer lying on the road to Jericho, stripped of his garments, covered with wounds? By original sin, we have all been stripped of grace; our personal sins have covered our soul with wounds, but Christ Jesus has been for us the good Samaritan; He came to heal us, to pour the balm of His Precious Blood upon our wounds, to take us into His arms and entrust us to the tenderness of His Church which is another Himself.

It is an excellent prayer to show our Lord all our miseries, all the deformities that still disfigure our soul. "O my God, behold this soul which Thou hast created and redeemed; see how it has been deformed, how full it is of inclinations displeasing in Thy sight. Have pity!" This prayer goes straight to Christ's Heart like the prayer of the poor leper in the Gospel: *Jesu praeceptor, miserere nostri.*[3] And Our Lord will heal us.

When we acknowledge that of ourselves we are weak, poor, miserable, infirm, we implicitly proclaim God's power, wisdom, holiness, loving-kindness; it is rendering homage to the Divine plenitude, and this homage is so pleasing to God that He stoops towards the humble soul to fill it with good things; *Esurientes implevit bonis.* As St. Bernard again says:[4] "Our heart is a vessel destined to receive grace; in order for

---

1 "As a father hath compassion on his children, so hath the Lord compassion on them that fear him: For He knoweth our frame," Ps. cii, 13–14.

2 Ps. xli, 8.

3 "Jesus, master, have mercy on us," Luc. xvii, 13.

4 P. Pourrat: *La Spiritualité chrétienne,* II, *Le moyen-âge,* p. 43.

it to contain grace in abundance it must be empty of self-love and vain glory.[1] When humility has there prepared a vast capacity to be filled, grace flows in, for there is close affinity between grace and humility": *SEMPER solet esse gratiae divinae familiaris virtus humilitas.*[2] Nothing then is more efficacious than this virtue for meriting grace; for retaining it in us, or recovering it if we have lost it.[3]

There exists yet another reason for God's liberality towards humble souls. God sees that the humble soul will not, as the proud does, appropriate to itself the Divine gifts, but will return all glory and praise to Heaven. And this is why, if we may be allowed so to speak, God has no fear in causing the abundance of His favours to flow into this soul; it will not abuse them; it will not use them otherwise than as God intends.

The nearer we would draw to God, the more deeply we must anchor ourselves in humility. St. Augustine shows us this very clearly in a familiar comparison. "The end," he says, "that we pursue is very great; for it is God Whom we seek, to Whom we would attain, for in Him alone is to be found our eternal beatitude. Now we can only come to this lofty end through humility. Dost thou wish to raise thyself? Begin by abasing thyself. Thou dost dream of building an edifice that will tower towards the skies? Take care first of all to lay the foundation by humility": *Magnus esse vis? a minimo incipe. Copitas magnam fabricam construere celsitudinis? de fundamento prius cogita humilitatis.* And the higher the building is to be, adds the holy Doctor, the deeper must the foundations be dug: the more so in that the soil of our poor nature is singularly shifting and unstable: *Ergo et fabrica ante celsitudinem humiliatur, et fastigium post humiliationem erigitur.* Now to what height dost thou aspire to raise this spiritual edifice? As high as the vision of God: *Quo perventurum est cacumen aedificii? Cito dico: usque ad conspectum Dei.* "See then," he exclaims, "to what a sublime height this edifice must be raised, what a thing it is to see God; but it is not reached by self-elevation, but by humility": *Videtis quam excelsum est, quanta res conspicere Deum, non elatione sed humilitate attingitur.*[4]

1 *In Annuntiat.* B.M.V. Sermo III, 9, cf. *Epistola* cccxciii, 2–3.
2 *Super missus est,* homilia iv, 9, cf. *In cantica,* Sermo xxxiv.
3 *In cantica,* Sermo liv, 9. Cf. *Epistola* ccclxxii, Sermo xlvi *de diversis.*
4 *Sermo 10 de Verbis Domini.*

II

Hence we easily understand why St. Benedict, who assigns us no other end than "to find God," founds our spiritual life upon humility. He had himself reached too near God to be ignorant that humility alone draws down grace, and that without grace we can do nothing. All the asceticism of St. Benedict consists in making the soul humble, then in making it live in obedience (which is the practical expression of humility): this will be for it the secret of intimate union with God.[1] "In the mind of the holy Patriarch, this chapter on humility views the spiritual life taken as a whole. He has marked out the stages of the soul's ascent to God, from the renouncing of sin to the plenitude of charity. Why does St. Benedict view this ascent from the angle of humility, granting to the development of this virtue the privilege of containing, so to speak, the increase of all the others? He could have claimed, and not without reason, that the ladder that leads to God is made up of degrees of patience, or else of a succession of graces of prayer: discursive prayer to begin with, then simplified, then mystically uniting the soul to God; or better still, he could have said that this ladder was a succession of degrees of charity. If St. Benedict preferred a conception of another kind, it is because, by tendency of character and the attraction of grace, he was predisposed to understand the ascension of the soul as characterised by a deeper and deeper submission of man before God. This conception is the reflection of an essentially religious and contemplative soul..."[2]

St. Benedict devotes a whole chapter to this fundamental virtue, but, as we shall see further on, he has a very sure and at the same time a very wide concept of humility; he does not envisage it simply as a very special virtue apart, linked to the moral virtue of temperance,[3] but as a virtue expressing the whole attitude the soul ought to have in face of God; an attitude wherein are fused the different sentiments that should animate us as creatures and as adopted children: an attitude on which

1 *Humilitas... praebet hominem subditum et patulum ad suscipiendum influxum divinae gratiae* (Humility... makes man submissive and ever open to receive the influx of Divine grace). Cf. St. Thomas, II-II, q. clxi, a. 5, ad 2.

2 D. I. Ryelandt, *Essai sur le caractère ou la physionomie morale de St. Benoit, d'après sa Règle,* in *Revue liturgique et monastique,* 1921, pp. 207–208.

3 Cf. St. Thomas, II-II, q. clxi, a. 4.

all our spiritual life is to be based. This proposition will be made clearer by what follows.

St. Benedict begins his chapter by recalling the law laid down by Christ Himself at the end of the parable of the Pharisee and the Publican. "Everyone that exalteth himself, shall be humbled, and he that humbleth himself, shall be exalted." "The intimate sense of the Divine hold upon human life causes a man to humble and submit himself, while simultaneously he is exalted in God by this very submission. The deep meaning of St. Benedict's idea is the assertion of the evangelical truth that the more a man progresses in true humility, the more he becomes absorbed in God and rises towards the heights of union with Him."[1]

The theory of humility is, with St. Benedict, exactly correlative with his conception of grace. The progress of the soul in God is the progress of God in the soul. The work, which by means of grace, belongs properly speaking, to the soul, is to open the way to God's action, to open itself to God. To every degree of ascension towards God, corresponds a degree of "the opening of self to God." How do we open ourselves to God? By more and more abolishing pride within us; by more and more deepening humility. And this is how, definitively, the ladder, in the negative sense, of humility can serve as the ladder, in the positive sense, of perfection and charity. Upon the ladder of humility can be marked a gradation which, doubtless admits of some convention and ingenuity, but which however well indicates all positive degrees in the supernatural life.

Borrowing the expressive image of the Psalmist, St. Benedict compares the proud man repulsed by God to an infant weaned too soon from its mother:[2] severed from the source of life the infant is doomed to perish. This is the great danger that the soul risks: to be separated from God, the sole fount of every grace. If then, continues our Holy Father, "we wish to attain to the summit of supreme humility, and speedily reach that heavenly exaltation to which we ascend by the humility of this present life, we must by the ever ascending degrees of our actions, erect that ladder which appeared to Jacob while he slept and by which he saw the Angels descending and ascending."[3] The holy Lawgiver next compares

1 D.I. Ryelandt, 1. c. 2 Ps. cxxx, 2.

3 Rule, ch. vii. This idea seems to have been borrowed from St. Jerome: but this holy Doctor understands it of interior ascension by the exercise of all the virtues: *Scalam...*

the two sides of the ladder to the body and the soul, for the body is to share in the inward virtue, and divine grace has placed between these two sides the divers degrees which we must climb.

Before studying these degrees with St. Benedict, let us first say what humility is. St. Benedict does not define it; he rather points out its different manifestations. We will therefore borrow the divers elements of the definition of humility from St. Thomas, who, moreover, in his *Summa theologica* comments on this chapter of St. Benedict and justifies the degrees of humility indicated by him.[1] God sometimes gives to a soul, all at once, a higher degree of humility, as He gives to another the gift of prayer; but in the ordinary way, He requires our co-operation; and

per quam diversis virtutum gradibus ad superna conscenditur (The ladder... on which one ascends the many steps of the virtues to the heavenlies) (Epist., 98.3); St. Benedict restricts the idea to the practice of humility. Let us add then that in the sixth century, St. John Climacus wrote his celebrated *Scala paradisi*, the "ladder that leads to Heaven," and that comprises thirty degrees, to recall the thirty years of Christ's hidden life.

1 II-II, q. clxi, a. 6, and q. clxii, a. 4, ad 4. However St. Thomas follows the inverse order in beginning by the last degree. In the body of the article he really takes up anew his teaching on humility beginning with the first degree: reverence towards God. It is known that St. Thomas was a Benedictine Oblate at Monte Cassino where he stayed nine years; he was obliged to leave the abbey in consequence of the political troubles raised by Frederick II, who, excommunicated by Gregory IX, drove out the monks from their monastery. During his sojourn at Cassino, the young Thomas studied the text of the holy Patriarch's Rule. "The writings of the future doctor"—thus says the most recent of the historians of St. Thomas, Père Mandonnet, O.P.—"bear testimony to his familiarity with St. Benedict's legislative monument." This same historian ends his study upon "St. Thomas, Benedictine Oblate" with these lines which I may be allowed to quote: "Thomas of Aquinas must have left the shelter of his youthful years with sorrowful regrets. Being a deeply religious soul, the wellspring of his life must have appeared to him to have run dry. However, throughout the events that might have seemed disastrous, he carried away with him, into exile, a great spiritual treasure. He had not only sheltered his years of childhood in the most illustrious monastery in Christendom; he also received a formation of which he never lost the unchanging benefit. To Benedictine spirituality he owed a sound and sincere mind. The monastic life, with the calm succession of days similar to one another, had already confirmed the admirable equilibrium of his temperament and faculties. The isolation of his life as oblate, and the development of the great Cassinian nature had awakened, if not matured, his profound power of recollection." *Revue des Jeunes,* 25th May 1919, pp. 241–242; cf. also 10th May, p. 145 sq.

since we only esteem and seek what we know, let us try to understand clearly what this virtue is.

Humility can be thus defined: a moral virtue that inclines us, from reverence towards God, to abase ourselves and keep ourselves in the place that we see is due to us.

It is a virtue, that is to say an habitual disposition. The virtue of humility is not constituted by a particular act; one can perform the acts without possessing the virtue; the virtue consists of an habitual disposition, promptly and easily manifested. It is like a furnace whence acts of humility arise as do sparks under a breath that stirs the flame.

Being a moral virtue, humility has assuredly all its premisses in the understanding, in the judgment. But we think that certain authors are wrong in placing it formally in the understanding; with St. Thomas we say that it dwells essentially in the will: *In IPSO APPETITU consistit humilitas essentialiter;*[1] *existit circa appetitum magis quam circa aestimationem.*[2] So, on the other hand, pride *predisposes* and *contains* ill-regulated self-esteem, but it consists more formally in self-complacency (the attitude of the heart) which follows the judgment. In humility, it is the goodwill, which aided by grace, humbles itself, out of reverence towards God, and urges the intellect and the whole man to remain in the place which he knows to be due to him.[3]

Now, what is this place? Let us consider the thing, not from the point of view of the world, which only esteems what is brilliant and assumes false appearances, but from the point of view of faith, from the point of view of God, Who is very Truth and is not deceived.

In the natural order, what have I of myself? Without any exaggeration, it must be replied: Nothing, neither life, nor health, nor physical strength, nor talents: "Thy hands have fashioned me... wholly." *Manus*

1 II-II, q. clxi, a. 2, co.

2 "Therefore humility has to do with the appetite rather than with the estimative power," Ibid.

3 The holy Doctor adds, of course, (Ibid.) that humility is based, as upon its directing norm, upon knowledge, whereby we do not esteem ourselves above what we are (Ibid. a. 2 and 6 :) an application to a particular case of this exchange of causality known to all psychologists and moralists, which is made between the reason and the will.

tuae, Domine, fecerunt me totum in circuitu.[1] And not only have I been formed by God, but my being relies wholly upon Him: In Him, "we live, and move, and are": *In ipso vivimus, movemur et sumus.*[2] The active preservation of things is, on God's part, a continual creation. If God withdrew His hand, I should instantly find myself without energy, without will, without reason, without life: *Omnis caro faenum; exsiccatum est faenum, et cecidit flos.*[3] I possess, it is true, the substance of my soul and body, their faculties and powers; but that is because I have received them from God. "For who distinguished thee?" says St. Paul. "Or what hast thou that thou hast not received? And if thou hast received, why dost thou glory, as if thou hadst not received it?"[4]

And in the supernatural order? It is true that by grace we are the children of God, the brethren of Jesus, called by God to be like unto Himself: *Ego dixi: dii estis.*[5] That is a wonderful condition, a sublime end, but God has called us to it gratuitously: *Non ex operibus justitiae quae fecimus nos, sed secundum suam misericordiam salvos nos fecit.*[6] And after God's mercy has endowed us with this Divine gift, we cannot use it without God; it is of faith, *de fide*, that we cannot have, by ourselves, in the order of grace, one good thought, meritorious for heaven. Our Lord has said speaking generally: *Sine me nihil potestis facere*;[7] "Without My grace you can do nothing." And St. Paul develops the same truth: "Not that we are sufficient to think anything of ourselves, as of ourselves: but our sufficiency is from God." *Non quod sufficientes simus cogitare aliquid a nobis quasi ex nobis, sed sufficientia nostra ex Deo est.*[8] Furthermore, he tells us that no man can supernaturally invoke the name of Jesus, except by the grace of the Holy Spirit.[9] As we see, all good comes from God; and if it is true that the merits of our deeds are our own, they are so because God allows us to merit.[10]

---

1 Job. x, 8. 2 Act. xvii, 28. 3 Isa. xl, 7.

4 I Cor. iv, 7. 5 Ps. lxxxi, 6.

6 "Not by the works of justice, which we have done, but according to His mercy, he saved us," Tit. iii, 5–6.

7 Joan. xv, 5. 8 II Cor. iii, 5. 9 I Cor. xii, 3.

10 *Absit ut christianus homo in se ipso vel confidat vel glorietur et non in Domino; cujus tanta est erga omnes homines bonitas ut eorum velit esse merita quae sunt ipsius dona.* (God forbid that a Christian either trust or glory in himself, and not in the Lord, whose goodness towards all men is so great, that He wills for the things which are His

Very logically then our Holy Father tells us that if "we see any good in ourselves we ought to attribute it to God and not to ourselves": *Bonum aliquid in se cum viderit Deo applicet, non sibi*; and, he at once adds, we ought, on the contrary to impute to ourselves all the evil that we do, and of which we know we are the cause: *Malum vero semper a se factum sciat et sibi reputet.*[1] Indeed what is in nowise from God, and is exclusively our own, is sin. If only once in our lifetime we have offended God mortally, we then deserved in all justice, to become an object of horror and hatred to this God Who is very Majesty and Goodness. And if we were not there and then struck down by death and doomed to everlasting punishment, if God, with His forgiveness, vouchsafed to restore to us His grace and friendship, it is again to His goodness that we owe it: *Misericordia Domini quia non sumus consumpti.*[2]

Such is the condition that the infallible light of faith shows us as being our own, when we consider all things from the point of view of Divine truth. Humility keeps us in an attitude conformable with this condition; the will, aided by grace, prompts us to keep in the place which is properly "our own."

III

St. Thomas says that the principal reason and motive of this self-abasement is: "reverence towards God": *Ratio praecipua humilitatis sumitur ex reverentia divina ex qua contingit ut homo non plus sibi attribuat quam sibi competat secundum gradum quem est a Deo sortitus.*[3] And the great Doctor recalls that St. Augustine links humility to the gift of fear as he links it to the virtue of religion: *Et propter hoc Augustinus humilitatem*

own gifts to be their merits.) *Conc. Trid.* Sess. vi, ch. 16.

1 Rule, ch. iv.

2 "The mercies of the Lord that we are not consumed," Thren. iii, 22.

3 "While the chief reason... is based on divine reverence, which shows that man ought not to ascribe to himself more than is competent to him according to the position in which God has placed him." II-II, q. clxi, a. 2, ad 3. Cf. a. 1, ad 5; *Humilitas praecipue respicit subjectionem hominis ad Deum.* (Humility... regards chiefly the subjection of man to God)—*Humilitas proprie respicit reverentiam qua homo Deo subjicitur* (Humility properly regards the reverence whereby man is subject to God).

atiribuit dono timoris quo homo Deum reveretur. We here touch on the deepest point, the very root of the virtue.

When, in prayer, we contemplate the perfections and works of God, when a ray of Divine light reaches us, what is the first movement of the soul touched by grace? It is one of self-abasement; the soul is lost in adoration. This attitude of adoration is the only "true" one that the creature, as such, can have before God. What is adoration? It is the avowal of our inferiority before the Divine perfections; it is the acknowledgment of our absolute dependence in face of Him Who, alone, is of Himself, the plenitude of Being; it is the homage of our subjection in face of the infinite Sovereignty. When a creature does not remain in this attitude, it is not in the truth. In Heaven, the Blessed are locked in God's embrace, an embrace surpassing all that the most ardent love can imagine; they are possessed by God, they possess Him in the essence of their soul; God is all in them; and yet they do not cease to be lost in deep reverence, the expression of their adoration: *Timor Domini sanctus permanens in saeculum saeculi.*[1] Should not the annihilation of self be likewise our law here below? When faith, which is the prelude to the Beatific Vision, makes us touch something of God's unfathomable perfections, we at once cast ourselves down in adoration. The soul understands, under a strong inner light, what a close contact there may be between itself and God; it beholds the infinite contrast of the two terms: littleness and lowliness contrasted with greatness and majesty; greatness and majesty contrasted with littleness and lowliness. The soul may moreover concentrate its attention the more upon the one or other of these two terms of the relation. Is it upon the term: "God"? It tends to *adore* Him. Is it the term of "self"? The soul tends to *humble* itself. It is at the precise instant of our self-annihilation in presence of the Divine Majesty that humility is born in the soul. As soon as reverence towards God fills the soul, it is like the source whence humility springs up: *Humilitas causatur ex reverentia divina.*[2] If this cause is lacking, humility cannot exist. This is a point which cannot be too much insisted upon. We see how eminently

1 "The fear of the Lord is holy, enduring for ever and ever," Ps. xviii, 10.
2 II-II, q. clxi, a. 4 ad 1.

humility is a "religious" virtue, permeated, as has been very well said,[1] with religion, and therefore essentially proper to our state.

We understand too, how important it is, in order to strengthen humility, to give ourselves up to the contemplation of the Divine perfections. God is Almighty: "He spoke and all things were made." With a word, He drew out of nothing a wonderful creation; and this creation which is so beautiful, these legions of angels, these nations of human beings, so great and numerous, are in regard to Himself, like an atom, as if they existed not: *Omnes gentes quasi non sint, sic sunt coram eo.*[2] He is eternal; all creatures pass away or pay their tribute to the order of succession, while He remains immutable in the full and sovereign possession of His perfections. So perfect is He that He has no need of anyone. His infinite wisdom attains all His designs with strength and sweetness; His adorable justice is equity itself; His goodness and power are unequalled; He has but to open His hand to fill every living creature with blessings.[3]

And what accents would have to be found to celebrate the Divine works in the supernatural order? We have many times spoken of the magnificence of the Divine Plan. God wills to make us His children by making us partakers of the very filiation of His Son Jesus,[4] and thus cause us to draw eternal beatitude at the very fountainhead of the Divinity. The Masterpiece of the eternal thoughts which is Christ, the wonderful mysteries of the Incarnation, the Passion, the Resurrection and the triumph of Jesus, the Institution of the Church and the Sacraments, grace, the virtues, the gifts of the Holy Spirit, all this marvellous supernatural order has come forth from this movement of the Heart of God as to make us His children: *Ut adoptionem filiorum reciperemus.*[5]

1 D. O. Lottin, in *L'Ame du Culte, la vertu de religion.* (Louvain, 1920, p. 40 sq.) In this little opusculе of condensed teaching, the author, an enlightened theologian, has shown "how after having linked humility to temperance and obedience to the observance, St. Thomas is brought by evidence of the reality, to relate these virtues to religion. The affinity is indeed undeniable. It was perceived by the ancient ascetical authors. The Rule of St. Benedict, for example, ignores the word *Religio;* but it is all embued with the spirit of religion. It is sufficient, in order to be convinced of this, to read the chapters 5–7 upon obedience, the spirit of silence and humility." (P. 49, n.).

2 Isa. xl, 17. 3 Ps. xcliv, 16. 4 Cf. Eph. i, 5.

5 "That we might receive the adoption of sons," Gal. iv, 5.

It is an admirable order, a work of power, of wisdom and love of which the spectacle ravished St. Paul.

When our souls contemplate these divine perfections and works, not according to a philosophy that would make of it an abstract, cold and dry study, but in prayer, and, when God touches us with His light, all terrestrial superiorities are effaced, all created perfections appear as nothingness, all human greatness fades away like smoke. Before this omniscient, this sovereign wisdom, this absolute power, this august sanctity, this justice into which not the least movement of passion enters; before this boundless goodness, this inexhaustible tenderness and mercy, the soul cries out: "Who is like to Thee, O my God?" *Quis sicut Dominus Deus noster, qui in altis habitat?*[6] And how profound are Thy thoughts! An intense reverence seizes us to the very depths of our souls, and we are lost in our nothingness: what are we, what are the celestial spirits, what are the human multitudes, in face of this wisdom, this power, this eternity, this holiness? *Omnes gentes quasi non sunt sic sunt coram eo.*

But let us be careful to remark, for this again is very important, that this sense of reverence in the soul, while yet being very intense and real, is not distinct from those of confidence and love.[7] Humility does not contradict any of the aspects of the truth. God is to be contemplated in all His perfections and in all His works; He is at once Lord and Father; we are at once creatures and adopted children; and it is from this *total* contemplation in the Almighty Power of a sovereign Lord and the Supreme Goodness of a Father full of tenderness, that reverence towards God, the root of humility, ought to arise.

St. Benedict's conception of humility far surpasses in amplitude those that have become classic with moralists; but it in nowise contradicts them. Humility remains for him, as for all, a virtue which restrains the inordinate tendencies of self-exaltation in the creature; but with him,—as appears above in the *Prologue* of the Rule,—on account of the "relationship" that he gives it with the virtue of religion, it is not complete unless blended with the love and confidence that should animate the heart of a child. Reverence towards God ought to make a soul lost in self-abasement, and at the same time, through this very self-abasement,

1 Ps. cxii, 5. 7 Cf. Collection "Pax," *La Mère Jeanne Deleloë.*

yielded up to the loving accomplishment of the Heavenly Father's desires. The virtue of humility is rather, with our Holy Father, the habitual attitude of soul which rules our whole relation with God in the truth of our twofold quality of sinful creatures and adopted children.[1]

If forgetful of our nothingness we come before God, full of confidence, but with little reverence; or, if, on the contrary, we are penetrated with fear, but have only a slight confidence, our relations with God are not what they ought to be. The self-abasement of the creature should not be to the detriment of the confidence of the child; the quality of child ought not to cause forgetfulness of the condition of creature and sinner. Humility thus understood envelops our whole being, and we understand why St. Benedict has made one of the most characteristic notes of the spiritual life to consist in this very precise and comprehensive attitude of soul. We shall not have grasped the holy Patriarch's teaching unless we have understood that the root of humility is an intense reverence of the soul before God; that this reverence itself is born of the contemplation of what God is and does for us in His two-fold character of Lord and Father; and that this two-fold reverence, once anchored in the soul, keeps it in the self-abasement befitting it as a creature stained by sin, but at the same time surrenders it entirely, in confident and grateful abandonment, to the will of the Heavenly Father.

In consequence, this reverence towards God extends to all that touches, represents or announces God: to Christ's Humanity, then to all the members of His Mystical Body. "We ought," St. Thomas well says, "not only to revere God in Himself; but also to revere, although in a different manner, what is of God in every man. Therefore," he concludes, "we ought, out of humility, to submit ourselves to all our fellow-creatures for God's sake." *Non debemus solum Deum revereri in seipso sed etiam id quod est ejus, debemus revereri in quolibet; non tamen eo modo reverentiae quo reveremur Deum. Et ideo per humilitatem debemus nos subjicere omnibus proximis propter Deum.*[2] When we have this spirit of

1 "The twelve degrees of humility (set forth by St. Benedict) form an astonishingly penetrating and harmonious whole, showing the blending of fear and confidence, of obedience and energy, of recollection and charity which ought to compose the attitude of the monk who advances in spiritual life..." D. Ryelandt, l. c.

2 *Non tamen eo modo reverentiae quo reveremur Deum.* (Although not with the same measure of reverence as we revere God.) II-II, q. clxi, a. 3, ad 1. St. Thomas says

reverence towards God, it bears upon all "that is of God" in creatures. Being unable completely to annihilate itself before God, the soul for God's sake, and out of regard for God, places itself at the feet of creatures. This reverence extends first of all to Christ's Sacred Humanity; united personally to the Word, this Humanity merits the worship and adoration that we render to God Himself. When we see our Lord upon the Cross, covered with blood, become the scorn of the multitude, *Dejectum et novissimum virorum,*[1] we fall upon our knees, we adore Him, because He is God.

All proportion guarded, we act in an analogous manner with all the members of Christ's Mystical Body, because God, through Christ's Humanity, is united to the whole human race. The humble monk, filled with reverence towards God, sees in every man with whom he comes in contact an apparition of God; and he devotes himself to serving this man because, in one way or another, the monk sees God in him. Such is truly the thought of our Holy Father when he ordains "to incline the head or even prostrate upon the ground before all guests at their arrival or at the moment of their departure, in order to adore in them Christ Who is received in their persons": *Omnibus venientibus vel discedentibus hospitibus, inclinato capite vel prostrato omni corpore in terra, Christus in eis ADORETUR qui et suscipitur.*[2] This is the attitude of humility. We prostrate before another, we serve him in all subjection, because we revere in him such or such a divine attribute; for example, the attribute of power in those holding authority. "It is in the reverence with which I encompass the plenitude of God's rights that I derive the ultimate motive of my obedience to all created authority."[3]

It is that humility of which St. Benedict treats with so much predilection that gives to Monastic spirituality its particular character of greatness, and invests it with a special splendour. The Holy Spirit harmonises

---

again with much justice: *Humilitas proprie respicit reverentiam qua homo Deo subjicitur, et ideo quilibet homo secundum id quod suum est, debet se cuilibet proximo subjicere quantum ad id quod est Dei in ipso* (Humility properly regards the reverence whereby man is is subject to God. Wherefore every man, in respect of that which is his own, ought to subject himself to every neighbour, in respect of that which the latter has of God's.) a. 3, in corpore. Cf. also a. 1, ad 5.

1 Isa. liii, 3. 2 Rule, ch. liii. 3 D. Lottin, *l. c.*

the two sentiments, the one of fear, the other of piety; and their accord causes the soul, selfless as it is before God and the neighbour, to be yet assured of the divine grace that comes to it through Christ, in Whom it finds everything which of itself it lacks. This invincible assurance fills it with the very power of God, and thus renders its life altogether fruitful. Knowing that without Christ it can do nothing, *Sine me nihil potestis facere*,[1] it knows with the same certainty that it can do all things, as soon as it leans upon Him: *Omnia possum in eo qui me confortat*.[2] Humility is the secret of its strength and vitality.

IV

It now remains for us to study the different degrees of this virtue, according to the teaching of the great Patriarch; and having done this, we will point out its beneficent effects, and the means of strengthening it within us.

The general classification of the degrees of humility, laid down by St. Benedict, has received the approbation of the Angelic Doctor.[3] Our Holy Father speaks first of all of interior virtue, and as the first degree he places the fear of God, reverence towards God. He rightly does so. St. Thomas shows us that the holy Lawgiver considered humility, set forth the teaching concerning it, and established its degrees, according to the very nature of the thing, *secundum ipsam naturam rei*.[4] "Exterior acts of humility," says the prince of theologians, "should proceed from the interior disposition": *Ex interiori autem dispositione humilitatis procedunt quaedam exteriora signa*.[5] But, he adds, the principle and root of interior humility itself is reverence towards God: *Principium et radix humilitatis est reverentia quam quis habet ad Deum*.[6] The fear of God is said to constitute the first of all the degrees: because without it humility cannot be born or maintained. Hence as from a living stem spring forth all the other degrees of humility—the virtue which lies within being naturally manifested outwardly.

The holy Patriarch therefore places reverence towards God as the point of departure: "The first degree of humility consists in having the

1 Joan. xv, 5. 2 Philip. iv, 13. 3 II-II, q. clxi. a. 6.
4 Ibid. a. 6, ad 5. 5 Ibid. a. 6. 6 Ibid.

fear of God ever before our eyes, without ever forgetting it": *Si timorem Dei sibi ante oculos* SEMPER *ponens, oblivionem fugiat.*[1] But there is a gradation in the fear of God. Of what fear is there question here? It cannot be question of servile fear, of the fear of chastisement, proper to the slave, which excludes love and paralyses confidence; it concerns first of all imperfect fear with which love is blended, secondly, reverential fear. Our Lord Himself tells us: "Fear ye Him, Who after He hath killed, hath power to cast into hell," *in gehennam*. This fear makes us watch unceasingly to avoid sin, in order not to displease God Who punishes evil: *Custodiens se omni hora a peccatis et vitiis*. This fear is good. Scripture places this prayer upon our lips; "Pierce Thou my flesh with Thy fear": *Confige timore tuo carnes meas.*[2] Our Lord in person enjoins this fear even on those whom He vouchsafes to call His friends.

Undoubtedly, as the soul progresses in the spiritual life, the aforesaid fear gives place, little by little, to love, as the habitual mainspring of action. It never ought, however, to disappear altogether; it is a weapon that we should constantly hold in reserve, in our spiritual arsenal, for hours of combat when love threatens to be overcome by passion. The Council of Trent insists forcibly upon the uncertainty in which we are left touching our final perseverance; our life is a continual trial of faith, and we ought never to part with, or fail to keep within our reach, the weapon of the fear of God.

This imperfect fear ought however to culminate habitually in the reverential fear whereof the ultimate term is adoration full of love. It is of this fear that is said: *Timor Domini sanctus, permanens in saeculum saeculi.*[3] "The fear of the Lord is holy, enduring forever and ever." It is the reverence that seizes every creature before the infinite plenitude of the Divine perfections, even when this creature has become a child of God, nay, even when admitted to the kingdom of Heaven; a reverence which makes the purest angels veil their faces before the dazzling effulgence of the Divine Majesty: *Adorant dominationes, tremunt potestates,*[4]

1 Rule, ch. vii. The texts of the Rule cited in this Conference in regard to humility being all from Chapter vii, we refer the reader to it once for all.

2 Ps. cxviii, 120. 3 Ps. xviii, 10.

4 "The Dominations adore, the Powers tremble," Preface of the Mass.

a reverence which filled the very Humanity of Christ: *Et replebit eum spiritus timoris Domini.*[1]

What does the great Patriarch say to us when he invites us in the Prologue to place ourselves in his school? That he wishes to teach us, as his sons, the fear of God: *Venite, filii... timorem Domini docebo vos.*[2] This God is a Father full of goodness, to Whose admonitions we ought to listen with the ears of the heart, that is to say with a lively sense of love, for this Father prepares for us an inheritance of immortal glory and eternal beatitude. St. Benedict would have us take care not to weary with our faults[3] the goodness of this Heavenly Father Who awaits us, *Quia pius est,* and, in His love, destines those who fear Him, to an ineffable participation in His own life: *Et vita aeterna quae timentibus Deum praeparata est.* This fear, this reverence towards God, the Father of infinite majesty, *patrem immensae majestatis,*[4] ought to be habitual and "constant," for it concerns the virtue, that is to say, an habitual disposition, and not an isolated act: *Animo suo semper evolvat.*[5]

Each degree of interior virtue is a step towards the profound adoration of God, the final term of our reverence. In fact, if we have this reverence towards God, we shall pass on, as it were naturally, to the submission of our own will to that of God; this is the second degree. True fear of God obliges a man to be solicitous as to what God commands him; it is a want of respect towards God not to think of what He enjoins on us. God's Will is God Himself: if we have the fear of God, we shall give ourselves up, from reverence towards Him, to the doing of all that He commands us: *Beatus vir qui timet Dominum, in mandatis ejus VOLET NIMIS.*[6] We shall have such reverence for God that we shall always prefer His will to our own; we shall immolate to Him this self-will which, in many souls, is an inner idol to which they unceasingly offer incense. The humble soul, knowing the sovereignty of God's rights which flow from the the plenitude of His Being and the infinity of His perfections, knowing too its own nothingness and dependence, does not wish to

1 Isa. xi, 3.
2 Ps. xxxiii, 12.
3 Prologue of the Rule.
4 Hymn *Te Deum.*
5 "And let him constantly turn over in his heart," Rule, ch. vii.
6 "Blessed is the man that feareth the Lord: he shall delight exceedingly in His commandments," Ps. cxi, 1.

find in itself the motive power of its life and activity; it seeks this motive power in the will of God; it sacrifices its self-will to that of God; it accepts the rulings of Providence towards it, without the least inward resistance, because God alone merits all adoration and all submission, by reason of His holiness and omnipotence: *Humilitas proprie respicit reverentiam* QUA HOMO DEO SUBJICITUR...[1] *Per hoc quod Deum reveremur et honoramus, mens nostra ei subjicitur.*[2]

V

These two first degrees belong, in substance, as much to the simple Christian as to the monk. But St. Benedict who wishes the monk to aim at the perfection of Christianity, has taken care to recall these degrees emphatically to his sons.

The third degree is already higher and is properly speaking monastic. "The disciple is to submit himself in all obedience to his Superior": *Omni obedientia se subdat majori.* The soul has such reverence towards God and His will, that it admits that God intimates His "good pleasure" through the voice of a man: *Pro Dei amore*; this is the motive pointed out by St. Benedict. To submit to God (2nd degree) is a relatively easy thing; but to obey a man in all things, and all one's life, is much more difficult to nature. It needs a greater spirit of faith and a deeper reverence towards God to see Him in a man who holds His place. God wills that, after having adored Him in Himself, we should render to Him the homage of our submission in the person of a man whom He has chosen to direct us. This man, however imperfect he may be in himself, represents God for the believing soul, because owing to his authority he participates in the divine attribute which is power; and the soul surrenders itself to him, for the sake of this communication that God makes of His sovereignty to the Superior. According to the expression of Blessed Angela of Foligno, the soul reads God's name on the man[3] who represents Him. Therefore the soul says to God: Thou art so great,

1 "Humility... properly regards the reverence whereby man is subject to God," II-II, q. clxi, a. 4, co.

2 "By the very fact that we revere and honour God, our mind is subjected to Him," II-II, q. lxxxi, a. 7, co.

3 *The Book of Visions,* ch. 63.

and I am so small a thing before Thee, that I wish out of love and reverence for Thee to obey, all my life, a man weak like myself, but who represents Thee: *Humilitas secundum quod est specialis virtus praecipue respicit subjectionem hominis ad Deum. PROPTER QUEM ETIAM ALIIS HUMILIANDO SE SUBJICIT.*[1]

And see how the self-abasement and adoration of the soul before God are increased at the 4th degree. The humble monk not only accepts the divine economy that wills he should be led by one of his fellow creatures, weak and imperfect; but he inviolably preserves this submission despite the difficulties he experiences in so doing, despite the injuries, contempt or affronts he may have to suffer in the exercise of his obedience, and this without a murmur arising from his heart: *Tacita conscientia*. Humility here blossoms out into heroic patience. What a contrast with pride! The proud man is assured of his perfection and so full of the idea of his importance that he at once bursts out with excuses.

Now on the day we made profession of our Rule, we promised to tend to this humility.

If so admirable a patience appears very difficult for us to possess, let us turn our gaze upon our Divine Model during His Passion. He is God, the All-Powerful, and His Soul is rich in all perfection. And behold, they spit in His Face; He does not turn away: *Faciem meam non averti ab increpantibus et conspuentibus in Me.*[2] He is silent before Herod who treats Him as a fool: *At ipse nihil illi respondebat*;[3] He submits Himself to Pilate who condemns Him to an infamous death, He submits Himself because Pilate, being the legitimate governor of Judea, represented, Pagan though he was, the authority that has its source in God: *Non haberes potestatem adversum me ullam nisi tibi datum esset desuper.*[4] Why does Christ Jesus submit without complaint to all these outrages? From reverence and love for His Father Who has fixed the circumstances of His Passion: *Sicut mandatum dedit mihi Pater.*[5]

1 "Humility, considered as a special virtue, regards chiefly the subjection of man to God, for Whose sake he humbles himself by subjecting himself to others," II-II, q. clxi, a. 1, ad 5.

2 Isa. l, 6, 3 Luc. xxiii, 9. 4 Joan. xix, 11. 5 Ibid. xiv, 21.

It is proportionately the same for the humble monk. Why does he accept all humiliation? Always for the sake of the reverence he has for God. As soon as he encounters a vestige of the Divine Majesty he surrounds it with respect; as soon as he sees God, under whatever form God presents Himself, he yields to Him: "And to show that the faithful servant ought to bear all things, however contrary, for the Lord, the Scripture says in the person of the suffering: For Thee we suffer death all the day long": *Et ostendens fidelem PRO DOMINO universa etiam contraria sustinere debere, dicit... PROPTER TE morte adficimur tota die.*

But love and confidence likewise animate the monk's soul in all these circumstances, painful as they are to nature. If he "remains steadfast, if he does not draw back or give in," *Sustinens non lassescat, vel discedat,* it is because a firm hope, full of love and spiritual joy, at the same time fills his soul and makes him say: "In all these things we overcome through Him Who hath loved us": *Et securi de spe retributionis divinae subsequuntur gaudentes et dicentes; sed in his omnibus superamus PROPTER EUM QUI DILEXIT.*

You see how in humility, our Holy Father never separates the confidence of the child who, through Christ's grace, invincibly hopes in the goodness of his Heavenly Father, from the reverence that possesses him on account of his condition as creature.

Monastic submission goes so far that we reveal to our Superior the state of our soul; here we have the 5th degree of humility. Pride prompts us to exalt ourselves and seek the esteem of others, and consequently to hide our defects from them. It is therefore an act of humility to reveal voluntarily to another man the true state of our soul:[1] and we do it because we revere God in this man: *Revela DOMINO viam tuam, et spera in eo.*[2] Notice the choice that St. Benedict here makes of this text. It is

1 In the terms of the ecclesiastical legislation actually in force, religious Superiors cannot in any way urge their inferiors to disclose their conscience to them; but on the other hand it is in nowise forbidden for subjects to open their hearts freely to their Superiors, and even, as is said in the text of the Code of Canon Law, "it is advantageous for religious to go to their Superiors with filial confidence and thus also lay open to them, if these Superiors are priests, the doubts and anguish of their conscience." Can. 530.

2 "Commit thy way to the Lord, and trust in Him," Ps. xxxvi, 5.

to the Lord, *Domino*, to the Lord Whom faith causes us to see in our Superior, that we unveil the state of our soul, assured that if we act as children, God will act towards us like a Father full of loving kindness: *Et spera in eo*. The fruit of this degree of humility is that God will lead us by a sure path, wherein we cannot go astray.

But in order that this degree may be truly attained, it is necessary for us to be always very sincere with ourselves before God and before the one who holds God's place, *Revela*. We ought to watch over the movements of our soul lest any falsehood in our attitude or dealings escape us; others must be able to say of us: *Qui loquitur veritatem in corde suo.*[1] We should be "true" in the sanctuary of ourselves in face of God, and be true with him to whom we yield our hearts for love of God: *Veritatem ex corde et ore proferre,*[2] says our Holy Father. This is a great duty. We should never tolerate the least insincerity with ourselves. If we did so frequently, we should end by obscuring and blinding our conscience. It would then be impossible for our Lord to make of our soul His own abiding place of predilection, because we have not revealed to Him the state of our soul such as it is; we have not that light of humility which shows us how little we are before God.

The two last degrees of interior humility are very high. Knowing we have offended this God, so great, so full of majesty, and that by our sins we have deserved to be under the feet of the devil, we are content with the worst of everything, and esteem ourselves, according to the spirit of the Gospel, as "unprofitable servants."[3] We are so small a thing before God, our actions are of themselves so defective that we are incapable of doing anything without the grace of Christ Jesus. It alone gives worth to our deeds. If, practically, we believe that we do a great deal by ourselves; that we have a right to consideration because we have rendered such or such service, we have yet not arrived at this degree. St. Benedict does not hesitate to deal rigorously, on occasion, with these persistent forms of the spirit of self-exaltation. If, he says, among those who exercise an art or craft in the Monastery, there be any who are tempted to pride themselves on their attainments and skill, or on the benefit that the

1 "He that speaketh truth in his heart," Ps. xiv, 3.
2 Rule, ch. iv. 3 Luc. xvii, 10.

monastery derives from them, they shall be forever forbidden to work at this art or craft[1] rather than expose their souls to spiritual detriment.

The 7th degree constitutes the summit of the virtue of humility: it is for a monk to believe himself, sincerely and from the bottom of his heart, the last of all men: *Si omnibus se inferiorem et viliorem intimo cordis credat affectu*. This is St. Paul's counsel: "In humility let each esteem others better than themselves": *In humilitate superiores sibi invicem arbitrantes.*[2] Few souls arrive at this height and live there habitually; it is assuredly a gift of God. For this it is needful that the light of the Holy Spirit should give the soul an intensely clear view of the Divine perfections, which makes it humble itself to its lowest depths; then, seeing the nothingness that it truly is in presence of the Divine greatness, and considering the gifts of God in others, the soul inwardly places itself at the feet of all.[3] Whoever mounts towards this degree, will keep himself, in every circumstance, from judging himself better than others and from being severe to them. If God had acted with rigour towards us, if He had treated us according to strict justice, what would have become of us? And are we so sure of ourselves? For we must also consider the possibilities of evil that are to be found in us. May not one whom we are tempted to despise today, soon become better than we are? Moreover, can we be sure of what our dispositions will be tomorrow? Within us all, poor creatures that we are, there is a constant principle of instability and deficiency that we have unceasingly to combat with the help of grace and the exercise of humility.

May God deign to allow us to rest a moment, at least in thought and holy desire, on the sublime summit towards which St. Benedict has traced the path and marked the stages! Thus beholding our ideal, let us be convinced of the truth of our nothingness and of the essential and constant need we have of help from above.

VI

From this interior humility of which St. Benedict has just shown us the ascending degrees, is derived exterior humility. The virtue resides

1 Rule, ch. lvii. 2 Philip. ii, 3. 3 St. Thomas, II-II, q. clxi, a. 3, ad 2.

principally in the soul: *Humilitas praecipue interius in anima consistit.*[1] Therefore the holy Patriarch speaks first of humility of soul. To wish to appear humble outwardly when one has not, and does not strive to acquire inward virtue, is a simulation in which there is something Pharisaical, and St. Benedict bids us beware of this,[2] or it is "immense pride," says St. Thomas.[3] We should first of all aim at acquiring the interior virtue. If that is real, sincere, alive, well anchored in the soul, it will quite naturally manifest itself outwardly, without difficulty as also without pretention. If we have interior humility, the body, by reason of the substantial unity of our being, will express the reverence that fills the soul before God. Outward humility is only of any value if it is the real expression of inward humility, or if it is the means employed to arrive thereat. A man must acquire and express humility by the movements of the soul and those of the body. We ought then to exercise ourselves likewise in outward humility even if we have not reached a high degree of the inward virtue.

On account of the close union between soul and body, every act of virtue often repeated, such as striking the breast, keeping the eyes lowered, going down on one's knees to make "satisfaction," has its echo in the soul and necessarily influences the interior life. "When," says St. Augustine, "we prostrate at the feet of our brethren, this humiliation of the body disposes and stirs up our heart to inward self-abasement, or, if it was already humble, strengthens it in humility."[4] It is then to help in the acquisition or in the strengthening of the inward virtue that the body should be humbled; otherwise, it would be Pharisaical to wish to appear humble in the eyes of men when pride reigns in the heart.

---

1 II-II, q. clxi, a. 3, Cf. a. 1, ad 2 and a. 6. St. Thomas very justly deducts from this principle that a Superior can perfectly well possess the virtue of humility without performing *exteriorly* certain acts of humility little compatible with his dignity.

2 *Non velle dici sanctum antequam sit, sed prius esse quod verius dicatur* (Not to wish to be called holy before one is holy; but first to be holy, that one may more truly be called so). Rule, ch. iv.

3 II-II, q. clxi, a. 1, ad 2.

4 *Cum enim ad pedes fratris inclinatur corpus, etiam ut corde ipso vel excitatur, vel si jam inerat confirmatur, humilitatis affectus* (Indeed, when the body is prostrate at the feet of the brethren, the disposition of humility either is stirred up in the heart, or, if it dwelt there already, is strengthened). *Tract. in Joan.* 58.

In this matter, however, there is need of a certain discretion with those who take their first steps in the spiritual life; humility is not acquired in one day, and novices ought not to wish to pass at the first onset from the free and easy manners of an undergraduate to the attitudes of an ecstatic. The important thing is to aim at inward humility, and to practise it, with discretion but fidelity, so as to acquire the outward degrees.

Another reason, which necessitates the outward practice of humility, is that this practice often serves as a diagnostic for knowing the reality of the virtue; it reveals to us whether we are actuated by secret pride. This is a great point, for it is already a step towards humility to know that we do not yet possess it. Ask the proud man if he has a high opinion of himself; most often he will at once reply in the negative; but, in practice, he will reveal himself as he is, in spite of himself, because from his secret pride will arise, as it were instinctively and often enough without his perceiving it, acts manifesting this pride. Thus you will see him, quite naturally, on account of the exaggerated sense of his importance, seek to impose his own opinion, and tend to act differently from others—when he does not look down on them—to make himself conspicuous and singular, even in small matters;[1] he worships his own person, his own ideas, his ways of doing things, although this is often unconsciously. Like the Pharisees he says: "I do this, I do that; I am not like other men": *Non sum sicut caeteri hominum*.[2] He begins to speak as soon as a discussion begins; you hear him raise his voice; he never resists the longing to speak, and he speaks unceasingly without enduring contradiction; he even imposes silence, often in a cutting tone. All this is a manifestation of pride, for our words are something of ourselves.

The manner of laughing is no less a sure sign of the inward dispositions of the soul. One might ask what there is in laughter, this attribute peculiar to man, that is opposed to humility? Our Holy Father does not condemn laughter; a monk habitually gloomy and morose would show that he does not "run in the way of the commandments with that sweetness of love"[3] which St. Benedict promises to those who are faithful. What the holy Legislator intends to proscribe first of all (this goes without saying) is the evil kind of laughter which has its source in an

1 See above, p. 88 what we have said of singularity as opposed to the cenobitical life.
2 Luc. xviii, 12. 3 Prologue of the Rule.

underlying coarseness of nature; it is the laughter of raillery which maliciously lays stress on the eccentricities and defects of others: all this is too contrary to the Christian spirit to be found in those who "seek God," those who ought to be the temple of the Spirit of all holiness; then St. Benedict above all condemns an habitual disposition to laugh readily, noisily, on all and every occasion: the habitual tendency to jest. If we have well understood that humility has its root in reverence towards God, a reverence itself resulting from the sense of the Divine Presence, we shall at once grasp how much reason the great Patriarch has in utterly condemning, *Aeterna clausura*,[1] this injurious tendency to buffoonery, this veritable dissolvant of inward recollection.

The failings we have been recalling are never to be found in the humble monk whose soul is full of reverence for the Divine Majesty always present to him. He does not try to make himself different from others, quite the contrary. Seeing in the common Rule the expression of the Divine Will, he fears to deviate from it however little; he does not speak on every occasion; he knows how "to keep silence," which is the atmosphere of recollection, "until a question be asked him." When he laughs it is not like the fool who "lifteth up his voice in laughter";[2] for reverence towards God is the antithesis, not of joy, but of the spirit of levity, of dissipation, of a bantering tone; he keeps in his very speech the gravity and sobriety of the wise man who "is known by the fewness of his words." Finally, his bearing, his gait everywhere express this inward humility, although without affectation; his soul is visibly possessed by God; the reverence for God that animates him inwardly makes him keep "his head bent downwards and his eyes downcast."[3]

We may ask ourselves why it is that the monk who has scaled the degrees of humility and has attained solid virtue is to keep the attitude of a culprit, why it is that St. Benedict, who yet writes nothing without reflection, places ever—*semper*—upon this monk's lips and in his heart

---

1 "Perpetual ban," Rule, ch. vi.

2 *Ubi timor et tremor est, ibi non vocis elatio sed animus flebilis, et lacrymosa dejectio* (Where fear and trembling are, there is no raising of the voice, but a lamenting soul and tearful purgation). S. Hieronym. Epist. 13. Virginitatis laus, P. L. xxx, Col 175.

3 *Extollentia oculorum est quoddam signum superbiae in quantum excludit reverentiam et timorem* (Lofty eyes are a sign of pride, inasmuch as it excludes respect and fear). St. Thomas, II-II, q. clxi, a. 2, ad 1.

the words of the publican: "My God, I am not worthy to raise mine eyes to Heaven"? It is because in prayer God has given this humble soul a light upon the greatness of His perfections; in this divine light, the soul has beheld its own nothingness, and its least faults appear as intolerable stains. A ray from on high has touched the monk, and whether he be with his brethren, or alone, in prayer, in his cell, in the garden, he knows that the eyes of the Sovereign Master penetrate into the innermost recesses of his soul; he lives in adoration, and his whole exterior bears witness to this adoration. "When the soul... understandeth that God is present, she is humbled exceedingly, and receiveth confusion at the thought of her sins. And here the soul receiveth an exceeding weight of wisdom, a great consolation of God, a great joy."[1] It is sufficient to look at the truly humble monk to understand that God's Presence, which is the source of his reverence, is familiar to him, and that he has a profound sense of what the gravity of divine union brings with it. These traits might assuredly have been taken from our Holy Father's portrait. His first biographer, Pope St. Gregory the Great, tells us that his life was nothing else than the faithful application of the Rule: "The spirit of all the just filled the soul of the Patriarch." There are however some virtues which particularly characterise him. Among the most salient of these traits is to be remarked an extraordinary spirit of adoration and reverence towards God.[2] Read, in fact, the Holy Rule; you will see it throughout imbued with the spirit of religion. Whether he speaks of the Divine Office, of the reading of the Gospel, of the *Gloria* that ends each Psalm, St. Benedict insists on reverence. This same spirit is extended to the monk's relations with his brethren, with guests, and even to the utensils of the monastery,

---

1 Bl. Angela of Foligno. *The Book of Visions,* ch. 27. *The Ineffable.* Translated by a Secular Priest.

2 "St. Benedict's gravity is essentially religious, that is to say that it results from an habitual and deep sense of the Divine Presence. The responsibilities of our present life, and the realisation that our eternal life is at stake, the love of Christ, the sight of God's judgments are ever present to him. All this inner life of his tends to make gravity a true recollection of soul, which radiates in the bodily attitude and behaviour. In St. Benedict's mind, it is the gaze fixed upon God, it is the sense of man's close relation with Him that banishes from life levity no less than dilettantism and begets humble and gentle gravity." D.G. Ryelandt, *l. c.*

which is the "House of God." In our Holy Father's sight, our whole life is bathed in an atmosphere of supernatural reverence.

And the Holy Patriarch was himself the model of what he requires of his sons; the picture of the humble monk which he draws in Chapter VII of his Rule, is without doubt, his own likeness. His soul, so dear to God that God granted to his prayers so many striking miracles, and vouchsafed to show him the entire world in a ray of light, was flooded with divine brightness; and in this supernatural light, he saw the nothingness of every creature: *Videnti Creatorem angusta est creatura*;[1] he saw that God alone is the fount of all good, that He alone merits all glory, and knowing thus that all comes from God, he returned to Him all praise and all honour.

VII

For—and here I approach an important point—humility is truth.

As St. Teresa says: "Some think it humility not to believe that God is bestowing His gifts upon them." Is this honouring God? Nothing is more unjustifiable. "Let us clearly understand this," adds the Saint, "that it is perfectly clear God bestows His gifts without any merit whatever on our part." What are we then to do in presence of divine graces? Recognise that God alone is the Author and Principle of them: *OMNE donum perfectum desursum est, descendens a Patre luminum*,[2] and thank Him for them with grateful hearts. "For if we do not recognise the gifts received at His hands, we shall never be moved to love Him. It is a most certain truth that the richer we see ourselves to be, confessing at the same time our poverty, the greater will be our progress, and the more real our humility... if we walk in simplicity before God, aiming at pleasing Him only, and not men."[3]

True humility moreover does not deceive itself: it does not deny God's gifts: it uses them, but returns all glory to Him from Whom they come. Look at the Blessed Virgin Mary chosen out from among all women to be the Mother of the Word Incarnate. No creature, after the Humanity

1 St. Gregory, *Dialogues.* Lib. ii, ch. 35. 2 Jac. i, 17.

3 *Life of St. Teresa* by herself, ch. 10. Translated from the Spanish by David Lewis. Cf. also St. Francis of Sales *Introduction to the Devout Life,* 3rd Part, ch. 5.

of Jesus, has been filled with graces as she was: *Ave, gratia plena.*[1] She was surely conscious of this. Now when Elizabeth congratulates her on her divine maternity, does the Blessed Virgin deny the signal favour of which she is the object? Indeed not. She even acknowledges that it is a unique privilege, that "He that is mighty hath done great things" to her, things so great, so marvellous that all generations shall call her blessed. But, if she does not deny these graces, neither does she make them an occasion of glorifying herself; she returns all the glory to God, the All-Powerful Who works them in her: *Magnificat anima mea Dominum.*[2] This is the way the humble soul acts.

Our Holy Father's teaching is inspired with exactly the same spirit. "Let the good that one sees in oneself," he says, "be attributed to God and not to oneself": *Bonum aliquid in se cum viderit Deo applicet, non sibi.*[3] St. Benedict does not deny that we may be aware of the Divine gifts within us; far from binding us to veil them from ourselves, he allows them to be seen: *Cum viderit*; having seen them we shall feel urged to use them on every occasion in the service of Him Who has distributed them to us: *Ei (Domino) omni tempore de bonis suis in nobis parendum est.*[4] Only we must not imagine they are due to us, but thank God for them. The holy Patriarch is still more explicit in his Prologue: Those who seek God, he says, fear the Lord (that is the root of humility,) they do not pride themselves on their good observance; knowing that the good which is in them does not come from themselves but from the Lord, they glorify Him for what He divinely works in them, saying with the Prophet: "Not unto us, O Lord, not unto us, but unto Thy Name give the glory":[5] *Operantem in se Dominum magnificant.* And St. Benedict adds: "So the Apostle Paul imputed nothing to himself of the success of his preaching, for he said: 'By the grace of God I am what I am,'[6] and again: 'He that glorieth, let him glory in the Lord.'"[7]

St. Paul's example brought forward by St. Benedict is extremely well chosen for none has been a better exponent of humility than the great Apostle. Does he then deny his good works? On the contrary he draws the picture of them as no other apostle has ever done. Does he despise

1 Luc. i, 48.
2 Ibid. 46–49.
3 Rule, ch. iv.
4 Prologue of the Rule.
5 Ps. cxiii, 9.
6 I Cor. xv, 10.
7 II Cor. x, 17.

God's gifts? Oh no. He says: "We have received... the Spirit that is of God; that we may know the things that are given us from God": *Ut sciamus quae a Deo donata sunt nobis.*[1] He knows these gifts, but it is that he may render thanks for them to the Father and His Son, Christ Jesus. It is in Christ's grace that he places all his glory, all his hope: *Ut inhabitet in me virtus Christi.*[2]

"It is contrary to humility," St. Thomas justly says, "for a man to tend to things too high for him, relying on his own strength; but if he puts his confidence in God and afterwards undertakes the most difficult things, this action is not contrary to humility, above all when he considers that he rises so much the nearer to God in proportion as he submits to Him the more profoundly by humility."[3]

When our Holy Father considers the contingency of "impossible things" that might be commanded by obedience, what does he tell the monk to do? First of all to receive the order in all meekness and submission. Then if after reflexion the monk is convinced that the thing enjoined really exceeds his capacity and strength, he may represent these difficulties to his Superior, but if the latter, after having heard the objections, persists in the order given, then, says St. Benedict, "let the monk know that the command is expedient for him, and putting his trust in God's help, let him obey for love of Him": *Et ex caritate confidens de adjutorio Dei obediat.*[4] God cannot fail a soul who acts thus.

What we now say of individual injunctions is likewise to be extended to the charges and employments to which authority has full right to appoint. The presumptuous, even if they have not the necessary capacity, desire posts that place them in full evidence: on the other hand, those who have false humility decline every function, even those that they naturally feel themselves capable of exercising well. Both go to extremes. What our Holy Father recommends is to accept out of reverence and love for God the charges given us, placing in God alone all our trust, while neglecting nothing in order to fulfil these charges with the greatest perfection possible. For in as far as He rejects those who exalt themselves, *qui SE exaltat humiliabitur,*[5] so He lavishes His help

---

1 I Cor. ii, 12.
2 II Cor. xii, 9.
3 II-II, q. lcxi, a. 2, ad 2.
4 Rule, ch. lxviii.
5 Luc. xiv, 11.

on those who knowing their own weakness, place their confidence in the support of Heaven.

"It is one thing," says St. Augustine, "to raise oneself up to God, and another thing to raise oneself up against Him; he who casts himself down before God is uplifted; he who rises up against God is cast down by Him."[1]

VIII

The chief fruit of humility is to make us so pleasing to God that His grace, meeting with no obstacles, abounds in us and brings us the assurance of remaining united to God by love: this is the state of perfect charity.

After having explained the different degrees of humility, St. Benedict concludes his comments with a phrase which although so short is one of great depth, and merits our special attention. "The monk who has ascended all these degrees of humility," he says, "will *soon*," *mox*—bear this word in mind—"arrive at that perfect charity from whence all fear is cast out": *Ergo his omnibus humilitatis gradibus ascensis, monachus* MOX *ad caritatem Dei perveniet illam quae perfecta fortis mittit timorem.*

You may have remarked that spiritual authors are sometimes at variance or in some uncertainty when they have to regulate the rank of pre-eminence among the virtues. It is beyond doubt that the queen of virtues is charity; but charity cannot exist in a soul without humility, which on account of our fallen nature is the condition *sine qua non* of the exercise of charity. Humility, then, is not perfection; perfection as we have said, consists in the love wherewith we remain, in all things, united through Christ to God and to God's Will. But humility, as St. Thomas well says, is "a disposition that facilitates the soul's free access to spiritual and divine goods": *Est quasi quaedam dispositio ad liberum accessum hominis in spiritualia et divina bona.*[2] Charity is greater than humility, as the perfection of a state is greater than the dispositions requisite to

1 *Aliud est se levare ad Deum, aliud est levare se contra Deum. Qui ante illum se projicit ab illo erigitur; qui adversus illum se erigit ab illo projicitur.* Sermo 351. *De utilitate poenitentiae.*

2 II-II, q. clxi, a. 5, ad 4.

reach this state; but humility, in achieving the work of removing the obstacles opposed to divine union, takes, from this point of view, the first rank. In this sense, St. Thomas[1] explicitly says humility constitutes the very foundation of the spiritual edifice; it is the disposition that immediately precedes perfect charity, so that without it and the work it does, the state of charity and of perfect union with God, cannot exist, still less be maintained.

Although humility is then in this sense a negative disposition, it is so necessary and so infallibly crowned by perfect charity, that in a soul that does not possess it, the spiritual edifice is ever exposed to ruin for lack of foundation; while he who possesses it attains in all surety to the state of union. This is what was said by Blosius, so versed in the science of union with God: "The humbler one is, the nearer he is to God and to perfection": *Quanto quis humilior existit, tanto Deo vicinior et in perfectione evangelica excellentior est.*[2]

It is the sublime recompense of humility to contribute, more than any other virtue, to prepare the soul to the outpouring of the Divine gifts which assure perfect union with God: *MOX ad caritatem Dei illam quae perfecta est perveniet.* "Nothing, in fact, is more sublime than this

1 *"Primum" in acquisitione virtutum potest accipi dupliciter: uno modo per modum removentis prohibens et sic humilitas primum locum tenet, in quantum scilicet expellit superbiam cui Deus resistit et praebet hominem subditum et patulum ad suscipiendum influxum divinae gratiae, in quantum evacuat inflationem superbiae. Et secundum hoc, humilitas dicitur spiritualis aedificii fundamentum* (The first step in the acquisition of virtue may be understood in two ways. First by way of removing obstacles: and thus humility holds the first place, inasmuch as it expels pride, which God resisteth, and makes man submissive and ever open to receive the influx of Divine grace... In this sense humility is said to be the foundation of the spiritual edifice). (a. 5, ad 2.) The holy Doctor next shows in what sense faith is said to be the first of virtues. Cf. *Faith, the Foundation of the Christian Life,* in *Christ, the Life of the Soul,* and supra p. 108. See too above, pp. 244–246 the teaching of St. Bernard. The Abbot of Clairvaux expressed the same idea as the holy Patriarch: "Oh! how great must be this virtue of humility seeing that it can so easily attract and draw down to itself even the Divine Majesty! How quickly the name expressive of reverence has been changed for the name inspired by love! With what celerity has He drawn nigh, Who awhile since was so far remote!" *CITO reverentiae nomen in vocabulum amicitiae mutatum est; et qui longe erat, IN BREVI factus est prope.* (In Cantica, xliii, translated by a Priest of Mount Melleray.) IN BREVI ET CITO can be coupled with the MOX of St. Benedict.

2 *Canon vitae spiritualis,* ch. 7.

way of union," says St. Augustine, "but it is only the humble who walk in it": *Nihil excelsius via caritatis, et non in illa ambulant nisi humiles.*[1] It is not by exaltation, but by humility that we attain to God: *Non elatione sed humilitate attingitur.*

A glance back will enable us to judge how simple, and at the same time sure and profound, is the way marked out by our holy Patriarch whereby to lead us to God. By humility, itself derived from reverence towards God, St. Benedict would have the monk destroy the obstacles that can prevent the soul's union with God. When this humility truly possesses the soul, then the Holy Spirit's action, being no longer opposed by sin or attachment to sin, to the creature, or to self, is all-powerful and fruitful. It is a remarkable thing that St. Benedict seems to have no longer any other direction to give his sons, once the degrees of humility are scaled by them. One would say that, for him, the end is attained: he leaves his disciple, as it were, to the action of the Spirit; for this soul anchored fast for ever in the fear of God and expecting all help from on high, is open to the divine effusions. Happy, thrice happy is the soul arrived at this state! God acts freely in it, and leads it by the hand to the highest perfection, to the summits of contemplation; for He wills our holiness, and His nature inclines Him to communicate Himself; the only condition that He lays down is that His gifts and His action meet with no obstacle: this condition is fulfilled by humility. "May the Lord vouchsafe by the action of His Holy Spirit, to bring us to this happy state of perfect charity, after having, by the ascension of the degrees of humility, cleansed our soul from sin and vice": *Quae Dominus jam in operarium suum mundum a peccatis et vitiis Spiritu Sancto dignabitur demonstrare!*

IX

It now only remains for me to point out some means of attaining this most indispensable virtue.

The first of all means is prayer: *Primo quidem et principaliter per gratiae donum.*[2] A high degree of humility is a gift of God, as is a high degree of prayer. "Our Lord Himself," says St. Teresa, "supplies (acts of

1 *Enarrat. in Psalm.* cxli, ch. 7.

2 "First and chiefly by a gift of grace," St. Thomas, II-II, q. clxi, a. 6, ad 2.

humility) in a way very different from that by which we could acquire them by our own poor reflections, which are as nothing in comparison with that real humility arising out of the light Our Lord here gives us."[1] God Who infinitely desires to give Himself to us will certainly not reject our prayer, if we beg of Him to take away the chief obstacle that is opposed to His action in our souls. Let us often beseech God for that spirit of reverence which is the very root of humility and is one of the most striking characteristics of our Holy Father's spirit: *Confige timore tuo carnes meas*.[2] Let us beseech Him to show us, in the light of His grace, that He is all and that without Him we are nothing; one ray of Divine light can do more in this way than any reasoning. Humility might be called the practical reflexion of our intercourse with God. A soul that does not frequently enter into contact with God in prayer cannot possess humility in a high degree. If, even once, God gave us to perceive, in the depth of our soul, in the light of His ineffable Presence, something of His greatness, we should be filled with intense reverence for Him; the groundwork of humility would be acquired and we should only have to guard faithfully this ray of Divine light for humility to be developed and kept alive in us.

Let us often give ourselves up to the consideration of the Divine perfections, not in a philosophic manner for the satisfying of the mind, but in a prayer and contemplation. "Believe me," says St. Teresa, "we shall advance more (the Saint is speaking of humility) by contemplating the Divinity than by keeping our eyes fixed on ourselves, poor creatures of earth that we are... I believe we shall never learn to know ourselves except by endeavouring to know God, for, beholding His greatness we are struck by our own baseness, His purity shows our foulness."[3] This is so true! The consideration of our own misery may produce a *passing* sense of humility, but the virtue, which is an habitual disposition, does not consist in this; reverence towards God is the one cause that can beget the virtue, and above all render it stable.[4]

1 *Life by herself.* ch. 15, translated from the Spanish by David Lewis.

2 See what we said above, p. 253–254 on the *religious* character of Benedictine spirituality.

3 *The Interior Castle,* first Mansions, ch. 2. Translated by the Benedictines of Stanbrook, p. 10.

4 "To keep our soul in the lowliness of humility, it is undoubtedly useful to consider

We monks find in the liturgy a great means of knowing God's perfections. In the Psalms, which form the groundwork of the Divine Office, the Divine perfections are displayed to the eyes of our soul by the Holy Spirit Himself with incomparable wealth of expression. We are therein at every moment invited to admire God's greatness and plenitude. When we say the Divine Office well, our soul little by little assimilates these sentiments expressed by the Holy Spirit on the perfections of the Infinite Being.

Finally, one of the most important means is the contemplation of the humility of Christ Jesus, and through faith, our union with the dispositions of His Sacred Heart. The great monk Blosius writes that "this contemplation is the most efficacious means for healing the wounds of pride."[1] Blessed Angela of Foligno says that when she saw the state to which Jesus was reduced as to His Manhood, she had an inkling for the first time of the greatness of her pride.[2]

More than once, in the course of the chapter that he consecrates to humility, St. Benedict recalls the example of Jesus Christ: he tells us to consider Him that we may find in Him the model of this virtue. Let us then contemplate our Divine Saviour for a few moments. In Him humility was rooted in the reverence that He had for His Father. The soul of Jesus, bathed in heavenly light, saw the Divine perfections in their plenitude, and this sight gave rise to intense and perfect reverence. Isaias says "the Spirit of the Lord shall rest upon Him," and you know how Our Lord applied to Himself this passage of the Prophet: *Et requiescat super eum Spiritus Domini.* But when he comes to speak of

---

what we are: the sight of our misery, our deficiencies, our faults is well calculated to put us in our right place and bring us back to the reality. However the consideration of God and His perfections is a more limpid and fuller source for maintaining our humility." D. Lottin, *L'âme du culte, la vertu de religion,* p. 43.

1 *Nullo alio efficaciori remedio ulceribus superbiae medeberis quam si humilitatem Salvatoris tibi ob oculos animi ponas. Neque enim ipse sine causa dixit: Discite a me quia mitis sum et humilis corde* (No remedy is more efficacious for healing the wounds of pride than to place the humility of the Saviour before the eyes of the soul. Nor, indeed, does He say without cause: "Learn from me, for I am meek and humble of heart"). *Canon vitae Spiritualis,* ch. 7. Saint Teresa said the same: (*l. c.*) "By meditating on His humility we find how very far we are from being humble." See also St. Bernard, *In Epiphania,* Sermo i, 7.

2 *The Book of Visions,* 13, i, ch. 30.

fear, the Prophet uses a more powerful expression: *Et* REPLEBIT *eum Spiritus timoris Domini*: "He shall be filled with the spirit of the fear of the Lord."[1] What is this fear that filled the soul of Christ Jesus? It was not terror; for it could not be question of the fear of chastisements. Neither was it the fear of offending God: Christ, enjoying the Beatific Vision, was impeccable. What then was this fear? Respect and adoration towards the Divine Majesty. And even now, although the Manhood of Jesus reigns *in gloria Patris*, His soul remains lost in perfect reverence. Christ is and remains the great, the only perfect adorer of the Blessed Trinity. His Humanity is that of a God, but this Humanity was created, and as a creature it ever humbled Itself before God in infinite reverence.

It was likewise to expiate our pride and to show us what our humility ought to be, that Christ descended to the lowest depths of humiliation. Christ does not tell us to learn humility from the Apostles, nor from the Angels; no, He tells us to learn it from Himself. In proportion to the height of His Majesty is the depth of His humility. "He gave Himself unto us as an example of humility... when He said 'Learn of Me for I am meek and humble of heart.'... Look deep down into the depth and usefulness of this doctrine and regard the sublimity and worth of this instruction."[2]

X

If we frequently contemplate Christ Jesus in His Passion, if we are united to Him by faith, we may be assured that He will make us participate in His humility, His reverence towards His Father, and submission to His Father's Will.

Neither let us forget this profound truth that the Sacred Humanity had its motive power only in the Word to Whom It was united. Its actions were truly Its own because the Human Nature in Jesus was perfect, but their value was derived only from the union of the Humanity with the Word. The Humanity referred to the Divinity the glory of all Its actions which were admirably holy.

1 Isa. x, 2–3.

2 Bl. Angela of Foligno, *L. c.*, ch. 63, translated by a Secular Priest. All this beautiful chapter should be read.

It ought to be the same for us in the domain of our spiritual activity. We can do nothing of ourselves; let us humble ourselves in beholding the Divine perfections and be penetrated with reverence. We should next place all our confidence in our union with Jesus Christ through faith and love. In Him, through Him, with Him, we are the children of the Heavenly Father. That is the source of this confidence in which our lowliness finds its counterpart, and without which it would be but imperfect humility and an occasion of discouragement. To imagine that, even with Christ's help, we are incapable of good actions, is to lose sight of the greatness of Jesus' merits; it is to lay open our soul to spiritual distrust and despair which are the fruits of hell. By true humility we have no confidence in ourselves, "as of ourselves": *Non quod sufficientes simus cogitare aliquid a nobis QUASI EX NOBIS*; our power comes from God Who, naturally and supernaturally, gives us being, life and movement: *Sed sufficientia nostra ex Deo est...*[1] *In ipso enim vivimus, movemur et sumus.*[2] And this power extends to all things, because we have boundless confidence in the merits of our Divine Head, Christ Jesus.

The proud who claim to draw their power from themselves, commit the sin of Lucifer who said: "I will ascend into Heaven, I will exalt my throne above the stars of God... I will be like the Most High."[3] Like Lucifer they will be overthrown and cast down into the abyss: *Qui se exaltat, humiliabitur.*[4] But what do we say? That without Christ, we can do nothing as He has Himself declared: *Sine me nihil potestis facere.* We declare that it is through Jesus, with Jesus that we can arrive at holiness and enter into Heaven; we say to Christ: "Master, I am poor, miserable, naked, weak, of this I am daily more and more convinced; if Thou hadst treated me, at certain hours of my life, as I deserved I should be under the feet of devils. But I know too that Thou art ineffably powerful, great, and good; I know that the Father Thou lovest so much hath given all sovereignty into Thy hands. I know that He hath placed in Thee all the treasures of holiness that men may desire; I know that Thou wilt never reject those who come to Thee. Therefore, whilst adoring Thee in the deepest recesses of my soul, I have full confidence in Thy merits and satisfactions; I know that altogether miserable as I am, Thou canst by Thy

1 II Cor. iii, 5. 2 Act. xvii, 28. 3 Isa. xiv, 13. 4 Luc. xiv, 11.

grace shower Thy riches upon me, uplift me even to the Divinity, that I may be made like unto Thee and may share in Thy Divine Beatitude!"

It is the Father's supreme desire that His Son be glorified: *Clarificavi et iterum clarificabo.*[1] Now, we never glorify Our Lord so much as when we acknowledge by our whole life that He is the sole Fount of every grace. Only true humility can render this homage to God and to Jesus, for humble souls alone feel the need of Christ's merits and have faith in them. Pride and false humility cannot nourish such sentiments. Pride looks for everything from itself; it does not feel the habitual necessity of having recourse to Christ. As to false humility, it declares itself incapable of everything, even in presence of grace; by this it does a wrong to the merits of Jesus: it casts down the soul without glorifying God.

Christ Jesus said one day: *Ego si exaltatus fuero a terra omnia traham ad meipsum.*[2] When I shall be lifted up from the earth, upon the Cross, My power will be such that I shall be able to lift up to Me those who have faith in Me. Those who looked upon the brazen serpent, in the desert, were healed: thus those who look upon Me with faith and love will be drawn to Me, despite their sins, their wounds and their unworthiness, and I will lift them as high as Heaven. I, Who am God, consented for love of thee to hang upon the Cross as one accursed. In return for this humiliation I have power to raise with Me even to the heavenly splendours whence I descended, those who believe in Me. I came down from Heaven, I shall ascend thither taking with Me those who hope in My grace. This grace is so powerful that it can unite thee to Me, and unite thee so indissolubly that no one can snatch out of My hands those whom My Father has given Me, those whom I have, through pure mercy, redeemed with My precious Blood.[3]

What a perspective full of consolation for the humble soul is that of one day sharing in the exaltation of Jesus, owing to His merits! St. Paul speaks to us in sublime terms of this supreme exaltation of Our Lord, the counterpart of His abasements. "Who being in the form of God emptied Himself... For which cause God also hath exalted Him, and hath given Him a name which is above all names: that in the name of Jesus every knee should bow, of those that are in Heaven, on earth, and under the earth: and that every tongue should confess that the Lord Jesus Christ

1 Joan. xii, 28. 2 Joan. xii, 32. 3 Cf. Joan. x, 29.

is in the glory of God the Father": *Semetipsum exinanivit... propter quod et Deus exaltavit illum.*[1] It is because Jesus humbled Himself to suffer the ignominy of the gibbet that God has exalted His Name to the highest heavens. Sublime is the glory, sovereign is the power which the Man-God enjoys seated at the right hand of the Father in eternal glory. And this incomparable triumph is the fruit of an incommensurable humility.

We here find again the whole teaching of our Holy Father. He too tells us that in order to arrive at that *exaltatio caelestis* where the soul is absorbed in God, it is necessary to pass through humiliations. Here below, humility leads us from the renouncing of sin to the fulness of charity: *Mox ad caritatem perfectam perveniet.* In the measure wherein the soul advances in humble submission, it is raised towards Divine union. It is also raised towards heavenly glory. The law recalled by St. Benedict at the beginning of the chapter is that laid down by Jesus Christ Himself, our Model. It is admirably verified in Him; but this law touches all the members whereof He is the Head, and Christ prepares a glorious place in His Kingdom only for those who upon earth have participated in His Divine humiliations: *Qui se humiliat exaltabitur.*

1 Philip. ii, 7 and 9.

BONUM OBEDIENTIAE[1]

SUMMARY.—Obedience is the practical expression of humility in the monk.—I. Christ brings humanity back to the Father by His obedience; every Christian must be united to this obedience in order to attain to God.—II. For the monk, too, obedience is the path that leads to God.—III. The high concept that St. Benedict has of this virtue.—IV. Why he calls it a "good": *Bonum obedientiae.*—V. How this virtue constitutes for the monk an ineffable means of acquiring perfection.—VI. Principal qualities that St. Benedict requires in the exercise of this virtue: faith.—VII. *Alieno judicio ambulare.*[2] Fruitfulness and greatness of obedience guided by faith.—VIII. Obedience should be sustained by hope.—IX. St. Benedict desires that above all it proceed from love.—X. Different deviations from this virtue; why St. Benedict is so strongly opposed to murmuring.—XI. The vigilance we must have in order to live perfectly according to this virtue.

THE foundation of spiritual life is, as we have seen according to St. Benedict and St. Thomas, constituted in some way by humility, this virtue being the preliminary and necessary disposition for the state of perfect charity to be established in the soul: *MOX ad caritatem Dei perveniet illam quae perfecta [est].*[3]

But, as our Holy Father has shown, the practical expression of humility, with the monk, is obedience. Indeed, when the soul is full of reverence towards God, it submits itself to God and to those who represent Him, in order to do His will in all things: *Humilitas proprie respicit reverentiam qua homo Deo subjicitur... propter quem etiam aliis humiliando se subjicit.*[4]

1 Rule, ch. lxxi. 2 "To walk by the judgement of another," Cf. Ibid. ch. v.
3 "The monk will presently come to that perfect love of God," Ibid. ch. vii.
4 St. Thomas, II-II, q. clxi, a. 3; a. 1, ad 5.

Now this is obedience. This virtue is the fruit and crown of humility.[1] Obedience, said the Eternal Father to St. Catherine of Siena, in one of the dialogues He vouchsafed to have with her "has a nurse who feeds her, that is true humility. Therefore a soul is obedient in proportion to her humility, and humble in proportion to her obedience... Without this nurse (which is humility) obedience would perish of hunger, for obedience soon dies in a soul deprived of this little virtue of humility."[2]

This obedience completes the work of abolishing any obstacles yet opposed to divine union. Poverty has removed the danger accruing from exterior belongings; the "conversion of manners" represses the tendencies of concupiscence and is careful to eliminate, in a general manner, all that, properly speaking, is imperfection; humility, going still further to the root of the matter, refrains all inordinate self-esteem. What yet remains to be overcome? Self-will. That is the citadel of the "ego." But once this will is surrendered, and it surrenders by obedience, all is given. The soul has nothing more belonging to it, nothing that it any longer possesses as its own; God can henceforward exercise His action over it in all plenitude: there are no more obstacles opposed to His Divine action.

By perfect obedience, man lives in the truth of his being and of his condition: that is why this virtue is so fundamental and so pleasing to God. God, Who is the plenitude of Being, Who has no need of anyone or anything, created man freely and by a movement of love. From this primordial fact, the essential relations between ourselves and God are derived; a creature is something essentially dependent upon God: "In Him we live, and move, and are": *In ipso vivimus, et movemur et sumus.*[3] Hence it would be going against the eternal law not to recognise this condition by our entire dependence in regard to God. What is the cry that should burst forth from the very depths of our being as creatures?

---

1 "The consideration of God's perfections is inseparable from that of His rights. Now is it not just that if God exercises His rights by enacting laws, man should respond to them by an active submission? Obedience will be born of humility as its eldest daughter, inclining us to submit ourselves not only to God, but to superiors and events, because in them we shall see reflected the perfections and absolute rights of the Creator." D. Lottin, *L'âme du Culte, la vertu de religion,* p. 44.

2 *Dialogue* translated by Algar Thorold, pp. 283-284, 302. The *Dialogue* contains an excellent treatise on *Obedience*. The Saint relates, in magnificent terms, the praise of obedience as she heard it from the Eternal Father.

3 Act. xvii, 28.

Venite, adoremus: "Come, let us adore the Lord!" And why? "For He is the Lord our God": and He has made us: *Est Dominus Deus noster*.[1] As reasonable creatures we ought to express our dependence by adoration and the submission of obedience. We see God requiring this obedience throughout the history of the human race, at each page of the Bible. The great saints of the Old Testament shine in obedience; we hear them ever renewing the cry repeated by Abraham, the father of believers: *Adsum*.[2] "Here I am!" Christ's coming upon earth renders us the children of God; henceforward our obedience has taken a new shade of meaning, a new character: it is an obedience full of love; but this special seal placed upon our obedience, while giving it a special splendour, takes away nothing of its fundamental character which links it to humility and imbues it with reverence and religion.

If obedience is infinitely pleasing to God it is no less beneficial to the soul. God reigns as Master and Sovereign in the obedient soul, but as a Sovereign Who is infinitely good and lavishes His gifts and graces upon it.

Obedience is named in the last place in the formula of our monastic profession; in our Vows it occupies supreme rank. Let us then study its source—its nature—the qualities it ought to have—and from what deviations it must be preserved.

I

The principle that makes obedience so necessary for us as monks is that this virtue resumes in itself the means of finding God. Why have we come to the monastery? What is our object in living here? There is but one: to seek God, to tend towards Him with all the energies of our being. But as we have often remarked, it is by following Christ Jesus that we find God, for it is He alone who brings humanity back to God: *Ego sum via; nemo venit ad Patrem nisi per Me*.[3] And how does Christ achieve this gigantic work? By His obedience.

He declares that He has not come to do His own will but that of His Father Who sent Him;[4] obedience is as it were His daily bread: *Meus*

1 Ps. cxiv, 6–7. 2 Gen. xxii, 1, and 11.

3 "I am the Way... No man cometh to the Father, but by Me," Joan. xiv, 6.

4 Ibid. vi, 38.

cibus est ut faciam voluntatem eius qui misit me.[1] During thirty years He obeys two creatures, Mary and Joseph: *Et erat subditus illis.*[2] Despite the transcendency of His Divinity, although He is the supreme Lawgiver and could have dispensed from His own laws, He will fulfil them even to the least detail: *Iota unum aut unus apex non praeteribit a lege, donec omnia fiant.*[3] We see Him seeking above all things to do always, under every circumstance, what pleases His Father: *Quae placita sunt ei facio* *SEMPER*.[4] He accepts the Passion because it expresses His Father's will: *Sicut mandatum dedit mihi Pater sic facio.*[5]

And see how this obedience especially shines out in His sufferings. During that terrible three hours' agony, all the sensitive part of His being shrinks from the bitter chalice: "Father if Thou wilt, remove this chalice from Me": *Pater, si vis, transfer calicem istum a me*; but His reasonable will remains submissive to the Divine decree: "Yet not My will, but Thine be done": *Verumtamen non mea voluntas,—sed tua fiat.*[6] He is presently arrested as a malefactor; he could deliver Himself from His enemies who at a single word from Him are thrown to the ground; He could, if He so willed, ask His Father Who would have given Him "more than twelve legions of Angels," but He desires only that His Father's will, as manifested by the Scriptures, shall be fulfilled to the letter: *Sed ut adimpleantur Scripturae,*[7] and therefore He gives Himself up to His mortal foes. He obeys Pilate because, although a pagan, the Roman governor represents the authority from above.[8] He obeys His executioners; at the moment of expiring, in order to fulfil a prophecy, He cries out: "I thirst": *Postea, sciens Jesus quia omnia consummata sunt,* UT *consummaretur Scriptura dixit: Sitio.*[9] He does not die until all has been consummated by a perfect obedience: *Dixit: consummatum est, et inclinato capite, tradidit spiritum.*[10] The *Consummatum est* is the most true and adequate expression of His whole life of obedience. It echoes the *Ecce venio* of the moment of His Incarnation.

---

1 Ibid. iv, 34. 2 Luc. ii, 51. 3 Matth. v, 18.
4 Joan. iv, 34. 5 Joan. xiv, 31. 6 Luc. xxii, 42.
7 Marc. xiv, 49. 8 Cf. Joan. xix, 11.

9 "Afterwards, Jesus knowing that all things were now accomplished, that the Scripture might be fulfilled, said: I thirst," Ibid. xix, 28.

10 "He said: it is consummated. And bowing His head, He gave up the ghost," Ibid. xix, 30.

Now, says the Apostle, as it was through Adam's disobedience that we became sinners and the enemies of God, so it was through this obedience of Christ that we are justified and saved. A great disobedience and a great obedience are the two factors of the loss and salvation of the human race. This is the explicit teaching of St. Paul: *SICUT per inobedientiam unius hominis peccatores constituti sunt multi, ITA et per unius obeditionem, justi constituentur multi.*[1]

This obedience of Christ is the means preordained by God for saving the world and restoring to it the heavenly inheritance; it was an expiation for the disobedience of Adam, our first father; and we go to God by uniting our obedience to that of Christ Jesus, become the Head of our race. All Adam's miseries have fallen upon us because we had solidarity in his sin; we have a share in all the blessings that overflow from the holy soul of Christ Jesus when we share in His obedience. All the economy of God's designs for our sanctification converge for us in a state of obedience. When the Father sent His Son upon earth, what did He say to the Jews? "This is My beloved Son. Hear ye Him." *Ipsum audite.*[2] As much as to say to them: Do what My Son bids you; obey Him: that is all I ask in order to give you My friendship.

Now that Christ has left us and ascended into Heaven, He has given His powers to the Church: *Data est mihi omnis potestas in caelo et in terra; euntes ergo docete omnes gentes servare omnia quaecumque mandavi vobis,*[3] "All power has been given Me by My Father; go then in virtue of this power that I delegate to you, teach all nations to keep My commandments. He who hears you, hears Me; he who despises you despises Me."

The Church is invested with the authority of Jesus Christ; she speaks and commands in Our Lord's name; and the essence of Catholicism consists in the submission of the intellect to Christ's teaching transmitted by the Church, and in the submission of the will to Christ's authority exercised by the Church.

It is in this that the difference lies between Protestants and Catholics. This difference indeed is not measured by the greater or lesser sum of revealed truths admitted by one or the other; certain Protestants accept

---

1 "For as by the disobedience of one man, many were made sinners; so also by the obedience of One, many shall be made just," Rom. v, 19.

2 Matth. xvii, 5. 3 Ibid. xxviii, 18–20.

materially nearly all our dogmas, and yet they remain Protestants to the marrow of their bones. The difference is much deeper and more radical. It practically lies in the attitude of dependence, of obedience of the intellect and of the will in regard to the living authority of the Church which teaches and governs in the name of Christ the Son of God. The Catholic accepts the Church's dogma and regulates his conduct according to this dogma because he sees in the Church, and her head the Sovereign Pontiff, another Christ. The Protestant admits such or such a truth because he discovers it—or imagines himself to do so—by his personal lights. Claiming the right of private interpretation and reading the Bible according to his reason alone, he takes or leaves what he will: each one then, keeping his faculty of choosing, is his own sovereign pontiff. The Protestant *admits*, the Catholic *believes*. As soon as the Church speaks, the Catholic submits in all obedience as to Christ Himself.

Recall the scene in the Gospel described by St. John in his 6th chapter. Jesus speaks to the multitude of people whom He had miraculously fed on the previous day. He announces to them the Eucharistic Bread: *Ego sum panis vivus*: "I am the Living Bread which came down from heaven. If any man eat of this Bread, he shall live for ever." At these words, His listeners are divided into two groups. The one begins to reason: these are the Protestants: *quomodo*, "How can this man give us His flesh to eat?" Now how does Jesus act in the face of this reasoning? Does He give any explanation? No, He contents Himself with affirming what He has just said with more insistency. *Amen, amen, dico vobis*. "Amen, Amen, I say unto you: Except you eat the Flesh of the Son of Man, and drink His Blood, you shall have not life in you." Then no longer finding this "reasonable," *Durus est hic sermo et quis potest eum audire*, they leave Christ: *Jam non cum illo ambulabant*.[1] But there is another group formed of the Apostles. In these same circumstances what is their attitude? Do these disciples understand any better? No, but having faith in Christ's word, they remain with Him to follow in His steps throughout all: *Domine, ad quem ibimus? verba vitae aeternae habes*.[2]

1 "This saying is hard, and who can hear it?... and [they] walked with Him no more," Joan. vi, 61, 67.

2 "Lord, to whom shall we go? Thou hast the words of eternal life," Joan. vi, 41–69.

Such is the attitude that procures salvation: to listen to Christ, to listen to the Church, to accept her doctrine and submit oneself to what she directs: who despises her, despises Christ. This is why Protestants do not belong to Christ's flock;[1] these sheep obey themselves, they follow their own personal caprices, and do not hear the Shepherd's voice.

Thus Christ does not recognise them: *Non estis ex ovibus meis.*[2]

Obedience of intellect and will is then the way of life for every Christian, for every soul: *Qui vos audit, me audit,*[3] *qui sequitur me, non ambulat in tenebris, sed habebit lumen vitae.*[4] We are the children of the Heavenly Father only on condition of hearing His Son Jesus; and, here on earth, we obey Christ in the person of the Church; this is the supernatural economy instituted by God Himself; apart from this way of obedience in the faith, there is no salvation possible. "No one," said the Father to St. Catherine of Siena, "can enter into eternal life unless he be obedient; for obedience was the key with which was unlocked the door which had been fastened by the disobedience of Adam."[5]

II

What is true of the Christian is, *a fortiori*, true of the monk. Christ Jesus brings humanity back to His Father by His obedience; every one must unite himself to Christ in His obedience in order to find God. Neither in this, as in anything else, does Christ separate Himself from His Mystical Body; the Christian must take his share in obedience and accept it in union with his Divine Head.

Our holy Legislator teaches no other doctrine than that of Christ and St. Paul. His words on this point are but the direct echo of the Gospel and the teaching of the great Apostle. At the very beginning of the Prologue he points out to us what is to be our end: "To return to God." Immediately afterwards he indicates the means: we must return to God *by obedience* since it was by the sloth of disobedience that we turned away from Him. "To thee therefore," he adds, "my words are now addressed

1 Reservation of course made in regard to those who, being in good faith, belong to the soul of the Church.

2 Joan. x, 26.

3 "He that heareth you, heareth Me," Luc. x, 16.

4 "He that followeth Me, walketh not in darkness, but shall have the light of life," Joan. viii, 12.

5 *Dialogue. On Obedience,* ch. 1.

that *renouncing thine own will* in order to fight for the Lord Christ, our true King, dost *take in hand the strong and bright weapon of obedience.*" St. Benedict knows but one way of leading us to God: this is by union with Jesus Christ in His obedience: "Let the brethren know that it is by the path of obedience they shall come to God": *Scientes PER HANC OBEDIENTIAE VIAM se ituros ad Deum.*[1]

This obedience certainly, first of all, has for its object the natural law and the strictly Christian law. We are only monks if we are first honest men and perfect Christians. The monk submits himself to Christ in the person of the Church as does the simple Christian. But he goes further. The obedience of the Christian while imposing certain sacrifices upon human nature, and certain duties to be fulfilled, leaves intact the free disposition that the individual has over his fortune, business, time and activity. Simply Christian obedience is limited to the precepts contained in the Decalogue, and the commandments of the Church, which are themselves completed by each one's duties of state. God asks nothing more in order to give His heaven: *Si vis ad vitam ingredi, serva mandata.*[2]

But there are souls whom love constrains to follow Christ more closely, *Qui nihil sibi a Christo carius aliquid existimant*,[3] that they may share His life of obedience more intimately. These souls hear the *counsel* of Jesus. "If thou wilt be perfect, go sell what thou hast... and come follow Me": *Veni, sequere Me.*[4] These souls have been more enlightened from above upon the Divine attributes, upon the greatness of a life of perfection, upon the sublimity of a complete imitation of Christ Jesus. "For love of God," *pro Dei amore*,[5] to give God greater glory, they seek a more exacting obedience than is imposed upon the simple faithful. An infallible supernatural intuition has revealed to them that it is more just, and they thereby give more adoration and more love to God.

By his profession, the monk strives to submit all that is in him to Christ; he does not wish anything to subsist that can be an obstacle to union between him and Christ; he wants to surrender to Him his whole being and every detail of his life, because his adoration and his

1 Rule, ch. lxxi.

2 "But if thou wilt enter into life, keep the commandments," Matth. xix, 17.

3 "Those who hold nothing dearer to them than Christ," Rule, ch. v.

4 Matth. xix, 21.

5 Rule, ch. vii.

love aim at being perfect. As long as we hold the citadel of self-will we have not surrendered everything to God; we cannot say to our Lord in all truth: "Behold we have left all things and have followed Thee."[1] When we give ourselves by obedience we accomplish a supreme act of adoration and love towards God. Indeed there is one thing that is sacred to us even in God's sight. God touches our goods, the beings dear to us, our health, our existence; He is the absolute Master of life and death; but there is one thing that He respects, namely, our liberty. He desires, with infinite desire, to communicate Himself to us, and yet the action of His grace is, if I may thus express myself, subordinate to our acquiescence: that is, in a very real sense, our liberty is sovereign. Now, in religious profession, we come before the altar, we take precisely what is most precious to us and out of love for God, in order the better to confess His omnipotence, we immolate to Him, in union with Christ, this "Isaac" this darling of our heart which is our liberty, and we give God full domain over our whole being and activity. Failing martyrdom which is not at our disposal, we immolate ourselves as far as it depends upon us, by the vow of obedience.

The sacrifice is immense; it is besides extremely pleasing to God. "To leave the world and give up exterior possessions," says that great monk, St. Gregory, "is perhaps something still easy; but for a man to give up himself, to immolate what is most precious to him by surrendering his entire liberty is a much more arduous work: to forsake what one *has* is a small thing; to forsake what one *is*, that is the supreme gift."[2] Without this gift, the sacrifice is not entire. "He is not detached from all," said another holy monk, "who still retains himself; moreover, it serves for nothing to relinquish every thing unless he relinquish himself": *Non enim relinquit omnia qui retinuit vel seipsum; imo vero nihil prodest sine seipso caetera reliquisse.*[3]

1 Matth. xix, 27.

2 *Et fortasse laboriosum non est homini relinquere sua, sed valde laboriosum est relinquere semetipsum. Minus quippe est abnegare quod habet; valde autem multum est abnegare quod est. Homil. 32 in Evang.* P. L. 76, 1233. Cf. St. Mechtilde, *The Book of Special Grace,* 4th Part, ch. 18. *How our Lord clasps in His arms those who vow obedience.*

3 S. Petr. Damian. *In natale S. Benedicti,* P.L. 144, 549.

III

It is to be remarked that the gift we thus make of ourselves on the day of our profession subjects us to a definite obedience; we vow obedience "according to the Rule of St. Benedict": *Promitto... obedientiam secundum Regulam S. P.N. Benedicti.*[1] Consequently, we must well understand the holy Patriarch's concept of religious obedience. For there is obedience and obedience; and as this virtue is one of the principles of our life, if the idea we form of it is erroneous, all our monastic existence will be falsified. There is an erroneous conception of obedience which no religious soul could accept. This conception makes of the superior a sage, an expert whom one has promised to consult, and to whom one goes out of prudence to learn what has to be done, and in order to avoid errors and mistakes. What the superior says is worth just what he knows, neither more nor less; his personal knowledge gives all the weight to his replies. This manner of seeing things, essentially rationalistic, would suit the spirit of Protestantism; the idea of submission, of homage paid to God in the person of a man is totally absent. The mere fact of mentioning this conception is sufficient to condemn it.

Neither could the Catholic sense of what is right be satisfied with a *merely* outward obedience, such as is sufficient in the army. Although in each particular case, the immediate object of obedience is exterior and the intention is not seen by the superior, yet perfection demands that the monk should animate the exercise of his obedience by interior submission.[2]

In religious obedience itself, such as it is conceived by Holy Church, there are different modes to be distinguished. Of cause it is not here a question of criticising any one or anything whatsoever: all the religious orders approved by the Church procure God's glory and are pleasing to Him; our intention is only to lay stress, by way of comparison, on what is special in Benedictine obedience. In some institutes, obedience is strongly marked with an economic character. Without ceasing to be the object of a vow and of a virtue, it is a means for arriving at a particular, special end, fixed by the constitutions of the said institutes. Thus such an Order or Congregation has for its special end the evangelising of the heathen, another teaching, a third preaching. Obedience concurs in

1 Ceremonial of Monastic Profession.

2 See further on § viii and ix.

carrying out the particular work to which these institutes are dedicated. Those who belong to these Orders and submit themselves generously to this obedience for love of our Lord surely attain holiness, because, for them, it is the vocation to which Christ has called them.

With St. Benedict, obedience has not this "economic" character. It is to be desired in itself as the soul's homage to God, independently of the nature of the material work which is its object. Let us suppose that the postulant in presenting himself at the monastery puts this question to the Abbot: "What do you do here?" He will be told: "We go to God by following Christ in obedience." That is the sole end pursued. Such is certainly the teaching of our Holy Father, from the first lines of the Prologue which we have recalled. To seek after God, *Si revera Deum quaerit*,[1] that is the characteristic of the Benedictine vocation. St. Benedict only writes his Rule for those who seek obedience that they may find God: *Ad te ergo nunc mihi sermo dirigitur quisquis abrenuntians propriis voluntatibus... obedientiae... arma sumis.*[2]

In instituting monasticism, the great Patriarch did not intend to create an Order exclusively destined to attain such or such a particular end, or to accomplish such or such a special work. He wished only to make perfect Christians of his monks and envisaged for them the plenitude of Christianity. Doubtless, as we have seen, it has befallen that in the course of ages, monasteries have become centres of civilisation, by preaching, the clearing and cultivation of land, teaching, art, literary work, but this was but the outward blossoming, the natural and normal outcome of the fulness of Christianity with which these monasteries were inwardly animated. Being vowed to God, the monks spent themselves in the service of the Church, and under every form that this service demanded. But what they *sought* before all, was to give to God, for love of Him, the homage of all their being in obedience to an Abbot, as Christ, in coming into this world, only sought His Father's will, leaving to His Father the determination of this will: *Ecce venio: ut faciam Deus voluntatem tuam.*[3]

1 Rule, ch. lviii.

2 "To thee my words are now addressed, whosoever thou mayest be that renouncing thine own will... take up the strong and glorious weapons of obedience," Prologue of the Rule.

3 Hebr. x, 7.

How is this will determined for the monk? By the Rule and the Abbot. It is for the Abbot, inspired by the Rule and respecting its traditions, to fix the direction of the activity of the monastery. Having, moreover, according to our Holy Father's saying, to govern the monastery "wisely," he will undoubtedly be watchful to see how he may utilise, for God's glory and the benefit of the Church and society, the talents placed by God in each of his monks. But as for the monk himself, he has nothing to arrange or determine in all this: he does not come to the Abbey to give himself to one occupation rather than another, to discharge such or such a function that he finds suitable; he comes to seek God in obedience. In this lies all his perfection.[1]

IV

You may perhaps say: Is not this inconceivable nonsense? Is it not folly to submit oneself entirely in this way? Yes, from the merely human point of view it is folly, as monastic life taken as a whole is folly: *Vitam illorum aestimabamus insaniam.*[2]

But, replies St. Paul in his energetic language "the sensual man," that is to say one who lets himself be guided by nothing but natural reason, "perceiveth not these things that are of the Spirit of God."[3] What is foolishness in the eyes of men is wisdom in the sight of God, and what is wisdom in the world's sight is foolishness before the Lord. And it has pleased God to confound the wisdom of the world with works of divine folly.[4] For the wise of this world, was it not a folly and a scandal—the Greek philosophers of St. Paul's time already judged it to be so—for a God to have been made man in order to redeem mankind and for thirty years to have lived a life of obedience in an obscure workshop, and have then consecrated three years to the labour of preaching before dying upon a cross? This was, however, the means chosen out of all others, by God, Eternal Wisdom, for the salvation of the human race. And this loving obedience which was the mainspring of this life—a life which closed as it had opened with a cry of obedience—had as its object an existence full of toil, of deep humiliation, and a death surrounded with

1 Cf. D.G. Morin, *The Ideal of the Monastic Life,* ch. 11, *Obedience.*
2 Sap. v, 4. 3 I Cor. ii, 14. 4 Cf. Ibid. i, 20–21.

indescribable sufferings. But it was by this that the world was redeemed; it is still thanks to this that the world continues to be saved, that souls return to God and are sanctified. God derives His glory from our submission to the Crucified; and it is by means of this submission that He gives us His grace: *Scientes per hanc obedientiae viam se ituros ad Deum.*

We can therefore understand why our holy Lawgiver calls obedience "a good": *Bonum obedientiae.*[1] What a remarkable expression! Does this mean we naturally like to obey? No, quite the contrary! Then why is obedience "a good," a thing that we ought to seek and hunger after? Because it is the path by which a God has passed, a path which leads us to beatitude. Obedience gives us God. When we do God's will, we are united to God; by obedience we embrace the Divine will; this will is God manifesting Himself to us as Sovereign Master, received by us with adoration and love. And as we come to the monastery to seek God and obedience gives Him to us, it becomes for us a precious good, for it gains us the sole Good.[2]

Thus our Holy Father strives, by his precepts or exhortations, to procure this good for us as abundantly as possible. He wishes us to go so far as "to obey one another,"[3] that is of course, if the orders of superiors are not in question. He asks that the monk should obey even in undertaking what is "hard and impossible."[4] He reminds us that we are not authorised to do anything without the command of the Abbot or of those delegated by him;[5] even good works and mortifications are of no worth for one who performs them unknown to the Abbot.[6]

Why so much insistence? Because the great Legislator is convinced that it is by the path of obedience we shall arrive at holiness. When the monk obeys in all things, for love of God and in union with Christ Jesus, *Pro Dei amore, imitans Dominum,*[7] he reaches the summit of perfection; for, as we have shown, there are no longer any obstacles opposed to the Divine action for a soul unreservedly given up to obedience; this soul is entirely open to the influence of grace. God, Who is the Fountainhead of all holiness, can act within it according to the plenitude of His

1 Rule, ch. lxxi.

2 See in the *Dialogue* of St. Catherine of Siena, (*Obedience,* ch. 10) in what an infinite measure obedience is a "good."

3 Rule, ch. lxxi. 4 Ibid. ch. lxviii. 5 Ibid. ch. lxxi.

6 Ibid. ch. xlix. 7 Ibid. ch. vii.

power.[1] Christ reigns in it undisputedly. He is the Sovereign Master of all the life and activity of the soul. Then perfect union results, filled with divine communications: *Dominus regit me et nihil mihi deerit.*[2]

And where a spiritual good is concerned, of what consequence is it whether it is found in doing one action rather than another? In the eyes of our holy Legislator, whether it be a question of a mission of confidence which places us in full view, or an obscure action known to God alone, what does it signify? It is the matter upon which obedience is exteriorly exercised; the essential is the virtue, the homage we pay to God by our submission. For—although there are evidently manifold degrees of intrinsic value among various actions, resulting from their very nature and their more or less direct relation with God's glory,—as regards our *personal* perfection and our own advancement in the way of holiness, the merit of an action is measured, at the last analysis, by the degree of love wherein our obedience is enveloped. Look at our Divine Saviour. Were those thirty hidden years He spent at Nazareth less pleasing to His Father and less fruitful for the world's salvation than the three years of His public life consecrated by preaching? We should not dare to uphold such an opinion. It was in obedience to His Father that Our Lord willed to remain thus hidden so many years, and this obedience was the obedience of a God.

Proportionately it is the same for us, since Christ is our Model. True wisdom, that which is the gift of the Spirit, is to obey, to render to God the homage of our obedience, whatever be the material work which is the object of this obedience and whereby it is manifested. For this reason our Holy Father says that true monks, those illumined with divine light, are only ambitious for eternal things, the things which alone are real: *Quibus ad vitam aeternam gradiendi amor incumbit.*[3] They "desire"—remark the word; St. Benedict does not say: "support,"—obedience, as one seeks after a precious good that one may take possession of it. *Abbatem sibi praeesse DESIDERANT*;[4] they are upon the watch for

1 See an extract from the writings of St. Teresa at the end of this conference.
2 "The Lord ruleth me: and I shall want nothing," Ps. xxii, 1.
3 "By those who are impelled by the desire of attaining life everlasting," Rule, ch. v.
4 "[They] desire to have an abbot over them," Ibid.

occasions of obeying, and are thus enabled to give to God the most effectual pledge of their love.[1]

V

Such is the lofty concept that St. Benedict forms of obedience. Now we have promised to follow his Rule that we may live according to his spirit. It is this view of the matter we must admit and put into practice in as far as we are able, because it is for us the path of perfection. In order to bring us to holiness, our Blessed Father does not require of us constantly repeated exercises whereby all our defects are attacked one by one, or great corporal macerations, or rigorous and continual mortifications; no, in this respect he is very discreet and full of moderation: *Nihil asperum, nihil grave.*[2] St. Gregory remarks that his Rule is of "admirable discretion."[3] But the holy Legislator has especially in view—and in this he goes as far as possible to the root of the matter[4]—to despoil a man of all that is an obstacle within him to grace and the

---

1 We at once see how obedience, as understood by St. Benedict, is permeated with religion, and is, like humility, an eminently religious virtue. Cf. above p. 253–254. "One who is truly obedient," said the Eternal Father to St. Catherine, "ever retains the *desire* of submission; continually and unremittingly, this desire is like an inward refrain of music." *Dialogue.*

2 "Nothing that is harsh or burdensome," Prologue of the Rule.

3 *Dialogues.* Lib. ii, ch. 36.

4 "Although carefulness never to go to extremes and to take account of circumstances characterises the Holy Rule, nevertheless when St. Benedict dictates to monks their duty of obedience, he shows himself categorical and it would be in vain to seek for any compromise from him on this point. How far the regulations are to be tempered in special cases, St. Benedict leaves to the discernment of the Superior alone; it is for the monk to obey and not to murmur… This categorical manner of conceiving obedience… brings us into touch with the cenobitical sense of St. Benedict's asceticism." D. I. Ryelandt, *Essay on the character or the moral physiognomy of St. Benedict according to his Rule.* See *Revue liturgique et monastique,* 1921, p. 203. "Monastic obedience, such as is prescribed by the Rule of St. Benedict, penetrates to the deepest fibres of the soul and sets itself to destroy the very root of self-love and self-judgment: this appears to be indeed the maximum of psychological penetration." D. M. Festugière. See *Revue Benedictine,* 1912, p. 491. Thus it may be said that the concept of religious obedience has made no further progress as to the substance of the matter since St. Benedict's time. It is enough, in order to be convinced of this, to read the chapters v, vii (3rd and 4th degrees of humility), xxxiii, lviii, lxviii, lxxi, etc. of the Rule.

Divine action; for this reason absolute detachment is required of him, by means of poverty and humility, the latter being chiefly manifested by perfect obedience. These virtues despoil the soul of all attachment to self and creatures, so that all liberty and plenitude may be left to the action of God. This is one of the salient characteristics of St. Benedict's asceticism. Without underrating, as we have seen, the value of personal practices of mortification in setting us free from vices that we may go to God, he insists above all upon poverty, humility and chiefly upon obedience. Full submission to the Superior and to the Rule is for the monk the way that leads most surely to God, because a like humble and constant submission in all things, such as our Holy Father requires, closes every outlet to bad habits and opposes them till in the end they are destroyed. Perfect obedience is the most authentic means for the monk of purifying himself to the innermost depths of his being. A monk who obeys perfectly, in the spirit indicated by the Rule, will quickly arrive at complete freedom from every trammel which holds him back from God. At the same time, he advances in virtue which, becoming stronger, renders him more pliant under the Holy Spirit's action. Now was it not this we came to seek in the monastery? In this way all the other virtues hence increase, and progress towards Divine union is assured.[1]

Obedience is then for the monk the surest way to holiness. St. Teresa calls it "the road that leads most rapidly to the summit of perfection"; "the most prompt and also the most effectual means of arriving at perfection."[2] When a man achieves the work of giving himself entirely by obedience, he receives the Infinite Good in an incomparable measure. This is what Christ Jesus said to that perfect nun who was so dear to Him—St. Gertrude. On the evening of Palm Sunday she was meditating on the reception given to Jesus by His friends at Bethany, whither He

1 St. Mechtilde "one day saw a train of virtues personified by virgins standing before God. One among them, more beautiful than her sisters, held a golden cup into which the other virgins poured a fragrant wine which the first virgin offered, kneeling, to the Lord. Astonished at this sight, St. Mechtilde was desirous of knowing its meaning when our Lord said to her: 'This virgin is obedience; she alone gives Me to drink, for obedience contains within herself the riches of the other virtues: one who is truly obedient must necessarily possess the whole of these virtues.'" Our Lord then enumerated the different virtues, showing how they are necessarily to be found in the perfectly obedient soul. *The Book of Special Grace,* 1st Part, ch. 35. 2 *Foundations,* ch. 5.

had withdrawn in the evening, and the desire burnt within her to offer hospitality to Him in her heart. Immediately Christ appeared to her: "I am here," He said to the saint, "and what wilt thou give Me?" "Welcome, Salvation of my soul, my one and only treasure," replied Gertrude; "alas! I have prepared nothing that can befit Thy magnificence, but I offer Thee all my being, desiring that Thou wilt Thyself prepare in me what shall best please Thy Heart." "Since thou givest Me the liberty," Christ said, "I will take it; but I need the key that My hand may find and may dispose of all that I wish." "What is this key of which Thou hast need and that must be given to Thee?" the saint asked. "It is thy self-will," replied our Lord.[1] Hence the Saint understood that Christ finds His delight in a soul wholly yielded up to Him, and keeping nothing back: it is by perfect obedience that one gives to Christ the key that He demands. He then knows Himself to be the Master of this soul because He holds the citadel which is its liberty.[2] He can do all that He wills; and as He desires nothing so much as our holiness, a soul thus given and who never takes back anything from this gift, is upon the most sure path of perfection.

You see how right our Holy Father is to insist so much upon this virtue: let us try to understand thoroughly the character he wishes to give to it. Obedience is a homage of perfect submission of all our being to God; it is a good which we must unceasingly strive to obtain, for in it we shall find what we came to seek in the monastery, namely, God. If we never lose sight of this capital point, our obedience will become easy, whatever be the command given; and, through it, we shall obtain, with God, peace of soul and joy and freedom of heart.

VI

However, in order that obedience may thus become for the monk the channel of Divine grace, it must be invested with certain qualities. Our Holy Father evinces a real complacency in detailing them, so much predilection has he for this virtue. What then are these qualities? There are three principal ones from whence all the others flow: the obedience

---

1 *The Herald of Divine Love,* Bk. iv, ch. 23.

2 God spoke in similar terms to St. Catherine of Siena: "I have made obedience the key of the whole edifice in very deed." *Life* by Raymund of Capua.

of the monk must be supernatural, trustful, and it must spring from love. It will then be a putting into practice of the three theological virtues of faith, hope and charity. As you see, we are especially speaking of inward qualities; for obedience, like humility from which it is derived, resides essentially in the soul. When we have analysed the conditions of the inward exercise of this virtue, we shall pass on naturally to its outward practice and note the qualities that accompany the material execution of the work commanded.

The first quality of our obedience is to be *supernatural*, that is to say accomplished in a spirit of faith: a man obeys the Superior as if obeying God Himself.

Our holy Legislator dwells much on this point, and with reason, for it is of capital importance. He tells us that the Abbot represents Christ: [*Abbas*] *Christi enim agere vices in monasterio creditur.*[1] Note this last word: *creditur*, which specifies that faith is the root of submission. The promptitude of obedience should, in the eyes of St. Benedict, be derived from this spirit of faith. We must obey, he says, "without delay": *sine mora*;[2] and "as if the order came from God Himself": *Ac si divinitus imperetur, moram pati nesciunt in faciendo.*[3] The order does, indeed, come from God, as the words of Eternal Truth, which the great Patriarch immediately recalls, bear witness: "He that heareth you, heareth Me." He would have us never forget that "the obedience which is given to Superiors is given to God": *Obedientia quae majoribus praebetur,* DEO *exhibetur: ipse* ENIM *dixit: qui vos audit me audit.*[4]

Hereby homage is paid to God, in the order of supernatural things that God has Himself chosen to establish here below to bring us to Him. God's ways are not our ways. We have more than once remarked that, especially since the Incarnation, God, in His relations with us, often acts through men. This is to be seen in the Sacraments; we can only draw from them the graces they contain by having recourse to men appointed by Christ to confer them upon us. Again this is to be seen in the love of our neighbour which is the sign of the reality of our love for God. It is the same with obedience. This Divine economy constitutes as it were a prolongation of the Incarnation. Since God has united Him-

1 Rule, ch. ii. 2 Ibid. ch. v. 3 Rule, ch. v. 4 Ibid.

self to humanity in the Person of His Son, it is through the members of His Son that He ordinarily enters into communication with our souls. Such being the Divine Plan, we shall walk in all security in the way of salvation and perfection if we adapt ourselves to it; to go aside from it is to withdraw ourselves from grace.

Why does God thus cause men to take His place with us? In order that our obedience inspired by faith may be a homage rendered to His Divine Son and may beget our merit. If God were to appear to us in all the glory of His power, where would be our merit in obeying Him? God wills then that we should adore Him not only in Himself, not only in the Humanity of His Son Jesus, but also in the men whom He has chosen to direct us. Doubtless it would be infinitely more agreeable for us if God were Himself to reveal what He desires of us in everything, or if He were to appoint an angel to do so. But what would be the result of this? Most often, an extraordinary increase of self-love,—or, in case of our refusal, a more evident culpability. God has not chosen to act thus. The means He has taken to imprint His initiative on our life is that which St. Benedict recalls to us in citing these words of the Psalmist, *Imposuisti homines super capita nostra,*[1] "Thou hast set men over our heads," men like to us, "men who are mortal frail, infirm" and feeling their powerlessness: *Homines mortales, fragiles, infirmi, lutea vasa portantes.*[2] This is vexatious and painful to nature, but such is the way of Divine wisdom. Why, once again, has God chosen these means, so humiliating for us?—for it is a humiliation to our pride and our spirit of independence to be subjected to another man, who is not without imperfections, every man belying his own ideal: *Omnis homo mendax.*[3] Why?—God has thus decided thereby to exercise our faith, our hope, our love.

Our *faith* first of all. You know it is befitting that the free creature should not enter into participation of infinite good without first undergoing the trial on which his merit is to rest. As for us, faith forms our trial: to live in the obscurity of a practical and active faith, such is the homage that God requires of us. Obedience gives us the opportunity of showing God our faith in Him: obedience is the practical manifesta-

1 Ibid. ch. vii; Ps. lxv, 12. 2 St. Augustine. *Sermo* lxix, ch. 1. P. L. 38, 440.
3 "Every man is a liar," Ps. cxv, 11.

tion of this faith. Indeed great faith, perfect faith, is needed, to maintain constant obedience to a man who, it is true, represents God but does so while still keeping his own imperfections. And this is the source of deep virtue and great merit.

One day when our own St. Gertrude besought Our Lord that He would Himself correct certain faults, alas! too apparent, in one of her superiors, Christ replied to her: "Do you not know that not only this person, but all who are in charge of this beloved congregation, have some defects? No one in this life is altogether free from imperfection. This is an effect of My goodness, and I allow it in order that the merit of all may be increased. There is far more virtue in submitting to a person whose faults are evident than to one who appears perfect."[1]

When we look upon the Sacred Host, our senses cry out to us: "That is not Christ: only bread is there." We see, we touch, we taste bread. But Christ has told us: *Hoc est corpus meum*,[2] "This is My Body." Then, we put aside all the testimonies of the senses and we say to Christ: "Thou hast said it, and I believe, *Credo*"; and to manifest our faith we fall down upon our knees before Christ, really and substantially present under these appearances; we adore Him, we give ourselves up to Him to do His will.

In the same way,[3] Christ veils Himself in our superiors. The Abbot, despite his imperfections, represents Christ for us. St. Benedict is formal upon this point. Christ is hidden under the imperfections and weaknesses of the man, as He is hidden under the sacramental appearances. But the Superior is placed *super candelabrum*.[4] By reason of our habitual contact with him, we naturally see his deficiencies and limitations, and then we are tempted to cry: "This man is not Christ; his judgment, limited as it is, is not infallible, he can be mistaken, he is mistaken; he cannot understand my point of view; he allows himself to be biassed." But faith says again: *Abbas Christi agere vices creditur*; whether Christ gives us, as His representative, a man with the wisdom of a Solomon, or a man without talent, it is, for faith, always Christ Who is represented. Faith discovers and touches Christ beneath the imperfections of the man.

1 D. G. Dolan. *St. Gertrude the Great,* ch. 5.
2 Matth. xxvi, 26.
3 This "in the same way" evidently implies only a simple analogy.
4 "Upon a candlestick," Matth. v, 15.

And then, if I have this faith, I say: *Credo*: "I believe"; and I obey this man whomsoever he be, because in submitting myself to him, I submit myself to Christ and remain united to Him: *Qui vos audit me audit.*[1]

Always thus to see Christ in the Superior, then, even if this Superior shows himself to us with all his failings, ever to obey him unfalteringly whatever be the circumstances, this requires of us very strong faith: because to be led *always* by this supernatural obedience without ever wavering is very hard and mortifying for nature.

But it is certain, with a certainty that I do not fear to call divine, that the Lord cannot fail one who obeys in this spirit of faith and is happy to offer Him the sacrifice of his abnegation. On the day of our monastic profession we make a contract with God. We say to Him: "My God, I have come here to seek Thee; for love of Thee, I have left all things; I come to lay at Thy feet my independence, my liberty; I promise Thee to submit myself to a superior, to obey him in everything, however contrary to my tastes and ideas his command may appear to me." And God Says to us on His side: "I promise you, despite the weaknesses or even the errors of the one who represents Me towards you, to direct you at each step of your life, and to bring you, through him, to the one thing necessary that you seek:—perfect love and the most intimate union with Me."

If we observe our part of the contract, it is absolutely beyond doubt that God will observe His part: He has engaged Himself to it, and His word is the word of a God: *Fidelis Deus.*[2] To think the contrary would be to deny the Veracity, the Wisdom, the Goodness, and the Power of God, it would be as much as to deny God Himself.[3]

VII

Our Holy Father, enlightened with the rays of divine light, is so convinced of the efficacy of this means of bringing us to perfection that, in obedience, he even requires of us "to follow the judgment and orders of another": *Non suo arbitrio viventes, vel desideriis suis et voluptatibus*

1 Luc. x, 16. 2 I Cor. i, 9.

3 See text of St. Teresa at the end of this conference.

obedientes sed AMBULANTES ALIENO JUDICIO ET IMPERIO.[1] There is need to insist here, for sometimes we come across upright, but simple minds that form an inexact idea of obedience. They believe that the Superior can never be mistaken. This is an error. Every man is fallible—and the merit of our obedience consists precisely in placing our initiative in the hands of a man whom we know to be fallible.

It may happen that the Abbot does not think as we do. If he always thought like us, where would be the submission of our judgment? We should be convinced that the Superior is very sensible... because he had the same ideas that we have! To obey, because we find what is ordered us is reasonable, is not obeying, but following our own judgment.

Does this mean that we must give up our judgment so far as to make all the judgments of the Abbot our own? No. We cannot abdicate the light of our reason. Only, the Superior is already, humanly speaking, much better placed than his inferiors for judging because of his knowledge of the case; moreover, for taking his decisions he possesses not only the elements that escape us, but also the lights that are wanting to us: the graces of state are not a myth. Let us suppose, however, that our reason evidently shows us things under an altogether different light and point of view from those under which the Superior sees them: we can then humbly expose to him our manner of looking at them; St. Benedict whose supernatural spirit is tempered by such just good sense does not fail to suggest this to us.[2] But if the Superior maintains his order, ought we, in order to realise the perfection of obedience, theoretically to see things as the Abbot sees them? No, that is not required. What must be done then? We may continue to see the thing speculatively under a different light from that under which the Abbot sees it; we may theoretically believe that our view is better and more reasonable than what is commanded us. But we must obey perfectly in action, in the execution of what we are told to do; we must besides be intimately persuaded that in the present case, *in concreto*, no spiritual harm will result from our obedience, either for the Divine glory nor for our own soul, but only

1 Rule, ch. v.
2 Ibid. ch. lxviii.

good will come from it. It is this intimate persuasion that is necessary to obedience of judgment.[1]

Now, this persuasion is born of faith. Again, is it that the Abbot is infallible or possesses infused knowledge? Assuredly not. The graces of state which he has the right to expect from God do not go so far as to accord him this privilege. He can be mistaken, he is in fact mistaken at times; but the one who is never mistaken is he who obeys: for him the path is certainly straight that leads to God. And if the spiritual good which results for him and for his personal perfection from his obedience appears to him to be less than it would have been if the Abbot had not been in error, this is only in appearance. Real harm cannot be done to his soul, for he gives an extremely pleasing homage to God. It is as if he said: "My God, Thou art so wise and so powerful, *fortiter et suaviter disponens omnia*,[2] and I am so convinced of Thy Divine attributes, that I affirm Thy power of drawing my soul to Thee, in spite of the errors that can creep in at times in the orders of my Superior." It is incontestable, indeed, that God leads us to His love through the very errors of men. He would intervene in a special way rather than allow His glory or our soul to suffer real spiritual harm in the case we have been considering.

In the course of our spiritual life, God will sometimes permit the Superior to command us things that appear to us unreasonable or not quite prudent, or less good than those we could imagine: He will thus give us the opportunity of rendering Him this very pleasing homage of obedience of judgment, and of hence renewing the tradition which we made to Him of our whole being on the day of our profession. At that blessed hour, in all the gladness of our donation, obedience appeared to us like child's play, although we had been forewarned of things, "hard and rugged," *Dura et aspera*,[3] whereby we go towards God. At that moment we pronounced the vow; but we were only entering on the path of the virtue.

This virtue is only acquired and strengthened by corresponding acts. Now, in the measure that we advance in maturity of mind or are inclined

1 Upon this subject we make our own the sentiments at once most safe and most moderate of one of the best modern ascetical writers, Mgr. Hedley, Bishop of Newport, in his excellent *Retreat*. See also the remarkable reflections expressed by Abbot Delatte in his Commentary on the Rule of St. Benedict.

2 Cf. Sap. viii, 1.

3 Rule, ch. lv.

to take more initiative, we realise the more the truth of these words of the Psalmist recalled by our Holy Father: "Thou hast placed men over our heads": *Imposuisti homines super capita nostra*. Our holy Legislator gives us moreover to understand that obedience can become very hard to nature; in his fourth degree of humility he speaks of "hard and contrary things, even injuries,"[4] which may befall us in the course of obedience: he warns us that "narrow is the way," but he adds—"which leadeth unto life": *ducit ad vitam*.[5] If indeed we submit with faith we may be assured, as St. Benedict guarantees, that each of our acts done under these difficult circumstances will turn to good, and our virtue will go on strengthening: *Sciat junior ita sibi expedire*.[6] God's glory triumphs precisely in using men's frailty and errors for the good of those who trust in Him: *Omnia cooperantur in bonum*.[7]

Our holy Father's words should then be ever before our eyes: *Abbas Christi agere vices creditur*. The more we see Christ in the Abbot, the more we enter into this life of faith, the more too will the Abbot become for us a "cause of eternal salvation" and of perfection: *Factus est obtemperantibus sibi causa salutis aeternae*.[8]

There is yet more. The man who yields himself up by a like obedience into God's hands can be compared to an arrow of election, shot by the hand of a mighty archer: *Sicut sagitta in manu potentis*.[9] The soul that possesses this supernatural suppleness of obedience is capable of great things, because if it can count upon God, God can count upon and be sure of it; and very often, God uses these souls for work wherein His

4 Rule, ch. vii. 5 Ibid. ch. v.

6 "Let the subject know that it is expedient for him," Ibid. ch. lxviii.

7 Rom. viii, 28. "As experience shows so often, compulsion is best for the individual and for the attainment of an object desired. Looking back on the years that have gone by, I can testify from personal observation that some course I was obliged by authority to take, against what in my own judgment at the time I held to have been a better way, has proved in the event to have been right. Even what I regarded as failures have under obedience had results which I afterwards came to acknowledge as distinctly providential. "...The real danger of failure comes when in moments of weakness or cowardice we try to withdraw ourselves directly or indirectly from the yoke of authority. Spiritual writers are unanimous in condemning as perilous in the extreme, from a spiritual point of view, an attitude even of passive opposition to constituted authority." Cardinal A. Gasquet, *Religio Religiosi*, ch. 12, *The Yoke of Obedience*.

8 Hebr. v, 9. 9 Ps. cxxvi, 4.

glory is particularly at stake. But He uses them through obedience, in order to preserve them in humility. However high be the aim, the fully obedient soul reaches it: however arduous be the work, it accomplishes it to perfection, for the strong God is with this soul which has at its disposition the very power of God.

We are therefore not surprised at the prodigies performed by those who, forgetting themselves and stripped of self, are invested by obedience with power from on high. A very remarkable example of this is given in the well-known episode recounted in the Dialogues of St. Gregory. The young Placid having fallen into the Lake of Subiaco, St. Benedict orders his disciple Maurus to go and pull the child out of the water, and St. Maurus, in the promptitude of his obedience, walks on the water, and brings back St. Placid safe and sound.

It is this faith alone that can assure the security of our monastic life. As long as we see Christ in the Superior, we shall participate, like St. Peter walking upon the waves,[1] in the Divine immunity; as soon as the breath of doubt touches our heart, we shall sink. The soul who obeys in faith in God's word is not supported solely by natural strength: *Hi in curribus et hi in equis;* it has the right of counting upon the very power of God: *Nos autem in nomine Domini.*[2]

Do not be astonished in that I have insisted so much upon the part that faith holds in religious obedience. It is a most important part. Faith makes our obedience safe and guarantees its fruitfulness; it also makes its greatness.

Men of the world sometimes reproach us religious for being characterless, servile or small-minded in face of authority. The world is always ready to throw stones, and very often just where it might itself be found at fault: we need not know much of the world in order to be aware how often is to be found in its midst that want of character with which it reproaches us. However is it always without reason that we are accused of it? Let us confess that unhappily the reproach might not be unde-

1 Matth. xiv, 29.

2 "Some trust in chariots, and some in horses: but we... in the name of the Lord," Ps. xix, 8. St. Catherine of Siena frequently comes back upon this point in treating of obedience.

served in regard to those who do not see God in the Superior. There is in fact something debasing for a man to obey another man, when the latter appears merely as a man, and not as representing, in some degree, divine authority. To obey the Abbot because we have the same ideas or the same tastes as he has, because we feel for him a natural sympathy, because he possesses talents that we admire, because we find his orders are reasonable, is unworthy of us and apart from the virtue of obedience. It is possible, in these cases, always to accomplish materially what is commanded us by the Abbot, and yet never to make a formal act of veritable obedience.[1]

None of these natural motives ought ever to affect us. Why so? Because as soon as we place ourselves on the natural plane, one man is worth as much as another, and the dignity of man commands him not to submit to another creature, considered as such; to do so would be to lessen and abase himself. Never would I obey a man, were this man a dazzling genius, if he had not received a participation in the Divine authority, in order to command me. But as soon as God says: "Such or such a man represents Me," were this man without talents, had he all the most crying natural defects, did this man belong to an altogether inferior race, I would yield myself to him,—as long as he ordered me nothing evidently contrary to the Divine Law; in this latter case, he would no longer represent God.

To obey thus is to raise oneself, for it is to acknowledge, in order to bow down before it, but a single authority, that before which all nations ought to lose themselves in adoration—the authority of God. To serve God is to reign: to serve God thus is to rise above all human considerations, above natural contingencies even as far as the Supreme and Sovereign Being, even as far as God; that is truly to be free, to be strong, to be great, for one is not the slave of any creature, however high he may be: *Servire Deo regnare est.*[2] But it is only faith, an intense, ardent faith, that can raise us to this level, and, above all, keep us there.

1 "A religious may obey through mere habit, by routine, for the sake of a quiet life, or through mere slavishness of disposition: such a one leads an outwardly obedient life; but he is not obedient. Much less is that religious obedient who obeys to the eye, but rebels inwardly." Bishop Hedley. *Retreat,* ch. 19. *Obedience.*

2 Roman Pontifical, ordination of sub-deacons; this expression is found in a letter attributed to St. Leo (*ad Demetriadem*) P. L. 55, 165. We see how the reproach of servil-

Does this mean that we must not love the Superior? Quite the contrary. Among the counsels that our Holy Father gives to the Abbot, is that "he should study to inspire love rather than fear": *Studeat plus amari quam timeri*;[1] to the monks, he gives the precept to "love their Abbot with sincere and humble affection": *Abbatem suum sincera et humili caritate diligant.*[2] But this love itself must already be of the supernatural order; this love should certainly be manifested by obedience, but obedience ought not to have as its motive power an affection that remains purely in the natural order. It is an obedience of faith that our holy Lawgiver requires of us: the commands of the Superior must be carried out "as if they came from God Himself": *Ac si divinitus imperetur.*[3] If this is a living faith, it will render obedience easy; whatever be the order enjoined, it will make us find God: that is the best recompense.

VIII

Born of faith, religious obedience is sustained by hope. We have indeed already touched on this subject so need not enlarge upon it, since, in a soul where faith is perfect, hope necessarily flourishes. We will therefore only say a little about this. What is the rôle of hope in the exercise of obedience? To render us full of confidence in God's help, especially in triumphing over the obstacles and difficulties that may be foreseen and encountered in the execution of the task commanded. God cannot leave to itself a soul that confides wholly in His grace. Look at Moses on Mount Horeb. The Lord appeared to him and entrusted him with delivering the children of Israel held in Egyptian bondage: "Come, and I will send thee to Pharaoh, that thou mayst bring forth My people." Moses is alarmed by the greatness of this mission: "Who am I that I should go to Pharaoh, and should bring forth the children of Israel out of Egypt?" And God answers: *Ego ero tecum*: "I will be with

ity falls to the ground as regards the obedient religious. Far more than this. The spirit of faith that animates this religious is the only moral force that delivers man from all servility in face of any superior whomsoever,—magistrate, military chief, prince—and it contains the secret of true human dignity. The Catholic is at once the most obedient and the least servile of men.

1 Rule, ch. lxiv. 2 Ibid. ch. lxxii. 3 Ibid. ch. v.

thee."[1] Henceforth intrepid, Moses went to the court of the Pharaohs and you know the prodigies that God wrought by his hands to deliver the Hebrews. *Ego ero tecum*: we often read these words in the lives of the Saints. Our Lord frequently repeated them to St. Catherine of Siena[2] and the Blessed Bonomo,[3] when He gave them commands: "Have no fear," said He to the latter, "I shall be with thee." He repeats these words to all of us, when obedience commands us to do hard or impossible things: *Noli timere quia ego tecum sum*.[4]

He gives us, with confidence, that virtue of patience without which obedience is not perfect. "The sign that thou hast this virtue of obedience," said the Heavenly Father to St. Catherine, "is patience; impatience makes known that thou hast it not... Disobedience has a sister given to her by self-love and this is impatience... Patience and obedience are inseparable; whoever is not patient has, by this very fact, the proof that obedience does not dwell in his heart."[5]

Obedience quickened by supernatural confidence, infallibly draws down help from on high. St. Benedict is explicit on this point: when the Abbot commands us to do things difficult or impossible, the order must first of all be accepted. Then if we see that the burden altogether exceeds our strength we must make known, patiently and at the seasonable moment, the reasons of our incapacity, showing neither pride, resistance, nor contradiction. If having listened to these representations, the Abbot still persists in his way of thinking and maintains his command, the monk, says our Holy Father, will know that this command is advantageous for him and he will obey for love, confiding in God's assistance: *Ex caritate confidens de adjutorio Dei obediat*.[6]

This admirable sentence concludes this chapter so lofty, so firm and at the same time so full of discretion, devoted to obedience in "impossible" things. The hope that God will be with us ought to sustain us, because it is "through love of Him" that we obey.

---

1 Exod. iii, 12. 2 *Life,* by Raymund of Capua.

3 *Une extatique au XVIIIe siècle. La Bienheureuse J.M. Bonomo, moniale bénidictine,* by D. du Bourg, p. 81–82, 141.

4 Gen. xxvi, 24. 5 *Dialogue. On Obedience,* ch. 1 and 2.

6 Rule, ch. lxviii.

IX

The expression "through love," which we have just quoted, marks the last of the fundamental qualities—and this especially in relation to the *motive*—of our obedience. Although he makes obedience the offspring of humility, and gives it faith as its first inspirer, you will however remark that the holy Patriarch always presents monastic obedience as an act of love: *Ut quis* PRO DEI AMORE *omni obedientia se subdat majori:*[1] it is for the love of God that we submit to the Superior in all obedience. Certain lines written by St. Benedict upon obedience (Ch. v, vii, xviii, xxii) reveal a deep-lying tendency in his soul to act for love. Within him burns as it were a restrained enthusiasm for God, for Christ, for love itself. According to his way of thinking, obedience is not only an inmost disposition which inclines the monk to execute every command with promptitude and devotedness because the moral order requires that the inferior shall submit to the superior; the obedience of the monk is to be an exercise or a perpetual effort of love... Obedience thus becomes the expression of an habitual dispusition of unitive life by the conformity or perpetual communion of the human will with the Divine Will."[2]

For, the Holy Lawgiver repeats to us that this virtue in its perfection is only to be found in those "who hold nothing dearer to them than Christ": *Haec convenit iis qui* NIHIL SIBI A CHRISTO CARIUS *aliquid existimant.*[3] St. Benedict wishes the monk's obedience to be the expression of love; and he adds that in this above all we shall imitate Christ: PRO DEI AMORE *omni obedientia se subdat majori,* IMITANS DOMINUM *de quo dicit Apostolus: factus obediens usque ad mortem.*[4]

The first act of the holy soul of Jesus in the Incarnation was to dart through the infinite space that separates the created from the divine. Resting in the Bosom of the Father, His soul contemplates face to face His adorable perfections. We cannot picture to ourselves that this contemplation could be, if I may so express myself, only speculative. Far from it. As the Word, Christ loves His Father, in very deed, with an infinite love surpassing all comprehension. But the Humanity of Jesus is drawn into this impetuous current of uncreated love and the Heart of Christ

1 Ibid. ch. vii.
2 D. I. Ryelandt, *l. c.* p. 209.
3 Rule, ch. v.
4 Ibid. ch. vii; Philip. ii, 8.

burns with the most perfect love that could ever exist. A member of the human race through His Incarnation, Christ falls moreover under the great precept: "Thou shalt love the Lord thy God, with thy whole heart, and with thy whole soul, and with thy whole mind, and with thy whole strength."[1] Jesus has perfectly fulfilled this commandment. From His first entering into the world, He yielded Himself up through love: *Ecce venio... Deus meus volui et legem tuam in medio cordis mei.*[2] I have placed, O Father, Thy law, Thy will "in the midst of My Heart." His whole existence is summed up in love for the Father. But what form will this love take? The form of obedience: *Ut faciam Deus voluntatem tuam.*[3] And why is this? Because nothing better translates filial love than absolute submission.[4] Christ Jesus has manifested this perfect love and this full obedience from the moment of the Incarnation "even to the death of the Cross": *Usque ad mortem.*

Not only has He never for an instant hesitated to obey, but love draws Him, despite the sensible shrinking that He feels, towards the consummation of His obedience: "I have a baptism wherewith I am to be baptised: and how am I straitened until it be accomplished?"[5] It is with intense desire that He desires to eat the Pasch with His disciples,[6] that Pasch which is to inaugurate the Passion. If He delivers Himself up to death, it is that the world may know that He loves His Father: *Ut cognoscat mundus quia diligo Patrem.*[7] And this love is unutterable because this perfect obedience is the very food of His soul: *Meus cibus est ut faciam voluntatem ejus qui misit me, ut perficiam opus ejus.*[8]

---

1 Marc. xii, 30.

2 "Behold I come... O my God, I have desired it, and Thy law in the midst of my heart," Ps. xxxix, 8–9. 3 Hebr. x, 7.

4 The Eternal Father said to St. Catherine, "I wish thee to see and know this most excellent virtue in that humble and immaculate Lamb, and the source whence it proceeds. What caused the great obedience of the Word? The love which He had for My honour and your salvation. Whence proceeded this love? From the clear vision with which His soul saw the divine essence and the eternal Trinity, thus always looking on Me, the eternal God, His fidelity obtained this vision most perfectly for Him, which vision you imperfectly enjoy by the light of holy faith. He was faithful to me, His Eternal Father, and therefore hastened as one enamoured along the road of obedience lit up with the light of glory." *Dialogue. On Obedience,* ch. 1, translated by Algar Thorold.

5 Luc. xii, 50. 6 Ibid. xxii, 15. 7 Joan. xiv, 31.

8 Joan. iv, 34.

A similar sense of love ought to inspire the monk "in all his obedience": *Ut quis pro Dei amore, omni obedientia se subdat majori.* Our Lawgiver is very explicit upon this point. The obedience of the monk, enlightened by faith, is to spring from the love that he bears to Christ, as the Model and mainspring of his submission. There is not after all any motive more essential and fundamental, more effectual also, for making us perfectly obedient than this ambition to imitate Christ Jesus our Ideal. Why have we left all things, renounced all things, even our own will, except to follow Him more closely: *Vende quae habes... et veni sequere me... Reliquimus omnia et secuti sumus te.*[1]

It is not an easy thing to follow Jesus as far as the death of the cross. Only those hearts inspired by an intense faith, hearts humble, steadfast and generous are capable of it. In order to march courageously in the footsteps of Christ Our Lord and King, as St. Benedict wishes, a man must renounce his own will and take up the most strongly tempered arms, the only ones that can lead us to glory: those of obedience: *Quisquis abrenuntians propriis voluntatibus, DOMINO CHRISTO VERO REGI MILITATURUS obedientiae fortissima atque praeclara arma sumis.*[2] Obedience may sometimes require heroic patience and self-abnegation. Our Holy Father himself forewarns us of this. But did our Divine Master find it agreeable to be delivered up to the Jews, insulted by the Pharisees, spat upon by the soldiery? No, all this filled Him with horror and disgust; and yet He accepted all to prove to His Father the love wherewith His Heart overflowed. His Father had willed that He should be treated as the last of men, the outcast of the people; that He should undergo the death of one cursed, *cum sceleratis.*[3] And so deep was His submission that He allowed Himself to be led to immolation as a Lamb that does "not open his mouth," *Et non aperiet os suum.*[4]

Now it is even as far as this that Christ Jesus is the Model of our obedience. None will ever make us suffer such things, nor ask of us such obedience. If God sometimes permits that obedience should crush us, let us, in those difficult moments, look at Christ Jesus in His agony

1 Matth. xix, 21, 27.

2 "Whosoever thou mayest be that renouncing thine own will to fight for the true King, Christ, doest take up the strong and glorious weapons of obedience," Prologue of the Rule.

3 Isa. liii, 12.

4 Ibid. 7.

or hung upon the Cross, and let us say to Him from the depths of our heart: *Diligam te et tradam meipsum pro te*:[1] "Because I love Thee I accept Thy will." Then divine peace—that peace which passes all understanding—will descend into our soul with the sweetness of heavenly grace. This alone will give us the strength and patience to endure all things in silence of heart and lips: *Tacita conscientia patientiam amplectatur*.[2]

But when a man has not this faith which shows God to be the one Good, when he is not carried on by this generous and ardent love for the Person of Christ Jesus, he seeks himself, he is attached to such or such a work, to such or such a charge, he goes no further than his own ideal. Does the Superior happen to touch this charge, this work, to oppose this ideal, then woe betide!... It cannot be said of these souls what our Holy Father declares of the perfect monk that he "leaves what is his own": *Relinquentes quae SUA sunt*.[3] When a man "truly seeks God," *Si revera Deum quaerit*,[4] and not self, he is content with whatever task obedience imposes upon him, however humble, obscure, painful or difficult this task may be; he even judges himself to be unworthy of it, as St. Benedict wills,[5] because all obedience, coming from God, leads us to God, and it is always a signal grace to be enabled to draw near to God in order to be united to Him.[6]

It needs great love to arrive at this degree of the virtue. In fact, to obey always without faltering, to submit in everything, *in OMNI obedientia*, to a frail and fallible man, is, I repeat it, very hard to nature: but it gives God a homage that is very pleasing to Him.

A pleasing homage, first of all because to allow oneself to be thus moulded by obedience, is to arrive—and "infallibly," *sine dubio*,[7] St. Benedict says forcibly—at perfectly reproducing in oneself the features of

1 Cf. Gal. ii, 20. 2 Rule, ch. vii. 3 Rule, ch. v. 4 Ibid. ch. lviii.

5 *Ad OMNIA quae sibi injunguntur velut OPERARIUM SE MALUM judicet et INDIGNUM* (Let him esteem himself, in regard to the work that is given him, as a bad and unworthy workman). Rule, ch. vii.

6 We are speaking here of the orders of Superiors, but this can be applied, all proportion guarded, to obedience to the Rule and to the traditions established by the Constitutions. We touched on this point of faithfulness to the Rule and the common life in the conference on "The Instruments of Good Works," and "The Cenobitical Society."

7 Rule, ch. v.

Christ. *Factus obediens usque ad mortem.*[1] Now this is all that the Heavenly Father wills, namely, that we should be conformed to His beloved Son. Never let us forget that the more we reproduce these features in us, the more will the Father place His delight in us and pour upon us the abundance of His grace: for God's love is divinely active in the soul.

A pleasing homage, secondly, because it is to surrender to God what is dearest and most sacred to us; it is to offer Him the most entire and religious sacrifice that we can bring to Him.[2] Therefore God draws straight to Him those who never let themselves be turned away from rendering Him this homage, those who aim at imitating the obedience of Christ Jesus, despite the difficulties and repugnances they experience: *Scientes per hanc obedientiae viam se ituros ad Deum*;[3] others, those who consider the man in the Superior, discuss the rightfulness or expediency of his orders, or are held back by difficulties and these come near God without ever fully finding Him: *In circuitu ambulant.*[4]

X

Let us often beseech God to give us that light of faith and strength of love which will render our obedience perfect. Thus supernaturally sustained, this obedience will become easy, generous, simple, prompt and joyous: *Non trepide, non tarde, non tepide, aut cum murmurio vel cum responso nolentis.*[5] It is important that all these qualities should accompany the exercise of our obedience. Our Holy Father wishes us to obey with a good will, *bono animo*, and he adds with St. Paul that "God loveth a cheerful giver."[6] Even when we always see Christ in the Superior it may yet happen that the Superior's character is the antithesis of our own, which may for the whole of our life render obedience naturally difficult for us, but our love for God should overcome these difficulties.

---

1 "Becoming obedient unto death," Philip. ii, 8.

2 *Quod obediatur praelato in quantum est Dei minister pertinet ad religionem qua quis colit et diligit Deum* (That he should obey a prelate inasmuch as he is a minister of God pertains to religion, by which someone worships and loves God). St. Thomas, *Quodlibet* VI, q. vi, a. 1, co. Cf. II-II, q. civ, a. 3, ad 1.

3 Rule, ch. lxxi. 4 Ps. xi, 9.

5 "Not done timorously, or tardily, or tepidly, nor with murmuring or the raising of objections," Rule, ch. v. 6 Rule, ch. v and II Cor. ix, 7.

If not, it is to be feared that our obedience will fall short some day, and that to our great detriment.

For there are many ways of allowing the spirit of obedience to be impaired, or even of losing it altogether.

The obedient monk, as St. Benedict wishes, places his needs, desires, aspirations and aptitudes before his Superior with all the simplicity, all the frankness, all the loyalty of a child with his father. To use artifice or address, to show only one side of a situation or affair, to circumvent the Superior so as to extract an authorisation from him, even under the pretext of the good of souls, runs counter to the spirit of submission required by the great Patriarch: in these cases, says St. Bernard, one simply deceives oneself.[1]

For certain souls, one danger is to feel urged to arrange their own little existence apart, so as to be disturbed as little as possible, and practically to live as if the Superior did not exist. This outlook may sometimes be covered under the pretext of safeguarding the soul's union with God. But this is only a fallacious pretext hiding a singular illusion full of perils.[2] And how contrary is this manner of acting to all that our vocation demands, to all that our Holy Rule requires: *Abbatem sibi praesse DESIDERANT*![3] St. Benedict certainly did not employ this last word haphazard; we may be assured, on the contrary, that he chose it designedly, as when he wrote that the monk ought "to walk according to the direction of another": *Alieno judicio ambulare.*[4] This is the spirit in which we ought to live, since this is the Rule we have vowed to observe "until death": *Usque ad mortem.* We must then in all that concerns our work, our personal occupations, our undertakings, place ourselves under the control of the Superior: *Cum VOLUNTATE abbatis OMNIA agenda sunt; vindictae regulari subjaceat qui praesumpserit... QUIPPIAM QUAMVIS PARVUM*

1 *Quisquis vel aperte vel occulte satagit, ut quod habet in voluntate, hoc ei spiritualis Pater injungat; ipse se seducit, si forte sibi quasi de obedientia blandiatur; neque enim in ea re ipse praelato sed magis ei praelatus obedit* (Whoever either openly or secretly fusses, so that the the spiritual father enjoins upon him the thing which he already has in his will; this one seduces himself, if perhaps he flatters himself as though it were by obedience; for in that matter he does not obey the prelate, but rather the prelate obeys him). St. Bernard, *Sermo de tribus ordinibus Ecclesiae.* P. L. t. 183, 636.

2 See note at the end of this Conference.

3 Rule, ch. v.

4 Ibid.

sine JUSSIONE abbatis facere.[1] Let every thing without exception, in our life, be marked with the seal of obedience: that is our greatness, that is our security. Otherwise it is to be feared that, on the day of judgment, we shall come before God with empty hands, because, having fulfilled *our* desires, realised *our* will, we shall likewise have "received *our* reward" here below: the vain satisfaction of our self-love: *Receperunt mercedem suam, vani vanam.*[2] "Self-will begets nothing in the spiritual life, except eternal need."[3]

We see other souls voluntarily surround themselves with a hedge of thorns through which the Superior can scarcely pass; it may happen that, for the sake of peace, he dare not command them such or such work, or employ them in such or such charge. Undoubtedly they would not refuse in so many words, but they cannot be counted upon. They are lacking in that spiritual docility which is the very essence of obedience; and this lack of suppleness often comes from want of faith. These souls are not practically convinced enough that what is important in obedience, is less the material work to be done than the motive that makes us submit all our being to God in order to please Him. They believe that the works in which they ensconce themselves are more important than the rest, while in reality everything, in the sight of God, Eternal Wisdom, is measured by the obedience and love that inspires it.

This state which we have been considering does great harm to souls; for they practically cease to advance in the way whereby we return to God; they are not drawn into the current of heavenly peace; they are not borne along by the impetuosity of the river of God; they amuse themselves upon the banks, going on indifferently, and they only reach the port with great difficulty,—if indeed they do reach it. For, to render oneself, wilfully, so little approachable that the Superior no longer feels free to express his will, constitutes, for one who has promised obedience, a breaking of his word and an act of sloth: it is the *inobedientiae desidia*[4]

---

1 "Everything is to be done with the approval of the abbot; let him undergo the punishment of the Rule who shall presume... to do anything however trifiling, without the permission of the abbot," Ibid. ch. xlix, lxvii.

2 Cf. Matth. vi, 5.

3 St. Mechtilde, *The Book of Special Grace,* 4th Part, ch. 19, *How useful it is to break our self-will.*

4 "Sloth of disobedience," Prologue of the Rule.

of which our Holy Father speaks when he says that it "separates from God." "Set aside your free will" says the Venerable Blosius, "and obey for God with humble readiness. Better to pull up nettles and weeds in the simplicity of obedience than by our own choice to employ our time in the contemplation of the most sublime heavenly mysteries, for the most pleasing sacrifice to God is the abnegation of self-will. He who resists his Superiors and will not obey, deprives himself of heavenly grace and can in nowise please the Lord, if he change not."[1]

It is true that to submit unreservedly to obedience may require great sacrifices. But to hesitate in obedience, is not this to hesitate before the one Good that we have come to seek in the monastery and which we shall only meet in the way of obedience? Is it not saying implicitly to God: "My God, I do not love Thee enough to make Thee this sacrifice, to render Thee this homage?" Were these the sentiments that inspired us on the blessed day of our religious profession?

Let us then in this matter be of great and vigilant delicacy of soul, for it is not all at once, but little by little, that one arrives at that state of living, practically, outside obedience—a state that cannot be without real danger for the religious.

It is also of extreme importance to watch over the avenues of our heart and never to permit murmuring to creep in. Murmuring is regarded by our Holy Lawgiver as one of the greatest perils in the life of a monk; he combats it forcibly and in every circumstance. We might ask why our Holy Father so strongly condemns all murmuring and all disobedience while he shows himself so unusually indulgent for faults of weakness. It is because his soul, bathed in divine light, saw that this diversity of attitude was according to God's own ways.

Let us open the Holy Scriptures; we shall therein find an astonishing revelation of the way God judges of sins. There is David. Elected king by the Lord, heaped with heaven's gifts, David forgets all these benefits from on high and allows himself to be drawn into murder and adultery. The Lord sends the prophet Nathan to the king to denounce the enormity of his crime. And David, immediately filled with repentance, utters these simple words: "I have sinned against the Lord": *Peccavi Domino*.

1 *Sanctuaire de l'âme fidèle*, § 1. *Œuvres spirituelles.*

Then the prophet replies: "The Lord also hath taken away thy sin: thou shalt not die; nevertheless... the child that is born to thee, shall surely die."[1] The expiation was great, but God's forgiveness remained assured to David in spite of the extent of his sin.

Let us now look at another scene which had come to pass a few years previously. There is Saul. Established as king of Israel by God Himself, he is good, chaste, simple; but he is attached to his own judgment. The Lord had commanded him to make war against the Amalecites and to exterminate these enemies of his people without sparing them. You know what Saul did: he spared the life the king of the Amalecites and reserved what was best in the booty. And remark that Saul's intention was, in itself, excellent: it was not for himself that he thus kept a part of the booty, it was in order to offer it in sacrifice to the Lord. Now how did God act in this circumstance? He rejected Saul forever, despite the king's repentance. "Doth the Lord desire holocausts and victims," said the prophet Samuel to Saul, "and not rather that the voice of the Lord should be obeyed? For obedience is better than sacrifices: and to hearken than to offer the fat of rams. Because it is like the sin of witchcraft, to rebel: and like the crime of idolatry, to refuse to obey. Forasmuch therefore as thou hast rejected the word of the Lord, the Lord hath also rejected thee from being king..." Saul then breathes forth his repentance, as David was to do later: "I have sinned... pardon my sin..." But it is in vain that he reiterates the expression of his repentance, that he beseeches Samuel: he is rejected—and rejected for ever.—So great is the horror with which disobedience inspires God, even when it seems to be justified by good reasons: *Melior est obedientia quam victimae.*[2]

We hence understand why our Holy Father is so strongly opposed to all disobedience, and why he so severely condemns murmuring which, like a canker, eats into the root of the spirit of obedience and makes all true submission impossible. Let us listen to his words, for they are grave. "If the monk," he says, "obey with ill-will, if he murmur not with his lips, but even in his heart, although he fulfil the order he has received, it will not be accepted by God Who seeth the heart of the murmurer;

1 II Reg. xii, 13–14.

2 "For obedience is better than sacrifices," I Reg. xv, 22.

and far from obtaining any grace for such an action, he will rather incur the punishment of murmurers, unless he amend and make reparation."[1] Such is St. Benedict's explicit teaching. And this doctrine is perfectly just. Murmuring is, in fact, like the indemnity that one takes for having obeyed when practically one cannot do otherwise than obey. The order is materially executed; but the essence of obedience, which is the loving submission of the whole being, is absent from the soul. Murmuring is the resistance of the soul which is must often manifested by words, by criticising the order given, its legitimacy or its expediency.

Our holy Father calls murmuring "an evil": *Murmurationis malum*,[2] quite the contrary of *bonum obedientiae*.[3] Why is it an evil? Because it turns the soul away if not always from the outward observance, at least from the inward submission of the heart, essential to the perfection of obedience; hence it turns away the soul from "the way that leads to God": *Scientes per hanc obedientiae viam se ituros ad Deum*; it turns the soul away from God, its supreme Good, in turning it away from the authority that represents God. It is a stratagem of the devil to make a soul doubt the legitimacy of the orders of authority; when this doubt has arisen, the devil has won his part: this is the history of the first fall and of all those that have followed it. Even when a man murmurs without any bitterness, when he pretends only to state objectively the errors, the weaknesses or the faults of authority, he can do considerable harm to souls; serving as an agent to the devil to do his business, he repeats to others what the serpent breathes in his ears. With poisonous breath he tarnishes the freshness of the "humble and sincere love" towards authority that St. Benedict requires of the monk.

The evil of murmuring is so much the more to be dreaded in that it has the power of infecting others: it is like a microbe capable of ravaging all the members of a community one after the other. However, in order to live and be propagated it needs a propitious soil. The Superior can do nothing directly against murmuring; it is in a sense beyond his grasp; it is for the organism to defend itself. If the murmurer finds no complaisant ear to listen to him, he loses his time and pains and has to keep his murmuring to himself; but it is a terrible evil because it is a sheer dissolvant of inward perfection.

1 Rule, ch. v. 2 Ibid. ch. xxxiv. 3 Ibid. ch. lxxi.

Whence comes the evil of murmuring? Almost always from lack of faith.[1] One sees the man in the Superior, and no longer Christ; faith no longer covering the weaknesses or imperfections of the man, his commands are judged because the man himself is judged. And by force of habit, the murmurer spares nothing, neither men, nor institutions, nor customs, nor works. Nothing escapes his criticism. If he was governed by an archangel, he would still find means of criticising his orders. Look at the Jews in the time of the Gospel. Our Blessed Saviour was assuredly perfection itself; and yet the Jews often murmured at what He said or what He did. If Christ heals on the Sabbath day, these men, full of bitter zeal and thinking themselves the guardians of the Law, murmur.[2] Does He eat with the Publicans? they murmur.[3] Does He enter the house of Zacheus? they murmur.[4] If He forgives sins, they are scandalised.[5] If He reveals the secret of His love for men, in announcing the gift of the Eucharist, they cavil.[6] Therefore Christ Jesus Himself says that nothing finds favour in their eyes: "Whereunto shall I esteem this generation to be like?... For John came neither eating nor drinking; and they say: He hath a devil. The Son of man came eating and drinking, and they say: Behold a man that is a glutton and a wine drinker, a friend of publicans and sinners."[7]

Let us then carefully and before all things keep ourselves from all murmuring, as our Holy Father warns us to do so insistently and earnestly; for nothing is more contrary to the letter and spirit of the Rule than murmuring: *ante omnia, ne murmurationis malum pro qualicumque causa in aliquo qualicumque verbo vel significatione appareat.*[8]

---

1 "The disobedient man," said the Eternal Father to St. Catherine, "is deluded by his self-love, because *the eye of his intellect is fixed with a dead faith,* on pleasing his self-will, and on things of the world... because obedience seems weariness to him, he wishes to avoid weariness, whereby he arrives at the greatest weariness of all, for he is obliged to obey either by force or by love, and it would have been better and less wearisome to have obeyed by love than without it." *Dialogue,* ch. 8. Translated by Algar Thorold.

2 Joan. v, 16. 3 Matth. ix, 11. 4 Luc. xix, 7.

5 Ibid. v, 21. 6 Joan. vi, 53. 7 Matth. xi, 16–19.

8 Rule, ch. xxxiv. "In St. Benedict's eyes, monastic peace is a benefit which surpasses all others, as murmuring seems to him the worst of evils." Abbot Delatte, *Commentary on the Rule of St Benedict,* translated by D. Justin McCann, p. 253. The whole passage should be read.

However, we must distinguish the difference between complaining and murmuring. Complaining is in nowise an imperfection, it may even be a prayer. Look at our Lord Jesus, the Model of all holiness. Upon the Cross, did He not complain to His Father of being forsaken? But what is it that makes the difference between these two attitudes? Murmuring evidently implies opposition, malevolence (at least transitory) in the will; however, it proceeds more formally from the mind; it is a sin of the mind derived from the spirit of resistance. It is a contentious manifestation. Complaint on the contrary, if we suppose it to be pure, comes only from the heart; it is the cry of a heart that is crushed, that feels suffering, but however accepts it entirely, and lovingly. We can feel the difficulties of obedience, experience even movements of repugnance: that may happen to the most perfect soul; there is no imperfection in this as long as the will does not adhere to these movements of revolt which sometimes get the better of the sensitive nature. Did not our Lord Himself feel such inward trouble? *Coepit taedere et pavere et maestus esse.*[1] And what did He Who is our Ideal say in these terrible moments? *Pater, si possibile est, transeat a me calix iste.*[2] "My Father, if it be possible, let this chalice pass from Me." What a plaint wrung from God's innermost Heart in the face of the most terrible obedience ever proposed here below! But likewise how this cry from the depths of crushed sensitive nature, is covered by the cry, far deeper still, of entire abandonment to the Divine Will: *Verumtamen fiat voluntas tua, non mea!*

From murmuring, on the contrary, love is absent: therefore murmuring separates from God; it destroys precisely what our holy Patriarch wishes to establish in us: that "amen" of every instant, that loving "fiat" coming more from the heart than the lips: in a word, that perpetual and incessant submission of our whole being to the divine will for love of Christ.

XI

Let us watch over ourselves. Obedience is too precious a good for us not to safeguard it with care. Let us love this good, this "bonum," as our

1 "He began to grow sorrowful and to fear and to be sad," Matt. xxvi, 37 and Marc. xiv, 33. 2 Matth. xxvi, 39.

Holy Father is pleased to call it, for it contains and gives God. Let us seek it with love and guard it jealously. Let us think of the example given us by those who seek for gold. They are told that in some El Dorado, in some region unknown to them, gold is to be found. They set off with gladness, upheld by the hope of riches; they leave country, friends, family; they embark, cross the seas, force their way through a thousand dangers, to the interior of unknown lands. Behold them at last, after many toils, perils and explorations, arrived at the place where lies the precious metal. Let us now suppose that after having extracted it from the ground, at the cost of many pains and labours, they prepare to return without taking back with them all the ingots they can, but content themselves with a few nuggets held in the hollow of their hands. What should we say of these men who have undergone so many sufferings, endured so many labours, overcome so many obstacles to content themselves finally with such meagre gain? That they are fools. And we should be right.

Now that is the portrait of a monk who, after some time spent in the monastery, suffers the loyalty of his obedience to be impaired. There is none amongst us that has not made great sacrifices before crossing the threshold of the cloister. We read one day in Holy Scripture, or we heard Christ give us in prayer, the counsel to leave all things and follow Him. "Come, follow Me and I will give thee life, I will be thy beatitude." This Divine Voice, full of sweetness, touched our soul to its depths; we understood the call of Jesus; and then, like the merchant in the Gospel, who, having found a treasure in a field, sold all that he had to gain this field and make himself master of the treasure, we left all things. We said farewell to all that was dear to us, we renounced the legitimate joys of hearth and home, the visible affection of our own dear ones. Why did we consent to all these acts of renunciation? To gain the treasure which is none other than God Himself. And where do we find this treasure? In eternity we shall find it in the ineffable and supreme bliss of God; here below in the obedience of faith. This is the treasure we seek and that obedience gives us. And after such great sacrifices, so often renewed, instead of appropriating this precious good in the greatest possible measure, shall we content ourselves with taking some small particles? Is it sufficient for us to obey from time to time, just enough not to fail in our vow? God grant it is not so, that we are not so foolish as thus to squander eternal treasures in advance!

Neither let us forget that our vow of obedience is a solemn promise made to God on the day of our profession. Each time that we deliberately exempt ourselves from obedience, in whatever way it may be, we "like cowards" (it is St. Benedict's expression) take back something from what we have given. On the day of judgment, God Who is not mocked, *Deus non irridetur*,[1] will require of us, with a rigorous judgment, the account of the fidelity we swore to Him.[2] We shall not be able to say to God: "I wished to attain perfection, but my Superior was an imperfect, annoying person with exaggerated ideas, who let himself be guided by paltry and partial motives, and opposed my plans." God will answer us: "The faults of your Superior only concern Me; it is before Me that he is responsible for them, as for all the orders that he has given; as to you, I was, by My wisdom and goodness, bound to make up for the imperfections and human errors of the one who represented Me towards you; and I would have done so abundantly if, having had faith in My word, you had placed your hope in My fidelity."

Let us rather live in obedience, let us make it "our food" as Christ Himself did: *Meus cibus est ut faciam voluntatem eius*.[3] Let us ask our Lord for this virtue of obedience in all its perfection, this virtue which surrenders the judgment, will, heart, the whole being to God and to His representative. If we are faithful in asking for this grace, Christ Jesus will certainly grant it to us. Each morning, let us join ourselves to Jesus in His obedience, in the entire submission that He made of Himself at the moment of the Incarnation: "Behold me, O my God, I give myself

---

1 Gal. vi, 7.

2 St. Bernard compares obedience to a coin which we have to render to God and that He will not accept unless it be entire and exempt from falsification. "If we argue, if we obey one precept and not another, the coin of our obedience is broken, Christ will not accept it, for we have all promised obedience simply and without any restriction whatsoever. If then we make a feint of obeying under the master's eye, while murmuring secretly, our coin is debased, there is lead in it, all is not silver, and we pay in leaden talents; there lies our iniquity. We defraud, but it is under God's eye; now, God is not mocked." *2nd Sermon for the feast of St. Andrew*, § I. P. L., 183, 509. See also Rule, ch. lviii: *Si aliquando aliter fecerit, ab eo se damnandum sciat quem irridet* (Should he ever do otherwise he will be condemned by him whom he mocks).

3 Joan. iv, 34.

to Thee, to Thy good pleasure. Because I love Thee, I will give Thee the homage that consists in submitting my whole being to Thy will whatever it may be. I wish to say in union with Thy Son Jesus: *Quia diligo Patrem, et sicut mandatum dedit mihi Pater, sic facio.*[1] This Will may perhaps be painful to my nature, to my tastes, it may be opposed to my personal ideal, hard to my spirit of independence, but I want to offer Thee this sacrifice as testimony of my faith in Thy word, of my confidence in Thy power, and of the love I bear to Thee and to Thy Son Jesus." We ought to renew this offering every day, even—and especially—if it happen that a work imposed or approved by the Superior responds to our personal tastes. Otherwise, it is greatly to be feared that the natural satisfaction we may find in it will carry us away and make us forget that *spirit* of obedience with which our works ought to be done in order to be pleasing to God.[2]

If we act in this way, our obedience will be sanctified by contact with that of Jesus. He, who infinitely desires that we be "one with Him,"[3] will grant us to reach little by little the perfection not only of the vow, but of the virtue. And through this virtue, He will finish the work of detaching us from ourselves to unite us entirely to Himself, since we shall no longer have any will but His own,—and, through Him, we shall be united to His Father.

Then all will become more and more pleasant and easy for us because we shall draw our strength from Jesus, Who, in order to communicate it to us, draws it Himself from the Bosom of the Father. Love upholding us, all will be indifferent to us; we shall have no preference for such or such a work, but we shall accomplish with equal perfection the little things as the great: all coming to us from God, all will likewise lead us to God.

We shall unceasingly increase that eternal inheritance which we came here to seek and that nothing, if we so wish, can take away from us, because we find it in God Himself. "O Lord, full of goodness, teach me, for the sake of this goodness, to keep Thy precepts, for the law that falls from Thy lips is infinitely more precious to me than heaps of gold and

---

1 Ibid. xiv, 31.

2 This is the counsel that St. Gregory gives us: *Obedientiae te sibi virtutem evacuat qui ad prospera etiam et proprio desiderio anhelat* (He makes void for himself the virtue of his obedience, who pants for successes with his own longing). *Moralia in Job,* Lib. xxxv, ch. 14. P. L., 76, 706.

3 Joan. xvii, 21.

silver": *Bonus es tu, [Domine], et in bonitate tua doce me justificationes tuas; bonum mihi lex oris tui, super millia auri et argenti.*[1]

NOTE

(See pp 296 and 316)

St. Teresa has upon the subject of obedience some words too significant not to be quoted here, and her testimony can sum up all the others: "It would be a strange thing," she writes, "if, when God clearly told us to betake ourselves to some work that concerns Him, we were to do nothing but stand still and gaze upon Him because that gives us a greater joy. A pleasant progress this in the love of God!—to tie His hands through an opinion that He can do us good only in one way.

"I know of some, and have lived among them—I put on one side my own experience, as I said before—who taught me the truth of this; when I was myself in great distress because of the little time I had, and accordingly was sorry to see them always employed and having much to do, because they were under obedience, and was thinking within myself, and even said as much to them, that spiritual growth was not possible amidst so much hurry and confusion, for they had then not grown much. O Lord, how different are Thy ways from what we imagined them to be! and how Thou, if a soul be determined to love Thee, and resigned in Thy hands, askest nothing of it but obedience; the sure knowledge of what is for Thy greater honour, and the desire to do it. That soul need not seek out means, nor make a choice of any, for its will is already Thine. Thou, O Lord, hast taken upon Thyself to guide it in the way most profitable to it. And even if the superior be not mindful of that soul's profit, but only of the duties to be discharged in the Community, Thou, O my God, art mindful of it; Thou preparest its ways, and orderest those things we have to do, so that we find ourselves, without our knowing how, by faithfully observing, for the love of God, the commands that are laid upon us, spiritually growing and making great progress, which afterwards fills us with wonder..."

And after having brought forward several examples illustrating her teaching, the great Saint stimulates us with one if those exclamations

1 Ps. cxviii, 68, 72.

so characteristic of her: "Well, then my children, be not discouraged, for if obedience employs you in outward things, know that even if you are in the kitchen our Lord moves amidst the pots and pans, helping us both within and without."

Then becoming grave again, she concludes with this conviction which can only be born in the light from on high: "I believe myself that when Satan sees there is no road that leads more quickly to the highest perfection than this of obedience, he suggests many difficulties under the colour of some good, and makes it distasteful; let people look well into it, and they will see plainly that I am telling the truth... What I aim at showing is the reason, in my opinion, why obedience furnishes the readiest or the best way for arriving at so blessed a state. That reason is this: as we are never absolute masters of our own will, so as to employ it purely and simply for God, till we subject it wholly to reason, obedience is the true means of bringing about that subjection; which can never be brought about by much reasoning, because our nature and self-love can furnish so much on their side that we shall never come to an end, and very often will make that which is most reasonable, if we have no liking for it, to seem folly because we have no inclination to do it." *The Foundations*, ch. V. Translated from the Spanish by David Lewis. All this chapter should be read.

THE LIFE OF UNION WITH CHRIST

...et secuti sumus te

THE OPUS DEI, DIVINE PRAISE

SUMMARY.—God has made all things for His glory; how the Divine Office procures this glory for God: St. Benedict rightly calls it the *Opus Dei*.—I. Ultimate basis of the excellence of the Divine Office: the canticle of the Word in the bosom of the Divinity and in creation.—II. The Word Incarnate has bequeathed to the Church, His Bride, the mission of perpetuating His canticle.—III. The Church confides a more important part of this mission to some chosen souls.—IV. The Divine Office becomes, through the heart and voice of man, the hymn of all creation.—V. It forms a particular homage of the virtues of faith, hope and charity.—VI. This homage is invested with a special splendour when it is offered in suffering: *Sacrificium laudis*.

WHEN we would judge of the absolute value of anything or any work we ought to try to do so from God's point of view. God alone is the Truth; truth is the light in which God, Eternal Wisdom, sees all things; these are worth what they are in God's estimation. That is the sole infallible criterion of judgment, outside which we expose ourselves to deception. It is a truth familiar to us that our holiness is of the supernatural order, that is to say above the rights, exigencies and powers of our nature; all then that relates to this supernatural order, of which God alone is the Author, surpasses by its transcendency, all our human conceptions. God's thoughts and ways are not ours; He Himself tells us so: *Non enim cogitationes meae, cogitationes vestrae: neque viae vestrae, viae meae, dicit Dominus.*[1] Between our ways and God's there is the infinite: *Sicut exaltantur caeli a terra.*[2] This is why, in order to know the truth about things of the supernatural domain, we must see them as God sees them, that is, with the eyes of faith. Faith is the light that reveals the Divine thoughts to us and makes us penetrate into God's designs. Lacking this light, there is but darkness and error in regard to spiritual things.

Now one capital truth God has granted us to know touching His designs is that He has created everything and done everything for His glory: *Universa propter semetipsum operatus est Dominus.*[3] God gives us all things; He gives Himself in the person of His Well-Beloved Son Jesus, and with Him He gives us all good things; He has prepared for us for all eternity an infinite beatitude in the fellowship of His adorable Trinity. But there is one thing that He reserves jealously for Himself, that He neither will nor can give us: that is His glory: *Ego Dominus; gloriam meam alteri non dabo.*[4]

This being so, things are of value only in the measure in which they procure this glory for God. There are some works which, of their own nature, have no direct relationship with this glory; for example, in the intellectual order, to devote oneself to literary work, to teaching; and, in the manual order, to sweep the cloisters or work in the garden or kitchen; transformed by the love wherewith they are done, these works become pleasing to God; however, they procure His glory indirectly, not of themselves, *fine operantis*, that is to say by reason of the right intention of the one who performs them in view of pleasing God.[5]

Other works go to procure this glory directly; they are agreeable to God not only on account of the love of the one who accomplishes

1 "For My thoughts are not your thoughts: nor your ways My ways, saith the Lord," Isa. lv, 8.

2 Ibid. 9.

3 Prov. xvi, 4; see what we have said on this subject in the conference on humility.

4 Isa. xlii, 8.

5 We are speaking, of course, of the *supernatural* order; it is evident that every upright act, morally good, gives of itself a certain glory to God, from the fact that it enters already into the natural order willed by Him.

them but in themselves: *fine operis*; their direct end, like the elements that compose them, are supernatural: such are Holy Mass and the administration of the Sacraments. It is quite evident that in themselves, abstraction made of the interior dispositions of the one who performs them, these works surpass, from God's point of view, all other works.

The Divine Office belongs to this second group. Not only in our intention, but by reason of its nature, its composition, and the elements of which it is constituted, it relates entirely to God; of itself, *fine operis*, it has God in view. With the Holy Sacrifice, around which it gravitates, it forms the most complete expression of religion; it is by excellence "the work of God," *Opus Dei, Opus divinum*: that is the beautiful name by which our Holy Father calls it.

Doubtless, the Divine Office contains petitions, prayers of impetration, but this is not its dominant element; before all, the Divine Office is praise, and this praise is perfectly summed up in the doxology which ends each psalm: *Gloria Patri et Filio et Spiritui Sancto*. The direct aim of the Office is to confess and exalt the Divine perfections, to delight in them, and thank God for them: *Gratias agimus tibi, propter magnam gloriam tuam*.[1] It proceeds from this principle: "Thou art worthy, O Lord, to receive glory and honour": *Dignus es, Domine, Deus noster, gloriam accipere et honorem...*[2] This is the cry of the elect in heaven: contemplating God's infinite perfections, they are necessarily lost in praise and adoration: *Magnus Dominus et laudabilis NIMIS*.[3]

Now we, as religious, are seeking God; it was for this we came to the monastery; what is more natural therefore than to adopt the Divine Office as our principal work, by which we especially devote ourselves to God's service? How are we "to seek Him truly,"—*si revera Deum quaerit*,[4] unless we occupy ourselves first of all with Him, with His perfections and His works? *Et laudabunt Dominum qui requirunt eum*.[5] But in return, the more that we find Him, and that He reveals Himself to us, the more we feel the need of celebrating His perfections and works: *Quaerentes enim invenient eum, et invenientes laudabunt eum*.[6]

---

1 *Gloria* of the Mass. 2 Apoc. iv, 11. 3 Ps. xlvii, 1.

4 Rule, ch. lviii.

5 "They shall praise the Lord that seek Him," Ps. xxi, 27.

6 "Searching for Him, they will find Him; and finding Him, they will praise Him," St. Augustine, *Confessions*. Lib. I, ch. 1. P. L. 32, col. 661.

Thus, after having pointed out the purpose of our life, after having established the authority of the head of the monastery and defined the cenobitical life, after having shown how humility and obedience achieve the work of removing obstacles from the path of perfection, St. Benedict speaks to us of the Divine Office. He devotes numerous chapters to regulating it; he makes the Divine Office, not the end nor even the exclusive nor characteristic work of the monk, but the principal work to which the others, in the order of estimation and action, are to be subordinate: *Nihil Operi Dei praeponatur.*[1] He establishes a school of the Lord's service: *Dominici schola servitii,*[2] and the Divine Office constitutes, in this school the first "service of our devotion": *Devotionis servitium.*[3] Doubtless, as we have already said, St. Benedict does not exclude other works, and history as well as tradition for which we ought to have a humble respect, shows us that in the course of ages our Order has filled many missions in the varied domain of Christian civilisation; but it remains none the less true that the work which first of all claims our attention and energies is the Divine Praise. This same Divine Praise is also, apart from the Sacraments, the surest means for us monks of entering into contact with God. The Divine Office which gives so much glory to the Lord becomes for each of us an extremely fruitful source of sanctification. We will reserve this second point for the next conference; let us now endeavour to see how the *Opus Dei* constitutes an infinitely pleasing homage of praise to God,

To comprehend its excellence, we have to form a concept of its source, its nature, its elements and its end. We must, of course, come to this study with eyes of faith; faith alone can help us to penetrate into the truth. St. Paul says that only the Spirit of God is capable of searching into the deep things of God;[4] while the natural spirit, not going below the surface of things, falls frequently into error.

Our love of the Divine Office depending moreover on the esteem we have tor it, and on our faith in its value, it is supremely useful to us that this faith should be enlightened and this esteem well and solidly grounded.

---

1 Rule, ch. xliii. 2 Prologue of the Rule. 3 Rule, ch. xviii.
4 I Cor. ii, 10–11.

I

It is in lifting up our minds by faith—a faith full of reverence—even to the heights of the Adorable Trinity, that we shall find the very fountainhead of praise. We have the right to seek our examples thus high, for by grace, we are no longer strangers but sons belonging, through Christ, to the family of God: *Non estis hospites et advenae, sed estis cives sanctorum et domestici Dei.*[1]

What has Christ granted us to know of this ineffable life of God in Three Persons?

The Word, says St. Paul, is "the brightness of His (Father's) glory, and the figure of His substance."[2] The Word, the Son, is essentially, the glory of His Father. From all eternity, this Son in a single infinite Word which is Himself, expresses the Father's perfection, and this is the essential glory that the Father receives. The Eternal Word is a Divine canticle singing the Father's praise. *In principio erat Verbum, et Verbum erat apud Deum, et Deus erat Verbum.*[3] From all eternity He gives, has given and will give, in this infinite and unique act which is Himself, eternal and adequate glory to His Father. This glory consists in the infinite knowledge that the Son has of His Father, of the perfections of His Father, and in the infinite appreciation that He utters concerning them: an appreciation equal to God, worthy of God; God has no need of any other glory.

The Word sees also in His Father the eternal decrees of His Wisdom and Bounty, all the merciful designs which are wrought in the creation, in the Redemption, in the institution of the Eucharist, and realised daily in the sanctification of souls: *Quod factum est in ipso vita est*;[4] He contemplates all these objects and glorifies His Father for them: *Quam magnificata sunt opera tua, Domine! omnia in sapientia fecisti.*[5]

This is the infinite hymn that ever resounds *in sinu Patris*[6] and ever ravishes the Father. The Word is the Canticle that God inwardly sings to Himself, the Canticle that rises up from the depths of the Divinity, the Living Canticle wherein God eternally delights, because it is the infinite expression of His perfection.

---

1 Eph. ii, 19. 2 Hebr. i, 3. 3 Joan. i, 1.
4 "... that [which] was made. In Him was life," Ibid. i, 3–4.
5 "How great are Thy works, O Lord? Thou hast made all things in wisdom," Ps. ciii, 24.
6 Joan. i, 18.

The mystery of the Divine Life which we have just searched into with all reverence, bears in itself the fundamental reason and value of the Divine Office.

"The Word was made flesh, and dwelt among us": *Et Verbum caro factum est, et habitavit in nobis.*[1] But never let us forget this truth that we sing at Christmastide: *Id quod fuit permansit; quod non erat assumpsit.*[2] In taking a human nature, the Divine Word is not lessened; He remains what He is—the Eternal Word, and consequently He remains the infinite glorification of His Father. However, as He has united a human nature to Himself, in the unity of His Divine Person, this Sacred Humanity enters, through the Word, into participation of the work of glorification. Christ's Humanity is like the temple[3] where the Word sings the Divine canticle which glorifies the Father; or rather, the Sacred Humanity is carried along in the current of the Divine Life. Did not the Word Incarnate, Christ Jesus say: *Ego vivo propter Patrem,*[4] "I live by the Father." All His activity tends to procure His Father's glory. This theandric activity remains that of a human nature; it glorifies God in a human fashion; but, as it emanates from a Divine "Person," as it depends upon the Word, the praises it supplies, human in their expression, become the praises of the Word, and acquire on this account an infinite value.

When Christ prayed, when He recited the Psalms, when, as the Gospel says, He spent the night in prayer: *Erat pernoctans in oratione Dei,*[5] these were the human accents of a God: of an absolute simplicity in eternity, the canticle of the Word was multiplied, detailed, upon the lips of His Manhood. Thus this same canticle which, from all eternity, the Word causes to resound in the sanctuary of the Godhead, was prolonged and sung upon earth when the Word became incarnate.

Henceforward it will be prolonged for ever in creation. Forever, Christ's Humanity will therein sing, to the glory of the Father, a canticle of human expression but of incommensurable price and consequently

---

1 Joan. i, 14.

2 "That which He was, He remained, and that which He was not, He assumed," Antiphon of Lauds for the Feast of the Circumcision.

3 This image is evidently only an imperfect comparison, for the union of the Word with a human nature is not accidental like that of the temple and the adorer; it is a personal and substantial union.

4 Joan. vi, 58. 5 Luc. vi, 12.

alone worthy of God: this is the *Opus Christi*. On the last day of His life, Christ summed up all His work in saying to His Father: *Ego te clarificavi super terram.*[1] His whole life was but a continual praise to His Father's glory. This was His essential work; for Him, nothing came before the glorification of His Father.

Certainly, He glorified Him by all His actions, in spending Himself for souls, in giving Himself to them as no apostle has ever done, in going about doing good everywhere; but these were secondary forms of His praise. Above all, Christ, the Word Incarnate, praised His Father in exalting the Divine perfections in ineffable communings. Who shall tell us how Jesus worshipped the Father and how full this worship was of profound adoration! What incense of praise was that which went up unceasingly from His blessed soul to God His Father! Jesus contemplates the Divine perfections in all their splendour and this is the source of ineffable praise. He rendered to His Father, in the name of the human race to which He authentically belongs, all the duties of adoration, praise and complacency which we owe to God. The perfect knowledge, the sublime comprehension that He had of the inspired canticles made His praise infinitely worthy of God.

Christ also contemplated the creation: in Him, the Divine Word, the creation was full of life: *In Ipso vita erat*. It was needful that the whole order of created things should be for once perfectly comprehended by a human soul: Christ Jesus exulted in looking upon the wonders of nature, as the Triune God in the days of creation contemplated the goodness and beauty of the work come forth from His hands: *Viditque Deus cuncta quae fecerat: et erant valde bona.*[2] With what joy did Christ, seeing in creatures the reflection of the Father's perfections, constitute Himself their High Priest, in order to bring all things back to His Father! Hence was born in the soul of Jesus that perfect worship which it behoved Christ to offer as the supreme High Priest in Whom the Father finds all His delight.[3]

1 "I have glorified Thee on the earth," Joan. xvii, 4.

2 "And God saw all the things that He had made, and they were very good," Gen. i, 31.

3 Cf. Mgr. Gay, *Elevation 99. Sing to the Lord a new song for He hath done wonderful things.*

II

But, as you know, Christ does not separate Himself from His Mystical Body. Before ascending into Heaven, He bequeaths His riches and mission to His Church. Christ, in uniting Himself to the Church, gives her His power of adoring and praising the Father; this is the *liturgy*. It is the praise of the Church united to Jesus, supported by Jesus; or rather it is the praise of Christ, the Incarnate Word, passing through the lips of the Church.

Seeing her, the Angels ask each other: "Who is this that cometh up from the desert flowing with delights leaning upon her Beloved?"[1] It is the Church, we reply, her beauty and charm come to her from the Bridegroom Himself, Whose arms uphold her; her voice is ever sweet and her face comely.[2]

Dowered with the riches of Christ, the Church, His Bride, is introduced by Him into the palace of the King of Heaven, into the Father's presence, and there, united to Jesus Christ, she sings—as she will do until the end of ages—the canticle sung *in sinu Patris* by the Word, and brought by Him to earth.

The Apocalypse shows us the elect adoring "Him that sitteth on the throne," and exalting His ineffable perfections: *Dignus es, Domine Deus noster, accipere gloriam et honorem et virtutem*;[3] that is the choir of the Church Glorious. Here below is formed the choir of the Church Militant, called also to take her place one day in the ranks of the blessed; but this choir is united, by faith and love, with that of Heaven, and resounds too before the throne of God; for the Church is *one* in Christ, her Divine Head. In Heaven, says St. Augustine, satisfied love sings the Alleluia in the plenitude of eternal enjoyment; here below, yearning love seeks to express the ardour of its desires; *Modo cantat amor esuriens tunc cantabit amor fruens*.[4] But it is the same choir in two parts, the choir of *one* Church, singing the unparalleled canticle of Divine glory animated, both here on earth and up in Heaven, by the same supreme High Priest, Christ Jesus.

1 Cant. viii, 5. 2 Ibid. ii, 14.

3 "Thou art worthy, O Lord our God, to receive glory, and honour, and power," Apoc. iv, 10–11; cf. v, 12–13. 4 Sermo cclv, 5. P. L. 38, 1183.

The office is the official voice of the Bride of Christ. The Church, by her faith, confidence and love and by her union with Jesus, bridges the space that separates her from God and sings His praise, like the Word Incarnate, in the bosom of the Divinity. She sings, united to Christ, under God's very gaze; because of her title of Bride, she always merits to be heard. The great work, the triumph of the Divinity of Jesus, is to raise us, poor mortals, even up to His Father. God has given to the Sacred Humanity of the Word the power of drawing us with It where this Humanity Itself is: *Ascendo ad Patrem meum et Patrem vestrum, Deum meum et Deum vestrum*:[1] "I ascend to My Father and to your Father, to My God and your God." And again: *Pater, volo ut ubi ego sum, et illi sint mecum*:[2] "Father, I will that where I am, they also whom Thou hast given Me may be with Me." After death, we shall be—we truly hope to be—in a real and immutable way, where the Saviour is; but even now we are there by faith. The Word dwells in us by faith: *Christum habitare per fidem in cordibus vestris*.[3] We are especially united to the Word Incarnate when we join ourselves to Him in order to sing, through Him and with Him, the glory of His Father.

Such is the fundamental reason of the transcendency of the *Opus Dei*, such is the incommunicable and untransferable privilege attached to this prayer, the Work of God, accomplished with Christ, in His name, by the Church, His Bride.

III

The Church associates all her children in this praise. There is a part of the public worship which ordinary Christians themselves must perform if they are to be counted among the disciples of Jesus. However, the Church has not contented herself with this worship common to all. In the same way as she chooses some from among her children to associate more particularly and preferably with the eternal Priesthood of her Spouse, so she confides to some chosen ones a more important and special share in her mission of praise: this phalanx is formed of priests and religious orders invested with the functions of the choir. The

1 Joan. xx, 17. 2 Ibid. xvii, 24.

3 "That Christ may dwell by faith in your hearts," Eph. iii, 17.

Church, in her name and that of her Bridegroom, deputes them as her ambassadors before God's throne.

An ambassador does not present himself in his own private capacity, he stands in the place of his sovereign or of his country; these are involved when he speaks in virtue of his mission. Therefore he has a right to all the honours and privileges which would be given to his sovereign, and there is a juridical obligation that these should be granted to him. The reasons and arguments that he brings to bear in his diplomatic interviews have not only a private value resulting from the qualities and talents of the man, but they acquire a special weight, more or less powerful, according to the greatness of the country or the rank of the sovereign represented by him. This is not a simple fiction, but is a moral and juridical reality which defines the very rôle of the ambassador.

It is proportionately the same with those whom the Church, the Bride of Christ, deputes in her name to hold her place before God, that is to say the priests and religious obliged to the Divine Office in virtue of the rules approved by ecclesiastical authority. They stand before the Father as ambassadors appointed by the Church, whose homage they offer, and whose interests they represent. And as the Church is Christ's Bride, these ambassadors share in the privileges conferred upon the Church by her supernatural dignity, as the Spouse of Jesus. When we are in choir, we bear a twofold personality: our own individual personality, that of our misery, our frailty, our faults, but also that of members of Christ's Mystical Body deputed by the Church. In this second capacity we have to guard the numerous and varied interests of Christendom. If we know how to use our power, we are sure, in spite of our imperfections, of being pleasing to God and heard by Him. For, when we are acquitting ourselves of our official functions, all our miseries are as it were veiled by the prestige with which the Bride of Christ invests us. The Father sees us, during these hours of the Divine Office, no longer as souls coming before Him with their private interests and personal merits, but as ambassadors of the Bride of His Well-Beloved Son, treating of the cause of souls with every right to do so; we are officially invested with the dignity and power of the Bride of Jesus, and with those of Jesus Himself. Moreover, Christ Himself is in the midst of us; He has formally promised to be so; He is the supreme Hierarch Who receives our prayers and gathers up our praises to bear them to the throne of God: *Ad thronum gratiae*.[1] Therefore, in God's sight, this praise surpasses, in value and efficacy, all other praise, all other prayer, all other work.[2]

This truth is absolutely beyond doubt, and the saints, who lived in God's light, so understood it. St. Magdalen of Pazzi put assistance in choir before all the private devotions that pious persons can make; and when one of her nuns asked to be dispensed from choir in order to give herself up to mental prayer, she replied: "No, my daughter, I should certainly deceive you in giving you such a permission, for it would be making you believe that this private devotion would honour God more and render you more pleasing to the Divine Majesty, while in comparison with this public office which you sing with your sisters, private prayer is but a small thing."[3] St. Alphonsus Liguori relates, while making this opinion his own, the saying of a wise religious: "If time is lacking to us, it is much better to shorten mental prayer, and give more time to the Divine Office that we, may be enabled to recite it with the devotion due to it."[4]

Such is the opinion of the saints, such is the language of faith. There is no work that comes anywhere near the Divine Office. All other works are *opera hominum*. This is truly "the Work of God" pre-eminently, because it is a work of praise that comes from God through the Word Incarnate and is offered by the Church, in Christ's Name.

IV

Another reason of the transcendency of the Divine Praise is that it directly tends to procure God's glory.

Doubtless, as we have said, God finds His essential glory in Himself independently of any creature: *Deus meus es tu, bonorum meorum non eges*.[5] But from the moment that there are creatures, "it is truly meet and just" that they should praise God, magnify His name and give thanks to Him; this is in the right order of things, it is justice; it is from this

1 Hebr. iv, 16.

2 Evidently supposing that the degree of love be the same, and setting apart the Sacraments.

3 *Life* by P. Cepari, S.J.

4 *L'Office meprisé; Œuvres complètes.* Paris, 1836, t. XI, p. 39.

5 "Thou art my God, for Thou hast no need of my goods," Ps. xv, 2.

principle that the virtue of religion is born: *Vere dignum et justum est, aequum et salutare, nos tibi semper et ubique gratias agere.*[1]

Now, in creation, there are many beings who do not know God. They assuredly praise Him after their manner by the simple fact of their obedience to the laws that He ordained for them on their coming forth from nothingness: *Caeli enarrant gloriam Dei et opera manuum ejus annuntiat firmamentum.*[2] However the heavens do not know their own canticle, any more than they know their Creator. Whence is the song of inanimate creation to take life? Upon our own lips, the lips of humanity. Hear what Bossuet so admirably says; the text is rather long but it renders the idea very clearly. "The inanimate creature cannot see, it is seen; it cannot love, it urges us to do so; and this God Whom it knows not, it does not allow us to ignore. Thus imperfectly and in its own manner it glorifies the Heavenly Father. But in order that it may consummate its adoration, man must be its mediator. He must lend a voice, an understanding, and a heart burning with love, to all visible nature that it may love, in man and through him, the invisible beauty of the Creator. This is why he is placed in the midst of the world, himself the world in brief... a great world in the little world, because although the world contains him, he has a mind and a heart greater than the world; in order that contemplating the whole universe and gathering it up in himself, he may offer, sanctify, and consecrate it to the Living God."[3]

We acquit ourselves of this sublime rôle each day at the Divine Office. The Church wills that every creature should take life upon the lips of the priest or religious, so that every creature may praise its Lord: *Benedicite omnia opera Domini Domino, laudate et superexaltate eum in saecula.*[4]

Upon our lips as in the Word, *in ipso vita erat*, all these creatures become animate that they may sing the Creator's perfections. "Come," we say to all these creatures, "come; you know not God, but you may

---

1 "It is truly right and just, our duty and our salvation, always and everywhere to give Thee thanks," Preface of the Mass.

2 "The heavens shew forth the glory of God, and the firmament declareth the work of His hands," Ps. xviii, 2.

3 *Sermon for the Feast of the Annunciation*, 1662, 3rd point. The great orator has taken up this idea again and developed it in his Sermon on the worship due to God, April 2nd, 1666.

4 Canticle for Sunday Lauds; Dan. iii, 57.

know Him through the medium of my understanding, and sing to Him through my lips. Come, sun, moon, stars that He has sown in the firmament; come, cold and light, mountains and valleys, seas and rivers, plants and flowers, come and magnify Him Who created you. O my God I love Thee so much that I would have the whole earth adore and praise Thee": *Omnis terra adoret Te et psallat Tibi!*[1] Through our lips, all the praise of creation rises up to God.

It rises up to Him because Christ, the Divine Word, makes His own this praise which we, guided by the Church, offer to Him. Man is the mediator of creation; but, says Bossuet again,[2] man himself needs a mediator and this Mediator is Christ the Word Incarnate. We lend our lips to Christ, so that, through Him, our praise may be accepted in the Bosom of the Father: *Per ipsum et cum ipso et in ipso est tibi Deo Patri omnipotenti in unitate Spiritus Sancti,* OMNIS *honor et gloria.*[3] All things are ours, and we are Christ's, and Christ is His Father's: *Omnia vestra sunt, vos autem Christi, Christus autem Dei.*[4] "Rejoice, O human nature, thou lendest thy heart to the visible world that it may love its Almighty Creator, and Jesus Christ lends thee His own Heart wherewith thou mayest worthily love the One Who can only be worthily loved by another Himself."[5]

Through the Divine Praise, we associate creation and ourselves, as intimately as possible, with the eternal praise that the Word gives to His Father. This participation in the eternal, thrice-holy canticle is realised above all in the doxology of the *Gloria*, repeated at the end of each psalm, and again in many other parts of the Office. As we bow down to give "glory to the Father, and to the Son, and to the Holy Ghost" we unite ourselves to that ineffable glory that the Holy Trinity finds in Itself from all eternity: *Sicut erat in principio et nunc et semper et in saecula saeculorum*. It is like the echo of the infinite mutual complacency of the Divine Persons in the plenitude and bliss of their adorable fellowship.

What work equals this in greatness? What work is more pleasing to God? None; let us be deeply convinced of this. The *Opus Dei* is what is

1 Ps. lxv, 4.
2 Continuation of *Sermon for the Feast of the Annunciation,* 1662.
3 Canon of the Mass. 4 I Cor. iii, 22–23.
5 Bossuet, *Sermon for the Feast of the Annunciation,* 1662.

most precious in the inheritance of our Order: *Funes ceciderunt mihi in praeclaris, etenim hereditas mea praeclara est mihi.*[1] There are no other hours when we can do more for God's glory than those we spend in choir, in union with the Divine Word praising His Father; *pernoctans in oratione Dei.*[2] There is no work more pleasing to the Father than that whereby we join, in order to glorify Him, in the canticle sung *in sinu Patris* by "the Son of His love."[3] There is no work that better pleases the Son than this which we borrow from Him and that is like the extension of His very essence as the Word, the splendour of infinite glory. Neither is there any work that glorifies the Spirit more: for by the formulas that He has Himself inspired, we express our love under its most delicate forms, admiration continually renewed, and unending complacency. *Gloria Patri et Filio et Spiritui Sancto.*

When this work is performed with all the faith, all the heart-felt confidence and all the love whereof our soul is capable, it surpasses every other work, and therefore our great Patriarch "filled with the spirit of all the just,"[4] wishes nothing to rank before this work: *Nihil Operi Dei praeponatur;*[5] without being exclusive, it comes before everything with us. Although we are not Canons Regular, we cannot put this work in the second place, because it concerns God directly and we came to the monastery especially to seek God. Ardent love of the Divine Praise is one of the most indubitable signs that we "are truly seeking God": *Si revera Deum quaerit... si sollicitus est ad opus Dei.*[6]

V

What further renders the Divine Praise extremely pleasing to God is that it constitutes a homage of those virtues of faith, hope and love which are the specific virtues of our state as children of God.

Everything here—let us repeat it—is to be judged from the point of view of faith. To gather together several hours day by day to praise God is a homage of our faith; we thereby confess and proclaim that this

1 "The lines are fallen unto me in goodly places: for my inheritance is goodly to me," Ps. xv, 6.

2 Luc. vi, 12. 3 Col. i, 13. 4 St. Gregory. *Dialogues.* Lib. ii, ch. 8.

5 Rule, ch. xliii. 6 Ibid. ch. lviii.

Unseen God is alone worthy of adoration and praise. The acts of reverence, thanksgiving and complacency that we accomplish in the course of this work consecrated solely to extolling God, are, above all, acts of faith. Faith alone gives its meaning to the Divine Office. Those whose faith is null, pity men who pass a part of their life in chanting God's praises; they do not comprehend how people can, at certain hours, occupy themselves solely with the Infinite Being: *Ut quid perditio haec.*[1] Where faith is weak, the Divine Office is undervalued and other works are preferred before it. Souls which, like that of our Blessed Patriarch, are bathed in "the deifying light"[2] of faith, give the first place to Divine Praise; they do so at least in their estimation, even if, in consequence of their state in life, they cannot devote themselves to it. Divine Praise becomes uninterrupted when the eternal light of vision succeeds the obscure light of faith: *Sine fine laudant.*

In the second place, our praise is a homage of hope. During the divine psalmody we rest upon the infinite merits of Christ Jesus. We hope for everything from the satisfactions of our Divine High Priest. In fact no prayer of the Office terminates without explicitly seeking its support in Our Lord: *Per Dominum nostrum Jesum Christum.* We make our claim through this All-Powerful Mediator Who "lives and reigns for ever with the Father," and pleads with Him unceasingly in order to render Him propitious to us: *Semper vivens ad interpellandum pro nobis.*[3]

In leaving everything in order to hasten to the choir, it is like saying to God: "There is nothing of which I am more certain than of Thy goodness; I come to praise and bless Thee, leaving in Thy hands the care of all the rest. I have nothing more at heart than to praise Thee, being persuaded that if I leave every other work for this, Thou wilt know how to take better care than I could do of my dearest interests; I want only to think of Thee, knowing that Thou wilt think of me." To go to the choir every day, and several times a day, in this disposition of soul; to put in practice the "one thing necessary," *Unum est necessarium,*[4] to lay aside all our cares, all that regards our personal work, so as to occupy

---

1 Matth. xxvi, 8. 2 Prologue of the Rule. 3 Hebr. vii, 25.
4 Luc. x, 42.

ourselves during several hours with Him alone, what an evident proof of our absolute confidence in Him!

Finally, our praise contains above all a homage of love. In it every form of love finds expression, especially in the Psalms which form the most considerable element of the Divine Office. Admiration, complacency, delight, the love of benevolence, contrite love, grateful love, all these affections find a place in an almost uninterrupted manner. Love confesses, admires, exalts the Divine perfections. Complacency whereby we rejoice in the joy and beatitude of the person beloved is one of the purest and most perfect forms of love. When we truly love, we find no sweeter joy than in praising and glorifying. St. Francis of Assisi composing his "Canticle," St. Teresa writing her "Exclamations," such is the soul overflowing with love, and seeking to express it. Such is also the love that transported the Psalmist. With the sacred writer, the soul passes in review all the Divine perfections in order to exalt them: *Exaltare Domine, in virtute tua, cantabimus et psallemus virtutes tuas...*[1] *Narrabo omnia mirabilia tua.*[2] "Exalt ye the Lord our God, and adore His footstool, for it is holy": *Exaltate Dominum Deum nostrum... quoniam Sanctus Dominus Deus noster.*[3] "Justice shall walk before Him";[4] "the searcher of hearts and reins is God."[5] "The mercies of the Lord I will sing for ever."[6] "O Lord God of hosts, who is like to Thee? Thou art mighty O Lord, and Thy truth is round about Thee."[7] "How great are Thy works, O Lord? Thou hast made all things in wisdom": *Quam magnificata sunt opera tua, Domine, omnia in sapientia fecisti.*[8] Then the soul turns to God to express its grateful love: "I will sing to the Lord Who giveth me good things": *Cantabo Domino qui bona tribuit mihi.*[9] "Bless the Lord, O my soul: and let all that is within me bless His holy name. Bless the Lord, O my soul, and never forget all He hath done for thee. Who forgiveth all thy iniquities; Who healeth all thy diseases. Who redeemeth thy life from destruction: Who crowneth thee with mercy and compassion, Who satisfieth thy desire with good things." Then feeling incapable of

1 "Be thou exalted, O Lord, in thy own strength: we will sing and praise thy power," Ps. xx, 14.
2 "I will relate all thy wonders," Ibid. ix, 2.
3 Ibid. mcviii, 5, 9.
4 Ibid. lxxxiv, 14.
5 Ibid. vii, 10.
6 Ibid. lxxxviii, 1.
7 Ibid. 9.
8 Ibid. ciii, 24.
9 Ibid. xii, 6.

glorifying God as He should be glorified, the soul invites the Angels to unite in praising Him: *Benedicite Domino omnes Angeli ejus, benedicite omnes virtutes ejus.*[1] At other times, together with the sacred singer, the soul convokes peoples and nations to join in this praise: *Regna terrae cantate Deo,*[2] for, "from the rising of the sun until the going down of the same, the name of the Lord is worthy of praise,[3] admirable... in the whole earth."[4] Yet again, the soul pours out its joy and gladness before God in being admitted to praise Him: *Exsultabunt labia mea cum cantavero tibi...*[5] *et labiis exsultationis laudabit os meum.*[6] This joy is so deep and overflowing that the soul asks God for power to praise Him unceasingly: *Repleatur os meum laude ut cantem gloriam tuam...*[7] *Psallam Deo meo quamdiu fuero.*[8]

Where could love find accents as burning and ever new as these? At every instant in the psalms this love is manifested and diffused. A truly extraordinary condescension of Divine Goodness has more than once shown to what an extent these praises are agreeable to God. We see Our Lord deigning with infinite kindness to teach ignorant souls the Latin tongue, so that having this knowledge they may be able to penetrate into the meaning of the sacred texts.

A like trait is met with in the life of a certain Benedictine nun, the Blessed Bonomo. "Often, during her ecstasies," says a biographer, "she was heard reciting the Divine Office; but a curious thing was that she pronounced the verses alternatively, as if the inhabitants of Heaven were repeating the psalms with her; she recited the whole without omitting a single syllable, whatever was the Office of the day."[9]

---

1 Ibid. cii, 1–5, 20–21.
2 Ibid. lxvii, 33.
3 Ibid. cxii, 3.
4 Ibid. viii, 1.
5 "My lips shall greatly rejoice, when I shall sing to thee," Ibid. lxx, 23.
6 "My mouth shall praise thee with joyful lips," Ibid. lxii, 6.
7 "Let my mouth be filled with praise, that I may sing thy glory," Ibid. lxx, 8.
8 Ibid. cxliv, 2.
9 Dom du Bourg. *Une extatique du XVIIe siècle, la Bse Bonomo, moniale bénédictine,* p. 11 and 52. We likewise see St. Catherine of Siena asking Our Lord to teach her to read in order to be able to chant the Psalms and praises of God during the Canonical Hours. Often, too, Our Lord walked up and down with her in her cell and recited the Office with the Saint. It was as two religious might have done. *Life,* Bl. Raymund of Capua.

Then, do not let us forget that in the Divine Office the soul exalts these perfections as is befitting, in a manner truly worthy of God, a manner which He has Himself ordained. Left to ourselves, we could not render due homage to each Divine attribute: God alone can tell us how we can and ought to praise Him; God alone knows how worthy He is of being magnified, blessed, glorified; and it is the Holy Spirit, the Spirit of Love, Who places upon our lips the very formulas we are to use in singing to God. These praises, in their origin, are not of earth, they come to us from Heaven, from the innermost depths of the Godhead and of Love. And when we appropriate them to ourselves with faith, above all when we recite or sing them in union with the Divine Word, our canticle becomes infinitely pleasing to God, because it is presented to Him by the Word in person.

St. Gertrude had the revelation of this truth in one of her visions. As Vespers were being intoned on the Feast of the Holy Trinity, Christ, holding His Heart in His hands like a melodious lyre, presented it to the glorious Trinity. Upon this lyre the fervour of souls and all the words of the sacred canticles resounded before the Lord in a hymn of heavenly delight.[1]

VI

One circumstance often occurs in our monastic life to enhance further this homage of love: it is when we have to offer it to the Lord in suffering.

Suffering gives to love a special splendour and a singular value; to love God in suffering is truly the height of self-oblation; our Divine Saviour loved His Father with immense love at each instant of His life, but this love shone out in an incomparable way during His Passion, when Christ endured His unutterable sufferings for love of His Father: *Ut cognoscat mundus quia diligo Patrem.*[2]

The Divine Office can become, and even frequently does become for certain souls, a veritable sacrifice. In this case the expression *Sacrificium*

1 *The Herald of Divine Love,* Bk. iv, ch. 41. St. Gertrude often expresses this idea. See Ibid. Bk. ii, ch. 23; Bk. iii, ch. 25; Bk. iv, ch. 48 and 51; cf. Dolan. *St. Gertrude the Great,* ch. 2. *The Divine Office.*

2 Joan. xiv, 31.

laudis[1] truly takes on a special fulness of meaning. This can happen in various ways; to begin with we must not spare ourselves; we must give all the energy we have. To use our voice unsparingly, to submit to the manifold and varied details of the ceremonial, willingly to accept and follow the indications of the cantor, even when our opinion differs from his on such and such a point of musical interpretation: all this requires continual attention. We must keep our imagination from wandering, and this requires generosity. Frequently renewed efforts are needed to overcome our natural apathy or levity; these are so many sacrifices pleasing to God.

Next come the sufferings that the common life necessarily entails. Certainly common life is a stimulus; the fact of being together in our stalls excites fervour, but it allows also of a number of inevitable small sacrifices, often repeated: *Sumus homines fragiles... qui faciunt invicem angustias.*[2] The possibility of tiny annoyances jarring upon us is inherent to our poor human nature; this is true even of prayer in common. A ceremony awkwardly performed, false movements of the choir, a melody badly rendered, discord in the rhythm with those around us, all this can set our nerves on edge, especially when, in addition, fatigue or an ailing state of health weighs upon the body and superexcites the sensibility. When we have to hymn God's glory under these conditions there is room for a real sacrifice, a veritable immolation. In Heaven, when we possess God, we shall praise Him in the eternal harmony of overflowing gladness; here below, in the valley of tears, it may happen that we have to praise Him in suffering; but our sufferings add a new degree of love to our praise, and prove the sincerity of our seeking after God.[3] Jesus sang the praises of His Father not only upon Thabor, but on the Cross. St. Augustine says explicitly[4] that upon Golgotha Our Lord recited the

---

1 "The sacrifice of praise," Ps. xlix, 23.

2 "We are weak men... who make difficulties for each other," St. Augustine. Sermo lxix, ch. 1. P. L. 38, 440.

3 *Laudemus et modo Dominum, quantum possumus, mixtis gemitibus; quia laudando eum desideramus eum, et nondum tenemus: cum tenuerimus, subtrahetur omnis gemitus et remanebit sola et pura et aeterna laudatio* (And now let us praise the Lord, as much as we can, with groans mingled; for in praising Him we desire Him while we do not have Him: when we will have Him, every groan will be taken away and only pure, eternal praise will remain). St. Augustine, *Enarr. in Psalm.* lxxxvi, ch. 9. P. L. 37, 1109.

4 St. Augustine. *Enarr. in Psalm* lxxxc, ch. 1.

Psalm that begins with these words: *Deus, Deus meus respice in me: quare me dereliquisti.*[1] This striking Messianic psalm expressed not only the circumstances of the Passion, but also the affections of Our Blessed Saviour's soul. In the darkness of Calvary, in the midst of indescribable tortures, Christ Jesus recited "the Office," and, at that moment, because He was suffering, he gave, much more than when on Thabor, infinite glory to His Father.

We too, following His example, must praise God, not only when the Holy Spirit replenishes us with His consolations, but likewise when we suffer. Loving souls follow Jesus everywhere, as well and even more willingly to Golgotha as to the Mount of the Transfiguration. Who remained at the foot of the Cross with Jesus? His Virgin-Mother who loved Him with a love into which not the least self-seeking entered; Magdalen whom Jesus had forgiven much because she loved much; St. John who possessed the secrets of the Divine Heart. These three stayed there near to Jesus; they remained "in their stalls" when the soul of Christ, the supreme High Priest, sang its sorrowful canticle for the world's salvation. The other Apostles, Peter himself, who had so loudly protested his love, would willingly have remained on Thabor, where it was good to be: *Bonum est nos hic esse: faciamus hic tria tabernacula*,[2] but not at the foot of the Cross.

Christ Jesus Who loves us, Who has chosen us in preference to so many others to associate us in His work of praise, allows us sometimes to feel, by the sufferings that prayer in common brings with it, by the desolations and aridities to which it may subject us, what it is to chant the Office with Him on Calvary. If really you seek God solely, that is to say His Holy Will, and not His consolations, prove it by continuing even then, and even especially at such moments, to sing *ex toto corde vestro;*[3] do not run away, stay with Christ as long as He will have it so, near the Cross. The Cross is raised, as a reminder, upon the altar that the choir surrounds. Let us then repeat with the Psalmist: *Benedicam Dominum in omni tempore, semper laus ejus in ore meo.*[4] "I will bless the Lord at all times; His praise shall be always in my mouth." Whether He fills my soul with the sweetness of His Spirit of Love, or leaves it like a

---

1 "O God my God, look upon me: why hast Thou forsaken me?" Ps. xxi, 2.

2 Matth. xvii, 4.

3 "With all Thy heart," Prov. iii, 5.

4 Ps. xxxiii, 2.

desert land where there is no water,[1] I will ever praise Him with all the energy of my heart, because He is my God, my Lord and my King, and is worthy of all praise: *Exaltabo te, Deus meus Rex et benedicam nomini tuo,*[2] *confitebor tibi Domine Deus meus in toto corde meo, et glorificabo nomen tuum in aeternum.*[3]

Recited in these dispositions, the Divine Office becomes the *sacrificium laudis* pre-eminently, the most agreeable sacrifice to God, because, united to Christ's Sacrifice, it constitutes the most perfect homage that the creature can offer Him: *Sacrificium laudis honorificabit me.* Moreover, God not allowing Himself to be out-done in generosity, the same sacrifice of praise becomes for the one who accomplishes it the way of salvation and beatitude: *Et illic iter quo ostendam illi salutare Dei.*[4]

1 Ps. lxii, 3.

2 "I will extol Thee, O God my King; and I will bless Thy Name," Ibid. cxliv, 1.

3 "I will praise Thee, O Lord my God: with my whole heart, and I will glorify Thy Name for ever," Ibid. lxxxv, 12.

4 "And there is the way by which I will shew him the salvation of God," Ibid. xlix, 23.

THE OPUS DEI, MEANS OF UNION WITH GOD

SUMMARY.—Divine praise, the *Opus Dei,* is likewise a means of union with God and of sanctification.—I. It furnishes excellent forms of prayer and impetration.—II. It provides opportunities of practising the virtues well.—III. It constitutes the best manner of being made one with Christ. Dispositions in which the Divine Office ought to be accomplished: immediate preparation; intentions to be formulated.—V. Attitude of the soul during the Divine Office: to pray worthily, with attention, and devotion.—VI. Final exhortation.

IF the *Opus Dei* were presented exclusively as a homage rendered to the Divine perfections in union with Christ Jesus, it would already, and on this ground, eminently merit all our fervour. In the last conference we tried to show what a lofty work the Divine praise constitutes; it is the *Opus Dei* by excellence, the voice of the Church addressing herself officially to the Father, being entitled, as Christ's Bride, to offer Him her adorations; it is the homage of a soul wherein faith is active, hope assured and love ardent. It is for these reasons that liturgical prayer is so pleasing to God: *Laudabo nomen Dei cum cantico, et placebit Deo super vitulum novellum.*[1]

Worship is also a conversation, an exchange; man, being full of needs, asks at the same time that he adores; and God gives more than He receives. This is why the *Opus Dei* is an abundant source of precious graces for the soul. After having said in the Psalm, that the sacrifice of praise

1 "I will praise the Name of God with a canticle... And it shall please God better than a young calf," Ps. lxviii, 31–32.

is pleasing to Him, God, Who is magnificence itself and ever bestows the hundredfold, adds that this sacrifice becomes for him who offers it, a way of salvation: *Et illic iter quo ostendam illi salutare Dei*. It is impossible indeed for a soul to come near to God, to come before Him in the name of His Son Jesus, and, finding strength in the infinite merits of this supreme High Priest, to offer unceasing homage to God, without the Father delighting in this soul and pouring special graces upon it. When He sees in us "the Son of His love,"[1]—and He sees Him during the Divine Office celebrated in the aforesaid dispositions—the Father from Whom comes down "every perfect gift,"[2] cannot but enrich us with heavenly favours. In one of her collects, Christ's Bride herself logically links together these two aspects of the Divine Office: "Grant, O Lord, to the people consecrated to Thee to find the *source of increase* in the affections of pious devotion, that, being taught by the sacred rites, they may be *filled with favours so much the more precious*, according as they become more pleasing to Thy Divine Majesty."[3] God, being moreover the first Author of our sanctification, the daily and repeated contact that we have with Him in the Divine Praise veritably constitutes for us an inexhaustible principle of union and holiness.

This principle is true for every soul, even for those of simple Christians; the faithful who, although in a more restricted manner, take part in Divine worship with faith and devotion, imbibe the Christian spirit as from its fount. This is what Pius X, of holy memory, has so explicitly said: "The active participation of the faithful in the sacred mysteries and in the public and solemn prayer of the Church is the first and indispensable source whence is drawn the true Christian spirit."[4]

But is it not manifest that this truth is to be applied still more appropriately to those who, like us, have the happiness of the monastic vocation? Besides the means of sanctification that are common to all the members of Christ's Mystical Body, such as the Sacraments, there exists, so to speak, in each Order, a special means corresponding to its institution and to which souls belonging to this Order ought preferably

1 Col. i, 13. 2 Jac. i, 17.

3 *Proficiat, quaesumus, Domine, plebs tibi dicata piae devotionis affectu: ut sacris actionibus erudite, QUANTO MAJESTATI TUAE FIT GRATIOR, TANTO DONIS POTIORIBUS AUGEATUR* (Saturday in Passion Week).

4 *Motu proprio* of Nov. 22nd, 1903.

to be attached, so as to arrive at perfection. Upon Christian predestination, God has engrafted for us the Benedictine predestination; we must not think indeed that God has left our monastic vocation to chance; every religious vocation, constituting a signal grace, is the fruit of the infinite and privileged love which Christ Jesus bears to a soul: *Intuitus eum dilexit eum*;[1] and it is only by an act of His sovereign and Divine will that the Word gives us this immense grace. We definitely responded to this call on the day of our profession; but do not let us lose sight of the fact that we have made profession *secundum Regulam S.P.N. Benedicti*.[2] The particular character like the singular splendour of the holiness that God expects of us, should be derived from the monastic code of our great Patriarch. It is not in following the Rule of St. Augustine or the institutions of the Carthusians, however great and lofty they be, that we shall arrive at the perfection that Christ demands of us. To a particular vocation, a special perfection, or rather a special form of holiness, ought to respond.

Now our Holy Father ordains that among all the positive[3] works of piety that his monks are to perform, none is to take precedence of the Divine Office: *Nihil Operi Dei praeponatur*.[4] Doubtless, it is right to repeat that this work is not in our case exclusive of the others; but being the one which, in the Rule of St. Benedict, is given the first place, it becomes by that fact, for us monks, a very sure and authentic means of attaining that form of perfection which God willed for us when He called us to the cloister. Thus if it is averred that we are pleasing to God in the measure that we give ourselves up to this work, it will not be less truly averred that the Divine Praise constitutes one of the most infallible means of realising in ourselves the eternal and special idea that God has of our perfection.

Let us then explain how the Divine Office is a means of union with God and of sanctification; it will next remain for us to point out the requisite conditions in order that this means may produce all its fruits in our souls.

1 "And Jesus looking on him, loved him," Marc. x, 21.

2 Ceremonial of Monastic Profession.

3 "Positive" in opposition to works of a rather "negative" character, such as the exercise of the virtues of poverty, humility, etc., which serve above all to remove obstacles.

4 Rule, ch. xliii.

I

One of the most important truths of the spiritual life is incontestably the necessity of prayer for obtaining the Divine help: "Ask," said Our Lord, "and it shall be given you; seek, and you shall find: knock, and it shall be opened to you."[1] Our needs are immense, and without Christ's grace we can do nothing. How are we to obtain Christ's help? By prayer: *Petite et accipietis;*[2] *omnis enim qui petit, accipit.*[3] Now, the Divine Office contains wonderful supplications as pressing as they are varied. Undoubtedly, as we have seen, it is first and before all a Divine Praise, the cry of the soul that, full of faith and love, admires and magnifies God's perfections: *Magnus Dominus et laudabilis nimis.*[4] We do not come to the choir primarily to beg; no; we come to praise God, to glorify Him, to think upon His glory, to lend material creation our lips with which to sing, and our heart with which to love God: The first and direct end of the Divine Office is the glory of the Creator: *Domine, Dominus noster, quam admirabile est nomen tuum in universa terra!*[5] The dominant idea of the *Opus Dei* is drawn from these words of the Psalmist, as it is summed up in the ever recurring doxology of the *Gloria*.

But the Divine Office contains, however, numberless forms of prayer and supplication. The psalms, for example, express not only admiration, joy, exultation of soul in presence of God's admirable perfections; all the needs of the soul are also found therein set forth as it were in God's sight. We can, with the Psalmist, beseech forgiveness of our sins: "Have mercy on me, O God, according to Thy great mercy. And according to the multitude of Thy tender mercies blot out my iniquity. Wash me yet more from my iniquity, and cleanse me from my sin... Turn away Thy face from my sins, and blot out all my iniquities... Cast me not away from Thy face; and take not Thy Holy Spirit from me.[6] The sins of my youth and my ignorances do not remember: *Delicta juventutis meae et ignorantias meas ne memineris;*[7] *ab occultis meis munda me, et ab alienis parce servo tuo.*[8] Out of the depths I have cried to Thee, O Lord... if Thou, O Lord, wilt mark iniquities, Lord who shall stand? Hope, therefore, O my soul, hope in Thy Lord, for His Redemption is abundant, and He

1 Matth. vii, 7. 2 Joan. xvi, 24. 3 Luc. xi, 10. 4 Ps. xlvii, 2.
5 "O Lord our Lord, how admirable is Thy Name in the whole earth," Ps. viii, 2.
6 Ibid. l, 3–4, 11, 13. 7 Ibid. xxiv, 7. 8 Ibid. xviii, 13–14.

shall redeem thee from all thy iniquities: *Et copiosa apud eum redemptio.*[1] Thou shalt wash me, and I shall be made whiter than snow. To my hearing Thou shalt give joy and gladness: and the bones that have been humbled shall rejoice... Restore unto me the joy of Thy salvation, and strengthen me with a perfect spirit... O Lord, Thou wilt open my lips: and my mouth shall declare Thy praise."[2]

When the soul is in trouble, in distress, when beset by temptation, when sadness overpowers it, when discouragement takes possession of it, it has but to open the inspired Book: "O God come to my assistance; O Lord, make haste to help me.[3] Why, O Lord, are they multiplied that afflict me? many are they who rise up against me. Many say to my soul: There is no salvation for him in his God. But Thou, O Lord, art my protector, my glory, and the lifter up of my head... Arise, O Lord, save me."[4] "Why art thou sad, O my soul? and why dost thou disquiet me? Hope in God, for I will still give praise to Him: the salvation of my countenance, and my God.[5] And let all them be glad that hope in Thee... O Lord, Thou hast crowned us, as with a shield of Thy good will": *Et laetentur omnes qui sperant in te... Scuto bonae voluntatis tuae coronasti nos.*[6] "In the Lord I put my trust, how then do you say to my soul: Get thee away from hence to the mountain?[7] Hear, O Lord, the voice of my supplication, when I pray to Thee; when I lift up my hands to Thy holy temple... Save, O Lord, Thy people, and bless Thy inheritance: and rule them and exalt them for ever."[8]

Does the soul need light? strength? courage? Words wherewith to invoke God flow endlessly to our lips: "My soul is as earth without water unto Thee.[9] Send forth Thy light and Thy truth, they have conducted me, and brought me unto Thy holy hill, and into Thy tabernacles. And I will go to the altar of God: to God Who giveth joy to my youth. To Thee, O God my God I will give praise upon the harp": *Confitebor tibi in cithara Deus, Deus meus.*[10]

Then, above all, the holy longings of the soul to attain one day to God rise ardently from the sacred poesy, the expression of its thirst for the

---

1 Ibid. cxxix, 1, 3, 5–8.
2 Ibid. l, 9–10, 14, 17.
3 Ibid. lxix, 2.
4 Ibid. iii, 2–4, 7.
5 Ibid. xlii, 5.
6 Ps. v, 12–13.
7 Ibid. x, 2.
8 Ibid. xxvii, 2, 9.
9 Ibid. cxlii, 6.
10 Ibid. xlii, 3–4.

divine meeting: "For what have I in Heaven? and besides Thee what do I desire upon earth?... Thou art the God of my heart, and the God that is my portion for ever": *Quid mihi est in caelo et, a te, quid volui super terram?...*[1] "As the hart panteth after the fountains of water; so my soul panteth after Thee... when shall I come and appear before the face of God?[2] I shall be satisfied when Thy glory shall appear": *Satiabor cum apparuerit gloria tua!*[3] Thus, the soul's most intense desires, its deepest aspirations, its most pressing and extensive needs find wonderful forms of expression furnished by the Holy Spirit. And each soul can appropriate to itself these forms as if they had been made for itself alone.

To the inspired texts are to be added the "Collects," the prayers composed by the Church herself, where are daily gathered up the supplications that the Bride of Jesus offers in her children's name, in union with her Divine Spouse. They are ordinarily very concise, but contain, in their brevity, the true pith of doctrine. As you know their structure is almost always the same: the Church addresses her homage to the power and goodness of the Eternal Father, then a petition in correlation with the Feast of the day, the whole under a condensed, but often profound form; finally, the invoking of the infinite merits of Christ Jesus, the Beloved Son, equal to His Father, Who lives and reigns with Him and the Spirit, in the heavens: *Per Dominum nostrum Jesum Christum Filium tuum, qui tecum vivit et regnat...*

How should a like prayer fail to be powerful with God? How could God refuse His grace to whomsoever beseeches Him according to the words He Himself has inspired?[4] God loves all that comes from Himself or from His Son, and so this prayer which we address to Him in the name of His Son is most pleasing to Him, and efficacious for us: *Pater ego sciebam quia semper me audis.*[5]

On this head, the Divine Office possesses great power of sanctification. I am certain that a monk who gives himself up to it with de-

1 Ibid. xlxii, 25–26. 2 Ibid. xli, 2–3. 3 Ibid. xvi, 15.

4 We evidently do not give the word "inspired" the same sense when it concerns the elements, of diverse origin, of the Divine Office.

5 "Father... I knew that Thou hearest me always," Joan. xi, 42.

votion cannot fail to obtain from it an abundance of divine help for every circumstance of his life. This is so much the more true in that the devout recitation of the Office familiarises us with these holy forms of prayer: spontaneously then, in the course of the day, these arise again from his soul under the form of "ejaculatory" prayers, short but ardent aspirations, whereby the soul is lifted up to God to remain united to Him. St. Catherine of Siena had a special devotion to the *Deus, in adjutorium meum intende*;[1] she often repeated it during the day.[2] So many verses of the Psalms, after having served us in choir can thus become, outside the Divine Office, bonds of union between God and ourselves, uprisings from the heart to beseech His help or to tell Him that it is our will never to turn away from Him: "It is good for me to adhere to my God, to put my hope in the Lord God.[3] Preserve me, O Lord, for I have put my trust in Thee. I have said to the Lord, Thou art my God.[4] When my strength shall fail, do not Thou forsake me.[5] My soul hath coveted too long for Thy justifications, at all times... I have stuck to Thy testimonies, O Lord: put me not to shame."[6]

Each soul can thus choose from among so many formulas those which most aptly express its innermost aspirations, those which best help it to remain united to Our Lord. Often it has no need to seek them. When the Divine Office is recited with fervour, it is the Holy Spirit Who throws His Divine light upon some text of the Psalms or of the Liturgy; this text then particularly strikes the soul, and by this vivid, penetrating and effectual action of the Spirit of Jesus, it hereafter becomes a principle of light and joy, and like a wellspring of living water where the soul may constantly allay its thirst, renew its strength, and find the secret of patience and inward gladness: *Psalterium meum, gaudium meum*.[7]

II

It is not only in itself and directly that the Divine Office is a means of sanctification; it also gives us the occasion of practising many virtues

1 "O God, come to my assistance," Ps. lxx, 1.
2 *Life*, by Drane, 1st Part, ch. 5.
3 Ps. lxxii, 28.
4 Ps. xv, 1–2.
5 Ps. lxx, 9.
6 Ps. cxviii, 20, 31.
7 "My psalter, my joy," St. Augustine, *Enarrat. in Psalm.* 137, n. 3, P. L. 37, col. 1775.

several times a day. Now this practice, according to the Council of Trent,[1] is a source of union with God and of progress in perfection.

When a soul is in God's friendship, each act of virtue it makes increases grace in it, and this is above all true of charity which is the queen of every virtue. Now, the Divine Office recited with fervour, is a continual exercise of the most varied virtues. We saw, in the last conference, the frequency with which acts of faith, hope, and charity occur in the course of the Divine Office; charity especially shines out in it; it finds the purest and most perfect expression in the Opus Dei, namely, complacency in God; and this complacency is manifested at almost each moment in accents of admiration and joy.[2] When, for example, we have recited Matins and Lauds with devotion, we have made numerous acts of perfect love.

To the theological virtues, which are the specific virtues of our state of children of God, must be joined the virtue of religion. Religion has no purer manifestation than the Divine Office gravitating around the Eucharistic Sacrifice which is its crown. The Divine Praise encompassing the altar, where the holy oblation is offered, is the purest expression of the virtue of religion; it is also the most pleasing to God, because this expression is determined by the Holy Spirit and by the Church, Christ's Bride; worship finds its plenitude in the Divine Office.[3]

It is in the Divine Office too that we learn reverence towards God; the Liturgy is the best school of respect: all within it is regulated by the Church herself in view of magnifying God's Sovereign Majesty. When the soul performs all the ceremonies, even the smallest, carefully and lovingly, it is gradually formed to that inward reverence which is, as we have said, the very root of humility. It is impossible for a monk to be devoutly assiduous at the "Work of God" without gaining in a short

1 Sess. vi, ch. 10–11.

2 "It is a great mistake to imagine that a sacrifice is only valuable and agreeable to God if it is sad and mortifying to nature. The Holy Bible gives testimony that God receives flowers and fruits as well as blood, and joy as well as tears. There are certainly many tears in the sacrifice of praise which is named the Psalter, but how joy overflows in it and how often one is made aware of a jubilant and ravished soul!" Mgr. Gay, *Entretiens sur les mystères du Rosaire,* I. pp. 80–81.

3 Cf. Lottin, *L'âme du culte, la vertu de religion.*

time a great knowledge of the divine perfections, and without that respect and reverence springing up in his soul from this contemplation.

We have likewise seen how the Divine Office is moreover a school where, on account of the common life, may be exercised the virtue of patience and self-forgetfulness.

Thus the virtues most necessary to our state as children of God, faith and confidence, humility, love, and religion, find each day not only the means of being exercised, but of being maintained, and strengthened; the Divine Office hence becomes an abundant source of holiness.

III

The sanctifying power of the Divine Office however goes further than this. Not content with being the best form of impetration for our spiritual necessities and giving us the opportunity of daily practising lofty virtues, this praise constitutes for us the best way of being made one with Christ.[1] We must never forget this capital truth of the spiritual life: all is summed up, for the monk as for the simple Christian, in being united, in faith and love to Christ Jesus in order to imitate Him. Christ being the very "form"[2] of our predestination, is at the same time the ideal of all holiness for us. He is the centre of monasticism as of Christianity: to contemplate Christ, to imitate Him, to unite our will to His will in order to please His Father, that is the sum total of all perfection. The Father has placed all things in His beloved Son; we find in Him all the treasures of redemption, justification, wisdom, heavenly knowledge, sanctification; for us everything lies in contemplating Him and drawing near to Him. For the thought of Jesus, the looking upon Jesus, are not only holy, but sanctifying.

And nowhere can we better contemplate Our Lord in His Person and in His mysteries, than in following the liturgical cycle established by the Church, His Bride, she herself guided in this by the Holy Spirit. From Advent to Pentecost, the liturgy is Christocentric; in it all leads back to Christ, all converges towards Him; it is a representation, but a

1 See a remarkable commentary on this thought in D. Festugière. *La liturgie catholique, essai de synthèse,* ch. 13. *La Liturgie comme source et cause de vie religieuse,* pp. iii, sq. 2 Cf. Rom. vii, 29.

living representation of His mysteries: His Incarnation, His most sweet Nativity, His hidden life, His public life, His sorrowful Passion, the triumph of His Resurrection, His admirable Ascension; the Mission of the Holy Spirit. The Church leads us by the hand in Jesus' footsteps; we have only to listen, only to open the eyes of faith: we are following Jesus.

The mysteries of Jesus thus contemplated with faith and love, give rise within us to the affections that we should have felt had we been present at the Birth of Jesus, had we followed Him to Egypt, been with Him at Nazareth, in His discourses, in the Garden of Gethsemani, upon the Way of Sorrows, and at Calvary; as we should have felt if we had been present at His Resurrection, and Ascension.[1] This is what was said by a holy Benedictine, Mother Deleloë: "At Christmastide, during all those solemnities of our Saviour's Birth, I received great favours; His Majesty often gave me a vivid light so that I knew these divine mysteries *as if they were then really taking place.*"[2]

Indeed, although Christ is no longer upon earth, although the historical reality of His mysteries has gone by, He ever remains our Head and the virtue of His actions and of His life is ever fruitful: *Jesus Christus heri et hodie: ipse et in saecula.*[3] It is as the Head of the human race, and for the human race, that He has lived these mysteries: therefore, simply by contemplating them with faith, the soul is moulded little by little upon Christ, its Ideal, and is gradually transformed into Him, by entering into the sentiments felt by His Divine Heart when He lived each of His mysteries. Jesus lives the reality of His mysteries in us, and when we have faith, and rest lovingly united to Him, He draws us with Him, making us partakers of the virtue proper to each of these states. Each year, as the soul follows the Liturgical cycle, it shares ever more intimately in these mysteries, and is identified more and more with Christ, with His thoughts, His feelings, His life. *Hoc enim sentite in vobis, quod et in Christo Jesu.*[4] Gradually it is transformed into the likeness of the Divine Model; not only because this Model is represented in each stage of His terrestrial existence, but above all because a divine virtue goes

1 See the development of this idea in our work: *Christ in His Mysteries,* 1st Conference: *Christ's Mysteries are our mysteries.*

2 *La Mère Jeanne Deleloë,* p. 247, Collection "Pax."

3 "Jesus Christ, yesterday, and today; and the same for ever," Hebr. xiii, 8.

4 "For let this mind be in you, which was also in Christ Jesus," Philip. ii, 5.

out from these mysteries to sanctify us, according to the measure of our faith, and to make of the soul the living reproduction of Him Who is our Elder Brother. Does not all our predestination, all our holiness consist in being made conformable to Christ for the glory of His Father?

It is this custom of following, under the Church's guidance, the mysteries of Jesus that gives to Benedictine spirituality such a specifically Christian character: the piety of the soul, traced upon the very piety of the Bride of Christ, becomes extremely lucid. It is a fact of experience that with souls, who say the Divine Office devoutly, who let themselves be replenished with the truths of the Psalms and follow Our Lord step by step in each of His mysteries, the spiritual life is very limpid, sane, and at the same time abundant and fruitful; in these souls piety is exempt from all complication, nor is there anything forced about it. If we try to create or arrange our own spiritual life, there is danger of putting much of ourself into it, much that is human, and there is the risk at times of not taking the way that God wishes us to follow in order that we may attain to Him. Walking in the footsteps of the Church, there is no risk of going astray. The secret of the safety, as of the simplicity and breadth, of Benedictine spirituality lies in the fact that it borrows not from ever fallible man, but from the Church, from the Holy Spirit, all its elements even to its framework, which is nothing else than the representation of the life of Christ.

This is a point of extreme importance. Our holiness indeed is of the supernatural order, absolutely transcendent, having its source, not in us, but in God. Now, says St. Paul, we know not how we ought to pray, we know not, in this unique affair of our sanctification, what is befitting; but the Spirit of Jesus, Who is in us since our Baptism, Who directs the Church, Who is as it were the Soul of the Mystical Body, prays in us with ineffable groanings.[1]

In the Liturgical Office, everything is inspired by this Divine Spirit or created under His action. The Holy Spirit, Author of the psalms, deeply ingraves in the docile and devout soul, the truths whereof they give admirable formulas, He fills the soul with the affections that the

1 Cf. Rom. vii, 26.

sacred canticles express. Little by little the soul lives on these truths, is nourished on these sentiments which make it see and judge all things as God sees and judges them; it lives constantly in the supernatural sphere; it cleaves to Him Who is the unique object of all our religion, the One Who is placed unceasingly before our eyes in the reality of His mysteries and the power of His grace.

There is no surer way than this of keeping united to Jesus, and consequently going to God. The Church, guided by the Holy Spirit, leads us to Christ, Christ leads us to His Father and makes us pleasing to Him: what incomparable security and what powerful fecundity of the inner life this spiritual way guarantees to us!

IV

The Divine Office will produce its precious fruits in us only if it be well accomplished; it does not act in the manner of the Sacraments, *ex opere operato*;[1] its fruitfulness depends in great part on the dispositions of the soul. It is a divine work, extremely acceptable to God; it is a privileged means of union and sanctification—on condition however that we bring the necessary dispositions. What are these dispositions?

Before the Office, we must first of all, prepare ourselves. The perfection with which we acquit ourselves of the Work of God depends in great part on the preparation of the heart; it is the heart which God looks at first of all: *Praeparationem cordis eorum audivit auris tua*.[2] "Whatever good work thou undertakest," our holy Patriarch says, speaking to us in general, "beseech God *with most earnest prayer* to vouchsafe to bring to a good end": *Quidquid agendum inchoas bonum, a Deo perfici INSTANTISSIMA ORATIONE deposcas*.[3] If this recommendation extends to all our undertakings, how much more expressly is it to be applied to a work which demands of us faith, love, patience, the sense of reverence, and which is for us the "work" by excellence, because it is "the Work of God"? If we do not beg the help of God before giving ourselves to the Divine Praise, we shall never accomplish it well. Not to recollect ourselves before the Office, but to let our minds wander, then begin

1 "By the doing it is done," *Conc. Trid.* Sess. vii, ch. 8.

2 Ps. x, 17.

3 Prologue of the Rule.

ex abrupto, and imagine that fervour will be born of itself in the soul, is to be under a singular illusion. Scripture tells us: "Before prayer prepare thy soul: and be not as a man that tempteth God": *Ante orationem, praepara animam tuam, et noli esse quasi homo qui tentat Deum.*[1] What is "to tempt God"? It is to undertake an action without being assured of the means of carrying it out. If we begin the Divine Office without preparation, we cannot recite it as is befitting; to expect the necessary dispositions to come to us from on high, without first using the means of producing them within us, is to tempt God.

The first disposition required of us then is that we prepare our soul by most fervent prayer: *instantissima oratione*. It is with this object in view that we assemble at the "station" in the cloister before entering the Church. The silence of the station ought to be inviolable. It is important that each one should respect the recollection of his brethren and not trouble (even by words which are necessary but might be said at other moments) the work of a soul that is preparing itself to be united to God. The moments which pass at the station are golden moments. Experience proves that fervour during the Divine Office is to be very exactly measured by the immediate preparation. Almost infallibly, if we do not prepare ourselves, we come out from the "Work of God" as we entered, with, moreover, the culpability of our negligence.

In what then does this preparation consist?[2] As soon as the bell calls us, *venite adoremus*,[3] we ought to leave every other work: *Mox exoccupatis manibus, et quod agebant imperfectum relinquentes*;[4] direct our thoughts towards God and say to Him by a movement of the heart: "Behold I come, O my God, to glorify Thee; may I give myself altogether to Thy work!" We ought secondly, if needs be by a generous and vigorous effort of the mind, to put from us every irrelevant preoccupation, every distracting thought, and gather up our energies that all may be concentrated upon the work about to begin: our intellect, our will, our heart, our imagination, in order that our whole being, body and soul, may

1 Eccli. xviii, 23.

2 We speak of the immediate preparation, supposing the remote preparation to be understood and admitted. The remote preparation is, in the moral order, purity of heart and the habit of the presence of God, and, in the intellectual order, knowledge of the sacred texts, of the rubrics and chant etc.

3 Ps. xciv, 6.

4 Rule, ch. v.

praise the Lord. We should be able to say in all truth: *Benedic anima mea Domino, et OMNIA, QUAE INTRA ME SUNT, nomini sancto ejus;*[1] to say like David, the sacred singer: *Fortitudinem meam ad te custodiam:*[2] I will keep my strength for Thee, O Lord, and for Thy service; I wish to consecrate to Thy praise every power within me.

Then let us unite ourselves, by a spiritual communion of faith and love, to the Word Incarnate. We must have recourse to Christ Jesus; in this as in all things He is our Model and our Head. Christ Jesus loved the Psalms. We see Him, in the Gospel, more than once making use of the inspired songs, for example, the magnificent psalm *Dixit Dominus Domino meo,*[3] wherein is exalted the glory of Christ, the Son of God, triumphant over His enemies. His Divine lips have recited these canticles "in such a manner that manifestly His soul took possession of the sacred poetry as belonging to Himself."[4] We then recited the Psalms in Him, as now He recites them in us,[5] in virtue of that marvellous union which grace establishes between Christ and His members. This is what Our Lord Himself made Saint Mechtilde understand. One day when she asked Him if He had really celebrated the Hours upon earth, He deigned to reply to her: "I did not recite them as you do; however, at these hours, I rendered homage to God the Father. All that is observed among My disciples, I Myself inaugurated, as for example Baptism. I observed and accomplished these things for Christians, *thus sanctifying and perfecting the works of those who believe in Me.*" Our Divine Saviour gave the following counsel to the Saint: "In beginning the Hours, let these words then be said with the heart and even with the lips: Lord, in union with the attention wherewith when upon earth Thou didst observe the Canonical Hours in honour of the Father I celebrate this Hour in Thy honour. Secondly let all our attention be kept for God. And when this practice having been often repeated has become a habit, *this exercise*

1 "Bless the Lord, O my soul: and let all that is within me bless His holy Name," Ps. cii, 1.

2 Ps. lviii, 10. 3 Ps, cix. 4 D. Festugière, *l. c.,* pp. 114–115.

5 *Oramus ergo ad illum, per illum, in illo, et dicimus cum illo et dicit nobiscum; dicimus in illo, dicit in nobis psalmi hujus orationem* (We pray, therefore, to Him, through Him, and in Him, and we speak with Him and He speaks with us; we speak in Him, and He speaks in us the prayer of this psalm) St. Augustine, *Enarr.* in Ps. lxxxv, 1 P. L. 37, col. 1082. All this § 1 should be read.

will be so lofty and noble in the sight of God the Father, that it will seem to make but one with that which I Myself practised."[1]

We must not forget that if Christ Jesus recited the psalms, it was "not only individually but, moreover, as the Head of humanity, morally identifying Himself with all Adam's race, being touched at Heart with every peril, struggle and fall, with every regret and hope of men, uttering to His Father, at the same time as His own prayer, the supreme and universal prayer of all humanity."[2] This truth applies to all the prayer of Jesus, to all His works, and to His sacrifice.

This is why, with its every movement, the Liturgy finds its support in Christ Jesus, the Son of dilection. All its prayers end in recalling Christ's merits and Divinity: *Per Dominum Nostrum Jesum Christum...* At the Mass, which is the centre of the liturgy and of all our religion, the "Canon," that most sacred part of the holy oblation, begins most solemnly by having recourse to Christ's mediation: "O Father most clement, we beseech Thee: accept these gifts through Jesus Christ Thy Son and Our Lord." It ends with the same thought, still more explicitly formulated: *Per Ipsum, et cum Ipso, et in Ipso*: it is through Christ, with Christ, and in Christ that we can render all honour and all glory to the Father. Why so much insistence? Because the Father has appointed His Son as the one universal Mediator. St. Paul, who penetrated so far into the mystery of Christ, exhorts us in these terms: "By Him therefore let us offer the sacrifice of praise always to God, that is to say, the fruit of lips confessing

1 *The Book of Special Grace,* 3rd part, ch. 31. Our Lord deigned still more explicitly to teach the same doctrine to another Benedictine nun, Mother Deleloë. "One day," this holy nun relates, "the Well-Beloved drawing my heart close to Him, it seemed to me that truly this most lovable Spouse plunged it with warm caresses and demonstrations of love into the recesses of His Divine Heart as in a furnace of infinite Love. It was then given me to understand how this favour was granted me by the Well-Beloved, in order that my soul which belonged entirely to His Majesty, should not come alone into the presence of the Eternal Father to confess and love Him, but that being accompanied by this Divine Saviour, united to Him, and as it were altogether transformed into the unique object of His eternal delight, it should love and honour the Divine Majesty the more,—with and by the most adorable Heart of His Only-begotten Son, my Beloved,—and be more acceptably received, through this means, by the Sovereign Bounty." *La Mere Deleloë,* p. 231. Collection "Pax, XVI."

2 D. Festugière, *l. c.* p. 115.

to His Name": *PER IPSUM ergo offeramus hostiam laudis semper Deo, id est fructum labiorum confitentium nomini ejus.*[1]

In Christ Jesus, we find our best support; He supplies for our deficiencies. Let us entreat Him to be in us the Word that praises His Father. In the Sacred Humanity, the personal principle of every work was the Word; let us entreat Him also to take the initiative in all our praises; let us unite ourselves to Him in the infinite love whereby, in the Trinity, He glorifies His Father, and in that immense love He bears to the Church, His Mystical Body, *Christus dilexit Ecclesiam.*[2] Let us further unite ourselves to Him, praising Him for the glory that He gives to the Church triumphant, which is without spot or wrinkle in His holy sight: *non habens maculam aut rugam;*[3] let us beseech Him to increase the glory of His Blessed Mother, of His Angels and of His Saints; then let us unite our love to His love for the Church suffering, in order that we may help those of His members who are waiting in the place of expiation; let us unite ourselves to Him in that prayer which He made at the Last Supper for all His Church here below: *Pater, rogo pro eis qui credituri sunt in me.*[4]

As the ages succeed one another, Christ leaves His Bride to accomplish a part of the prayer that He recited when on the point of offering His Sacrifice. Although this prayer is of infinite efficacy, Our Lord wills us to join our own to it. One day our Divine Saviour, casting His gaze upon the multitude of souls to be redeemed, said to His Apostles whom He was about to send to preach the Gospel: *Rogate dominum messis ut mittat operarios in messem suam,*[5] "Pray ye therefore the Lord of the harvest, that He send labourers into His harvest." The Apostles might have replied: "Lord, why dost Thou tell us to pray? Does not Thy prayer suffice?" No, it does not suffice: *Rogate*: "Pray," you also. Christ Jesus chooses to have need of our prayers as of those of His Apostles. Let us think, at the moments when we are recollecting ourselves at the "station" that from the depths of the tabernacle, Christ is about to say us: *Rogate Dominum messis*: "Lend Me your lips and hearts that I may prolong My prayer here below while in Heaven I offer My merits to the

---

1 Hebr. xiii, 15. 2 Eph. v, 25. 3 Cf. Ibid. 27.

4 "Father... I pray for them who... shall believe in me," Joan. xvii, 20.

5 Luc. x, 2.

Father. Prayer first of all: the labourers will only come afterwards and their work will bear fruit only in the measure that My Father, attentive to your prayer, which is Mine, will pour down the heavenly dew of His grace upon earth."

Before beginning the Divine Office, let us then cast a glance over the world: the Church, the Spouse of Christ, is ever in travail of redemption. Let us behold the Sovereign Pontiff, the pastors of dioceses and parishes, the religious Orders, the missionaries who carry the good word to the heathen in order to extend the Kingdom of Jesus; let us behold, in spirit, the sick in the hospitals, the dying whose eternal salvation is about to be decided at this very moment; let us think of prisoners, of the poor, of those who suffer, of souls in temptation; of sinners who wish to return to God but are weighed down by the burden of their chains; of the just who ardently long to advance in divine love. Is it not this that the Church herself does on Good Friday? Remembering the sacrifice for the redemption of the whole world, and feeling herself strong in the very strength of the Saviour, the Church lets her motherly gaze travel over the diverse series of souls who have need of help from on high, and she offers special supplications for each. Let us imitate this example of our mother and approach God with confidence, for at this moment we are the mouth of the whole Church: *Totius Ecclesiae os.*[6]

I was saying in the preceding conference that, in choir, we are the Church's ambassadors. Now what is the most fundamental quality of an ambassador? To be clever? powerful? to have a large fortune at his disposal? to have influence? to shine by his personal talents? to be *persona grata* with the sovereign to whom he is sent? All this is useful and necessary; all these qualities would contribute without any doubt to the success of his mission, but they would be insufficient and sterile, they would even deviate from the end in view did not the ambassador identify himself first of all, and as perfectly as he possibly could, with the intentions and opinions of the sovereign who sent him, with the interests of the country he represents. The Church deputes us to the King of kings, to the throne of God. We must then identify ourselves with her views and wishes; the Church confides to us her interests, which are those of souls, those of eternity. This is not a trivial matter! Let us then

6 S. Bern. Senen. *Sermo* xx.

take into our hearts all the needs, all the necessities of the Church—so dear to Jesus since she is purchased by His Blood—the anguish of souls in pain, the perils of those who are at this moment grappling with the devil, the anxieties of those who have to direct us; in order that all may receive God's help. This is what was done by the holy Sister Mechtilde of Magdebourg. She took all Christendom in the arms of her soul to present it to the Eternal Father that it might be saved. "Let be," said Our Lord to her, "it is too heavy for thee." "No, Lord," replied the Saint, "I will lift it up and bear it to Thy feet with Thine own arms, that so Thou mayest bear it Thyself upon the Cross!"[1] An example of the faith of great souls which constrains them to put the dogma of the Communion of saints into the highest and most perfect practice.

Let us imitate these models, and we may be assured that light, consolation, help, and the grace of forgiveness will flow down abundantly from the throne of mercy upon the whole Church. Remember what Our Lord Himself said: "Amen, amen, I say to you; if you ask the Father anything in My Name, He will give it you."[2] Rely upon this promise, ask much, ask in all confidence, and the Father from Whom "every perfect gift comes down,"[3] will open His hands to fill every soul with blessings.[4] For it is not we who pray, who intercede at this moment; it is the Church, it is Christ, our Head, the supreme High Priest Who prays in us, and stands before His Father to plead the cause of the souls He has redeemed: *Ut appareat vultui Dei pro nobis...*[5] *Semper vivens ad interpellandum pro nobis.*[6]

It is true that men of the world shrug their shoulders when they learn that we stay such long hours in choir praising God. For them, nothing is worth anything unless it is exterior, unless the results can be touched or felt, unless it is something that is talked about, that is successful and brilliant; but, says St. Paul, in his inspired energetic language, the sensual man, whose natural reason is his only guide, cannot understand the things of God: *Animalis homo non percipit quae sunt Spiritus Dei*;[7] the supernatural sense is lacking to him. For him, these hours are lost and

1 *The Light of the Divinity,* Bk. ii, ch. 12.
2 Joan. xvi, 23.
3 Jac. i, 17.
4 Cf. Ps. cxliv, 16.
5 Hebr. ix, 24.
6 Ibid. vii, 25.
7 I Cor. ii, 14.

wasted hours; but to the eyes of faith, in the sight of God,—and who is just and true as God?—these hours are rich in graces for the Church, and of great weight for souls as regards eternity. It is at these hours we fulfil the most excellent apostolic work, even towards our neighbour; we obtain for him the grace of God, we give him God: this is the greatest good for a soul. St. Bernard, that great monk and apostle, consumed with zeal, says, "all apostleship demands three things: the word, example, prayer. But of these three prayer is the most important, because it is prayer which obtains the grace and efficacy of the word and example."[1] Indeed "unless the Lord build the house, they labour in vain that build it. Unless the Lord keep the city, he watcheth in vain that keepeth it."[2] It is truly God Who holds the eternal destinies of souls within His hands: *In manibus tuis sortes meae*;[3] and when we fervently recite the Divine Office for the whole Church, in union with Christ Jesus, we labour for the salvation and sanctification of souls in a measure we cannot compass.[4]

The "Work of God" is an eminently apostolic work, although this does not appear outwardly; this character of the Office is perceived by faith alone, but for those who have faith, how much the value of this work is enhanced! A Sister of Charity can count the number of sick persons she has assisted, the number of the dying for whose conversion she has laboured; a missionary can verify the success of his preaching, take into account the good that he does, and therein find encouragement for his efforts and motives for thanksgiving. We cannot keep any such register. It is in the obscurity of faith that, during the Divine Office, we work for souls; it is in heaven alone that we shall see all the glory we have given to God by devoutly singing His praises, all the good we have gained for the Church and for souls; below we cannot gauge it; this is one sacrifice the more that faith asks of us. But although the apostolic efficacy of the Work of God well performed does not appear to our bodily eyes, it is no less deep and far-reaching.

---

1 *Manent tria haec: verbum, exemplum, oratio; major autem his est oratio; nam, etsi vocis virtus sit opus, et operi tamen et voci gratiam efficaciamque promeretur oratio. Epistola,* 201, n. 3. P. L. 182, co. 370. A disciple of St. Bernard, Dom Chautard, Abbot of Sept-Fons, has written on this subject a most valuable work translated into English under the title of "The True Apostolate," which we cannot sufficiently recommend.

2 Ps. cxxvi, 1. 3 Ps. xxx, 16.

4 See *La Vie contemplative et son rôle apostolique,* by a Carthusian monk.

Let these great thoughts occupy our minds at the moment of beginning the Divine Office; they enlarge the horizon of the soul; they increase its energies tenfold, they prevent routine. When we habitually act in this spirit of faith, when we thus forget our personal pain and troubles, in order to occupy ourselves with the needs and interests of souls, we go out of self; we praise God with fervour, in spite of the weariness that may befall us, in spite of the repugnance which God sometimes permits us to feel; and let us be assured that if we think, before all things, of God's glory and of Christ's Mystical Body, Jesus will think of us and will pour down blessings upon our souls surpassing all our hopes and desires. Has He not promised this Himself? "Give—and it shall be given to you": *Date, et dabitur vobis.*[1]

V

After having formulated our intentions, in a few rapid but intense acts, let us ask God "earnestly" *instantissima oratione*, to open our lips that we may praise His holy name; to cleanse our hearts from vain, perverse, or simply irrelevant thoughts; to enlighten our understanding, to enkindle our love, that we may praise Him worthily, with attention and devotion. This is all contained in the prayer *Aperi* which we recite before each Office; we should endeavour to say it with humility and fervour, for it points out the dispositions that we ought to have during the work of God: *Digne, attente et devote.*

To pray worthily—that is to observe faithfully the ceremonial, the rubrics, the rules of chanting, all that forms the protocol imposed by the King of kings upon those who present themselves before Him. If, being admitted to the court of an earthly sovereign, we did not trouble ourselves about etiquette, we should be quite reasonably taxed with being guilty of great disrespect. The Church, under the Holy Spirit's action, has arranged the ceremonial of her prayer with extreme care. By this she manifests the reverence she bears to her Divine Spouse. Under the Old Covenant, God Himself gave the details of the worship to be paid to Him, and we see that He shed blessings upon the Jewish people in the measure that they observed His ordinances. And yet, what was the

1 Luc. vi, 38.

immediate object of this worship? The ark of the covenant, containing the tables of the Law, and the manna. It was but a figure, a symbol, an imperfect shadow—*egena elementa,* to speak in the language of St. Paul.[1] Ours is the true tabernacle, for it contains the true Manna of souls; it contains the One Who alone is holy: *Tu solus sanctus, Jesu Christe.*[2] The Divine Office is celebrated around the tabernacle, under the eyes of Christ. The Father lovingly beholds a soul who seeks to procure the glory of His Beloved Son Jesus: *Et clarificavi, et iterum clarificabo;*[3] therefore all is pleasing to Him that composes or enhances the worship whereof Jesus is the centre. Let us then take care not to exempt ourselves from the ceremonial nor to recite or chant the Office according to our own fancies or caprices; this would be wanting in respect to God; it would be exposing ourselves to a wrong kind of familiarity which could only be harmful to us. God remains God, that is to say the Infinite Being, full of incommunicable majesty, even when He admits us to praise Him. Neither let us say that the rubrics are small matters; yes, these things are materially small; but they are great by reason of the love with which we should observe them; great because they so closely concern God's honour; a soul who loves Our Lord shows this love by putting as much fidelity into small things as into great actions, for nothing is really small which is according to the Divine good pleasure.

Let us pray *attentively*. Attention must be distinguished from intention, although the one is not without influence on the other. We have just now pointed out the intentions we ought to have in the course of the divine psalmody. Attention, too, is very necessary, for the Divine Praise is a human action, performed by a being endowed with reason and will. Failing this attention, we should fill the mechanical rôle of a series of well tuned phonographs; we should be like the praying-wheels of the monks of Thibet.

But what is the kind of attention required? St. Thomas distinguishes first: the *attentio ad verba*, the mental application to pronounce the words well; it is this that beginners have to strive after first of all; secondly, the *attentio ad sensum*, attention to the meaning of the words;

1 Cf. Gal. iv, 9. 2 *Gloria* of the Mass. 3 Joan. xii, 28.

finally, the *attentio ad Deum*; this is, according to St. Thomas, "the most necessary": *Quae quidem est maxime necessaria.*[1]

Our holy Lawgiver combines the whole in a sufficiently synthetical manner in his beautiful chapter *De disciplina psallendi.* He first of all lays down the principle: *Ubique credimus divinam esse praesentiam, maxime tamen... cum ad Opus divinum assistimus*: "We believe," he says, "that God is present everywhere, but especially, *maxime*, when we are assisting at the Divine Office." From this principle he draws two conclusions; we must sing God's praises with the greatest reverence: *Ideo semper memores simus quod ait propheta: servite Domino in timore*; with understanding, knowing well what we are doing and saying; *Et iterum: Psallite sapienter*. Then at the end of the chapter, he links together the two dispositions with these words: *Ergo consideremus qualiter oporteat in conspectu Divinitatis esse, et sic stemus ad psallendum ut mens nostra concordet voci nostrae*:[2] "Let us consider with what reverence we ought to behave in God's presence, and so assist at the psalmody that our mind be in accord with our lips." We should weigh this teaching carefully.

We are first of all told that during the Office, we ought to remain interiorly prostrate in adoration before God. God is Infinite Holiness, "the Lord God of all things," our Blessed Father reminds us in the chapter *De reverentia orationis.*[3] When Abraham, the father of believers, spoke to the Lord, he called himself dust and ashes.[4] When Moses conversed with God, such was his profound sense of the Divine Majesty that he durst not raise his eyes to look upon Him: *Non audebat respicere contra Deum;*[5] and yet Scripture tells us, God spoke to him "as a man is wont to speak to his friend."[6]

From the time of the dedication of Solomon's Temple, "the Majesty of the Lord" filled the temple so exceedingly that the priests dare

1 *Triplex attentio orationi vocali potest adhiberi: una quidam qua attenditur ad verba, ne aliquis in eis erret; secunda qua attenditur ad sensum verborum; tertia qua attenditur ad finem orationis scilicet ad Deum et ad rem pro qua oratur* (There are three kinds of attention that can be brought to vocal prayer: one which attends to the words, lest we say them wrong, another which attends to the sense of the words, and a third, which attends to the end of prayer, namely, God, and to the thing we are praying for). II-II, q. 83, a. 13.

2 Rule, ch. xix.

3 "Of Reverence in Prayer," Rule, ch. xx.

4 Gen. xviii, 27.

5 Exod. iii, 6.

6 Ibid. xxxiii, 11.

not cross the threshold.[1] Even under the law of love, even in the Beatific Vision, which is the absolute perfection of intimacy with God, adoration does not cease. St. John shows us the Angels and the Elect casting themselves down before the Infinite Majesty: *Et ceciderunt in facies suas.*[2] Now, during the Divine Office, we are introduced by the Church into the presence of the Father; we are, it is true, the children of this heavenly Father, but His adopted children; we ought not to forget our first condition of creatures. The *Invitatory* psalm which is repeated daily at the beginning of Matins and is like the prelude to the "Hours" of the whole day, is very expressive of this attitude. "Come, let us praise the Lord with gladness... let us come before His presence with thanksgiving; and make a joyful noise to Him with psalms. For the Lord is a great God, and a great King above all gods. For in His hand are all the ends of the earth: and the heights of the mountains are His... For the sea is His, and He made it: and His hands formed the dry land. Come, let us adore and fall down. Let us weep before the Lord that made us, for He is the Lord our God."[3] What a magnificent opening! "Come," says the Psalmist, and at this moment, we bend the knee, to manifest our adoration, our reverence. Our fear is not that of the slave, unworthy of us and of God; nor even an imperfect fear, like that of a servant; but it is the fear of children in their heavenly Father's house, for we are really *His* people, the sheep of *His* pasture: *Nos autem populus ejus et oves pascuae ejus.*[4] It is an intense reverence, like that which even now in Heaven fills the Sacred Humanity of Jesus Himself: *Timor Domini sanctus, permanens in saeculum saeculi.*[5]

This inward reverence for a "Father of infinite majesty," *Patrem immensae majestatis,*[6] should from time to time be manifested outwardly. Let all, says our holy Patriarch, incline at the *Gloria Patri* which follows each psalm, and is the doxology wherein we translate our adoration, *ob honorem et reverentiam sanctae Trinitatis;*[7] let us, he says again, listen to the reading of the Gospel, at the end of Matins, standing in reverence

1 II Par. vii, 2. 2 Apoc. vii, 11. 3 Ps. xciv, 1–7.

4 Ps. xciv. We here give the text of the Breviary and not that of the Vulgate.

5 "The fear of the Lord is holy, enduring for ever and ever," Ps. xviii, 10.

6 Hymn *Te Deum.*

7 "In honour and reverence to the Holy Trinity," Rule, ch. ix.

and awe: *Cum honore et timore.*[1] These are some of the outward manifestations of inmost reverence, but we ought to be watchful to keep ourselves in this reverence throughout all the Office without however making violent efforts of mind or imagination.

Nothing hinders us, while thus inwardly prostrate in adoration, from attending to the meaning of the words, to the affections that the Holy Spirit makes the Psalms express. This is what our Blessed Father asks of us when he tells us, in a lapidary phrase, to put our heart in unison with our lips: *Mens nostra concordet voci nostrae.* "If the Psalm prays, pray; if it weeps, weep; if it rejoices, rejoice; if it hopes, hope; and if it fears, fear. All that is contained therein is our mirror."[2] We remain in adoration during all the time of the psalmody; it is a fundamental attitude; but over this reverence which holds the depths of our being in awe surge movements of love, joy, praise, complacency, confidence, intense longings, earnest supplications. All these modulations rise up from the Psalms, to the glory of our Father in heaven, and for the good of souls, in the measure that the Holy Spirit touches the chords of our heart. Our soul ought to be like a harp docile to the fingers of this Divine Artist, that so our canticle may be pleasing to God.

Under an apparent divergency, there is perfect accordance between the views of St. Thomas, quoted above, and those of St. Benedict. The angelic Doctor does not in any way teach that "attention to God" is exclusive of "attention to the sense" (of the words); he only wishes that the soul shall not be bound to follow word for word, that it shall be free to soar Godwards, in short that the means shall not become an end. And this is exactly how St. Benedict understands things; he does not say that the soul ought to be tied down to each word we pronounce (*verbis*); he says that it ought to be in harmony with our voice, that is to say it ought to go towards God by using the wings that the liturgical theme offers. This is what the elect do in heaven's liturgy; they unceasingly remain in contemplation before God in most perfect adoration, without this contemplation hindering them from praising each of the Divine attributes.

---

1 Rule, ch. xi.

2 *Si orat psalmus, orate; et si gemit, gemite; et si gratulatur, gaudete; et si sperat, sperate; et si timet, timete. Omnia enim quae hic conscripta sunt, speculum nostrum sunt.* St. Augustine, *Enarrat. ii in ps. 30. Sermo 3,* N° 1. P. L. 36, col 248.

This moreover is what our Saviour, our Divine Model, did here below. The soul of Jesus was always plunged in the contemplation and adoration of the Father's perfections. When He spent the night in prayer, *in oratione Dei*,[1] when His Divine lips murmured the sacred canticles, His understanding sounded all their depth, exhausted all their plenitude.

In the same way when the monk, united to Christ Jesus, enters the oratory, bearing in his soul the deepest and most precious interests of Jesus' Mystical Body, when his heart is filled, and then overflows with the varied affections to which the Holy Spirit successively gives rise by means of the words uttered by the lips,—he offers God an extremely pleasing homage, while torrents of light and love, flowing at his prayer from God's munificence, are poured out upon the world of souls.

The last disposition required for acquitting oneself well of the work of God is devotion: *devote. Devovere* means "to consecrate." Devotion is the consecration of our whole self to God; it is the most delicate flower and the purest fruit of love, for it is love giving itself wholly to the beloved being; it is the literal fulfilment of Christ's words: *Diliges Dominum Deum tuum ex TOTO corde tuo et ex TOTA mente tua.*[2] It is this totality in love which is the mark of devotion. When we love with all our heart, we do not count the cost, we willingly spend ourselves without measure for the sake of those we thus love. In regard to God and in the Work of God, these dispositions constitute devotion.

We must not confound this devotion with certain of its effects. It does not consist in feelings of sensible consolation; however frequent these may be, they are not the less accidental, depending as much on temperament and circumstances as on Our Lord. It is good to feel sweetness in God's service. The inspired singer says himself, *Gustate et videte quoniam suavis est Dominus*,[3] but it does not constitute the essential of devotion. We must thank God if He allows us to experience that His service is full of sweetness, for that encourages us and stimulates love;[4]

---

1 Luc. vi, 12.

2 "Thou shalt love the Lord thy God, with thy whole heart, and with thy whole soul," Marc. xii, 30.

3 "O taste, and see that the Lord is sweet," Ps. xxxiii, 9.

4 This is what we say to God in the Postcommunion of the Mass of the Rogations; "Vouchsafe, O Lord, favourably to receive our vows; that receiving Thy gifts in the

however we must not cling to these consolations as if they formed the very basis of devotion.

To be truly devout in the Divine Office is to strive with all one's being to celebrate it well; it is to go to the choir every day and several times a day, with all the zeal, strength and energy that we can bring, in order to accomplish the Work of God as perfectly as possible; it is to persevere in doing this, not only when feeling consolation, but whatever be the state of our mind, the weariness of our body, the inward repugnance that God sometimes allows us to experience. These are sacrifices to be accepted during the hours of praise; we have mentioned several of them in the preceding conference. To accept them requires self-abnegation and much generosity. From whence will this generosity arise? What will nourish it? Love; for devotion is love put into practice. When one possesses this fervour which is born of love, he truly gives to God a sacrifice of praise: *Tibi sacrificabo hostiam laudis.*[1] Devotion is to praise God with one's whole being, to make of one's self a holocaust to God: *Confitebor tibi Domine in* TOTO *corde meo.*[2] A monk who does not sacrifice every thought foreign to the occasion, who, during the Work of God, does not concentrate all the forces of his intellect and will upon God, and assists at the office of praise scarcely moving his lips, neglecting the points of the ceremonial established by the Church for the glory of God, does not fulfil his duty as a monk in a satisfactory manner. This negligence, this indolence, is unworthy of a monk. While so many religious in purely active Orders, so many missionaries spend themselves without counting the cost in ministering to souls, it would be inadmissible that a monk should perform without fervour the lofty work devolving upon him. When we are in choir, we ought to be able to say in all truth: "O my God, I can now glorify Thee, in union with Thy beloved Son; I can do much for the interests of souls redeemed by the Blood of this Son; without my prayer, which is that of Thy Son, there might perhaps be some at this moment who would be lost for eternity. Let all within me sing Thy praise; let there be nothing in me which is not Thine!" God loves generosity in His service, but, according to the

---

midst of our tribulation, we may, from the consolation Thou givest us, increase in Thy love": *de consolatione nostra in tuo amore crescamus.*

1 Ps. cxv, 17. 2 Ps. ix, 2.

energetic expression of Scripture, He "vomits the tepid,"[1] those who are indifferent to the interests of His glory and those of souls.

Let us then give ourselves wholly to this work of capital importance, after the example of so many holy monks who have found it the best means of showing their love to God and souls. It is related of St. Mechtilde that "it was her custom to use all her strength in praising God with fervent love; it seemed that she would never be stayed even if it were at the cost of her last breath. One day when she was weary with singing, as often happened, she felt ready to swoon. It then appeared to her that she drew all her strength from Christ's Divine Heart, and could thus continue to sing, less by her own strength than by Divine virtue. In this union, she seemed to sing with God and in God, and Our Lord said to her: "Thou dost now appear to draw thy breath in My Heart; in the same way, every person who shall sigh after Me with love or desire, shall draw his breath not in himself, but in My Divine Heart."[2]

VI

For the Divine Office to be accomplished with the fervour entirely worthy of it, great faith and generous love are needed. If we have not this living faith and this ardour of love, it may happen that after some time we do not sufficiently esteem the Divine Office; that we no longer have a high enough idea of its immense value for God's glory and the welfare of souls, and we end by considering other works more important. Without owning this to ourselves, we may perhaps feel some satisfaction if it happens that for such or such a reason we are dispensed from presence in choir.

On the contrary, to a soul inspired with a living faith, the *Opus Dei* always appears incomparably great and inexhaustibly fruitful. Joined to the Holy Sacrifice which it encircles, it appears as the most perfect homage we can offer to God, as an extremely effectual means of union with Him. Routine takes no hold on such a religious; every day the Divine Praise has fresh attractions for him; every day it is a "new canticle" *canticum novum*[3] that all his being, body and soul, sends up to God to

1 Cf. Apoc. iii, 16. 2 *The Book of Special Grace,* 3rd Part, ch. 7.
3 Ps. xcv, 1; xcvii, 1; cxlix, 1.

glorify Him. For example, at the oft repeated words of the Invitatory: "Come, let us adore the Lord," all heads are bowed, like a field of corn bending beneath the breeze. If this inclination is made by routine, without attention to the meaning the action expresses, it is an almost valueless ceremony, but if the soul, full of devotion, casts itself interiorly before God and gives itself entirely to Him, what magnificent praises then rise up to God! The Angels alone can admire all the beauty of this action. In the same way, when we incline at the *Gloria Patri* at the end of each psalm, let us gather up into this action all our praise and all our devotion, and strive to penetrate ourselves with devotion at the thought of the oblation we ought to make of ourselves to the Holy Trinity in chanting these words.

If it happens that despite all our ardour to praise God in choir, we are there assailed with distractions, what are we to do? Distractions are inevitable. We are all weak; so many objects solicit our attention that our mind easily wanders. We need not be anxious about those distractions which are the result of our frailty. "As for the distractions you experience in reciting the Divine Office," St. Teresa wrote to one of her correspondents, "I am subject to them as you are, and I advise you to attribute them, as I do, to weakness of the head; for Our Lord well knows that, since we pray to Him, our intention is to pray well."

This last phrase of the great contemplative is one to bear in mind. Inasmuch as we ought not to trouble ourselves about the distractions that arise during the Divine Office owing to the instability of our imagination, so, before the Work of God, ought we to do our utmost to prepare ourselves, in order to show "our intention is to pray well." Otherwise, having made no effort before the Office to turn our mind towards God, to recollect ourselves in Him, to fill our soul with deep reverence and great devotion, it will be very difficult for us not to have those distractions which are to be imputed to negligence. We can appeal to our own experience; the greater number of our distractions would be avoided if we gave the proper care to the immediate preparation; and if, going through the Office in a mechanical manner, we let many lights and graces escape us, it is our own carelessness we have to blame.

But if, before offering our homage to God, we recollect ourselves with fervour; if we unite ourselves, in an intense act of faith and love, to Christ Jesus, the Incarnate Word, that we may lend Him our lips, in order to praise His Father and draw down the lights and gifts of His Spirit upon all His Mystical Body, we may be at peace on the subject of the distractions that arise; they are the result of our infirmity; as soon as we are aware of them, let us recover possession of our mind, but let us do so gently without any violent effort. In particular, let the *Gloria Patri,* by its frequent recurrence, be an opportunity of reawakening our vigilance. In pronouncing it, we bow in order to give to God the homage of our reverence and adoration; it is the easiest moment for bringing back the soul to the sense of the Divine Presence. Distractions will thus serve to reanimate our fervour; and if we continue to do our utmost to observe all the rites carefully, our praise will remain none the less pleasing to God and fruitful for the Church.

This is what Bossuet admirably says in terms which we will borrow as the conclusion of this conference. "Religious soul! The fruit of Jesus Christ's teaching upon prayer should principally be to be faithful to the hours consecrated to it. Were you to be distracted inwardly, if you lament being so, if you only wish not to be so, and remain faithful, humble and recollected outwardly, the obedience you give to God, the Church and the Rule, by observing the genuflexions, the inclinations and all the other exteriour pious observances, maintains the spirit of prayer. We pray then by state, by disposition, by will: but especially if we humble ourselves for our dryness and distractions. Oh! how pleasing to God is this prayer! How it mortifies body and soul! How it obtains graces and expiates sin!"[1]

1 *Meditations on the Gospel,* Sermon on the Mount, 44th day.

MONASTIC PRAYER

SUMMARY.—I. The place that prayer holds in the life of the monk.—II. Qualities that St. Benedict requires of prayer; necessity of preparation.—III. Character of monastic prayer in the purgative way.—IV. In the illuminative way.—V. How the *Opus Dei* is the pure source of abundant illumination.—VI. State of prayer in the unitive life.—VII. Means given by St. Benedict for maintaining the life of prayer within us.—VIII. This life constitutes the normal state of a religious in his cloister; the precious fruits it produces.

THE representation of the life of Christ forms the principal basis of the Liturgical Cycle. But Christ is not alone; we also celebrate those members of His Mystical Body who already make part of His glorious Kingdom, the elect who are the noblest purchase of the Blood of Jesus and the most beautiful fruit of the Church's union with her Divine Spouse. The Saints form Christ's cortége throughout the Liturgical Cycle, and when we praise their virtues and chant their merits, we exalt and celebrate the One Who, being their Head, is now likewise their Crown: *Ipse est corona Sanctorum omnium.*[1]

There is great variety among these saints; each according to his or her vocation, and the measure of the giving of Christ's grace, *secundum mensuram donationis Christi,*[2] reproduces one of the aspects of the plenitude of the Man-God's perfections. The same Spirit, says St. Paul,[3] has given to each a special grace which, being engrafted upon nature, makes each one of the elect shine with a particular glory. In some, strength has dominated; in others, prudence; again in others, zeal for God's glory; in one, faith has especially shone out, in another, purity. But whether

1 Invitatory at Matins for the Feast of All Saints.

2 Eph. iv, 7. 3 I Cor. xii, 4.

they be the Apostles, Martyrs or Pontiffs, whether it concerns Virgins or Confessors, one common character is to be found in them all. This character is stability in seeking after God and in love of Him. And this is a great virtue, for inconstancy is one of the most redoubtable perils that menace mankind.

The Saints sought God indefatigably. Whatever the circumstances wherein they were placed, the temptations with which they were buffeted, the difficulties they encountered, the seductions that surrounded them, the Saints all remained steadfast and faithful. Therefore on the day of their entrance into the Eternal Kingdom, God crowned them with glory and inebriated them with joy: "Good and faithful servant, because thou hast been faithful over a few things, enter into the joy of thy Lord": *Euge, serve bone et fidelis, quia super pauca fuisti fidelis... intra in gaudium Domini tui.*[1] Because, in seeking after the unique Good, they did not allow themselves to be turned back, the Saints have attained the glorious goal.

And what is the intimate reason of this stability in good? What is the secret of the Saints?

This secret is the life of prayer. The soul that leads a life of prayer, remains united to God; it lays hold upon God, it shares in the Divine immutability and eternity, and therefore it is not moved whatever be the circumstances. A child who in the tempest clings to the rock is stronger than a man abandoned to the caprices of the waves.

The firm adherence of the soul to God is the fruit of prayer. The Saints in Heaven cannot but remain united to God and to His will because they contemplate God and see in Him the fulness of all perfection and the fountainhead of all sovereignity. To live a life of prayer is to abide habitually in contact with God in faith, and, in this union, the soul finds the necessary light and strength to do the Divine good pleasure in all things. And as God is for it the principle of all holiness, the soul that lives by prayer finds in this habitual union with God Who created prayer the fruitfulness of its supernatural life.

Let us examine the place that prayer holds in our monastic life;—what characters St. Benedict wishes to give to it;—what means are put within our hands by the Rule for safeguarding and maintaining the life of prayer within us.

1 Matth. xxv, 23.

I

Prayer should occupy a very large place in the life of the monk. Those who read the Rule of St. Benedict for the first time are a little astonished to see that he does not assign to his monks any special length of time to consecrate to private prayer. He says simply that the monk should frequently apply himself to prayer: *Orationi frequenter incumbere.*[1] He says furthermore that a brother who wishes to pray by himself after the recitation of the Divine Office shall have leisure to do so.[2] Again he writes a very beautiful though short page upon the qualities which prayer ought to have.[3] Nowhere, however, does he fix for his monks one hour rather than another to give themselves to private prayer. There are people of a certain turn of mind who cannot refrain from evincing their surprise at this: but they are wrong. The existence of the monk, such as St. Benedict has organised it, with its separation from the world, its solitude, the Divine Praises, holy reading, is in view of creating, and at the same time supposes, a *life* of prayer. The holy Legislator did not therefore feel the necessity of determining one hour or half hour for the *exercise* of prayer. Monks who live in perfect obedience to the prescriptions enacted by St. Benedict necessarily attain to the life of prayer. In the conception of the holy Patriarch as in that of all monastic tradition, prayer is not simply a transitory isolated action accomplished at such or such an hour and having only a virtual relation with the other actions of the day; it should be the very breath of the soul without which there is no true inner life. But when a man lives this life of union with God, he quite naturally consecrates an interval of specified time during the day for communing specially with God, for the soul that loves God wishes to be united with Him in a more exclusive manner at certain moments. This hour of prayer is as it were the intensifying of the life of prayer in which the soul habitually moves.

No day should pass without our applying ourselves to this prayer, for our holy Father desires that "daily in prayer" *cotidie in orationi*,[4] we should confess our sins to God. Even "frequently" in the day, the monk should turn to God to commune with Him, *Orationi frequenter incumbere*. Moreover, according to the Rule, the monk is to consecrate two

1 Rule, ch. iv. 2 Ibid. ch. lii. 3 Ibid. ch. xx. 4 Ibid. ch. iv.

to four hours a day to "holy reading."[1] This last expression has, with St. Benedict, a very elastic meaning, allowing of the possibility, foreseen for certain souls, of devoting a very long time to prayer.

We know too how the holy Patriarch has himself set us the example. Each day he poured out his soul before God in sublime prayer which was the well-spring of magnificent graces. It was assuredly whilst he was in prayer that God one day showed him the entire universe gathered up as it were in one ray of light;[2] it was as a sequel to his prayer that he raised to life a monk crushed by the falling of a wall,[3] and, at another time, the son of a peasant;[4] again it was during prayer that he saw the soul of his sister St. Scholastica ascend to Heaven under the form of a dove.[5]

If then we want to be true disciples of the great Patriarch, we must often give ourselves to prayer, in view of that life of prayer which he certainly desires each one of us to lead. Our Blessed Father, in fact, has no other aim than to help us to find God: *Si revera Deum quaerit.*[6] As we said in our first conference where we tried to show the greatness of this aim, we shall only attain it by the entire gift of ourselves. We quoted the words uttered by St. Catherine of Siena on her death-bed; we cannot truly possess God, said she, save by giving ourselves to Him by an undivided love. But the Saint immediately added that she had also recognised "that without prayer one cannot arrive at that state where the whole heart is given to God without ever taking anything back."[7] There is nothing in this that ought to astonish us. Man is naturally weak and unstable, and it is only in habitual contact with God by means of prayer that he practically learns the emptiness of created things in themselves; and the plenitude of God Who, alone, is worthy of the whole of our love. Therefore our Blessed Father wishes us to give ourselves frequently to prayer in order never to lose sight of the Sovereign Good nor let ourselves be turned away from Him by the ephemeral attraction of the creature.

We have need of prayer to keep ourselves constantly at the height of that seeking after God which constitutes our vocation. When Our Lord called us to the monastic life, He illumined us with the light of His Spirit; we understood in this Divine light that He is the Supreme

1 Ibid. ch. xlviii.
2 St. Gregory, *Dialogues.* Lib. ii, ch. 35.
3 Ibid. ch. 2.
4 Ibid. ch. 32.
5 Ibid. ch. 34.
6 Rule, ch. lviii.
7 *Life* by Bl. Raymund of Capua.

Good and we left all to follow Him. On the day of our profession, we, in the simplicity of our hearts, "joyfully offered all these things" upon the altar: *In simplicitate cordis mei, laetus obtuli universa.*[1] We vowed stability, conversion of our manners and obedience: this act constituted a supreme homage of love and adoration, extremely pleasing to God. If throughout life we could maintain ourselves in the dispositions we had at that moment, we should become real saints. This is absolutely beyond doubt. Now, only an intense life of prayer can keep us unfalteringly in this attitude of unreserved self-donation. Two reasons will convince us that this assertion is well founded.

First of all, the life of prayer makes us live constantly in that Divine light whereof a ray enlightened us on the day of our monastic vocation and profession. Shut out from this light, we should come little by little to have no longer any esteem for the thousand details of religious life, which is meaningless if it is not supernatural; and, on the other hand, religious life is too much opposed to fallen nature, for a man to be able to bear it long without Divine help. It is from this light that we draw the strength and joy for the practice of the abnegation of which our life is composed; that we nourish our hope of one day attaining to God; that we find the love which makes us love Him here below in faith.

The second reason which flows from the preceding is that the means we have of ever tending to God and remaining united to Him—the Sacraments, Mass, Divine Office, the life of obedience and labour—only attain the *summum* of their efficacy if we lead a life of prayer. All these means are valuable and fruitful only if we do not put any obstacle in the way of their action, but bring to it the interior dispositions of faith, confidence, love, compunction, humility, and abandonment to God's will. Now it is above all by the life of prayer, by habitual union with God in prayer, that we gather strength to thrust obstacles aside and keep ourselves in dispositions favourable to grace. A soul that does not live this habitual life of prayer needs a great effort each time it wants to be recollected and to arouse the affections upon which, generally speaking, depend the fruitfulness of the supernatural means that we have for sanctifying ourselves. On the other hand, a soul that leads a life of prayer never lets the Divine fire go out but keeps it ever smouldering; and when

1 1 Par. xxix, 17.

the regular hours of prayer or moments of inspiration arrive where this fire is put more directly or more exclusively in contact with grace—as occurs in the Sacraments, the Holy Sacrifice, the *Opus Dei*, the orders of obedience, the trials sent or permitted by God—these smouldering embers burst into flame and become a glowing furnace wherein the soul sees its love for God and the neighbour increased and transformed, sometimes in a very high degree. Love of God being the only source, and its intensity being the only measure of the fruitfulness of our acts, even of the most ordinary ones, the life of prayer which maintains and increases this love within us, becomes the secret of holiness for us.

You see how right our Blessed Father is in telling us to apply ourselves *often* to prayer. It is by the faithful and frequent exercise of prayer that we come gradually to lead this life of habitual union with God in view of which St. Benedict has established everything in his monastery: *Dominici schola servitii.*[1]

II

I have elsewhere commented at length[2] on the nature of prayer and pointed out the elements that constitute it. Taking it for granted that we have grasped the substance of the teaching on prayer let us content ourselves here with touching upon some points that concern the characteristics of prayer, such as we find them in the letter and spirit of the Rule of the holy Patriarch.

Prayer, as we have said, is the intercourse of the child of God with his Heavenly Father; thereby we adore Him, praise Him, tell Him our love for Him, learn to know His will, and obtain from Him the necessary help for the perfect accomplishment of this will. Prayer is the normal outcome, under the Holy Spirit's action, of the affections resulting from our divine adoption.

This definition affords us a glimpse of the primary qualities which prayer ought to have. If prayer be the conversation of the child of God with his Heavenly Father, it will bear the impress both of a high degree of piety and of a deep reverence. Indeed for the child of God, for the brother of Christ Jesus, no tenderness, no intimacy is too great, but on

1 Prologue of the Rule.

2 *Christ, the Life of the Soul,* 2nd Part, ch. 10, *Prayer*.

the condition that it be always accompanied and sustained by a sense of unutterable reverence before the immense majesty of the Father: *Patrem immensae majestatis.*[1] This is to adore the Father in spirit and in truth.[2]

And it is this double character St. Benedict requires in his Rule. What does he tell us, in fact, in that chapter on the reverence we ought to have at prayer? He would have us first of all "offer our supplications to the Lord God of all things with all lowliness and purity of devotion": that is the note of reverence. We are to draw near to God with that sense of respect before His infinite perfections which is expressed by a humble attitude and the longing to be pure in the presence of holiness itself. St. Benedict knows of and wishes for no better manifestation of this reverence than tears of compunction shed in remembrance of faults whereby, miserable creatures as we are, we have offended a God full of majesty—tears accompanied by entire purity of heart.

He wishes our prayer to be "pure and short" "unless" he adds,—and here comes in the note of submission of heart proper to an adopted child of God—"it be perchance prolonged by the inspiration of Divine grace": *Nisi forte ex affectu inspirationis divinae gratiae protendatur.*[3]

Our holy Patriarch requires then that we come before God with respect and humility, as befits creatures, and creatures who have sinned; but this deep reverence which holds us prostrate before Him in all submission, does not prevent the heart from opening out, under the movement of the Holy Spirit, in confidence, love and tenderness. This confidence is so much the surer in that it rests exclusively on the goodness of our Father in Heaven.

In the Prologue, our Blessed Father recalls these Divine words:[4] "My eyes will be upon you, and My ears will be open to your prayers, and before you call upon Me, I will say unto you: 'Behold, I am here!' What can be sweeter, dearest brethren," the great Patriarch immediately adds, "than this voice of the Lord inviting us and shewing unto us the way of life?"

Thus appears the double aspect of piety as St. Benedict understands it. These affections are both necessary; they are inseparable, as our condition of creatures and our character of children of God are inseparable. If an unrestrained familiarity, forgetful of reverence, is perilous, fear,

1 Hymn *Te Deum.*
2 Cf. Joan. iv, 23.
3 Rule, ch. xx.
4 Cf. Ps. xxxiii, 16; Isa. lxv, 24; lviii, 9.

separated from confidence, is not less so; each of these two attitudes is a wrong done to God: irreverence, to His infinite sovereignty: servile fear, to His boundless goodness.

This reverence and this confidence are possible and are maintained only if we take care to prepare ourselves for our intercourse with God. Some might say: Since it is the Spirit of Jesus Who prays within us, we can come into God's presence without preparation. To think in this way, would be to make a great mistake; we cannot expect the Holy Spirit's action to be forthcoming in our souls independently of certain interior conditions. You know the Protestant sect of Quakers. Very respectable people are to be met with among them, but their religion is rather singular. The principal religious act consists for them in assembling in their meeting-houses, large square halls with white-washed walls; men and women sit upon benches which are the only furniture in the edifice; silence is established, all await until "the spirit moves." All at once, sometimes after long waiting, one of those present, a man or woman, boy or girl, cries out: "The Spirit moves me." And immediately she or he rises and begins to say "what the Spirit breathes." All listen attentively to the words, which are, most often, only disconnected ramblings. When the speaker has finished, the "prayer" is at an end and the assembly disperses. These Quakers expect everything from the Spirit; their whole religion consists in this desire for the moving of the Spirit which makes the soul vibrate and agitates the body, whence the name of "quakers." No interior preparation is required, no exterior action is asked for.

It cannot be the same for us; our prayer is not the result of nervous troubles or illusion. "The Spirit Himself asketh for us," says St. Paul,[1] but the same Apostle warns us not to "grieve"[2] nor "extinguish" the Spirit.[3] Now, how do we extinguish the Spirit? By mortal sin, which forces Him to separate Himself from the soul. How do we grieve Him? Certainly not by the frailties we deplore, the faults that take us by surprise, but we grieve Him by our infidelities and our deliberate resistance to divine inspirations. We must, then, if we would make the life of prayer possible and prayer itself fruitful, watch over the purity of our heart. St. Benedict holds much to this quality. It is "the purity of our devotion" which

1 Rom. viii, 26. 2 Eph. iv, 30. 3 I Thes. v, 19.

is to be the condition of our supplications: *Puritatis devotione supplicandum est*; "let us know it is only for our purity of heart and tears of compunction that we shall be heard": *In puritate cordis et compunctione lacrymarum nos exaudire sciamus.*[1] The soul that does not strive to purify itself of its faults by compunction, to avoid as far as possible all that could be displeasing to God, cannot attain to a life of union with Him through prayer: it wilfully grieves the Holy Spirit Who must uphold the soul in prayer. It is in this purity that the preparation of the heart consists, a remote preparation, but always necessary.

Another preparation, of a more intellectual character, is likewise demanded. The Holy Spirit guides us according to our nature: intellect and will. Before entering into prayer we ought to possess some knowledge of the things of faith which will serve us as elements for this communing with God. You may say that God sometimes gives a soul the gift of prayer even before it has acquired great knowledge of the mysteries of faith and dogma, or is completely purified. Undoubtedly this is so, but it is not the general way. We here find a certain analogy between the manner in which God governs the natural world, and His mode of action in the order of grace. See how things come to pass in the domain of creation. God could produce effects without the concourse of secondary causes; He could create bread and wine without man having to sow and reap, plant and gather the grapes. Did He not change the water into wine at Cana? and multiply the loaves in the desert? He is the Sovereign Master of all the elements, but His glory requires that the habitual course of things be ruled by the laws which His eternal wisdom has established. God wills that the vine shall be planted and the leaves bud forth, that the fruit shall ripen and be gathered by man and go through the wine-press, before the wine is poured out into the cup. After the same manner in the supernatural order there are laws fixed by Divine Wisdom and shown by the experience of the Saints. God undoubtedly is not enslaved by His laws. Thus He makes certain souls pass in an instant from the state of sin to a state of perfect love. Magdalen, by the disorders of her life, was at the antithesis of love; it needs but a word from Our Lord to change her life into one of glowing charity. Again look at Saul; he is a persecutor of the Christians, *spirans*

1 Rule, ch. xx.

minarum,[1] "breathing out threatenings and slaughter," hating the disciples of Jesus and blaspheming Christ: he is overthrown on the road to Damascus, and our Divine Saviour makes of him, in an instant, "a vessel of election,"[2] an Apostle full of fire who preaches Christ from Whom nothing can henceforth separate him. In the same way, we read in the life of St. Teresa[3] that, in one of her Carmels, a novice received the gift of prayer without anything having prepared her for this grace. But these are exceptional gifts or extraordinary prodigies whereby God manifests His sovereign power and reminds us of the infinite liberty of His Spirit and of His Spirit's action. God's ordinary way in leading souls to Himself is to have respect to the laws of which He is the Author.

But God excludes no one from benefiting from these laws about which we will say a few words. He calls all baptised souls to be intimately united to Him. Are we not, by grace, His children? the brethren of the Son of His love? the living temples of His Spirit? All the mysteries of Jesus, all the marvellous supernatural organism that He has established in His Church, to what do they tend, if not to open to upright, generous and faithful souls the way of love and of most intimate union with Himself? And if this be true of Christians in general, how much more must it be so for those whom, by a singular predestination, Christ has chosen to consecrate especially to His service? It is of them above all that He says: "I have called you friends" for I have made you enter into the secrets of My love.[4]

III

In speaking of the instruments of good works, we already said a word about the three stages that, in the ordinary way, the soul must pass through before coming to perfect union. It is necessary to return to this subject because the degree of our prayer is practically determined by the degree of our inner life.

As you know, spiritual authors mark out three states of the inner life; the purgative, the illuminative, and finally the unitive way. Although these three stages are real, they are not in contradistinction to one anoth-

---

1 Act. ix, 1. 2 Ibid. 15.
3 *History of St. Teresa,* according to the Bollandists. 4 Cf. Joan. xv, 15.

er; there exists between them a reciprocal penetration, a certain affinity; these denominations result only from the predominance of such or such an element, a predominance which cannot go so far as to exclude the other elements. Thus a soul who is in the way of purification likewise accomplishes, and it may be often, acts of the illuminative way and acts of union. In the same manner, a soul that is in the state of union cannot say: "I no longer need the thought of hell and the practice of mortification." We cannot then in this matter assign such or such impassable limits, or rather, we cannot geometrically fix souls in one state distinct from another; these stages are not separated by fixed boundaries passed once and forever; they more truly comprehend and sustain and complete one another, but with one predominating element: here purification, there illumination, finally, habitual union. With this reservation, let us say a word on each of these three "ways."

In the *purgative* way, the soul is chiefly occupied in the work of purification. It has come from the world to which it was more or less given up; more or less it has offended the Divine Majesty; it comes for its "conversion" says our Blessed Father: *Veniens quis ad conversionem*:[1] "conversion" here being taken in the wide sense of the word, and meaning detachment from every creature in order to seek God unceasingly. The Sacrament of Penance has remitted the sins of this soul but the scars of sins and evil tendencies remain; the attraction towards creatures is not entirely corrected; the soul is yet full of spiritual imperfections. It is doubtless in a state of grace and seeks God, but has not yet reached that state of purity and stability in good which is to make it worthy of the embrace of the Divine Spouse: the soul is not yet *paratum sicut sponsam ornatam viro suo*.[2]

God requires of this soul to take the last place at the feast. It must above all exercise itself in the first degrees of humility and in reverence towards God. It is not becoming, especially when one has greatly offended God, to expect to enter into familiarity with Him at the beginning of the spiritual life. We must remain at the end of the banquet table until our Lord calls us "to go up higher."[3] What ought to be the prayer of the soul in this state? Not having any acquired habit of prayer, nor possessing within itself the material elements of intercourse with God, it must

1 Rule, ch. lviii. 2 Apoc. xxi, 2. 3 Luc. xiv, 10.

perforce borrow them from such or such a work that will provide these elements and of which it will make use until the heart be touched and the will be made subject to God. Otherwise mental prayer may degenerate into a vague barren reverie. If in the course of prayer, God draws the soul to Him, then it can lay aside every book. Our Blessed Father compares prayer to an audience.[1] Now when we beg an audience with a great personage that we may present to him our homage and respect, we are careful to come prepared in order not to be taken unawares; but if in the course of the interview, this personage takes the direction of the conversation, we make it our duty to follow his lead without thinking any more of ourselves. In the same way we ought, especially at the beginning of the spiritual life, to have recourse to the help of such or such a practice, such or such a method, but without attaching so great importance to it as would leave us no liberty of spirit; the danger of illusion will moreover be avoided by submission to the direction of the Father Master.[2]

In this we should imitate the discretion of which our holy Patriarch gave proof. He was certainly a true contemplative; he possessed a great gift of prayer and a wide experience of the ways of union with God: none can doubt this on studying his life and Rule. In the latter we might expect to find long pages upon prayer. We find barely two short chapters; and in neither of them is any special method laid down; some principles, fundamental and characteristic, but briefly formulated, are all that he has left to us. Why is this? It is because our holy Legislator shines in discretion; he knows that nothing is more narrowing for souls than to regulate their intimate relations with God in too rigid and imperious a manner. He contents himself with indicating the fundamental *attitude* of the soul in presence of God, the dispositions that are the condition of the fecundity of the divine action in the soul: purity of heart, humility and compunction.

---

1 Rule, ch. xx.

2 "Before beginning your prayer," wrote a holy Benedictine nun, favoured with heavenly gifts, "try to realise God's presence in your soul; then make your proximate preparation; if in the continuance of your meditation the Lord inspires you with some special affections, follow the light that He gives you, and I pray Him to grant you the grace to keep the fruit of it for His glory." *An Ecstatic of the XVIIth Century. The Blessed Bonomo.*

As to the habitual subject of mental prayer in the purgative way, what is it to be? It ought to be chiefly taken from the Last Ends, Christ's Passion caused by our sins, the Divine perfections of which the sight fills the soul with fear and reverence. Prayer ought then to resolve itself before all into acts of compunction and most humble confidence. It is chiefly of a soul in this state that St. Benedict is speaking when he says "one ought daily in prayer to confess one's past sins with tears and sighs": *Mala sua praeterita cum lacrymis vel gemitu cotidie in oratione Deo confiteri.*[1]

Such is the dominant note, not however the exclusive note, of this stage. The monk who is in this way ought often to cast himself at the feet of God, as did the Prodigal Son, to ask pardon of Him and soften his own heart at the sight of the Divine Majesty he has offended and at the thought of the sufferings of Jesus; he ought to incline his will in all humble submission before the Divine will and that of his Superiors. The last fruit of this stage is submission, deep and generous because humble and contrite, to God's holy will whatsoever it may be, and whatsoever be the manner in which it is manifested.

The duration of this stage is more or less extended: it much depends on the manner of life previous to entering the monastery, the strength of bad habits, the degree of generosity that the soul brings to the work of self-purification. It is for a prudent and enlightened director to judge of this. However it is not presumptuous to believe that those who, during the Novitiate, have allowed themselves to be moulded by humility and obedience, who have been generous and full of ardour, who made their monastic profession with great love and great purity of intention, will on that day reach the threshold of the illuminative life. Monastic profession is indeed like a second baptism; to one who has been constantly faithful to grace during the time of probation, God certainly gives a great purity that enables him to advance in spiritual ways.

IV

As the name indicates, the *illuminative* way is characterised by the spiritual lights that God causes to abound in the soul, thanks to which it is filled, if we may thus speak, with the knowledge of divine things.

---

1 Rule, ch. iv.

God leads beings according to their nature. We are intellect and will; now we only love the good that we know. If then we wish to cleave fully to God, we must first know Him as perfectly as possible. Therefore, as the soul begins to be purified from all sin, from all negligence, God enlightens it little by little in order to bring it entirely to Himself. God has only to show Himself and the soul is drawn by His infinite wisdom, beauty, goodness and mercy. In return God requires of the soul who seeks Him that it should also give itself, and even for a long time, to the study of divine truths. This extremely important work was already begun in the preceding stage, but it must be intensified as one advances. The soul must go deeply into the truths of faith. Some might say: What is the use of so much searching into the truths of faith? What is the use of so many theological notions? What advantage do we reap from them? It would be dangerous to reason after this manner. Listen to these words of our Lord: O Holy Father, eternal life consists in knowing Thee, and in knowing Him Whom Thou hast sent here below, Jesus Christ: *Haec est vita aeterna: ut cognoscant te solum Deum verum, et quem misisti Jesum Christum.*[1] Thus it is Christ Jesus, the Infallible Truth, Who makes eternal life consist in the knowledge of His Father and of Himself, certainly not a knowledge purely theoretical but a practical knowledge which surrenders us wholly to the service of God and of His Beloved Son.

For there is knowledge and knowledge. There is a knowledge of Christ which is purely intellectual, limited to the understanding alone; one might thus know all that is treated of in the Gospel, the history of its composition, of its sources, of its text, all the commentaries that have been made on it; but this knowledge will remain cold and sterile if love be absent from it.

There is another knowledge of which the motive is neither curiosity of mind nor intellectual pleasure, but love seeking the beloved object with the view of being united to it, love striving to know more in order to love more. This is the knowledge that turns to love, practical knowledge. Study thus comprehended is the expansion of our faith; it becomes prayer, contemplation. This knowledge is necessary to us; it is important that it be developed, because it then becomes the principle of an ardent love.

1 Joan. xvii, 3.

God has not left us the treasures of revealed truth for us to keep them buried *in sudario*,[1] as if they were not worth the trouble of being studied. The deposit of revelation was delivered to us in order that, with humility and with eyes on the Church's teaching, we should exercise our intelligence in fathoming this deposit and in extracting from it all that is precious, glorious to God, and fruitful for our souls. The lives of the Saints show us that God loves this seeking after the truth, the starting point of a more generous charity. When He wishes to lead to a higher degree of union a soul that is, naturally speaking, little instructed, like St. Catherine of Siena, He Himself takes the charge of enlightening it by His Spirit and of giving it in an infused manner the knowledge of the deepest mysteries that it may therein find the secret of a more extensive love. Let us then be persuaded that studying the truths of faith makes the "talent," confided to us, fructify, and we thus labour at our sanctification.

Our faith should seek to be enlightened: *Fides quaerens intellectum*, said the great monk, St. Anselm.[2] According to our holy Father, the monastery is a school where we learn to serve the Lord: *Dominici schola servitii*:[3] but our service will be so much the more perfect and pleasing to God in proportion as our knowledge in matters of faith—whence love is derived—is the wider and deeper: *PROCESSU FIDEI... curritur via mandatorum Dei*.[4] It is therefore not a small thing to apply ourselves to nourish the faith within us.[5] The monk who is called by his vocation to a great union with Christ cannot content himself with a faith ignorant of the marvels wrought by God for our sanctification. Let us seek as St. Paul says, "to comprehend... what is the breadth, and length, and height, and depth" of the Divine mysteries, that we "may be filled unto all the fulness of God": *Ut impleamini in OMNEM plenitudinem Dei*.[6] Such is the goal of our efforts in this way of illumination:—to fill our souls with the truths of faith that they may become for us the principle of a closer union with God.

---

1 "In a napkin," Luc. xix, 20.

2 St. Anselm, *Meditat.* xxi, et *Epist.* i, ii, ep. xli.

3 Prologue of the Rule.

4 Prologue of the Rule.

5 Innocent XI condemned this proposition of Molinos: *Theologus minorem dispositionem habet quam homo rudis ad statum contemplativi* (The theologian has less disposition to the state of the contemplative than does the common man). Denziger-Banwart, *Enchiridion sumbolorum*, p. 363.

6 Eph. iii, 18, 19.

Now how are we to carry into effect this part of the work that God requires of us, whereby we may live in this state of illumination? The result may be obtained in different ways. There are souls who lay up and appropriate to themselves supernatural knowledge by reflection and meditation. This is an excellent means for souls who are engaged the most part of their time in what we agree to call the active life; for them, this is often the only means of entering deeply into the notions of faith and being permeated with supernatural truths.

Other souls incapable of giving themselves to this discursive labour, set apart a regular time for spiritual reading, either in the Gospels, or a *Life* of Our Lord, or an ascetic treatise on His mysteries, frequently interspersing this reading with aspirations of the heart towards God, towards Christ. This is for many the only possible manner of getting light on Divine things and of holding intercourse with the Heavenly Father.

For us, monks, this "illumination" finds its principal source in the Divine Office; therefore it is quite natural that after having spoken of the *Opus Dei* we should pass on to the subject of mental prayer. It is an immense advantage to be able to link our mental prayer to liturgical prayer, but to be enabled duly to appreciate this advantage it is necessary to understand it well. We have often encountered the truth that in the spiritual life all leads up to Christ Jesus. When St. Paul speaks of the understanding of the mysteries of faith that we ought to have, he sums all up in the knowledge of Jesus. He writes to the Ephesians that he does not cease to pray for them "that the God of our Lord Jesus Christ, the Father of glory," may give them a spirit of wisdom and of revelation in order to know Christ that so the eyes of their hearts may be enlightened.[1] Christ, is the great revelation of God; He is God interpreted to our souls. Jesus first makes known to us the Divine secrets; secondly He shows us how a God lives among men to teach them to live perfectly; He is the purest, the most living manifestation of the Divine perfections. When the Apostle Philip asks Our Lord to show him the Father, what does Christ reply? "He that seeth Me seeth the Father,"[2] for he makes only one with His Father: *Ego et Pater unum sumus*.[3] He is the image of the invisible God.[4] Therefore to be filled with the knowledge of God[5] we

1 Eph. i, 16–18.
2 Joan. xiv, 9.
3 Ibid. x, 30.
4 Col. i, 15.
5 Cf. Eph. iii, 19.

have but to look at the Person of Our Lord, to listen to His words, to contemplate His mysteries.

Now where shall we find the account of what Christ said and did? In the Gospel. But the Gospel is to be found admirably set forth, enshrined and commented upon in the Liturgy. From Advent to Pentecost, the Church places the entire life of her Divine Spouse under our eyes, not only as it appears in the Gospel, but illustrated, we may say, by the prophecies, the letters of St. Paul and the commentaries of the holy Doctors. The Church makes us contemplate, one by one and link by link, all the mysteries of Jesus; all that He said, all that He did, all that He fulfilled in His person, all that He willed for us, is there presented by the Church, in its proper place. Nowhere can we better learn the actions of Christ Jesus, the words that fell from His lips, the affections of His Divine Heart; it is the Gospel lived over again at each of the stages of the terrestrial life of Christ, the Man-God, Saviour of the world, Head of His Mystical Body, and bringing with Him to our souls the virtue and grace of all His mysteries. Nowhere so much as in the Liturgy does there exist a narration as complete and simple, as ordered and profound, of all the wonders that God has wrought for our sanctification and salvation; it is a revelation of what is at the same time most perfect and most appropriate for our souls; it is a setting forth that speaks to the eyes of the body and of the imagination, and that touches the attentive soul to its very depths.

The Liturgical Cycle is an incomparable source of supernatural illumination. But furthermore—and this is a truth of paramount importance for our sanctification—we can therein obtain the special fruit that Our Lord willed to attach to each of His mysteries in living them for us here below, as our Head.

To this source, then, our prayer may go for its elements. The monk ought to follow the Church, the Bride of Christ, in Christ's footsteps, listen to His words, contemplate His actions in order to imitate His virtues. Never let us weary of returning to these themes in our prayer: each action, each state in Christ's life is not only a teaching, but in the wide sense of the word, a "sacrament." To approach Christ thus is to walk in a path which is one of the surest and most fruitful.[1]

1 See the *Note* at the end of the Conference.

We may be easily convinced that this path is truly that wherein St. Benedict leads his sons. The holy Legislator in fact speaks of mental prayer immediately after having treated of the Divine Praise;[1] he links it closely to "the Work of God."[2] According to his life written by St. Gregory, we see that the monks gave themselves to prayer "after the office": *expleta psalmodia*.[3] Like the Egyptian monks[4] it was after each psalm that they prayed for a few instants in silence, first standing then prostrating themselves on the ground as they poured out before God their souls enlightened and touched by the sacred verses. This custom has disappeared, but St. Benedict has kept the idea that inspired it; and we must keep it after him. Our holy Father wishes likewise that the time which according to the regular horarium remains available after Matins should be spent in meditating on the psalms or lessons: *Quod vero restat post vigilias... psalterii vel lectionum... meditationi inserviatur*. We know that it was the custom of the monks, anterior to the great Patriarch, to fill the interludes of the Divine Office with meditation on the eternal truths; St. Benedict gathered up this precious tradition and made it his own.[5]

We should then take from the Divine Office, of which Christ is the centre, the elements of our prayer, whether we have retained some text that struck us during the recitation, in order to meditate upon it, or whether after the Office we speak to Our Lord with the help of a Breviary or other book appropriate to the feast or the mystery.[6] Our prayer should be like the flower of the psalmody. We know how the ancient monks, St. Gregory, St. Bede, St. Anselm, St. Bernard and so many others lived this life of prayer; we know that it was by drawing at this source that St. Hildegarde, St. Elisabeth of Schönau, St. Gertrude and St. Mechtilde rose to such heights of contemplation and love. So sure and fruitful is this way which is that of the Church herself.[7]

---

1 Rule, ch. xix and xx. 2 Ch. lii. 3 *Dialogues*. Lib. ii, ch. 15.
4 Cassian, *Institut*. ii, 7. 5 Rule, ch. viii.
6 For example, the *Meditations upon the Gospel*, or the *Elevations upon the Mysteries*, by Bossuet; *Elevations upon the Life and Doctrine of Our Lord Jesus Christ*, by Mgr. Gay, etc.
7 Cf. D. Besse, *Les Mystiques Bénédictins*. See also D. Festugière, l. c. p. 86.

V

Like those who have gone before us, we too shall find in the *Opus Dei* a pure and unfailing source of illumination, extremely fruitful for the inner life. When we are faithful in reciting the Divine Office *well*, the Holy Spirit—Who inspired the Psalms and directs the Church in the organisation of the worship of Jesus—gives us little by little a deep knowledge, full of unction, *sapida*, of God's perfections and the mysteries of Christ; a knowledge more fruitful than any we could gain by study and reasoning; the Holy Spirit illumines with His Divine light some truth, some word or mystery of Jesus; He deeply engraves them in the soul.

This knowledge, altogether heavenly, supernatural and sweet, fills the soul with humility and confidence, and thus illumined with divine splendours, it annihilates itself before God and surrenders itself entirely to His holy will. The Holy Spirit, as has been justly said, "suggests the attitude of sincere souls,"[1] the inward attitude which places the soul before God in full truth.

For you will remark that the sacred texts are not taken from man; they come to us from Heaven; and as none but the Holy Ghost, Who inspired them, can make us know their depth, so none but He alone, as Christ Himself said, can make us understand the words that fell from the lips of the Incarnate Word, the actions accomplished and the mysteries lived by the Saviour's Sacred Humanity: *Ille vos docebit omnia et suggeret vobis omnia quaecumque dixero vobis*.[2] The Holy Spirit presents these truths in a divine light to the soul; they hence become as it were the elements of our own life, without there being need of reasoning. The passing vividness of the first impression fades, it is true; but the truth has been deeply perceived and remains in the soul like a principle of life: *Verba Christi Spiritus et vita sunt*.[3] The Divine Office is truly a "granary," *promptuarium*, prepared by God Himself, and those who recite the Office *devoutly* abound in the lights of the Holy Spirit; after a few years, prayer becomes an easy habit to them. The novice who for the first time hears this fact affirmed may be, for want of experience, astonished at it.

---

1 D. I. Ryelandt, *Bréviaire et Méditation*, 1912.

2 "He will teach you all things, and bring all things to your mind, whatsoever I shall have said to you," Joan. xiv, 26.

3 "The words [of Christ] are spirit and life," Cf. Ibid. vi, 64.

But, if he is fervent, he will learn for himself, and quickly enough, that assiduous and daily acquaintance with the inspired word is a sure and easy way of conversing with God.

"How can it be that a soul prepared and formed by the Holy Spirit should not know better than any other how to converse with God in the intimacy of her heart returning as she does to her solitude laden like a bee with honey from so many flowers? How can she be ignorant of the right language in which to address the Divine Majesty, when she enters into the secret chamber of her heart, all replenished with the Divine Word? What is contemplation in its highest form but the opening out of the beautiful affirmations which the prayer of the Church puts upon our lips? When a soul borrows her expressions from human language, she will never find any words that more exactly convey the truths which she has contemplated than the forms of liturgical prayer, lending themselves, as they do, with equal ease to the lispings of the soul beginning to seek God and to the enraptured outpourings of the soul that has found Him."[1]

Do we not grasp how well founded is this doctrine when we examine things with the eyes of faith, and view everything in a supernatural light? What is the aim of prayer, of all prayer? To unite ourselves to God in order to do His will. If prayer does not tend to this, it is a mere amusement of the mind, mere child's play of the soul. Now what is "the will of God"? Our sanctification: *Haec est voluntas Dei sanctificatio vestra.*[2] These are St. Paul's words. But this same Apostle does not cease to repeat to us under a hundred different forms that our sanctification is of the supernatural order, that it is God alone Who has created this order and established the means of realising it in us; that our sanctification amounts to the entire reproduction in us of the features of Jesus. The Father has no other will for us; indeed, the very form of our predestination—and holiness is but the realisation of predestination in its plenitude—is the conforming of ourselves to His beloved Son: *Praedestinavit [nos Deus] conformes fieri imaginis Filii sui.*[3] All prayer, the whole life of prayer, ought then to tend to form Christ within us more, until we shall be able to say

1 *Spiritual Life and Prayer According to the Holy Scripture and Monastic Tradition* by Madame Cecile J. Bruyère, Abbess of Solesmes. Ch. 10, translated by the Benedictines of Stanbrook. This work is excellent in every point; unfortunately it is too little known.

2 I Thess. iv, 3. 3 Rom. viii, 29.

in all truth: "I live, now not I; but Christ liveth in me": *Vivo autem, jam non ego: vivit vero in me Christus.*[1]

Now what better way could be found of forming Jesus in us[2] than to contemplate His mysteries, and thereby obtain the strength to imitate them? The soul, faithful in following Christ step by step as the Church presents Him, infallibly arrives at reproducing within itself the character (in the deep meaning of the word) of Christ Jesus. The Church, in her Liturgy, is guided by the Holy Spirit, and it is this Spirit Who not only enlightens us as to Christ's mysteries, but forms in us—for He is the *digitus Dei*[3]—the features of Christ. St. Paul tells us that without the Holy Spirit we cannot even pronounce the name of Jesus;[4] with much greater reason, we are incapable, without the help of this Divine Artist, of reproducing in our souls the features of the heavenly Model, the form of our predestination and the Ideal of our perfection. Undoubtedly, we see souls succeed, by force of will and effort, in forming within themselves the human character, the natural virtues; but in order to form within us the Divine character, to engrave within us supernatural traits, the only ones that make us pleasing to God, it needs the action of the Holy Spirit, and this action is unceasing in the Liturgy.

Thus a life of prayer which is like the continual echo of the liturgical life that each year makes us walk closer, by faith, reverence and love, in the steps of Christ Jesus, from His Birth to His Ascension, besides having a very sure and supernatural foundation, possesses incomparable efficacy and fruitfulness.

From the fact that our prayer as monks takes its elements from the Liturgy, it becomes, I do not say exclusively but mostly, affective.[5] Our soul expresses desires rather than forms reasonings. We no longer need to reason in order to be convinced of the Divine truths: we find them ready set before us by the Church in their fulness and splendour; we have only to open our eyes, to put out our hand, to dispose our heart in order to appropriate these truths; the attentive and faithful soul that lives in

1 Gal. ii, 20. 2 Ibid. iv, 19.

3 "The finger of God," Hymn *Veni Creator.* 4 I Cor. xii, 3.

5 We do not say: sentimental. The remainder of the text sufficiently explains our thought.

solitude is spared the labour of discursive reasoning. What is necessary is to be well prepared, as we have said, to accomplish "the work of God"; when the soul is recollected, the Holy Spirit enlightens it little by little and fills it with those *Verba Verbi* which become well-springs of life and principles of action. It is a law of experience that one who recites the Divine Office in the necessary dispositions goes out from the choir replenished with truths, and is thereby placed in an altogether favourable atmosphere for prayer and the inner life.

The soul is inclined above all to express its desires. It is in holy desires which come from the heart and not in the multitude and arrangement of words that prayer lies. When we have this inward thirst of conversing with Our Lord, when we feel the need of speaking with Him, we do not make phrases; we tell Him how much we love Him, how much we desire to love Him; we listen to Him; we stay looking at Him, praising Him, adoring Him, were it only by a humble attitude, full of reverence and confidence. Commenting on these words of Job: "Who would grant... that the Almighty may hear my desire," St. Gregory the Great tells us: "Remark these words: my desire. True prayer is not in the sound of the voice, but in the desires of the heart; not our words but our desires give power to our cries in God's most secret hearing. If we ask for eternal life with our lips without desiring it from the bottom of our heart, our cry is a silence; if, without speaking, we desire it from the bottom of our heart, our silence cries out."[1]

The words of this great monk, who was at the same time a great Pope and a great contemplative, are but an echo of those of our holy Father. "Let us remember," says St. Benedict—who himself echoes Our Lord's own words[2]—"that it is not for our much speaking, but for the purity of heart, and tears of compunction that we shall deserve to be heard..."[3] A monk may remain in the oratory after the Divine Office and there pray "not in a loud voice for fear of disturbing his brethren praying beside him,

1 *Moralia in Job,* Lib. xxii, ch. 17, n. 43. p. L. t. 76, col. 238. St. Augustine says the same: *Ipsum desiderium tuum oratio tua est, et si continuum desiderium continua oratio... continuum desiderium tuum continua vox tua est... Flagrantia caritatis clamor cordis est* (Your desire itself is your prayer, and if you have continual desire you have continual prayer... your continual desire is your continual voice... The blaze of charity is the cry of the heart). *Enarr. in Ps. xxxvii,* n. 14. P. L. 37. col. 404.

2 Matt. vi, 7. 3 Rule, ch. xx.

but with tears and fervour of heart": *Intret et oret, non in clamosa voce, sed in lacrymis et intentione cordis.*[1] The monk pours out to Him the desires with which the liturgy has inflamed his soul, desires which are all summed up in that prayer taught to us by Jesus Christ, our Master,[2] and that occurs so frequently in the Divine Office: "Father... hallowed be Thy name, Thy kingdom come, Thy will be done on earth as in Heaven..."

To speak thus to the Father is to adore Him "in spirit and in truth," *in spiritu et in veritate*, it is a prayer that rises up to Him like fragrant incense; when we recite the Office with piety and devotion, this prayer becomes very easy. As soon as the soul comes in contact with a Divine truth or one of Christ's mysteries, it overflows in pure but fervent desire, and "sees" in the truth of God what God asks of it. The soul has reached the fountainhead of a life of intense union.

VI

When a soul is thus faithful in following Christ Jesus step by step, in allowing itself to be replenished by the Holy Spirit with truths from on high and in conforming its life to them, God leads it little by little to the *state* of prayer. This is the third stage: that of the unitive life, where the soul clings solely to God, to Christ. It can make the words of the Apostle its own: "Who shall separate (me) from the love of Christ?" *Quis me separabit a caritate Christi?*[3] There are many degrees in this state, but it is certain that the day will come when God will raise us to that degree which He wills for each one of us, if we continue to be generously faithful in seeking Him alone: *Ego merces tua magna nimis.*[4]

Indeed in the measure wherein a soul is stripped of self, God acts more and more within it; He draws to Himself all the faculties of the soul that He may simplify their exercise. Prayer becomes more simple, the soul no longer feels the need of reflecting much, of thinking much, of speaking much; the direct action of God is made deeper; the soul is motionless before God, as it were, knowing that He is there; it is intimately united to Him by an act of loving adherence, while yet this act is enveloped with the shadows of faith. This union can be compared to that

1 Ibid. ch. lii. 2 Matt. vi, 9. 3 Rom. viii, 35.
4 "I am thy reward exceeding great," Gen. xv, i.

of two souls who each know what the other is thinking, even without speaking, and are in complete union of sentiment, without needing to express themselves. Such is contemplation: the soul looks at God, loves Him and is silent. And God looks at the soul and fills it to overflowing. This is what persons do who are knit together by a deep love: when they have said all they have to say, they are content to be silent; a simple glance tells all their love and tenderness. The soul remains in this prayer of faith, united to God, to Christ Jesus, without any intermediary. The soul puts aside all that the senses, the natural intelligence, even revealed truths, say of God: it rests in pure faith.

It can say to God: "Since I am unable to see Thee such as Thou art, I want no types or images; I prefer to identify my intelligence with that of Christ and to contemplate Thee through His eyes, for He seeth Thee, O my God, as Thou art." In this tryst of the soul with its God, in this immediate contact with the Beloved, the soul gives itself and finds all good, for God also communicates Himself in revealing Himself. This contact of faith and love is sometimes very short, lasting only a few instants, but it is sufficient to fill the soul with light; the life of God becomes its own, the Divine activity transforms its own.

This union with God in faith is very simple but very fruitful. For the soul who lives in it, these words of the Lord in the Scriptures are fulfilled: "I will espouse thee to Me in faith: and thou shalt know that I am the Lord": *Sponsabo te mihi in fide: et scies quia ego Dominus.*[1] What ought the soul to do? To give itself up, to let itself be taken; God touches the soul, He seizes its every fibre to make them all converge to Himself as to their centre; it is a Divine embrance, in which the soul, despite aridity, or darkness, or its own powerlessness, has nothing to do but yield itself up into the Divine Artist's transforming hand.

The fruitfulness of this prayer merits for it the name of transforming. It is said that in Heaven we shall be like to God, "because we shall see Him as He is": *Similes ei erimus, quoniam videbimus eum sicuti est.*[2] Immediately the blessed soul sees God, it is identified with Him in the intellect by truth, and in the will by love. In the measure possible, the soul is—not equal evidently—but like to God: the Beatific Vision works this transformation, rendering the soul like to God, to such a degree

1 Ose. ii, 20. 2 I Joan. iii, 2.

that it is united to Him in unity. Now, during this life, what is the prelude to the vision that the elect enjoy? Prayer through faith. The soul by contemplating God, through faith, in prayer, sees His perfections in all truth, it surrenders itself to this truth; and thus beholding in God the Sovereign and Unique Good, its will is united to this Divine will, fount of all beatitude for the soul: and the more powerful this adherence is, the more the soul is united to God. This is why prayer in faith is so precious for the soul. We ought to wish to reach a high degree in this prayer, that is to say to attain to this union full of love and simplicity, which results in an outpouring of the most pure Divine light.

The value of this union is very great, for it sometimes transforms a soul in a very short time. Plunge an iron bar into the fire; without delay, the iron shares in all the qualities of the fire. God is a furnace; the soul that plunges in God through prayer is wholly filled with light and heat, its love increases in immense proportions, and this is a great grace. God then acts in the soul much more than the soul itself acts. He works in it, the Holy Spirit takes it in hand. We then accomplish with great ease and much better what was hitherto done very imperfectly. God Himself brings forth the virtues which before we had toiled painfully to acquire. This state is therefore exceedingly to be desired; the Fathers of the Church have always regarded it as perfection, the normal crowning point of the whole spiritual life. Far from producing pride, it gives birth in the soul to the deepest sense of its nothingness, for it is impossible for the creature to comprehend God's greatness without realising at the same time its own littleness.

However it would be an error to think that we can attain to a high degree of this prayer without having laboured much and suffered much for God and His glory. Under the ordinary conditions of His Providence, God does not give Himself to the soul with this plenitude until the evening of life, when the soul has proved, by a constant fidelity to the inspirations of grace, that it belongs wholly to God and in all things truly seeks but Him alone: *Si revera Deum quaerit.*[1]

We ought to tend to this blessed state, to which many religious souls are certainly called; it is to this life of union that the monk's whole existence should tend; otherwise it is useless. This is truly what our Holy

1 Rule, ch. lviii.

Father proposes to us:—to be so far stripped of self, and cleansed from all sin that God may fully act in us as Master through the action of His Spirit: *Quae Dominus jam in operarium suum mundum a vitiis et peccatis Spiritu Sancto dignabitur demonstrare.*[1] It is this state of perfect charity that is reached by the generous and constant ascension of the degrees of humility which resume in themselves the whole work of purification: *His omnibus humilitatis gradibus ascensis, monachus mox ad caritatem Dei perveniet illam quae perfecta foris mittit timorem.*[2] Happy state wherein the soul that is all for God finds the prelude to that eternal union of endless beatitude![3]

VII

The best means of stimulating within ourselves the holy ambition of a like state is to maintain with vigilance our life of prayer. Our holy Lawgiver organised his monastery so that this life might become easy for us: separation from the world, solitude, silence and recollection, holy reading, the Divine Office are so many elements that are of a nature to create and favour the life of prayer.

We must first of all seek solitude and silence. We see our Blessed Father in his youth leave the world: *recessit.* What is his aim? "To please God alone": *Soli Deo placere desiderans;*[4] but there is no true solitude that is not bathed in an atmosphere of silence. Noise, in fact, disturbs the soul's inward recollection; to walk noisily, to shut the doors in the same way, to hold loud conversations, can hinder our brethren from giving themselves up to prayer; upon this point, each one should have it at

1 Ibid. ch. vii. 2 Ibid. ch. vii.

3 This is how a nun of a wonderful mystical life, the Blessed J. Bonomo, characterised the three stages: "The purgative way leads to the feet of Christ (this signifies humility feeling its misery and imploring grace and pardon); the illuminative way leads to the side of Christ, wherein are contained the divine secrets which the beloved disciple learnt at the Last Supper as he leaned upon his Master's breast; the unitive way leads to the kiss: supreme testimony of that union which begins upon earth to be consummated in Heaven." *Life* of D. du Bourg, pp. 38-40. This comparison is already to be found in the writings of St. Catherine of Siena. *Dialogue,* ch. 10. St. Bernard speaks of the kiss of the Feet, of the Hand and of the Mouth of the Lord which signify the three stages of the soul's progress (*In cantic. Sermones* iii, iv, P. L. 183, col. 794, sq.).

4 St. Gregory, *Dialogues.* Lib. ii, ch. 1.

heart to respect the inner life of his brethren, to facilitate it by carefully avoiding all that could be an obstacle to it. Little things, yes, but pleasing to God, for they favour His intimate work in souls.

More than outward noise, indulgence in useless conversations divert the attention of the soul and destroy recollection. Whenever, apart from the time given to recreation, we speak without authorisation, unless urged to do so by the motive of the love of God or of our neighbour, we commit an infidelity, we put an obstacle in the way of our intimate union with God; with culpable levity, we allow the perfume of the Divine visit received in that morning's Communion to evaporate. As St. Benedict says, we do harm to ourselves and are a distraction to others: *Non solum sibi inutilis est, sed etiam alios distollit.*[1] Where silence is not observed, it can be affirmed that the inner life is lacking in intensity. Therefore our Blessed Father rarely concedes to his disciples the faculty of speaking together.[2] Is it not remarkable that after having pointed out a great number of "instruments of good works" he reserves three of which to treat more specially, thus signalising that these are, in his eyes, particularly precious, namely, obedience, silence, humility? He warns us to keep what he calls by a word of deep meaning: "the gravity of silence," *taciturnitatis gravitas.*[3] He knows and repeats that a multitude of words is often the source of sin. Silence is, for him, the atmosphere of prayer; when he invites us to give ourselves frequently to prayer,[4] it is only after, having laid down the preliminary conditions: "To keep our mouth from all evil words. Not to love much speaking. Not to speak vain words apt only to provoke laughter. Not to love excessive laughter."[5] Does then our great Patriarch condemn joy? Quite the contrary! He extols that "dilatation of heart" the fruit of a joy of which the sweetness is unspeakable;[6] but he condemns, with a severity which is only too well justified, all that dissipates the soul and the interior life, particularly words out of season, buffooneries, mere jesting, the habitual tendency to levity of spirit: things which he wishes to see forever banished from his monasteries: *Aeterna clausura in omnibus locis damnamus.*[7] So sure is he that a soul which pours itself out in a torrent of words cannot hear within itself the Divine voice of the interior Master.

---

1 Rule, ch. xlviii. 2 Rule, ch. vi. 3 Ibid. ch. vi. 4 Ibid. ch. iv.
5 Ibid. 6 Prologue of the Rule. 7 Rule, ch. vi.

Silence of the lips would be of small use unless silence of the heart were joined to it: "To what serves material solitude," says St. Gregory, "if the solitude of the soul be lacking?" *Quid prodest solitudo corporis si solitudo defuerit cordis?*[1] We might live in a Carthusian monastery and not be recollected, if we allowed our imagination to wander over an immense field of memories and insignificant things, if we dreamt of these futilities and opened our mind to vain thoughts. It is distressing to see how lightly we often squander our thoughts. In God's sight, a thought is worth more than all the material universe; heaven may be gained, it may be lost by a thought... Let us then watch over ourselves; let us guard our imagination and our mind, which we have consecrated to God, from all tendency to run after deceptive mirages and unwholesome or useless thoughts: as soon as they appear let us dash them, as St. Benedict wishes, against the rock which is Christ: *Cogitationes malas cordi suo advenientes mox ad Christum allidere.*[2] It is by this vigilance, says our Blessed Father again, that we shall remain exempt at every hour from sins of thought[3] and safeguard within ourselves the precious good of interior recollection. A frivolous, superficial soul, wilfully and habitually distracted by the disordered agitation of sterile thought cannot hear God's voice. But happy that soul that lives in inward silence, the fruit of a calm imagination, of the rejection of vain solicitude and heedless haste, of the quelling of the passions, of progress in solid virtue, of the concentration of the faculties upon the constant seeking after the Only Good! Happy this soul! God will speak to it frequently; the Holy Spirit will make it hear those words of life which do not strike the bodily ears, but which the attentive soul gathers up with joy within itself as the nourishment of its life.

Was it not in interior recollection that the Blessed Virgin lived? The Gospel writes of her that she kept the words of her Divine Son in her heart, so that she might meditate upon them: *Maria conservabat omnia verba haec conferens in corde suo.*[4] The Blessed Virgin did not speak many words: filled with grace and light from on high, inundated with the gifts of the Spirit, she remained silent, in the adoration of her Son; she lived on the contemplation of the ineffable mystery wrought in her and

---

1 *Moralia in Job,* Lib. xxx, ch. 16. P. L. 76, col. 553.

2 Rule, ch. iv. 3 Ibid. ch. vii. 4 Luc. ii, 19.

through her; and from the sanctuary of her immaculate heart a hymn of praise and thanksgiving rose up unceasingly to God. Our monasteries are like other Nazareths where, in virginal souls, divine mysteries should likewise be wrought. Let us then live in recollection and try to remain closely united to our Lord.

It is not enough to keep outward silence, to put away vain and profitless thoughts from mind and heart; this inward solitude must be filled with reflections that help the soul to rise towards God. Our Patriarch provides for this by "holy reading"; he wishes the monk to listen to it willingly: *Lectiones sanctas libenter audire.*[1] Numerous hours are set apart by him for what he calls the *lectio divina*;[2] he wishes this holy reading to be taken especially from Holy Scripture, the works of the Fathers, and the conferences of the monks of ancient times.[3] Our Blessed Father knew by experience that no source of contemplation is purer and more fruitful than the Holy Scriptures. Indeed what is contemplation but the movement of the soul that, touched and illumined by light from above, enters into the mystery of God? It is true that no one has ever seen God,[4] for He "inhabiteth light inaccessible,"[5] says St. Paul. How then are we to know Him? By His words. "Would you enter into the very heart of God?" says St. Gregory. "Listen to His words": *Disce cor Dei in verbis Dei.*[6] With a being as essentially true as God, His words manifest His nature. Have we not here the very mystery of the Eternal Essence? God expresses Himself in His Word, in an infinite manner, so perfect and so adequate that this Word is Unique.

And see how this Word, Who is Light, veiling His native splendour under the infirmity borrowed from our flesh, reveals Himself to us in the Incarnation: *Illuxit cordibus nostris ad illuminationem scientiae claritatis Dei in facie Christi Jesu.*[7] This Word makes us hear the words from on high, which He alone knows because He alone ever dwells in the Father's Bosom: *Qui est in sinu Patris ipse enarravit*;[8] being "One with the Father," He gives us the words which the Father has given to Him,[9] so

1 Rule, ch. iv. 2 Ibid. ch. xlviii. 3 Ibid. ch. ix and lxxiii.
4 Joan. i, 18; I Joan. iv, 12. 5 I Tim. vi, 16.
6 Lib. iv. *Epist.* 31. P. L. 77, col. 706.
7 "For God... hath shined in our hearts, to give the light of the knowledge of the glory of God, in the face of Christ Jesus," II Cor. iv, 6. 8 Joan. i, 18.
9 Cf. Ibid. xvii, 8.

that the words of Jesus, sent by the Father, are the words of God Himself: *Quem enim misit Deus, verba Dei loquitur.*[1] Manifold words of the One Word, as the human words that translate them are manifold and likewise the generations that are to hear them in order to live by them.

These words of God are words of Eternal Life: *Verba vitae aeternae habes.*[2] Our Lord tells us: "This is eternal life [O Father]: That They may know thee, the only true God, and [Him] Whom Thou hast sent."[3] The words of Jesus, the Incarnate Word, reveal God to us, His Nature, His Being, His Perfections, His Love, His Rights, His Will. Being the utterances of the Word, the utterances of Wisdom, they make the soul penetrate into the light from above; they transport us into these holy splendours where God dwells. The soul, therefore, that, full of faith, hearkens assiduously to these words is wonderfully enlightened upon the plenitude of the Divine mystery, and is able, with perfect safety, to remain in contemplation of this mystery.

Where shall we find Jesus' words, these words that should be for us "fountains of water springing up into everlasting life?"[4] In the Gospel, first of all. There we listen to Jesus Himself, the Word Incarnate; we see Him revealing in human words that which is ineffable, translating the invisible into deeds comprehensible to our feeble minds; we have but to open our eyes, to prepare our heart, in order to know and rejoice in this light of glory: "The glory which Thou hast given me," says the Saviour in speaking of the Apostles to His Father, "I have given to them."[5] To the Gospels are to be added the letters of the Apostles especially those of St. John and of St. Paul: both repeat to us the divine words into the meaning of which they had penetrated, the one while resting his head upon the Master's Heart, the other in those visions where Christ Himself gave him to hear the *arcana verba*,[6] "secret words" containing His mystery.

And as Jesus Christ was "yesterday" as He is "to-day" and will be to-morrow,[7] even the Old Testament itself reveals Him to us. Did He not say that it was of His Person that Moses spoke? Did He not frequently bring to mind the prophecies concerning Him? And as for the Psalms, are they not overflowing with Him, to the point of being, according

1 Ibid. iii, 34.
2 Ibid. vi, 69.
3 Joan. xvii, 3.
4 Cf. Ibid. iv, 14.
5 Cf. Ibid. xvii, 22.
6 II Cor. xii, 4.
7 Hebr. xiii, 8.

to Bossuet's beautiful expression, "a Gospel of Jesus Christ turned into canticles, affections, acts of thanksgiving, and holy desires?"[1]

The whole treasury of the Scriptures, then, reveals Christ to us; on each page we read His name. These pages are full of Him, of His Person, His perfections, His deeds; each repeats to us His incomparable love, His boundless goodness, His untiring pity, His ineffable wisdom; they unveil the unfathomable riches of the mystery of His life and sufferings, they recount to us the supreme triumphs of His glory.

We understand what St. Jerome wrote: "To be ignorant of the Scriptures, is to be ignorant of Christ": *Ignoratio Scripturarum, ignoratio Christi est.*[2] The first Christians did not incur the reproach of ignorance; not only did they lavish upon the book of Scriptures a special veneration, which has passed into the Liturgy, but they read Holy Writ assiduously; they put into practice the Apostle's exhortation: "Let the word of Christ dwell in you abundantly": *Verbum Christi habitet in vobis abundanter.*[3] It is said of St. Cecilia that she always carried the Holy Gospel in her heart. She therefore remained united to God by an unceasing colloquy, by an uninterrupted prayer: *Et non diebus neque noctibus a colloquiis divinis et oratione cessabat.*[4]

But that this word may be "living and effectual"[5] in us, that it may really touch the soul, and truly become the fount of contemplation and principle of life, we must receive it with faith and humility and a sincere desire of knowing Christ and uniting ourselves to Him in order to walk in His footprints. The deep and intimate knowledge, the supernatural and fruitful perception of the meaning of Holy Writ is a gift of the Spirit, a gift so precious that our Lord Himself, Eternal Wisdom, communicated it to His disciples in one of His last apparitions: *Tunc aperuit illis sensum ut intelligerent Scripturas.*[6] To souls that have obtained this gift by great humility and earnest prayers,[7] the Scriptures

---

1 *Elevations upon the Mysteries,* 10th Week, 3rd Elev.

2 *In Isaïam Prologus,* P. L. 24, col. 28.

3 Col. iii, 16.

4 Antiphon of the Office of St. Cecilia.

5 Hebr. iv, 12.

6 "Then He opened their understanding, that they might understand the Scriptures," Luc. xxiv, 45.

7 *Tenemus libros et legimus, sed spiritualem sensum non attingimus, et ideo opus est lacrymis et orationibus indesinentibus postulare, ut Dominus aperiat oculos nostros* (We have the books and we read, but we do not attain the spiritual sense, and therefore it is

disclose abysses unsuspected by other souls. These souls rejoice in the possession of these divine testimonies as those who have "found great spoil": *Laetabor ego super eloquia tua sicut qui invenit spolia multa.*[1] They truly discover therein "the hidden manna," *manna absconditum*,[2] which has a thousand different tastes, contains all sort of delights[3] and becomes their daily food, full of savour.

What is the innermost reason of this fruitfulness of God's Word? It is that Christ is ever living; He is ever the God Who saves and quickens. What was said of Him during His earthly life? "Virtue went out from Him, and healed all" who came near to Him: *Virtus de illo exibat et sanabat omnes.*[4] All proportion guarded, that which is true of the Person of Jesus is true also of His word; and what was true yesterday is still true in our days. Christ lives in the soul of the just; under the infallible direction of this inner Master, the soul, humbly seated like Magdalen at His feet to hear His words, penetrates into the Divine Light; Christ gives it His Spirit, the first Author of Holy Writ, that it may there search into the very depths of the Infinite: *Omnia scrutatur etiam profunda Dei*;[5] it contemplates God's marvels in respect to men; it measures, by faith, the divine proportions of the mystery of Jesus, and this wonderful spectacle, whereof the splendours enlighten and illuminate it, touches, draws, enraptures, uplifts, transports and transforms the soul. It experiences in its turn what the disciples of Emmaus felt when Christ Jesus Himself vouchsafed to interpret to them the sacred Books: "Was not our heart burning within us, whilst He spoke in the way, and opened to us the Scriptures?" *Nonne cor nostrum ardens erat in nobis—dum loqueretur in via et aperiret nobis Scripturas?*[6]

What is there astonishing, then, in the fact that the soul, charmed and won by this living word "which penetrates even to the marrow," makes the prayer of these disciples its own: *Mane nobiscum*,[7] "Stay with us!" O Thou, the incomparable Master, indefectible Light, infallible Truth, the only true Life of our souls! Forestalling these holy desires, "the Holy Spirit Himself asketh for us with unspeakable groanings,"[8] which

---

necessary to ask with unceasing tears and prayers that the Lord would open our eyes). Origen, *In Genes.* ch. 21, homil. 7.

1 Ps. cxviii, 162. 2 Apoc. ii, 17. 3 Sap. xvi, 20. 4 Luc. vi, 19.
5 I Cor. ii, 10. 6 Luc. xxiv, 32. 7 Ibid. 29. 8 Rom. viii, 26.

constitute true prayer, these vehement desires to possess God, to live no longer save for the Father's glory and for that of His Son Jesus. Love, become great and burning by contact with God, takes possession of all the powers of the soul, renders it strong and generous to do perfectly all the Father's Will, to give itself up fully to the Divine good pleasure.

What better or more fruitful prayer than this? What contemplation can be comparable to it?

Hence we understand why our Blessed Father, heir to the thought of St. Paul and the first Christians, wishes the monk to consecrate so many hours to the *lectio divina*, that is to say to the reading of the Holy Scriptures and the works of the Fathers which are their echo and commentary. We understand how it is that a monk, attentive to gather up daily in the liturgy this substantial nourishment of the Scriptures given to him with perfect fitness by the Church, Christ's Bride, could not be better prepared to converse intimately with the Divine Master.

Oh! if we knew the gift of God![1] If we knew all the value of our share of the inheritance! *Funes ceciderunt mihi in praeclaris, etenim hereditas mea praeclara est mihi!*[2]

VIII

In truth, the monk whose soul, pure and faithful, is attentive to keep the silence of the lips and heart, who listens devoutly to holy reading day by day, is excellently prepared to live in God's presence. We are not yet in Heaven, where by the Beatific Vision we shall be forever in the Eternal Presence; let us, at least, often place ourselves under the gaze of God: "In Him we live, and move, and are."[3] Let us render His Presence actual by the free movement of a recollected soul; this Divine Presence will thus become the atmosphere in which we move. Like St. Benedict of whom it is said: "He dwelt alone with himself under the eyes of the Sovereign Beholder," *Solus in superni Spectatoris oculis habitavit secum*,[4] we shall abide continually in presence of the thrice-holy God, not by

1 Joan. iv, 10.

2 "The lines are fallen unto me in goodly places: for my inheritance is goodly to me," Ps. xv, 6.

3 Act. xvii, 28.

4 St. Gregory, *Dialogues*. Lib. ii, ch. 3.

means of ceaselessly renewed prayers, or violent efforts of mind or imagination, but by a deep and peaceful sense of faith which everywhere keeps us before God. We shall put in practice the precept of our Blessed Father: "To hold for certain that God sees us everywhere": *In omni loco Deum se respicere pro certo scire*;[1] we shall seek the gaze and smile of our Father in Heaven; we shall often repeat to Him: O Father, cast a ray of light upon Thy servant, become Thy child: *Faciem tuam illumina super servum tuum!*[2]

When we are faithful thus to keep habitually the sense of God's Presence, the ardour of love is constant; all our activity, even the most ordinary, is not only kept pure from all stain, as our Lawgiver wishes, *Actus vitae suae omni hora custodire*,[3] but, moreover, raised to a supernatural level. Our whole life is irradiated with heavenly light, "coming down from the Father of lights" *descendens a Patre luminum*,[4] and this is the secret of strength and joy.

This habit of the presence of God disposes the soul for the divine visits. It may happen, and to certain souls it happens frequently, that they find a real difficulty in making their prayer at the hour assigned; weariness, sleepiness, a state of ill health, distractions, hinder, in appearance, all efforts to attain prayer: this is spiritual dryness. Let the soul, however, remain faithful and do what it can to stay near the Lord, even if it is without sensible fervour: *Ut jumentum factus sum apud te, et ego semper tecum.*[5] God will draw near to it at another moment. It can be said of these visits of the Lord what the Scripture declares of His coming at the close of our earthly life: "You know not at what hour your Lord will come": *Nescitis qua hora Dominus, vester venturus sit.*[6] If everywhere, in the cell, in the cloister, in the garden, in the refectory, we live recollected in the Divine Presence, Our Lord will come, the Trinity will come, *Et ad eum veniemus*,[7] with hands full of light and glory which will possess us to our very depths and have sometimes a considerable repercussion upon our inner life. There is then produced, as it were, an indelible imprint of God upon the soul; a divine touch which becomes the starting point of a new orientation of our soul towards God, and strengthens,

1 Rule, ch. iv. 2 Ps. cxviii, 155. 3 Rule, ch. iv. 4 Jac. i, 17.
5 "I am become as a beast before Thee: and I am always with Thee," Ps. lxxii, 23.
6 Matth. xxiv, 42. 7 Joan. xiv, 23.

in a more radical and absolute manner, our seeking after God. By our recollection, let us then be "like to men who wait for their Lord," *Similes hominibus exspectantibus Dominum suum;*[1] the Lord finding us ready will make us enter with Him, *cum eo,*[2] into the festal hall...

Thus, little by little, the soul mounts towards God and prayer becomes its very breath; habitual union, full of love, is established, a very simple but steadfast contact with the Lord: God becomes the life of the soul. If the monk keeps silence, it is to converse inwardly with God; if he speaks, it is in God, of God, for His glory. Such was the practice of a holy monk, Hugh, Abbot of Cluny: *Silens quidem, semper cum Domino; loquens autem, semper in Domino vel de Domino loquebatur.*[3]

The monk who lives this life does not waste his time thinking of himself, of what others are doing, of the wrongs that may have been done to him, or that he imagines have been done to him; he does not turn over in his mind all these littlenesses, all these trifles, but he seeks only God; whenever he can do so, at every free moment left to him by work, the functions of his charge, the ministry of souls, his heart turns towards God to cleave to Him, to express to Him his desires, brief but ardent: that is the tendency of his soul. The soul withdraws into its own depths there to find God, the adorable Trinity, Christ Jesus Who dwells in us by faith. Christ unites us to Himself; we live with Him *in sinu Patris*;[4] and there we are united to the Divine Persons; our life becomes a communing with the Father, Son, and Holy Spirit; and in this union we find the well-spring of joy. We meet sometimes with sorely tried souls who yet by a life of prayer make within themselves a sanctuary where the peace of Christ reigns. It is enough to ask them: "Would you not like to have some diversion in your life?" to hear them at once reply: "Oh, no, I wish to dwell alone with God." Happy state of a soul living the life of prayer! It everywhere finds God,—and God suffices for it, because it is filled with God, the Infinite Good.

But the soul feels the need of consecrating one hour exclusively to communing with God, that, this may be, as it were, the intensification of the soul's habitual life. This hour is at once a manifestation of and a

1 Luc. xii, 26. 2 Matth. xxv, 10.
3 *Vita Hugonis,* ch. 1, P. L. 159, loc. 863. 4 Joan. i, 18.

means of attaining the life of prayer. It is impossible for a soul to have arrived at a state where prayer is its life without giving itself in an exclusive manner, at certain hours of the day, to the formal exercise of prayer but this exercise is only the natural expansion of its state: this is why our holy Lawgiver, who has regulated everything to establish and maintain this life of prayer in his monasteries, has not thought it necessary to fix determined times of prayer for his sons. He wants the monk to seek God; and if this desire of seeking Him be true and sincere, the monk will try to find these hours where he may be alone with Him Who is the One and Sovereign Good of his life.

Thus animated, monastic life necessarily becomes an ascending pathway towards God. The virtues are nourished by the frequent contact of the soul with the fount of all perfection: *Ibunt de virtute in virtutem.*[1] Prayer brings down the dew that fructifies the earth of the soul. Without prayer, the soul is dry "as earth without water": *Anima mea sicut terra sine aqua tibi*;[2] the divine seed of grace, sent to us through the Sacraments, the Mass, the Divine Office, the exercise of obedience, may fall abundantly, but it may fall upon ground hard as a rock, and touch only the surface without penetrating the depths; it then "withers away": *Semen cecidit supra petram et aruit.*[3] To fructify our soul, prayer must descend upon it "as a shower upon the herb, and as drops upon the grass": *Quasi stillae super gramina*,[4] it must soak through and soften the soil of the heart, and make it ready to profit as much as possible from the manifold means of sanctification to be met with in our life; prayer is the secret of great supernatural fruitfulness and the very condition of the soul's progress.

Do not let us say that these are mystical heights to which a few privileged souls alone can attain; no, it is the normal state of a religious in his monastery, of a nun in her cloister; it is the necessary expansion of our grace of adoption, of our monastic vocation. This life of prayer is our most excellent inheritance; *optima pars*. We can and ought to give ourselves, and to give God to souls; but this ministry should be the natural radiation of our innermost life in God. Let nothing turn us away from

1 "They shall go from virtue to virtue," Ps. lxxxiii, 8.
2 Ibid. cxlii, 6. 3 Cf. Luc. viii, 4. 4 Deut. xxxii, 2.

it: *Non auferatur ab ea*,[1] but rather let us strive to become souls of prayer. Our condition as monks is a magnificent one for attaining this lofty end. We live in solitude, far from the vain noise of the world; we sit down daily, and are served by the Church herself, at the splendid table of the liturgy where we find in abundance that bread of God's Word which is the soul's best food. Everything in the monastery, even the stones, the archways, the architecture bears us towards God. The Lord thus draws us to Him, for it was not for nothing that He brought us into monastic solitude; He wished that we should be able to listen more easily to Him. God is doubtless everywhere, even in the tumult of great cities, but His voice is only to be heard in silence. He Himself has told us so: "I will lead her [the soul] into the wilderness: and I will speak to her heart": *Ducam eam in solitudinem et loquar ad cor ejus*.[2] Religious vocation is the expression of a singular love of God and of Christ Jesus towards each one of our souls: God wills to be for us the Only Good and our sole reward; He contains all good, all joy, all beatitude, but let us be persuaded that we shall only find Him fully by a life of prayer.

Happy the humble and obedient monk who seeks but to listen to God in the sanctuary of his soul, with deep reverence and unutterable tenderness. God will often speak to him, even when least expected; He will fill him with lights to rejoice his soul, even in the midst of his tribulations and trials. "For Thy word, O my God, is sweeter to the soul than is the most delicious honey to the mouth";[3] it contains all light and all strength; it gives the secret of patience, and is the source of all joy.

NOTE

(See p. 397)

We have said elsewhere (*Christ, the Life of the Soul*, conference on *Prayer*) how the contemplation of the Sacred Humanity of Jesus is the source of prayer even for the most perfect. We there gave a very explicit text of St Teresa. Let us add thereto the following passage. Having, in *The Interior Castle*, taught that it must be truly admitted that the soul raised to perfect contemplation cannot meditate in discoursing inwardly, the Saint however adds: "Souls... would be wrong in saying that they

1 Luc. x, 42. 2 Ose. ii, 14. 3 Cf. Ps. cxviii, 103.

cannot dwell on these mysteries (of the Life and Passion of Jesus Christ) nor frequently think about them, especially when these events are being celebrated by the Catholic Church. Nor is it possible for the soul which has received so much from God to forget these precious proofs of His love, which are living sparks to inflame the heart with greater love for our Lord... Such a soul comprehends these mysteries... in a more perfect way than do other people." *The Interior Castle*, 6th Mansion. ch. vii. Translated by the Benedictines of Stanbrook.

THE SPIRIT OF ABANDONMENT TO GOD'S WILL

SUMMARY.—The spirit of holy abandonment is the crowning point of the way of detachment.—I. Objective basis of this abandonment: the Divine Will.—II. This spirit of abandonment is found in a high degree in the Rule of St. Benedict.—III. Practice of this virtue.—IV. Above all in trials.—V. Holy abandonment constitutes a very pleasing homage to God.—VI. Special blessings flow from it for the soul.

THE end of the whole life of the monk is "to seek God": *Si revera Deum quaerit*;[1] and on the day of our Profession, we promised to pursue with constancy this high and great end. In order to attain it we have left everything; we have all made sacrifices; like St. Peter we can say to our Lord: *Ecce nos reliquimus omnia et secuti sumus te*:[2] "Behold we have left all things, and have followed Thee."

The motive power of these sacrifices and acts of renunciation is love which drew us in the footsteps of Christ Jesus. We said to Him: "Good Master, Thou callest me, and I am here: I believe that Thou art so great, so powerful, so good, that Thou wilt not confound any of my hopes: *Non confundas me ab exspectatione mea*. I believe that Thou wilt make me to find in Thee the fount of all beatitude and of all life: *Et vivam*!"[3] This is, on our part, an act of faith in Jesus Christ. We leave all, persuaded that in Him we shall find all. Faith is already, of itself, the giving of our whole being to the Truth Who is Jesus, the Incarnate Word. And

---

1 Rule, ch. lviii. 2 Matth. xix, 27.

3 "And I shall live," Prayer borrowed from the Psalmist, and that St. Benedict ordains to be sung thrice by the novice at the moment of his monastic profession.

our monastic existence is only to be the extension to our entire life of an initial act of faith and abandonment.

This act received its official consecration in the offering that we made of ourselves to God on the day of our religious profession.

When our whole life is maintained in this spirit of holy abandonment whereby we were animated when we pronounced our Vows, it becomes true and extremely pleasing to God. All those virtues of which we have spoken until now: poverty, humility, obedience, are like the fruits of the monastic profession; their practice is the logical consequence of that deed which yielded us up entirely to Christ under the Rule of the holy Patriarch; all our Benedictine perfection flows from that as from its source. That donation to God on the blessed day of our profession can only be true, entire, complete, absolute, if it is afterwards manifested during our whole existence by these virtues of detachment, reverence and submission; but these virtues, to be living and fruitful, must constantly draw their sap from that loving abandonment which marked our donation.[1]

It is now the moment to speak of this spirit of abandonment: not only does it explain our existence, because, being at the very basis of religious profession, it inspires all the acts that are derived from this profession as from their point of departure; but it also gives them their supreme fecundity. Indeed holy abandonment is one of the purest and most absolute forms of love; it is the height of love; it is love giving to God, unreservedly, our whole being, with all its energies and activities in order that we may be a veritable holocaust to God: when the spirit of abandonment to God animates a monk's whole life, that monk has attained holiness. What in fact is holiness? It is substantially the conformity of all our being to God; it is the *amen* said by the whole being and its faculties to all the rights of God; it is the *fiat* full of love, whereby the whole creature responds, unceasingly and unfalteringly, to all the Divine Will: and that which causes us to say this *amen*, to utter this *fiat*, that which surrenders, in a perfect donation, the whole being

1 The spirit of holy abandonment can be considered as being the last expression of detachment or the summit of the life of union: these two aspects are correlative, but it is chiefly the first that we are here considering.

to God is the spirit of abandonment, a spirit which is the sum total of faith, confidence and love.[1]

Let us try to see what is the basis of this spirit of abandonment; how it constitutes one of the characteristics of the inner life as it is understood by our Blessed Father St. Benedict; we shall then show how we can practise it, and the excellent fruits to be gained from it.

I

The objective basis of holy abandonment is the Divine Will. All that God decides, all that He decrees, is absolutely perfect: *Judicia Domini vera, justificata in semetipsa.*[2] Now God *wills* our holiness and our beatitude, but this holiness and this beatitude are not of some indefinite kind. There are two Divine utterances—and these two utterances are the completing of one another—which make known to us the ways of Providence as regards ourselves, and in the light of which we may comprehend the wherefore of the spirit of abandonment.

Christ Jesus pronounced the first of these utterances: "Without Me, you can do nothing": *Sine me, nihil potestis facere.*[3] We have often meditated upon these words, but it is sovereignly useful to penetrate into them anew. All the reunited efforts of nature cannot produce one supernatural act, one act which has any proportion with our end, which is the beatifying Vision of the Adorable Trinity.

This end is the only one assigned to us; outside this one there is only damnation. God could have disposed things otherwise if He had so willed: He might have asked of us only a natural religion and a natural morality; but He did not establish things thus. God is Master of His operations and of His gifts; His will is supreme and it is in this will that our salvation and sanctification find their principle: *Secundum beneplacitum ejus.*[4] It is from God that our sanctification first of all comes, because it is His infinitely free will which has fixed its laws; and these laws make of our sanctification a supernatural work. It is impossible to

1 In the beautiful book by the Right Rev. Abbot Lehodey, *Le Saint Abandon,* 1919, is to be found a complete exposition of the teaching relative to this important subject.

2 Ps. xviii, 10. 3 Joan. xv, 5. 4 Eph. i, 9.

attain perfection without acknowledging this Divine Plan established from all eternity.

But God, Who accomplishes all His works with infinite wisdom, has given us, in grace, the means of realising within ourselves His Divine designs. Without grace, which comes from God only, we are incapable of doing anything whatsoever in order to reach our supernatural end; St. Paul tells us that without grace we cannot have a good thought to be counted worthy of eternal beatitude: *Non quod sufficientes simus cogitare aliquid a nobis* QUASI EX NOBIS.[1] This is the echo of Christ's words: "Without Me you can do nothing," you cannot attain the supreme end; you cannot become saints. Christ Jesus Himself has commented upon this truth: He has told us that He is the Vine and we are the branches; to bring forth fruit, we must abide united to Him through grace, in order that, drawing supernatural sap from Him, we may bring to His Father fruit pleasing to Him.

You hence see the necessity for the soul of not separating itself from God, the Fount of grace, without Whom we can do nothing. But, much more than this, we ought to give ourselves to Him without reserve, for with this grace we can "do all things": this is the second of the two utterances that show the reason of holy abandonment: *Omnia possum in eo qui me confortat.*[2] There is no honest deed, however commonplace it be, that, done under the inspiration of grace, cannot contribute to make us reach that supreme exaltation which is the Beatific Vision, for all things work together unto good, to such as God calls to live in union with Himself: *Omnia cooperantur in bonum iis qui secundum propositum vocati sunt sancti.*[3] But why does God ordain all unto the good of His elect; why does He grant to them, through His grace, to do all things whereby they may reach Him? For several reasons.

God's Will towards souls is full of love: "God is Love": *Deus caritas est.*[4] Not only does He possess love: He *is* Love, boundless, unfailing, indefectible Love. It has not entered into the heart of man to understand what is Infinite Love. Now the weight of this infinite love draws God to give Himself: *Bonum est diffusivum sui.* All that God does for us has love as its motive power, and as God is not only Love, but Eternal Wisdom and Almighty Power, the works that Love causes this Wisdom and

1 II Cor. iii, 5. 2 Philip. iv, 13. 3 Rom. viii, 28. 4 I Joan. iv, 16.

this Power to accomplish are ineffable. Love is at the foundation of the Creation and of all the mysteries of the Redemption.

This love bears moreover a particular character: that of being the love of a father for his children: *Videte qualem caritatem... ut filii Dei nominemur et simus.*[1] God loves us as His children. He is the Father essentially: all paternity is derived from His: *Ex quo* OMNIS *paternitas in caelis et in terra nominatur.*[2] This is not a meaningless word. And as, in God, all is active, this paternity in relation to us is all that is most great, most solicitous, most constant: God *acts* with us as with His children, and leads us during our whole life in the light of His incomparable fatherly love.

How has He manifested this fatherly love? In having destined us to His own beatitude as our inheritance. He loves us to the point of adopting us as His own children, of giving us a share in His own bliss; of making us enter into the fellowship of His Blessed Trinity. All the graces given to the elect, all the mercies granted to sinners, all the blessings that raise, beautify and rejoice souls, had their dawn in this eternal act of our divine adoption: *OMNE datum optimum et omne donum* PERFECTUM *desursum est, descendens a* PATRE *luminum.*[3] It is the first link in that interrupted chain of heavenly graces granted to souls throughout the centuries. Now this predestination comes forth from the Heart of God: *Videte qualem* CARITATEM *habuit in nos Deus ut filii Dei nominemur et simus.*

This is not all: for the marvels and manifestations of God's love for us are inexhaustible. Divine Love shines out not only in the *fact* of our adoption, but in the admirable *way* chosen by God of realising it in us. God loves us with an infinite love, a fatherly love; but He loves us *in His Son*. To make us His children, God gives us His Son Christ Jesus: that is love's supreme gift. "God so loved the world, as to give His Only-begotten Son": SIC *Deus* DILEXIT *mundum ut Filium suum unigenitum* DARET.[4] And why does He give Him to us? That He may be our Wisdom, Sanctification, Redemption, and Justice; our Light and our Way; our Food and our Life: in a word that He may be the Mediator between Him and us. Christ Jesus, the Word Incarnate, fills that chasm

1 Ibid. iii, 1. 2 Eph. iii, 15.

3 "Every best gift, and every perfect gift, is from above, coming down from the Father of lights," Jac. i, 17. 4 Joan. iii, 16.

separating man from God. It is "in His Son" and through His Son, that God pours down from Heaven upon our souls all divine blessings of grace that make us live as children worthy of this Heavenly Father: *Qui benedixit nos IN OMNI benedictione spirituali in caelestibus IN CHRISTO.*[1] All graces come to us through Jesus, and God loves us in the measure in which we love His Son Jesus and believe in Him. Our Lord Himself tells us these consoling words: "The Father Himself loveth you, because you have loved Me, and have believed that I came out from God": *Ipse enim Pater amat vos, quia vos me amastis et credidistis quia ego a Deo exivi.*[2] When the Father sees a soul full of love for His Son, He showers His most abundant blessings upon it. That is the order, the plan established from all eternity: Jesus has been constituted Head and King over all God's heritage because it is He Who, through His Blood, has restored to us the rights of this heritage: "The Father... hath given all things into His hand": *OMNIA dedit Pater in manu ejus.*[3] We abide in Him by faith and love; He abides in us by His grace and merits: He offers us to His Father, and His Father finds us in Him.

Such are the foundations upon which holy abandonment rests. God wills our sanctification: *Haec est voluntas Dei sanctificatio vestra*;[4] this Will in God is efficacious and full of love, therefore He has multiplied the means of sanctification. God grants us to find in the Son of His delight the well spring of *all* grace and *all* perfection: "How hath He not also, with Him, given us all things?" *Quomodo non etiam cum illo OMNIA nobis donavit?*[5] Shall we not, therefore, abandon ourselves in all confidence to this all-powerful Will, which is love itself and has not only fixed the laws of our perfection but is the principle and source of it? Grace goes before, aids and crowns all the acts that we do. For, says St. Paul, "I can do *all* things in Him Who strengtheneth me": *OMNIA possum in eo qui me confortat.*[6] This *qui me confortat* shows us that holy abandonment does not consist in doing nothing; let us guard ourselves against that false quietude, that "*far niente*" falsely esteemed as mystical passivity. "By the grace of God, I am what I am," says the Apostle again, "and His grace in me hath not been void."[7] Grace acts sovereignly, it leads to a high degree of holiness, but only where it meets

1 Eph. i, 3. 2 Joan. xvi, 27. 3 Joan. iii, 35. 4 I Thess. iv, 3.
5 Rom. viii, 32. 6 Philip. iv, 13. 7 I Cor. xv, 10.

with no obstacles to its action; the Spirit of God acts powerfully but only where it is not opposed, "grieved,"—speaking still in the language of St. Paul[1]—and where the created powers are surrendered to Him.

What is the part left to us in our seeking after God? To put away generously—of course, with the help of grace—all the obstacles that are opposed in us to the action of this same grace, and to keep ourselves constantly in the dispositions required by God in order that He may and will act. For supreme as is God's will, wide as is His power, infinite as is His love, God expects of us that we should remove all that impedes His grace, that the soul should remain in that attitude of humility and confidence whereby it hopes for everything from God. When the soul has reached that state where it is freed from obstacles: sin, imperfections, attachment to created things, and to itself; where it has emptied itself of all that is not God; where it no longer truly seeks anything but God; then God, finding it entirely given up to His will, acts freely within it. Happy the soul to whom God grants such light and such generosity: the Lord will bring it, by His own ways, to the highest perfection.

II

The spirit of holy abandonment is to be found in a high degree in the Rule of our holy Patriarch.

It is true that all religious life leads the faithful soul to this constant union of its will with the divine will, a union which forms one of the chief elements of holy abandonment; but this abandonment is particularly realised in the form of life regulated by the holy Lawgiver; his concept of poverty, humility, obedience, leads the faithful soul by a very sure path, to detachment from the creature and from self, in order to look for all good from God alone.

Call to mind what poverty is in this respect, and to what a radical degree our Blessed Father carries this virtue which detaches us from creatures. The monk is to have nothing of his own, since he has not power even over his own body.[2] To this stripping of self, St. Benedict clearly links the idea of holy abandonment: the monk should hope to receive all that is necessary from the Abbot, the Father of the monastery: *OMNIA*

1 Eph. iv, 30. 2 Rule, ch. xxxiii.

vero necessaria a patre SPERARE *monasterii*.[1] The practice of monastic poverty, as I have tried to show, is a very high form of the virtue of hope, without which there is no virtue of abandonment.

Does not humility, in its turn, lend its "ladder" to the virtue of abandonment?[2] Its divers degrees are so many ever-widening acts of abandonment to God's Will. We have seen that the very root of this virtue is reverence towards God, "the Father of incommensurable majesty": *Patrem immensae majestatis*. This reverence towards God, the Sovereign Master of all things and unique Fountainhead of every good, keeps the soul in habitual submission to all that God wills. It consequently leads the soul to avoid all that can displease God (1st degree); constantly to seek after the Divine Will (2nd degree); to abandon oneself to this will in the person of a Superior (3rd degree); even if this man's will imposes upon us hard things, contrary to our tastes, exposing us to the worst injuries: this is the 4th degree in which abandonment goes as far as heroism, for everything is to be accepted silently, *tacita conscientia*, as with victims destined for the slaughter: *Aestimati sumus ut oves occisionis*. Abandonment is to go even to the yielding up of the secrets of the heart to the one who holds the place of God with us (5th degree); to be contented with the worst of every thing, to perform the meanest tasks, because of the feeling of unworthiness which makes one humble himself before God (6th degree) and before men (7th degree). Is not this recognition of God's rights the underlying reason of entire self-surrender and complete detachment? Each degree of humility itself only increases with faith and confidence in God. With every degree of inward humility, our Blessed Father gives hope of a special correspondence of Divine grace. Have we not shown how with him humility finds its completion in invincible confidence in the merits of Christ Jesus Who brings grace to us? It is for God then to direct us by His will, by that of His Church, by events; it is for us to do this will each time that it is manifested to us, trusting ourselves to God, for the rest, and holding ourselves assured that we shall infallibly come to perfect charity: *Mox ad caritatem Dei perveniet... perfecta[m]*... This is the whole aim of the asceticism of humility.

---

1 Ibid. 2 Ibid. ch. vii.

The practice of obedience, such as St. Benedict understands it, has no other aim. Why does the monk come to the monastery? Is it to accomplish such or such special work? To give himself to some occupation that he prefers? No, it is solely to follow Christ in obedience, relinquishing all that is his own: *Relinquentes statim quae sua sunt.*[1] The monk, faithful to the spirit of his Rule, "relinquishes" himself literally by obedience; he gives up his will to that of God. He says to God: "I lay down my will into Thy hands; I wish henceforward to listen only to Thee." To act thus is to follow Him Who, by essence, is the principle of all things; it is to will to be guided by Eternal Wisdom.

We make this act of self-surrender on the day of our religious profession, which is the most perfect expression of the full surrender of ourselves into God's hands. The inner life of the monk who remains faithful to his vows infallibly evolves into this spirit of abandonment which is one of the greatest graces for the soul.

This is because, in a soul thus yielded up unreservedly, God's action, the source of all holiness, is supreme. The Rule which we promise to follow is like a sacred and beneficial mill-wheel: when we allow ourselves to be taken up into this "mill of God," the soul is ground like wheat and set free from all that is displeasing in God's sight. Our holy Legislator gives us to understand this in remarkable terms, at the end of the chapter on humility. When he has led his disciple, by successive acts, to the last degree of self-abnegation, he no longer gives him any direction: he leaves him to the action of the Holy Spirit, Who makes the soul altogether yielded up to Him, His abode full of delights, and brings it, if such be His design, to the most sublime perfection, to the height of contemplation; in this soul there is no longer, as it were, any other life than that of love.[2]

We see how St. Benedict leads the soul to the spirit of self-surrender. For him this is not a negative state of immobility or mistaken indifference. To arrive at holy abandonment, the soul labours to put away a crowd of obstacles, then to keep itself faithfully in this fundamental disposition of humility and of submission in regard to grace; it accepts all the Divine Will, even in things most contrary to its tastes, even those that

1 Rule, ch. v. 2 Rule, ch. vii.

make it suffer the most; but, this done, the soul has fulfilled its task, it no longer looks to anyone except God for what is necessary to enable it to come to Him, and it looks to Him with invincible confidence and unshaken faith in His word, in His power, in His goodness, and in the merits of Christ. This state of abandonment is the purest and sweetest fruit of the practice of humility and obedience, upon which the holy Patriarch has founded our inner life.

III

It is from the very nature of holy abandonment that the means we have of practising it are derived.

Abandonment is first of all the consecration of one's self, in faith and love, to God's will. The will of God is not distinct from Himself; it is God intimating to us His wishes; it is as holy, as powerful, as adorable, as immutable as God Himself.

In relation to us, this will is in part manifested, and in part hidden. God's will is revealed, is manifested to us by Christ. "Hear ye Him": *Ipsum audite*;[1] this is what the Father said in sending us His Son. On His side, Our Lord tells us that He has made known to us all that His Father has given Him to reveal: *Omnia quaecumque audivi a Patre meo nota feci vobis*.[2] The Church, the Bride of Christ, has received the deposit of these revelations and these precepts, whereto are joined the voice of Superiors, the precepts of the Rule: these are so many manifestations of the Divine will.

What ought to be the attitude of the loving soul with regard to this will? The soul ought to feel itself fire and flame to fulfil it. Every energy of our being should be employed, with fidelity and constancy, to carry out this will. The more intimate we are with anyone, the more careful we are not to displease him; in regard to God, our fidelity ought to be absolute: "I do always the things that please Him": *Quae placita sunt ei facio* SEMPER.[3] Such ought to be the passion of a soul that seeks God solely; his eyes, as the Psalmist says, should be "ever towards the Lord": *Oculi mei* SEMPER *ad Dominum*,[4] thereby to learn His will and to do it.

1 Matth. xvii, 5. 2 Joan. xv, 15. 3 Joan. viii, 29. 4 Ps. xxiv, 15.

Souls differ from one another in the fulfilment of the Divine will, in the intensity of love wherewith they acquiesce in it. None of us would do what God forbids, act in opposition to the Divine law, transgress, however slightly, the Lord's commandments. But can we testify that we do everything solely because God wills it? Are we totally detached from ourselves and given up unreservedly to the good pleasure from on high? Are we always ready to bow down before the Divine will, however painful it be to our nature? As far as it depends upon us we ought always to be ready to execute this will perfectly, whatever it be, with the greatest love possible. Is it not written: "Thou hast commanded Thy commandments to be kept most diligently"? *Tu mandasti mandata tua custodiri nimis.*[1] Whenever this Divine law commands, we must be ready to let ourselves be cut in pieces rather than hesitate, for to transgress this will is to wish that God did not exist. Love serves as the measure of this self-surrender, and the deeper love is, and the more intense and active, the more complete and absolute it renders self-surrender. St. Benedict intends to carry us to the furthest limits of self-surrender. Do we not see him bidding the monk whom the Superior commands, in the name of God, to do impossible things "to obey for love, trusting solely in the help of God": *Ex caritate confidens de adjutorio Dei obediat?*[2] That is perfect abandonment which, for love's sake, totally forgets self, and confides only in the Divine Power and Goodness.

The loving soul does not only adhere to the will of God manifested; it yields itself also, and especially, to the hidden will of God: this enwraps our natural existence and our supernatural life, in the whole as in detail. The state of health or sickness, the events in which we are involved, the success or failure of our undertakings, the hour and circumstances of our death, the degree of our holiness, the particular means which God wills to employ to lead us to this degree, these are so many things whereof we are ignorant, that God wills to keep hidden from us.

In regard to this will, two attitudes are possible.

There is that dictated by the wisdom of the world, merely human wisdom, which always wants to be ruled by itself, to do everything only according to merely natural lights; it wants to arrange life in *its own* fash-

---

1 Ibid. cxviii, 4.　　2 Rule, ch. xlviii.

ion; it is irritated by all that is contrary to what it seeks, contrary to the conceptions of perfection that it forms for itself. But what is "the wisdom of this world" in God's sight? "Foolishness," replies St. Paul: *Sapientia enim hujus mundi stultitia est apud Deum.*[1] It has not understood that God willed to redeem the world not by riches or brilliant deeds, nor by the prestige of science or of eloquence, but in taking the weakness of our nature, and in leading a poor and hidden life; it has not comprehended that during thirty years God put "under a bushel" that ineffable plenitude of perfection which is the Sacred Humanity of Jesus; it has not comprehended that it behoved Christ to die a bitter death upon the gibbet. The Cross is "a stumbling-block and foolishness"[2] to the world's wisdom. But God has willed to confound this wisdom by the folly of His impenetrable decisions.

We must not let ourselves be guided by this natural wisdom. God's thoughts are not our thoughts; His ways are not ours. What are our ways, those that we should ourselves suggest? What would be our own ideal? To be the master of our life, to arrange our existence, even supernatural; not to suffer, never to be subject to temptation, never to feel any repugnance in obedience. Human ways are these, leading up to an extraordinary increase of our pride. What are God's ways? the thoughts of Eternal Wisdom? "Without Me you can do nothing;[3] if any man will come after Me, let him deny himself, and take up his cross;[4] no man... looking back, is fit for the Kingdom of God;[5] blessed are the poor in spirit, the meek, the pure, the merciful, those who mourn, those who suffer persecution for justice' sake."[6] And so many other thoughts that each page of the Gospel yields to us! But their application to each one of us often remains veiled.

In face of God's designs, our attitude will be one of abandonment; to give ourselves to God, to place within His hands our personality, our own views, in order to accept His, in all humility: such will be the order we follow. In this matter, true wisdom is not to have any wisdom of our own but to trust entirely in the infallible word, the eternal wisdom and ineffable tenderness of a God Who loves us.

---

1 I Cor iii, 10. 2 I Cor. i, 23. 3 Joan. xv, 5. 4 Matth. xvi, 24.
5 Luc. ix, 62. 6 Matth. v, 3–11.

At present God hides from me certain of His designs over me; I ought to find it well that He hides them from me, without troubling myself as to wherefore. I do not know if I shall live a long time, or if I shall die soon; if I shall remain in good health, or if sickness will weigh me down; if I shall keep my faculties, or if I shall lose them long before my death; I do not know whether God will lead me by one particular path or by another. In this domain God keeps the sovereign right of disposing everything both as concerns my natural existence and my supernatural perfection; for He is the Alpha and Omega of all things. And what am I to do? To lose myself in adoration. To adore God as Principle, as Wisdom, as Justice, as Infinite Goodness; to throw myself into His arms, like a child in the arms of its mother, letting itself be swayed with her every movement. Are you afraid of throwing yourself into your mother's arms? Certainly not, for what mother, unless a monster, has ever betrayed the confidence of her child? And where has a mother derived her tenderness, her goodness, her love? From God. Or rather, these virtues of a mother are but the pale reflection of the perfections of goodness, love, and tenderness, that are in God. Has He not compared Himself to a mother? "Can a mother forget her infant... and if she should forget, yet will I not forget thee."[1] Therefore whether this Divine will leads me by wide paths strewn with roses, or draws me along rugged ways bristling with thorns, it is still the adorable and loving will of God, of my God.

But I *know* that this Will wills my holiness, that, guided by love, it works ever and mightily to this end; beyond the means that God has officially established to lead me to perfection, such as the sacraments, prayer, the practice of virtue, He possesses a thousand particular means for realising in me, little by little, the special form of holiness that He wills to see in my soul. The whole thing for me, in this hidden domain, is to surrender myself entirely to His action, with faith, confidence, and love. All is salutary for me that comes from God:—joys and sorrows, light and darkness, consolations and aridities, for "all things work together unto good" for those whom God calls to holiness.[2] This is what our Lord said to His faithful servant, St. Gertrude: "Make an act of abandonment to My good pleasure, leaving Me the full disposal of all that concerns thee, in the spirit of obedience which dictated to Me this

1 Isa. xlix, 15. 2 Cf. Rom. viii, 28.

prayer: 'Father, not My will, but Thine be done.' Be resolved to receive adversity or prosperity from My hand for My love it is that sends them to thee for thy salvation. In all things, unite thy thoughts and desires to those of My Heart. My love it is that gives thee days of dilatation and of joy, out of indulgence to thy weakness, and in order to raise thine eyes and hopes towards Heaven; welcome these joys with gratitude and unite this gratitude to My love. Again it is My love that sends thee days of weariness and sadness that they may gain for thee everlasting treasures; accept them, uniting thy resignation to My love."

IV

It is above all on days of weariness, sickness, impatience, temptation, spiritual dryness, and trials, during hours of sometimes terrible anguish which press upon a soul, that holy abandonment is pleasing to God.

More than once we have considered this truth, namely, that there is a sum total of sufferings, of humiliations and sorrows, which God has foreseen for the members of Christ's Mystical Body in order to "fill up those things that are wanting of the sufferings of Christ."[1] We cannot reach perfect union with Christ Jesus unless we accept that portion of the chalice which our Lord wills to give us to drink with Him and after Him.

Our Lord knew all about the terrible way along which His Father had ordained that He should travel; did He refuse to accept the Divine Will or refuse to fulfil it? No, He embraced it. "Behold I come, O Father; I have placed this law of suffering in My Heart, and I accept it for love of Thee." The Word of God, Eternal Wisdom, Christ likewise foresaw the part that we should have in His Passion. What is there better than to surrender ourselves, with Him, to our Father and accept this participation in the sufferings and humiliations of His Son Jesus? "O Father, I accept all the sorrows, all the humiliations, all the sufferings that it shall please Thee to send me, all the misunderstandings to which it shall please Thee to subject me, all the painful obediences that it shall please Thee to impose upon me; and all this for love of Thee, in union with Thy beloved Son."

---

1 Col. i, 24.

If we could always keep ourselves in these inward dispositions, never stopping at secondary causes, never asking, murmuringly, when annoyed and contradicted: "Why has this happened? Why do they treat me in this manner?" If we could lift ourselves up to that supreme Will which permits everything, and without the permission of which nothing happens; if we could always look up above creatures with hearts uplifted, *sursum corda*, to see only God, to abandon ourselves to Him, we should constantly abide in peace.

A great nun, the Blessed Bonomo, wrote to her father, at a time when she was exposed to sharp persecution through an unenlightened confessor: "I say to the Lord, all is for Thee, I will not be troubled: *Fiat voluntas tua in aeternum*. I let everything pass, as the water passes returning to the sea; if things come from God, I at once return them to God; and I live in my state of peace; if I am tempted, I commend myself to God and await His help and light; and thus all goes well. Let your Lordship then have no trouble on my account, even when you hear that I am sick and in anguish; for I know not what trouble is, because all is love, and I fear but one thing: to die without suffering."[1]

A like state of soul requires strong and generous faith. If we only had this faith! If we could hear our Lord saying to us: "I, Who know the Divine secrets; I, Who see all that My Father does, say to you that not a hair of your head falls without the permission of your Heavenly Father. Solomon, in all his glory, was not arrayed in splendor to be compared to that of the lilies of the field. The birds of heaven sow not, neither do they spin, and your Father does not leave them without food. And you, with your immortal souls, who have been purchased with My Blood, you think that God does not concern Himself about you? *Modicae fidei*, men of little faith, what do you fear? All the sufferings, all the humiliations and annoyances that may come upon you, come from the hand of your Father Who knows what is most expedient for you. He knows by what road, by what winding paths, He will bring you to beatitude; He knows the form and the measure of your predestination. Give yourself up to Him, for He is a Father full of goodness and wisdom Who wills to lead you to closest union with Himself."

1 D. du Bourg, *La Bienheureuse J. M. Bonomo, moniale bénédictine*, p 134.

Do not then let us be afraid of the sufferings, humiliations, temptations and desolations that come upon us; let us try to "support God," *Sustine Dominum,*[1] that is to say to accept everything, absolutely everything, that He would have us accept. The Father is the Vinedresser Who purges the branch, says Christ Himself, "that it may bring forth more fruit."[2] He wishes to enlarge our capacity; He wishes to make us sound the depth of our weakness, our insufficiency, so that, convinced of our powerlessness to pray, to work, to advance, we may place all our trust in Him. Only let us remain docile, generous, faithful: *Viriliter age;*[3] the hour will come when having emptied us of ourselves, God will fill us with His own fulness: *Ut impleamini in omnem plenitudinem Dei.*[4]

One of the most important and most fruitful practices of the virtue of abandonment is to have immediate and persevering recourse to God, to our Lord, in our sorrows and tribulations, in order to confide them to Him.

It is recounted of St. Mechtilde that in her sorrows, she had the custom of taking refuge with our Lord and of abandoning herself to Him in all submission.[5] Christ Jesus Himself had taught her to do this: "If a person wishes to make Me an acceptable offering, let him seek refuge in none beside Me in tribulation, and not complain of his griefs to anyone, but entrust to Me all the anxieties with which his heart is burdened. I will never forsake one who acts thus."[6] We ought to accustom ourselves to tell everything to Our Lord, to entrust to Him all that concerns us. "Commit thy way to the Lord," that is, reveal to Him thy thoughts, thy cares, thy anguish, and He Himself will guide thee: *Revela Domino viam tuam, et spera in eo, et ipse faciet.*[7] How do most men act? They talk over their troubles either within themselves, or to others; few go to pour out their souls at the feet of Christ Jesus. And yet that is a prayer so pleasing to God, and so fruitful a practice for the soul! Look at the Psalmist, the singer inspired by the Holy Ghost. He discloses to God all that happens to him; he shows Him all the difficulties that beset him,

1 Ps. xxvi, 14; Rule, ch. vii.
2 Joan. xv, 2.
3 "Do manfully," Ps. xxvi, 14.
4 Eph. iii, 19.
5 *The Book of Special Grace,* 2nd Part, ch. 8.
6 *The Book of Special Grace,* 4th Part, ch. 7.
7 Ps. xxxvi, 5.

the afflictions that come to him through men, the anguish that fills his soul. "Look upon my weariness, my miseries, my sufferings! Why, O Lord, are they multiplied that afflict me? *Domine quid multiplicati sunt qui tribulant me...?*[1] Look upon me, and have mercy on me, for I am alone and poor. The troubles of my heart are multiplied: deliver me from my necessities...![2] Bow down Thy ear to me: make haste to deliver me. Be Thou unto me... a house of refuge to save me...[3] I am afflicted and humbled exceedingly... my groaning is not hidden from Thee...![4] Withhold not Thou, O Lord, Thy tender mercies from me,... for evils without number have surrounded me... I am a beggar and poor, but the Lord is careful for me..."[5]

Whether our troubles come from men, from the devil, or arise from our fallen nature or from circumstances, we ought to confide everything to God. Let us recall our own experience. Is it not true that when we pour out our heart into that of men, to every comer, or turn over within ourselves our difficulties, especially those that arise from obedience, we are enervated, weakened, and each time feel our heart more empty? While if we address to God "those plaints full of reverence that a sorrow full of submission pours out before Him in order to make them die away at His feet,"[6] or if we confide our difficulties to the one who represents Our Lord in our regard, we find light, strength and peace. Evidently, we may also at times open our heart to a faithful and discreet friend; did not our Blessed Saviour, the Divine Model of every virtue do so Himself, in the Garden of Olives? Did He not confide to His Apostles the supreme anguish of His Sacred Heart? "My soul is sorrowful even unto death": *Tristis est anima mea usque ad mortem.*[7] This is not forbidden; but to be ever craving from creatures what they are unable to give us,[8] leaves us weak and restless; while there is no light and strength that we cannot find in Christ Jesus: He is the surest Friend; He is, as He Himself

1 Ps. iii, 2. 2 Ps. xxiv, 16–17. 3 Ps. xxx, 3. 4 Ps. xxxvii, 9–10.
5 Ps. xxxix, 12–13 et 18. 6 Bossuet. 7 Matth. xxvi, 38.

8 "The heart," writes St. Francis of Sales (*Love of God,* Bk. ix, ch. 3 and *letter* 391) "is permitted by love to bemoan itself... and to sigh out all the lamentations of Job and Jeremias, yet with the condition that a sacred place be still preserved in the depths of the heart, in the highest and most delicate point of the spirit." But the holy bishop blames us "if we do not cease lamenting, if it seems as if we cannot find enough people with whom to bewail ourselves and recount our sorrows in detail."

said again to St. Mechtilde, "essential fidelity."[1] Let us then say to Him: "Lord Jesus, behold I come to Thee, with such or such a sorrow, difficulty, suffering, or affliction; I unite it to those which Thou didst endure here below, when Thou wast in Gethsemane; I abandon myself to Thee, assured that Thou wilt accept this sacrifice in expiation of my sins: *Vide humilitatem meam et laborem meum, et dimitte universa delicta mea.*[2] In return Thou wilt give me strength, constancy and joy." This confidence will not be deceived; a virtue goes out from Christ Jesus which heals all the wounds of those who unite themselves to Him in this way: *Virtus de illo exibat et sanabat omnes.*[3] Indeed, says St. Teresa, "this Divine Master will behold you with those eyes, so beauteous and compassionate, big with tears; He will forget His own sorrows to comfort yours, and that only because you went to seek consolation from Him and turned to look upon Him."[4]

Once more we shall experience how, in every circumstance of our life, it is good for the soul to keep the eyes ever fixed upon the Divine Ideal. Is He not moreover the most perfect example of holy abandonment?

When the Precursor announces to the world the coming of the Saviour, in what terms does he designate Him? "Behold the Lamb of God": *Ecce Agnus Dei.*[5] And is it not the characteristic of the lamb to let one do with it as one will, to let itself be immolated without resistance? It was thus that the prophet Isaias symbolised the Messias. And how truly Christ verified this symbol especially during the time of His Passion! He does not seek to escape from the unheard-of treatment of which He, Eternal Wisdom and Sovereign Master of all things, is the object. He keeps silence: *Jesus autem tacebat*;[6] He is "dumb as a lamb before his shearer": *Quasi agnus coram tondente se obmutescet.*[7] But in the sanctuary of His blessed soul, what a prayer of abandonment to His Father! What an entire donation of Himself to justice and love!

1 *The Book of Special Grace,* 3rd Part, ch. 5. All the last part of this chapter should be read; Our Lord shows the saint how pleasing abandonment and confidence are to Him.

2 "See my abjection and my labour; and forgive me all my sins," Ps. xxiv, 18.

3 Luc. ci, 19.

4 *Way of Perfection,* ch. 26.

5 Joan. i, 29.

6 Matth. xxvi, 63.

7 Isa. liii, 7.

"Christian," Bossuet admirably says, "imitate this God; adore the decrees of the Father, whether He strikes or consoles; whether He crowns or chastises thee, adore, embrace His holy will. But in what spirit? Ah! there lies perfection: in the spirit of the Incarnate God... Let there be accord, consent, eternal acquiescence, an eternal "yes," so to speak, not of our lips but of our heart, in response to His adorable Will..." But it is especially when it concerns hard, humiliating, painful things, that this "yes" ought to come from the bottom of the heart, that our eyes ought to be kept fixed on Christ nailed to the Cross. Then, continues the great orator, "imitate, O Christian, this Man-God, our Exemplar, desolate and forsaken, Who after His bitter complaint, "My God, My God why hast Thou forsaken Me?'[1] casts Himself once more, with a last effort, into the hands that repulse Him: 'Father,' he says, ' into Thy hands I commend My spirit."[2] Thus, be obstinate, Christian, with a holy obstinacy, however forsaken, in throwing thyself again with confidence into the hands of thy God; yea, even into these hands that strike thee with their thunder-bolts; yea, even into these hands that repulse thee, that they may draw thee the closer. If thy heart does not suffice thee in the making of such a sacrifice, take the Heart of an Incarnate God, of a God overwhelmed with sorrow, of a God forsaken; and with all the strength of this Divine Heart, lose thyself in the abyss of holy love. Ah! this losing of thyself is thy salvation, and this death is thy life."[3]

V

In this spirit of holy abandonment there is a perfect and continual homage of faith, confidence and love; "it is composed of a rich store of acts of most perfect faith, most entire and trustful hope, the purest and most faithful love."[4] Therefore God is truly delighted by it.

It is an act of *faith*. To put our confidence in God, is it not indeed to believe in His word? to be assured that in listening to Him we shall attain to holiness, that in abandoning ourselves to Him, He will bring us to beatitude? This faith is easy when we meet with no difficulty, and walk in a way of light and consolation: it is a little like the case of those

1 Matth. xxvii, 46. 2 Luc. xxiii, 46.y
3 *Sermon for the Feast of the Annunciation.* 4 Bossuet, *États d'oraison,* x, 18.

who read the account of expeditions to the North Pole while comfortably sitting by the fireside. But when we are struggling with temptation, with suffering and trial, when we are in dryness of heart and spiritual darkness, then it needs a strong faith to abandon ourselves to God and remain entirely united to His holy will. The more difficult the exercise of this faith is for us, the more pleasing to God is the homage that flows from it.

Holy abandonment likewise bears with it an act of *confidence* in God's goodness and almighty power. Sometimes, it seems to us as if God does not keep His promises, that we are mistaken in confiding ourselves to Him. Let us however learn how to wait patiently. Let us say to Him: "My God, I know not where Thou art leading me, but I am sure that if I do not separate myself from Thee, if I remain generously faithful to all that Thou askest of me, Thou wilt be solicitous for my soul and for my perfection. Therefore, though I should walk in the midst of the shadow of death, even if all should seem to be lost, I will fear nothing for Thou art with me, and Thou art faithful."[1] This is an admirable, heroic act of confidence in God, suggested by the spirit of abandonment; an act which glorifies God's Almighty Power, and forces from Him, as it were, the most precious favours. Of this faith and hope, of which abandonment is composed, we find a memorable example in Abraham. God had promised him a numerous posterity; yet the years pass by; Abraham reaches extreme old age, still without having any children. But, as St. Paul, who glorifying the faith and confidence of the father of the faithful, says so well: Abraham "against hope believed in hope." His faith unshaken, he did not consider that he was almost a hundred years old and that Sara was beyond the usual age for having children; but "in the promise also of God he staggered not by distrust; but was strengthened in faith, giving glory to God; most faithfully knowing, that whatsoever He has promised, He is able also to perform. And therefore it was reputed to him unto justice."[2] Later, when Isaac was grown, God commanded Abraham to go forth and immolate this only son upon a mountain. And Abraham immediately obeyed, without murmur or complaint. He did not ask: What posterity will then be given me if I must sacrifice my only son? No, he abandoned himself to God, to His truly mysterious ways, convinced that God is able to fulfil His promises, despite all appearance to the con-

1 Cf. Ps. xxii, 4. 2 Rom. iv, 18–22.

trary: *Contra spem in spem credidit.* What glory this full abandonment gave to God! Therefore God rewarded him by saving Isaac and keeping His most magnificent promises: the Father of believers truly received a posterity numberless as the stars of heaven.

Holy abandonment also and especially includes deep and entire love; it is love's last word. Consider how brides behave in the world. They very rarely know what the future has in store for them; and yet they leave all to give themselves up to the one they love; this affection honours the bridegroom: he is proud to see this confidence. What is the motive of this confidence? Admiration, love. And the object of this love is but a poor human creature who may sometimes deceive the confidence placed in him. Yes, this trustfulness of the bride who leaves family and home to follow one who perhaps but a short time ago was unknown to her, is absolute. But admirable though this trust may be, how groundless is it compared to ours: the One to Whom we give ourselves we have long known, even from the first awakening of our intelligence and our power of loving; we have already received in profusion the pledges of His love; He is God, a God Who cannot deceive us, Who is wisdom itself, boundless power and infinite tenderness. Who is there amongst us who cannot appropriate to himself the words of St. Paul: "I know Whom I have believed": *Scio cui credidi*?[1]

The love which this abandonment supposes, is so great that it honours God perfectly. Is it not equivalent to this declaration: "I love Thee so much, O my God, that I want none but Thee; I only want to know and do Thy will; I lay down my will before Thine, I wish to be directed only by Thee. I leave to Thee all that is to befall me. Even if Thou shouldst leave me the choice of Thy graces, the liberty of arranging all things according to my will, I would say: No, Lord, I prefer to commend myself wholly to Thee; dispose of me entirely, both in the vicissitudes of my natural life, and in the stages of my pilgrimage towards Thee; dispose of everything according to Thy good pleasure, for Thy glory. I desire one thing alone: that all within me may be fully subject to Thy good pleasure, to Thyself and to those who hold Thy place,—and this, whatever be Thy will, whether it leads me by a flower-bordered path, or makes me pass by the way of suffering and darkness." Such language is the transla-

1 II Tim. i, 12.

tion of perfect love; the spirit of self-surrender which is nourished with such dispositions of love and complacency and makes us find in them the rule of all our conduct is likewise the source of a continual homage to the wisdom and power of God.

It is related that during the last days of St. Gertrude's life when she "was sick of a violent fever," our Lord came to her radiant with beauty and holding health in one hand and sickness in the other. He bade her choose between them. But she would have neither. She only cast herself upon His Sacred Heart, desiring nothing but what He chose to give her. And turning her face away from Him she said: "'See, dear Lord, I turn my face away from Thee, desiring with my whole heart that Thou wilt not consider my wishes but wilt accomplish Thine own adorable Will in all that concerns me.' In return for her generosity our Lord caused two streams of grace to flow from His Heart to hers, saying: 'From the moment when, in turning your face from Me, you renounced your own will, I have poured out upon you all the sweetness of My Heart.'"[1]

VI

Such indeed is the way God leads the soul that gives itself entirely to Him. He pours out singular and immense blessings upon it; we can never repeat often enough how sovereignly God acts in such a soul and how it advances in holiness. He leads it by sure ways to the height of perfection. Sometimes, it is true, these ways appear to go quite in a contrary direction, but God attains His ends, ordering all things with strength and sweetness: *Attingit ergo a fine usque ad finem fortiter, et disponit omnia suaviter.*[2] "All things," said Christ Jesus again to His faithful servant Gertrude, "are ordered by the wisdom of My Providence."[3]

Is not the story of the Patriarch Joseph a striking example of this Providence which leads men by wonderful ways, wherein God makes all work together for the good of the soul? Jacob sends Joseph, his beloved son, to find out how his brothers are faring. This is a detail, an act of slight importance; it becomes precisely the first link in a chain of memorable events. Joseph goes to his brethren; but they are jealous

---

1 D. Dolan. *St. Gertrude the Great,* ch. 13, *The Joy of Pain.* p. 208–209.

2 Sap. viii, 1. 3 D. Dolan. l. c. p. 218.

of him because of Jacob's affection for him. They want to be rid of him, by means of a crime if need be; however, at the entreaty of one of them, they content themselves with casting him into a dry cistern; then some merchants happening to pass by on their way to Egypt, they sell Joseph to them. Human wisdom would think that this man's destiny is now fixed; nothing more would be heard of him, but it is just the circumstance that God awaits to make him the saviour of Egypt and of his own brethren. In Egypt, after being for some time in favour with his master, the chief captain of Pharaoh's army, the youth is thrown into prison. We might still think that now his career is broken; but no, from this circumstance, God brings all success to Joseph; he is to come forth from his adversity that he may reach the very step of the throne of the Pharaohs, and all Egypt is to be subject to him.

It is thus that God acts. Even when all seems lost, He shows Himself and comes to our aid. God leads the just man through right ways, and shows him His kingdom; and gives him the science of the saints; He makes him glorious in his labours and crowns his works: *Justum deduxit Dominus per vias rectas et ostendit illi regnum Dei; et dedit illi scientiam sanctorum; honestavit illum in laboribus, et complevit labores illius.*[1] These words may be perfectly applied to the soul that gives itself utterly to God.

Per vias rectas: God's ways are straight, however winding and crooked they may appear to human eyes. Is not God infinite wisdom and power Whom nothing holds back? "All things are equal in My sight," He said to Catherine of Siena, "for My power equally reaches to them all. It is as easy for Me to create an angel as a worm; it is written of Me that all that I have willed, I have done... Why trouble thyself as to how? Thinkest thou that I know not or cannot find the way of carrying out My plans and My decrees?"[2] Let us then trust God. Our own ways seem to us to be sure and certain, but, says St. Benedict, "there are ways which to men seem right, but the ends thereof lead to the depths of hell." Only souls who let themselves be led by God as children do not go astray.

Ostendit illi regnum Dei. There are many souls in the world who have not understood the Kingdom of God. They have formed a kingdom of their own; but it is God Who is to show us *His* Kingdom: He is the architect of our spiritual edifice. What is this kingdom? The perfect union

---

1 Sap. x, 10. 2 *Life,* by Bl. Raymund of Capua.

with God in our heart: *Regnum Dei intra vos est.*[1] In the concrete, the souls wherein God is entirely the master compose His Kingdom. Believe me, if we did but embrace God's will in its entirety, Our Lord would take upon Himself the care of uniting us to Him despite our miseries, despite our absorbing occupations and all that we deem to be distractions and obstacles. While if we do not give ourselves up entirely to God's Will and to His ways, we shall never reach intimate union with Him. Souls who do not give themselves do not understand this; they put obstacles in the way of God's supremacy; while a soul who surrenders itself to Him recognises in all things no other power than His own.

Dedit illi scientiam sanctorum. What is this "science of the saints" that God gives to the soul whom He leads? It is the knowledge of the truth of things. Every man is a liar, Scripture says.[2] When a man leads himself, by the wisdom of the world, by ways that are merely human, he goes astray because he follows false maxims which are so widespread in this world of darkness. But when he gives himself to God, God enlightens him, because God is the Truth and the Light. The soul comprehends the truth concerning God, itself, and the world; little by little, it sees all things as Eternal Wisdom sees them, it possesses this science which is the only true one, because it leads us to our supernatural end.

Honestavit illum in laboribus suis et complevit labores illius. Wisdom enriches the just man in his labours and crowns his works. The more we come in contact with souls, the more we see that God is our holiness. We shall never be holy if we wish to become so in our own way, and not in God's way. We do not altogether know what is good for us; we do not understand the utility of temptations, trials and sufferings. But God is wisdom and He created us. He sees everything in our soul. He beholds with an infinite intensity and in light incomparable. The soul that leads itself by its own sense of what is fitting, easily thinks that all it does must be right, and is very astonished that others do not think the same. This soul builds up its own plan; but what would happen if all succeeded according to its views and desires? It would grow so full of self that it would become insupportable to God and the neighbour. When God sees a soul, He sees its good will, but also its miseries. He allows this soul to be tempted. What is the result of this Divine treatment?

1 Luc. xvii, 21. 2 Ps. cxv, 11.

That self-love begins to die in the soul in order to give place to the Love of God. We may speak in analogous terms of sufferings or of success in our work. Certainly we must do everything as perfectly as possible, for the glory of God, and, for our part, neglect nothing in order to do so; but we must not wish for success for the sake of success: this is often to meet with a stumbling block. A soul left to itself wishes to succeed, but God permits that it does not succeed, so that it may say to God: "Take me and guide me." Then God replies: "Very well, now that you know how weak and powerless you are, I will lead you." And the more this soul gives itself, the more God acts and blesses its works, doubtless not always according to human foresight, but according to the good of this soul and the interests of His glory. The influence of such a soul in the supernatural world is immeasurable, because its action participates in some way in the very infinity of God's action.

God acts towards us as we act towards Him; God, as it were, measures His Providence according to our attitude in relation to Him: and the more we give ourselves to Him, the more we look upon Him as our Father, as the Spouse of our souls, the more His Providence enters into the least details and circumstances of our life. For a soul totally surrendered to Him, God has ineffable delicacies which show that His gaze is ever fixed upon it; never has mother cared for her child, never has friend gladdened his friend, as God cares for and gladdens this soul.

When God sees a soul utterly given up to Him, He would move the whole world for it, He encompasses it with a special and intimate protection. Read the Psalm, *Qui habitat in adjutorio altissimi*,[1] and you will have an idea of the singular protection with which God covers a soul who "dwelleth"—*habitat*—in absolute confidence in Divine aid.

This soul is perfectly free and detached from self and from creatures. It is the captive of nothing whatsoever, neither of an employment, nor of a charge. It seeks and desires God, *Revera quaerit Deum*, and when it has found Him, its every desire is fulfilled. God is the sovereign Master

1 "He that dwelleth in the aid of the Most High," Ps. xc, 1. See also Ps. xxvi, a true song of confidence for the soul that is given to God: "*The Lord is my light and my salvation; whom shall I fear?... For He hath hidden me in His tabernacle; in the day of evils, He hath protected me in the secret place of His tabernacle. He hath exalted me upon a rock.*"

of this soul; nothing in it disputes this sovereignty: it procures Him incomparable glory by the continual homage of utter self-surrender; the Lord works great things through it, and its life has the most wonderful repercussion in the spiritual world.

The liberty possessed by souls thus given to God, brings them great peace and deep joy: they know that God is a Father full of goodness, that He loves them and wills to bring them to Himself. What have they to fear? God guides them, nothing is wanting to them, neither light nor grace: *Dominus regit me, et* NIHIL *mihi deerit.*[1] They live in the abundance of Divine gifts and in an inward peace passing all understanding. It is enough to come near them to feel the sweetness of the influence which flows from them and has its well-spring in their unshaken confidence in God, and in the close intimacy which unites them to Him. The Lord has become for them their wisdom, strength and glory, and even "in the midst of the shadows of death," they taste the peace of God and an inalterable joy, because they know they are in the hands of the best of fathers, the most faithful of friends, the most tender of spouses: *Et si ambulavero in medio umbrae mortis, non timebo mala, quoniam tu mecum es.*[2]

1 Ps. xxii, 1.

2 "For though I should walk in the midst of the shadow of death, I will fear no evils, for Thou art with me," Ps. xxii, 4.

GOOD ZEAL

SUMMARY.—The life of prayer and of union with God is the source of zeal.—I. St. Benedict begins by condemning bad zeal.—II. Forms of good zeal which he wishes to see us practise towards our brethren in the cloister: respect.—III. Patience.—IV. Promptitude in rendering service.—V. Diversity of faults committed against charity.—VI. Good zeal ought to be extended to the whole Community.—VII. Divers forms of good zeal towards souls living in the world.—VIII. How all this holy fervour has its principle in the love of Christ Jesus: *Christo omnino nihil praeponant!*[3]

ONE of the most precious results of the life of union with God is the keeping alive of the fire of love in the soul, not only the fire of divine love, but also of charity towards our neighbour. By frequent contact with the furnace of substantial Love, the soul is set on fire for God's interests and glory, and for the extension of Christ's reign in hearts. The true inner life makes us give ourselves to souls as well as to God: it is the fount of zeal. When one truly loves God, one desires that He be loved, that His name be hallowed, His Kingdom come in souls and His will be done in us: *Sanctificetur nomen tuum, adveniat regnum tuum, fiat voluntas tua sicut in caelo et in terra!*[4] The soul that truly loves God, deeply resents the injuries that are done to the object of its love; "a fainting takes hold of it because of the wicked that transgress the divine law": *Defectio tenuit me pro peccatoribus dereliquentibus legem tuam.*[5] It suffers at seeing the empire of the prince of darkness extended by sin; for Satan "as a roaring lion goeth about seek-

3 "Let them prefer nothing whatever to Christ," Rule, ch. lxxii.

4 Matth. vi, 9–10. 5 Ps. cxviii, 53.

ing whom he may devour,"[1] and he has accomplices into whom he breathes an incessant ardour, a zeal of hatred against the members of Jesus Christ.

The soul that loves God sincerely is also devoured with zeal, but it is for the glory of the house of the Lord: *Zelus domus tuae comedit me.*[2]

What in fact is zeal? It is an ardour that burns and is communicated, that consumes and is spread abroad; it is the flame of love—or of hatred—manifested by action. The soul inflamed with holy zeal spends itself for the interests of God without counting the cost, it strives to serve them with all its powers. And the more glowing this inward fire is, the more it radiates outwardly. This soul is animated with that fire which Christ Jesus came to cast upon earth, and so ardently desires to see kindled in us.[3]

Every Christian who truly loves God and Christ, who wishes to respond to the desire of the Heart of the Divine Master, ought then to be inspired with this zeal. But this ardour ought above all to be enkindled in those whom Christ has rendered participants of His Priesthood. The priest is called, by his function and dignity, to work more than any other for the extension of the Kingdom of Jesus; he can fully accomplish his mission only by unceasing mediation between souls and God.

Let us then see, in the cloister itself to begin with, what form the exercise of this zeal towards our brethren ought to take. Indeed, if we must be zealous for the salvation of our neighbour in general, there are, however, evident degrees in spiritual "proximity." Our neighbour is first of all he with whom we live in community of vocation and life. To be enlightened in this matter, we have only to read over together the magnificent chapter wherein our Holy Father has condensed in truly lapidary formulas how "good zeal" is to be manifested. We will next consider the divers manifestations of this zeal outside the cloister;—we will finish our comments by showing in what furnace the fire of the love of souls is nourished.

1 1 Petr. v, 8. 2 Ps. lxviii, 10; Joan. ii, 17. 3 Cf. Luc. xii, 49.

I

Our holy Father declares first of all that there is "an evil zeal that leads to hell."[1] It is the zeal of the agents of Satan who are intent on snatching from Christ's hands, by every means, the souls redeemed by His Precious Blood. This baneful ardour constitutes the most bitter form of evil zeal: the devil keeps it alive with his breath; this is why the holy Patriarch says it ends in the eternal abyss.

Other forms of evil zeal, taking the appearance of good, are to be met with. There is, for example, the zeal of Pharisees, strict observers of the outward law. This "bitter" zeal, as our holy Lawgiver styles it, has its source, not in the love of God and of our neighbour, but in pride. Those who are tainted with it are filled with inordinate esteem for their own perfections; they do not conceive of any other ideal than their own; all that does not accord with it is necessarily blameworthy; they want to bend everyone to their own way of seeing and doing; hence arise dissensions. This zeal tends to hatred. See with what acrimony the Pharisees, moved by this zeal, pursue the Lord Jesus, putting insidious questions to Him, setting snares to entrap Him, seeking not to know the truth, but to find Christ in fault. See how they press Him, how they try to induce Him to condemn the woman taken in adultery: "Now Moses in the law commanded us to stone such a one. But what sayest Thou?" *Tu ergo, quid dicis?*[2] See too how they reproach Him for healing on the Sabbath day;[3] how they complain of the disciples for rubbing the ears of corn in their hands on the day of rest;[4] how they are scandalised at seeing the Divine Master sit down to table with sinners

---

1 Rule, ch. lxxii.

2 Joan. viii, 5. "The Pharisees were urged not by the zeal of justice which fears the contagion of evil example, but by the impatience of a bitter zeal, or the ostentatious pride of an affected piety." "We exert a species of tyranny over our brethren, we are moved by a spirit of bitterness or a spirit of disdain against them, and become censors to such a degree that we forget we are brothers. Such was the vice of the Pharisees: it was not compassion for our common weakness that made them reprove the sins of men: they held themselves to be beyond compare; and as if they alone had been impeccable, they always spoke disdainfully of publicans and sinners: they set themselves up as public censors, not to heal wounds and correct sin, but to exalt themselves above others, and arrogantly display their proud justice." Bossuet, *Sermon on the Woman taken in adultery*.

3 Luc. vi, 7; Joan. v, 16; ix, 16.

4 Matth. xii, 2.

and publicans.[1] These are so many manifestations of this "bitter zeal" into which hypocrisy so often enters.

There is also excessive zeal, ever strained, ever restless, tormented, agitated; nothing is ever perfect enough for souls possessed by this ardour. Our holy Father carefully forewarns the Abbot against this unseasonable zeal. "Let him not be turbulent and over anxious, not impatient and self-opinionated, not jealous and prone to suspicion, or else he will never be at rest": *Non sit turbulentus et anxius, non sit nimius el obstinatus, non zelotypus et nimis suspiciosus, quia nunquam requiescet.*[2] "Even in his corrections, let him act with prudence and not commit any excess, for fear that in being too eager to scrape off the rust from the vessel and make it too clean, he break it... Let him never lose sight of his own frailty..."[3] In a word he is "not to let a false zeal of envy or bitterness be kindled in his soul": *Ne forte invidiae aut zeli flamma urat animam.*[4] What he says of the Abbot, the holy Legislator repeats to the monks: they must "not give way to animosity and envy": *zelum non habere; invidiam non exercere.*[5] This is a wise precept. Religious are to be met with who frequently criticise what is done; they believe themselves to be full of zeal, and it is true: zeal animates them, but it is a contentious zeal, a zeal of bitterness.[6] And why is this zeal "bitter"? Because it is impatient, indiscreet, and wanting in sweetness.

It is of this zeal that our Lord speaks in the parable of the sower, when the servants ask the master of the field if they may go to pull up the cockle sown by the enemy, not thinking how they run the risk of also rooting up the good grain. "Wilt thou not that we go?" *Vis emus?*[7] It is this zeal that carried away the disciples with indignation and made them want to call down fire from heaven upon the city of Samaria in

---

1 Ibid. ix, 11. 2 Rule, ch. lxiv. 3 Ibid.

4 Ibid. ch. lxv. 5 Rule, ch. iv.

6 "The important point is to know what we have in our hearts. Perhaps we should have to answer: 'I love myself much; scarcely anyone else counts. I possess a very keen self-assertiveness; I belong heart and soul to my own views—that is to my delusions. And since I am not alone in the world and there is a multitude of other selves around me who limit me and try to check me, my zeal easily becomes impatience, anger, contentiousness and rebellion: *Zelus amaritudinis malus.*'" Abbot Delatte, *Commentary upon the Rule of St. Benedict,* translated by Dom Justin McCann, p. 487.

7 Matth. xiii, 28.

punishment for not having received their Divine Master. "Lord, wilt Thou?" A word would suffice: *Domine, vis dicimus ut ignis descendat?* But what does Christ Jesus reply to this headstrong ardour? "You know not of what spirit you are": *Nescitis cujus spiritus estis.* "The Son of man came not to destroy souls, but to save."[1]

II

Good zeal knows not this excess; it is not eager to impose its personal conceptions of perfection upon others, nor is it full of the sense of duty accomplished, nor of inconsiderate, violent impulses, but of the love of God, pure, humble, full of sweetness. Let us see how the holy Patriarch would have us manifest it.

As for the forms of the good zeal of the monk towards his brethren, St. Benedict reduces them to three: respect, patience, and promptitude in rendering service.[2]

Our Lawgiver requires first of all respect: "Let monks prevent one another with marks of honour."[3] These words are borrowed from St. Paul: *Honore invicem praevenientes.*[4] There are some who think that respect acts as a constraint to love, while in fact these two sentiments can be perfectly allied to one another: respect safeguards love. We are souls consecrated to God; that is the first source of our mutual love. "I pray for them," said Jesus in speaking to His Father of His Apostles, "because they are Thine": *Quia tui sunt.*[5] Christ loved His disciples because, while being near to Him, they were still nearer to His Father. We are all "one"[6] in Christ's Mystical Body; we have all been called by Him to the same monastic vocation; therefore we ought to love one another. But, as this Christian and religious vocation gives us first of all to God, to Jesus Christ, as our souls are the temple of the Holy Spirit, we ought to respect what is divine in our neighbour; our love, however fervent it be, should never degenerate into familiarity; far from drawing closer

1 Luc. ix, 54–56.

2 We have had already to touch rapidly upon these three points so as to give a general view of the cenobitical society; we must now return to them here more in detail on account of the importance given to them by the Gospel and the Rule.

3 Rule, ch. lxxii. 4 Rom. xii, 10. 5 Joan. xvii, 9.

6 Ibid. 21; cf. I Cor. x, 17.

the bonds of affection, this wrong kind of familiarity ends by breaking them; far from keeping charity alive it ends by exstinguishing it. Our love should be supernatural; that is what Our Blessed Father indicates by these words: "Let all exercise fraternal charity with chaste love": *Caritatem fraternitatis caste imbendant amore.*[1] He does not wish the brethren to call each other by their simple names, but he requires that the name be prefixed by a term expressing respect;[2] he wishes that the young should show to their elders a respect that has in it something of veneration: he carefully determines the forms.[3] In all these precepts, we see manifested that spirit of religion that the holy Patriarch brings to bear in all the articles of his Rule.

Never let us permit a creature, however holy in appearance, to turn us away in the slightest degree from the object of our love. All sensible or too natural affection ought to be pitilessly rejected. Our heart is insatiable for love, but once it is consecrated to the Divine Spouse it is no longer permissible to go begging from the creature for the wherewithal to satisfy it.

You may say: Must not we then love one another, not even in the bosom of the monastic family? Are we to be for each other like abstractions? Certainly we must love one another, really, intensely, but in God, and for God. Our love for others must be supernatural, and this character, which keeps our affection in all purity, also gives it invincible strength. We see that Christ Jesus, our Divine Model, had very real affections. With a truly human Heart, He loved His Mother, St. John, His friends at Bethania, Lazarus, Martha and Mary, and His disciples. At the tomb of Lazarus, He did not fear to let His tears flow, so that the Jews, who witnessed this touching spectacle, could not refrain from exclaiming: "Behold, how He loved him!" *Ecce quomodo amabat eum.*[4]

Our affections ought to be the reflection of His; He Himself said: "Love one another, as I have loved you": *Sicut dilexi vos.*[5] His affections were divinely human: divine in their source and mainspring, human in their expression.

1 Rule, ch. lxxii. 2 Ibid. ch. lxiii. 3 Ibid.
4 Joan. xi, 36. 5 Ibid. xiii, 34.

You know too with what tenderness St. Paul addresses his dear disciples of Philippi; he calls them his "joy and his crown";[1] he declares that he has them all in his heart; he takes God to witness that he loves them all tenderly. And whence does the great Apostle find the secret of this love? In the Heart of Christ: *in visceribus Jesu Christi.*[2]

It is especially when a soul has arrived at a high degree of veritable detachment, where God is really its *all*, that it can love with a holy liberty, because its affections, being rooted in God, serve to increase its charity. The history of St. Teresa shows us this. At the beginning of her spiritual life, Our Lord reproaches her for loving creatures too naturally; when, later, Teresa is entirely dead to all created things, the Divine Master restores to her all her affections, but supernaturalised. We are astonished to see the exquisite tenderness with which her letters overflow, but we feel truly, by a thousand details and expressions, that it has its source in God.[3] In the same way, in no correspondence does affection overflow as it does in that of St. Anselm with his friends; we have no longer any conception in our days of such outpourings, such depth and fervour of affection; but his great heart was all for Jesus, and it was in his love for the Word Incarnate that he found this wealth of affection.

Our love for our brethren must then be true, sincere, fervent, but it must come from on high, depend upon God, and be subordinate to Him.

III

The second form of "good zeal" is patience with one another: "Let the brethren most patiently bear with one another's infirmities whether physical or moral": *Infirmitates suas sive corporum sive morum patientissime tolerent.*[4]

Not one of us is exempt from infirmities and defects; even souls who sincerely seek God, who are very near to Him, who are the object of His particular favours, keep their limitations and imperfections. God leaves them these miseries, says St. Gregory, in order that these souls may always be kept humble: *Etiam quibus magna dona tribuit, parva*

1 Philip. iv, 1. 2 Ibid. i, 7–8.
3 Cf. *Life by Herself*, ch. 24 and 27; letters 180, 227 and 312; *History of St. Teresa*, according to the Bollandists. Vol. I. 4 Rule, ch. lxxii.

quaedam reprehensibilia relinquit, ut semper habeant quod mentem non erigant.[5] To be astonished at the presence of these frailties betrays a lack of experience; we show that we are still imperfect if we are troubled by them; it belongs only to saints to understand all miseries and to compassionate them. Our defects may also be accentuated by the lack of education, by bad habits, or aggravated by the painful train of infirmities that age brings with it; they may be born of natural antipathy; the very presence of a person may be sometimes sufficient to cause annoyance, or even aversion.

Now, what will throw a veil over all this? What will prevent coldness from gaining the heart, and repugnance from manifesting itself outwardly? The warmth of charity. Indeed charity alone will bring about this marvel of causing us to overcome nature and to love all our brethren as we find them.

Is it not thus that God treats us? Unquestionably He loves each one of us in an individual manner; He loves us, taking us as we are, with that something which makes each one himself and not another; with all the gifts of nature and grace that He Himself has placed within us; with all that human weakness admits of limitations and defects. And of what pitying patience has He not given us the proof while we were for Him as enemies, "children of wrath"?[6] If He had then treated us with all rigorous justice, where should we be now? And how many times has not God forgiven us? With what truly Divine magnanimity has He not often waited for us like the Father of the Prodigal, enlightening us in our darkness, bearing with our resistances, and opening out His arms to us as soon as we return to Him?

We shall find in our holy Father St. Benedict an admirable example of this condescension and patience. His great soul, arrived at perfect holiness and so near to God, overflowed with indulgence and compassion. Is not the Good Shepherd the ideal especially cherished by him and presented as model to the Abbot?[7] Like the Good Shepherd, like the Patriarch Jacob whose conduct St. Benedict brings forward, he must not cause his flock to be overdriven but have consideration for those among

5 *Dialogues.* Lib. iii, ch. 14, P. L. col. 249.
6 Eph. ii, 3.
7 Rule, ch. ii, xxvii.

his sheep whose progress is more painful.[1] The Abbot has not always to do with heroic souls. While striving to remain himself at a high level, he must know how to stoop towards souls who mount slowly, sustaining them by his example as well as by his encouragement and charity.

And what astonishing indulgence the holy Patriarch manifests in regard to delinquents! He is not scandalised, he is not angry; like a kind physician he does all he can to save them, and to console the wavering and troubled culprit "lest he be overwhelmed with excess of grief."[2] It is not until he has duly proved that his efforts and prayers are unavailing and that the offending brother's will is obstinately anchored in evil that St. Benedict cuts him off from the monastic flock.[3] Up to this point he bears with everything; he even wishes that the door of the monastery shall be re-opened to fugitives as many as three times from the moment they show sincere repentance.[4] See too with what thoughtful tenderness, what almost maternal solicitude, he concerns himself with the weakness of children, the infirmities of the aged,[5] with what ingenious love he wishes the sick to be borne with and nursed.[6] It truly seems that no other religious rule demands such perfect patience from those who follow it.

"Have we ever read elsewhere anything to compare with this for generous compassion? We might search all traditions from the end of the sixth century to this time, when ecclesiastical discipline appears most to take human weakness into account, without finding anything to surpass, or even to equal, the merciful large-mindedness shown by St. Benedict. Only perhaps to some exceptionally great soul, an Augustine or a Gregory, has it been given to share this immense treasure of condescending charity. If it be true that the Benedictine Rule is a compendium—'a mysterious abridgment' of the whole Gospel—and that the Gospel itself may be reduced to the one word 'charity,' it may be said that the Rule has found means (at least, in most cases) to epitomise still further; it is all compassion."[7]

The Rule is here truly the pure reflexion of the Gospel. It is remarkable that wherever St. Benedict speaks of this charity towards our brethren,

1 Rule, ch. lxiv; cf. Gen. xxx, 13. 2 Ibid. ch. xxvii. 3 Ibid. ch. xxviii.
4 Ibid. ch. xxix. 5 Ibid. ch. xxvii. 6 Ibid. ch. xxxvi.
7 D.G. Morin, *The Ideal of the Monastic Life Found in the Apostolic Age,* ch. 10. *Discretion and Breadth of View*, translated from the French by C. Gunning, p. 165.

he recalls Christ to our minds.[1] Our Blessed Saviour Jesus is in truth the most perfect Example of this wonderful patience. He wishes us especially to learn that He is "meek of heart."[2] The Evangelist applies to Him that beautiful text of Isaias—a text that the holy Legislator repeats in order to apply it in his turn to the Abbot—"The bruised reed He shall not break, and smoking flax He shall not quench."[3]

Far from extinguishing the smoking flax, He awaits the hour of grace, the hour when it will burst forth in a magnificent flame of pure love. Thus it was with Magdalen and the Samaritan woman and so many others. What indulgent loving kindness He manifested to misery under every form, including that of sin which is most hideous in His Divine sight![4] And what unwearied patience He shows with His disciples! He sees and hears them dispute among themselves, and express their ambitions; He sees the weakness of their faith; He witnesses their impatience: one day, they want to send little children away from Jesus;[5] more than once, even after His Resurrection, He has to rebuke them for their hardness of heart, their slowness to believe in Him,[6] despite so many miracles wrought under their eyes. He is the Model of admirable patience even so far as to endure having near Him the one He knows is to betray Him.

Whence comes the indulgence of Christ? From His love. He loves His disciples, because He sees in them the nucleus of that Church for which He gives His life, *Dilexit Ecclesiam et seipsum tradidit pro ea;*[7] and, because He loves them He bears with them with infinite sweetness.

Such is our Model. Let us keep our eyes ever fixed upon Him, and we shall learn, by His example, to be "meek and humble of heart." Far from being scandalised at our neighbour's faults, we shall see in each of our brethren all that God has put in him that is good and noble, and we shall bear willingly, with inexhaustible patience, *patientissime*, all the imperfections of character, all the physical infirmities that may be found in him. We shall know how to remain in the company of our brethren, at recreation for example, even if this exercise of the common

1 Rule, ch. xxviii, xxxvi, liii.
2 Matth. xi, 29.
3 Ibid. xii, 20; Isa. xlii, 3; Rule, ch. lxiv.
4 For the further development of this idea, we refer the reader to the conference, *Some Aspects of the Public Life of Jesus,* in our work: *Christ in His Mysteries.*
5 Matth. xix, 13.
6 Marc. xvi, 14; Luc. xxiv, 24.
7 Eph. v, 25.

life is burdensome to us; not only shall we never seize a vain pretext for dispensing ourselves from it, but we shall bring to it a spirit of cordiality: this is one of the precious occasions when fraternal charity may be manifested in its every form. Neither shall we look with a severe eye on the exceptions granted to our brethren; when one's own health does not need any special exceptions, one is easily inclined to see in the dispensations granted to others concerning rest, food or work, concessions granted to their self-indulgence, and one is tempted to criticise the conduct of the Superiors.

I would say to you with St. Paul: "Put ye on therefore, as the elect of God" as those who tend towards charity and are dear to the Lord—"the bowels of mercy, benignity, humility, modesty, patience: bearing with one another."[1] And how right St. Paul is! He who is humble does not consider himself as the only one who is perfect, he is not exacting towards others, he does not lay stress on the weaknesses of his neighbour in order to criticise them with malignity and hardness; he has not that "bitter zeal" which, arising in the soul from the sense of one's own perfection, so easily becomes imperious and intransigent. As patience is the daughter of humility, so pride often gives birth to impatience.[2]

"I therefore beseech you," St. Paul says again, "that you walk worthy of the vocation in which you are called, with all humility and mildness, with patience, supporting one another in charity, careful to keep the unity of the Spirit in the bond of peace."[3]

The reason the great Apostle gives for these earnest exhortations is that we are all one in Christ, that we are all members one of another in the Mystical Body of Jesus: we ought therefore to bear with one another, thus imitating our Head, the Lord Jesus, Who gave His life for each one of us; so that by this charity which makes us to be of one mind, we may, with one mouth, glorify God, the Father of our Lord Jesus Christ.[4]

1 Col iii, 12–13.

2 This is what the Eternal Father several times repeated to St. Catherine of Siena. See *Dialogue, Passim* and especially where it treats of *Obedience.*

3 Eph. iv, 2–3; Cf. 32 à I Thess. v, 14: *Patientes estote ad omnes.*

4 Cf. Rom. xv, 1–7.

Thus bearing with one another, we shall fulfil, in its plenitude, all the law of Christ: *Alter alterius ONERA portate, et SIC ADIMPLEBITIS legem Christi.*[1]

This humble and patient charity, which is "the bond of perfection," is at the same time the source, for us, of God's gifts: it brings us in abundance that most excellent gift of our common vocation "the peace of Christ": *Caritatem habete, quod est vinculum perfectionis, et pax Christi exsultet in cordibus vestris, in qua et vocati estis in uno corpore.*[2]

IV

To respect and patience, St. Benedict adds promptitude in rendering mutual service; he would have emulation in this matter: *Obedientiam sibi certatim impendant.*[3] This is the faithful echo of St. Paul's counsel: "By charity of the spirit serve one another": *Per caritatem Spiritus servite invicem.*[4] And again: "Let every one of you please his neighbour unto good, to edification," *Unusquisque vestrum proximo sua placeat in bonum.*[5]

Naturally, this is not a question of orders properly so called, nor demands which might be against the commands of the Superiors, but of small services of which each may have need. In such a matter, we must be very generous. God looks with pleasure upon a soul that forgets itself to think of its neighbour: this is what St. Benedict wishes. "Let no one follow what seemeth good for himself, but what seemeth good for another": *Nullus quod sibi utile judicat sequatur, sed quod magis alio.*[6] It is the precept of the Apostle to the Philippians: "Each one not considering the things that are his own, but those that are other men's": *Non quae suae singuli considerantes sed ea quae aliorum.*[7] To think more of our neighbour, of his interests, his satisfaction and his joy, than of our-

---

1 Gal. vi, 2. 2 Col. iii, 14–15.

3 "Let them vie in paying obedience one to another," Rule, ch. lxxii.

4 Gal. v, 13. 5 Rom. xv, 2.

6 Rule, ch. lxxii. St. Anselm wrote the same to his disciples: "Let the love that you have for one another cause you to live in peace and concord; and in order to cherish this love let each study to do the will of others rather than his own": *Ad invicem pacem et concordiam per mutuam dilectionem habete, quam dilectionem sic nutrire et servare poteritis si unusquisque non ut alius suam, sed ut ipse alterius voluntatem faciat studuerit. Epistol.* 49, L.III, P. L. 159, col. 80–81. 7 Philip. ii, 4.

selves is the unequivocal sign of true charity: for to act in this way, not once, not ten times, but always, under every circumstance, towards all our brethren without distinction, one must love God truly; a like love of the neighbour requires too much abnegation to be sustained for long for his own sake: it can only be so if it is born of God. Therefore charity towards the neighbour is given by Jesus in person as the special sign of God's presence in the soul. This is what St. Gregory wrote to St. Augustine of Canterbury whom he had sent to preach Christ to the pagans of Great Britain. Augustine had addressed to the holy pontiff an account of the marvels God wrought by his hands for the conversion of these pagans: "Think that the gift of miracles is not given thee for thyself," the great Pope replied to him, "but for those whose salvation is entrusted to thee. There are miracles wrought by the reprobate, and we know not if we are of the number of the elect. God has given us only one sign whereby to recognise His elect: it is that we love one another."[1]

What indeed is charity? It is the love of God enfolding in a single embrace God and all that is united to Him: the Humanity of Christ, and, in Christ, all the members of His Mystical Body. Christ is afflicted in the afflicted, He suffers in those who suffer, He is sad in those overwhelmed with sadness. Are not these the words of Infallible Truth: "As long as you did it to one of these My least brethren, you did it to Me"?[2] In becoming incarnate, Our Lord took upon Himself all our infirmities: *Vere languores nostros ipse tulit.*[3] In ministering to these infirmities, it is Himself to Whom we minister.[4]

---

1 *Epistol.* xxviii, Lib. xi, P. L. 77, 1140–1141.

2 Matth. xxv, 40. 3 Isa. liii, 4.

4 "You cannot render Me any service," God said to St. Catherine of Siena, "but you can come to the help of your neighbour, and if you seek the glory and salvation of souls, it is the proof that I dwell in your heart by grace. The soul enamoured of My truth, allows itself no rest while ever seeking to succour others. It is impossible for you to render Me personally the love I exact, but I have given you your neighbour that you may be enabled to do for him what you could not do for Me: to love him disinterestedly, without looking for any gratitude or any advantage from him. I then consider as done to Myself what you do for your neighbour." *Dialogue,* ch. 7, 64, 89. Our Lord several times used the same language in speaking to St. Mechtilde; cf. *The Book of Special Grace,* 2nd Part, ch. 41 and 4th Part, ch. 49.

The lives of the Saints are full of traits verifying this teaching. St. Gregory the Great recounts to us the history of the monk Martyrius who met upon his way a leper weighed down with misery and exhaustion. Martyrius wrapped the sick man in his cloak and carried him upon his shoulders as far as the monastery. But, behold, the leper appeared as Christ Himself Who, before disappearing from the monk's gaze blessed him in saying: "Martyrius, thou hast not been ashamed of Me upon earth, and I will not be ashamed of thee in Heaven."[1]

So St. Gertrude, that worthy daughter of St. Benedict, showed inexhaustible charity throughout her life. It is related[2] that during the last days of Holy Week, her soul remained so united to Christ, Whose sorrowful mysteries were then being renewed, that it became almost impossible for her to tear away her thoughts from Jesus and apply her senses to exterior things. However, if it concerned acts of charity, she recovered her liberty and performed them without any hesitation; an evident proof, adds the Saint's biographer, that the Guest to Whom Gertrude inwardly clung in the ecstatic repose of those days was He of Whom St. John wrote: "God is charity: and he that abideth in charity, abideth in God, and God in him."[3]

These examples of charity show us how important it is to give ourselves to our brethren, in the measure that is permitted by obedience to the Rule and the orders of the Superiors. God loves one who is happy to give himself. Such a disposition is the contrary of official charity, which is so often but the simulation of love that an English proverb says: "Cold as charity." Our charity ought to be warm, ready to adapt itself generously, lovingly and always, to all our brothers' needs. Let us behold Christ Himself in the brother who comes to knock at our door and we shall then serve him with delight. If we think it is Our Lord Who comes to ask this service of us, shall we say: "Yes, Lord, but wait till I've finished what I am doing"? Quite the contrary! Applying to this fraternal obedience what our holy Lawgiver says of obedience to the Abbot, we shall immediately leave our own occupations in order to serve Christ with

1 *Hom. in Evangel.* Lib. ii *homil.* 39. P. L. 76, 1300. See an analogous trait in the life of St. Wandrille, (D. Besse, *St. Wandrille,* pp. 38–40).

2 *The Herald of Divine Love,* Bk. iv, ch. 25.

3 I Joan. 16, 16.

joy: *Relinquentes statim quae sua sunt, mox ex occupatis manibus...*[1] If we have these views of faith, our love will always be zealous, disinterested, and we shall not complain if we have often to give ourselves to others.

Christ Jesus will not leave our generosity unrewarded. Was it not He Himself, the source of all grace as of all truth, Who said: "Give, and it shall be given to you": *Date, et dabitur vobis*?[2] He who gives to his neighbour receives in his turn from God. There are souls who do not advance in the love of God, because God acts sparingly towards them; and God shows Himself sparing because they are selfish and will not give themselves to Christ in His members. It is not always on account of the lack of affictive mortification that inward progress is retarded in so many souls; this cause must often be sought for in the selfishness that makes them indifferent to the needs of their brethren, in the stiffness that they show towards them: "With the same measure that you shall mete withal, it shall be measured to you again": *EADEM quippe mensura, qua mensi fueritis, demetietur vobis.*[3]

Herein lies the secret of the spiritual sterility of more than one soul; God leaves in their isolation those who surround themselves with precautions to safeguard their selfish tranquillity: by shutting themselves up from their neighbour these souls close themselves to God.

And as God is the Fount of every grace, as without Him we can do nothing for eternal beatitude, what can a soul hope for that thus voluntarily closes the avenues of grace? God lets Himself be touched by our miseries, but on condition that we are ourselves sensible to the miseries and needs of our brethren.

Let us then give, as Christ; this is His own precept: *Sicut dilexi vos.*[4] Our Divine Saviour has no need of us; and yet He has given Himself, Heart, Blood, Life; He still delivers Himself up daily in the Eucharist. Every day, Christ Jesus gives Himself to all those who wish to receive Him, whatever be the state of their soul: "Both the wicked and the good" receive Him: *Sumunt boni, sumunt mali.*[5] Let us too give without reservation, let us listen to our Lord Who tells us: "I Who am God, have loved this neighbour, I have given Myself for him, I call him to the same

1 Rule, ch. v.
2 Luc. vi, 38.
3 Luc. vi, 38.
4 "As I have loved you," Joan. xiii, 34.
5 Sequence *Lauda Sion.*

eternal beatitude as yourself; why do you not love him, if not in the same measure that I have loved him, at least as ardently as you can for My sake, and in Me?" That is our ideal, and it is by ever striving to reach this ideal that, according to the precept of St. Benedict, we shall fully pay off the debt of fraternal charity: *Caritatem fraternitatis impendant amore.*[1]

V

As to faults against charity, they are of two kinds.

The first are faults of weakness, whereby the will is taken by surprise: movements of temper or impatience, unkind words, heat in discussion. It is such as these that the great Patriarch so well names "thorns of scandal": *Scandalorum spinae.* These slight frictions "are wont to arise," he adds: *Quae oriri solent*,[2] above all in a rather numerous Community. Such faults are not grave, because they generally arise without premeditated intention.

On these occasions, when we are the object of them, we ought not to be touchy, and think that a crime of *lèse-majesté* has been committed against us. If we take these little failings in a high and mighty way, if we turn over in our mind the offence that has been done to us, we shall always live in trouble; even to think of it once is once too often. Our holy Legislator wishes, like St. Paul,[3] that we should very readily forgive one another these small offences; he wishes the Abbot, the Father of the monastic family, to sing the *Pater Noster* from beginning to end in the choir, twice a day during the Divine Office, in order that in asking God to forgive us our faults, we may thereby be ready likewise to forgive our brethren.[4] Our holy Father St. Benedict also wishes that in case we are at variance with anyone we should be reconciled before the setting of the sun: *Cum discordante ante solis occasum in pacem redire.*[5]

Other faults which in the long run can become grave, because they are deliberate, are those of wilful coldness towards anyone, the cher-

1 Rule, ch. lxxii. 2 Ibid. ch. xiii.

3 *Donantes vobismetipsis, si quis adversus aliquem habet quaerelam sicut et Dominus donavit vobis, ita et vos* (Bearing with one another... if any have a complaint against another: even as the Lord hath forgiven you, so do you also). Col. iii, 13; cf. Eph. iv, 32.

4 Rule, ch. xiii. 5 Ibid. ch. iv.

ishing of resentment, prolonged indifference, and other forms of evil which St. Benedict names in order to combat them, in his list of the instruments of good works: "Not to give way to anger; not to harbour a desire of revenge; not to foster guile in one's heart; not to give insincere tokens of friendship." Such faults are too contrary to the spirit of Jesus for it to be necessary to insist more upon this.

Only let us give a forcible reminder that such failings in charity paralyse the soul and hinder spiritual progress. And what is the reason of the greatness of the wrong thus done to oneself? It is that Christ Himself is the object of this coldness, this resentment. If you wound me in one of my members, the eye or the hand, it is myself you wound. Now, says St. Paul, "you are the body of Christ, and members of member": *Vos estis corpus Christi, et membra de membro*.[1]

This language is that of faith. Do we live by this faith? Do we always reflect that all we think, all we say, all we do against our neighbour, we do and say against Christ Himself? If our faith is weak, we do not live by these truths; we easily offend our neighbour and, in him, Christ in person.

When a person thus fails in charity, and receives Christ in Holy Communion, he cannot say to Him: "My Jesus, I love Thee with all my heart." It would be a lie, since he does not envelop Christ and His members with a self-same love. He has not accepted the mystery of the Incarnation in its totality; he stops at Christ's individual Manhood, and forgets the spiritual prolongation of the Incarnation which is the Mystical Body of Jesus. So, then, when we communicate, we ought ever to be ready to embrace, in one and the same charity, Christ and all that is united to Him; for the measure of the giving of Christ to our souls is that of our own donation to our brethren. The Eucharist is a Sacrament of union with Christ, and of union between souls.[2]

Thus a soul who draws near to our Lord, in Communion, in these dispositions of unreserved love towards the neighbour is very pleasing

---

1 I Cor. xii, 27.

2 *Symbolum unius illius corporis, cujus ipse (Christus) caput existit, cuique nos, tamquam membra, arctissima fidei, spei et caritatis connexione adstrictos esse voluit, ut idipsum omnes diceremus nec essent in nobis schismata* (A symbol of that one body, of which He is the head, and to which He willed that we would be as members, bound by the strictest bond of faith, hope and love, so that we might all speak with one mind, and there might be no schisms among us). *Conc. Trid.* Sess. xiii, ch. 2.

to the Sacred Heart. Christ showers magnificent gifts upon it; moreover, faults and shortcomings in respect to the other virtues are at once forgiven, because of this fervent love it bears towards the members of Jesus. This is what Christ Himself made St. Gertrude see one day during Mass. She suddenly beheld her soul adorned with precious stones of marvellous brilliance: it was the reward for an act of charity towards an infirm nun. But this adornment revived St. Gertrude's sense of her own unworthiness; she remembered several slight faults which she had not been able to reveal to her confessor, then absent from the monastery; and she was troubled at not being able to accuse herself of them before Communion. Then Jesus said to her: "Why lament these shortcomings since thou art so gloriously apparelled in this mantle of charity which covers a multitude of sins?" The Saint replied: "How can I be consoled in that charity dissimulates my faults, when I still see myself all sullied with them?" "Charity," replied the Saviour, "not only covers sin, but like to a burning sun, it consumes and effaces all venial sins; moreover, it fills the soul with merits."[1]

When, on Maundy Thursday, the Abbot has communicated all the members of the monastic family, the Angels who behold us see that we are all one in Christ, each one being united to Christ Jesus, and Christ being one, we are then truly one in Him. We thus fulfil the dearest desire of the Word Incarnate.

Indeed, at the supreme farewell hour, when Christ Jesus spoke for the last time with His Apostles before entering into His sorrowful Passion and sacrificing Himself for the world's salvation, what is the exclusive theme of His discourse and the first object of His prayer? Spiritual charity. "A new commandment I give unto you... by this shall all men know that you are My disciples... Father... that they may be one, as We

1 L. c. b. iii, ch. 61. Our Lord said likewise to St. Mechtilde, the companion of St. Gertrude: "If anyone wishes to make Me an acceptable offering, let him be careful never to forsake his neighbour in need or distress; let him ever be ready to extenuate and excuse his brother's failings and sins as much as he can. I promise to be attentive to all the necessities of the one who so does, and to cover his sins and negligences in excusing him to My Father... This practice is so pleasing to Me as to pay every debt that he may have contracted towards his neighbour." *The Book of Special Grace,* 4th Part, ch. 7.

also are one, I in them, and Thou in Me, that they may be made perfect in one."[1] That is the testament of Christ's Heart.

Our Blessed Father St. Benedict, in concluding his Rule, also leaves us as his last testament, his magnificent teaching on good zeal. After having set forth in detail the ordering of our life, he sums up all his doctrine in this short chapter. And what does he tell us? Does he speak to us of prayer? of contemplation? of mortification? Undoubtedly, the holy Patriarch forgets nothing of all this, as we have seen; but having reached the end of his long life so full of experience, at the moment of closing the monastic code which contains for us the secret of perfection, he speaks to us, before all else, of mutual love; he wishes, with that intense desire which was that of Jesus at the Last Supper, to see us excel in most fervent love: *Ferventissimo amore exerceant.*[2] This chapter is the worthy crowning of a Rule which is but the pure reflection of the Gospel.

VI

The exercise of good zeal ought not to be limited distributively to the person of each of our brothers in particular; the character of the cenobitical society requires that it be extended likewise to the Community whereof we are members, taken as a whole. We ought to love this community to which the vow of stability binds us for ever. To love is to wish well;[3] we should then desire, and, in the measure of our power, procure the spiritual welfare, and, according to the views of Providence, the material well-being of this community.

In this domain, we may have duties to fulfil in the capacity of "officials." As soon as obedience entrusts us with a function to fulfil in the monastery, we are responsible, before God and before the Abbot, as to the manner in which we acquit ourselves of it. Good zeal here consists in acquitting ourselves of this function according to the instructions given by the head of the monastery, and with the utmost perfection possible. In this matter, the field of zeal may be boundless; the acts of self-abnegation, patience and devotion are numberless. Let us devote ourselves to the accomplishment of this charge even if it absorbs our

---

1 Joan. xiii, 34–35; xvii, 22–23.
2 Rule, ch. lxxii.
3 St. Thomas, I, q. xx, a. 2.

time and makes painful demands on us. We must not fall into a false mysticism which would make us substitute prayer for the accomplishment of our duties. "Believe me," writes St. Teresa on this subject, "it is not length of time that enables a soul to make progress in prayer; if it is given up to active works also, [by charity and obedience] that is a great help whereby the soul in a very short time may attain to a greater enkindling of its love than it could attain to by many hours spent in meditation. All has to come from His hand."[1] Do not let us think we only approach God when we pray; we are near to Him and find Him when we do the work obedience has laid upon us so that we may come to the help of our brethren.

Even when obedience does not lay any charge upon us, there still remain to us many opportunities of exerting good zeal towards the Community to which we belong. What form ought this zeal to take?

We ought to love our monastery with an ardent indefectible love, never allowing ourselves, especially when with outsiders, to throw the least shadow upon it by mentioning the imperfections which human weakness ever bears in its train; such indiscretion and evil speaking moreover shock the ears upon which they fall, as we are all hurt by hearing anyone speak unkindly or to the disadvantage of our own family.

We ought especially, within the monastery, to labour with all our might, each for his own part, to render the monastic Community less unworthy of God's loving kindness, more skilled in serving Christ's interests in the Church;—we ought to avoid all that, even remotely, can diminish the fervour of the Community, impair its spiritual health, lessen its supernatural radiation: in a word, we must be entirely faithful to observe all the details of the code which rules the cenobitical life. Experience shows that the least breach in this matter can bring disaster. Nothing is more lamentable than the decadence of great monasteries, founded by saints, inhabited by souls dear to God, souls who throughout the centuries have embalmed with the fragrance of their virtues the cloisters where they lived. How are such downfalls brought about? Is it at one blow that institutions at first so vigorous have fallen away? More than once, undoubtedly, exterior circumstances, rav-

1 *The Book of the Foundations,* ch. 5. Translated from the Spanish by David Lewis.

aging wars, decimating plagues, revolutions by which the very walls were destroyed, have hastened these downfalls; but more than once also, ruin has come from within, and was prepared long in advance. The decadence began with slight failings; these failings became habits, they took root and were propagated; soon the dikes thrown up by monastic discipline were destroyed, relaxation entered in, and, with it, the principle of destruction.

Let us be strict on these points, let us beware of infringing the least of our observances, however insignificant they may appear. Let us jealously and lovingly safeguard the traditions, the customs, which form the very physiognomy of the monastery. This is the best form of zeal that we can exert in our community; it is also the principle of our perfection.

In fact the more we endeavour to practise our rule and our observances, the more we shall enter into the spirit of our holy Patriarch, and realise the destiny God has for us. This is because a very real relation exists between our spiritual vocation to the Order of which we are members, and our sanctification. It is evident that the Divine call outwardly manifests God's special design and that to each soul He distributes His lights and gifts according to the measure in which that soul responds to its own particular vocation.

We should often ask our holy Patriarch to make us live according to his spirit; God was pleased to pour signal graces upon him; but he received them as head and lawgiver in order to make them overflow upon all those who, living under his Rule, seek to be imbued with his spirit. As in the Old Testament, the blessing of the Patriarchs was a pledge of the protection of Jehovah for their descendants, so the blessing of the founders of different Orders is the source of favours from on high for those of their disciples who walk in their footsteps. The wide mantle of the Patriarch of monks preserves and safeguards those who take refuge under its folds, while awaiting that they in their turn and in his train may ascend by that magnificent luminous way by which his great soul went up into heaven.[1]

---

1 St. Gregory, *Dialogues.* Lib. ii, ch. 37.

VII

Of its nature, zeal is ardent, it tends to diffuse itself. From the cloister, monastic zeal has naturally spread itself abroad in manifold manifestations which we cannot pass over in silence: they form part of our history and constitute an intangible and inalienable part of our purest traditions.

We have seen that the time at the monk's disposal, apart from the hours of the Divine Office, is consecrated by St. Benedict to manual labour or to the *lectio divina*.

Among manual labours was included, as the Rule itself insinuates,[1] the transcribing of manuscripts; to copy a manuscript was as meritorious as to sow a field or exercise a craft.[2]

Little by little, by a quite natural evolution, which has its principle in the monastic code, and has been accentuated since the elevation of monks to the priestly dignity, brain work has taken the place of the labour of the hands, and the abbeys have thus become important centres of intellectual life and Christian civilisation. How many names it would be necessary to cite among so many monks who have placed their knowledge at the service of truth, either to defend it against its adversaries, or to elucidate it, or to guide souls in the path of the inner life from St. Gregory the Great and the Venerable Bede, Alcuin, Rabanus,

1 Ch. xxxiii.

2 The monks were moreover applied to this work with a wonderful broadmindedness, transcribing with the same fervour, upheld by obedience, not only Holy Scripture and the works of the Fathers, but also the writings of profane antiquity: in their libraries the manuscripts that contain the works of Cicero and Livy are side by side with those where are to be read St. Paul's Epistles, the treatises of St. Augustine and the homilies of St. Gregory. Read on this subject the discourse delivered in September 1910 on the occasion of the 10th centenary of Cluny, by an eminent member of the Institute, M. E. Babelon: "There is one side of the activity of the monk which ought to be sufficient to assure to them, as long as the human race lasts, the gratitude of every man who thinks and reflects. This is that they have passed down from century to century, and bequeathed to us, the inestimable treasure of ancient literature. The monks of the Middle Ages are the bond of intellectual union between antiquity and the modern spirit. They prevented, in the normal evolution of the human mind, a complete rupture, a solution of continuity suddenly taking place which would have swamped civilisation and thrown it back for an incalculable number of centuries... Deprived of the literary treasure of the Greeks and Romans, the principal foundation of our modern culture would have been wanting to us: who would dare to estimate the consequences in which a like catastrophe would have involved the human race?"

St. Anselm and St. Bernard, down to the Ven. Blosius, Dom Mabillon and Dom Martène, Dom Guéranger, Dom Maurus Wolter, Bishop Ullathorne and Bishop Hedley. Doctors full of wisdom,[1] theologians or consummate scholars, ascetics full of doctrine, they have rendered inestimable service to the City of God. The scientific study of Holy Scripture, of the Fathers of the Church, of the Liturgy and ecclesiastical and monastic history: all these forms of zeal and activity are justified by the most ancient and constant tradition, the interpreter of the Rule;[2] they have found and still find in the cloister fervent representatives who have had and still have it at heart to put their talents and the fruit of their labours at the service of the Church and of souls.

The education of youth likewise takes an important place in the series of the works of monastic zeal. One of the greatest monks of the last century, Dom Maurus Wolter, called attention to this work which he declared to be especially confided to monks and is, moreover, several times indicated in the Rule itself. He calls it, in all truth, "an ancient and traditional mission."[3] Not indeed that it is a question here of vast over-peopled colleges of which the care would absorb all the vital strength of the abbey; but of schools where the limited number of students is favourable to education, at the same time that it permits those devoting themselves to this work to safeguard habitually the regular life of Benedictine cenobitism.

Another form of apostolic zeal dear to sons of St. Benedict is the exercise of hospitality. One of the most beautiful chapters of the Rule is devoted to this subject. It is here that St. Benedict reveals the great-

---

1 We know that four conditions are requisite in order to be inscribed in the catalogue of "Doctors" of the Church: purity of orthodoxy, eminence of doctrine, holiness, and, what consecrates all, the express declaration of the Church. The number of "Doctors" for the entire Church is at present twenty three, among which the Order of St. Benedict numbers St. Gregory the Great, the Venerable Bede, St. Peter Damian, St. Anselm and St. Bernard.

2 Cf. D. Mabillon, *Traité des Etudes monastiques,* and the beautiful book of D. Besse: *Le Moine bénédictin.*

3 *La Vie monastique, ses éléments essentiels,* ch. 6. Cf. D. Berlière. *L'Ordre monastique des origines au XIIe siècle.*

ness of his soul; he rises above any narrow point of view to embrace all mankind in the charity of Christ Jesus. One of the greatest reproaches that the Word Incarnate made to the Pharisees was for preferring *their* human traditions to the most explicit precepts of the Divine law, above all, the precept of charity. Religious are to be found who, by a small and superficial way of understanding the exigencies of the cloister, would exclude their brethren in the world from the monastery. But do they not thereby shut out Christ Himself from the sphere of their charity?

Did not Christ Jesus say: "As long as you did it to one of these My least brethren, you did it to Me"?[1] This is the supernatural principle held by our holy Father St. Benedict, always so penetrated with the pure spirit of the Gospel.[2] For if he desires that his sons shall not seek contact with the world, he well knows that in order to be a monk, one does not cease to be a Christian, and that the basis of the true Christian spirit is not only the love of God but also love of our neighbour. Thus he wishes that far from closing the door to the poor, to pilgrims and guests, "all those who come shall be received as if they were Christ in person, for He will say to us one day: I was a stranger, and ye took Me in": *Omnes supervenientes* TAMQUAM CHRISTUS *suscipiantur, quia ipse dicturus est: Hospes fui et suscepistis me.*[3] The great Patriarch secondly ordains that guests shall be treated with all respect and charity. He even goes so far as to enjoin on the Superior to break his fast out of consideration for the guest who arrives,—unless it be a fast day of the Church.

True sons of St. Benedict in nowise fear to imitate their Father's example and to let Christ enter their monastery in the person of guests. St. Teresa pleasantly jests at those who during prayer dare not stir nor make the least movement for fear of interrupting the union of their soul with God.[4] All proportion guarded, it may be said that he who, under

---

1 Matth. xxv, 40.

2 We know too how St. Paul insists upon the duty of hospitality: see Rom. xii, 13; Tit. i, 8; I Tim. v, 10. Hebr. xiii, 1–2.

3 Rule, ch. liii.

4 *Her Life written by herself,* ch. 15; see above all *The Interior Castle* 5th Mansion, ch. 3, translated by the Benedictines of Stanbrook. "When I see people very anxious to know what sort of prayer they practise, covering their faces and afraid to move or think, lest they should lose any slight tenderness and devotion they feel, I know how little they understand how to attain union with God, since they think it consists in

pretext of preserving tranquillity, wished to exclude guests from the cloister, would understand nothing about charity and his pietist recollection would be very fragile and propped up on a very artificial basis.

Experience proves that where monastic hospitality has been exercised in a spirit of true Christian charity, surrounded moreover with the safeguards St. Benedict himself prescribed, the monks, far from suffering from these visits of Christ, have received abundant blessings from them because they have known the Divine Guest in *fractione panis.*[1]

This love of the neighbour, the fruit of true love of God, has necessarily led monks to occupy themselves directly with the care of souls. This is one of the most fruitful aspects of monastic zeal.

The normal and habitual place of the monk is in his monastery. It is there that he was hidden with Christ[2] on the day of that second baptism which is the religious profession; it is there that he diligently works out his sanctification; there is properly speaking the workshop where he is to spend his activity: *Officina ubi haec omnia diligenter operemur claustra sunt monasterii.*[3] Thus St. Benedict desires that the monks shall be able to find in the enclosure all that is necessary to their existence and occupations.[4]

However if we study the question in the light of the example that our holy Father St. Benedict himself gives us, we see that this "cloistered" or "enclosed" life is not to be understood in too absolute and too exclusive a sense. St. Benedict was the perfect imitator of Christ. Christ is before all things the Adorer of the Father, and this is why the great Patriarch wills that no work be preferred to the *Opus Dei*. But he does not forget that Christ is also the Saviour of men, that He consecrated to them three years of preaching, that He shed for them the last drop of His blood; and therefore St. Benedict also, so steeped in the true Christian spirit, wished to devote himself to the salvation of the neighbour. He tells us that the

such things as these. No, sisters, no; our Lord expects *works* from us! If you see a sick sister whom you can relieve, never fear losing your devotion; compassionate her; if she is in pain, feel for it as if it were your own, and, when there is need, fast so that she may eat, not so much for her sake as because you know our Lord asks it of you. This is the true union of our will with the will of God."

1 Luc. xxiv, 35. 2 Cf. Col. iii, 35. 3 Rule, ch. iv.
4 Ibid. ch. lxvi. Cf. above p. ### sq.

Abbot ought to instruct his community especially by his example, and that he ought not to do anything that he teaches his brethren to avoid in their own conduct: *Omnia vero quae discipulis docuerit esse contraria in suis factis indicet non agenda.*[1] St. Gregory assures us that St. Benedict's own life was the authentic commentary on his Rule,[2] and he adds how "The man of God by continual preaching, converted many of the people thereabout": *Vir Dei commorantem circumquaque multitudinem praedicatione continua ad fidem vocabat.*[3] And elsewhere the great Pope remarks that in a certain town not far from the monastery, no small number of people, by the exhortations of Benedict[4] were converted to the faith of God. The Saint himself therefore evangelised the neighbouring populace. We read too that he sent certain of his monks "often," *crebro*, to instruct some nuns who were at a distance from the monastery.[5]

What St. Benedict taught his monks by word and example, the best traditions of the Order have consecrated by the practice of centuries.[6] Without touching the integrity of the community, nor the essential exigencies of stability, the monastic Order has exerted this fruitful apostolate which has converted so many nations to the light of the Gospel and extended the boundaries of Christ's Kingdom. None can deny the title of true sons of St. Benedict to those great monks, full of the love of souls, such as were St. Gregory, St. Augustine of Canterbury and his companions, St. Boniface, St. Anscar, St. Willibrord, St. Adalbert and, nearer to ourselves, Mgr. Marty, Bishop Polding and Archbishop Ullathorne, Bishop Salvado and so many others, "men powerful in word and deed," according to the expression of Dom Guéranger, "illustrious Saints of the monastic order, great religious souls who were at the same time by their whole life the most vivid expression of the spirit which our great Patriarch has laid down in his holy Rule."[7] The zealous life of these great monks constitutes one of the most beautiful pages of mo-

1 "And whatever he has taught his disciples to be contrary to God's law, let him show by his example that it is not to be done," Rule, ch. ii.

2 *Dialogues.* Lib. ii, ch. 36: *Vir sanctus nullo modo potuit aliter docere quam vixit* (The holy man could teach in no way otherwise than he lived).

3 Ibid. ch. 8. 4 *Dialogues.* ch. 19. 5 Ibid.

6 Cf. *L'Apostolat Monastique,* in Berlière, *l. c.*

7 *Notions sur la vie religieuse et monastique.*

nastic holiness; they are themselves the purest glory of a past singularly fruitful for the Church of Christ.[1]

One of the most remarkable characteristics of the life of these great monks is their boundless devotion to the Apostolic and Roman Church.[2] This union with the Apostolic See "was, to our fathers, always an assured pledge of vitality and glory. Wherever the Benedictine monk turned his steps, he was considered as the born representative of Roman influence. Whether he is called Augustine in England, Willibrord in Frisia, Boniface in Germany, Adalbert in the Slav countries, it is always Rome who sends him, who blesses his beginning, seconds his efforts, hallows his success. Having lent its concourse to the great liturgical work of Rome, and, side by side with the Roman faith, introduced civilisation to the farthest boundaries of Europe, the Monastic Order [whose power was then concentrated at Cluny] will be called to a still higher mission. Identified for the time being with the destinies of Rome, it will furnish, inspire, and support in every way those great Popes of the eleventh and twelfth centuries, the heroic defenders of the sanctity and independence of the Church."[3]

"After this epoch it begins, from various causes to play a less important part. Nevertheless, it is an established and significant fact that the Popes have never ceased their efforts to protect and uphold it, and to attach it to themselves as the principal member to the head—*velut principalia capiti suo membra*[4]—to use the expression of Pope Gregory VII." Have we not ourselves had the happiness and consolation of witnessing the attachment of the last Pontiffs to our Order?[5] It is to the princely mu-

---

1 See at the end of this conference a quotation from Dom Maurus Wolter and one from D. Guéranger, too long to be inserted here.

2 Of these great monks may be said what G. Kurth wrote of St. Boniface: "Perhaps no part of his correspondence places the greatness of his character in a more striking light than his letters to the Sovereign Pontiffs. It is known with what devotion, faith, and tenderness, his heart turned towards St. Peter's See. He never loved anything here below so much as the Holy See, and all the glory that he coveted consisted in being the minister of the Vicar of Jesus Christ." *St. Boniface*, p. 119.

3 Cf. Mgr. Baudrillart, *Cluny et la Papauté*.

4 St. Gregory, p. vii, *Epist.* 69. P. L. 118, 420.

5 D. Morin, *The Ideal of the Monastic Life Found in the Apostolic Age*, translated from the French by C. Gunning, p. 74.

nificence of Leo XIII, of glorious memory, that we owe the erection in Rome of the international college of St. Anselm; and without speaking of other facts, the Roman Church has asked the monks of the French Congregation to place at her disposal the results of the admirable work they have done for sacred music, that all Christian assemblies may benefit by it: she has confided to St. Benedict's sons the arduous and delicate task of the critical revision of the biblical text of the Vulgate. These are undubitable marks of singular confidence. Let us see that we respond to it, "ever remembering that the monk to be faithful to his mission, must show himself 'St. Peter's man,' the servant and the devoted son of the holy and Apostolic Church of Rome."[1]

And what was the source of this zeal? Where did these holy monks find the secret of becoming, when God called them by obedience or circumstances, great apostles and wonderful men of action? Whence did they obtain that irresistible ardour, that generous and indomitable strength which enabled them to accept every labour, confront every difficulty, endure every suffering for the extension of the Kingdom of Jesus Christ? The love of God and of Christ was the inward furnace where the living flame of zeal was enkindled.

It was the great monk, and at the same time great apostle, St. Bernard, who wrote these lines: "It is the characteristic of true and pure contemplation that it not only inflames the soul with the fire of divine charity, but it also occasionally fills her with such zeal and desire to gain others to God who shall love Him as she loves Him herself, that she gladly interrupts her contemplative repose and devotes herself to the labour of preaching. Afterwards, having satisfied this longing at least to a certain extent, she returns to her solitude with all the more eagerness in proportion as she knows that her apostolic efforts have been fruitful. Then when she has recruited her strength once more with the sweet food of

1 D. Morin, *l. c.* p. 75. Let us say by way of completing these statements, that, given the extreme variety of Benedictine works, not only does the Abbot proportion and distribute tasks to each monk, but each monastery has in some way its own part in this vast inheritance; and furthermore, we have seen and still see Benedictine Congregations, according to the period and the country, specialise, here in the direction of colleges and of the sacred ministry, there in matters of Liturgy and sacred learning, etc.

prayer, she again issues forth with renewed zeal and energy to resume her work for souls."[1]

This was also the opinion of St. Gregory: "If it is a good thing," he writes, "to pass from the active to the contemplative life, it is generally also useful for the soul to return again to the active life: the ardour obtained in contemplation allows the works of the active life to be all the better accomplished..."[2]

St. Teresa does not speak otherwise: "Oh, the charity," she writes, "of those who truly love our Lord and who understand their own state! How scanty the rest they will be able to take if they but see they can in any degree help a single soul to advance, and to love God more, or be able to comfort it in any way or rescue it from any danger! How ill at ease such souls will be when they are at rest! And when they cannot help them in act they have recourse to prayer, beseeching our Lord on behalf of the many souls whom it grieves them to see going to ruin; they abandon their own comfort, and look on it as well lost, for they think not of their own rest, but only how they may more and more do the will of our Lord."[3]

For us, who must do all things in obedience, the outward exercise of this zeal has its limits fixed by the kind of activity assigned to the monastery by traditions, circumstances, and above all by the orders of the

---

1 *In cantica,* Sermo lvii, translated by a Priest of Mount Melleray. And again: *Zelum tuum inflammet caritas* (Let charity inflame your zeal). *In cantica* Sermo xx, 4. Ibid. col. 868; *Est enim tantum lucere vanum, tantum ardere parum, ardere et lucere perfectum* (It is indeed vain to shine only, likewise vain to burn only, but to burn and shine it is perfect). Sermon on the Nativity of St. John the Baptist.

2 *In Ezech.* Lib. ii, Homil. ii, no ii. Cf. also Ibid. Lib. i, Homil. v, no 12,

3 *The Foundations,* ch. 5. Translated from the Spanish by David Lewis. All this remarkable chapter should be read. The Saint seeks to discover "whence comes that inward dissatisfaction which we generally feel when we have not passed the greater part of the day alone and absorbed in God." This dissatisfaction proceeds, according to the Saint, from two causes: "One, and this is the chief, is self-love, which thrusts itself in here in a most subtle way, and accordingly escapes detection; that is, we would please ourselves rather than God... The second source of this dissatisfaction, in my opinion, is that the soul seems to live in greater purity when left in solitude, because there are fewer opportunities therein of offending God." The Saint admirably shows how this second cause itself, is not always sufficient and how one may have illusions on this point.—The Eternal Father likewise showed to St. Catherine of Siena how, in this matter, spiritual self-love may be a deception for the soul. *Dialogue,* ch. 39.

Abbot. But each one of us, in the sphere given to him, ought to become Jesus' apostle. Although we ought deeply to love and eagerly to seek solitude, recollection, the hidden life, we must, when obedience imposes charges upon us or active offices to fulfil in the monastery or outside, give ourselves wholly up to them. It is not to leave Christ when we give ourselves to His members by obedience. Quite the contrary! All that we do for the love of our brethren—of *His* brethren—touches Christ Himself. This is what He Who is the infallible Truth and unique Fount of our perfection has told us in His own words.

VIII

Does not St. Benedict himself give us to understand this capital truth that good zeal springs from the love of God and of Christ? Indicating the different forms which good zeal ought to take in regard to our brethren, the great Patriarch adds, in the same page of the Rule, three precepts concerning the exercise of this zeal. He repeats to us once more, as if he wished to sum up his thought before leaving us, "to fear God, to love the Abbot with a humble and sincere affection, finally, never to prefer anything to Christ." A passion for the rights of God, the Sovereign Master; obedience to His representative; the love of Christ: have we not here the most life-giving and purest springs for the nourishing of zeal?

We need not come back to the two first points; we have seen, in other conferences, what an important place they occupy in the monk's life. Let us insist only, like our Blessed Father himself, upon the last phrase of this chapter "of Good Zeal," with which the great Patriarch has chosen to close the holy Rule: "Let monks prefer nothing whatever to Christ": *Christo omnino nihil praeponant.* It will be good for our soul to stay a few seconds to consider this *absolute* love which we ought to bear to the Person of Christ Jesus.

Our heart, as you know, is made to love; it is a necessity of our life; hence we shall love either the Creator or the creature. Did not our Lord say that a man cannot serve two masters? And this love will be so much the more ardent as our capacity for affection is the more profound. Now our Blessed Father St. Benedict tells us that Christ is to hold the first place in our heart: *Christo omnino nihil praeponant*. Notice how absolute are these two terms: *Omnino nihil.* And why is St. Benedict so forcible in expressing this precept? It is because we are consecrated to Christ; on the day of our profession, we lost the right of giving our soul to creatures. There is—always supposing the essential order of finality secure—a division that God allows to persons in the world; He does not ask of them that entire, complete, dominating love; but as for us, we have promised to love God *solely*, to seek Him *always*, and Him *alone*, and to love creatures only in Him. We have said to Him: "My God, I know that Thou art so great, so powerful, so good, that Thou alone canst content all the aspirations of my soul and the needs that lie the deepest in my heart, therefore I want only Thee, I want to live only for Thee."

God is pleased with such an act of faith; we made it gladly on the day of our monastic profession. We should remain always at the height of this faith. Now this is very difficult for the human heart. In His immaterial nature, God is so far above us that, to keep ourselves in the love that seeks Him uniquely, we need an objective, concrete, tangible support. God knows this need, and He satisfies it through the Incarnation. The Incarnate Word is God made visible and living in our midst, and the love we manifest to Jesus Christ reaches God Himself.

So we should have the most absolute, burning and constant love for Christ Jesus.

How is this love to be expressed? We must first strive to know the Saviour, to render ourselves familiar with His Person, His works, His mysteries. All that touches Him ought to interest us, not to increase a coldly intellectual knowledge, but to become a source of prayer. The more we know Him in this way, the more we shall be attached to Him.

There is one affection which we ought chiefly to have in presence of the person and mysteries of Jesus; it is that of admiration. Indeed it is an excellent way of honouring these mysteries "to remain before God in great admiration and great silence, at the sight of His loving kindness and wonders... In this kind of prayer, it is not a question of producing many thoughts, nor of making great efforts: we are in God's presence: we are filled with wonderment at the graces He gives us: with David we repeat a hundred times without ever speaking a word: *Quid est homo?...* What is man that Thou deignest to be mindful of him?... One is lost in astonishment and gratitude without thinking of wishing to frame, either within or without, the least word, as long as this blessed and most simple state lasts... This admiration is an act of love. The first effect of love is to make us admire what we love, to make us always regard it with complacency, to bring it before our eyes, not to lose sight of it. This way of honouring God is marked in the saints of early times... It is David's way when he says: *Quam admirabile! quid homo! Quam magna multitudo dulcedinis tuae, Domine!* How wonderful is Thy Name! What is man! How great is the multitude of Thy sweetnesses! It is the canticle of all the Saints in the Apocalypse... We are silent then, not knowing how to express our tenderness, reverence and joy, nor in fine what we feel of God. And there is 'silence in Heaven, as it were for half an hour': a wonderful silence, which cannot last long in this turbulent and tumultuous life."[1]

This way of loving and honouring Him in His mysteries is acceptable to our Lord. Did He not Himself give us the example when He exulted with holy enthusiasm at the sight of His Father's adorable perfections and His wonderful ways with souls? *Exsultavit Spiritu Sancto.*[2]

This admiration and this attachment find their practical expression in frequently seeking Christ's company. When the heart is overflowing with love for anyone, the mind is always occupied with the same object. And we shall find our Lord wherever we will, in the oratory, in the tabernacle, in our cell, in the sanctuary of our soul. We shall find Him as He was seen by His contemporaries: the Shepherds and Magi at the Crib, the multitudes upon the roads, Martha and Magdalen at Bethania, the disciples in the Upper-room; the same Christ Who spoke with the Samaritan woman at Jacob's Well, and said to her: "If thou didst know the gift of God";[3] the same Who healed the lepers, Who calmed the angry waves; the same Christ Jesus, Son of the Father, our Saviour, become our Redeemer, our Wisdom, our Holiness. We shall find Him in the plenitude of His Almighty power, in the virtue of His Divine mysteries, in the infinite superabundance of His merits and satisfactions, in His love's ineffable mercy. And this contact established between us and Himself by faith will bring to our souls help, light, strength, peace and

1 Bossuet, *Elévations sur les Mystères,* XVIIIe semaine, IIe Elévation.

2 Luc. x, 21. 3 Joan. iv, 10.

joy: "Come to Me, and I will refresh you": *Venite ad Me et ego reficiam vos.*[1] He is, in truth, a faithful, compassionate, magnificent Friend; He receives us that He may bring us to His Father and make us partakers, in the holy and beatifying splendours, in the eternal glory of the Only-begotten Son, the object of infinite delight.

Finally, the most indubitable token of our love will be that in all things we seek to do His will and that of His Father: "Whosoever shall do the will of My Father," said Jesus Himself, "he is My brother, and sister, and mother."[2] And elsewhere: "If you love Me, keep My commandments": *Si diligitis me, mandata mea servate.*[3] When we love anyone are we not ingenious in giving him pleasure?

There cannot be a more sure means of pleasing Jesus, of manifesting to Him that absolute love which He alone merits, than in ever seeking "with most fervent love" to do the will of His Father Who is also ours; in keeping united to Him, the Father's Beloved Son; and in striving to reproduce in ourselves the dispositions of reverence and love for His Father, of charity for our brethren, of humility and obedience, which animated His blessed soul here below.

The exercise of this most fervent love: *ferventissimo amore*, will provide us with the secret of being among these souls of ardent zeal, such as our holy Patriarch requires us to be. It is in giving ourselves up fervently throughout our life to this exercise that we shall find the assurance of seeing fulfilled the wish expressed by St. Benedict at the end of the chapter upon good zeal: May Christ, the supreme object of our love, "bring us all alike to life everlasting": *Christo omnino nihil praeponant, qui nos* PARITER *ad vitam aeternam perducat.*

NOTE

(See above p. 471).

The founder of the Congregation of Beuron, Dom Maurus Wolter, a learned and pious monk, whose monastic spirit was imbibed at the purest sources, thus summed up his teaching, on the subject of the monastic apostolate: "The monk being by excellence God's son, His liege-

1 Matth. xi, 28. 2 Ibid. xii, 50. 3 Joan. xiv, 15.

man and His vassal... as soon as the king or His Church calls a monk or an army of monks, they intrepidly come forward, and whatever be the fierceness of the combat, their invincible courage carries off the victory... Ready for every work of zeal, monks show in action a sovereign scorn for every human consideration and place so much magnanimity, firmness and valour at the service of the Church that to see them combat, we at once recognise in them, in all its fulness, the very strength of God and the power of the Holy Spirit. This is what has brought forth from the cloister that wonderful phalanx of apostles, confessors, doctors and martyrs, whose labours have so powerfully contributed to found, preserve, and multiply the great Christian family. Enkindled with this zeal, innumerable legions of monks have not hesitated to give themselves entirely to this task, to sacrifice to it their very life, and consummate it by the shedding of their blood. The Gospel in one hand, the Rule in the other, they penetrated into the most distant regions and by the new peoples they have constantly added to the Christian family, they founded, extended and strengthened the Kingdom of the Cross throughout almost all the universe..."[1]

Dom Maurus Wolter had been in the school of D. Guéranger who helped him in the establishment of the *Constitutions* of the Beuron Congregation. The illustrious restorer of the order of St. Benedict in France wrote in his *Notions sur la vie religieuse et monastique* (Solesmes, 1885), destined for the formation of novices: "Although one of the essentials of monastic life is separation from the world, we must, nevertheless, beware of the idea that the monk may possibly arrive at the perfection proper to his state without including zeal for his neighbour in his intentions and mode of life... Monastic life tends to draw man nearer to God by submission and love. So the monk, entering into the spirit of his vocation, should be carried away by a holy zeal for the welfare of his neighbour, the great and eternal occupation of God, for which end He delivered up even His only-begotten Son.

"Let no one imagine that monastic life consists exclusively in working out our own perfection, regardless of the sanctification of our neighbour... Nothing can be more contrary to charity, which is the distinguishing mark of every true disciple of Christ, than a petty occupation with self,

1 *La Vie monastique, ses principes essentiels,* pp. 131, 132 sq.

which would conceal from the eyes of the monk the needs of those who will always remain his brethren…

"Husband the time before your holy profession and prepare yourselves well for those works of zeal which may be entrusted to you by obedience, be they employments within the monastery, or works which have for their object the propagation of the truth in writings destined for the public, or the exercise of the sacred ministry, preaching the word of God and administering the Sacraments…

"We will magnanimously recommend to God the works of zeal performed in our Order. Let us often entreat Him to accept our endeavours, whether they regard our own deeds or those of the public, or serve directly the sublime object of the salvation of souls. Ask Him frequently that for His divine glory and service our Order may be filled with men powerful in word and deed, men after the pattern of the many illustrious Saints of the monastic life, who became all things to all men and knew so well how to serve the Church and the souls ransomed by Jesus Christ. The whole life of these great religious souls was, at the same time, the most vivid expression of the spirit which our great Patriarch has laid down in his holy Rule."[1]

1 Translated from the French by Rev. Jerome Veth, O.S.B., under the title of *Religious and Monastic Life Explained.*

THE PEACE OF CHRIST

Pax Christi exsultet in cordibus vestris.[1]

SUMMARY.—The gift of peace to souls sums up all Christ's work in regard to us; peace also sums up the harmony of the monastic life.—I. Peace is the tranquillity of order.—II. How we are to conform to the Divine order.—III. The peace that the soul finds in God is unchanging.—IV. St. Benedict has ordained everything in his Rule towards the finding of this peace.

IN all the preceding conferences, I have sought but one thing: to place the Divine figure of Christ Jesus before your eyes, that contemplating this unique Ideal you may love and imitate It. This is in fact the whole of monasticism, as it is the very substance of Christianity. The integral seeking after God, the entire gift of self, poverty, humility, obedience, abandonment to the Divine will, the spirit of religion towards our Heavenly Father, charity and good zeal towards our neighbour, all these virtues which, if carried to a certain degree of perfection are characteristic of the religious life, have their first Exemplar in Jesus.

The one aim of monastic life is to make us perfect disciples of Christ; we are truly monks only on condition that we are first of all Christians. Our holy Patriarch wrote his Rule only as an abridgment of the Gospel; this is why, in ending as in beginning the code destined for his sons, he tells them nothing else than "to follow Christ";[2] "That they should prefer absolutely nothing before Christ Who will bring us to everlasting life": *Christo omnino nihil praeponant, qui nos pariter ad vitam aeternam*

1 "And let the peace of Christ rejoice in your hearts," Col. iii, 15.
2 Prologue of the Rule.

perducat.[1] It is with these words that the holy Legislator takes leave of us in the last chapter.

Now when we seek to sum up the whole of Christ's work, to see in brief the extent of His mystery, what do we find to say? Is there one word in which can be gathered up the whole substance of the mystery of the Man-God? Yes, there is such a word.

When Christ appeared upon earth, after thousands of years of waiting and anguish, what was the first message that fell from heaven, the message wherein man could discover in advance the secret of the ineffable mystery of the Word Incarnate, and, as it were, the plan of all the work of Jesus? It was the message brought by the angels sent by God Himself to announce to the world the good tidings of the Birth of His Son: "Glory be to God in the highest; and on earth peace to men of good will!"[2] The Word becomes incarnate to give all glory to His Father, and bring peace to the world. To seek His Father's glory is the supreme aspiration of Christ's Heart in regard to Him by Whom He is sent, and of Whom He is the Beloved Son; the gift of peace condenses in itself every good which the Saviour brings to the souls He comes to redeem.

Christ's life upon earth has but this one aim. When that is attained, He looks upon His work as finished. In the presence and hearing of His Apostles, He says in that wonderful prayer to His Father when about to consummate His life by His sacrifice: "I have glorified Thee on the earth; I have finished the work which Thou gavest Me to do": *Ego te clarificavi super terram; opus consummavi quod dedisti mihi ut faciam.*[3] And at this same moment, what does He say to His disciples to show that in regard to them too, He has "finished His work"? He leaves them peace, His own peace, not that which the world promises, but that which He alone can give.[4] It is the perfect gift He leaves to His Apostles, as to all souls redeemed and saved.

This gift is so precious and so necessary for the preservation of every other gift that Jesus bids His disciples greet one another with this wish of peace as their salutation of rule.[5]

---

1 Rule, ch. lxxii.
2 Luc. ii, 14.
3 Joan. xvii, 4.
4 Ibid. xiv, 27.
5 Luc. x, 5.

All the letters[1] of St. Paul—the herald of the mystery of Christ—begin with this salutation: "Grace to you and peace from God our Father, and from the Lord Jesus Christ": *Gratia vobis et pax a Deo nostro et Domino Jesu Christo*. The Apostle associates grace with peace, because grace is the primary condition of peace, "without grace," says St. Thomas, "it is impossible to have true peace": *Sine gratia non potest esse vera pax*.[2]

This peace, like other every good gift, comes from God the Father as being its first principle.[3] This is why St. Paul throughout his Epistles often designates the Heavenly Father as "the God of peace."[4] This peace comes, too, from Christ: did He not gain it for us in giving, through His immolation, full satisfaction to Divine justice? Then, as says St. Paul,[5] peace comes to us from the Holy Spirit: it is one of the fruits of the Spirit of Love, as much so as is joy. Peace is an essentially supernatural, an essentially Christian gift.

We cannot then be astonished that the holy Lawgiver places it before us as a gift that we should eagerly seek after, and that the word "*pax*" has become one of our dearest mottoes. It adorns the front of our monasteries. Inscribed on the threshold of our cloisters, it ought above all to be engraved in the depths of our hearts and emanate from our whole being. It is the word that best sums up, even in the eyes of seculars, the characteristic harmony of our life.[6] Peace, the supreme result of the practice of virtue in a heart given wholly to God, is the first good we wish to those who come to us; faithful to the Gospel precept and inheritor of the first ages of the Church, our Holy Father wills that the prior and brethren shall give the kiss of peace to all guests who arrive at the monastery.[7]

---

1 Except that to the Hebrews which, as we know, was probably not written by Paul's own hand.

2 II-II, q. xxix, a. 3, ad 1.

3 Cf. Jac. i, 17.

4 Ps. xv, 53; xvi, 20; I Cor. xiv, 33 etc.

5 Gal. v, 22.

6 This is one of the reasons why Newman has characterised the monastic life as "Virgilian." But the great Cardinal is totally mistaken in making what is poetical a sort of attribute and a dominating and almost exclusive attribute of the Patriarch of monks and Western monasticism. Newman's knowledge of St. Benedict's character is incomplete and inexact; his psychology of the great Patriarch is fantastic; the idealogist, in Newman, has misled the psychologist and the historian. We see with what reservations *The Mission of St. Benedict (Historical Sketches II)* must be read.

7 Rule, ch. liii.

But how can we truly wish this good to others if we do not possess it in ourselves? Let us then see what this peace is, what are its characteristics, and what is the source whence it is to be derived.

If we are to be worthy disciples of Christ and of St. Benedict we must seek this good as a great treasure. In the Prologue where he traces the broad outline of his institution, the holy Legislator recalls these words of the Psalmist:[1] "Seek after peace, and pursue it": *Inquire pacem et persequere eam.* It is remarkable that he associates the seeking after peace with the seeking after God, as two ends which become but one. Indeed they who strive to find this peace for themselves and others are truly the children of God: He Who is the Infallible Truth tells us: "Blessed are the peacemakers: for they shall be called the children of God": *Beati pacifici, quoniam filii Dei vocabuntur.*[2] Our Holy Father who wishes, throughout his Rule, to bring us to God and make us perfect children of the Heavenly Father by the grace of Jesus, has ordained everything in the monastery in such a way "that all the members may be at peace."[3] With this conference on peace we shall therefore finish determining the characteristics that mark the physiognomy of the monk, the disciple of Christ.

I

What then is peace? It is not here a question of exterior peace, that which results for us from solitude and silence. This peace is certainly a great thing, for silence and solitude help the faithful soul to be recollected, the better to turn to God.[4] However, as we have said, this outward peace is profitless if the imagination is wandering and the soul is troubled and disquieted. It is of inward peace that I wish to speak to you. You know the definition that St. Augustine has given of this peace: "Peace is the tranquillity of order": *Pax est tranquillitas ordinis.*[5]

To understand the force of this sentence let us carry our minds back to the days of the creation of Adam. It is said that God created man "right," in perfect rectitude of nature: *Fecit Deus hominem rectum.*[6] He had given him, moreover, sanctifying grace, original justice. All Adam's faculties

1 Ps. xxxiii, 15. 2 Matth. v, 9. 3 Rule, ch. xxxiv.
4 See above p. 408 sq.
5 *De civitate Dei*, Lib. xix, ch. 13. P. L. 41; col. 640. 6 Eccle. vii, 30.

were perfect and perfectly harmonised. In this virgin nature, come forth from the hands of God, there was a magnificent subordination of the inferior powers to reason, of reason to faith, and of the whole being to God; a harmony which was the divine radiation of original justice. The order was perfect in Adam, complete concord reigned between all the faculties, each of which rested in its object: hence was born unalterable peace. As St. Thomas says, it is "from the union of the different appetites in man tending towards the same object that peace results": *Unio autem horum motuum est quidem de ratione pacis.*[1]

Sin came into the world: all this admirable order was overthrown; there was no longer union between man's different appetites; diverse and contrary tendencies, generally in conflict, are henceforward to be encountered in him; the flesh conspires against the spirit, and the spirit wars against the flesh.[2]

To find peace again, the desires must be brought back to order and unity. Now this order consists in the senses being dominated by reason and the reason being subject to God: until such order is re-established, peace cannot exist in the heart. "Thou hast made us for Thyself, O Lord, and our hearts are ever restless until they rest in Thee."[3]

But how are we to rest in God if sin has made us His enemies? In consequence of sin—Adam's sin and our own—far from being able to approach God, we are separated from Him by an abyss. Is man then forever to be robbed of peace, is all his sighing after this lost possession to be in vain? No. Order is to be re-established, and peace restored; and you know in what an admirable manner. It is in Christ and through Christ that both order and peace are to be found again. "O God," we say in one of the prayers of the Mass, "Who in creating human nature, didst wonderfully dignify it; and hast still more wonderfully renewed it": *Deus, qui humanae substantiae dignitatem mirabiliter condidisti, et mirabilius reformasti.* A wonder that consists in the Word being made Man, in having taken our sin upon Himself in order to offer befitting expiation to His Father, in having restored to us God's friendship and given us His own infinite merits whereby we may retain this friendship.

1 II-II, q. xxxix, a. 1. 2 Ibid. a. 1 and 2.
3 *Confessions.* Lib. i, ch. 1. P. L. 32, col. 661.

St. Paul wrote to the Ephesians: "Now in Christ Jesus, you, who some time were afar off, are made nigh by the Blood of Christ. For He is our peace."[1] He says again: "God indeed was in Christ, reconciling the world to Himself, not imputing to them their sins."[2] Christ is the holy Victim, perfectly pleasing to God and in Him God has forgiven us.[3] As the Psalmist so well says, in Him, justice at length satisfied and peace at length restored have given each other the kiss of reconciliation: *Justitia et pax osculatae sunt.*[4]

Christ is "the Prince of peace": *Princeps pacis.*[5] He has come to fight against the prince of darkness and snatch us from the power of the devil and to make peace between God and man. And this Prince of Peace is so magnificent in His victory that He gives us a share in all His merits in order that we may for ever keep this peace won by His Blood. When the Psalmist announces the coming of the Messias, he says, as characteristic of His visitation: "In His days shall justice spring up, and abundance of peace, till the moon be taken away": *Orietur in diebus ejus et justitia abundantia pacis, donec auferatur luna.*[6] In the weeks following His Resurrection, it is peace that Christ wishes to His Apostles each time He appears to them. His Passion expiated everything, paid off everything; therefore this salutation of peace, henceforward restored by His grace, falls continually from His Divine lips.[7] Is it not remarkable that this same wish of peace should be heard at the two extremities of His earthly career: when the Angels announce the opening of His mission of salvation and when, this being accomplished, He enters into His glorious life? "Peace be with you": *Pax vobis.*

Look at St. Paul. Tormented by the inward warfare of the flesh against the spirit, he cries out: "Who shall deliver me from the body of this death?" And what answer does he give to his own question? "The grace of God, by Jesus Christ Our Lord." For, he adds, Christ by His death has freed us from all condemnation; His grace has been given to us that we may live, not according to the desires of the flesh but according to those of the Spirit; and he concludes, the desires and affections of the flesh bring forth death, the desires and affections of the Spirit bring

1 Eph. ii, 13–14. 2 II Cor. v, 19. 3 Cf. Eph. iv, 32.
4 Ps. lxxxiv, 11. 5 Isa. ix, 6. 6 Ps. lxxi, 7.
7 Luc. xxiv, 37; Joan. xx, 19, 26.

life and peace: *Nam prudentia carnis mors est: prudentia autem spiritus, vita et PAX.*[1]

It is then in the grace of Christ Jesus that the principle of peace is to be found; this it is which makes us pleasing to God and gives us His friendship, which makes us see that other men are our brethren, which subdues perverse tendencies in us and makes us live according to the Divine Will.

And this grace comes to us only through Christ. For such is the Divine order, the essential order: Christ Jesus has been established King over Sion. He is King by right of conquest, having delivered Himself up to death for the souls He wills to bring back to His Father; He is this peaceful King Who shows His magnificence in coming down from Heaven to bring us pardon: *Magnificatus est rex pacificus*;[2] the Father has given Him all power: *Data est mihi omnis potestas in caelo et in terra*;[3] in order that He may be our justice, our sanctification, our redemption, and hence, "our peace": *IPSE est pax nostra*.[4]

Such is the admirable order established by God Himself: Christ, the Head of all the elect, is, for each one of them, the source of grace, the principle of peace. Outside this order there can only be trouble and insecurity for the soul. Those who want to do without God, those whom Scripture calls "the impious" cannot have peace: *Non est pax impiis*.[5] Doubtless, certain of their desires can be satisfied, fulfilled even. They can satisfy to a certain point their thirst for pleasures and honours. But, says St. Thomas,[6] this is an apparent and false peace; the impious are ignorant of man's true good: they put the contenting of their desires in apparent, relative, fugitive good; thus these souls who appear happy are never truly so; the heart remains empty even after having exhausted all the sources of joy that the creature can give, because our deepest desires exceed all sensible good. All we can do is in vain, our heart is created for God: this is one of the principles of order; our heart has a capacity for the infinite, and no creature can satisfy it perfectly. Except in God there is only ephemeral joy and illusive peace; the heart is agitated in vain in running after the creature. "Why," says St. Augustine, "do you persist in

1 Rom. vii, 24–25; viii, 1–6.
2 Antiphon for 1st Vespers at Christmas.
3 Matth. xxviii, 18.
4 Eph. ii, 14.
5 Isa. xlviii, 22, lvii, 21.
6 II-II, q. xxix, a. 2, ad 3.

ever traversing painful and wearisome paths? Rest is not where you are seeking it... you pursue happiness in the sojourn of death; it is elsewhere. How shall a happy life be found where there is not even true life?" *Non est requies ubi quaeritis eam... Beatam vitam quaeritis in regione mortis, non est illic. Quomodo enim beata vita, ubi nec vita?* And the holy Doctor concludes: "He Who is Life, our Life, has come down amongst us": *Et descendit huc ipsa vita nostra.*[1] In Christ Jesus alone is to be found the principle of life, the source of peace.[2] To enjoy true peace, we must then not only "seek God," but moreover we must seek Him in the way He wishes us to seek Him, that is to say in Christ. This is the fundamental order, established by God Himself, according to the good pleasure of His sovereign will: *Ut notum faceret nobis sacramentum voluntatis suae, secundum beneplacitum ejus quod proposuit in eo... instaurare omnia in Christo.*[3] Outside this order fixed by Infinite Wisdom, we can find neither holiness, nor perfection; we can find neither peace nor joy.

II

How are we to conform ourselves to this Divine order of things?

First of all by an act of practical faith which surrenders our whole being to Christ that we may follow Him.[4] An act of faith in the Divinity of Jesus Christ, for we cannot give ourselves entirely to Him unless we have this deep conviction that He is the Son of God and that He is everything for us. We must have this absolute faith in the Almighty power of Jesus, in His sovereign bounty, in the infinite value of His merits, in the inexhaustible abundance of His riches. When the Father sent Him to us to be the ambassador of Divine peace, He told us nothing else than to hear this Son in Whom He has placed all His delight: *Ipsum audite.*[5] It is on this condition that the Divine grace and friendship are restored to us. Our first attitude is therefore faith: "Yea, Heavenly Father, Jesus

1 *Confessions.* Lib. iv, ch. 12. P. L. 32, col. 701. 2 Rule, ch. lviii.

3 "That He might make known unto us the mystery of His will, according to His good pleasure, which He hath purposed in Him... to re-establish all things in Christ," Eph. i, 9–10.

4 "Peace between man and God, is obedience well ordered in faith under the eternal law." St. Augustine. *De civitate Dei,* Lib. xix, ch. 13. P. L. 41, col. 640.

5 Matth. xvii, 5.

is Thy Well-beloved Son; this I believe, and I adore this Son." Then the Father regards us with the same look of love with which He regards His Son. Does not Our Lord Himself assure us of this? "The Father Himself loveth you, because you have loved Me, and have believed that I came out from God."[1] And when He pleads for His disciples and for us, when upon the point of quitting earth He confides us to His Father's goodness, He brings forward no other reason for His request than the faith that His disciples have in His Divinity. Let us listen to Him in that ineffable discourse He has with His Father when about to reconcile the world with God by His sacrifice: Father keep them, save them, for they have truly known that I am Thy Son and that all I have comes from Thee: *Pater, serva eos... cognoverunt quia omnia quae dedisti mihi, abs te sunt... cognoverunt vere quia a te exivi.*[2]

This act of faith marks the dawn of peace for us.

Is not this natural, since it is through faith in Jesus Christ that we enter into the Divine order of grace, the foundation of peace? "Being *justified therefore by faith*, let us have peace with God, through Our Lord Jesus Christ, by Whom also we have access through faith into this grace... and glory in the hope of this glory of the sons of God."[3]

This faith ought to be practical; it ought to extend to all our being, and have for its object all that touches Christ.

Souls are to be met with who truly wish to adore Christ, but they confine their submission to His Person alone, refusing to extend it to His Church. When these souls cannot lay claim to be in good faith, they cannot find peace: they are not according to the Divine order. We must then give ourselves entirely to Jesus Christ, surrender to Him our soul, our understanding, our will, our body: everything in us ought to be subject to Him; all that is withdrawn from the action of His Spirit is withdrawn from the Divine order. Outside the light of the Word, there is only darkness; outside the way which is Himself, we find only error; without His grace, there is only powerlessness. And indeed what peace can be given to us by darkness, error and powerlessness to go to God, the only true Good, the only true End of our life?

Let us then yield ourselves up to Our Lord by an act of living faith, of deep adoration, of perfect submission and entire abandonment. Let

1 Joan. xvi, 27. 2 Ibid. xvii, 11, 7–8. 3 Rom. v, 1–2.

us ask Him to direct all our life, to be the object of all our aspirations, the principle of all our actions. He is "the Prince of Peace," "the pacific King": *Rex pacificus*: may He be really the King of our Souls. We say to God every day: "Thy Kingdom come": *Adveniat regnum tuum*. What is this Kingdom of God which we desire? It is the Kingdom of Christ, for God has apointed Him King upon earth and in heaven: *Postula a me, et dabo tibi gentes hereditatem tuam!*[1]

When we thus submit ourselves entirely to Christ Jesus, when we abandon ourselves to Him, when our soul only responds, like His own, with a perpetual *Amen* to all that He asks of us in the name of His Father; when, after His example, we abide in this attitude of adoration before all the manifestations of the Divine Will, in face of the least permissions of His Providence, then Christ Jesus establishes His peace in us: His peace, not that which the world promises, but the true peace which can only come from Himself: *Pacem meam do vobis; non quomodo mundus dat, ego do vobis.*[2]

Indeed, such adoration produces in us the unity of all desires. The soul has but one thing in view: the establishing in her of Christ's Kingdom. Christ Jesus, in return, satisfies this desire with magnificent plenitude. The soul possesses the perfect contentment of her deepest tendencies because the satisfaction of her supernatural desires has been reduced to one; she is in the right order of things; she lives in peace.

Happy the soul who has thus understood the order established by the Father, that soul who seeks only to be conformed by love to His admirable order, where all leads up to Christ Jesus: she tastes peace, a peace of which St. Paul says that it surpasses all understanding[3] and defies an expression. "It is impossible," says Blosius, "to explain the abundance of this peace in the soul altogether given to God and seeking Him alone."[4]

III

And this peace is a lasting peace. What indeed can trouble it? The devil? He is a powerful enemy, without doubt, who seeks to devour us;

1 Ps. ii, 8. 2 Joan. xiv, 27. 3 Philip. iv, 7.

4 *Canon vitae spiritualis,* ch. 14. *Perfecta pax et quies animarum* (The perfect peace and rest of souls).

but if the dog, when he is chained up, barks; he can only bite those who go near him: *Latrare potest, mordere non potest, nisi volentem.*[1] Christ has conquered him, we shall be conquerors in our turn, for Christ Jesus is more powerful than he. Moreover, does not God surround the soul with a special protection, if, seeking Him alone, it likewise puts all its confidence in Him? He commands His Angels to keep it in all its ways in order that it shall not stumble;[2] He Himself keeps it "in the secret of His face."[3] What enemy shall be able to trouble it? What terror shall be able to come near it?

Neither can the world destroy this peace. "Fear not," said our Lord to His disciples; and He repeats this to us: Fear not; you shall have tribulations in the world, but I abide with you. "Have confidence, I have overcome the world": *Confidite, ego vici mundum.*[4] If you remain faithful to Me, I will give you, with My grace, My own peace. My all-powerful grace shall indeed make you victorious over the solicitations of the world. The world may offer us its pleasures, vent its sarcasms upon us; it no longer touches us; we have left all to follow Christ; our peace, founded upon the truth of Jesus, cannot be broken into by the world's weapons.

Shall our peace be destroyed by temptation? by contradictions? by sufferings? Again no. Doubtless, here below, peace is not always sensible; upon earth we are in a condition of trial and, most often, peace is won by conflict. Christ has not restored to us that original justice which established harmony in Adam's soul, but the soul that lays hold on God alone participates in the Divine stability; temptations, sufferings, trials touch only the surface of our being; the depths where peace reigns are inaccessible to disturbance. The surface of the sea may be violently agitated by the waves during the tempest; the deep waters remain tranquil. We may be slighted, opposed, persecuted, be unjustly treated, our intentions and deeds may be misunderstood; temptation may shake us, suffering may come suddenly upon us; but there is an inner sanctuary which none can reach; here is the sojourn of our peace, because in this innermost secret of the soul dwell adoration, submission and abandon-

1 Appendix to the Sermons of St. Augustine, xxxvii, 6.
2 Ps. xc, 11. 3 Ibid. xxx, 21. 4 Joan. xvi, 33.

ment to God. "I love my God," said St. Augustine, "no one takes Him from me: no one takes from me what I ought to give Him, for that is enclosed within my heart... O inward riches which no one or anything can take away!"[1]

In the centre of the soul that loves God there rises up the *civitas pacis* which no noise of earth can trouble, that no attack can surprise. We may truly say that nothing which is exterior, outside us, can, unless we so will, touch our inward peace: this essentially depends on only one thing, namely our attitude towards God. It is in Him that we must trust. "The Lord is my light and my salvation, whom shall I fear?"[2] If the wind of temptation and trial arises, I have only to take refuge with Him. "Lord, save me, for without Thee, I perish." And our Lord, as formerly when in the ship tossed about by the waves, will Himself calm the tempest with a single gesture; and there will come "a great calm": *Et facta est tranquillitas magna.*[3]

If we really seek God in everything, by following in the footsteps of Christ, Who is the sole way that leads to the Father; if we strive to be detached from all, that we may only desire the Master's good pleasure; if, when the Spirit of Jesus speaks to us, there is in us no inflexibility of soul, no resistance to His inspirations, but only docility and adoration, we may be assured that peace, deep and abundant, will reign in us; for, O Lord, "much peace have they that love Thy law": *Pax multa diligentibus legem tuam.*[4] Souls that do not wish to give *all* to Our Lord, and to bring all their desires to *unity* by this *total* donation, cannot taste this true peace. They are divided, tossed to and fro between themselves and God, between the satisfaction of their self-love and obedience; they are the prey of trouble and disquiet.

"Let us ever cleave to God; let us have Him within us; in Him every object of our love is stable and immutable."[5] "There only is sure peace to be found where love remains faithful": *Et ibi est locus quietis imperturbabilis, ubi non deseritur amor, si ipse non deserat.*[6]

---

1 *Enarr. in Psalm,* lv, n. 19. P. L, 36, col. 659.

2 Ps. xxvi, 1. 3 Matth. viii, 26. 4 Ps. cxviii, 165.

5 St. Augustine, *De musica.* Lib. vi, ch. 14, n. 48. P. L. 32, col. 1188.

6 St. Augustine, *Confessions.* Lib. iv, ch. 11. Ibid. col. 700.

Even its past sins do not trouble the soul established in peace. Certainly it feels profound sorrow in having offended the Heavenly Father, in having caused the sufferings of Jesus and grieved the Spirit of Love; but this sorrow is not mixed with agitation and fever: the soul knows that Jesus is the Ransom for sin, and a Ransom of infinite value; that He has become "the propitiation for our sins, and… for those of the whole world";[1] that now, He is at the right hand of His Father, ever living, a compassionate High Priest Who unceasingly pleads in our favour: *Semper vivens ad interpellandum pro nobis.*[2] Nothing gives such peace to a contrite soul as to be able to offer to the Father all the sufferings, expiations, satisfactions and merits of His beloved Son; nothing gives the soul such confidence as to be able to render to Him, through Jesus, all glory and praise. For this homage of Christ, which the soul makes its own, is full, adequate, leaving nothing to be desired; thus it gives deep peace to the soul that finds in Jesus the perfect means of repairing all its negligences and all its faults.

Neither can discouragement penetrate into this soul to trouble it; it knows something of "the unsearchable riches of Christ": *Investigabiles divitias Christi.*[3] Doubtless, of itself, it can do nothing, nor even have a good thought, but it submits to the order willed by God, the Author of the supernatural life, and it knows that in this order is likewise contained the power the soul has of appropriating to itself the riches of Jesus: "I can do all things in Him Who strengtheneth me": *Omnia possum in eo qui me confortat.*[4] It knows that, with Him, through Him, in Him, it is rich with the very riches of Christ, "so that nothing is wanting to [it] of any grace": *Divites facti estis… ita ut nihil vobis desit in ulla gratia.*[5] Its confidence cannot be shaken, because the soul belongs to Him Who is for it the Way, the Light, and the Life; He Who is the Master above all others, the Good Shepherd, the charitable Samaritan, the faithful Friend. Our Lord revealed to a soul that one of the reasons of His bounteous gifts to St. Gertrude was the absolute confidence that this great nun had in His goodness and His treasures.[6]

1 I Joan. ii, 2. 2 Hebr. vii, 25. 3 Eph. iii, 8. 4 I Cor. i, 5, 7.
5 *The Herald of Divine Love,* Bk. i, ch. 10. 6 Joan. xi, 25.

Finally, neither can death trouble the soul that has only sought God. Has it not confided itself to the One Who says: "He that believeth in Me, although he be dead, shall live," *Qui credit in Me, etiamsi mortuus fuerit, vivit*?[1] Our Lord is the Truth; He is also the Life; and He brings us, He restores to us, the life that is unending. Even though the shadow of death falls upon it, this soul will abide in peace, *Nam etsi ambulavero in medio umbrae mortis, non timebo mala, quoniam tu mecum es.*[2] Does it not know in Whom it has trusted: *Scio cui credidi*?[3] And this presence of Jesus reassures the soul against every terror.

In one of her "Exercises," St. Gertrude allows her assurance, which the infinite merits of Jesus give her, to overflow. At the thought of the divine tribunal of which the image rises up before her mind, she makes the most moving appeal to these merits. "Woe, woe unto me, if, when I come before Thee, I had no advocate to plead my cause! O Love, stand thou forth on my behalf, answer for me, sue out my pardon. If thou undertake my cause, I know that I still have hope of life. I know what I will do, I will take the chalice of salvation, even the chalice of my Jesus. I will lay it upon the empty scale of the balance of Truth. So shall I supply all that is lacking, and outweigh all my sins. That chalice will raise up again the ruins of my hope, for therewith I shall infinitely overbalance all my unworthiness... Come Thou with me to judgment," says St. Gertrude to our Lord; "there let us stand together. Judge me, for the right is Thine; but remember Thou art also my Advocate. In order that I be fully acquitted, Thou hast but to recount what Thou didst become for love of me, the good Thou hast decreed to do unto me, the price wherewith Thou hast purchased me. Thou hast taken my nature to this very end, that I might not perish. Thou hast borne the burden of my sins, Thou hast died for me, that I might not die an eternal death. Thou hast willed to make me rich in merit, and so hast Thou given me all. Judge me, then, at the hour of my death according to that innocence and that purity which Thou didst bestow on me in Thee when Thou didst pay all my debts, when Thou wast Thyself judged and condemned in my stead; that, all poor and destitute as I am in myself, I might have all and abound."[4]

---

1 Joan. xi, 25. 2 Ps. xxii, 4. 3 II Tim. i, 12.

4 *Exercises of St. Gertrude,* Seventh Exercise: Reparation. Translated by Thomas Alder Pope, M. A., of the Oratory.

For souls moved by such sentiments, death is but a transition; Christ comes Himself to open to them the gates of the Heavenly Jerusalem, which, much more so than that of old, deserves to be called the "Blessed vision of peace": *Beata pacis visio.*[1] There will be no more darkness, trouble, tears, or sighs; but peace, infinite and perfect peace. "Peace first becomes ours with the longing and seeking for the Creator; it is in the full vision and eternal possession of Him that peace is made perfect": *Pax enim nostra ex desiderio Conditoris inchoatur, ex manifesta autem visione perficitur.*[2]

IV

Let us then ask Jesus to bring us, to give us this peace which is the fruit of His love. "O Lord God, give peace unto us," as St. Augustine so well says at the end of his *Confessions,* that wonderful book where he shows us how he had sought peace in every possible satisfaction of the senses, the mind and the heart, without finding them elsewhere than in God. "Give peace unto us... the peace of the Sabbath, a peace without any evening," *Domine Deus, pacem da nobis, pacem quietis, pacem sabbati, sabbati sine vespera.* "For Thou, the Supreme Good, that needest no good, art ever at rest, because Thou Thyself art that rest. And what man is there that can make another man to understand this? Or what Angel, an Angel? Or what Angel, a man? Let it be asked of Thee, let it be sought in Thee." And the holy Doctor who had made the experience of all things, who had felt the vanity of every creature, the frailty of all human happiness, ends the book with this cry: "So shall it be received, so shall it be found, so shall it be opened."[3]

Let us ask this peace for each of our brethren who dwell with us in the same spiritual Jerusalem, *Rogate quae ad pacem sunt Jerusalem;*[4] this peace

1 Hymn for Vespers for the Dedication of a Church.

2 St. Gregory, *Moralia in Job,* Lib. vi, ch. 34, P. L. 75, col. 758.

3 *Tu autem bonum nullo indigens bono, semper quietus es; quoniam tua quies tu ipse es. Et hoc intelligere, quis hominum dabit homini? quis angelus angelo? quis angelus homini? a te petatur, in te quaeratur, ad te pulsetur; sic, sic, accipietur, sic invenietur, sic apertetur. Amen.* Lib. xiii, ch. 35 and 38. P. L. 32, col. 867, 868. Translation of Sir Tobie Matthew, Kt. Revised and amended by Dom Roger Huddleston. O.S.B.

4 Ps. cxxi, 6.

will be given to us; but we shall especially obtain it by an attitude of soul full of adoration, of submission and abandonment to Our Lord. Here, as I repeat, is the source of the only true peace, because here is the Divine order and consequently the true satisfaction of the innermost desires of our souls. On the day of our Profession we relinquished everything, we gave ourselves to Jesus that we might follow Him: *Reliquimus omnia, et secuti sumus te.*[1] We have but to continue in this disposition and we shall taste peace. Everything in the Holy Rule is ordered in such a way as to procure this peace, all leads us to it; and the monastery, where men live according to this Rule is indeed, even here below, a "vision of peace." Each one who lets himself be fashioned and moulded by humility, obedience, the spirit of abandonment and confidence, those foundations of the monastic life, becomes a city of peace.

This is because our Holy Father has marvellously understood the Divine plan, the order established by God. Our souls are made for God; unless they are set towards this end, they are perpetually in agitation and trouble. Now St. Benedict wishes that we should have but this one and universal intention: That we should seek God: *Si revera Deum quaerit*;[2] he makes all converge to this: this is the centre of his Rule. By the unity of this end, he brings unity into all the manifold actions of our life, and especially into the desires of our being; and this is, according to St. Thomas, one of the essential elements of peace: *Tranquillitas consistit in hoc quod omnes motus appetitivi in uno homine conquiescunt.*[3] Our souls are troubled when they are torn by desires that bear upon a thousand different objects: *Sollicita es, et turbaris erga plurima*;[4] when we seek God alone by an obedience full of abandonment and love, we sum up all things in the one thing necessary; and it is this that establishes strength and peace within us.

Secondly, penetrating more deeply into the Divine order, the holy Patriarch tells us that without Christ we shall not attain to this end: He alone is the way that leads us to it. Therefore, in opening his Rule, he shows us no other means than the love of Christ: *Ad te ergo nunc mihi*

1 Matth. xix, 27 2 Rule, ch. lviii. 3 II-II, q. xxix, a. 1, ad 1; a. 3.
4 "Thou art careful, and art troubled about many things," Luc. x, 41.

sermo dirigitur, quisquis... Domino Christo vero Regi militaturus;[1] it is by giving Christ full dominion over our hearts, that we shall be true disciples of St. Benedict. And when he takes leave of us, he repeats this to us once more under the form of an urgent counsel of which he shows us the value: "Prefer nothing whatever to Christ": *Christo omnino nihil praeponant, qui nos pariter ad vitam aeternam perducat.*[2]

Such is, in brief, the whole of the Divine order shown forth by the holy Legislator with an admirable simplicity of outline. To return to God by Christ, to seek God in Christ, to tend towards God in the footsteps of Christ. And so as to prove that this seeking after God is sincere, absolute and total:—separation from the world, humility, loving obedience, the spirit of abandonment and confidence, the preponderance given to the life of prayer, the love of our neighbour. These are virtues of which Christ Jesus has given us the first example; their exercise proves that we truly seek God, that we prefer absolutely nothing to the love of Jesus Christ, that we make Him our one and only Ideal.

Happy the monk who walks in this path! Even in the greatest sufferings, in the most painful temptations, in the most trying adversities, he will find light, peace and joy. Everything is ordered in his soul as God wills it, and all his desires are unified in the one sole Good for Whom he is created.

St. Benedict, who spoke from experience, could likewise guarantee to us the obtaining of many and great things. In the measure, he says, that the monk goes forward in the way of faith and the practice of the virtues, it is "with heart enlarged that he runs with unutterable sweetness of love in the way of God's commandments": *Dilatato corde, inenarrabili dilectionis dulcedine curritur via mandatorum Dei.*[3] Happy, once again, is this monk! Divine peace dwells in his soul, it is reflected upon his countenance, it is shed around him. He is essentially what our Holy Father wishes the monk to be:—the child of God through Christ's grace, a perfect Christian: *Beati pacifici, quoniam filii Dei vocabuntur.*[4] Blessed, indeed, because God is with him; and at every moment, he finds in this God, Whom he came to the monastery to seek, the greatest and most

1 "To thee are my words now addressed, whosoever thou mayest be... to fight for the true King, Christ," Prologue of the Rule.

2 Rule, ch. lxxii.

3 Prologue of the Rule.

4 Matth. v, 9.

precious good, because He Himself is the Supreme and Unchanging Good Who never disappoints the desire of those who seek Him in the simplicity and sincerity of their hearts: *Si revera Deum quaerit.*

That in all things God may be glorified.
RULE OF S. BENEDICT

About The Cenacle Press at Silverstream Priory

An apostolate of the Benedictine monastery of Silverstream Priory in Ireland, the mission of The Cenacle Press can be summed up in four words: *Quis ostendit nobis bona*—who will show us good things (Psalm 4:6)? In an age of confusion, ugliness, and sin, our aim is to show something of the Highest Good to every reader who picks up our books. More specifically, we believe that the treasury of the centuries-old Benedictine tradition and the beauty of holiness which has characterised so many of its followers through the ages has something beneficial, worthwhile, and encouraging in it for every believer.

cenaclepress.com

Printed in the USA
CPSIA information can be obtained
at www.ICGtesting.com
LVHW052321161023
761015LV00003BA/11

9 781915 544179